T0142506

Translational Systems Sciences

Volume 12

In 1956, Kenneth Boulding explained the concept of General Systems Theory as a skeleton of science. He describes that it hopes to develop something like a "spectrum" of theories—a system of systems which may perform the function of a "gestalt" in theoretical construction. Such "gestalts" in special fields have been of great value in directing research towards the gaps which they reveal.

There were, at that time, other important conceptual frameworks and theories, such as cybernetics. Additional theories and applications developed later, including synergetics, cognitive science, complex adaptive systems, and many others. Some focused on principles within specific domains of knowledge and others crossed areas of knowledge and practice, along the spectrum described by Boulding.

Also in 1956, the Society for General Systems Research (now the International Society for the Systems Sciences) was founded. One of the concerns of the founders, even then, was the state of the human condition, and what science could do about it.

The present Translational Systems Sciences book series aims at cultivating a new frontier of systems sciences for contributing to the need for practical applications that benefit people.

The concept of translational research originally comes from medical science for enhancing human health and well-being. Translational medical research is often labeled as "Bench to Bedside." It places emphasis on translating the findings in basic research (at bench) more quickly and efficiently into medical practice (at bedside). At the same time, needs and demands from practice drive the development of new and innovative ideas and concepts. In this tightly coupled process it is essential to remove barriers to multi-disciplinary collaboration.

The present series attempts to bridge and integrate basic research founded in systems concepts, logic, theories and models with systems practices and methodologies, into a process of systems research. Since both bench and bedside involve diverse stakeholder groups, including researchers, practitioners and users, translational systems science works to create common platforms for language to activate the "bench to bedside" cycle.

In order to create a resilient and sustainable society in the twenty-first century, we unquestionably need open social innovation through which we create new social values, and realize them in society by connecting diverse ideas and developing new solutions. We assume three types of social values, namely: (1) values relevant to social infrastructure such as safety, security, and amenity; (2) values created by innovation in business, economics, and management practices; and, (3) values necessary for community sustainability brought about by conflict resolution and consensus building.

The series will first approach these social values from a systems science perspective by drawing on a range of disciplines in trans-disciplinary and cross-cultural ways. They may include social systems theory, sociology, business administration, management information science, organization science, computational mathematical organization theory, economics, evolutionary economics, international political science, jurisprudence, policy science, socio-information studies, cognitive science, artificial intelligence, complex adaptive systems theory, philosophy of science, and other related disciplines. In addition, this series will promote translational systems science as a means of scientific research that facilitates the translation of findings from basic science to practical applications, and vice versa.

We believe that this book series should advance a new frontier in systems sciences by presenting theoretical and conceptual frameworks, as well as theories for design and application, for twenty-first-century socioeconomic systems in a translational and trans-disciplinary context.

More information about this series at http://www.springer.com/series/11213

Pierre-Léonard Harvey

Community Informatics Design Applied to Digital Social Systems

Communicational Foundations, Theories and Methodologies

 Springer

Pierre-Léonard Harvey
Department of Social and Public Communication
of the Faculty of Communication
University of Quebec in Montreal (UQAM)
Montreal, QC, Canada

Translated by Virginie Bucco

ISSN 2197-8832   ISSN 2197-8840   (electronic)
Translational Systems Sciences
ISBN 978-3-319-88010-5   ISBN 978-3-319-65373-0   (eBook)
DOI 10.1007/978-3-319-65373-0

Printed on acid-free paper

This Springer imprint is published by Springer Nature
The registered company is Springer International Publishing AG
The registered company address is: Gewerbestrasse 11, 6330 Cham, Switzerland

*To my wife, Véronique, and my family
(Monique, Léonard, Michel and Ginette,
Sylvie and Yohann) and to my in-laws, Elsa
and Aloïs, Frantz, Gothard, Wolfgang,
Konrad, Hans Peter, Elizabeth and Éric,
I would like to express my admiration
and gratitude.*

Preface

The past 3 years has been very inspiring for me and the members of the Université du Québec à Montréal's Applied Community Informatics Lab (ACIL) whose core researchers include the following: Marie-Kettlie André, Gilles Lemire, Guy Gendron, Hassane Beidou, Abdel Ourahou, Guylaine Lavoie, Jean-François Roussy, Michel Brière, Marina Palarchevska, Lionel and Pascal Audant, Geoffroi Garon and several students from UQAM's Communication Faculty. As jointly responsible of the research entitled "My Portal Col@b and Community Informatics Design", we have met with tens of people coming from the corporate world, academics, government, civil society and community and association sector to partake in workshops and discussion groups called "COLAB's Get Together". From the beginning of the project, the government of Quebec and its *ministère des Services gouvernementaux* wanted to have a better understanding of the emergence of a culture participating in Internet communities' importance. The emergence coincided with the desire of Quebec's scientific community to better master the way information and communication technologies (ICT) interlock with politics, economy and the society in general to generate innovation. In 2012, the *Secrétariat du Conseil du Trésor* took over the initiative program called *Appui au passage à la société de l'information (APSI)* while maintaining the same present partners in the project, thus assuring monitoring. Several major events here and overseas have impacted these works.

In particular, various European Community programs surround the Living Labs initiatives and the desire to assure a better governance of the complex articulation between technology, innovation and society. It gave place to a never before seen excitement in the effort to evaluate the effects of technology promotion on society (quoting the vast FuturICT project initiative). In addition, we have seen an entire group of high-level researchers structure itself around the recent American National Science Foundation policies as part of the "Technology-Mediated Social Participation" (TMSP) concept/program (Shneiderman 2011). The current context, influenced by the proliferation of collaborative Web and by "user/designer" notions and "innovative communities", leads the Fonds de recherche du Québec on "social sciences and technologies" to position itself as a major actor in the transfer of knowledge and technologies validation. The growing innovation overlap in priority sectors and the technological complexity lead the actors to a better understanding of the impact networks and collaborative technologies can have on the broader economy. Canada and Quebec's governments rely on developing partnerships between universities, companies, government research centres and civil society to contribute to technological transfer in order to improve the companies' innovation capacity in our country. The appointment of Mr. Rémi Quirion in 2011 as Quebec's chief scientist officer already seems to be a promising initiative.

Also on June 1, 2011, during a speech at Queens University, the Science and Technology Canadian Minister Gary Goodyear declared that the government of Canada will invest 29,6 million dollars through the CREATE Program to help young scientists and engineers acquire professional skills, leadership and the entrepreneurial abilities they need to transition into the workplace and to ensure the growth of the Canadian economy. As part of another initiative, Minister Goodyear and the Industry Minister, Christian Paradis, received the second report on the situation published by The Science, Technology and Innovation Council (STIC) entitled *De l'imagination à l'innovation—Le parcours du Canada vers la prospérité*. This report focuses on Canada's productivity in terms of innovation and provides references allowing to measure innovation on a global scale. The *De l'imagination à l'innovation* report is centred on companies' innovation and the way participants establish partnerships within the innovation system. It also studies product innovation, process innovation and organizational innovation as well as investments in ICT.

The current ICT and its relationship towards innovation have such extent that it reminds me of the collaborative movement centred on the introduction of computers in schools and companies in the 1980s. This movement rallied all sorts of subjects and partners helping us understand the ICT social impacts on our societies. They went from the timid technological determinism in the 1980s to the social and community appropriation of the new information and communication technologies (NICT) movement for discovery and innovation. The potential gains for society are huge, and Quebec's civil society makes no mistake and demands a digital platform for the entire province. The "My Portal Col@b" research project has been developed according to a new reference model called "community informatics design". It seeks to contribute to a thrilling era since it is part of the international innovation movement, which until now was only reserved for the "pure sciences" through networks (systems) and scientific collaborative platforms like mathematics, biology and physics. Today, it expands to the fields of communication sciences and social sciences through new expressions and cybernetic languages: cyber communication and social cyber sciences.

The work we have accomplished until now is only a modest contribution and a sort of prelude to an international research program that will stretch over several years. On the shorter term, our UQAM research group has developed a road map that stretches until 2020 and aims to vitalize Quebec's pure sciences and social science communities around complexity, collective intelligence and collaborative intelligence, in a reference framework we call "community informatics design science" (CID) for innovation. This book is also a contribution to the implementation of the "Quebec digital platform" under construction.

Supporting transdisciplinary researches is far from being an easy task in any creative and active environment. And, defining a reference framework that gathers design thinking concepts as well as science, digital arts, complexity and social sciences is even harder. In the medium term, this lengthy work widely exceeding our own works will involve hundreds of people in tens of "collaboratories", here and all over the world. To emphasize the validation effect technology has on society, our project wanted to suggest strong conceptual bridges between practical communities and innovation, complexity and social science theories. With new research policies' support, we hope our project will be reflected in various government levels to obtain its future financing and unfold in the innovation communities. The report we are presenting to our sponsors, partners and future knowledge "co-designers" represents a unique occasion for Quebec's economy. We should not miss this opportunity. Why? Because we are entering a new creativity and reflexivity era around imagination worlds and more sustainable socio-economic development.

The Ubiquitous Imagination Paradigm

Ubiquitous imagination is a concept serving as a creativity platform at UQAM's Applied Community Informatics Laboratory. This concept supports the idea that knowledge and participatory innovation culture production are omnipresent in our advanced societies and they are now producing a paradigmatic shift which transports us towards an age where creativity, imagination and collaborative design take over the economic and cultural scene. These concepts take precedence over analysis, critical thinking, doubt and general cynicism of the last two or three decades. This deep innovation movement in our "massively collaborative" societies is what we call "design society". It becomes the first employment and economic value creator in the so-called fourth industrial revolution. The imagination supported by telepresence tools and intervention methodologies and sociocultural innovation replace the information reducer paradigm and its treatment. It is completed with knowledge and critical thinking concepts, without, however, allowing to be imprisoned by it. Questioning and giving criticism are, of course, healthy activities when we want a clearer picture of a socio-economic process and we wish to re-establish confidence in democracy. Furthermore, cynicism is sometimes used for protecting oneself against issues that exceed our comprehension. They are to social change what immobilism is to a train with a defective engine. Those positions or attitudes have a function of supporting change, just like the train's innate function to move forwards. But in reality, they simply do not have the capacity to ensure that function anymore. The CAPACITÉS evaluation model (page 132, Chap. 5) refers to the operational and digital skills in communication and information technologies that enable generic design and social design with ubiquitous media (*everyware*) for user's generated content and needs assesment in the context of "socially responsible communication design". These concepts refer to a brand new situation of social interaction and communication between humans. All citizens, massively and at a large scale,

have the operational capacity to contribute to the organizations' design development, virtual social systems and various services and applications that help to
update them in a ubiquitous and decentralized manner. The "ubiquitous media" key
concept translates the current progression of immersive and collaborative environments of creative cyberspace and innovation meta-universes that have the potential
to increase and spread the imagination culture usually reserved for intellectuals,
software engineers, artists, screenplays and creatives, by shifting it towards a sociocultural group of users/designers whose global movement is only beginning.
Contrary to analytical and rational culture at the age of information, the ubiquitous
imagination era will establish creativity as a priority foundation for culture and
economy. Will each one of us become a designer or innovator? Maybe not. But we
would be mistaken to underestimate this trend.

In a few years, we will witness massive innovation and collective creation
phenomenon never been seen in history. Young generations will progressively
become active participants in the ubiquitous imagination era. They become ambas-
sadors of the Canadian and Quebec culture by introducing ideas, customs, traditions, rituals and beliefs to the "global scientific conversation". In the past, these
were reserved to micro-environment experts or mass media members. Ubiquitous
current users, the ubimedia, can contribute to build, share and convey contents subject to collaborate in the construction of a brand new humanism in the cyberspace.
They can contribute to cultural identity development ("indentics") while validating
a reciprocal interdependency with other cultures' wealth. The cultural transformation and economic development supported by technologies are complex evolutive
and creative processes ("imaginatics") we cannot entirely allow to develop according to laws of fate, current contingencies or external factors. In the absence of a
good ethical comprehension of the sustainable development mechanism as well as
the influence technology has on identity, collaboration between foreign cultures and
the resolution of natural disasters or insecurity, we condemn ourselves to experience
even more uncertainty, better yet serious conflicts. The "ubiquitous imagination in
the design society" aims to combine one of the greatest human beings' cognitive
functions: the imagination, with organized complexity theories thanks to ubimedia
at the service of human development. But the appropriation of ubimedia without the
will of orientation by users' conscious design is also a bearer of threats. Here is a
huge social science and communication science research program that will have to
increase their insertions in the international movement of sustainable development
over the next few years.

Therefore, ubiquitous imagination characterizes a design society whose culture
is the "imaginatics", such as omnipresent socio-economic innovation, continuous,
open and in real time, supported by collaborative Web design tools. This culture
is made possible by the ubimedia we should better define towards a more
human-friendly world. The idea reflected is, as any agrarian society has produced
some types of culture and artistic forms and the industrial society has seen the rise
of political organizations (democracy, fascism, militarism, communism) with their
own media (radio, television, records, newspapers, books), the design society

creates new social forms, more specifically, virtual organizations and virtual social systems supported in their development by socio-collaborative ubimedia (artificial intelligence, Internet of Things, cyber-physical systems, modeling and social simulation tools). For better or for worse, these new media forms create new organizations and institutions we should count on for our future prosperity. Strictly speaking, they are not coming soon, but they are currently multiplying all over the world.

This design society brings about the creation of a "design for all and by all" circular economy, which requires new ICT skills. But there is more, an advanced digital knowledge society will help an innovation economy emerge, which becomes more intangible, more abstract, requiring new civic and professional skills for sustainable development. It is more or less a crisis recovery strategy when our economies allowed outsourcing and offshoring of the logical and rational thinking of the industrial era towards emerging economies. Our economies go from industrial and informational jobs to an imagination economy. All publication employment are declining, while architecture, software creation, computer consulting, production strategies, cinema and mostly video game sectors are in exponential growth. The ACIL team sees this digital advanced knowledge as a hierarchy made of at least three levels:

1. The appropriation of basic tools (e-mails, social media use)
2. Production and organization of audio-scripto-visual contents targeting various audiences and markets with a micro-, méso- and macrosocial added value
3. The informatics design and adapted collaborative tool configuration, configured and personalized to groups and communities in a relocated manner

This individual and collective skills hierarchy is highlighted in our researches and in this study carried out as part of the APSI program. It illustrates the fact that digital skills represent the first crucial resource in our economies, a resource starting from basic skills in the value creation to high-level skills necessary to intuitive, emotional and sensory intelligence as well as ubiquitous imagination's collective digital skills that become vital to the communication society. The intervention hypothesis is that each upper tier provides an excess of value creation at a lower level and the result of globalization and design skills generativity makes it more available to a large group of knowledge workers who, in return, create even more value. Currently, these skills are developing everywhere in the world in all kinds of collaborative communities, in small cultural creative groups as well as large engineer groups established in collaborative networks as well as the association and the municipal sectors. All these design activities revolve around the imagination of new technical solutions, the user's experience, collaborative experience and the imagination of sustainable digital social systems supported by a more responsible communication design. According to our group, the understanding of global issues our country and our planet face creates the need to intervene in a more appropriate way. The re-election of President Obama largely demonstrates this concern. This challenge we face goes through reinforced social science integration, communication sciences, complexity sciences, computer sciences and community information systems.

Tribal Imagination of a New Global Scientific Narrative

What can we learn from one of the oldest cultures in the world about design for all and knowledge sharing put at the service of more sustainable social systems?

During my last sabbatical year, I had the privilege of travelling to Australia. The scholars there believe the first inhabitants of Australia came 50,000 or 80,000 years ago. Some even believe they never actually came but have inhabited the continent without interruption for 130,000 years. Therefore, the indigenous Australians' culture probably represents the oldest surviving culture on the planet. When we think about the British who arrived on the continent in 1788, the imagination is impacted by the surviving force of these communities, who despite their weak technical means have put in place a great survival and sustainable governance model. This assessment prompts us to get inspired by the best practices and lessons the Australian Aboriginals' experience can provide to the current sustainable development discussion.

I was immediately intrigued by the Aboriginal culture's image of longevity during my first stay in Australia in 2006 with my UQAM colleague Albert Lejeune. While on a mission to participate in an international conference on health knowledge management, I met Professor Karl Erik Sveiby and Mrs. Dorothy Leonard Barton, respectively, knowledge management and empathic design specialists. Both were main speakers for the Australian government and its national health and medical research council. Professor Sveiby's conference, in particular, drew my attention since it was announcing the writing of a future book about how the traditional Aboriginal tales and their artistic practices were used to relay knowledge from one generation to the other, whether it was about the environment, laws, human relationships or even interconnectivity between communities. He stated the important role of stories and community tales on four levels:

1. Stories told to children about the natural world and animal behavior
2. Relationships, knowledge sharing and the distribution of roles between peoples and within the community
3. Relationships between the community and the larger environment; the importance of nomadism to preserve the resources
4. Psychic skills, practice and experience that explained how the hidden art of "tales and life lessons" were used in knowledge sharing, thus building the learning basis of a sustainable society

I was deeply interested by these words, but the book was not yet available at the time, so I forgot the upcoming publication announced by the speaker. It is only recently, while I was staying in Australia during the winter of 2012, that I was able to get my hands on the famous book in a bookstore in Sydney. Sveiby's book, published in 2006 in collaboration with Tex Skuthorpe (a painter, educator and tales specialist), tells how the Nhunggabarra Aboriginal people and their culture were able to implement mechanisms that made this civilization one of the strongest cultures and the most sustainable of our era in the full sense of what we call a knowledge economy today.

The main thesis of the book is based on the fact that while several societies outside of Australia have emerged, prospered and died, the Australian Aboriginal communities have resisted and proven their sustainability over tens of millennium, through very dramatic events like the arrival of the British only 225 years ago. According to Sveiby, the Australian Aboriginal communities' sustainable development model is the one of the earliest whose trace we found on Earth.

This model conveyed by dialogue, conversations and intergenerational tales is at the origin of the Ubiquitous Imagination Paradigm. The vision of a sustainable society shared by these communities, their capacity to imagine a long-term future, their innovation capacity and their responsible use of resources and the balance of their development convinced us of the creative power of life stories and the citizen dialogue in the organizations and future sustainable communities' collective imagination. Through the power of language, dialogue and communication, we are able to convey phenomena and the most intangible as well as the most practical processes that increase our understanding of the future while helping to guide it. This attitude is related to the power of tales, to imagine and inspire more responsible New Worlds. It is through vision exchange and dialogue that young generations learn hope and the desire to imagine our societies "differently".

During this captivating trip, I had the great pleasure of spending several days with my partner, Véronique Larcher, in the beautiful little town of Alice Springs, built in the heart of the Australian continent. There, far away from the hustle and bustle of Melbourne and Adelaide, the fascinating vastness of the desert and the reading of the book led me to these two questions: Why build all these socio-technical systems, virtual communities and these social media platforms? How can we guide the ICT research towards sustainable imaginative development?

In order to answer the first one, we need to recognize the essential role of communication, not only at certain human affair levels but for the culture and environment as a whole. Scientists, experts, governments, companies and the civil society must validate the more sustainable New Worlds' current power of imagination thanks to a better control of socio-technical cognitive phenomena on a large scale supported by digital platforms.

One of the first commentators on the matter, Fritjof Capra, uses the expression "the invisible connections" in his 2002 book (the title of his book) translating this proactive attitude by showing the links between phenomena, as disparate as environmentalism demonstrations, problematic biodiversity technologies introduction, social movements for green energies, university research in biotechnology and human development partnerships. Media and social media should be, first and foremost, communication and conversation devices putting into play symbolic languages, cultural dialogs, power relations and global consensus building regarding social responsibility and digital environment design at the service of complex co-design of a sustainable society. The often invisible dimension of sense and meaning emerging from these synthesis tools shows they are only supports for a "computer publicized global conversation". It illustrates the mobilizing power and real learning capacities of these new ubimedia tools we can try to use for all human beings' survival. Consequently, it invites us to better ethically guide the development at all tiers of our society.

The second question refers to the "how": where should we start our interventions and how? At the beginning of humanity and the basis of our modern societies, people made sense of their world through the tales they were sharing. The tale is the basis of all sciences as a discourse on reality. The Australian Nhunggabarra people is only an example of oral tradition that has developed the practice of the tale, but we find several others all through discursive practices within the native people of Quebec, Canada or elsewhere. Over time, these tales and life stories have become more complex, and some even gave birth to sciences, organizations and institutions that are very complex in their organization and knowledge legitimization, such as universities. They taught us that man is not outside of nature, but part of it and the universe. The separation of the observer and the science object is based on restrictive and reductive imaginative concepts applied to living system complexity such as the first phase of science was practicing it (Bausch and Flanagan 2013). In the second phase, we learned to ask better questions and to build better objects. If the first phase of science was locating the object outside of man, the second one tried to negotiate in a more flexible manner with subjectivity and cognition of the researcher in the observation of phenomena. While trying to reduce reality to an external object, the second phase tried to locate its observation in a wider context, less restrictive. However, it had to go further. Our society promotes the co-building of a third phase of science, a "citizen science", emerging from the integration of multiple points of view, transdisciplinary research partnerships and intersectorial commitment in new knowledge production process.

In this book, we introduce you to a new scientific field based on the third phase of science, inspired by the discovery of the tale as a world apprehension mode, as a learning method and collective design where various dialogue worlds suggest a vision that re-establishes the role of humans in the world, nature and technology: the community informatics design science. We consider this applied science as a means of understanding and adapting complex social situations of our time while freeing ourselves from reductive scientific silos of the two first phases of science. We will come back to it in various chapters of the book. Rising collaborative communities of the social Web are the actor of this third phase of science, where the object is observed according to a confrontation/tension/balance dialectical between realistic, subjective and individual points of view on one hand, collective and interactionist on the other. We observe in these new plural and communication contexts the explosion of various language modes and "scientific tales", where the reciprocal interdependence of millions of users/designers allows to share transdisciplinary, transcultural and paraprofessional perspectives around global interest issues. However, we would be wrong to believe this new science that includes observers' communities would only be founded in tales, common sense, legends and myths, even a lack of rigor, where the absence of formalism or systematization would be the norm. Quite the contrary. The global scientific discussion, thanks to the Internet's socio-technologies, calls out all social groups. This is why we approach new collaboration situations allowed by technology to better build our research objects, to document issues by multiple angles of observation and to deepen our examination of mechanisms often difficult to understand because of large-scale social change, as well as the acceleration of innovation through a new reflection of socio-scientific dialogue and global action representing the priority role of the community informatics design field: accompany cultural and citizen validation of intentional social change according to sustainable development values.

However, despite its activities' systemization effort, the ubiquitous imagination supported by informatics design is not conceived as a new triumph of reason over myths and tales of the planet's first communities. It rather suggests to get inspired by it metaphorically as a new mode of scientific evolution, supported by a humbler vision of the world, while inviting us to capture this precious moment in recent history where we all experience for the first time the potential of ubiquitous imagination in the design of solutions better suited to global issues. The Western philosophical and scientific tradition seems to rediscover this force inspired by the First Nations indigenous people, the sitting of a tribe around the fire, forming an effervescent circle where imagination catalyses itself by the tale, the fire of creative spirits inspiring multiple solutions from various dialogues. It is strange that our societies have only recently discovered this form of powerful ancestral wisdom, animated by our desire to observe the world, to better understand it in order to solve large-scale socio-technical problems together and to better confine large dimensions related to the challenges that distinguish our time. In this preserved tradition of tribal social system practices, could we find a new social and scientific communication situation and a new paradigm for the study of complex digital social system development? Away from social media excesses rightly highlighted and condemned by the local and international press, would this new collaborative culture make us think about a new humanist and global scientific discussion based on the collective and ubiquitous imaginations of our future?

Montréal, Saint-Henri-de-Taillon, Alice Springs
2012–2013, 2016–2017

Pierre-Léonard Harvey

Acknowledgements

I would like to thank the Secretariat Treasury Board of Quebec and their APSI fund for supporting my research from 2011 to 2014 and the University of Quebec in Montréal and in particular my colleagues at the Communication Faculty, my academic home for nearly three decades, for giving me the required university freedom for intellectual exploration and transdisciplinary imagination. Thank you to my colleagues at the Hexagram Institute, an international network dedicated to research creation in arts and technology, for encouraging the birth of a social science and communication design thinking perspective.

I am deeply grateful to Marie-Kettlie André for the numerous meticulous proofreadings of the book and chapters' revision, not to mention the long hours of discussing concepts and the work's general organization over the years. I thank her as well as Hassane Beidou for their collaboration on two chapters. The creation of a reference book in any new scientific field requires efforts related to several types of collaboration. And so, my gratitude extends to UQAM's Applied Community Informatics Lab (ACIL) team of students and collaborators, in particular my colleague Gilles Lemire, my research partner for over 15 years now, and Guy Gendron, a communication PhD student, a great techno-pedagogic teacher and one of the best social counsellors in Quebec, especially with Atikamekw communities from Wémotaci, for his unfailing support regarding my work since 2005. Thanks to Geoffroi Garon Epaule, one of our Ph.D student in the Doctoral Communication Program at UQAM, anthropologist and Community Informatics Design specialist, for helping me in the creation and revision of many of the book's figures and for his ongoing support for many years in our classes and conferences; and also, to Michel Brière and his CCA team, in particular his colleagues Guylaine Lavoie (project manager) and Jean-François Roussy (multimedia creator). Thanks also to Abderrahman Ourahou, for his computer expertise, and Marina, for her work in visualization and her evaluation chart of the information visualization tools. Thank you to all the collaborators from UQAM's Service de l'audio visuel (SAV), in particular Louis Guérette, Nathalie Lavoie and Anne-Marie Sauriol for creating our websites related to this book. Thanks to Samuelle Ducrocq-Henri, for her doctoral work regarding the application of video games scenarios to serious learning, and to

Pierre Bérubé, who opened several perspectives on communication approaches applied in a crisis and chaos context. Thank you to my partners Lionel and Pascal Audant, Yves Lusignan, Gilles Guay, Éric Grimard and Alexandre Gravel and to Monique Chartrand and her organization's team at *Communautique*.

My acknowledgements also to all my colleagues who participated in our research works in different ways through various forms of dialogue: more specifically Louis-Claude Paquin, Carmen Rico de Sotelo, Mireille Tremblay, and her doctoral student Nadine Martin, Isabelle Mahy, Jean-Marie Lafortune, Gaby Hsab, Christian Agbobli and Michèle Isis Brouillet. Thanks to Martin Lussier, for his reflections and collaboration on cultural intervention strategies; to Albert Lejeune from UQAM's *Management et technologie* Department, for recommending us books on organizational modeling and enterprise architectures; to Marc Trestini, for welcoming us in Strasbourg, and Professor Jean-Paul Pinte from Lille, for participating in our seminar on socio-technical design in Sherbrooke in 2011; to Pierre-Michel Riccio and Jean-Michel Penalva for welcoming us at the Mines d'Alès School in 2006 and for allowing us to publish one of the first articles on community informatics design in France; and to Dotty Ager Gupta, Kjell Erik Rudestam and Judith Schoenholtz-Read from the Fielding Institute in California for allowing a larger diffusion of our work on community informatics design published in English by Sage and allowing to develop basic concepts of this book.

My acknowledgements also to Robert Proulx, rector of UQAM, Magda Fusaro and Marcel Simoneau who, with several colleagues from UQAM's *Comité Institutionnel sur les Environnements Numériques d'apprentissage (CIENA)*, contributed to the book's several reflection elements especially regarding the application of socio-technical higher education platforms like Moodle. My gratitude to Professor Jurgen E. Mueller from the University of Bayreuth in Germany with whom we have developed a master's class and a partnership on community informatics design research in their Media Management Department. Thank you to the successive deans from the Communication Faculty, Marquita Riel, Enrico Carontini and Pierre Mongeau, for supporting our work and for granting us an important physical space for our research. My gratitude to colleagues like Serge Proulx and Florence Millerand who placed their trust in me by allowing me to evaluate several master's and doctoral papers in information technology and communication. In the same spirit, thanks to my doctoral colleagues from *Informatique Cognitive* and *Téléuniversité*, who allowed me to sit on several evaluation committees, and also to Anne-Marie Field for trusting us and for accompanying us in our future informatics design research.

Several curious and critical generations of graduate students have raised interesting questions and drawn my attention to relevant publications. A large number of social media readers spread over the Internet have asked questions, provided information and offered criticism. Finally, a good number of universities and scholarly organizations in half a dozen countries gave me the opportunity to speak and share my thoughts, our hopes and our fears with prestigious researchers and bright students from various fields. More recently, we would like to thank the colleagues at the MIT Media Lab and their European colleagues from the FuturICT project, especially Dirk Helbing in Zurich and Markus Eisenhauer in Bonn, for welcoming us within workshops and partner discussions about the idea of an international collaborative platform in digital humanities and social computational science.

Last but not least, I would like to especially thank my colleague Ms. Danielle Maisonneuve to have welcome us in her collection called "Communication" at the *Presses de l'Université du Québec, for the first edition of the book in French in 2014*. Thank you to all the PUQS team, Ms. Céline Mercier, Director General; Ms. Nadine Elsliger, Publishing Director; and their computer graphics and editing team. I would also like to thank my new international editor, Springer Nature, especially Christopher Coughlin, Senior Editor, Fan Ho Ying, Assistant Editor, Jeffrey Taub Project Coordinator/Book Production, and Aishwarya, Chandramouleeswaran, Project Manager SPi Content Solutions – SPi Global. Thank you for trusting us in editing a transdisciplinary reference book in the new "Translational Science" collection. We really hope and wish that this book, will help our future generations of students and young researchers in designing a sustainable world. Last but not least, all my gratitude goes to Virginie Bucco for the translation of this book during the last year. I have appreciated her discipline and great professionalism.

Pierre-Léonard Harvey

Contents

List of Figures

List of Tables

Chapter 1
Global Transformation and Design Principles in the Knowledge Society

We live in a communication and information society that has become a global and evolutive force in our everyday lives.

But the promises of significant benefits of this transformation, for too long qualified as a revolution by technology experts, will not get created without a global planning and a generic design of information and communication systems effort. These have become an integral and emergent part of the participative users'/designers' culture. In sociocultural terms, information and communication systems must be put at the service of people and communities. They must be reliable, user-friendly, intuitively significant and available everywhere at all time. In this important phase of the information age, the "design for all" becomes essential.

In this context, this book represents a development effort of foundations and the reference framework of a collaborative design form that is more and more practiced by various users' communities in Quebec: community informatics design. It relies on the report of a research conducted by the UQAM's Applied Community Informatics Lab and offers some answers to the Secrétariat du Conseil du Trésor du Québec program called *Appui au passage à la société de l'information* (APSI), regarding ubimedia appropriation levels and collaborative tools by various communities spread all over our vast territory. Between 2010 and 2012, our lab's team of professors and students asked the following questions while formulating three general hypotheses. The "community informatics design and My Cola@b portal" project's main objective was to lead case studies, write questionnaires to evaluate design practices and discover interactional and organizational trends for the following purpose:

1. Explore infrastructures, platforms or portals, which have existed for several years, within various organizations to identify the structure and process.
2. Help with the design and production of a multiplatform portal model adjustable to the needs of various organizations from the projects' several life cycles' analysis. We have combined knowledge from numerous projects and multiple

© Springer International Publishing AG 2017
P.-L. Harvey, *Community Informatics Design Applied to Digital Social Systems*,
Translational Systems Sciences 12, DOI 10.1007/978-3-319-65373-0_1

studies to present a high-level reference framework that inspires other researches and practices in the field of modeling virtual networking organizations (hypothesis 1).
3. Experiment an "organizational information systems design" (or community informatics design) aiming to lead virtual communities while encouraging trans-disciplinary studies involving computer specialists, communication experts, sociologists and artists.

We have developed a reference framework, an instantiation strategy and a fundamental verification list necessary to the technological, communication and organizational modeling functionalities, to ensure that future organizations and digital social systems would be off to a good start (hypothesis 2).

Virtual organizations are co-built as social and technological systems (a socio-technical system.) They *simultaneously* include:

1. Human factors (people or subjects)
2. Worlds of knowledge to share (contents)
3. Socio-collaborative platforms adjustable to each organization's needs (tools or cloud and ubiquitous computing instruments.)

On an epistemological scale, the APSI research will contribute to define the "community informatics design" scientific bases which is organization and virtual communities' design as socio-technical environments supported by ubiquitous media: the ubimedia (Greenfield 2007.) These environments are received as new socio-economic ecosystems (hypothesis 3). The community informatics design and My Col@b Portal research project lead several case studies, here and internationally, in order to transform experiences with Internet and information and communication technologies (ICT) in a typical case. These activities were executed by organizations (ACIL, CCP, CA, among others) and more particularly by enterprises and people. These research approaches should shed an epistemological light upon imposed transformations by recent Internet evolution. They touch its instrumentation, its forms of communication and community informatics organization, as well as the planning of social networks made of people, organizations or communities of all kinds. It represents many systems that become more complex and specialized in the multiple relations to tools and contents in the digital world.

In the past decades, social computer science's main objective was to make people work in virtual spaces and allow them to achieve a better productivity with tools that were encouraging information digital uses, such as texts, images, sounds and videos. The recent social, ubiquitous and user-friendly computer science emergence, like new Web 2.0 media (LinkedIn, MySpace, YouTube, Flickr, Facebook), collaborative platforms (Ning, Google Group, Vox, Apprendre 2.0) and collective design platforms (CIEL Project, Laboranova, Service design from Roberta Tassi, Habitats from Wenger and Smith), allows the world of citizen Internet to enter in a new creative phase of socio-technical systems development (Whitworth and De Moor 2009; De Moor 2005; Barab and Kling 2004; Barab et al. 2004). And the module or platform configurations in diversified environments, often mobile, are required: My Col@b Portal research project will contribute to the design, script writing and the production of customized portals by prototyping a virtual social systems community informatics' assistance portal. This implies that users – organizations and people – to various degrees and different tiers of society, by positioned uses and by current ubiquitous social media, will develop new needs for autonomy and participation in the information and communication society.

In order to do so, our ACIL team had to develop a new support methodology for the development of communities' users that became necessary through the desire to make the general process and the life cycle more systematic. My Col@b Portal research project aims to erase doubts related to the evolution of the Web's uses, considering the information flow, relations to the worlds of knowledge and more participative usage of tools put forwards by socio-technical systems operations and generalized ubimedia appropriation. The verification and evaluation of past and current uses (case studies) as well as the observation of new uses (questionnaires) related to My Col@b Portal script writing and production (discovery matrix), personalized and operated by this research-associated partners, brought us elements disconfirming or confirming our hypothesis and building our models.

1.1   The Sociohistorical Context

Large-scale environmental concerns, natural and meteorological disasters, the current financial crisis, the wars all over the world, the social divide intensifying within democracies, the accelerated growth in Asian countries' population, the continuous reforms in national health and education systems and the epidemic progression of cybercrimes and cyberattacks prove that humanity is facing unprecedented challenges. These changes touch everyone's everyday life, each family, each community and each country and define the human being's future.

However, we are entering the second decade of the third millennium with organizations designed for the most part in the nineteenth century. The improvement or restructuring of existing systems founded in the industrial age of the machine does not work anymore. The population realizes that the massive society changes and current global transformations are reflected in the new realities of post-industrial age, of the knowledge and information economy society. Only an ubiquitous imagination and a massive innovation effort will allow us to face requirements of our era's new realities and aspirations and contain the generalized risks of youth's disillusionment and massive cynicism.

Some questions arise: What role each citizen plays in those massive changes? Is he without a voice or means? How can he switch from one social innovation vision centred on closed local innovations' structure to a new vision oriented towards the new interaction ICT systems that would allow us to understand complex social systems we created in cyberspace and the emerging collective phenomena typical to their evolution? How can we switch from a geocentric vision of the world to a heliocentric one allowing us to grasp the world of economics and the society transformations? How can we grasp the socio-dynamic of the digital culture and the transitions between various change paradigms? How can we orientate our future by developing a science, technology and society approach that aims to ensure the distributed governance of these complex worlds and analyse new human organizations in global interconnectivity?

With the present book, we would like to answer these questions. The "My Col@b Portal community informatics design" project, in development, will combine the power of creative and information technology and communication tools with the knowledge of the complexity sciences, social systems and social science theory as well as computer science. We will show that a research attitude too exclusively founded on the critics of the "community informatics design" existing systems, a research orientation combining critical analysis strengths and the conception/simulation of multiple aspects of evolutive phenomena, will make social sciences leap forwards towards the new era of complex information systems' design. Complexity and emerging digital social systems sciences will shed new light on phenomena like virtual communities and innovation communities, as well as a multitude of networked organizations, virtual enterprises and interactive social structures where the knowledge that will influence our future is produced at a speed never seen before in history.

In that context, we will explore the emerging needs of online social systems, digital skills necessary to their development, possible means to create collective and collaborative intelligence to contribute to the advent of a better future for our children and for ourselves and our emerging new social needs for digital social systems and for our growing innovation communities. The present research's basic idea is that community informatics design – as large-scale communication and collaborative digital social systems methodology, like virtual communities building that we can perceive as socio-technical systems design – is a human creation activity of the future. These digital social systems and virtual communities and individual and group partners commit to the design in a way of distributing tasks and roles in the implementation of corresponding innovation systems that catalyse desirable changes. Or even they can improve and restructure existing systems according to what they believe to be a more favourable system that matches their collective values. Complexity sciences will shed substantial light on emerging phenomena like interactive social media. Social sciences and more particularly social and public communication sciences will improve our understanding of perspectives and risks related to strongly interconnected social systems, especially the Internet community information systems. We will see that those analyses will create new theoretical approaches, new methods and new tools allowing to apprehend the twenty-first-century transformations. Furthermore, they will create communication society's new employment.

Thus, building on the needs of the skill and practice study we have achieved on the Quebec territory, we analyse what we call the community informatics design "8C". They represent the main concepts of our APSI research: cognition, communication, conversation, cooperation, collaboration, coordination, skills (*competences*) and contracts. In an era where speed, intensity and complexity of change increase constantly and exponentially, the ability of human communities to mould this change instead of being the spectators or victims depends more and more on digital analysis, synthesis, production and network knowledge sharing skills. A generic design skill, multi-skills and a great motivation to guide our digital social systems intentional evolution will become one of the Western nations' education priorities in a few years, to all tiers of society organization.

The digital social systems co-design program and similar endeavours could become in the short term certain of the most important scientific programs of our time just like artificial intelligence and operational research were for pure sciences in their time. Why? Simply because this program will reveal the structures, processes, values, skills and ethical principles that will allow interactive and networked social systems to be oriented by the citizens. By inspiring the appropriation and the social creation of new innovation tools that enable the exploration of "invisible connections" (Capra 1997, 2004), we will be able to collectively anticipate and influence our future. And by establishing an age of "socially responsible communication design" through many kinds of innovation portals we will mobilize the collective intelligence of many actors to create new collaborative networking organizations and institutions. The program will build the knowledge base necessary to its support: the philosophy, the theories, the methodologies and the applications and the online social systems design instrumentation.

Thus, we note five major interdependent transformations:

- *The Explosion of Digital Communication*: This phenomenon becomes the new central field of information and communication theories; its validation effects on society and organizations are still little known. It promotes human activities by inviting us to configure ourselves and our artefacts with new small digital tools that form the basis of the community informatics design in a ubiquitous imagination society.
- *Mobile and Ubimedia Network Generalization*: We are headed towards what Marc Weiser, researcher at the famous Xerox PARC laboratory, predicted over 20 years ago – computer science without computers, where knowledge sharing extends to the opposites through minuscule devices interconnected with everyday life elements. The word "ubiquitous" does not only mean "everywhere" but also "in everything". A more and more invisible computing but omnipresent is emerging and gives us the tools of autonomy in the creation. It comes with the birth of a movement of designers and developers who produce their own functional modules likely adaptable to other devices or existing platforms.
- *The Appropriation and the Acquisition of Design Skills by Network Practices*: This appropriation becomes a priority in regard to simple access to technology. Even if the access to technologies and new media issue has been a social priority for 20 years, it is shifting towards design activities making them possible. We have to promote a new digital literacy to all tiers of the education system. Just like people love to tend their own garden themselves despite the existence of large produce markets, they like to configure their own creativity and design tools from existing platforms. Programming becomes the users'/designers' new first role, which encourages their organization autonomy in facing greater threats of state surveillance, cybercriminals and spies, social control and the everyday life gadgets from superficial applications. These new society self-organization

possibilities by design redefine citizenship, democratic institution participation, innovation ecosystems and work methods.

- *The "Design for All" Generalizations*: Design is more and more distributed; therefore, in Quebec, in Canada and across the world, it becomes a common practice that is trivial to society as a whole, more a way of life than a separate profession reserved to the creative elite. In fact, this affirmation goes much further: design cannot be left to designers alone. Here is a new face of the citizen's principal liberties. The designer becomes a virtual ethic and democratic environment programmer, and "to program or being programmed" (Ray Kurzweil), in a society of communication opulence (Moles 1967, 1990; Moles and Jacobus 1988; Moles and Rohmer 1986, 1998), becomes the new modus operandi of the enlightened citizen and competitive economies.

- *The End of Technology-Centred Design:* While being aware of its glory, this form of design is, in a certain way, near its decline. Indeed, the community information systems co-construction needs a wider reference framework that concedes a part of the national innovation technological platform to human, social, cultural and economic dimensions. We currently all participate, through networking design practices and activities, in a wide communication turn ("dialogual", semantics and semiotics) in design, which, as a priority, becomes centred not only on the individual user but simply on the human. Moreover, alongside this major colossal challenge, we witness the international emergence of new partners for innovation that demand new scientific, methodological and applicative approaches. This open science, more collaborative and largely supported by "conversational" ICT, tries to unify aspects of computer sciences and complexity sciences. Above all, it invites social and communication sciences to make a qualitative leap towards a better online theorization/modeling of digital social systems, made to serve great issues related to the needs for innovation of our time. It calls for a motivating vision of the future and new development principles as well as training programs to face the challenge.

1.2   The New Design Principles Emerging from Our Works

One of the largest orientations that guided our research, for nearly 5 years now, was to explore the principles that will rule the design of virtual environments dedicated to innovation in the future. We have, however, explored other avenues in order to give our works another scale that will have positive impact on collaborative design over the next 30 years. Our group appointed itself to evaluate the elaboration means of necessary governance mechanisms to support Quebec's national efforts towards a global digital platform construction to serve the economy. Our report is supported by discussion groups, case studies and an evaluation questionnaire on design practices of various Quebec innovation communities and enterprises. It recognizes a radical change in practices that go from an industrial mode of production of knowledge reserved for experts to a ubiquitous imagination and collaborative intelligence context. Their tools and applications are not, strictly speaking, support tools nor mirror sites of existing organizations. New practices go much further. Our research results indicate that we are co-building, with the help of virtual environment tools, brand new intelligent organizations from social and informational architectures that question the basic knowledge we should pass on to the youth and to all citizens in a design for all society. The design society users/designers need to better understand the complex process of social and public communication and to think about the principles and values associated with the development of community information systems, ubimedia and devices likely to improve our quality of life. The ten design principles emerging from our works first apply to:

- To future users/designers of the civil society, who need more training suitable to the knowledge society.
- To the practitioner designers who have the intention of partnering with important works on digital social systems and the development of communication and collaborative artefacts, co-design will become a priority in the next decade.
- To educators and trainers issued from social and communication sciences who want to better prepare students facing new professional practices that require new higher-level digital skills.
- To enterprises looking for qualified workers in generic tools, applications and services as well as governance and performance indicators of superior quality.
- Finally, to financing institutions and to government foundations supporting scientific research, the education system and its training initiative as well as the support platforms' development towards an information society. They should include these principles in their actions and encourage their adoption in order to contribute, even modestly, to improve insertion of all in this constant sociotechnical revolution.

Here are the ten principles, which are research-intervention hypothesis, we support throughout this book:

First Principle We recommend that the construction of artefacts and collaborative platforms supported by ubimedia makes more sense for the users. This sense resides in the way the stakeholders are partnered with a project and invest their values and skills to improve living conditions. In terms of operational practices, the sense and understanding require the designer to be more attentive to the social and communication foundations of their practices and to intervention parameters related to ideologies, beliefs, ontology, epistemology, theories, methodologies and applications.

Second Principle We recommend that the design focuses on the development of collaboration interfaces and actions between humans and technologies. The current ubimedia tools became unthinkable, considering the acceleration of their production and obsolescence. Without a design oriented towards interfaces that translate more the various human worlds, we run the risk of getting trapped by a causal, linear computing, instrumentalizing human activities' universes in an algorithmic way. This aspect of "ethical" computing, with its human and social factors, has been considered as a "secondary employment" of specialists. The progression of the social Internet now makes it a priority; no modern society can keep its population away from technological orientation and its various manifestations. A new communication and networking empirical domain arises that we call *community informatics design*.

Third Principle We recommend that the diverse types of socio-technical design extend their object and traditional preoccupations for the auditive, the visual and the textual to all senses, to the entire body, in different spaces (physical, virtual) like any important elements evacuated by numerous contemporary communication approaches. Furthermore, in addition to an object-oriented approach in the design of information systems, we recommend and greatly document a brand new approach oriented towards aspects (dimensions) that suggest a much more holistic intentional social change, oriented towards change. Taking into account the multi-sensoriality and the multiple aspects related to information systems design could suggest the development of systems, products or improved applications such as digital social systems. The persons and communities with specific needs and workers who need a work ergonomics better adapted to their cultural and psychosocial characteristics could see their work interfaces improve.

Fourth Principle One essential achievement of innovation communities associated with the co-creation through open-source code interfaces was to ensure the variability adaptation to users' needs. We recommend the ubimedia artefacts and the collaborative tools to be designed in a variable way, adjustable and customizable. These tools will be "multi-aspectual" to support users without trespassing their skills, while respecting the capacities of the various stakeholders, their needs, their communication requirements, their world vision and their conception about the worlds to be built. Interfaces must be open and flexible; they must encourage fluidity and speed of knowledge appropriation while avoiding the information overload. We must be able to differentiate the products and the services, to reconfigure and personalize the interfaces, to instrument the more destitute ones, to implement several types of multimedia and ubimedia interfaces and to adapt new tools easily.

Fifth Principle We recommend, in our societies based on individualism, the conception of all design artefacts dedicated to the ubiquitous imagination of solutions and actions be supported by design tools. Also it should encourage collaboration and cultural diversity respect and it should help resolve social conflicts. Current social media created an explosion of a sort of cooperation between individuals: communication. But these communication activities are too simple to significantly support and validate certain types of collaboration activities necessary to the construction of organizations and digital social systems dedicated to innovation in all sorts of Internet communities. Our approach, just like numerous authors who write about innovation through economic development validation, insists on the development of creativity and imagination ability. We must be able to transcend the present state of systems to imagine better ones. Designers everywhere can act as social catalysts; knowledge appropriation organizers of a larger number of people can exploit the innovative power of ubimedia in their everyday life. In the long term, winning societies are not exclusively the ones that rationalize socio-economic processes but also the ones that optimize them while imagining new ones. The discovery does not come from the status quo nor the denial of favourable change either but from conceptual bifurcations that combine memory, rationalization, reflection and imagination.

Sixth Principle We recommend virtual organizations and digital social systems to be more than information systems or knowledge management. They have to be designed to include several points of view; they have to be integrated in a horizontal (bottom-up) manner and not exclusively hierarchical (top-down), according to the standardization model and the control concept of traditional computing management. Their design must include common languages and semantics we can combine with specialized languages proper to engineers and programmers. The natural language can serve as a base of collaborative design for the most part. It provides dialogue modes to a design thinking that suggests exploratory spaces and widens anticipated uses, and, above all, it is not limited to only one functionality. These modes promote activities of numerous virtual communities and are not limited to the closed circle of experts. In the knowledge society, the activity of collaborative artefact co-creation is not only similar to a language in the sense where different ubimedia tools are freely customizable, reconfigurable and reproducible. In the stronger sense of digital communication, design is the power to collectively generate new practices by natural langue use. Our approach aims to create a bridge between natural languages and expert languages, while lifting the barrier of codification and mathematics programming languages. We must be aware of the fact that a design mandate is given by the spoken and written language and that the stakeholders' roles are evaluated and negotiated by diverse dialogue modes. The instructions given to computer engineers are written that the projects are presented in the form of charts, diagrams, figures and text. The decision-making is elaborated with the help of scenarios and synthesis software encouraging deliberations, that needs are caught by tales and that the participants' requirements are evaluated from tales of exemplary practices, etc. Throughout the book we emphasize on the fact that the community must be able to use its own language to contribute to the projects' orientation and to ensure its values' respect, while following the evolution of various projects. Each design or scientific field specialty asked to contribute to an innovation project contains, of course, its "specialized jargon". However, even if these jargons are necessary, the various stakeholders must have access to their own speech and literature, assuming, of course, we are convinced of the necessity of their democratic participation in these innovation projects. The community informatics design semantics issue, as mainly communication design instead of exclusively centred on experts' languages, possesses its own discourse.

We recommend to researchers from different backgrounds, practitioners or designers, from pure sciences, human science or the artistic field, to recognize the mainly communication and linguistics nature of their effort so the projects are more debated in public and recognized worldwide and that they benefit from evaluative techniques understood by all. This is why we suggest (Harvey 2017 online) a first collaborative technologies and cyber-collaboration lexicon. The dialogue allowed by the list of these first terms thus becomes a citizen participation tool in the creation of platforms and artefacts. To this effect, our group suggests long methodological developments around discovery matrix and strategic alignment, various types of users can build together, in a convivial and rigorous way, to better understand the complexity of digital systems they suggest to build.

Seventh Principle Throughout the book, we put forwards the idea that design must be "centred on the human being" and achieved by networking innovation communities inside these communities and through them. This means design is formed according to a second-class systemic evolutive culture, namely, the understanding the designer has regarding the user's comprehension. In this spirit, designers from social sciences, pure sciences or different artistic disciplines should be concerned by the first instance and not by technology itself but by the way technologies are understood and utilized by various stakeholders. The understanding engineers from all backgrounds bring to the world is generally very different from the users. Community informatics designers must apprehend both at the same time, according to different design contexts. All design activity is a communication activity understood as a "contextualization" of human activities supported by technology, to paraphrase our colleague Mucchielli (2005, 2006). All the effort of the present book consists of clarifying and listing elements and components related to technology in terms of infrastructural characteristics, architecture and product/service/application functionalities of digital social systems. Furthermore, without having to be a communication and social sciences specialist, computer specialists and engineers must better understand the role of key concepts such as relations, reports, interaction, interactivity, socio-technologies, socio-communication factors, social architecture, socialization, collaboration, cooperation, coordination, etc. from the various scientific field standpoint. The research must mobilize all stakeholders and not only engineers, computer specialists or software creators. For example, in the next years to come, it will be more and more usual to see different types of engineers collaborating with different types of social scientists.

Eighth Principle Design and more specifically socio-technical designs – interactive, participative, empathic, emancipator, collaborative, semantics and community design – are a body of disciplines and methodological processes, a body of expertise that must constantly be expanded. This is why they suggest a collective duty of training young people, a distributed training made available to millions of users. It is the participative democratic philosophy that underlies the massive expansion movement on the Internet but also the need for new learning they generate. The word processing and electronic publication tools have made traditional graphic arts obsolete. Web design is often done by non-professionals who do not have a specific training. The computer fiddler succeeds better at certain website projects than designers that are trained in a school or university. The analysis of our online questionnaire results widely that Web design has become an increasingly universal human activity. Designers cannot stay, for a long time, far or in front of users, especially when we mention organizations or digital social systems. If we deeply want these design skills to serve improvement and prosperity for all, we will have to speak not only a language understood by all but also encourage the training of many regarding understanding and implantation of design processes dedicated to innovation. The community informatics design discipline and its foundations have a lot to offer to collaborative processes – pragmatic, epistemology, evolutive systems theories, plural analysis methodology, instantiation and co-creativity. It possesses a unique world vision and approach to our global issues related to our connected and interconnected societies. It suggests a way of validating individual autodidactic principle and self-organization of communities and users/designers. But to collectively benefit from these advantages of this major cultural movement, we have to encourage this process at all tiers of the education field. How?

Ninth Principle Design education must adopt a wider vision of design centred on the human being. Therefore, it must expand by leaving the design and engineering faculties to extend to all fields and professions most likely to benefit from it:

(a) The education ministries, government agencies and universities have to encourage the training of transdisciplinary research teams and community informatics design development to support the birth of new social and organization structures in all activities where they seem relevant to validation or change.

(b) Financing agencies like the *ministère de l'Enseignement supérieur, de la Recherche, de la Science et de la Technologie du Québec (MESRST)*, as well as the industry in the broader sense should play a more important role in the assignment of budgets according to socio-technical large-scale projects that centralize their efforts towards building organizations and digital social systems equipped with better technical and psychosocial qualities. These environments should experiment with partnerships, not only bipartite like the companies-universities but multipartite, like the ones we call the "five helix partnerships". They dynamically include the complementary complexity of at least five stakeholders: citizens, entrepreneurs, government agencies actors, universities and environment and sustainable development specialists.

(c) We must establish courses that prepare various professionals, including designers, to better understand the communication, cognitive, social, cultural and technological factors at different levels of society, global networking individuals as well as groups, communities and organizations in different space-time. Visualization, modeling and evaluation methodological tools should be taught as a priority in social and human sciences and become an integral element of all education programs, from primary school to university. This transdisciplinary challenge has very important implications for remote education everywhere on our territory: the dissemination of results, the access to remote publics, mentoring and supervising techniques, tutorials and online facilitation are particularly targeted sectors.

(d) At the end of their community informatics design projects, students should be encouraged to present their logbooks, reviews, reports, summaries and case studies that document their practice and suggest feedback. Eventually, these activities of reflexive practice, promising development gathering, collective tale writing, content editing and application design and imagining new solutions to large-scale issues could contribute to rekindle the desire for a well-structured thinking, well-written and well-tailored reports, a deep logic in the organization of ideas and the dissemination of better practices to the largest number of people possible.

(e) The dissemination and appropriation of ideas of collaborative informatics design could benefit greatly to national strategic design workshops at the disposal of economy and innovation. An annual international symposium on design validation effects in all economic activity sectors could be held in various cities in Quebec via telephone and video conferencing, according to the global and local development issues and contexts. The profile of future designers suggested by Ostrom and Hess (2011), Robbin (2011), Hofkirchner (2010), Fuchs (2008), Siemens (2005a, b), Kling (2002) and Schön (1992), to name only a few, could be widened and extended to sciences that have no real ties with the design field yet, from the principles that are emerging from our introduction.

Tenth Principle The APSI program should be accompanied by other subsidy programs and supported by a transdisciplinary research that, in addition to suggest products and infrastructure production programs, will also make this type of design a partner of all socio-economic innovation stakeholders, according to the collaborative culture philosophy of "community informatics design centred on the human being" and the structuring perspective of sustainable development.

Seven research orientations could contribute to rephrase the reference framework of socio-technical systems and activate the fields of knowledge that will guide Quebec towards the ongoing revolution. These seven fields call on the institutional commitment of several partners and include various operational action propositions. Here are the five most important:

(a) A support to preliminary research through the organization of various national strategic workshop
(b) The opening of strategic funds for exploratory research in order to stimulate the R-D applications and concrete propositions
(c) The creation of an implementation funds, to instantiate and deploy flourishing projects in the development of virtual organizations and digital social systems through community informatics design
(d) Workshops to evaluate projects and exemplary practices to create evaluation and validity tools and to compare the results obtained with the use of ubimedia and collaborative tools
(e) Establishment of new structured partners in multiple stakeholders' helix, in order to create new institutions like the Quebec digital platform and the democratic and participative knowledge platforms in numerous fields

When governments and industries decide to sponsor researches on the creation of new high school and university classes or research programs, they should specify the work must be executed by integrated teams in partnership with several disciplines. Each one should be relevant and able to face the numerous issues related to the development, planning, production, implementation and validation of ubimedia projects. This way, we would encourage a change in the paradigm of research project conduct. The traditional scientific paradigm emerged during the Enlightenment. It was engaging researchers in the idea of mechanism and analysis of past facts. Research meant "re-search", and it meant search the past, the already there, again and again, to find rules, laws and empirical constraints that would help us survive in the present while helping determine our future. In contrast, "the communication design thinking" suggested by the current community informatics design movement described in our works on "ubiquitous imagination" suggests a future vision while researching present orientations. This requirement would send a clear message to university researchers and encourage new approaches and the creation of new research structures in community informatics design. More specifically, our group recommends the systematic articulation and elaboration of a new research paradigm: the "imaginatics". This could lead to a generalized national effort towards the creation of a unifying reference framework based on the crossing roads between computer sciences, social and communication sciences and complexity sciences. This program would suggest methodological approaches and would give a logical and economic justifications to a research in community informatics design committed to action around ideas like research activities oriented towards the future and the creation of new artefacts helping the design of digital social systems (DSS) that would create new infrastructures based on this paradigm, especially in information and communication sciences.

Government agencies such as the *Secrétariat du Conseil du Trésor* or ministries like the MESRST, as well as the media, electronic and telecommunication industry, should play an important role by sponsoring major transdisciplinary projects to develop a second-order design science, a sort of science of the artificial, in the design sciences sense, as understood by Herbert Simon (1960, 1962, 1969, 1974, 1996). Half a century ago, he wrote that technology and information developments were beyond the horizon of all citizens. These design sciences must be extended by all sorts of means to a very wide socio-scientific whole, in a way to better understand the various uses of technology by diverse stakeholders, as well as users/designers and engineers from various fields, and the determination of what each one can bring to the ubimedia universe and collaborative platforms. Qualitatively, the research aiming for the comprehension of cultural and technological socio-dynamic put at the service of social and economic innovation is very different from the research on technology itself, as it is practiced in pure sciences.

Together, under the direction of its scientist in chief, the Quebec scientific community could put the shoulder to the wheel and establish a second-order and *third-phase design science*" (Bausch and Flanagan 2013) that could combine the following concepts: an imaginatics, in the sense of The Club of Rome, aiming to introduce a new thinking, supported by networking and ubimedia, that would consist of taking into account all patterns ubiquitous imagination rely on to design a new conceptual and pragmatic order of new organizational initiatives like the Quebec digital platform. Clearly said, the simplistic sequencing of integrator concepts in a dictionary, even Wikipedia, or even showcasing the values of the first and second phase science is not suitable to all research situations. Currently, sociohistorical conditions encourage the integration of creativity tools of collaborative ubimedia in this imaginatics and their interaction models and design put at the services of the *sharing economy*, which will meet an obvious need. This integration and its patterns resonate in a "polyphonic" way, much better adapted to the complex reality such as apprehended by new generations of researchers. We observe everywhere the enthusiasm the social Web, collaborative technologies and the future ubimedia provoke throughout the world. But we also notice their potential perverse effects. This is why we simultaneously create a "resolutics" that suggests Quebec's approach be integrated at all levels of society, inside an environment with global perspectives that command interactive solutions and collaborative news to resolve our local issues. The global intervention methodology suggested by the community informatics design includes an "imaginatics" that allows to harness the massive knowledge production towards the needs of our society, while "resolutics" accompany it while creating a richer representational bridge between the conceptual framework and multi-aspect instantiation strategies. Thus creating the need to have more researches on a new domain called "Identics", following an expression created by The Club of Rome (and taken up by Anthony Judge 2008a) to define imaginative metaphors, standards and procedures, the culture and identities of innovative communities of practice and their specific ways of organizing work and to understand imaginative patterns and particular innovation modes in a given society, all this will facilitate the planning of more original digital strategies in a specific country. New online social systems and organizations we create in Quebec refer to ways of learning, learning to do, to be and to live together that are proper to the Quebec society and that contribute to the dissemination, sharing and the production of a whole new digital cultural identity: the digital Quebecer "identics".

At this time of globalization of cultures and economy, the ways of living together are not exclusively defined inside a territory but throughout the multiple learning enterprise networks in the Peter Senge's sense (1990, 2006, 2013) through new learning practices and research whose boundaries are not confined to well-defined spaces like research centres, universities, schools or companies. While contributing to keep the intellectual leadership of existing institutions, the new knowledge society institutions are blasting through their boundaries' limits to project outside and practice the communityship by helping citizens of all horizons to increase their digital knowledge and skills in all fields. We must understand the way the cultural and social governance is influenced by innovation communities like wiki, DSS and virtual organizations of all kinds. How is our culture influenced by new artefacts and collaborative culture born in global networks and social Web? How is our society evolving dynamically *between* different spaces (physical, mental, social cyberspatial), with regard to its structures and operating in the new "identics" process framework? We must collectively channel and orientate these new participative behaviours in a sense that will be strategically favourable in the long term. We cannot remain confined in the appropriation of the Anglo-Saxon culture without risking to remain imprisoned in it. We must pay attention to Quebec's global image that is created in the world collaborative networks and to symbolic and imaginative devices of all sorts issued from our culture and that innervate the planet. The unawareness or ignorance facing these new socio-communication situations and the emergence of these new international identity expression systems of at various levels of society can have unexpected socio-economic consequences.

This new international identics of such complexity we cannot predict in one workshop or in one symposium only. We can, however, better define it if we consider it as a particular initiatives' attractor/unifying, if we understand it like a fifth discipline (Senge 1990, 2006) added to the fourth other pillars of the new research paradigm: the problematic, the community informatics design, the imaginatics and the resolutics. This requires the elaboration of a national director plan that allows to understand the perspectives in all their complexity.

These five pillars of research and development (problematic, community informatics design, imaginatics, resolutics and identics) rest upon a brand new research paradigm of the second-order systemic and a third-phase collaborative intermodal science. They command a whole new semantics and communication approach of the human-computer interface, which becomes the fourth big research focus on which the Quebec digital platform can rely on to ensure its future. The socio-communicational and semantics design of DSS relies on a natural, user-friendly, motivating approach that does not require specific computer or mathematics skills. We believe we have widely supported this argument in our study, and we strongly wish this approach becomes the chosen way to grasp the multiple modalities and aspects related to the community informatics design centred on the human being. Figure 1.1 illustrates this socio-dynamic process aiming at the maturation of the third-phase science five pillars: the community informatics design.

Therefore, we suggest the seven research orientations and axis development, articulated on a generic platform of collaboration and social creativity to be determined:

1. Develop an evolutive and interactive semantics link networks, a sense and meaning theory that emerges from the application arena and grounds at the same time as visual information representation systems such as Stella.
2. Co-build a stakeholder's theory replacing the old consumer/user model to reframe it in a partnership network (partnership helix) of proactive users/designers well informed, well trained and intrinsically motivated by certain types of innovation or applications supported by networking and the elaboration of resilient social systems, self-organized and well adapted to the new socio-economic situation of the knowledge society. We must conduct workshops that will unite scientists of various horizons, business people, people who define government policies and citizen communities interested in this challenge.
3. Extend the suggested vocabulary in this book to products, applications and services in order to make it "applicable or usable" in an appropriate way by large segments of the population coming from diverse domains or sectors of activities such as information, organization, social or virtual.
4. Continue the effort we undertook in the formalizing of DSS instantiation process and semi-formalizing socio-technical design by discovery matrices and strategic

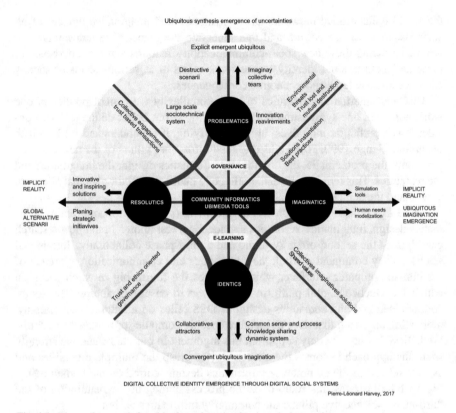

Fig. 1.1 Lines of research for ubiquitous imagination in a design society

alignment. We absolutely must try to computerize the multiple domains of community informatics design that will help stakeholders to better understand the DSS activities and the design process.

5. Improve social media analytics techniques and collaborative and ubimedia tools to reach a level of strictness comparable to the one found in architecture or applied sciences.
6. Organize conventions and workshops in person or via tele-presence and produce new reports according to a new formula that favours action for the future instead of past assessments.
7. Publish books, manuals and journals on community informatics and semantics innovation.

Throughout the APSI research, transdisciplinarity is made for one of the key problematic of our partnerships, our workshops and questionnaires. The information applications are so complex that they can simply not be designed or created without a collaboration that would go outside the disciplinary borders. Therefore, we recommend, and it is also in line with the *Secrétariat du Conseil du Trésor du Québec's* policies, to intensify the multidirectional and multimodal research effort on the major projects of the twenty-first century that, while remaining largely preoc-

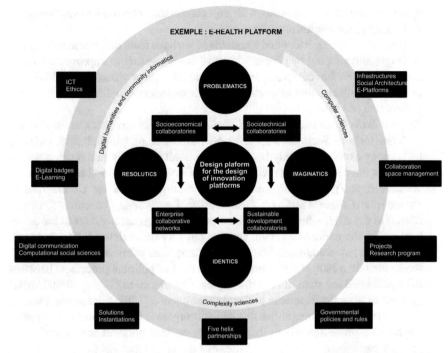

Fig. 1.2 Quebec's digital society governance platform

cupied by science and technology, is in line with the reflection and social imagination solutions for major socio-economic projects defined by the Science Technology and Society Sector (STS) and the *Finances et de l'Économie du Québec* ministry. Once again, we illustrate the great research axis by orientations likely to guide the policy planning (Fig. 1.2), by taking as an example our healthcare system, articulated around the five pillars previously mentioned (problematics, community informatics design, imaginatics, resolutics and identics) and its multi-domain governance mode.

To develop projects focused on thematic related to sciences, technologies and great twenty-first-century social projects and the five pillars' synthetic vision of informatics design and imaginatics, we suggest the following innovations:

1. *Create Collaboratories Articulated in Innovation Network Design Centres.* A proposition would be to develop a virtual design studio; another one would be to link education programs in order to improve the general quality of educational resources for all participants around the innovative projects involving various types of design.
2. *Increase the Collaborative Software Creation.* The current collaborative tools are more and more abundant, but they are not adapted to the various users'/ designer's complex tasks. More specifically, the effort should focus on accompa-

nying specialized collaboration with experts/creators who work in smart organizations around complex projects.

3. *Develop Procedures.* Rules and standards as we have them in our research should be taught and adopted by people who must work together to improve collaboration, whether within complex partnerships of all sorts or virtual teams dedicated to creating collaborative tools based on their experience in different spaces and places, real or virtual.

4. *Explore Techniques to Appoint and Facilitate Stakeholders in a Design Process with the Help of Socio-collaborative Media.* Often, people with an interest in technology express it openly but will not commit implicitly in reflection activities about the design process without facilitation or sociocultural facilitation.

5. *Validate New Types of Citizenship in the Future, Around the Co-creation of Democratic Citizen Platforms Dedicated to Innovation.* The current notions related to the citizenship concept in the public arena generally refer to the act of "voting" in the name of a known concept but very badly defined: "democracy". Information technologies and the social participation publicized by Internet networks contain a radical transformation potential of political processes, between the market and the state. It is of the highest importance to develop digital social systems in what the American political researchers call "the third sector", within which groups and communities that can self-organize in "Commons" and recreate flexible processes where they can become real political actors again and actively participate in diverse activities of various government tiers.

We recommend cutting-edge research that will take into account conceptual frameworks better suited to information, communication and collaboration's current reality. The old consensus on the Shannon and Weaver transmitter receiver's paradigm theory left us speechless for the portals and virtual organization design. The semantics and semiotics models presented in this research, like the semio-pragmatic communication star and the CAPACITÉS model, are there to correct the situation. They help us to better define concepts like information and knowledge and to consider the multiple disciplines that help design and document as well as the various modalities of knowledge sharing through new digital social systems. Throughout this book, we suggest to build solid conceptual pillars, like the evolutive system theory, social systems design, the theory of activity and conversational design, to name only the most important ones. We propose an in-depth research that conceptualizes, again, the information and knowledge notions through new virtual organizations semantics, networking institutions and the digital social systems that update them every day in all sorts of human activity systems. We must better understand the way ICT and technology are related to their users/designers.

The current blur that conceals information notions and shared knowledge put at the service of human development invites us to consider creativity and design tools from another angle. Instead of confining them in specific disciplines or specialized niches, we should consider them like prodigious innovation tools in cyberspace and inter-enterprise collaborative networks. These new technologies and social platforms are not there only to validate everyday human relations and communications, this task being of a great social benefit in itself. Their strength resides in their potential for the collaboration in complex projects and the support of governance and coordination processes of numerous semantic link networks. Coordination of individual citizen activities, of people, of groups and of communities is made of collaborative networks and virtual social systems of all sorts. Also, it could sustain the coordination of material and social entities in different spaces like in the growing Internet of Things, creating new socio-technological ecosystems like the telecommunication industry. The coordination of collaboratories is dedicated to the development of new economic models that numerous organizations can benefit from, when they are struggling with creating new economic models. This new understanding of governance and coordination possibilities through ICT, human activities and innovation ubimedia is new and must be explored at all levels of society. We recommend developing around the concepts such as governance, semantics, ethics and coordination, from theories like social and communicational sciences, complexity sciences and computer sciences.

To justify the role of community informatics design at the service of our society well, we must propose a new vocabulary and logical arguments likely to convince various stakeholders so they will find their interest and benefit. Better-established disciplines like computer sciences and information sciences have developed an entire intellectual technology to instantiate their models and implant their projects. Others, like engineering and medicine, put their propositions to the test and have developed techniques to evaluate their products and applications. The creation of a vocabulary, standards and evaluation tools for the design of future digital social systems represents a considerable intellectual challenge, and our research reveals certain bases and numerous applications. Because the development and co-design of such collaborative online social systems require the participation of several people and users'/designers' communities, at levels never seen before and including spaces of activities of higher risks, the need for technical instantiation and evaluation becomes a priority. In this context, we recommend developing analysis and design criteria up to the challenges we are identifying as well as rigorous and relevant evaluation techniques for all interested groups by promoting a motivating evaluation that does not divert from the values of community informatics design centred on the human.

1.3 New Skills, Social Creativity and Innovation

In this section, we organize our remarks according to two main reasoning lines:

1. *A Succinct but Virulent Critique of the Current Theory Deficiency Explaining the Relation Between Technology and Society*: Everything remains to be done regarding the collective design skills awareness that can help having a real democratic participation in the orientation of current social changes.

2. *Social and Communication Sciences as an Essential Basic Necessary Knowledge Source to Orientate Change*: If we seriously consider increasing the collective design skills, as an emancipating human activity system, we must demonstrate how it works and how it can be applied in the context of our lives and social, technological and economic systems. We direct our attention towards ten researchers that seem to be making innovative ways.

We will show how the "8-C" theoretical framework can meet the needs of new knowledge production for the analysis and development of digital social systems while providing basic concepts to create the community informatics design foundations. Community informatics design aims to respond to the pressing need to create a new complexity and co-design science regarding the evolution of technologies and digital social systems. This new face of social sciences and applied communication sciences cannot only provide a new interpretation of ongoing social transformations but also orientate them at various levels of society.

We will define a theoretical framework for the analysis of new online virtual organizations and social architecture likely to help model and evaluate them. To deepen questions related to potential links of new social structures in line with the economy and society, we must explore the complexity of collaboration mechanisms and their validation effects on human capital, organizational, technological and relational of our societies. The "intermodal architecture" notion is part of the array of creativity tools made available for future researchers in social sciences.

Finally, we will show the perspectives presented to us with the Web 3.0, the innovation Web. The new knowledge produced by community informatics design and the orchestration of a stakeholders' plurality, of architectures and of methodologies and creativity tools implies a new knowledge production paradigm through which innovation is channelled in a new research plan, where the five partnership helix model is socially inserted in networks, meaning spheres, a programming of community information systems oriented towards semantics aspects instead of object only. This plan of action is based on needs, skills, activities and typologies of the virtual communities we have discovered during our research by sociological survey and by case study:

1. Continuing education in the knowledge society (Chap. 2)
2. Virtual communities as socio-technical systems: reference model, management and methodology implementation theoretical framework

By using a life cycle inspired by the information systems design field and by extending it to the community information systems, our first task was to review the virtual community research and to suggest a succession of phases aligned with the development phases of the social systems design theory, allowing us to present successful conditions of the implementation of innovation communities in various socio-economic environments. The basic idea of our approach was to observe all the community development phases from initiation until metamorphosis or dissolution, for the purpose of increasing their chances to become dynamic and healthy communities, whose members actively participate in content and design creation of various elements and their process.

At the beginning of the second decade of the twenty-first century, the Internet is the dominant media for information exchange and social communication. For over 15 years, millions of Quebecers, Canadians and Americans use it daily for various information researches and communication activities at work, at home and in their community. They read the news, check the weather forecast, visit health websites, exchange in diverse communities, play all sorts of games and refer to maps and research travel destinations. Several play additional roles and become information providers, beyond traditional professional barriers. With their new skills, they contribute to arrange contents on a wide array of topics in networks blogs, wiki and more recently in the new complex spaces of the Internet of Things and Places. Today in 2017, social interaction is the most popular one for the majority of Internet users. For 150 million of Internet users in the United States, 91 % go online to stay in touch with friends, colleagues and people they know in the physical world. This majority also includes people who use the Internet and collaborative networks to co-build new forms of relationships online with people they have never met in person but with whom they have common interests. Users play games of all sorts, visit all sorts of websites where they can chat, participate in discussion forums or meeting spaces and visit social network websites to meet different people. All these people contribute to the collaborative network design of all sorts in multiple semantics link network, which go from the interest community to the socio-economic innovation community through a wide variety of organizations such as virtual teams, strategic alliances, technology parks, emerging digital social systems and business ecosystems.

As a matter of fact, collaborative semantics networks currently emerge according to an array of configurations and sociometric forms that create numerous digital social systems such as virtual organizations, virtual communities, virtual collaboratories, living laboratories, network-enterprise partnerships, more or less sustainable industrial clusters, experimental social environments and digital social systems support (Camarinha-Matos and Afsarmanesh 2004, 2005; Afsarmanesh and Camarinha-Matos 2005, 2008). These "new organizational forms" are not new. In our PhD work (Harvey 1993) as well as in Harvey's 1996 book dedicated to the emergence of virtual communities in the cyberspace, we were asking the following question: "Were Free-Nets at that time prefiguring an emerging and sustainable phenomenon or only short-lived social organization forms according to a more or less important trend"? In the present book, we will try to provide a more systematic answer. The starting point of our research is anchored in the transdisciplinary questioning that went to research fields we find under various designations: social computing, community computing, collaborative networks and now social Web or social media, Internet of Things and cyber-physical systems. Domain names are not lacking to qualify these new social life and organizational environments. Even if search results show that all virtual communities do not have a high structure degree, most collaborative networks necessarily involve a type of organization in their activities and their entities (things and places) that create new forms of social systems we call "digital social systems". Digital social systems know how to identify the roles of their participants, their member's status, deliberation procedure, a division and a coordination of work and certain governance rules. Some may have set up very specialized mechanisms for socio-economic innovation support. In this case, they cannot only form collaborative networks but generate business organizations and new networked institutions. These new collaborative network organizations have been the object of many research projects as well as national and international initiatives everywhere in the world, and a large data and empiric knowledge package is accessible on the subject. However, our documentary researches show us the urgency to consolidate this knowledge and to build better disciplinary foundations to optimize the development of this research sector.

The lack of reference models to apprehend network collaborative organizations as well as their manifestations in the form of various online social structures (like virtual enterprises, virtual professional communities, learning by project communities) represents a common concern for the research groups in the related fields like community informatics, social computing and the STS sector. This shortcoming in terms of theories, models and theory/practice (Harvey 2008) is highlighted as an obstacle in the consolidation of the studies we referred to as research on the Internet and society, in the broad sense of the ICT impact, the uses and the design in the society, the economy and the knowledge in particular in the community information systems sector.

In Quebec, for a few decades now, we have developed and operationalized certain technological development models around notions like technology parks, industrial clusters, enterprises incubators, strategic alliances and e-commerce or multimedia cities. These models appeared in common "socio-territories" or administrative regions by promoting the aggregation of diverse groups of organizations with the will to cooperate/collaborate to take advantage of business opportunities or potential markets that would never have seen the day or would have been too expensive if tackled individually. These long-term strategic alliances were often limited to the geographic proximity to their members, who saw a way of creating an economic force, industrial reconciliation and more intangible benefits such as a shared culture facilitating expertise exchanges and a sense of community belonging.

Alongside these private/public economic development initiatives, an entire movement we have identified in 1992 and 1993 under the name of "virtual communities", following the works of Howard Rheingold (1993), and that we had developed in Quebec under the name of "community informatics" since 1984, almost 10 years before our American and European colleagues, as part of our research work with Michel Cartier (2002) and Kimon Valaskakis (1988, 2010), quickly showed that the notion of community and network had to be clarified as a complex system containing communication, sociological and technological dimensions. Despite the language barriers or the absence of international diffusion in English, the Quebec expertise quickly crossed the borders to reach countries like France, Belgium, the United States and some African countries (Harvey and Bertrand 2004; Harvey 2004b). The impact of the first Electronic Bulletin Boards (BBS) and now the Web collaborative tools also called "social media" on virtual communities training must be not only revised with respect to theories and practices specific to the field (Fuchs 2010; Hofkirchner 2007, 2008, 2013; Wellman 2002; Benkler 2006; Castells 2011; Shneiderman 2002; Preece and Shneiderman 2008; Preece and Maloney-Krichmar 2005; Preece et al. 2004; Shneiderman and Preece 2008; Sunstein 2006; Lovink 2007; Gurstein 2008; Wilson 2006) but also to perspectives like the collaborative semantics networks and platforms that open to the social creativity fields (Romero et al. 2008; Molina et al. 2007; Fischer and Konomi 2007; Camarinha-Matos and Afsarmanesh 2005, 2006, 2008; Camarinha-Matos et al. 2005a, b) and to community informatics design. The ubiquitous imagination and collaborative intelligence's promotion in virtual communities design are currently inviting consumers and users to become content producers and users/designers of their own virtual communities, to contribute to the various phases of co-creation by crowdsourcing (finding collective solutions to common problem trend) open-source code design networks and practice communities.

For a few years, with the rapid ICT progression, accompanied by the market turbulence, economic chaos and business globalization, new forms of strategic alliances and collaborative networks of all kinds are emerging more and more on the differentiation/integration basis principle in terms of practice communities or communities of common interests. However, this principle must be completed by another important systemic principle: the unity of action in the diversity of organizational cultures and spaces. This generic theoretical principles and several other integrator concepts of these new organizational realities can help us characterize new social information flows that take place in the socio-economic life of the networked knowledge society. These new economic realities and the global markets influenced by ICT have a deep influence on all global social systems organizations, in particular small- and medium-sized enterprises which account for our basic industrial social fabric by giving the possibility to transgress traditional geographic borders and to form all kinds of "action communities", which we outline in another section of this present book.

These action communities can take many forms and may belong to one or several local or international networks, in order to increase or consolidate their influence on global markets. The phenomenon is so quick and important that it requires wording of new theoretical and methodological transdisciplinary concepts, not only to ensure its cognitive mastery but also and mostly to allow the development and co-building of new social and virtual economics architectures. Therefore, we must propose an improved explanation of the social networking and innovation network phenomena resulting from it to better answer the business perspectives that arise on the global scale. The famous McLuhan's global village is not at our door anymore but inside our homes. The new wealth of nations (Smith 2006) has become the wealth of networks (Benkler 2006). These new networks have to provide the necessary conditions (e.g. human, social, financials, infrastructural and organizational) to quickly ensure, in a fluid and safe way, the establishment of new collaborative networks dedicated to innovation. The development of innovation communities we have observed for many years mainly focuses on co-creation of virtual environments appropriate for collaboration, the fulfilment of cooperation contracts and the redaction of common operations and actions principles. Also, the accelerated development of collaborative and participative architectures that allow the implementation of common interoperable knowledge infrastructures, the co-building of collaborative ontologies and the sharing of knowledge, the development of trust and the sharing of many other resources, is actually exploding all around the world. The sharing of resources has the objective of preparing members, organizations, institutions and partner local communities to collaborate in virtual innovation communities that will allow to realize a business opportunity, a new social relation or strong interactions around collaborative common projects.

Within these new contexts, community informatics design takes a growing importance while presenting new challenges to research in several relevant fields. Also, the creation of digital social systems by community informatics design allows to put into perspective new organizational structuring possibilities that aim to validate different types of digital skills or to integrate new basic skills (analyse and synthesize information, arrange and share contents, configure software). All while observing the real effects of validation of these creation activities on learning new E-skills, acquiring knowledge or reducing some costs associated with particular projects such as the improvement of the services provided to the users' and consumers' online practices. Once its particular mission is accomplished, the social system or the networked practice or digital innovation community will dissolve or will transform into a lasting structure different from the original one. This new social structure entangled in many different physical and virtual assemblages (Foucault) will be able to extend in time and in space by always integrating in its deployment more people, resources and data supported by the computer networks and social media.

1.4   Why the Design? Its Emergence in Communication Sciences

The principal aim of this book is to promote the design's abductive thinking in all its multiple aspects as a mode of learning and acquiring skills in the information and communication fields (Aakhus 2007), in order to extract theories, practices and applications related to the communication process involved in the co-creation of environments, organizations and digital social systems. Design is a central element in communication and interconnective social action disciplines (Bennett and Segerberg 2013), and digital humanities under construction (Rosenbloom 2013) as well as several trades and professions are related: research/creation, research/intervention, facilitation, project management (Johannessen and Olsen 2011), marketing and public relations. And yet, the designer's work remains widely invisible in the field of teaching and research. The design work as such, whether it is media, publishing, graphic, visual or social coverage is often treated as a product of research, an application even a cultural product instead of a learning, creation, composition, imagination or inspiration act (Aakhus 2007, 2010, 2013). We can quote many examples: the construction and development of effective health promotion campaigns, the network collaboration in the social Web, the numerous works done to create new work organization forms, the recovery of organizational process design, the development of problem-solving methods or settlement of disputes and all the efforts dedicated to environment design for remote education and citizen platforms or sociocultural intervention promoting dialogues and debates. All transdisciplinary works related to work on information systems, to computer-based and to human-computer interfaces are skyrocketing. Nevertheless, the attentive examining of literature on the topic offers us many examples of studies carried out to evaluate design products and applications, but there are very little written about concrete principles and processes leading to the completion of such products in social and communication sciences. With the present book, we would like to contribute to fill part of these shortcomings. This book is an invitation to reflect upon foundations, theories, methodologies and applications of the design thinking in a communicational context and to join our future efforts to appreciate the impact on our practices, in order to suggest new conceptual frameworks in all spheres of social, public and digital communication.

1.5   The Detailed Presentation of the Book's Chapters

The book is divided into two main parts: the first one is entitled "The field of community informatics design science: theoretical foundations of digital social systems design". Throughout this first part, we seek to set the fundamental and communication basis of analysis and digital social systems of community informatics design.

The first part is divided into five chapters. This chapter presents universal anteriorities and the third-phase science. We lay the foundations of an exploratory research on ways to configure scientific knowledge and digital social systems' design practices in the context of innovation by the co-design on the Internet. In order to guide this exploration through the jungle of fields, concepts, theories, methodologies and applications, our team resorted to a piece of work very little known by communication and social sciences practitioners. In our opinion, it is essential for the understanding of the foundations of this scientific domain, *The Domain of Science Model*, presented by John Nelson Warfield in 1986, and that will inspire several significant researchers in the field of social systems design such as Bela Banathy (1996), Alexander Christakis (1987, 2010), Kenneth Bausch (2006), Heiner Benking and James Rose (1998), Thomas Flanagan (Flanagan et al. 2012; Flanagan and Bausch 2011; Flanagan and Christakis 2010), Alexander and Kathia Laszlo (2007) and many more. This model is at the basis of the masterful work of Warfield (1994), entitled *A Science of Generic Design: Managing Complexity through System Design*. Socio-technical networks give light to a third-phase science, a participative science where all citizens can contribute democratically to socio-economic innovation.

In Chap. 2, after having presented the philosophical foundations of digital social systems' community informatics design, we introduce "the community informatics design's general theoretical basis" that help understand some important orientations of community informatics design as a "socio-technical science". A typology of principles that is behind this type of design is also presented, as well as a certain number of laws and axioms that accompany its development. We thus try to bring a general reference framework out as wells as a socio-technical design perspective anchored in strong traditions of a society of participative, collaborative, sharing, durable and responsible information similar to the Scandinavian participate design tradition. Our approach is semi-normative, because it does not encourage any type of information society but a society aiming at the values supported by both World Summit on the Information Society (WSIS) in Geneva in 2003 and in Tunis in 2005, which includes desirable qualities by a set of countries, fields and professions concerning management and knowledge sharing and quality of life.

The community informatics designer's task is to develop and anchor in the foundations presented in our two first chapters a "socially responsible communication design science", like Victor Papanek and his successors.

Chapter 4 features ways to put "community informatics design in action". We thus review several modes of operational thinking to start a design process. The field of science model (FOSM) allows us now to provide theoretical and practical foundations of an operational collective imagination process, "community informatics design". We show here that it is an exploratory travel through numerous thinking and action modes supported by transdisciplinarity and pragmatic, no more, no less. We suggest seven reflection modes that represent a very concrete way to operationalize design thinking (Burnette 2009; Ranjan 2007), and they can help the uninitiated or students in social and communication sciences to start a design process. These seven reflection modes constitute an operating model that can intervene at any stages of the FOSM, his life cycle and design project phases. Each reflection mode is articulated in different natural or specialized languages and takes into consideration a different aspect of the FOSM (foundations, theories, methodologies and various applications). Each contains characteristics allowing to provide specific information and knowledge suitable for each instance, procedures or actions related to FOSM. In fact, this concretely means that each reflection mode allows to operationalize different users'/designers' intentions, their behaviours, standards, architectures, role identification, resource and management modes, values, etc. Going forwards, these reflection modes could help to reconcile computer science and social science vocabulary.

Chapter 5 presents a generic communication model adapted to community informatics design called the "semio-pragmatic communication star". This seven-pointed star allows to analyse and design socio-technical systems in a more exhaustive way than traditional communication models that neglect several important aspects of human behaviour. After the model presentation, we attempt to integrate it afterwards to an experimental evaluation model in the form of "hierarchical stairs" of interdependent fields we call CAPACITÉS: (*Constellation d'attributs pour l'analyse et la construction interactive des technologies éducatives standardisées*)

Constellation of Attributes for the Analysis and the Interactive Construction of Educational Standardized Technologies.

Our analysis of the elements related to the development of communication processes involved in the co-creation of socio-technical platforms seeks to result in useful norms (like basic architectures in Chap. 6) at various types of collaborative design. The implementation of standardized rules, transcultural and transdisciplinary, provides a bridge between learning processes performed with the help of different languages (animated images, symbols, diagrams, figures, natural or specialized languages), first moments of a communication and learning platform deployment by community informatics design and, transdisciplinary communication operationalized by these different languages, second moment of a learning platform deployment considered as an eloquent digital social system. It relies on our previous works (Harvey 2010; Harvey and Bertrand 2004; Harvey and Lemire 2001) dedicated to establishing a "dynamic appropriation" communication model as well as the APSI works realized with our partner Lionel Audant from Unimasoft. We use the education sector and learning communication platforms as an example in order to make the abstract platform reality more accessible to the reader.

Chapter 5 outlines the major points of a collaborative design scientific approach and suggests the first transdisciplinary architecture norms of a community informatics help system SADC *(système d'aide au design communautique)* as a collaborative platform development support we call digital social systems. Collaborative design has become one of the main challenges in several fields of study, especially social sciences, communication, physics, computer sciences and even biology and ecosystems. Designers want to create systems where several entities (organizations, communities, groups and individuals) can collaborate in an autonomous way, onsite, in their respective work sphere on various society projects. This process takes place as part of "collaborative networks". The goal of collaborative design is to allow stakeholders to work in a more efficient way by producing collaborative actions beyond cultural, disciplinary, geographic and temporal barriers. However, for the system to work, we have to configure it in a way it meets the needs of social demands and changes. Researches on collaboration have met many opposition caused by traditional sciences determinist followers also resulting from some misunderstanding caused by previous works lacking precision. This chapter proposes the first draft of the community informatics design ecosystem creation and suggests several types of appropriate architectures. It also provides a methodological framework, even multi-methodological (Mingers and Brocklesby 1997), as a diverse virtual co-design environment support. In other words, we attempt to test the design of community information systems (or to present a generic architecture for collaboration software, the "the design for open collaboration"). The SADC of socio-technical systems is essentially a frame and a platform framework offering design modalities adjustable to users' needs. It is the starting point for organizations and virtual communities that wish to implement new collaboration solutions. As an adjustable socio-collaborative platform, the SADC covers both community informatics design scientific basis and socio-technical aspects of collaboration design. It connects both to facilitate the information flow, the access to knowledge and users' communities coming together. The SADC also wants, to a lesser extent, to serve as a reference model, a conceptual framework, allowing to define a common ground and terminology for communication studies. It is intended as an open-service platform prototype, expandable and adaptable for the structuring and integration of all sorts of online activity systems, socio-technical systems and personalized portals and even all sorts of collaboration platforms like virtual communities or virtual enterprise campus.

The SADC also contains a series of models offering a complete definition of the whole desirable characteristics of a collaborative work environment: a governance architecture accompanied by general architecture principles and collaboration design strategies like resource sharing and service group financing. This presumes an ethical framework containing rules of conduct, commitment, responsibilities and code of ethics. Therefore, we attempt to extract the first norms of the fields:

- *A Social Architecture*, provided with collaboration services norms, as well as a collaboration model that underlies organizational aspects of collaboration aiming at supporting new socio-technical or community informatics in their virtual environment design activities
- *Community Information Architecture Systems* that defines a logical framework for collaboration software deployment showing how different implementation projects cover various aspects of digital social systems design thinking and that clarifies interfaces with components like work spaces and Web services
- *A Technical Architecture* that connects information system components to the applicative underlying framework reflected in standard reference models for the SADC design
- *A Production Architecture* identifying formal or semiformal of collaboratories and their use by various application components

In other terms, it is about suggesting a new methodological orientation aiming to help designers of these new virtual environments (digital social systems) discover products, applications and functionalities and design help devices that meet their needs. We also want to indicate how the methodological configuration presented in the second part of the book can be applied to create reference architectures towards the co-building of virtual communities taken in a constant evolution environment, for the purpose of collaboration activities, problem-solving as well as all sorts of online human activity systems like governance of virtual communities dedicated to open innovation.

The second part of the book is entitled: "From modeling to implementation: the reference framework, the instantiation methodology and the strategic alignment and discovery matrix". In Chaps. 6, 7, 8, 9, and 10, we present a digital social systems building guide (virtual communities, practice or innovation communities) that contains several reference models, which are translated by a series of guidelines and support measures for processes and activities involved in the co-design (large-scale collaborative design also called "community informatics design") of these new virtual environments. The community informatics design guide (the SADC to be implemented) is a design management system, a governance model catalysed by an iterative cycle of seven flexible phases called "design space". It is intended to provide creators of various types of virtual social systems, to virtual environment design experts, a better understanding of development needs and conditions as well as a series of mechanisms, functionalities and creativity tools to manage and operationalize in a semiformal way their entire life cycle and diverse actors' and partners' roles.

In Chap. 6, we describe digital social systems that can develop within several economic fields aiming to transform the physical vision of organization creation and traditional social systems (architecture co-building of "well-defined borders buildings", linear process of enterprise value chain, universities or government institutions) in a structure represented by a multiform and multifunction network, in order to increase the actors' chances to get involved in the "collaborative activities". The new virtual environments co-design to help digital social system design (like the SADC as a virtual help environment for the creation of services portal or innovation communities) systematically uses network infrastructures and socio-digital media. We believe community informatics design will considerably grow in the next years because the notion of "participative social architecture" PSA we are developing in the present book adds a "sense of place (following Joshua Meyrowitz) and moment" as well as an added value to the traditional physical space and social time notions where human activities used to take place. The Web 3.0 digital social systems (DSS) are emerging through collaboration mechanisms in place in the social Web structure (LinkedIn, Facebook, Moodle) that must be understood as new spaces built in the service collaborative social architectures. In fact, digital social systems apply common networking infrastructures and ICT with the objective of freeing itself from the restrictive barriers of geographical and territorial determinism, without missing the tangible character in human or inter-organizational relations. However, the infrastructure aspect (technologies, software, platforms) does not affect the structure work of the community informatics expert in developing collaborative spaces. Besides, we insist on the fact that mediatized computer collaboration and communication contain more complex and abstract processes related to belonging, identity, trust, cohesion, resource mutualization, governance and ethics.

In Chap. 7, we affirm the necessity of making an openness effort by observing the language of compartmentalized disciplines that must make their specialized boundaries explode (a reference to Henri Laborit in his "new chart") to transcend boundaries and zones of uncertainty regarding the unique linguistics of each field. Whether it is psychology focusing on cognitive aspects, sociology for social action-related aspects, communication for interaction and collaboration, economy for aspects related to operating costs and development budgets, operational research studies on risks and performance and aesthetics for issues related to interface harmony, balance or beauty, or even the systems governance, we must be attentive to these dialogues if we want to develop common visions and actions and avoid to succumb to a never-ending solipsism. These multiple aspects, examined several times throughout the book, must be described and harmonized in the design and implementation of systems centred on the human being. The contribution of several is a crucial condition of the essential social systems dimension description and several subsystems of activities that evolve interacting through discourses, languages, artefacts and methods. We will see a first attempt at this type of effort in the transdisciplinary dimension definition effort that community informatics design suggests and in the articulation of these dimensions as a "fundamental verification list" that constitutes the hearth of our instantiation strategy.

We will see that we can carve the diverse aspects of the digital social systems' world into many "shared meaning worlds" that intervene in the community informatics systems design. To do so, we have developed an original tool, the "community informatics instantiation methodology", with the main objective to support the community informatics design process by the meticulous deconstruction of its multiple aspects, as meaning or shared activities spheres, whether it is management mechanisms, design models or process, architectures, methodologies and resources allowing to operationalize the community informatics reference model in its different virtual and real application environments. The development of an instantiation methodology represents a great challenge for a small team of researchers like the ACILs. This activity, which is not very present nor validated in social sciences but exists in some fields like marketing, the action research or management, requires a combination of a variety of models developed by a large number of authors from various fields.

Chapter 8 reminds the challenge software engineers, technology managers and ICT users/designers will have to face, in considering technological platforms, social media and collaborative technologies as being part of larger systems containing not only technical aspects but also social and human aspects. Current conceptual models, originating from software engineering systems as well as social sciences (human-computer interaction (HCI), computer support cooperative system (CSCW), communication mediatized by computers (CMC), Scandinavian participative design, interactive design, digital design, media design and more recently technology-mediated social participation (TMSP)) are limited in their perspectives, more particularly in their ability to represent information and virtual complex systems' architectures. This chapter presents a conceptual structure and a modeling framework that aims to improve existing socio-technical system design architectures. By coming back to the social architecture notion, we suggest an analysis and design framework that allows to optimize jointly, to operationalize and instantiate the architectures defined in the previous chapters (technological, organizational, informational, participative, collaborative architectures, etc.) for digital social systems design as human activity systems mediatized by ICT (social media, collaborative platforms, creativity and design tools).

The value of our theoretical and practical effort will be to allow digital humanities, computational social sciences and digital communication practitioners to have for the first time tools and means to visually design and arrange the social and collaborative structure of their online activity systems, while allowing engineers, managers and computer programmers to widen their respective field view in order to structure various types of conversations and languages to facilitate socio-technical systems design like digital social systems. This chapter represents a way to increase existing documentation by suggesting a clear and concise generic structure for the construction of human activity systems on the Internet, like healthcare digital social systems, learning communities in education, enterprises-virtual campuses and universities and intervention and cultural strategies. It does not require any particular formal computer programming or code language expertise. Based on discovery matrices, the morphological analysis technique (Godet), the heuristics questioning matrix in imaginative and creative thinking (Moles 1992), as well as multi-field and multi-aspect matrices (BASDEN), our approach aims to provide social sciences researchers with a qualitative and quantitative methodology that will be used by communication students and citizens/designers to identify, name and organize community information systems in a way to better capture, memorize, treat, analyse and design complex data related to community informatics information systems that will evolve according to a socio-communicational character growing stronger in the near future.

Chapter 9 is strongly anchored in the practices' orientation. From the framework detailed in the previous chapters and the set of entities defined as modalities, meaning spheres or aspects to take into consideration in a DSS instantiation/implementation, we present in this chapter the definition of the multi-aspectual and multimodal discovery and strategic alignment matrix (2MDSAM) for digital social systems design. The 2MDSAM provides an operational reference framework to organize and model the DSS interactive elements and dynamic components, as well as a way to describe the design process and activities. Its objective is to close the gaps of current modeling systems with the input of various disciplines and fields related to modeling virtual social systems. The evolution of the Web over the last 10 years had us to form information and communication systems design dedicated to content production and organization (websites) to support digital social systems for action and transformations at the community, family, organization and social life level at different scales and from different worldviews. This is a new social creativity situation put at the service of change. Social sciences have remained very quiet until now in front of this major phenomenon of the beginning of the third millennium. In this chapter, and in the spirit to contribute to the challenges posed by the so-called Fourth Industrial revolution, we seek to fill this gap by suggesting a concrete representation and modeling tool while showing the potential of universal design centred on the human being. The 2MDSAM operationalize the DSS conceptualization (its instantiation) while taking up the challenge of addressing the limits of design frameworks existing in the organizations and digital social systems design. It provides a way to organize information on various modalities and numerous aspects of digital social systems, in order to facilitate co-creation and cognition distributed for a better DSS development.

In Chap. 10, we continue the community informatics design operating description, by following the life cycle of the seven design spaces that allow, by iteration, to identify the entities and elements to model and instantiate in the SADC. We can define the SADC as an innovation network with open-source code or user network support, where online community managers obtain DSS design helping tools. In the long run, it will become a platform that will promote strategic alliances between organizations wanting to offer multimodal conditions (human, financials, social, infrastructural and organizational) to support the rapid and fluid configuration of collaborative platforms useful to organizations, large and complex stakeholders' network and society.

Thus, the SADC that will be implanted online in the next years to come can be defined, according to the ACIL works (UQAM) as a "socially responsible communication design platform combining physical and virtual spaces" that mainly focuses on the creation of support environment that can guide various types of participative design appropriate to the establishment of a good governance, creativity tool appropriation, a continuous cooperation and an optimal collaboration through different means of technological supports helping users in the creation of their own efficient and effective collaboration environment adapted to their different online practices.

However, we must keep in mind that DSS are often coalitions and short-term organization dynamics less well adapted to a maturation and collective environment (reunification, incubation or learning environment) to answer to a collaboration opportunity between designers and users of a virtual environment while integrating skills or basic skills and necessary resources to reach, even go beyond the quality frameworks, delays and costs expected by recipient users whose cooperation is supported by computer networks (Camarinha-Matos and Afsarmanesh 2007). However, once it is successful, the DSS can extend its lifespan over many years.

So, this chapter suggests a tool framework (a verification list as the science first stage that will evolve over the years) made of a socially responsible design (community informatics design), a reference model, a management framework and an instantiation methodology, as a set of guidelines providing means to support the process and activities involved in the creation and operations of new virtual environments. The community informatics design kit (the SADC) aims to provide design initiators and managers with the understanding of the demands as well as foresight mechanism regarding the functionalities management while co-building virtual environments and DSS. With this tenth chapter, we close the iterative cycle allowing the SADC to offer all resources to support the DSS creation, while remaining an essential tool to update the third-phase science that is community informatics design science.

Our conclusion is not a real one, because it is dedicated to the description of a future research program. The ubiquitous imagination in a complex design world is only in its early stage. The concrete FOSM contribution to community informatics design, of its seven iterative design spaces and 2MDSAM in the apprehension and implementation of digital social systems, still remains to be developed. We will need several important socio-technical projects to validate its foundations, theories, methodologies and its applications. Even if we believe the conceptual scaffolding, the reference framework and instantiation strategies presented in this book are sufficient to describe several complex social systems that are interesting for our society. To produce its modeling and design, we still do not know yet to what extent the seven design spaces and the seven preferred modeling fields represent an appropriate design methodology for the DSS development. We do not know their future validation effect on our society either. We simply call for more and more studies and the creation of dynamic research programs in the future.

Part I
The Field of Community Informatics Design Science: Digital Social Systems' Theoretical Foundations

Chapter 2
Universal Anteriorities and Third-Phase Science

In this chapter, we outline an exploratory research on the configuration of scientific knowledge and practices of digital social systems' design in the context of innovation by co-design on the Internet. In order to guide this exploration through the jungle of fields, concepts, theories, methodologies and applications, our team mainly resorted to a text not well known by communication experts and social science practitioners but, according to us, that is fundamental for the understanding of the foundation of any scientific field, *The Domain of Science Model*, presented in 1986 by John Nelson Warfield, and that inspired many important researchers in the field of social systems design.

Warfield is committed to the creation of a generic design science (1994) likely to integrate the management and collaborative design of large-scale systems like the ones we find in inter-enterprises collaborative networks or scientific practice communities transbordering the Internet. Warfield (1986) feels that, for better or for worse, our societies have accepted the idea of complex systems at a large scale. If we want to step up to the challenge of guiding them socially and ethically, we need to acquire the necessary skills to manage and coordinate them. An excellent way to do so is to learn to design them. In the present chapter and all through this book, we will examine the foundations of a community informatics design's generic science that relies on this idea of great complex systems with the angle of several fields such as the design of socio-technical systems and social systems design as the base of construction of digital social systems. The "collaborative network co-design"(our generic designation for collaborative design, interactive design, participative design, design centred around the user and the design centred around the human) currently presents great difficulties of modeling and integration of human factors and technologies that overcome designers' skills while threatening them to quickly lose the cognitive and practical systems control they help developing. The implementation of a community informatics design generic science as an applied science of great socio-technical systems currently born on the Internet is founded on the most important elements of universal knowledge gathered in several fields of design for decades

© Springer International Publishing AG 2017   35
P.-L. Harvey, *Community Informatics Design Applied to Digital Social Systems*,
Translational Systems Sciences 12, DOI 10.1007/978-3-319-65373-0_2

by the best practitioners and becomes one of the conditions for the deployment of sustainable development designs of humanity.

Warfield's entire works can help us to build the bases of a community informatics design's generic and transdisciplinary science and to articulate it in a clear and simple way through multiple ramifications of a complex systems science. In his publications, Warfield explores the science basis according to the pragmatic attitude of the great philosopher Charles Sanders Peirce. By doing so, he integrates dimensions that are usually missing from the science philosophy and articulate them logically in a "science theory". Indirectly, his effort shows us that his science notion is more appropriate than traditional representations.

Warfield defines simultaneously the roles of formal language objects and the ones from natural metalanguages. As we will see, this opens up the door to transdisciplinary collaboration, for example, between computing and social and communication science practitioners. In this regard, Warfield develops important qualitative reality relational descriptions and incorporates them in mathematics digital dimensions. We will see in Chap. 4 that this attitude is salutary for researchers that wish to integrate precision in their analysis of complex social phenomena, even if they do not possess the theoretical and practical baggage of quantification specific to pure science and different engineer sciences. Therefore, Warfield integrates these qualitative mathematics to universal antecedents to create a "generic design science".

The Peirce philosophy that influences Warfield in the first instance incorporates the topic knowing the knowledge definition. Warfield examines the retroactive loops between the object, the concept and the subject and not only between the object and the concept or between the subject and the object. He invites us to an exhaustive conception of science. This conception is interested first by empty locations and spaces left by the conventional Cartesian science, at the origin of a permanent separation between the objective worlds, "what is there in the reality", and the subjective world of "cognitive universes" that perceives and explores them. Warfield decompartmentalizes the observer and the objective world by integrating the notion of knowledgeable subject. He does not make the counterfactual distinction with a "disembodied cosmic observer" that could adjudicate ex cathedra regarding the objectivity of a fact, truth or falseness.

In this tradition, Warfield was one of the pioneers in the design of social system in proposing questions raised by ontology, epistemology and communication connections between foundations of a science, theory, methodology, applications and project governance. He speaks expressly of the "knowledgeable subject" observer in the production of realities as well as the psychosocial nature of human participation at all stages of activities and design process. In this sense, Warfield can help us participate in the ongoing construction of the "third phase" of science. The works of Kenneth Bausch (Bausch and Flanagan 2012; Flanagan and Bausch 2011) and of Thomas R. Flanagan (Flanagan et al. 2012), inspired by Gérard de Zeeuw (1997), the design's semantics turn (Krippendorff 2007) and the entire current movement of conversational and dialogue in design that includes the interactive movement, the science of dialogic design and the language/action perspective represent a way to establish the third-phase science as a means to understand and adapt complex social systems. First, let us see the previous phases.

Very schematically, let us say that de Zeeuw (1997) maintains that in the first phase of science, there is no separation between the observer and the object. However, the connections are often so thin that the separation postulate is often justified and still produce valid results. In this first phase, this detachment of the observer and its subject is specially applied to physics and biology. Still according to de Zeeuw, in the second phase of science, the acknowledgment of an object depends on the point of view of the observer. This second phase is required in quantum physics, in medicine and more particularly in psychology and social sciences. The objects in the second phase of science are defined as grouping of defined qualities in terms of standard deviations with respect to a statistical median. The social science researchers are facing important problems when they research constant evolution systems in this second phase. Argyris (1993a, b) reminds us that during this period, researchers are facing a problem lying in the fact that they do not consider the influence of the subject on its observation object; it is a problem that can contaminate the entire research project. The independent observation of an informed observer, according to Merton, apprehends the world through the glasses of an individual observer. In the first phase, this lens is polished, and its angle is sharp to allow several researchers to see an object in a more precise way. In this phase, a non-material observer and the material world are understood in terms of essences, meaning it corresponds to the natural tendency the human has of distinguishing what constitutes the exterior world, its own nature (observation of exterior things) and its being, the true nature of the cognitive subject watching it.

Broadly, these hypotheses do not pose any problem for science routines in the fields of physics, chemistry and biology. They can, however, cause dismay when, in a thorough researcher, we discover that the "opposite of a deep truth is a deep equal truth" (Neils Bohr, quoted by Bausch and Flanagan 2013). In subatomic physics, a researcher can discover a particle if he observes a certain way, whereas another one can discover an undulation if he looks at it differently.

In the paradigm of dissociation of the observer and its object, we also use the lens of only one observer, but we recognize the observer and its object are part of the same reality level. The second-phase science continues to see reality through only one pair of glasses while making sure to provide only one abstract definition of its object, while understanding, however, that its definitions are built by the observer. Reality does not read like a text. During this phase, scientists suggest the hypothesis of a plurality of individual observers with their individual glasses to understand the world and its objects. The granted efforts to precise the orientation of any type of glasses or vision angle and to create consensual definitions can lead to vision conflicts regarding the "pair of glasses" we are using to look at the world as well as disagreements on the nature of the study's object. These disagreements can in some cases be contained or "made up" by a group of relatively homogenous researchers who have a common research program and who, eventually, resort to statistics methods to describe social or cultural situations. However, these disagreements can become very important when heterogeneous researcher groups with varied programs try to describe the social and cultural worlds. These difficulties associated with the "World Vision" and the view angles can become insurmountable if experts try to resolve problems or intervene in the organizational, social or cultural change.

De Zeeuw (1996, 1997) shows that, for several years, a third phase of science suggests another way of building the object with the dialogue and conversation between interdependent observers. As the observers share their perspectives (World Vision, object definition, prescribed roles in the research, transdisciplinary dialogue), they build a common context that constitutes the object of their deliberations. It is the third-phase method used by researchers like Warfield (1994, 1999), Gibbons (1994), and Nicolescu (1996). This method promotes the visions borrowed from various types of "glasses" and vision angles in order to use in the co-building of "combination lenses" that are shared by an epistemic community while it matures the concept sharing to examine the object at the heart of its researches. Through this meta-glance, a community of practitioners from various disciplines is gaining a common understanding of a situation in which practitioners are collectively submerged to make decisions on the way to study it or intervene. We are not far from defining transdisciplinarity here. In a very recent collective work, *Transdisciplinarity: Bridging Natural Science, Social Science, Humanities and Engineering*, published in memory of John Warfield in 2011 with contributions from authors like Basarab Nicolescu, we can find the following definition of transdisciplinarity:

> With respect to what is between disciplines, through disciplines and beyond all disciplines. Its objective is to understand the present world, in which imperatives affect the knowledge unity. (Nicolescu 2011, p. 26)

Thus the third-phase science adopts the deep principles of transdisciplinarity by searching and by respecting the reference frameworks in order to perform observations from multiple points of view and observers to better understand the object inclusive context. The specialized language or languages that help determine the "discussion object" are established through the interaction of involved observers. The third-phase science specifically negotiates the modalities of behaviours and social change, such as self-organization of group activities by social action and intentional social change. The third-phase science as such does not try to give the researcher additional control over the human dimensions. It does not manipulate its users nor does it try to antagonize participants' attitude. According to de Zeeuw (1997), it allows everyone to answer the people and communities' request that act as interactive users in a given situation (e.g. a diagnostic on a social design situation). It allows them to learn collectively, socially and systematically and to develop required resources to improve their own development. This common task, this socio-construction of the object and worlds to build, is not a task we can perform appropriately with a desk review, as exhaustive it may be.

The generic design science favoured by Warfield falls into line well with social systems design initiated by Churchman (1971, 1974) and by Checkland and Banathy (1996, 2000, 2005), as well as with different dialogic modes that come with it (Christakis and Bausch 2006; Christakis 2005; Christakis and Harris 2004; Judge 1995, 2007, 2008a; Jenlink 2004, 2006, 2009; Jenlink and Banathy 2008; Laszlo et al. 2010; Laszlo and Laszlo 2007, 2004). These systemic conception approaches (Simon 1996, 1974, 1969, 1960) show us several ways to ensure the co-building and the co-design of complex socio-communication issues according to various points of view. This science, much more philosophically articulated than contemporary definition of design thinking, is built on the basis of an inclusive attitude, a design culture that suggests a descriptive and normative language and that is in line with different design situations and social change. It stipulates the necessary stages and phases to develop multimodal and multi-aspectual objects that are the subject of this present book. These analysis, synthesis, design, intervention and implantation processes include not only system users but all the stakeholders that rely on their own language and not only expert languages belonging to pure sciences, to their "laws" and to their "objective facts". How? Let us come back to Warfield's works.

In the generic design science, it is important to look in a critical way at ontology, epistemology, methodology and communication questions. If these ideas that we defend in our methodology classes for years were meticulously applied in the information and communications sciences, as well as in social and human sciences, they would contribute to alleviate a deep misunderstanding and to increase the capacity of reflection according to models and their foundations. A meticulous application and more generalized of these sciences shows that it is not necessary to quantify social and communication sciences to make them rigorous, nor to quantify the construction of information systems such as social media, collaborative platforms, service portals or enterprise intranets, for them to exist or to implant new systems. Rather, like Warfield says, even if the "scientific approach" requires precision, it does not necessarily require quantification. This fact is of major importance for the practice of several social and human sciences that have tried to emulate observation modes of the first phases of science, with substantial epistemological gaps, and that now can define and position an object in an analysis and non-mathematical reasoning space, not to mention that social science researchers never really possessed the necessary mathematical basis to elaborate quantifiable issues. Initially, this seems to be an unsurmountable epistemological barrier in the first and second phases of sciences. It is not the case in the third phase where even if the quantification force remains appropriate in various situations, the transdisciplinary work can fill the gaps through several skills that articulate hard science and soft science in a new way.

As a matter of fact, social and communication sciences deprive themselves of a space notion used in hard sciences, except for some researchers like Abraham Moles, who knew how to show the benefits in *Psychosociologie de l'espace* (Moles and Rohmer 1998). They were restrained by the convention according to which the space notion should be quantifiable (mathematically). Because sciences face the realities that are rarely quantifiable in their fundamental characteristics, they were deprived of the obvious idea of organizing power of "space concept". The notion of space contains a usage generality that goes beyond the idea of dimensions. Warfield (1986) tells us it defines a series of relations in reference to an imagined space that integrates them. A (reasoning) space includes all the components of a field (e.g. actors' roles, functionalities of technologies in use, characteristic and properties of a socio-technical system). The space is a universal relation that contains all the possible relations between entities or elements found in it. In this space, it is not necessary for relations between elements to be quantifiable for them to provide explicit arrangement between those elements. These short definitions' conclusion is that in social and communication sciences, the series of aspects, dimensions and elements of a field, their relations and their interactions do not require quantifiable elements to be apprehended in their complexity.

Warfield and Christakis (1987) demonstrate, for example, that quantification of the dimension concept is not a necessary condition for its use. For 25 years, we have taught students that the dimension concept, introduced in social sciences by researchers like Katz and Lazarsfeld (2006), Lazarsfeld and Merton (1971), Moles (1990) and Moles and Jacobus (1988), constitutes one of the major contributions to pure and social sciences. The conceptual analysis and the decomposition of concepts in variables, states, attributes, factors and indicators have shown the prodigious impact of what is called the operationalization of concepts in social communication research (conceptual analysis and articulations). By decomposing concepts in quantitative dimensions (e.g. socio-demographic characteristics) and in qualitative dimensions (the relation between social appropriation of technologies and quality of life), we give ourselves the concrete possibility to discuss systematic relations between concepts or components of a socio-technical system without having to resort to mathematics. This definition of dimensionality in a qualitative reasoning space transcends classic reductionist interpretations of the space notion. It allows us to expand the use of space and qualitative dimensions to much broader classes of situations. We will see, in different chapters dedicated to methodology, that these concepts allowed us to adopt a pluri-methodological attitude (mixed methods) and that the entire instantiation strategy of community informatics design of organizations and digital social systems can greatly benefit from discovery matrix methodology. We will also see that the dimension creation process, like in the field of alignment between collaborative tools and the needs of a community, can later be computerized and then used in complex socio-technical modeling systems on a large scale. Dimension lists and elements to factor in can be done by researchers in social sciences and their students. These participants can answer important questions on dimension contents, document them and classify them (e.g. the role of various stakeholders of an innovation project and relations with other fields, especially collaborative tools they wish to appropriate). Once the dimensions and fields are taken in inventory by these members who are not computer specialist nor mathematicians, computing experts can then transform (translate) them in programming algorithms and solutions in a way to organize them in more customized modeling and visualization tools, the way to facilitate the understanding of diverse evolutive properties of a complex social system.

The important thing to know here, for the establishment for conceptual and methodological basis of community informatics design, is that a dimension is a technical term that refers to the "natural and specialized language" of social and communication sciences and their qualitative aspects. As we will see in the community informatics design instantiation strategy where we have to fulfil tasks of establishing and arranging the various components related to the major fields to model and understand (roles, functionalities, socio-technologies), the notions of space and dimensions can help determine relations between the characteristics of a practice community. "A is in the same category as B", "A is influenced by B", "A and B are in a reciprocal interdependence", "A is in conflict with B", "A must precede B temporally", etc.

In this spirit of theoretical imagination (Weick 1995; Weick et al. 2005) aiming the qualitative representation of various design fields through the relations reasoning, Warfield distinguishes four universal antecedents of a design science: the human being, the language, the reasoning by relations and the modes of archival representations. By developing these concepts and linking them to each other, he provides the essential concept that fills the gaps of several sciences, like applied information systems and communication sciences as well as the major socio-technical systems sciences developed in collaborative networks on the Internet. Warfield connects these antecedents to the "cosmic partition" of Pierce: Library, Phaneron, and Residue. He manages to suggest an essential basis to "design sciences" that must be composed with numerous aspects of social systems, such as the one we propose in defining the "digital social systems design" field we build throughout this book. Therefore, according to this scientific approach, we must "observe", "infer", "establish" and "archive".

The Cosmic Partition Library is the integration of all the information contained in human media. The Phaneron is the entirety of ideas that exist in the spirit of people. The Residue represents the rest of the universe after we have subtracted the elements contained in the Library and the Phaneron. The science process consists of transforming the Residue elements in entities represented by the Library and the Phaneron, to recycle them and to examine their results in an evolutive way. The design science or "design sciences" juggle with the use and transformation that come from the Residue and the Phaneron, through various media in spectra of theory, methodology, technology and management. Traditionally, according to disciplinary synthesis, we have performed for 5 or 6 years design deals with a context, a situation, objectives' knowledge and intentions as well as a design process (see Chap. 4). With the current digital (computational) media explosion and the proliferation of data bases in all human life sectors coupled with design activities of large-scale systems and transborder sociocultural community systems, we must take into account at least six other dimensions. They are (1) behavioural norms, (2) exemplary practices and lessons learned when systems fail, (3) learning related to human limitations in the mastery of complexity, (4) knowledge about design intentions of several stakeholders, (5) the design process and (6) the context. The entire aim of our theoretical and practical effort resides in the possible deeper realization of these dimensions whose prioritization in our architecture and our infrastructures will allow to avoid certain disasters related to badly defined issues and to eliminate obstacles considered unavoidable until now.

2.1   The Human Being

The first universal antecedent is the human being. Because human participation is omnipresent in knowledge and community informatics design's management, the nature of the participation should be explicit to all stages of science under construction: in its foundations, its hypothesis, its theories, the selection of criteria of construction and evaluation, methodology, roles and environments. To do so, the relevant and appropriate information to each design context must come from social and communication sciences as well as philosophy.

The researches we are leading for several years show us people approach communities' behaviour according to two orientations: activities and emotions. In non-organized groups and communities, the behaviour is relevantly organized with the following verbs: brainstorm, regulate and perform tasks that, even if interesting, cannot, on their own, totally ensure the activities to accomplish. Often, practice communities realize the simulated consensus that social psychologists have named "groupthink", through which members of a work group or a practice community take decisions without having access to substantial information. Generally, all groups experience problems, whether with communication, evaluation, control, decision-making, tensions management, transactional equity, consolidation or leadership maturation. As John Warfield reminds us, "the incredible is normal, the bizarre is the social norm, and what we could reasonably expect from a society that adheres to a reasonable behavior is abnormal each time major systems are involved" (Warfield 1986, p. 51).

According to Warfield, the social groups' strange behaviours originated in our digital worlds (in reference to cognition instead of cyberspace). A digital world is unattainable to those who possess it; in that sense it constitutes a sort of an unwavering cognitive overload (according to Pierce's expression, quoted by Bausch 2001) that the individual carries with him through his life experiences. It is as if in this digital world of each individual, there could be value components (of World Vision) specific to any design situation that can involve the person in a way or another. Also, each individual carries with him, in the same container, components that represent the digital world and that can be damaging to the same design situation. This is why, beyond the perceptual prisms related to expertise coupled with the digital world's phenomenon, it is important to have members that represent a wide array of disciplines, knowledge, disposition, interests, general attitudes towards the world, skills, operational capacities, etc.

Another very important dimension for the understanding of complex design situations is our poor capacity to develop deep logical patterns. This poor aptitude is an aspect highlighted by one of the conception sciences founders, Herbert Simon (1969, 1960, and 1974). It is defined by "a rationality limited to master the complexity" or is translated by our incapacity to understand a complex project or design situation in all its interrelations. In Chap. 8, we present the discovery matrix method that allows to reduce complex situations in their more significant components for a project's stakeholders. The key aspect to take into consideration is our human incompetence to retain more than height items in our short-term memory. In other words, we cannot reason appropriately and simultaneously about interactions between more than a small number of dimensions and factors. For this reason, online social systems like "blockchain", cyber-physical social systems, enterprise portals, communities of practice and living labs must be modularized in order to deal with this cognitive limitation of real and virtual communities in the apprehension of design structures and process. Our team has defined a large number of design concepts (design context, socio-technologies, design process) and has reduced them to a few definitions judged essential to the decision-making for large complex systems design. These large dimensions represent essential fields to model, for example, in the tasks consisting of aligning design and modeling tools with design activities to be accomplished in order to build digital social systems containing very large and numerous dimensions. In practice, each dimension or module related to the problem contains more than three interactive elements. These three elements each contain four combinations, which gives a total of seven elements and combinations.

2.2 Language and Dialogue Modes

The second universal antecedent is language. We use various languages in our everyday life. There are also language experts like computer experts and specialized discipline languages that facilitate the operations' synergy between humans and software tools. We call "object languages" the ones specifically dedicated to computing. The aspect languages are the transdisciplinary languages used for various aspects of the world (cognitive, social and cultural) and that help the transdisciplinary configuration of all dimensions retained by a community to build its DSS and its virtual community. Thus, community informatics design programming becomes the configuration of technological modules of a DSS through languages oriented towards the aspects. For example, aesthetics, ethics and cognitive ergonomics aspects refer to world visions and practices containing their own languages. It is why we must build metalanguages to speak of these local specialized languages. The object languages cannot provide their own metalanguages to speak about it, says Godel. Therefore, we must combine object languages, computing expert languages with the natural language that serves as metalanguage. This does not mean that we should use the common language. All our efforts over the past 4 years have been on language use, field ontologies and glossaries in order to precise the theorization field and community informatics design application. In fact, we should be aware that a good science and a good design created in transdisciplinary collaboration require meticulous language objects, explained and negotiated by communication and natural language. The great theoretical physicist David Bohm (1965, 1996), Professor Emeritus at the University of London, well known for his physics works, has also been very interested in the role of language and dialogue in the evolution of society. He describes the dialogue process like a communication system that has the potential to bring new world visions. Anthony Judge (1995, 2007, and 2008a) has dedicated a major part of his life to study the way different dialogue modes could contribute to establish peace in the world and the way to participate in these modes. His works show it is more and more necessary to build common world visions while better mastering, cognitively and socially, the great issues related to sustainable development and global governance supported by technology. It is also important to be able to present its colleagues with motivating projects. This is done through speech and language. While keeping in mind the huge roles that cultural facilitation and social media platform design play in globalization, we must remember that social and public communication sciences will be up front in the co-building of new collaborative governance modes in the next few years. We will come back to it in the following chapters.

For now, suffice it to say that in addition to the oral and written prose language, we possess other types of basic languages that are necessary to community informatics design: mathematics, diagrammatic and animation and linear prose in its emission and its reception. It is necessary to organize our thoughts but often deficient in suggesting new forms in the world pedagogically. Animation presents significant forms by combining the text and image. It can use all sorts of languages which require the understanding of generative grammar of the functional image (Moles 1990; Moles and Rohmer 1986, 1998): music, sounds, schematic videos, animated cartoons, drawings and symbols. Mathematics produce forms by condensing formal language prose or signs of the natural language in programming algorithms that translate representations and intentions of human design projects. An illustration of the possibility of using various languages in the programming of an e-learning network platform based on animation will be presented in Chap. 4 when we will describe in detail our CAPACITÉS design model and the communication star model.

The diagrammatic (graphic mode) that community informatics design uses in the discovery matrix (Chap. 8) presents a sort of descriptive landscape of the "communication action" in the design activities. These exploratory matrices in modeling and design try to reduce the complexity of design situations by calling upon the eye and the human visualization capacities to appreciate chosen implicit structural relations between social architecture platforms and design activities to accomplish. Considering our limited rationality in the individual and collective apprehension of complex social systems, the diagrammatic and graphic modes are usually widely used in our works, for example, in the present book, and are necessary to help people and communities to understand the social systems and to mentally master different complex network digital organizations. In the dawning science of "community informatics design", design intentions call upon a combination of graphics and prose, but the production and configuration of social media and collaborative platforms require the collaboration of analyst and systems integrators who master programming, quantification and mathematics.

A good hybrid language like the "oriented towards aspects programming", suggested in Chap. 8, can combine computing object languages, a precise prose coming from social and communication sciences, well-scripted graphic and animation representations and can undoubtedly contribute to express systemic and complex organizational relations during the building of future digital social systems. All these specialized languages can be consolidated with the help of dialogue and natural language. A glossary and an enlightened use of various dialogue modes must be an integral part of any research program on human-computer interfaces (computer-assisted teamwork, computer-mediatized communication) aiming at making socio-technical design of large-scale systems possible. The methodology we will present in Chap. 7, the definition of concepts and the multi-aspect hybrid languages that we will suggest to describe the properties and attributes represent an important effort in that sense. These descriptive efforts aim to tackle the difficulties related to our limited rationality by looking to help us in the cognitive mastery of complex social systems by making the systems visually feasible and easily modeled by validating a "frame of reference transparency" (Warfield) in the rigorous description of community informatics design process (Chap. 9, section 9.2.6). The multi-aspect hybrid language produced to accompany community informatics design science is called "multimodal dialogue integrated system and multi-aspect languages".

2.3 Reasoning Through Relations

The third universal antecedent is the reasoning through relations. This discovery related to the complexity of qualitative and quantitative results of our research is associated with the extension of analytic philosophy done by Warfield. We will see that this type of reasoning does not compel us to necessarily quantify design phenomena and that they inspire the two chapters we dedicate to community informatics design instantiation using discover matrices and strategic alignment of various design fields, their components and properties. Warfield (1986) examines the following analytical thematic: the types of inferences and their respective roles in reasoning, the types of logical patterns, the relations generation and certain structural metrics.

Pierce's four kinds of inferences are the perceptual judgement, the abduction, the induction and the deduction. The perceptual judgement is an internal cognitive process that interprets sensations to transform them in perception; it provides the largest part of the individual virtual world. According to Pierce's words, the abduction is the process through which our intuitions execute all sorts of theories, conjectures, hypotheses and explanations about the world. According to us, it is the fundamental process of new structure imagination, phenomena or events that do not exist in the world yet. We would say it is one of the great sources of human being creativity dealing with the imagination of the future's social systems. It is a process that, after analysing new ideas related to phenomena, contributes to synthesize and pour them into the digital world. The induction interacts within the abduction to test new ideas on empiricism, experience and field observation basis. Deduction uses intuitive abduction elements as research hypothesis to produce a logical interference system through a formal or semiformal reasoning. By using interferences, a practice or scientific community will extend towards doubt and reassessment as well as confirmation and belief.

The models of mathematics logic negotiate with relations patterns that exist within generic concepts explicitly defined. Qualitative logic negotiates relations patterns existing within "blurry or inaccurate" concepts we find in the methodology of an uncertain science that we are developing in the context of community informatics design. Let us note that through this point of view that discriminates the exact and uncertain knowledge, we can ask ourselves if social and communication sciences would not be more advanced than exact sciences since they are precisely more able to concretely integrate the vague, the semiformal and the inaccurate problems related to the creation, design and applied sciences that are interested in vague issues. A real effort of deconstructing the topic in this book, first with a vast methodology of digital social systems' analysis and design and then with examples of sectorial methodologies with scientific creation in the everyday work of the researcher or designer (activity theory, technological, organizational and social architecture, conversational design, Leonardo's case analysis, questionnaire, group discussion, dialogue), suggests, no more no less, a methodology of the creative spirit and massive sociological imagination in open innovation communities.

Contrary to the individual discovery process or the solitary genius invention, the "variation innovation" relies on combinations and alignments of logical relations and optional choices from design rules already known or elements defined by their properties and attributes: community informatics design's methodologies can be used in the next years by transdisciplinary expert groups and uninitiated civil society ones and by open innovation user groups. Even for data entry in a modeling software like a visualization tool, as long as the analysis of the architecture components and the design process are known, which makes it a case of finding how to put collective artificial intelligence at the service of the community.

Therefore, logic helps us going around the limitations of the human memory. However, its success goes through the good specific operations' conduct. When it is well handled, it can create structures of deep and profound logic extended to numerous design fields described by a researcher or a team that allows to make the relations existing within a digital social system transparent.

Logic and mathematics are two exemplary types of transparent methodological structures. Mathematics has the precision that is universally accepted. However the "vague logic", the one we use in the present community informatics design works, often deals with qualities and values that are not numerically quantifiable. For this reason, community informatics design is rigorously accompanied by a logic that relies on semantics, semiotic and pragmatic precision and the evaluative feedback of action.

The semantics precision (Krippendorff 2007) requires some definitions. This is why in 2017, we will provide the readers with the book a list of terms and glossary. It is only the beginning of our effort to describe structures and design processes. This task can be carried out in four different ways: "naming", "extending", "conceptualizing" and "linking". "Naming" is a simple operation we are all familiar with; it is the more elementary definition form. "Extending" consists of defining a class mane in terms of examples within a class, for example, the classification of canine species include several dog races. "Conceptualizing" corresponds to the classic mode of definition that aims to define concepts according to properties (attributes) that seem to be an integral part. This is what we will do in Chap. 7 by defining the different concepts belonging to various aspects whose properties we try to outline. To define a concept or a class by "relations", we try to describe its relationships with other factors, whether it is operational, conceptual, antithetical, by inclusion or exclusion, by par hierarchical or systemic relations or by priority relations, between other examples. All these ways of proceeding leave a space for dialogue and discussion. Thereafter, we can examine the environment, the context or the situation or even provide a conceptual map of the relational process that defines it. This process contains several stages.

To produce an appropriate relations' cartography, we must define both the types of relations and their extension (analytical prolongation). In order to succeed, we must define both the terms "link" (relationship between concepts) and the "relation" (their nature). For example, there is a relationship between two concepts belonging to the same class. Warfield uses the term "link" to represent an interpretive concept from the everyday language like the ideas of "life world" languages of Habermas (1984, 1973), who expresses the relationships between two entities (elements having each its components and properties). The term "relation" is not exclusively reserved to more formal concepts like mathematics ones. Interrelations and associations between those two concepts are rarely taken into account. We can only presume that logic relations model relationships. In the community informatics design of complex social systems, each conceptual association, logical basis and the implicit mission must be considered collectively and openly to overcome local subjectivities and lean towards a referential framework that is satisfying for a given practice community.

Warfield distinguishes six major categories of interpretive relationships we should consider in our analysis of context and DSS design process: the definitive link, the comparative link, the influential link, the temporal link, the spatial link and the mathematical link. In a definitive link, the entity A is a component of B; this link is expressed in terms of "included", "imply", "contain" or "is in the same category as". A comparative link evaluates relations between entities A and B on the basis of "common grounds" like "is larger than", "is preferable to", has a "higher priority" than or must "prevail on". An influential link describes how B is affected by A. In other words, it describes the way A causes B, increases it, validates it, diminishes it, supports it or is related to it. A temporal link indicates if A arrives before B, if it precedes it or follows it in time and if it requires more time than the other. A spatial link indicates a relative position: under or above, through a plan, in 2D or 3D, from left to right, towards East or West, the way to make a cartography of the element, its sequential position on a plan and the way to read it. A mathematical link is expressed by a symbolism that reflects if one or the other logical condition involving A and B is present or if a mathematical representation of A or B can be executed, for example, "A is B squared" or "A is a function of B". A mathematical link can be expressed in terms like: "A is a function of B", "A affects the occurrence probability of B", "is executable or translatable in algorithms in a server or software", "is disjointed" or "is concomitant".

Contrary to the relationships between entities, that in practice are very few, the elements or entities sensitive to interact in a social systems are countless. It is this phenomenon our team is facing by wanting to define and describe the elements and components of the community informatics design's digital social system's structure and process (Chap. 5). In this "normal social science" situation, we have deemed appropriate to focus on relationships our intuition considered important and that we could best understand a priori for the building of the COLAB. It is pointless to focus too much on relationships between elements that are not obvious, and we do not master cognitively. The relationships between entities, for example, interactions between available socio-digital media and design activities to be accomplished in a given context, can be simply identified in a "paired-down" way, according to their aspects, their components, their qualities, their properties and their attributes. The elements (social and human aspects) and entities (technological objects like infrastructures and software architectures) can be limited in numbers (which often requires a cognitive and collective effort) to make a choice between secondary elements and prominent ones in a context where the mind if not helped by computer or by modeling software. The discovery and strategic alignment matrix we present in the present book represent an effort of establishing relations between several elements/entities in the context of dynamic development that often staggers over long periods in delocalized telepresence spaces with vague borders. They can be widely used by non-initiated people and by our students in their university work.

With this in mind, among the relationships we have examined, the most important ones to notice are the ones whose interaction logic involves transitions in time and space. They are evolutive relationships in constant change. We were inspired by the state-transition systems theory while "relieving" them of their mathematical layer for a use by social and communication sciences practitioners. That type of relation "entails … ", "provokes the emergence of … " or "springs the following elements" is transitive in the following case: if A implies B and B implies C, so A implies C. The propagation and emergence relationships have a direction or an intention that provokes mutations or transformations. The transitivity relationships also contain expressions like "precede" or "follow", "is more complicated than … ", "is more West to … ", "evolves towards … ", and "provokes a change such as … ". However, let us note that all relationships are not implicitly transitive; for example, the fact that A likes B and that B likes C does not necessarily imply that A likes C or even that such a relationship from A to B will automatically create the same one with C.

In large-scale complex systems like the digital social systems of "strategic alliance collaborative network between several regions and countries" type, we notice a tendency towards long chains of relationships that evolve and propagate in time and space and are very difficult to seize by a mind whose cognitive operations are not supported by appropriate tools or methodology. For this reason, relationships established with the help of natural language that operates through institutions, postulates and hypotheses will have to be supported by associative processes of established relations through formal computer languages. The integration of several relational dimensions with the help of modeling software, community informatics design's help tools, collective creativity help tools, visual grammar or software like Excel that facilitate the organization of complex data, can free social and communication practitioners from disciplinary constraints related to hard sciences or even constraints related to the narrow entities of the word because of object languages that are too formal. In the future, in the image of more and more groups of researchers in social digital sciences throughout the world, we will try to associate the exercise of modeling process and social systems with the help of digital tools. Thus, we wish to face the challenge of working in large partner groups to this deep, dynamic logic extended in time that will benefit from a computerized treatment for documentation, qualification of information and simulation.

The deep logic according to Warfield (1986) refers to four or five similar propagation relationships that follow each other in a rather predictable sequence we can frame thanks to qualitative identification of certain emergent interaction patterns likely to contribute to that evolution of system's components towards very varied results, even unpredictable. In visual modeling languages like the ones the Stella software use (documented by Anthony Judge on his site *Laetus in Praesens*), we can describe complex psychosocial relationships like trajectories in a graphic or diagrammatic space. The simple problems involve a simple or less articulated logic. But complex problems, introduced in the last 10 years to build environments, organizations and virtual systems more and more complex, are difficult to apprehend with a surface logic. In fact, we introduce the idea of deep logic, colleagues are often discouraged, which contributes to the socio-technical systems' representation to be often deprived of deep analysis. We can sweep them aside by saying that they are soulless systems, determinist, controlling and inhuman. We are wrong because these systems are already everywhere. We have to apprehend them with a more powerful conceptual equipment because the lack of deep logic in the DSS analysis will have a consequence on the creation of systems more or less favourable for the human being, like we see every day with Facebook, Twitter and YouTube. These systems propagate at the speed of light and have considerable psychological and sociological consequences. It belongs to us, artists, researchers, practitioners and citizens not to let computing to computer specialists even if they are the first artisans of the information society. The sub-conceptualization, sub-theorization and large-scale communication pathologies could be the direct consequences.

2.4   Archival Reproduction Tools

The fourth universal antecedent is the representation by archives and digital libraries that refer to the different ways to reach, record, process, manipulate, file, manage and share new knowledge by communities of practice. In the social Web context and the progression of large virtual libraries like Wikipedia, the mass collaboration becomes a science, the "wikinomics" (Tapscott and Williams 2008, 2010).

Observing the exponential explosion and growth of the number of blog followers and the emergence of massive virtual communities dedicated to innovation and knowledge sharing, Tapscott and Williams conclude that massive innovation is the result of millions of connected individuals who can actively contribute to the information society and the capitalization of knowledge. Massive innovation that several researchers like Chesbrough et al. (2008) and Von Hippel (2007, 2005) associate to the creation of collective wealth, knowledge improvement and social development was only a dream until now. When the masses contribute to projects like the ones we illustrate in Chap. 10, they can make the arts, education, culture, science, democratic governance and the economic progress in an innovative and constructive way. Organizations and society that currently get involved in the creation of these technology-mediatized social systems on the social Web discover the real meaning of the "social capital" concept in appropriation, exchange, memorization and knowledge filing activities personalized to all sorts of groups, communities and strategic networking alliances. This is why the increase of knowledge and skills in the design of these vast socio-technical systems becomes a national priority.

Even if, more and more, the functions we are describing in this section are automated by agents and "smart librarians", the future orientation of these systems and the "thought sovereignty" requires that we develop these generation skills and bringing together the knowledge. This could considerably alienate the current critique of social media platforms that represent a social situation that any education systems must contain or eliminate. The critique is only one of the two necessary faces for the creation of future social systems that aim to make the world a bit more favourable for the human being. The other is the real capacity to orientate change, where lies the importance of design training at all levels of teaching: primary and secondary school, college and university. Mass socio-technical system design beyond the simple generation of content by users and the co-building of a universal database of emerging practices, as they are presented in the next chapters, represents one of the largest dimensions of our freedom in our society of knowledge.

2.5　The Validation of a Community Informatics Design's Generic Science

Warfield (1986, 1994, and 1999) introduces a validation law and its corollary. He affirms that the validity of all science depends on a substantial meaning agreement, at its highest degree, within a scientific community, through shared meaning of relations and interaction definition. Its corollary is that validity of all science depends on the capacity of a scientific community to build definitions within the frame of relationships' definition for the entire complex concepts that are involved in the new science. This law and its corollary are very difficult to achieve in the present research. They establish necessary conditions but insufficient to validate an approach. Therefore, other laws must be put to contributions.

It has become a habit, in social sciences, to resort to quantification of any research to answer the scientific models. Certain specific attributes of numbers and statistics calculus give quantification an air of respectability. Numbers, because they are universally understood, can help to quantify computers of a school, the degrees of appropriation of social media in an enterprise or the learning curve of a social modeling platform. They help lay the foundations of the validity agreement when it is time to specify magnitude orders, proportions and differences between data units. However, we all know that in social and communication sciences, important qualities and properties of our systems cannot be distinguished by quantification. The sweet clarity associated with numbers cannot systematically be transferred to these social systems qualities (ethics, aesthetics, emotional, conflictual and psychological) by giving them quantification modes. If quantification can impart a value or enrich the validation in connection with the scientific process, it does not implicitly give them validity. According to Warfield, validity is obtained thanks to "referential transparency", which commands a "deep logic". If a science possesses the "referential transparency", we are able to trace the logic in both directions through its structure and process. To achieve the referential transparency (not like the Holy Grail but like a certain rigor ideal to be achieved), our researchers team at the ACIL has tried to precise the foundations, theories and applications of community informatics design for 2 years. We have also made a systemic effort to try to show the feedback relations between these different stages of science according to Warfield's prescriptions:

- The hypothesis that intervenes in the pragmatic DSS' design foundations and underlying theories
- The selection of criteria, dimensions, aspects and fields we have used to create our modeling methodology and instantiation from the theories of social systems and socio-technical systems involved in the DSS co-design
- The roles of stakeholders and the environment (the exostructure or exogenous elements) in which DSS design methodology is applied (virtual environments to support DSS community informatics design)
- The evaluative feedback that applications provide by creating instruments for the analysis of social media uses and creativity tools in the DSS design modeling.

The component of interactive methodology and community informatics design's applications constitutes the arena where different types of "participative research action", sociocultural interventions or operational modeling of business models are organized and take place. The foundations and theory (concepts, principles and abstract prose) represent its corpus. The corpus represents as a whole, in limited principle, pieces, written documents or scientific conversations on the Internet and documentation elements relative to community informatics design. The constant circulation between the corpus and the arena create a living, open, dynamic science; it allows to feed the practice, and theories can, in turn, direct practices. It produces theories/practices where abstract separation between theory and practice disappears, both being intrinsically linked. It avoids sterile debates between practitioners and theoreticians and between quantophrenia scientific approaches (following the expression of Pitirim Sorokin) and research action without theoretical progress.

The absence of constant feedback between the corpus and the arena limits the community informatics design in its impact and its validity. It is true that the research action, for example, as a very generic methodological position, can discover valuable solutions to certain problems in certain intervention environments. But without the "conceptual weaving" related to the lessons learned from constraints and difficulties, the research action remains insufficient from the standpoint of the creation of a new science like the community informatics design. The community informatics imagination, the aptitude to imagine and make hypothesis on systems that do not yet exist, should be based on strong ontological principles (like pragmatism and systemism) and a creative and inspiring corpus if it wants to continue to imagine solutions to problems more and more complex at a very large scale. In the absence of an ontology and epistemology made explicit in the foundations and corpus, the research action condemns itself to drive its intentions at a small-scale instead of large-scale environments like the "network society" well highlighted by Manuel Castells (2011).

Warfield explains as follows the fact that physical sciences, for example, can almost perfectly negotiate their success in the arena of methodological and applicative fields without referencing to their foundations and theories. By making it a computing representation of deep logic implied in physical sciences oriented towards practice, it problematizes their "action landscape" through issues like the human being's nature, made of skills, language, integrator concepts and arithmetic and representations systems. He discovers how the measuring system "blocks" the interaction between applications and universal antecedents. Normalization that has been available in physical sciences for a long time dispenses the scientist to resort to constant foundations. Social and communication sciences, which occupy the largest part of information systems' foundations and community information systems modeling, do not benefit from such normalization. Warfield tells us that as long as sciences will not find universally approved measuring systems, they will have to be accompanied by a disciplined management of universal antecedents to ensure their validity.

The implications of this affirmation are important. Among other things, the social science language must be continually confronted to the task of defining terms and concepts that are implicitly present in physical and pure in general. It is clear that whims and the "vague" aspect of the language make obvious the idea that creative representations that want to distinguish relations and interactions between concepts and fields are one of the necessary conditions of validity and rigor in social and communication sciences. Community informatics design and related sciences on which they rely (especially computer-assisted collaborative work, HCI, computer-mediatized communication, computer-mediatized social participation, human-computer interfaces, the STS sector, Critical Research on Internet, the Internet Research domain and Sustainable Democracy development) often require "hard science" contributions, like the ones from physics, biology and computer science. But they also widely borrow from the imprecise sciences (Moles 1990), and they must widely call upon a creative and rigorous language use, which requires definitions by relations/links and semiformal representations towards a prose/ graphic.

We use this attitude throughout this book, by recognizing with humility that our effort is well incomplete but is, nevertheless, a contribution in that sense. This is why we give a lot of space to the more normalized definition possible of certain terms like "model", "reference framework", "open innovation" and "instantiation", and two chapters focus on the discovery of "quasi-standards", meaning relations, the discovery and strategic alignment matrix method, to try to standardize our approach as well as to master the inherent conceptual complexity.

Even those precautions are not sufficient for the dawning community informatics sciences we outline in this book. In keeping with exercising a control over the quality of production of science or generic interventions, community informatics design needs an additional orientation mechanism. For this reason, we will examine an exploratory research conducted as part of the APSI that explores the basis of large-scale socio-technical systems co-design on the Internet. To do so, we will use the Warfield "science field model" as an analysis guide of construction and design of online social systems.

At the image of our Professor Abraham Moles who, as early as 1954, was giving examples of a way to introduce a rigorous thought in the sciences of vague (sociology, psychology, communication, ethnology, anthropology, etc.), Warfield and an entire American movement that still goes on today (social system design researchers), wanted to show us that even if social and communication sciences are generally considered imprecise by essence (not as a consequence of a lack of objectivity), we can develop means to introduce a rigorous thought to deal with imprecise phenomena like networking intercultural relations, socio-technical design of collaborative platforms, planning and modeling of digital cities and the definition of policies on democratic participation by digital platforms (Moles and Rohmer 1986).

2.6   The Object of Community Informatics Design's Field of Science

Community informatics design as a systemic science of construction of digital social systems is still in its early phases of creation: it contains a very large diversity of points of view, approaches and very diverse concepts regarding its nature, its reach, its formalization/standardization degree and its applicability. One of its most promising current theories on systems is the social systems design theory (G. S. Metcalf 2014; Churchman 1974, 1971, 1968; Banathy 1996, 1992, 1991, 1986; Giddens 1984; Fuchs 2008, 2004, 2003; Hofkirchner 2013. 2008), which seems particularly well adapted since it is possible to link them to Giddens (1984), Habermas (1984) and Luhmann's sociology (1995, 1989) and to socio-cybernetics. After reviewing diverse definitions of science (Bunge 1998; Campbell 1952; Chalmers 1999; Kerlinger 1973), as well as several other works related to our practice and our methodological teaching for 25 years, we have observed and retained certain concepts common to science: (1) an object or a field of study, (2) a series of concepts defined by a specific language, (3) a philosophy/theory and (4) a method for applications. According to Warfield (2006, 1986), the science of systems and, a fortiori, a generic community informatics design's science should be covering four groups of activities for which he suggests fundamental components that integrate science of design and social systems and the socio-technical component we are adding to it within the unifying and transdisciplinary community informatics design's frame. Here are the five sciences and their components we adapt to our specific field:

1. *A description science*, which aims to describe problematic situations of any nature within the field of activities, for example, the description of components of a digital social system taking social aspects and technological aspects, accompanied by the description of their fields and integrated properties.
2. *A generic design science*, for the design of social systems by means of various transdisciplines applicable through different disciplines, cultures or organizational forms that take into account the human being in all his dimensions, thinking, ethics, language and systemic concepts oriented towards a sustainable society. For example, community informatics design is currently built on multiple bases: design thinking, the complexity sciences, human-computer interfaces (HCI), computer-assisted collaborative work (CSCW), evolutive social systems design, socio-technical approaches, social and communication sciences, virtual communities formal approaches, collaborative networks and living labs, the theory of activity, conversational design, participative culture movements and design centred on the human, computer-mediatized communication, computer-mediatized social participation, knowledge management, political governance and collaborative project management. All these disparate fields could be conceptually consolidated around the idea of Internet research.
3. *A complexity science*, with the objective to develop dimensions and their qualitative and quantitative measures and to model theoretical principles facilitating the understanding and interpretation of the complexity of problematic situations as well as the digital social systems design and their methodologies.
4. *An action science,* to specify methodologies that allow to resolve complex issues within the community informatics design's science field. We resort to an ontology/epistemology of action that allows not only the construction of virtual communities of all sorts but also the interactive management, the modeling of dialogic design's science, living labs, fab labs, colabs, social platforms and democratic and participation platforms for digital diplomacy.
5. *A communication and language science*.

The five italicized terms represent the five major components of the social systems theory. These five sciences and subdisciplines integrated their perspectives to contribute to the knowledge basis of the community informatics design and to resolve the problematic situations of any nature, especially those of the large-scale digital social systems development dedicated to sustainable development. The five meta-sciences provide "objective" bases for the definition of large-scale systems design, involving technological and social components, for example, virtual communities or strategic inter-enterprise alliances. To adapt them to today's world, our team has decided to define them, following Warfield and Christakis (1987), like systems of socio-technical nature. Such systems involve the evolutive emergence of subsystems that combine social systems (*soft*) and technological systems (*hard*). We can say that any pair of elements derived from science (S) and technology (T) is emerging/evolutive in a context C or a design situation D, if an S+T fusion reveals the generation of a new element V that does not preserve the individual identity of any original elements. For example, when the social appropriation of a technology from a collaborative platform merges with an organization, it may result in a new community information system allowing network innovations that could not occur within the ancient system of human activities. This new socio-technical system has to be analysed according to its emerging properties, from its social and technical components.

A social system is a configuration of actors in interaction. According to Anthony Giddens (1984), a social system is a set of interactions located in time and space. Giddens distinguishes several social systems: organizations, groups, social movements and societies as widen social systems. Peter Checkland (1981) presents a complete definition of the social system as a human activity system. While natural systems and engineer systems cannot be anything other than what they are, the human activity systems manifest themselves through the perception of human beings, who are free to assign a variety of meaning to what they perceive. There is never a unique way to report human activity systems; we observe a series of possible configurations, all valid according to a particular world vision. Considering the human being and its abilities, we have an important array of human activity systems on a continuum that goes from the individual handling a computer to international network political platform and enterprise portals (perspective of an observation continuum observation that goes from micro to macro through meso). A social system model is a configuration of roles that, together with the help of a script, report the interaction between different roles played by individuals or partners of organization stakeholders. Community informatics design of a social system consists of developing scripts and its roles as human activity systems aiming at producing technical or social artefacts.

A technical system is a series of artefacts, like communication, collaboration or coordination tools that interact in a DSS design project, according to intentions of a practice community and design activities it plans. Socio-technical information systems researchers instruct us to increase our knowledge about Web tools and their interactions with human activity systems. Cognitive mastery and collective design skills as well as human activities' tool configuration become the new conditions of our freedom and imagination in the innovation and democratic participation of the future. We must ethically direct their contents and design. The European living labs and the American colabs are recognized for helping many groups of non-expert users to come together in order to generate their content and create the design and the personalized applications that meet their needs. A socio-technical system is born and grows with the dynamic fusion of a social system S and a technical system T, to produce a socio-technical system V. From the moment when we recognize that a social system is dynamic and evolutive and that any dynamic system integrates another dynamic subsystem, we say that any socio-technical system is a dynamic and evolutive system. The integration of the social system and the technical system results in a socio-technical system. With the current social Web and the future Internet of Things, we have the possibility of building not only mirror sites but all new online institutions (Ostrom and Hess 2011) such as scientific communes mediated by ICT or the entities of the Internet of Things, we have a complex permanent socio-technical system. We have a mission and duty to direct them in a direction that is more favourable to the human being rather than the one illustrated in the tyranny and the abuse we see in the current social media. We call them "digital social systems"; they will be co-built with a whole new social media interactive and participative design: the community informatics design.

The script of a digital social system, like a virtual community, will be built thanks to community informatics design using the following definition of community on three levels according to a conception inspired by socio-technical design:

1. A socio-dynamic system supported by computer collaborative networks and applicative programs (like network infrastructures, educational platforms like Moodle, wikis and blogs).
2. The continuous collaboration validation through computer-mediatized communication and computer-mediatized social participation. The digital communication is regulated and structured by general interaction procedures, common interests and particular collaborative modes instrumentalized (Lemire 2008) by creativity, design and modeling tools and general interaction intentions such as knowledge management and social networking we find on Wikipedia or Facebook.
3. Collaboration and emotions related to the being and to the birth of multiple and shared identity and common values that can be born from computer-mediatized communication and the appropriation of computer-mediatized social participation tools emerge in activities of the community. This level is far from being reached in all virtual communities because several DSS are currently built on competition, the accumulation of identity differences and overrated reputations or a lack of ethics.

Community informatics, a recent face of communication's applied sciences, has been traditionally developed under the social informatics label (Kling 1973, 1996, 1999, 2007; Kling et al. 2001, 2005) and is also designated by expressions like "community networking", "social Web", "social media", "cybercommunities", "networking electronic communities", "socio-digital networks", "community-oriented technologies", "collaborative networks", "computer-mediatized social participation", "participative design", "participative research action" and "co-design". According to Gurstein (2006), one of the founding fathers of the field, community informatics refers to a series of principles and practices including the use of information technologies and communication for the social, cultural, political and economic development in the communities, by the communities and by their intervention. Community informatics, as a new academic discipline, has, until now, been developing within older disciplines like information systems and social computing. With living labs and colabs oriented on vast communities and large-scale massive innovation, the notion of design oriented towards users has occupied a substantial place in documentation dedicated to the subject. We will see that currently, with the meta-design and the human oriented design (Krippendorff 2007), the virtual communities movement promote, more and more, collective practices oriented not only on the production of contents but also on all sorts of fields related to design thinking[1] at the service of innovation, human development and the democratic conscience of the majority.

In addition, today, community informatics is associated with terms like "social intelligence" and "collaborative intelligence" in fields like social psychology; sociocultural animation by community media; communication sciences; located or distributed cognition; artificial intelligence; complex systems modeling; the Internet of the future; the Web 2.0, 3.0 and even 4.0; and critical approaches of the social Web. We can consider it like a transdisciplinary approach that uses ICT to create, in a participative and collaborative way, the design of all sorts of action communities aiming the innovation creation like living labs, practice communities, collective intelligence processes, learning organizations, assisted design social platforms, health grids, knowledge-building communities, open innovation communities and mutual design help communities. We will see that as an applied discipline, it can benefit from several disciplines to guide its actions on the field and suggest concrete instantiation methodologies of people and communities' intentions. In this context where social and communication action gives it a field practice character oriented on digital social systems co-design of the future, we call it "community informatics design".

However, community informatics design goes beyond the simple tool configuration on a website. In addition, it is not only interested in the generalized improvisation in the establishment of DSS by non-initiated communities. While recognizing the dynamism of certain practices, it rather validates the use appropriation of technologies to develop in a systematic and rigorous manner digital social systems like the communities that transcend the creation of unbridled social platforms and opposite to ethics, to rather try to engage people in processes and communication activities that are socially responsible. For example, develop common intentions and visions through different types of language that do not only speak of innovations and artefacts but that give them their shared meanings. Sharing objectives, values, value beliefs and a responsible ethics regarding others analyses the activity flow in collaborative network at work, at home and in the local or global communities. Also, evaluate the stakeholders' roles and partners in the co-creation of a future digital social system and facilitate groups and resolve conflicts with the help of modeling and representation tools. Plan collaborative networks projects of all sorts in the service of human development and their ethical governance.

---

[1] See the IDEO site (<www.ideo.com>).

In the next section, we will deepen the social and socio-technical principles that should guide the users/designers in their creation of future social systems. For the moment, let us simply mention that the community informatics designer needs to develop an excellent understanding of what is socially desirable, technically and economically feasible, legitimate, transparent and ethical in the creation of online interactions of all sorts. The community informatics designer also needs to understand well all technology affordances tool functionalities and their constraints. He must learn to align the tools with the community needs and objectives, how tools can be related to each other, inter-operationally configured and integrated in new evolutive ecosystems: the digital social systems. In short, the entire effort of the UQAM's applied community informatics lab consists of showing that, beyond the current improvisation in the Internet structuring, a semiformal approach does not aim to stifle users' creativity or imagination, quite the contrary, but to direct practically and ethically.

The websites, hubs, portals and virtual organization's co-design cannot be left to chance, without taking into account the several skills that allow it to involve governments, universities, enterprises and civil society in motivating projects for the economy and society. The context and virtual work environments become more and more complex, and they provoke more and more indignation, a loss of trust and fears because of not appropriate uses. We have the unique desire and opportunity to massively guide the change with the support of new information and communication technologies and technologies that are in a constant state of change and evolution. Community informatics design aims to optimize social and technological change and to represent a new intelligence technology that requires a deep understanding of logic (relations, links, strategic alignment between tools and social needs). This requirement has become necessary by the constant innervation of the social global tissue of social media, regarding the training of young people who will know that in an evolutive world, the community informatics design represents a promising contribution of orientation and cognitive, social, cultural and economic support of our societies.

2.7   Community Informatics Design's Field of Science

Now, let us come back to the structuring of the community informatics design field of science according to Warfield's works that will allow us to describe the essential elements we must establish in accordance with Charles Sanders Pierce's orientation philosophy. The model explains the interaction concepts such as the foundations, the theory, the methodology and the applications of the community informatics design while making sure we describe their reciprocal links we believe it is possible to integrate parts of disciplines in the new community informatics design transdiscipline. The Warfield model can help us with this task because it offers an attempt to classify sciences in general and conceptual sciences in particular.

Warfield tells us that to ensure the referential transparency of a generic design science, and this applies to community informatics design in particular, we must strive to propose three communicational interfaces. One is the interface between researchers/producers of the new science and the users/practitioners of problem-solving and planning of the digital social systems design. A second interface must be suggested between community informatics experts involved in the co-creation of the future digital social system and the administrative partners and project managers that provide governance modes and appropriate orientations for the objectives. A third interface consists of setting up interactions between the administrative personnel and citizens. We add a fourth interface the Europeans would call a "partnership helix" between governments, universities, enterprises and citizens. This helix offers an identification systemic of different partners' roles. Furthermore, in the current globalization context, where the problem of resource scarcity and sustainable development becomes the world's priority, we add a fifth interface that contains all the others: the environment and the ecosystems that contain experts and non-initiated humans; social, cultural and technological dimensions; ecological environments; and multi-profession partner helix around the director concept of sustainable development. Current global issues command these new communication structures in the information society. Figure 2.1 illustrates this partnership helix model. (Source: Carayannis and Campbell own conceptualization based on Etzkowitz and Leydesdorff (2000, p. 112), Carayannis and Campbell (2009, p. 207; 2012, p. 14; 2013) and Danilda et al. (2009))

The complexity governance brought by these new interfaces organized in the Internet networks and the "partnership helix" metaphor represents one of the main community informatics design contributions to the cognitive mastery of new social systems and their collaborative management in the new virtual environments. The multiplication and structuring of new social links of vast turban issues, related to risk situations or ecological disasters, force society to equip itself with means of quick understanding of global issues by suggesting interfaces and innovative partnerships, while maintaining a cooperative management through the flexible cycles of life and adapted to different design situations.

Besides the complexification of new problems our societies are facing more and more the necessity to make the new governance modes' design to face it, we have to manage complexity in other fields. We must reduce the "virtual cognitive world" information overload from the individuals and find appropriate dialogue modes to create necessary consensus for action in various types of communities. We must find new projects' life cycles, adaptable to this complexity that requires united behaviours and communities ready to face global changes.

Current design situations exceed the perception of individual problems and the capacity of human communities to face the set of their components. All sorts of collaborative tools are currently available to help individuals and groups to master this complexity, to model it, to simulate it for the purpose of social action and intentional social change. Warfield can help us to synthesize the functionalities relative to a correct community informatics design. These functionalities are validation and improvement tools for the design process. They take into consideration the design

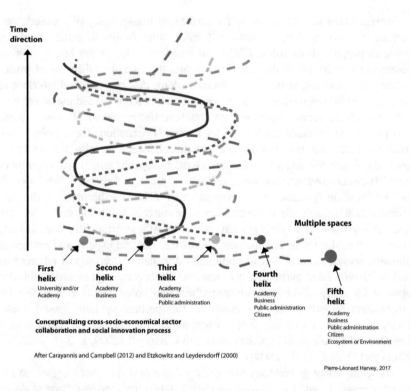

Fig. 2.1 "Partnership helix" model as an interface between various actors

and environment description process, identification of roles, governance criteria, leadership and the quality control by paying special attention to the sociocultural environment. We add a value table and an ethic design approach to it. We will come back to it at length in the sections dedicated to community informatics design instantiation strategies.

2.8   Community Informatics Foundations

As we have seen, Warfield distinguishes four universal antecedents of a design science: the human being, the language, the reasoning by links and the archival representation modes. By developing these concepts and by linking them to each other, he provides the essential context that fills the gaps of several sciences, especially information and communication systems applied sciences and major socio-technical systems developed in collaborative networks on the Internet. The universal antecedents' science and community informatics object serve as the foundations of the community informatics design generic science. In the present section, we propose a detailed presentation of the science model foundations according to Warfield.

According to Christakis and Flanagan (2011), the field of science models (FOSM) presented by Warfield in 1986 was not sufficiently appreciated for its heuristic value in the creation of a new scientific field like the community informatics design. The FOSM cannot only provide useful knowledge to better understand the intentions of a science but also highlights the foundations of this science, nominally the objects of a scientific field like the community informatics design that can analytically extend itself to various aspects of its development, the application ontology and the theories as well as their links with methodology. As we have already mentioned, today's human beings must live and work with large-scale systems where technology applications largely exceed an individual capacity to analyse these systems and intervene upon them (e.g. large artificial intelligence systems or cyber-physical social systems). It becomes important to put into perspective the way the scientific actors build a field and interact between them and with practitioners, engineers or computer experts. How do they perform cultural mediation between this science and the applications grounds? How do sponsors and subsidy organizations mediatize between them this science to other researchers and various concerned audience? In order to shed light on these partnership interactions, we will describe the FOSM by trying to present a few restrictions and some extensions to the community informatics design field.

• The restrictions refer to a conceptual knowledge base that incorporates only a part of the FOSM's elements.
• The extensions contain knowledge bases that go beyond community informatics design to expend to fields related to science's universal antecedents.

This conceptual exam will cause us to conclude that today, the construction of democratic user/designer platforms that is dedicated to large-scale human and sustainable development can be submitted to restrictions related to formal operating fields (applied aspects appliqués of interventions in the field), while other restrictions are the fruit of an incompetence to relate community informatics design's foundation (the FOSM applied to our field) universal antecedents of all sciences. Our will to shed light on these problems go beyond the framework of this present chapter. This study on its own could be the object of an entire other book. However, even by retaining a schematic writing, we believe this discussion on community informatics design's foundations supported by 40 years of application is indispensable for a dawning science.

Our intention is to briefly show the community informatics design's foundations, as a science that relies on various modes of dialogue, and to make connections between these modes and complex digital social systems design, in order to make them more transparent in referential terms and to make it a helping tool for our students and users/designers of all horizons that would be interested in these foundations for their sustainable development and intentional social change works. This effort represents a first step in the identification commitment entries and the mobilization of members of a practice community and users/designers of living labs in front of the extent of some DSS projects. The Warfield approach adopted by our team as an analysis guide and the FOSM systemic orientation use are appropriate to all sciences and community informatics design, in particular in their conceptual, methodological and applicative aspects. They are relevant to the extent of several stakeholders and R-D partners form an innovation community where it is important to define the role of each one, which is far from being an easy task.

The referential transparency study of community informatics design of digital social systems stems from years of theorization in the design science and in the practice of the dialogic design (Christakis and Bausch 2006; Christakis 2005, 1987; Christakis and Harris 2004). It is useful to recall axioms and main components of these sciences too often considered like sciences without foundations having a large practice field. The field feeds theories and the theory guides the praxis. Furthermore, we must recognize that the most influential communication and contemporary dialogic "design thought" belongs to the field of the design sciences applications in situ and not by telepresence and sociocultural animation modes of today. The FOSM requires that from the applications developed for years in workshops in person, meaning without the generalized help of technology, we could evaluate if, in view of the important evolution of living labs, colabs and other forms of Internet democratic participation/creation, our current practice communities possess ways and the necessary tools to revise the validity of its basic axioms. Such a foundation revision is now mandatory by the great current society debates that question the role and power of social sciences in the evolution of the current network society as diverse design sciences find themselves in a generalized evolution process of in-person accompanying towards more and more complex accompanying of practice through means of collaborative tools and social Internet platforms.

The FOSM possesses the virtue of illustrating the distinctions of four fields specific to any science, the distinctions between the corpus and the field (arena) in the generic framework of a science activities. Figure 2.2 shows that this model created in 1986 will help us to understand the evolution of the community informatics design as well as the potential impact of its current development stage on social sciences. The model contains the foundations that guide the theories, the theories that guide the methodologies and the methodologies and techniques that we can put into practice when a design context or situation demand it, as well as applications that are specific to today's collaborative design (participative platforms, agoras, living labs, colabs). First of all, we will present this model with its restrictions and its possible extensions to communication design sciences and socially responsible networking. And second, we will present its application to community informatics design.

Within the community informatics design's field of science, we distinguish four "open" blocks specific to the model, which start with the applications foundations and go to the theories and methodologies. Each block literally feeds its successor and acts retroactively on its predecessor in a never-ending evolutive spiral that goes from science to its applications and from applications to science.

Combinations The combination of blocks constitutes the science under construction (Fig. 2.2 science). The corpus of science is a subsystem that only involves foundations and theories. The arena only involves methodologies and applications.

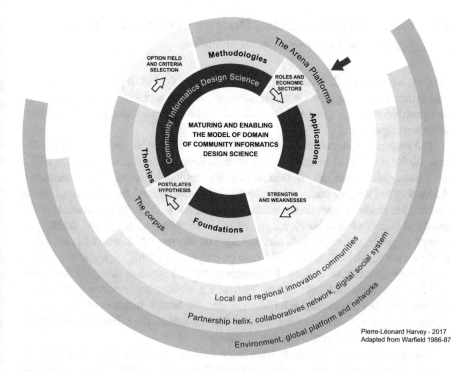

Fig. 2.2 Maturation and validation of the community informatics design field model

If the methodology is presented by Warfield as an integral part of science, it is nevertheless clearly possible to suggest, to develop and to use a methodology that does not have a clear connection with the corpus and that is strictly produced for the purpose of satisfying the needs of the arena or an explicit field. It is without a doubt one of the most obvious characteristics of the current design of sciences (sciences of conception according to Simons 2005) in all sorts of application fields, products, services, artefacts and social systems. For example, most current large-scale projects in the field of ubiquitous computing and social Web, guided towards applications and methodologies, do not draw their existence nor their orientation from a corpus nor an explicit and transparent conceptual framework. Rather, it is drawn from limited and volunteer initiatives of methodological transfers more or less appropriate between disciplines from the will of sponsors of enthusiastic consultants' discourses.

Connections The four connections in Fig. 2.2 represent the links between the blocks we can identify as a feedback cycle between 1-Foundation/Theory, 2-Theory/ Methodology and 3-Methodology/Applications and the feedback end of cycle with 4-Applications/Foundations or with the abbreviations FT, TM, MA, AF. They correspond to the four following block's orientation and organization functions, which allows to create an iterative virtuous circle benefitting the improvement of a science quality.

2.9   Community Informatics Design's Four Fields and Its Application to DSS: General Vision

Like so, we will use the constituent elements of the FOSM to present the community informatics design like a "design-for-all" science and like a type of systemic and practice research that involves both the social systems theories and the socio-technical approaches.

The systemic research centred on design of digital social systems includes the four Warfield's FOSM interdependent fields (1986; Warfield and Christakis 1987): the philosophical foundations, the theories, the methodologies and the applications. According to Banathy and Jenlink (2005), the philosophical foundations of social systems are made of three dimensions: ontology (that defines the components of the reality to be analysed or built), epistemology (a knowledge theory) and axiology (a system of goals, values, beliefs and ethics). The ontology dimension lies on a systemic vision of the DSS to be built, based on pragmatism (philosophy of action) and praxeology (science of action). It transcends the DSS vision designed like static systems (e.g. the Internet of "Things") towards a social systems vision (educational system, healthcare system, enterprise model, as Social Internet of Things), as dynamic and open living systems, a vision that recognizes the primacy of relational-organizing-self-organizing-evolutive processes.

The epistemology contains at least three fields of research. First, it studies the change, co-design or co-evolution process of a social system within which the research and development take place (a system called "design system research space"). In this design exploratory space, it produces knowledge to understand how the design systems will transform the work activity system (Engeström 1999), community networking practices, interpersonal relations and collaborative network organizational interrelations. We introduce a third space within the framework of principles and values of socio-technical approaches in organizational communication like human-computer interfaces (Hochheiser and Lazar 2007) that correspond to the "universal design" values (Fuchs and Obrist 2010) valorizing the appropriation of social technologies, the contents generated by the user and the design centred on the human being (Krippendorff 2007; Hofkirchner 2007; Fuchs and Obrist 2010). These approaches valorize the Technology Mediatized Social Participation (TMSP) domain (Preece and Shneiderman 2009), the collaboration and sustainable development field (Rico de Sotelo 2008, 2011; Agbobli and Hsab 2011) and similar approaches we find in the work on social design theories and also, the whole field of "Community Networking" that the International ICT community put forward during the two World Summits on Information Society (WSIS) in 2003 (Geneva) and 2006 (Tunis). The systemic research axiology dedicated to community informatics design of digital social systems that are favourable to men and civil society puts forwards a preoccupation for moral qualities, ethics and systems' aesthetics. It is particularly interested in social justice, equity and tolerance, to intercultural relations, to the facilitation of a social consensus through various dialogue modes, to social media development at the service of the community, to sustainable development through responsible development as well as to participative democracy.

The theories (the corpus) result from this philosophy and adopt a transdisciplinary approach that articulates the numerous concepts and principles of the theories of change in social and communication sciences, as well as the ones from diverse types of Internet domains previously mentioned in this book: for example, the commitment of users in digital ecosystem planning, the cultural intervention strategies supported by social media, the user's involvement in contents and design, the use of open-source code technology for socio-economic innovation, the social appropriation of collaborative and creative tools, the participation in the decision-making and democratic governance of ecosystem, the construction of virtual communities of all types and with various intentions, interconnected sociability, co-design and the improvement of all citizens "digital skills" as well as the pleasure of being together and playing videogames at home. Collaborative intelligence, motivation, trust, well-being, quality of life and generalized collaboration for the benefit of all citizens are fundamental concepts in community informatics design. Community informatics design aims to adapt these principles and articulate them in a transdisciplinarity to intentional systemic change of our real/digital social systems or as human activities in cyberspace systems.

The methodological system includes three fields of study:

1. The study of methods by which knowledge and the community informatics design's knowledge basis are generated, the identification and description of applications strategies, information collection tools (ethnographic methods, qualitative research, questionnaire, discussion groups, case studies), collaborative tools and platforms (socio-collaborative media), DSS configuration and instantiation methods like discovery and strategic alignment matrices of DSS objective tools, cooperative management and the organization of development principles
2. The study of the models used to build a support model for community informatics design research and the co-building of DSS according to stakeholders' objectives and the consolidation of their intentions/orientations through various modeling and visual representation modes
3. The evaluation and appropriation of various reflection modes (Ranjan 2007; Burnette 2009) and dialogues (Bohm 1998, 1996) to facilitate user/designer practice communities and the diverse languages used for the tool configuration or the programming of a particular collaborative platform in accordance with an objective.

The application field (the arena) has close links with methodology. It takes place in functional contexts of intentions' realization in relation with the design of a complex solution through the DSS instantiation strategy created from a reference model. In fact, it refers to the interaction dynamic and the foundation's translation (the philosophy), theory (the corpus) and methodology (the arena) in a social action system catalysed by the DSS and thanks to it. In the present book, we describe for the first time the entire set of fields that allowed us to build a DSS model through a transdisciplinary and multi-methodological process. It is a community informatics design helping systems of other DSS with its norms and concrete instantiation strategy through means of reflection modes and an iterative imagination process.

Through dialogue and languages, we not only observe the world, we "blend it into the practice" (Craig 1999, 2006; Krippendorff 2007; Morin 1982, 1985). This way, philosophy, theory, methodology and the applications of social systems come to life as varied transdisciplinary discourses that blend community informatics design into the four fields and that applies it in the functional and operating context of research on theory and systemic design just like the communication and social science systemic approaches used and applied in the DSS. It is in the practical context of action and systemic research applications in social systems design and virtual organizations that the philosophy, theory and methodology are confirmed, readjusted, modified and disputed. The systemic pragmatic philosophy, at the base of community informatics design, provides the values, beliefs, the hypothesis and the perspectives that guide us into the action by defining and organizing the "relational arrangements" of concepts and principles that constitute it. The systemic philosophy and theory dynamically interact to guide us in the co-building, the decision-making and the organization of choices for the approaches, strategies, languages, methods and collaborative tools related to the epistemology frameworks of digital social systems action. The systemic methodology and its socio-constructive applications interact to guide us in the confirmation of our intentions, the necessity to reorientate our activities or to stay the course, to transform or modify the theory or the systemic epistemology. Each of the four fields acts retroactively on the others and on the whole community informatics field of science. These four described fields constitute the conceptual system of the systemic research in digital social systems' design. As we will see further along, this influence relation of a field on another is recursive, commanding an iterative approach; it is multi-aspect and multimodal.

2.10   Community Informatics Design Science: A Specific Vision According to the Four Fields (Blocks)

Since the introduction of the FOSM and the presentation of social systems design 10 years later, in 1996,[2] until the current emergence of colabs and living labs, all sciences and all sectors of society and organization living have been affected by socio-technical innovations resulting from the progression of the Internet, social networks and now computer-mediatized collaboration social technologies. This context promotes the emergence of a transdisciplinarity in several fields, which in turn commands a certain basic philosophical positioning. This represents an intellectual challenge.

---

[2] Bela Banathy's works (1971, 1986, 1992, 1996; Banathy and Jenks 1991)

2.10.1   The Foundations (Block 1)

The applied community informatics lab (ACIL) is basing its works on a general philosophy of transdisciplinarity that has been developed by Francis Heylighen (2007) and his colleagues by creating, over 20 years ago, the group on evolution, complexity and cognition (ECCO). The conceptual framework of the ECCO group leans upon philosophical foundations based on an action ontology that considers that constituents of reality are the actions and the agents (actors or techniques) producing them. With the birth of a network society (Castells), more and more phenomena and projects are designed like self-organized and evolutive networks that develop to become systems more and more complex, adaptive, intelligent and collaborative. The result is a world vision that allows us to integrate the more fundamental problem of the science philosophy we have previously presented (like in Banathy's work) in addition to suggesting three others, ontology, epistemology and axiology, already presented in Warfield's FOSM as fundamental foundations components, with the help of Heylighen's works (2007) and his colleagues, we add metaphysics, praxeology and futurology.

This vision tackles more particularly problems surrounding the duality of mind/ matter, or cognition/society, including the intentional origins and the subjective experience as well as the relations between perspectives of the first person (the world observer of the first phase science), the second person (two observers confronting their world visions, second phase of science) and the third person (Basarab Nicolescu "included third" several observers acting on the world in the third phase of science). It succeeds by extending the intentional position from the simpler agents, elementary particles like the Higgs boson and atoms from the standard physics theory. In addition, according to Heylighen (2007), a world vision based on action can support a diversity of applications, including the design of self-organized technological systems like the digital social systems that aim to mobilize people to work in a motivated and coordinated way and any system supporting collaborative development and socio-construction of knowledge networks.

The clarification of this conceptual framework has two main advantages. First, it suggests a world vision that gives the community informatics design's foundations as a self-organized system. Second, it gives us a practice method to create collaborative Web systems, the "digital social systems", like Wikipedia, the living labs, the colabs and the participative science portals. Furthermore, it provides a collection of methods, stigmergy strategies and technologies capable of supporting the self-organization of virtual communities and the collaborative intelligence, especially the self-organization of the interaction between people, who, together, will develop innovation communities or complex management and knowledge sharing systems.

Without getting into the details of the ECCO group philosophy, we will try to offer a few definitions and to examine its process with a few adaptations.

The ECCO group's ontology maintains that the fundamental components of reality are actions and agents. It is the elementary processes or transitions between interdependent states of eternal matter components. Therefore, their ontology is fundamentally holistic and dynamic and reductionist. Interactions contribute to the emergence of organizations, social systems, virtual organizations and digital social systems. As these organizations and social systems emerge on the Internet, they manifest more and more perfected forms of distributed cognition, shared understanding and collective and collaborative intelligence; in other words, they develop collective skills to make enlightened choices between the actions. This ontology rejects the traditional dualist hypothesis that sees the mind and the matter as two separate entities, like two constituents of realities interdependent on one another. The matter and the mind are simply two aspects of the same basic actions network.

2.10.1.1 Metaphysics

If we could go back in time to the origins of the universe, we would see the agents and systems becoming more and simpler until losing all forms of complexity or organization. The organized forms we see around us are explained by a process called "blind variation" that produces random combinations of agents and actions and the natural selection process that retains only the "strongest" combinations, the ones that adapt or internally align best one with each other and externally with their environment. We will see that this adaptation process continues today on the Internet, in the context of natural and specialized languages that serve to establish and guide actions within digital social systems.

Futurology is a generic process that postulates that this complexification/adaptation can be extrapolated towards the future. It allows us to try to predict that, in the medium term, conflicts and frictions between human communities will decrease or increase, the cooperation and collaboration will expand worldwide and the quality of life will grow. Also, individuals will become more and more integrated in the socio-technical systems surrounding them, while human cognition and collective intelligence will increase significantly. In the long term, this prediction faculty will intensify with the social action and interaction between organization simulation and digital social systems, sciences and human development tools like the community informatics design. This will bear resemblance with the simulation in environmental sciences, while social sciences will use different simulation tools to better understand and intervene on social phenomena. In fact long-term survival of our specie depends not only on prediction and projective studies but also on the development of human capacities to consciously realize systems co-design that will be more favourable. This capacity and these anticipatory skills in the social appropriation of collaborative technologies are an alternative solution to traditional futurology that has always faced the natural evolution process with trial and error. This process in its essence is nonpredictable since we have to be ready to face large-scale unexpected issues that will punctuate the human evolution through the next decades.

Axiology postulates that evolution's internal engine, or the implicit value that governs life, is the adaptation/alignment, which is survival, growth and development. The ECCO group agrees with the fact that in the current situation, this fundamental value can translate into a universal and sustainable quality of life or a generalized *joie de vivre*. In the present book, we will see that these values can translate into the evolutive and systemic design of social systems as advocated by community informatics design in the context of social theories, theories on computer-human interfaces and the theory of systems that will allow the contribution of a series of other values in support of this major value that invites us to orientate our future towards the adaptation of a more human-friendly world which is necessary to our long-term survival. These values are the openness, the connectedness, the tolerance, the discovery of the positive properties of social systems, freedom, harmony, collaboration, knowledge, self-control, health and a coherent world vision with these too often neglected aspects in our large-scale socio-technical systems. In the long term, this means that the capacity of alignment of the man with the world has to increase our capacity of generative and evolution alignment capacities beyond our living conditions that currently prevail in our societies. Actions and human activity systems that will favour a better integration of all in the world will be considered like good; the other actions will have to be progressively removed.

Praxeology allows us to update these values in concrete life and to avoid various obstacles. Information sciences, systems theory and cognitive and social sciences have adopted several of these attitudes by suggesting various tools and strategies to take on the challenge of building large-scale complex systems like socio-technical systems. Today, computer-assisted collaborative work and the field of human-computer interfaces use it to reflect on their practices in the action. According to Alexandre Lhotellier and Yves St-Arnaud (1994), who introduced Donald Schön's work on "knowing in practice" in Quebec, praxeology is an approach built on (aim, method, process) empowerment and the awareness of the action (at all levels of social interaction) in its history, in its everyday practices, in its changing process and in its consequences. The praxeological approach finds its foundations in the nature of the action (activities aiming a result ordered by intentions). Everything begins by reflecting on the sense of the communication act that contains an intention, an effectiveness, a symbolic, a meaning and an individual and social transformation. Praxeology cannot be integrated to pragmatism, only focusing on success, and even less to utilitarianism, that is guided by its actors' interests. It is a contribution to society's well-being that seeks to become more conscious of itself while guiding more consciously its future and its development.

Praxeology offers an important contribution to social and communication sciences and implicitly to community informatics design because it reconciles, for action efficiency reasons, both poles that applied science nor research action has been able to integrate. In accordance to evolutive design theories conscious of our societies, it is a contribution to social empowerment of groups and communities to the well-being togetherness of a society that is built more consciously. We cannot mention theory without linking it to practice, because it would only be an abstract discourse plated on something concrete, nor can we ignore the feedback of the practice on theory. The community informatics design approach (feedback, collaborative design, anticipation, description and relations, interaction and hierarchical decomposition, heuristic research, stigmergic coordination, discover and strategic alignment matrices, socio-technical approaches, social systems design) is a fundamental praxeological approach. It is reflexive and not only conceptual: it is not just a practice's conceptualization.

2.10.1.2 The Epistemology

To resolve problems and plan the action, we need the appropriate knowledge. Knowledge is not limited only to and objective reflection on reality nor to a simple model only useful to make predictions. Different problems can require different models of a same reality, without any providing the ultimate truth, the true representation. However, models containing a greater explanatory extend or that improve our understanding of a phenomenon are intrinsically better. Models stemming from cognitive or social sciences can help us better comprehend how our budding social systems grow and die. We should favour those who help distinguish interaction patterns between various components of a socio-technical system and develop collaborative tools more and more adapted to the online social systems modeling/simulation.

Needless to say, the FOSM can help us reduce the divide between fundamental sciences and applied sciences. It also helps to characterize the "orientation functions" that link the axiomatic foundations to the praxis. It is important for all sciences to explicitly recognize the axioms on which they are founded, because discovery disparities in the applications can be understood as the manifestation of a deficient axiomatic comprehension or a gap in the basic theories' considerations. Regarding the corpus of science or basic science, the community informatics design of digital social systems already possesses an axiomatic foundation based on more than 40 years of practice around the comprehension of evolutive systems of the "reality" experienced in the arena of participative and interactive design practice. It is the theory that inspires those axioms, in particular approaches like dialogic design, conversational design, cognitive sciences, social systems design and the theory of relations. The arena where applied science shares the methodology includes praxeology allowing to act and reflect upon practice or theories from science. It puts this methodology in the applications with which it has "action interfaces" that engage the science practitioner (the subject). In the arena, the individual and stakeholders are represented by communities of practice, living labs and colabs discovering the relations between concepts, performing the action design and planning and modeling their future ideals through creativity and collaboration technologies that review the basic axioms.

2.10.2 Community Informatics Design's Axioms

Christakis and Flanagan (2011), followed by Bausch and Flanagan (2012), remind us seven fundamental axioms related to social systems design in the context of wide users/designers' communities take over open-source code software during the third phase of science's emergence. We add several semiformal great axioms, some inspired by Abraham Moles' works (Moles and Rohmer 1986, 1998; Moles 1990; Moles and Jacobus 1988) and some others come from our recent works performed within the framework of our research under the APSI program's aegis.

Let us quickly remind ourselves the definition of the axiom. In philosophy, the *Petit Robert* tells us it is an "indemonstrable truth, but obvious to anyone who understands its meaning". It is a great hypothesis that common sense can admit, provided that the proposition that articulates it be clear. It is an intellectually obvious statement from which we draw logical consequences towards the elaboration of a system (here, the FOSM system is applied to the creation of community informatics design's science). For example, we could say that "people have different ways to appropriate the Internet and the collaborative tools according to their cultural affiliation", or even that "the current social Web progression and the ethics drift it creates need the development of values and norms aiming to guide its evolution and its design". These general beliefs are encoded in the form of a proposition or a statement postulating a relation/link between two entities, components or concepts. They serve as a guide for the action, in particular in the search for links between transdisciplinary concepts within an instantiation strategy of several fields related to the establishment of a socio-technical system.

Within the context of our research, we could adopt the following work definition: "a socio-technical axiom combines social and technical elements to account for various hypotheses potentially generalizable concerning individual behavior towards ICT, collaboration between social networking groups, evolution of virtual organizations and DSS design, assistance virtual environments for collaborative design and creativity tools that support and accompany them". An axiom generally possesses the type structure "A is related to B". A and B can be any entity or component and the entities can be causal or correlational. For example, the statement "the well-designed sites are developed by people with the right digital skills" presents the characteristic structure of an axiom.

The values are different, because they have the following form: "A is desirable or right for the citizen. A is a value or an objective". In fact, several researchers see values like evaluative beliefs. When an evaluative belief becomes more specific (such as validated in part, either empirically through documentation or other means), it becomes an axiom. For example, statements such as "social system design is good", or even "community informatics design is good for the education system", are evaluative propositions we would classify among values instead of axioms. However, if we say that "social system design is good and has become necessary to meet the challenges of our civilization", or even that "community informatics design will produce competent and winning students in the knowledge society", we make them axioms, because these statements suggest a relation and concrete interactions between two entities.

Let us start by presenting the seven axioms favouring the emergence of the third phase of science such as community informatics design, as suggested by Zeeuw (1996, 1997) and supported by Warfield (1986), Christakis (1987, 2007, 2010), Banathy and Jenlink (2005), Banathy (1996), Laszlo (1972), Laszlo and Laszlo

72 2 Universal Anteriorities and Third-Phase Science

(2007, 2004), Laszlo et al. (2002, 2010), Laszlo (2001), Laszlo et al. (2002), Checkland (1981, 1976), Checkland and Holwell (1998), Checkland and Scholes (1990), Ackoff (1974), Ackoff and Emery (1972), Nadler (1981, 1985), Argyris (1982, 1993a), Schön (1983), Christakis and Bausch (2006), Flanagan and Bausch (2011) and Flanagan and Christakis (2010) and several other great researchers (with our socio-technical framework adaptations).

1. *The complexity axiom*: Social systems design is a multidimensional challenge. It requires an observational variety to be respected when two stakeholders or observers take part in a dialogue while ensuring their cognitive limitations are not at odds with our efforts aiming to improve understanding (Warfield 1986; Warfield and Christakis 1987).
2. *The commitment axiom*: Social systems design like healthcare, education, smart cities and virtual community or inter-enterprise collaborative networks, without the authentic commitment of stakeholders, the establishment of projects is impossible (Özbekhan 1970, with adaptation).
3. *The investment axiom*: All stakeholders are involved if the collaborative design of their own social system must make their own investment in trust and faithfully commit in order to be ready to discover a mutual understanding and collaborative solutions (Flanagan et al. 2012; Flanagan and Bausch 2011; Flanagan and Christakis 2010).
4. *The logical axiom*: The appreciation of distinctions and complementarities through one inductive, deductive, "abductive" and "retroductive" logic is essential for the future creative comprehension of the human being. The abductive logic leads us to imagine new systems, and the retroductive logic makes "imagination leaps" to the extent that it is capable to stock up on values and emotions in research and development, within the diversity of stakeholders (Romm 1996, 2002, 2006).
5. *The epistemological axiom*: An exhaustive science around the human being should perform its researches from the human life in the totality of its thoughts, its desires and its feelings, like the indigenous people of Australia, the Athenians, are able to do. It should not be dominated by the Western epistemology which reduces science to intellectual dimensions (Harris and Wasilewski 2004).
6. *The border transgression axiom*: A community informatics design science engages stakeholders into action beyond geographical, cognitive and cultural borders in order to create symbiotic social systems that allow people of all social backgrounds to have a discussion beyond all borders, cultural, religious, racial or professional barriers, as components of a mutual enrichment of their way of perceiving, feeling and acting (Christakis 1993; Romm 2006, 2002, 1996).
7. *The power conciliation axiom*: The social systems' community informatics design seeks to reconcile individual and institutional power relations that are persistent and inherent to any stakeholders' group according to their own preoccupations while honouring the required distinctions and perspective variety that occur in the action arena (Jones 2010).

8. *The self-organization axiom*: In the technological society, individuals and communities become able to self-organize by configuring, making, adapting, putting to service and mastering any technical device regardless of its complexity level. In other words, complexity is not an obstacle or an objection anymore to the creation of any collaborative technical device. The creation of transdisciplinary teams where members master the open-source code contributes to creating more and more complex digital social systems that are highly reliable (Moles and Rohmer 1986, 1998; Moles 1990; Moles and Jacobus 1988; with our adaptation).

9. *The dispersal axiom*: Society in its whole possesses the will and the capacity to make available open-source code devices to publics and users who are prodigiously spread out demographically and geographically, to the extent that these publics feel a propensity to communicate and a "communicativity" strong enough to create a critical mass of users or an intense enthusiasm to justify a technically commercial effort supported by an innovation digital social system (Moles and Rohmer 1986).

10. *The proxemics axiom*: The society of communicational opulence has been breaking the proxemics law for a long time (Hall 1962; Hall and Hall 1969; Hall et al. 1984), and according to which, historically, human relations have been built on a spectre of close sequence, meaning, that relations between individuals, groups and communities obey to a general evolution diagram where human beings influence each other more if they are closer in time and space. In this context, each action sequence determines more or less the following one. This law is disputed in its generality by the current progression of the social Web. The current social systems are not exclusively developed from relations between neighbour elements but also between elements that are geographically and socio-demographically distant. This situation gives rise to a new factor of socio-economic development based on new action and interaction forms that future social systems design must collectively support and orientate. (Moles and Rohmer 1986, 1998; Moles 1990; Moles and Jacobus 1988; Harvey 2003, 2004a, 2005, 2008; Harvey and Bertrand 2004).

11. *The digitization/personalization axiom*: It is possible to do more with smaller work modules and collaborative devices capable of personalizing and manipulating all sorts of knowledge at the speed of light. The current living labs and colabs have made this factor their modus operandi on the scale of several countries. In Quebec, the CEFRIO studies echo it largely. This possibility has dramatically increased the human capacity to massively implant algorithms formerly reserved to experts and that now distorts the world of objects, applications and services like online social systems implantation. This factor is currently exploding the exploratory design space (e.g. the number of options of available devices for the civil society and of creativity tools with open-source code supporting them). This axiom, well documented by our questionnaires and our case studies, shows that all sorts of groups, communities and organizations in Quebec are facing new ways of innovating that are reaching not only expert but also citizens in their everyday lives. New forms of social life and

social systems are born and command fulfilment criteria and norms we are not very familiar with (Harvey 2003, 2004b, 2005, 2008; Harvey and Bertrand 2004).

12. *Social systems' design skill axiom*: DSS are not only the mirror of already existing institutions and organizations. Brand new forms of social systems and virtual organizations are born from these new modules and devices, through global time and space at a pace never seen before. Never in the history of humanity were so many citizens able to learn so much from each other, to answer everyone from such great distances and to give advice on solving a problem through transborder knowledge. The traditional library or the university one is more and disputed in their roles of exclusive producer and keeper of the human knowledge. The metaphor of the *Universal Encyclopaedia* is more and more replaced by social systems of living and self-learning appropriation of knowledge and by multi-user designers' networks and content producers (participative sciences are eloquent current examples). In this context, institutions in the field of education must reflect on their roles in the information society. They must face "new digital literacy" that largely exceeds the appropriation of tools and the content production that questions their roles by taking over collective skills in design at the service of the innovation's ubiquitous imagination (Harvey 2003, 2008).

13. *The equity of technology's access and information democratization axiom*: This axiom is no longer a priority dimension in the Western world. With the social Web and collaborative platform generalization, these are replaced by the equity of new digital skills to be acquired in design. These skills must become basic tools in a knowledge society where ethics are maltreated and where threats of control over our lives are becoming greater. The progressive ICT infiltration progressive in all human activity spheres and the threat of "gadgetization" of everyday life by social media call for a radical turnaround of the present social informatization period where, from a global influence of technology on culture, we must put the human and the culture at the centre of human development: the citizen in the driver seat. The major design task of the upcoming decades is to become a "design centred on humans" and not only on the users (Harvey 2008, 2013).

14. *The globalization design axiom*: This axiom becomes the corollary of freedom, prosperity and innovation, while an increasing number of people become engaged in multimodal processes, like our evaluation questionnaire of design practices reveals (see annex for the APSI report on our website). These practices go from content production to new online social systems forms with all sorts of productions and innovations previously unseen at the time of mass media. This generalized social Web development has virtually replaced the ideal of the solitary discoverer or the inventive genius who works from the bottom of his laboratory. This ideal gives way to mass users who in the networks and large-scale social systems create practice communities of passionate people who take charge of the unprecedented activities through new forms of communication action. They prepare the Internet of the future. In the design society,

a brand new economy is seeking innovative models. Programming or being programmed, making design or having our own social systems design made – such are the maxims of autonomy, democratic participation and the necessity to favour the generalized appropriation of digital skills in the design of the future. The present book wishes to offer the outlines, the legitimacy of the spreading of this fundamental cultural attitude by showing some directions to designers, by giving some suggestions to people in the education field and by suggesting concrete orientations to granting organizations. In the information society, designers can no longer master all aspects of the design and the innovative aspects of research alone. They must become socio-technical facilitators, expert guides able to work within delocalized transdisciplinary teams at the service of socio-economic development and massive innovation (Harvey 2003, 2004a, 2005, 2008; Harvey and Bertrand 2004).

Chapter 3
Community Informatics Design's Theoretical Basis

The proper study of mankind is the science of design.
Herbert Simon (2005)
Our future will be above all a design matter.
Vilém Flusser

Taking the premise of second-order cybernetics seriously and applying the axioms of human centeredness to designers and users alike calls on designers to conceive of their job not as designing particular products, but to design affordances for users to engage in the interfaces that are meaningful to them, the very interfaces that constitute these users' conceptions of an artifact, for example of a chair, a building or a place of work. Taking, moreover, seriously the above-mentioned experiences that different people may bring a diversity of meanings to a design, meanings that are especially different from how designers conceptualize their designs, calls on designers to apply considerable cultural sensitivity to different users' epistemologies. Designers who intend to design something that has the potential of being meaningful to others need to understand how others conceptualize their world – at least in the dimensions that are relevant to their design.
Klaus Krippendorff (2007)

3.1 Theories and Principles Related to the Corpus (Block 2)

After having presented the foundations of science in the previous chapter, we will now succinctly present a few theoretical general bases that help understand fundamental community informatics design orientations as a socio-technical science. A typology of principles that underlies this type of design will also be exposed as well as a certain number of laws supporting its development. Our objective is to suggest a synthesis from Warfield (1986) and other theoreticians' model. Several other models will be presented in the following chapters.

This presentation of community informatics design's aspects related to the "theory and corpus" block aims to extract the general framework of a perspective of a socio-technical design anchored in solid traditions of a society of participative, collaborative, sustainable and responsible information, similar to the Scandinavian participative design. Our approach is normative because it encourages a particular information society, very much in line with the values supported by both world

© Springer International Publishing AG 2017   77
P.-L. Harvey, *Community Informatics Design Applied to Digital Social Systems*,
Translational Systems Sciences 12, DOI 10.1007/978-3-319-65373-0_3

summits on information society held in Geneva in 2003 and in Tunis in 2005. This information society includes qualities that are desirable for a group of countries, fields and professions on matters relating to management and knowledge sharing.

The community informatics designer's task consists of developing and anchoring in the foundations of a "science of communicational design socially responsible", previously presented, a certain number of principles, theories and concepts that help build community information systems and then aligning them on democratic principles of participation, collaboration, coordination and fair networking governance and sustainability that become major notions related to the information society concept. Our approach incorporates the general social science theories, design thinking and socio-technical approaches related to "Internet research", like the computer-mediatized communication and other activities from the sectors of science, technology and society (STS). Let us closely examine the works of our research group from the Applied Community Informatics Lab (ACIL) at UQAM and the characteristics of our approach.

Community informatics design (or socio-digital media design) is an intervention and support strategy that presents itself like an evolutive orientation model of social media and collaborative platforms, operating a change of significant paradigm for the acquisition of skills in the world of information and communications. It transcends individual communication theories and traditional mass media culture by proposing a cooperative vision of human activity and a pragmatic orientation mode belonging today to the "computer-mediatized social participation" movement (Fischer 2013b; Shneiderman and Fischer 2011) and to the interactive design (Preece and Maloney-Krichmar 2005; Preece et al. 2004) supporting it. As a strategy, community informatics design represents a specific ICT integration mode (social media and collaborative devices) to organizations, digital social systems and to virtual communities' activities. As a practice, it supports the co-construction of reasoning spaces associated with conceptual design (the design space), to network knowledge management and the co-design of virtual environments currently multiplying in cyberspace: virtual campus, corporate universities, virtual organizations, Web-mediatized work groups, institutions portals, fun spaces and multiplayer games. Finally, it initiates an emerging, sociocultural and communication process of production of new social forms and social networks of the Web within which users value cooperation, responsible citizen commitment, knowledge sharing and the accumulation of information capital dedicated to social change. Figure 3.1 represents successive skill levels currently evolving in the social system. At the first level, we find the mass of users who possess different degrees of design skills with diversified uses. We illustrate these design uses by increasing order of specific skills at various levels. The sixth and last levels characterize the community informatics designer of large-scale socio-technical systems. Inspired by the works of Gerhard Fischer, this simplified model of the mediatized social evolution by socio-digital technologies accompanied us in the construction of our analysis tools (questionnaires, case studies) aiming to better understand who the co-design users are, the object of their design and their current skills level.

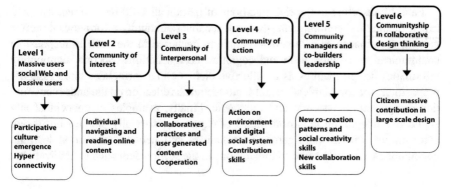

Pierre-Léonard Harvey, 2017

Fig. 3.1 Evolution of collaborative ecosystems and skills level

In the context of the present book, "co-design" extends from collaborative design in a partner's community possessing various types of expertise in different fields of practice and research, contributing this way to the development of online social systems design, interactive scriptwriting of large-scale sustainable development projects and the creation of network collaboration interfaces. This evolution occurring at various levels of society requires new collective skills.

3.2   Towards a Community Informatics Design Communication Model

Our research group, working at the UQAM's ACIL, provides an important research effort to develop a new theory of collaborative design of digital social systems (digital environments) supported by the Web 2.0 and 3.0 social participation platforms: community informatics design.

In a world of continuous information and communication flow, the social systems appear and disappear at a speed never seen before in history. In a context of information overload, solving large-scale socio-economic problems and the "digitalization" emancipation of human activities, learning in virtual environments and knowledge sharing all become survival conditions of our societies. Socio-digital media and modern information technologies and digital communications are an integral part of our everyday lives, work and our communities. They pose a challenge to the theories of communication and traditional media. Since 2007, a new communication design thinking (Krippendorff 2007; Crilly et al. 2008; Mehlenbacher 2008, 2009; Storkerson 1997, 2006, 2008; Aakhus 2007, 2010, 2011; De Moor 2005; De Moor and De Cindio 2007) proves to be one of the strongest trends of the international theoretical and practical development regarding innovation and the necessity to develop more responsible social systems.

First, by resorting to the rich traditions of participative design – direct user and expert facilitators' commitment – we will see that community informatics design is gaining prominence as a rhetorical paradigm anchored in the socially responsible communication, collaboration and cognition design notions. Second, community informatics design matures as a collective dialogue that formulates three essential propositions for communication and socio-technical reflection on the under construction design: ethic, systemic and pragmatic. Finally, examples of conceptual and applicative integration in various fields of expertise, especially practice healthcare communities, online multi-gamer communities and network animation learning communities, will help serve as illustrations in the section dedicated to applications.

3.3   Understand, Validate and Support Collaborative Cultures

Since antiquity, world cultures have defined themselves largely by their media and their communication tools integrated with their way of thinking, working, learning and collaborating. In the last decades, most media design has adopted a linear conception that was making a very clear distinction between producers and consumers, between designers and users (Harvey 1995; Benkler 2006). Radio, books, records and, especially, cinema and television illustrate this orientation that has been analysed in our communication departments as the couch potato phenomenon. During several decades, for the vast majority of mass-media "couch potato" viewers, the remote control has represented the most important device of cerebral and behavioural activity. This situation does not refer to a real democracy of users in the sense that we understand it today in the field of "Design Thinking" and "Open Innovation" where users of social media are also producers of the applications or program (the idea of "producers"). Likewise, for over a century, public relations systems cultivate a certain type of approach the "hypodermic bite" (Balles) to socialize enterprise's and organization's activities just like our mass education systems have favoured behavioural approaches considering the learners as "knowledge consumers" instead of knowledge producers and creators capable of generating socio-economic innovation. Governments have also transformed the citizen into a "beneficiary" instead of an actor able to resolve problems and orientate social systems of the future. All these approaches harm the sustainable development of our societies and taint a culture of "chronic passivity" that stays with them forever. The results can be disastrous regarding motivating people to actively participate in their society and transforming their way of life, to become entrepreneurs and innovators. Students, workers and citizens are often kept aside of decision-making mechanisms, the political class or education systems: instead of developing their skills in terms of autonomy, recreation of our social systems and active roles in the socio-economic evolution, we cultivate their aptitude to criticize and beg for services.

The recent expansion of the social Web and social media ecosystem has generated several practical and spectacular outcome of the works relying on a scientific movement started 30 years ago in the field of "Social Computing" (Kling 1973), and about 15 years ago with the development of "Community Informatics" (Harvey 2008 and Gurstein 2003), that is now facilitating the emergence of a "participative culture" paradigm for-co-design (Fischer 2011; Jenkins 2009; Preece and Shneiderman 2009) and a massive and historical "Citizen Science". This participative culture, whose lack of conceptual foundations or enthusiasm has been deplored, proposes no less than a deep change of the passive consumer culture to an active citizen committed culture (Etzioni 2009). We progressively go from one culture where artefacts and devices are industrially made to a participative culture (Jenkins 2009) of large-scale handiwork where individuals, groups and communities voluntarily contribute to the evolutive process of social information and massively collaborate to solving large-scale problems. These developments that may create all sorts of ethical, political and strategic problems represent no less than one of the perspectives of priority socio-economic development for Quebec, Canada and the world.

The world is changing and technological means are also transforming themselves. Recent developments of social media, ubiquitous computing, collaborative platforms and cloud computing arouse occasions we must seize within the framework of national innovation strategies. Quebec and Canada must put in place a cutting-edge research for mediatized collaboration systems design through information technologies and communication (DeSygnCoMéTIC). We must lead researches of national and international scale on socio-technical design approaches (combining social and technological systems) and a computing approach more centred on the human and society. As we evolve towards participative social and virtual worlds that free us from traditional worlds where only a small number of experts were defining politics, designing systems and rules and creating work artefacts, an entire field of new perspectives and large-scale challenges are opening to us: large projects of production and knowledge sharing of the twenty-first century in action and socio-economic innovation communities.

Our research program explores theoretical and practical foundations of collaboration and co-creation of systems and online social networks in order to understand, value and support participative cultures emerging in the Internet virtual communities. Our basic hypothesis consists of saying that new Web collaborative platforms facilitate socio-economic innovation, while recognizing it is far from being sufficient. The participative culture we find in virtual communities and in emerging social systems of the social Web, such as virtual campus, corporative universities, militant communities, living labs, colabs and online learning environments, are socio-technical systems since their development does not rely only on technology. They contain two types of process: technological systems that provide the possibilities of desirable and reliable interactions between users' systems and social systems (Luhmann 1989, 1995; Giddens 1984; Habermas 1984; Banathy 1996; Fuchs 2004, 2008) that are dynamic, emerging, contingent and transitory in their interactions that are socio-technical entities, socio-constructive subjects and evolutive objects. All these types of social Web emerging systems are the results of transformations in the groups, the communities and behaviours observed in the social organization where contributors (Preece and Shneiderman 2009) actively commit, at various levels, in the production of content and design of massive innovation, dynamic ICT appropriation (Harvey 2004a), the reconfiguration of technologies to their specific needs and the collaborative construction of knowledge.

Our analytical and conceptual framework relies on a large diversity of application contexts such as the co-creation of an open-source code software, support technologies for collaborative computer-assisted work (TCAO), multiplatform creation, community informatics environments (Harvey and Lemire 2001), community facilitation and hypermedia facilitation in media design, urban planning and project management, distance education and community informatics, sustainable development and communication for responsible development, meta-design, participative and collaborative design as well as the socio-construction of virtual worlds (Lemire 2008). These different analysis and design perspectives, which we will define further along in terms of research axis (Sect. 2.5), allow us to jointly articulate guidelines for human collective design and non-human (Latour 2008), as well as to articulate and incorporate multiple perspectives capable of guiding socio-technical platform design and especially to explore the conceptual framework capable of orientating the action into social computing and community informatics on social and organizational participation and collaboration assisted by computers.

3.4 Collaboration Mechanisms: The ACIL's 8C Approach

It is important to understand how collaborative technologies and platforms of the social Web allow the emergence of a participative culture where cognition, cooperation, collaboration, coordination and communication concepts (the first five C) can account for important and relevant processes translating a wide diversity of important challenges our society is faced with and the way to resolve them, for example:

- Large-scale communication problems that force us to reflect on new adaptable and evolutive models since the transmitter-receiver interpersonal model represents only a part of a global context where relations between individuals and society must be re-evaluated in terms of action in the world and double contingency between the various actors involved in a specific communication situation in complex environments.
- Cognitive master problems and the necessity to create methodologies that can understand the governance modes at never-seen-before scales, requiring new information visualization tools, for example, to visualize all catastrophes and threat situations through the world such as the modeling Google Earth, 3D Warehouse and Google SketchUp.
- Systemic and transdisciplinary problems that require the collaboration of several experts from different fields of knowledge, especially the creation of collaborative platforms and virtual environments dedicated to various types of collaborative and participative design of online social systems like the ones developed by the ACIL in the context of its My Portal Col@b initiative at UQAM's faculty of communication.

- Problems of politics orientation and partnership development, in terms of research program creation and grants, as well as partnership initiatives able to promote massive social innovation and contribute to "support to information society transition", the same name of the program suggested by the Quebec government and its ministry of *Services gouvernementaux*.
- Problems of personalizing collaborative and modeling DSS platforms (like virtual communities) in a changing world (Banathy 1996), systems that must rely on open architectures like the ones of living labs that are on the rise everywhere throughout the world (e.g. get equipped with generic design techniques to create data bases and digital libraries in order to answer the particular needs and the communicational requirements (Feenberg 2002) of underprivileged communities or handicapped people. We will come back to it in the Sect. 3 on methodology).
- Problems related to the self-organization of virtual communities, problems that are impossible to define well once and for all and requiring levels of social commitment and mobilization because the co-design of social systems we are mostly interested in cannot be entrusted to organizations outside the community.
- Lifelong learning problems and the creation of distance education platforms capable of transgressing not only geographical borders but also the ones related to ethnic division, intercultural affiliations and language barriers which are the focus of our partners' work Lionel and Pascal Audant, from UNIMASOFT, who have created a new language for distance learning within the global interconnectivity: learning through hypermedia animation supported by community networking (mentioned in Chap. 5). We also continue important work in partnership with the native Wemotaci community in the fields of learning communities, Web radio and sustainable development with Guy Gendron, a member of the ACIL and a PhD student at UQAM, as well as with Yves Lusignan, engineer, pioneer of complex systems and technical functional modeling applied to sustainable development. As well as several professor researchers of the UQAM's faculty of communication who have joined our efforts to develop a model for a collaborative platform, a type of social architecture tool kit for the community informatics design (SADC).

Today, the development of what we now identify as a "circular" or a "sharing economy" or better, as a "Fourth Industrial Revolution", is based on a "collaborative culture" supported by a vast diversity of products, applications and services: social media and networks, design tools, creativity devices, digital environments for learning, MOOCs and digital object libraries, information democratization tools, learning analytics, socio-technical co-creation methodologies, business platforms and open innovation in living labs. Many of these generic digital design environments are oriented by different fields of knowledge and assessment, allowing human and social sciences to progressively take part in the construction of new living and working environments by promoting the creativity "of all for all". Knowledge sharing and the increase of collaboration capacities within the new users' practice communities are progressively becoming contributors (Preece and Shneiderman 2009). These users' communities allow the accelerated democratization of design and socio-economic innovation by placing the creators' power (engineers, artists, multimedia designer, computer graphic designer, experts, architects) in the hands of widen users' communities. These communities transform themselves into active innovation actors, the "prosumers" (Harvey 2009) of the online social systems design. New social systems (networking work groups, practice communities, virtual organizations, new institutions, economically innovative partnerships, cyber-physical social systems) are created each day to co-build products or create events, plan projects and draw a new platform, all that in real time, without any distinction of distance or borders. Thousands of websites and portals can currently testify the accelerated increase of this mass creativity movement. Hundreds of new environments are created each day by different participation and collaboration cultures.

One of the fundamental challenges of the living labs and the colabs dedicated to innovation, like the UQAM's ACIL and My Portal Col@b, is to catalyse and capture the incredible creative of collaborative cultures. A second challenge consists of conceptualized virtual environments, to make the design and to make these environments evolve. In addition to technically promote and increase the creative capacities of users' communities, they will also systematically favour the members' commitment and the good collective governance of these new cyber-infrastructures. Collaboration is often influenced by individual efforts in the use of tools and by the validation of other users' contribution. This effort of digital literacy and common production can be considerably reduced by providing the right tool and methodology at the best moment and location by enticing people to participate in the social innovation efforts through collective force and by favouring the best alignment (fit) for the users' needs, their vision of the future and their skills in the innovation context. This alignment idea is extremely important in the organizational design theories, because they seek to show that beyond literacy, interested in media writing (Cartier 2011), we must insist on the capacity of self-creation of communities in regard to a specific communicational intention (teleology). One of the UQAM's My Portal Col@b priority objective is to align (adapt) collective aspirations of groups according to functionalities and collaborative tools that accompany and individual and collective skills that help updating them. These skills will have to attract the explicit attention of all involved actors in the socio-economic development, because in the knowledge economy, a real skill in participative culture is not only a social life and leisure one but a collaborative skill oriented towards social innovation. Since all individual efforts can greatly vary from one person or organization to another, we must now tackle the co-design (collaborative design) of educational and training programs within innovative partnerships.

The Northern Plan, announced in Quebec in May 2011, almost abandoned in 2013, could greatly benefit from this participative culture and virtual organization, provided we can build responsible ecosystems where we will be able to better define the roles of each actor and the necessary skills according to our socio-economic development objectives. This coordination skill and collective efforts is what is lacking today in Quebec, Canada and in the Western world. After two decades of individualism, how to convert the incredible energy and participative culture into a socio-economic emancipation force and sustainable development?

The history of media teaches us that for millennia, the biggest cultural changes coincide with the birth of new media and new knowledge production devices. One of the questions raised by history regarding the current world participative cultures consists of trying to analyse if the current growth of virtual worlds and meta-universe will disrupt human activities like reading, writing and reprography have done in their day (Cloutier 2001). Will the power of the collective brain (symbiotic man, planetary brain, distributed cognition, collective intelligence and community informatics ubiquitous imagination) favour the emergence of a planetary conscience of urgent problems humanity is currently facing and the discovery of solutions that save the specie? Or shall we expect still unknown adverse effects like global computer crashes, a decline of civilization and cultural disadvantages such as the ones currently condemned by several communication specialists, heirs of Socrates, Baudrillard or Derrida? Are we deconstructing the world or rebuilding it as a mirror in cyberspace without a good knowledge of global issues, advantages and disadvantages of these new media and technologies for our future? Can we identify the major validation effects of information technologies and communication and try to reduce their negative effects? Which security issues will we be facing within the next few years?

3.5   The Various Aspects of a Theoretical Framework and Our Lines of Research

All these questions surrounding social media and the current collaborative culture can be thrilling, but it must not eclipse a fundamental phenomenon: the evaluation of various ways of dealing with numerous difficult and urgent problems. Through these ways, the appropriation of new media and the co-building of virtual environment for collaborative design and social systems can create winning economies for the future.

In this section, we will describe several concepts as well as research lines that are related to our theoretical and methodological emerging framework. This conceptual effort is culminating in a research program relying on 15 years of work supporting the creation of remarkable progress in the fields of communication and information sciences, the STS sector, information systems, community informatics, meta-design and design oriented on communities, programming-oriented aspects and community informatics design as well as the socio-construction of virtual worlds. All these fields and approaches contributed to recognize the fundamental role of ICT within and information society (or communications, a knowledge community, etc.). However, we can only note the current theoretical poverty that accompanies the popular doxa surrounding social media. Already well-established fields, like social computing and other newer ones like Internet research, citizen research and new media study, have produced an important historical documentation on information society theory (Brier 2000, 2008, 2013; Hofkirchner and Fuchs 2008, 2003) that provide us with several analytical frameworks and a wide diversity of approaches.

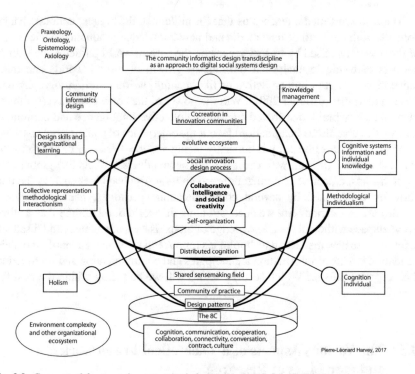

Fig. 3.2 Conceptual frame and community informatics design foundation theories

The objective of the present book is to develop the beginnings of a taxonomy and the definition of these approaches that would help, on one hand, to recognize challenges, weaknesses and perspectives of the current social media approach and, on the other hand, to contribute to the elaboration of substantial thinking lines and essential points of view. In short, a conceptual reference framework is on the rise. Before defining the most important terms of our research program and its development lines, we think it is useful to succinctly present the reference framework we have built for the beginning of the APSI research.

Figure 3.2 allows to visualize a part of the starting conceptual framework used for the APSI research. On the top right are the philosophical foundations of our approach. If the FOSM showed the process of the new science, this image illustrates some of its content. The spherical image shows the disciplines that intervene in the co-creation of virtual environments called "digital social systems", especially innovation communities. At the centre are the objectives related to collective intelligence and to the needs of social creativity. At the top of the sphere, we find the needs related to virtual communities and at the bottom are presented three major dimensions of the ACIL's 8C approach: cognition, communication and cooperation. On each side of the sphere, we try to give a clear picture of the confrontation and complementarity between cognitive points of view, between holism and reductionism or between the fields of psychology and social and communication sciences. We rediscover several of these concepts in various chapters of the book, and we will define the terms within the framework of various co-design processes like instantiation of innovation communities considered like digital social systems.

3.6   The Community Informatics Design Program: Methodologies (Block 3) and Applications (Block 4)

Our funding request for the APSI program (under the *ministère des Services gouvernementaux*) was aiming to elaborate a research program on the collaborative Web spreading over several years (from 2010 to 2016). We were coveting the integration of human, organizational and technological perspectives by means of collaborative design models. The significant challenge of this program was to facilitate the access of social media for the citizens by facilitating the co-construction of platforms through computer-mediatized cooperation and collaboration within co-designer communities by means of collaborative devices and community tools we can describe like community and organizational information software systems (Harvey and Lemire 2001). We were aiming the progressive elaboration, through analytical extensions and successive application "collaboration's heuristic" and a co-design platform capable to serve several fields.

While user graphic interface's design is accompanied by several design tools and individual creation software suites, it is largely renowned that few interfaces or technological integrated and universal platforms exist to facilitate information sharing, design cooperation (co-design) and social sciences and information and communication sciences co-creation. Most existing tools lack conviviality or are not equipped with work modules necessary for design and networking co-creation. The existing CAD (computer-aided design) systems and other types of design assistance platforms (e.g. AUTODESK) traditionally help engineers, architects and computer and experts in their creative tasks. Similarly, is it possible to create different CAD platforms for social system design? It is becoming obvious that community informatics and socio-technical designers need support for the collaboration of innovation project's development in the short and long term with partners contributing to the production and integration of new knowledge from various disciplines. This way, they can improve meta-design (design for designers) and community informatics design while developing diverse interactive applications. Therefore, the project and efforts suggested in our future program seek to build a flexible and modular infrastructure, a cyber infrastructure supported by a digital knowledge library, collaborative devices and cooperation evaluation tools between creators of community informatics design interfaces and devices.

3.6.1   The Applications (Block 4)

The present project and our general objectives seek the creation of a large collaborative and sustainable development research centre with the mission of training young people about community informatics design, at different levels of the education system. The objectives of the research centre are the following:

(a) Build a research and development infrastructure aiming to explore the potential and application of community informatics design and complex social modeling systems as a reference framework allowing to face fundamental challenges related to the creation of community informatics and collaborative platforms supporting the research-creation communication sciences, in social sciences and in Arts and letters.

(b) Create the best possible alignment between support software systems dedicated to social systems design, the *Réseau d'informations scientifiques du Québec* (RISQ) platform, the high-performance calculus national Canadian platform and the e-learning systems, serious multi-user online games, problems, fields and communities of users in constant evolution which requires the use of large-scale collaborative platforms.

(c) Define scientific, transdisciplinary and methodological foundations of applied sciences in the *cyber collaboration* with the objective to create design platforms and collaborative software systems as socio-technical environments (Moodle portal and its social learning environments at UQAM). They mobilize users like responsible and "owners of problems" that involve them actively and collaboratively in a perspective of continuous development of software tools. The goal is to personally and collectively support design and modeling activities that are significant and structuring in line with their emerging needs in fields where cyber collaboration is important.

3.6.2   The Challenge and the Applied Vision

Over the last decades, most software systems had the objective of optimizing the productivity of architectures and the system's reliability. Incidentally, software engineer research has made enormous efforts and has acquired tremendous expertise to meet these goals. However, we are currently entering a new phase of software development that, in addition to involving human and social factors, also suggests a brand new socio-pragmatic and communication paradigm: from computer codification to the participative-ecological-contextual configuration of software tools in information and communication sciences through complex partnerships that include civil society. In fact, more and more people, beyond the status of content producers or software users, also intervene by their design, in a wider optic of improvement of life conditions where socio-technical design and software implantation contain levels of collective commitment never seen before. (Only in the United States, we estimated at 13 millions of people who were user designers in 2012).

The current socio-digital media's collaborative application explosion on the Internet and the swift progression of virtual communities of open-source code creators constitute powerful levers of a participative culture that aims to develop a "global expertise of ecosystemic analysis and software creation contextualized by social communication". Existing software development, mainly centred on productivity in well-defined activities contexts, is insufficient to face the accelerated and increasing emergence of use centred on the human, at a large scale. This seeks to satisfy the fluctuating needs we meet more and more in the generation of new network participation modes and the acquisition of collective design expertise in the extent of open possibilities by massive innovation practice. We need a new class of users and participative creation methodologies and collaborative software that does not end with implantation phase and deployment but that owe their success to the continuous participation of users' communities (we particularly think about Moodle), under penalty of letting the "massive amateurism" expand and the generalization of "anything goes".

3.6.3 A Research Program Issued from The UQAM's Communication Faculty Aiming to Improve Digital Skills in Quebec

The program pursues the development of a reference framework in community informatics meta-design in order to guide developers and improve citizens' digital skills in the design of collaborative software systems oriented by the communicational and democratic development context. Supported by professors' researches from social and public communication's department and few professors from the school of media regarding an important documentary study on design theories as well as the analysis of exemplary practices and the systematic evaluation of factors related to collaborative systems in several fields, our transdisciplinary research program started with a partially articulated reference framework called "community informatics design" (Harvey 2006b). This reference framework is founded on the hypothesis that the design of several collaborative social systems like multi-user games, virtual learning communities and social science simulation games can be supported by our meta-model in the context of collaborative construction of a community informatics design's assistance systems (SADC). The research program identifies and correlates technical, social and communicational characteristics involved in the design and development of collaborative software systems inviting users to collaboratively commit to the design of applications and innovations that will help solve their own problems. The noted characteristics (interaction and collaborative design methodology patterns in various disciplines) serve as orientation parameters to guide the development of the SADC, which is an assistance platform

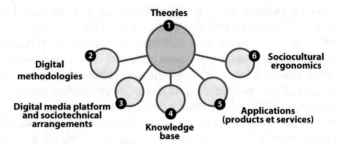

Pierre-Léonard Harvey, 2017

Fig. 3.3 The six lines of research

for the development of software between several partners. A real and virtual development co-laboratory is dedicated to the discovery and massive innovation of the "synerspace". The SADC has been built in the Colab (sponsored by UQAM's ACIL) in order to progressively generate the "synerspace" of My Portal Col@b as a catalyser of real users' efforts committed in the collaborative solving of complex problems of the social world in several design fields. Our researches have led us towards several research lines whose contexts we are presenting in the application below (Fig. 3.3).

3.6.4   The Suggested Six Research Lines and Their Applications Contexts

Research Line 1: Theory Transdisciplinarity, social systems design theory and community informatics systems' methodology

> *The adaptation and development of crossing paths between several different points of view constitute the success in the development of human centred interactive systems and its numerous contexts of collaborative lives.*

3.6.4.1   Description

This transdisciplinary research centre project will contribute to build a new academic discipline from the consolidation/integration of many disparate works we can temporarily group under the terms "applied sciences cyber collaboration" or "community informatics", for example, the human-computer interface design, the human-computer interaction, the multimedia-interface design and educational multimedia, computer-mediatized communication and collaborative computer-assisted work, social media design centred on the user and participative research action, social and distributed cognition, digital social systems analysis and collaborative cultures. The development of collaborative interactive systems requires the contribution of several people possessing different professions, playing different roles with different objectives and points of view in the development's life cycle, that extend from participative design to knowledge engineering through business processes and several types of users.

As the communicational, contextual, emotional and cultural factors gain importance in the development of interactive and collaborative systems, within organizations and general affairs, the transdisciplinary, informational and communicational knowledge management becomes critical for the evaluations of needs and experiences of users and for the coherent and consistent realization of relevant business process and innovative architecture services. We have developed an analysis and implantation conceptual framework, the SADC, as a general platform for the integration of different points of view and activities, the sharing of design resources, the monitoring of conceptualization and design conception channels, the development of new methods and devices (e.g. communityware and digital objects libraries) and the capitalization of community informatics design knowledge. The centre's research program will continue to build and expand the SADC and will create other methods and tools to support development in interactive and collaborative systems. Like users' profiles and organizational studies' contexts, modeling, simulation and visualization systems, generation of interactive scripts, communicational evaluation of interactive processes, distance collaboration and business processes as well as the development of Web service architecture and social systems design is dedicated to sustainable development.

3.6.4.2   Application Example

Basic Transdisciplinary Studies on Collaboration

- R-D in knowledge management, in a plurality of disciplines, projects, co-laboratories and organizations
- Development of description and context analysis tools in the development of interactive and collaborative uses
- Development of planning, design and communicational evaluation methods of interactive and collaborative systems
- Assistance in the implementation of user/context study programs (like the short communication and risk program) in our classes in healthcare and human relations, the alignment of communicational processes with business processes and strategic management of the cyber collaboration through the creation of new Web service architectures, scientific communication program, animation and cultural researches, marketing and communication/health as well as the new profile of the socio-digital media masters
- The massive innovation by social science simulation and its applications in the analysis and design of complex social phenomena (pandemic, ecological mobilization, collaborative design of social systems dedicated to sustainable development)

Research Line 2: Methodology Community informatics design: contextualization by communication

> *The understanding of use by the analysis of communicational processes in place is essential to the massive social innovation and design centred on users; social innovation, contents, contexts and information and communication devices jointly generate a communicational use experience.*

3.6.4.3   Description

The appropriation and performance of an information and communication device widely depend on the communicational context in which it is used. Activities strongly focused on the extensive and expansive knowledge like mobile work, collaborative work, distributed learning and the decision-making field contain contexts and communicational processes particularly dynamic and complex. Our research centre program will propose a communicational theory and a socio-pragmatic methodology and community informatics design that will systematically value and incorporate the communicational and transdisciplinary context in the design of devices and will allow to manage this context with the aim of enhancing the system's performance in terms of emancipation, human development and added value use experience.

The development of embedded technologies and ubiquitous computing requires a deep understanding of mediation mechanisms and interaction patterns as well as the incorporation of the "communicational context" concept that intervenes in the design of interactive and collaborative systems. Our program will develop mixed methods (Creswell) to observe, capture, describe, analyse, evaluate, manage and accompany the implantation of communicational processes able to intervene and be used in the research on community informatics design, interactive systems and collaborative environments (micro-, meso- and macrosocial levels). This global approach will pave the way for the development of reconfigurable architecture interfaces, which will facilitate the personalization and adaptation of interfaces, modules and materials to the needs of different projects, their contexts and their respective uses. We expose the first elements of our design research methodology in the next section dedicated to the methodology of community informatics design.

3.6.4.4   Application Example

- Mobile communications and intelligent interfaces in the transport systems
- Knowledge management in physical spaces physiques (in person), media and information and communication devices (remote)
- Learning, social networking, collaborative work and inter-organizational environments

Table 3.1 Research design and observation procedures

Phases	Procedures	Products
1. Collection of qualitative exploratory data through case studies	Colab case study. Autoscopy of design and ICT use design. Content analysis and categorization of functions and collaborative tools	Content analysis of used process diagrams (verbs), functionalities, products
2. Discussion group	Content analysis of partners' needs (Francosourd, community informatics, Wemotaci, Unima, Colab)	Discussion group report
3. ICT and social media calibration	Analysis of technology by the ACIL/ Colab technical group	Report identifying the collaborative technologies on Internet Schémas
4. Quantitative data collection	Survey sampling inter-portal and online practice communities. Portal analysis chart developed and applied by the design analysis. Description, frequencies, SPSS software	Statistical analysis. Reports on uses and practices (tool description). Integration with qualitative data. Chart. Sampling plan
5. Connection between quantitative and qualitative phases	Selection by the reasoned choice (and intentional) of a participant in the designer groups accounted for on the Web at the previous phase, according to answers indicating a knowledge of socio-technical design	Email, telephones and follow-ups for the recruitment. Interviews, word-for-word transcription, description of design artefacts and devices, images, videos
6. Analysis of qualitative data	Codification and thematic analysis. For each case and between the cases: crossed thematic analysis. Use of the Chartier method (Leray)	Multiple case analysis models. Convergence and divergence in practices. Construction of an inter-mathematics analysis matrix
7. Integration of quantitative data and qualitative results	Interpretation and explanation of the quantitative and qualitative phase's results	Result discussion. Explanation for the community informatics design. Future research programs

- Large-scale social systems design (cyber democracy, social cyber sciences, access and co-creation charts, communication and health co-laboratories, ecological chart grille and economic development)
- Methodologies that are relevant to our field can come from social science methods like ethnography and sociological investigations as well as the ones originating from fields like human-computer interfaces and information systems. The understanding of use and appropriation processes of creativity tools now requires mixed research strategies like the ones proposed by Creswell (2008). Table 3.1 offers an example of mixed methods we have used for the APSI research and their dynamic articulation (Table 3.1).

Research Line 3: Socio-digital Devices and Media Physical interaction and reconfigurable open-source code interfaces: devices, applications and collaborative interfaces architectures

Network and embedded technologies value the integration of physical spaces and media spaces thus creating an unexplored space of support to the design dedicated to new applications in marketing, business, health and education, cyber-physical social systems *and valuing the collaborative creation of new socio-communicational products and services.*

3.6.4.5 Description

Physical objects and the material carry a rich information that can excite the imagination and enrich our experience. This research line seeks to develop socio-pragmatic communication conceptual frameworks and co-design and co-creation methodologies to develop applications, products and services in open-source code according to the paradigm of the collaborative reconfigurable architecture. This type of architecture facilitates the implantation of concepts such as "communicational contextualization," by allowing a system to change its structural and parametric configurations and to adapt them to the emergent and evolutive users' needs according to new interaction and design patterns in varied use contexts. It also introduces a new dimension in the collaborative systems design where users directly commit at various levels to the exploration of interactive methodologies, innovative communication processes and the modification of software and material architectures to better adapt to their own needs. It encourages an increased number of users, experts and uninitiated, including people with physical or mental handicap, to commit creatively to the co-design tasks, collaborative work, self-organization of learning activities in physical and media spaces.

3.6.4.6 Applications Example

- Interactive learning and serious games for self-learning and acquiring digital skills for the co-creation of virtual learning communities.
- The experimentation and communication and social science simulation for the formulation of theories, the creation of "artificial societies" for the study and representation of social interactions and the analysis of social systems representations, organizations and emerging institutions
- The construction of architectures for the development of networked and interactive products, applications in interactive management and collaborative interfaces design.
- The design of multimedia, reconfigurable and multimodal community informatics interfaces.

Research Line 4: Knowledge Basis Interactive environments of knowledge representation

Collaborative knowledge workers need the right content in the right format at the right time and in various locations and materials dynamically answering the evolution of tasks in varied contexts according to evolutive needs in continuous transformation. We will explore the relation between the location, the time, the information and communication.

3.6.4.7   Description

The embedded and networking technologies (e.g. the USB stick), socio-digital media and many other types of networked information and communication devices promote the delivery of information in every situations, spaces and places where the user is located. Working environments of the knowledge workers like interactive knowledge management environments, research co-laboratories and digital online health and education platforms require efficient information and transmission access forms in compliance with contextual and organizational changes. However, no standard design process allows to visualize and present the information dynamically according to multiple modes. This research line focuses on the following perspectives:

1. The fundamental dynamics and communicational processes that intervene in the communicational/media design and the information presentation
2. The ways of describing the dynamic visualization of information and interactions with users
3. The situational topology for the space and time presentation and community informatics of knowledge and behaviour
4. Boarding knowledge techniques in physical objects and collaborative environments

The methods developed in this research line will constitute a practical operational guide for the ubiquitous computing applications in the fields like learning organizations, health practice communities, great sustainable development projects, collaborative virtual work environments, home automation, cultural learning exhibitions, cyber learning, virtual interactive museums and collaborative human-computer interfaces.

3.6.4.8   Application Example

- Informational environments design in various fields
- Industrial simulation and collaborative solutions prototyping
- Sociocultural and urban animation and computer graphic design innovation
- Decision-making support environments
- Interface design for product creation and network applications
- Knowledge management with the help of digital shared libraries and specialized collaborative ontologies

Research Line 5: Applications (Products and Services) The definition of a new socio-economic holonic and fractal paradigm

> *The integration of the physical world and media spaces is the opportunity to develop, for people and communities, products and services with new network innovation paradigms containing several actors that make different levels of society intervene and promote transversality as well as hierarchy by disrupting the traditional value chain and the positivist, sequential and linear business processes.*

3.6.4.9 Description

We are witnessing an increasing need to ensure the co-creation of products, virtual environments and shared documents. More and more, this need knocks down the traditional boundaries between the world of information and communication (media spaces and collaboration devices) and the one of physical spaces of human experience and the creation of sustainable manufactures products. With the new mobile technologies and the network communication technologies, both spaces were separated until now into two distinct universes which tend to merge creating links between physical objects, media entities and human experience of creation in various socio-economic sectors. According to the orientation of this line, we could investigate three emerging issues:

1. The development of new transdisciplinary paradigms and products integrating physical and media spaces
2. The incorporation of computing and community informatics functions into physical products by promoting the integration of organizations' various life cycles of services and knowledge to the users and vice versa
3. Position users through appropriation and network marketing as strategic partners and resource persons in the development of products and business models

3.6.4.10 Application Examples

Holonic and fractal design for products manufacturing

- The planning and decision-making support environments
- Smart home automation development
- Interfaces design for the co-creation and co-design of network products
- The development of network business models

Research Line 6: Sociocultural Ergonomics (Alignment Between Needs and Social Media) The evaluation of sociocultural and communicational factors in interactive and collaborative media systems

> *Cultures create artefacts; artefacts create culture. Social systems influence the creation of technologies; technologies influence the evolution of social systems. Values, beliefs, concepts and interactive and collaborative systems (ICS) performance must be an integral part of socio-cultural life cycles and creation cycles of social systems. This is an important challenge for communication sciences that would like to not only evaluate and analyze interactive and collaborative systems but also contribute to ensure its design and implantation at various levels of society in different social change contexts.*

3.6.4.11 Description

The understanding of cognitive and sociocultural factors related to users' communities and the culture of diverse use has become critical to meet the communication requirement needs and psychosocial needs of users of interactive and collaborative systems. This research line seeks to develop models and methods to evaluate, capture and represent cultural interaction and communication patterns that intervene in the community informatics design and modeling of artefact-human interactions. Our first approach will be the socio-pragmatic model of communication and the SADC that will integrate multiple points of view in the composition of a "polyphonic design" and various layers of training and cultural creation intervening in the description and creation mechanisms of collaborative and interactive systems.

3.6.4.12 Application Examples

- The construction of serious multiroles electronics and multi-user games
- The development of virtual and real social systems' devices and interfaces
- The creation of inter-, multi- and transcultural interfaces
- The planning and creation of methods and communication and cultural evaluation charts for application products intended for the international within the globalization of services and sustainable human development
- The study and production of guidelines for studies on the user context, appropriation mechanisms and cultural and communicational factors that influence them

3.6.5 A Call for Action and for Socially Responsible Communication Design

Thanks to this research program, we introduce a new knowledge technology applied to communicational action that allows the co-creation of social-virtual systems ethics (socio-technological) through community informatics design. It validates the users'/designers' participative culture for the creation of socio-technical systems that possesses the "emerging strategic alignment" virtue, taking into account the new socio-economic realities of the communication society. At a critical era where speed, intensity and complex expansiveness of the Web's changes constantly increase, our emancipation and skills should guide this change instead of being the victims or expropriated spectators ("who are distracted to death", said Porter (Norman and Porter 2007; Porter and Kramer 2006]) depending on our capacity of giving desirable orientations to changes we all aspire collectively in our communities and our society. Social sciences and information and communication sciences are on the brink of an important paradigm change, the digital communication one at the service of evolutive design in society. We believe the acquisition of community informatics design and communicational skills can mobilize actors of the Quebec society in the exercises of participative and entrepreneurial democracy.

We really wish that, in a near future, all the partners of our current social system scan are really convinced of the emancipating powers of the community informatics design in the socio-economic development in order to collectively and consciously orientate the creation of more favourable virtual institutions organizations. Social change does not operate only through the government or industry's critique. In fact for some, design and its learning would be limited to certain professions or certain sectors of activities like software, engineering or architecture development. We have to develop a new design and social learning network culture in the education world. Community informatics design focuses only on the remarkable perspectives offered by the participative culture and the wealth coming from new forms of production and collaborative tool creation to promote desirable social changes. Community informatics design is not exclusive to experts; it concerns the entire society.

At the time, sciences like biology created medicine and surgery, physics gave birth to engineering and architecture, chemistry promoted pharmacies and its clinical study, sociology produced social work and the research action, just like psychology create psychiatry and psychoanalysis, mathematics created computer sciences and political science management and governance modes. It is now time to give to applied communications and information planning their intelligence technologies and their digital social systems design strategies by putting in common our ubiquitous imagination transdisciplinary practices, collective creation large-scale intervention and massive innovation.

If we are serious about the idea of committing more and more to people in the massive social innovation culture, we must develop a design culture at all levels of the education systems, in the business sector, government and non-government organizations as well as in the entire Quebec society. Members of My Portal Col@b project believe we must provoke concrete learning opportunities in community informatics design to develop the necessary skills for innovation at a time when Web technology is infiltrating all sectors of society. The transition to information society is not only an observation or Internet critique transition which is very useful university tasks. It is also a transition by the application of generic design skills for socio-economic innovation, individually and collectively, in various contexts of our life, at all levels of society.

Chapter 4
Community Informatics Design in Action: Towards Operational Ways of Thinking in Order to Start a Design Process (Block 3)

4.1 Exploration Through FOSM and the Seven Design Spaces

As we have previously seen, the field of science models (FOSM) provides the theoretical and practical foundations of a collective operational imagination process called community informatics design. It is nothing less than an exploratory voyage through several thinking and action modes relying on transdisciplinarity. We will now see that these thinking modes are a very concrete way of operationalizing the community informatics design thinking by seven thinking modes (Burnette 2009; Ranjan 2007) likely to help the uninitiated or social and communication science students start a design process. These seven thinking modes constitute an operational model that can intervene at different stages of the FOSM, a life cycle or a design project. Each thinking mode is articulated in several natural or specialized languages and takes into account a different aspect of the FOSM (foundations, theories, methodology or the several applications). Each contains characteristics that allow to provide specific information and knowledge appropriate to each of the instances, procedures or actions related to the FOSM. Concretely, it means that each thinking mode allows to operationalize the different users'/designers' intentions, their behaviours, the norms, the architectures, the role distribution, the resources, the management modes, etc. These thinking modes conciliate material thinking modes (hard) and software (soft). Let us examine how these thinking modes allow to explore "imaginary territories" of an innovation culture suggested by the FOSM.

The design process begins with the collective exploration of the "design space", which resembles the trajectory of explorers searching for an unknown territory, the one occupied by an unbuilt ecosystem, innovation community, the specification of a product or an application or a service to the partners' community. The research is led within the context of a great motivation from the actors, their desire to understand and imagine new knowledge universes with all the curiosity and open mindedness necessary for the creation of new ways to act, share and live together.

© Springer International Publishing AG 2017   99
P.-L. Harvey, *Community Informatics Design Applied to Digital Social Systems*,
Translational Systems Sciences 12, DOI 10.1007/978-3-319-65373-0_4

This voyage is also an interior one that does not only take place with cognitive representations or mental images of the project but also along a process we call "oriented sensualization" through a common intention, context and particular environment design. It is made of different stimuli that take turn at the forefront of the creator's mind, containing various sensorimotor sources, captured by the five senses as well as by feelings (emotions and intuitions) coming from different languages (gestural, non-verbal) with a deep sensitivity for the surrounding environment.

The exploration of the design space is accompanied with a series of perceptual and sensitive inputs oriented towards a goal (vague or precise) and that together provoke a certain amount of learning integrated with each other. This process constitutes a sort of "complexity radar" and of the unknown, an expression seeking to translate the abductive capacities and collective imagination that, once combined together, will produce the degree of interest and tendency to the necessary commitment to meet the communities' objectives. The nature of the community informatics design's thinking instantiates through a plurality of technological tools, creation process and thinking modes that evolve through the design process, life cycle or design phase in a certain given context/environment.

In the image of the systemic FOSM's process (Chap. 1) and the seven iterative space model of community informatics design (Chap. 6), various thinking modes and their respective languages are coiled and iterative, and users/designers are generally comfortable in the uncertainty and have a great tolerance towards ambiguity. This allows them to face the type of exploration and sensualization commanded by innovation design, for example, the production of new collaborative open-source code modules. For example, in the space of design 1 of the FOSM's block 3, a practice community clarifies its intentions; formulates its first objectives; examines the architectures, applications and existing modules; and then carries out a high-level analysis on the feasibility and potential obstacles. This "vagrant" and systematically unstructured exploration is progressing in space 2 towards the establishment of more specific analysis and synthesis categories introducing by successive observation levels (our CAPACITÉS model, presented in this chapter). This process is executed by sections of brainstorming, collective imagination collective of more or less intuitive solutions and categorization of design activities until a reference framework and a structure of the design space are developed and modeled.

In our case, the seven design spaces that define part of the methodology of our FOSM in community informatics design can be increased or decreased according to the requirements of a specific project representing an open process. It is a scaffolding we have created following the observation of numerous projects' life cycles in various fields like research action, software engineering, open innovation process design and collaborative networks or architecture. The idea is not to confine in the creation process and collective imagination in a closed algorithm but to show that we can orientate the iterative design space process in a way to guide the community's efforts and to validate them at various stages and mostly to evaluate them. Without direction, we go nowhere. With too much direction, we subdue the social Internet process which is our dynamic global innovation model.

As we have mentioned in our introduction, UQAM's ACIL tries to semi-formalize a design process that will be capable of associating and putting together skills usually found in the creation of infrastructures and software engineering platforms to combine them with the flexibility required by uninitiated communities from all horizons with needs to meet according to their experience and adaptability found in social and communication sciences.

The strict improvisation or spontaneous initiatives give extraordinary results in the social Web. But with the exponential increase of spontaneous design practices, evolutive and non-expert, research has a certain delay on what makes the success of these composite infrastructure initiatives at the basis of digital social systems. This formidable complexity can hardly be apprehended without the addition of quite complex philosophical and theoretical models, to understand them, model them, implant them and mostly, evaluate them. The current open innovation explosion and the new collective design modalities at a large scale command this effort. Will this be worth it? Only well-led empirical researches accompanying numerous cases of implantation will tell us.

We need to see in the semiformal design process an action-guiding process instead of a break to creativity and in the open innovation, a conscious process facing the future like the fluid currents and informational meanders of an action landscape (Barker 1968; Moles and Jacobus 1988) in which actors explore together the situation, context, design process, possible trajectories, promising scripts, the most efficient human activity systems and the human-centred digital social systems. Whether it is at a micro level like the work team or at the meso level like the community organization, or even at the macro level like the networks in the global society, the possibilities are identified and the options are explicit, which facilitates the collective decision-making.

Our team took an inventory of a good amount of collaborative and analytical tools used by the designers from all backgrounds to design and model the community information systems that support the digital social systems. These transdisciplinary, technological or methodological tools intervene in different stages of the project's life cycle. Their appropriation or adoption depends on the project's specific task and activities, the knowledge field and its relevance in various evolution phases as well as what the team finds appropriate to include in each one. Accessibility is important, but also the acquisition costs, individual and collective design skills in content planning, access codes and licenses, programming difficulty levels and the capacity of integration, compatibility and systems interoperability. These explorations and sensualization of the design space activities will continue until the moment the innovation community is comfortable with all the concepts, until components and quantitative and qualitative properties met, until the decision-making deadline or until quality concepts have been captured in a creative way by the collective imagination of the actors who will then submit them to common exams, evaluations and validations.

These exploratory processes are executed according to a series of unique thinking patterns that, through each project's personalized life cycle, evolve towards generative design patterns supported by various heuristic methodologies such as discovery matrices, a concept we will develop largely in the following chapters. In the exploration and interaction patterns proper to each design process, we examine relations and links between the roles of each partner according to project objectives, functionalities and socio-technologies of a portal in relation to the community needs or the management modes and governance according to ethical criteria and different stakeholders. Our contribution, in this chapter, consists of showing that at the current level of socio-technical project of the collaborative Web, these processes are rarely documented even if they help the creative thinking and imagination of new systems. Substantial learnings can be obtained by the collective creation of double identity matrices that, in a combinatorial of dimensions and properties not always quantifiable, help evaluate alternatives and create a sort of incubator for the research of interaction and design patterns, thus provoking substantial qualitative leaps for the imagination and innovation.

Various thinking modes channelled in dialogue modes used in an explicit or diffuse way in instantiation and discovering relation strategies allow the community to go from abstract fields (functionalities, technologies) to very tangible fields in their forms and treatment (the configuration of a digital social system). For example, a complex co-creation process of a complex social system can emerge from very simple expressions striped of collaborative social media alignment on an uninitiated community needs to evolve towards perfected forms of explicit diagrams and three-dimensional exploration matrices. These help to script complex architectures that take the abstract social sciences model or neophyte towards concrete diagram expressions like the one we are presenting in our chapter on technological, organizational and social architectures.

Numerous decisions are taken throughout these exploration activities. We will show further along in this book that they can support highly strategic decisions, whether they are technological or with social and cultural dimensions. Successive decisions are taken throughout this trajectory, the first strategic ones are followed by decisions of a more tactical nature contributing to precise or modify an objective or examine in detail a series of problem-solving that makes a starting better aligned with the intentions or objectives of the community. However, once the design activity process is set in motion and enters a collective reflection space, it usually escapes the initial design team, and only the consequences are assignable to the designer in charge. The final result can be a success or a failure in complex contexts where radical changes create a loss of control regarding the expected results.

All these explorations remind the designer at all levels of perception, representation and senses, because the team's highs and lows, the hesitations and the lack of skills, good or bad decisions, the loss of trust or the collaboration difficulties destroy each other's trust. Sometimes, even the conduct and facilitation of a community can be a very united work especially if the team members do not benefit from the external representation of the project by the team or the designer in charge. In other words, if the participants do not have the possibility to access the designers' imagination at the basis of the coordination and action committee, the communicational action becomes difficult at all stages of a project's life cycle. The impact of the results of a design can be positive or negative, just like a fire can warm up campers, but, if not controlled, it can burn the forest surrounding it. It is the same substance, but it can have disastrous consequences if the project's dimensions are not well managed or if no collective or consensual representation emerges. The decisions and judgments sometimes result in compositions that offer good development options, but other times, these compositions bring the stakeholder to make a bad decision. It is preferable to vary the decision-making tools, to consider problems from every angle and to reject options that are little relevant before continuing the DSS development cycled, the application or the service.

4.1.1 Community Informatics Design and Its Seven Thinking and Dialogue Modes

The design thinking, the communicational action and the design activities channel different thinking and dialogue modes; each puts to contributions in an appropriate project phase. One can be called to the rescue of a task or activity, and the other can help make a decision regarding the mobilization of creativity tools. In a design project, these thinking modes are not necessarily sequential: we can easily go from one thinking mode to another as long as the mind or the collaborative team judges appropriate to use it throughout the activities that correspond to the different stages of an iterative life cycle or a design process. It is important to point out here that the appropriation of these diverse modes of collective creation and imagination applied to the FOSM and operationalized through the seven design spaces will allow the community informatics design to become an evolutive "doctrine" in a universal design science in the process of creation.

We will now examine each of these modes and the way we can assign them to the design activity articulation. The description of each mode is accompanied by a short development centred on several skills identified to the culture and design professions as well as on its applications to real-world design situations as the processes are "sensualized" and integrated to the collective imagination of new social worlds.

Following Burnette (2009) and Ranjan (2007) with adaptation by us, the seven thinking modes are (1) intentional thinking, (2) categorization thinking, (3) analytical thinking, (4) exploratory thinking, (5) abductive thinking, (6) synthetic thinking and (7) reflexive thinking. Each thinking mode contains its own dialogue activities.

4.1.1.1 Intentional Thinking

Intentional thinking is a series of operational reflections seeking to manage problem-solving, satisfying a need or a desire, for example, the construction of a digital social system like a health service. It serves to make a design project's goals and orientations explicit. It can also be inspired by the experience, interest, a "stroke of genius", the learning of a situation or even the idea of improving collective life. These thoughts can be animated by a sense of motivation for the intentional social change and documented by a particular philosophy like the improvement of an organization performance, a cultural intervention strategy or the sustainable development in a particular field. In some cases, the motivations, instead of being explicit, are more dormant and are really only consciously oriented when users/designers or innovation communities have explored them with the reflexive practice thinking modes and made them visible and tangible in order to orientate the collective action.

A need's perception, which is usually motivated by the imagination of a new world to build or universe to explore, gives birth to the vague notion of a "community informatics design opportunity", which is cognitively represented or collectively "sensualize" like a "thing it is possible to do" or "a thing that must be realized.". Often, the prerogative of one individual at the beginning, his thoughts remain until a form of a dialogue takes shape between actors and a question is asked, "what if we could do this differently?", an affirmation would be made, "we can only continue like that!", a visual expression scribbled would serve as an action plan surrounding a motivating question, a 3D drawing would illustrate a change of process to be planned, etc. The trigger can be a gesture or a non-verbal expression, a wave of the hand, a role play, a choreography, an involved song and a theatre performance showing new roles to adopt and act as a symbolic, metaphorical or iconic system. Expressions, communicational action verbs and phrases illustrating various modes of dialogue (Judge 1998, 2017) like "propose a vision", "involve members", "review", "state a mission ", "motivate a team", "establish our beliefs", "share our information", "open a dialogue", "set objectives" and "consult its members" are examples of discourses susceptible to support this thinking mode. These expressions translate, at the beginning, diverse modes more or less intuitive of a design situation perception that progressively improve the understanding of the field where the particular dialogue mode or expression can anchor itself. Diverse models and dialogues can be put to contributions to explore limits and boundaries of a starting design project, boundaries that are not immediately and necessarily obvious at the origin but that become so as the discovery and learning relations explore its outlines by an appropriate dialogue mode.

4.1.1.2   Categorization Thinking

This type of thinking is used like a heuristic mode to discover and organize various specific properties and functionalities of a design project in the context of a particular design situation. Thinking by categorization serves to identify facts, events, objects, structures and infrastructures and relevant and appropriate aspects of a given design situation. Brainstorming and classification are key processes that serve to structure a design situation throughout the FOSM and the seven spaces life cycle by exploring the interactions between a design process foundations, its theories, its methodologies and its applications on the ground. The systematic exploration of facts and design structures through the discovery matrix methodology allows a practice community to identify fields like social technologies and their functionalities, to relate them to the practice community needs by multiple iterations and successive grindings. The clarity of the activities to realize emerges only once the entire project structure is discovered (its goals, its stakeholders' roles, the infrastructures and architectures, the evaluation modes).

The identification, definition and classification process of fields with the help of the discovery matrix, exploration or strategic alignment allows to structure or model various types of facts or structures we already know and to confirm them but also to note hidden or intangible facts that until now were escaping the members' comprehension. The collective development of visual structures organized like discovery matrices and their translation into 3D dynamic matrices allow teams to spread on vast territories to co-criticize and analyse individual works of a designer or collective works of a collaborative team involved in the project. The consolidation of known and unknown zones constitutes one of the most important discoveries of a direction in a given design situation or in the future research on the community informatics design science according to several feedback loops suggested by the FOSM.

These discovery matrix exploration or communication research general methodologies take place in the real world, through an instantiation strategy of various fields to be modeled. However, they allow a team of experts and users to open to a series of constraints like resources access, the identification of appropriate skills in a design situation, knowledge appropriation, the availability of necessary budgets for the action, the time feasibility as well as infrastructures and social media essential to the realization of experiences and trials susceptible to help shed light on a certain number of questions in the mind of the users/designers. These questions appear serious and will be taken into account and will need imperative answers in order to ensure the project's success.

This thinking mode contains a dialogue mode that is articulated around expressions like "assess what the team favours as design facts"; "focus our attention on what emotionally resonates with the team"; "lift human, material and financial obstacles"; "develop an argumentative line for the project's funding"; "evaluate several replacement scripts"; and "open a dialogue with new stakeholders around priority issues", knowing that the establishment of a common program requires the knowledge sharing between actors, professions and disciplines. Certain well-executed explorations, but useless to an immediate project, will be kept in the digital library for a future application or other exploratory, local or delocalized activities.

4.1.1.3   Analytical Thinking

Current creativity tools and collaborative design assistance platforms can contribute to the exploratory design if it is possible to organize large quantities of data they generate in order to map them in the models. This way, it will help them to reveal, in a pragmatic and useful way, new knowledge within the framework of a juxtaposition and compared analysis process of relations between the aspects and concepts of an issue. Numerous analysis tools can be adopted and adapted by a community to manage a great diversity of data and types of information.

The material data analysis can be done from a point of view of their relevance regarding certain values or certain subprojects, according to their structural and functional viability in planning or according to their access or acquisition costs. With the formal and semantics data, one can adopt the social sciences or diverse cultures' point of view from their ethical acceptability founded on several other properties and attributes to study, according to a series of parameters (skills, functionalities required by a community), through conception tools and process appropriate to the type of data, information or knowledge required within the project's framework and design context.

Experts and users/designers from all horizons largely borrow from all fields of knowledge and currently learn to use many creativity tools and design assistance platforms to conduct several types of explorations and analysis. Quebec's users'/designers' communities we have surveyed between December 2011 and February 2013 mainly learn from experts coming from various knowledge fields in order to lead well a collaborative portal project if the delays, budgets and members' commitment allow. However, our case studies reveal that they face several difficulties in the analysis tasks because of a lack of time, budget or skills. The required clarity degrees for the exploratory design task analysis are rarely achieved which makes it difficult to resort to external consultants or outsourcing, lacking the capability of "naming" the phenomena and the activities involved in the project. We often say: "we want a portal". However, the lack of skill in the adequate analysis of the study's phenomena often ends up approximately even with the help of a computer expert or designer. Also, physical boundaries or dimensions related to a design project are rarely clearly defined, so it becomes very difficult to define a first budget and action plan knowing the limits of the related activities, the exploratory analysis being more often impressionist or under-documented.

The present book, which might seem complex at a first glance, seeks to suggest a simple way of performing the analysis of activities and boundaries inherent to any design situation and to express support requests that are more rationally dedicated to specialists when a project's pre-planning and planning time comes. Like quantitative studies and surveys today which do not obligate the social science researcher to possess high-level statistics knowledge to make his calculations, since he can resort to a statistician, today's researcher must possess enough basic knowledge of tools and design analysis methods to collaborate with a specialist or obtain his help. Because of these difficulties, many projects that are half-improvised dare not complete or cannot ensure their own longevity. The absence of exploratory analysis regularly ends up in the computer experts executing the tasks that are completely out of their fields of expertise, not knowing what to leave to the social science researchers or because they do not have the appropriate vocabulary to delegate a task. Currently, everywhere on the Internet, we seek to correct this situation as the social and communication researchers try to appropriate the vocabulary of their opposite in pure sciences and as they work within transdisciplinary teams to appropriate ontologies outside of their disciplinary comfort zone, according to a law of variety required in terms of terminology, an attitude, that will allow to face the challenge of the complexity of the tasks to execute in order to build transcultural digital social systems.

4.1.1.4   Exploratory Thinking

Many portals, websites or virtual environment projects take the shape of a trip to the unknown and should be led in an open way and form an administration stand point and the users/designers who currently participate in the global open innovation movement. This testing mind, this collective imagination culture of economics solutions and volunteering participation to large-scale projects, needs encouragements at all levels of the social system because such mind is susceptible to provoke accidental arrangements and unexpected discoveries that lie at the heart of the "community informatics imagination".

These often improvised synergies can seem insignificant for many observers, but they are in fact a very critical and productive part of the current social Web innovation. The type of research that takes place in the community informatics design's process is reasonably centred on project collaboration and governance, but its results are largely unpredictable due to multiple emerging aspects that contain online digital social systems design.

Experienced designers who practice the design thinking understand very well that we can start from the known to escape in the unusual and less familiar spheres proper to the innovations of all kinds. Unpredicted results, surprising facts and unexpected discoveries can emerge when we can take the unbeaten paths. For that, one must be attentive to his creative colleagues, to ideas that provoke a new reflection, to conceptual explorations that help develop new sensibilities and to new attitudes that contribute to the discovery of new properties of organizations and innovative social systems. Such explorations can be repeated and articulated at various levels of society, at various fields of knowledge, at various scales going from the details of microsociology to macro-systems like international social systems and at the meso level of enterprises and virtual organizations. We can discover interaction and design patterns that allow to establish new scripts and contribute to the maturation of a strategic and tactical thinking in the planning and execution of projects, thus feeding the imagination and the cascading decision-making inherent to all sorts of projects. These new directions can be re-evaluated and its patterns verified, once in a while, under various angles. This maturation of new ideas and feedback actions on patterns can be done iteratively in different design spaces as well as in various phases of the project at different times. They feed the oriented reflection on the possible, the feasible, the conceivable and the modelizable in the desired directions that go from the most abstract process to the most tangible and realistic expressions forms and from the simple drawing to the perfected forms of social, organizational and technological forms of the DSS.

4.1.1.5   Abductive Thinking

The exploratory design space is characterized by a sort or projective epistemological process where the community informatics expert and the users/designers propose hypothesis from the observation of homogenous elements and by the intuitive discovery of action patterns where the objective is to validate these forms of activities, to realize dreams and collective aspirations or to cultivate hope through their realizations. This form of thinking, guided by the perception and the future's conscience, by its hopes and dangers, allowed Bateson (1972) to formulate ethics and aesthetic fears regarding human interventions in the world, for example, the identification of mistakes susceptible to happen again. This epistemology brings him to identify contact points between the words that help naming things and their mapping modes, whether it is solutions, problem ecosystems or conflicts, not as "concrete reality" (realism) but as a reality built and co-built by the mind mapping these entities. Bateson is interested in the mapping process rather than their simple specific existence. The mapping methodology, which he calls the ecology of the mind, allows to apprehend "ecology" in the larger sense we give it today, meaning the interaction of several species of messages, technologies and resources in a given cognitive context (brain/cyberspace relation, e.g.), by trying to balance and integrate the potential "destabilizor" of conscious intentions of actors when they know to make place to different representations that do not only follow the original project mandate.

Bateson (1972) says the abduction is the word Pierce uses to designate the part of the research process where we bring forward a series of phenomena and often represents an occurrence of few rules previously laid down (e.g. a pattern that connects life stories), but we would not stop here. According to this epistemology, the discoveries made in the FOSM arena can be faced with foundations and the theory in terms of logical level or abstraction, by comparing the relations between the word and the thing, between the map and the territory and between a new concept and the phenomenon or activity it represents. The correlations discovered in the ground, faced with the existing theories (patterns and models), allow to create feedback loops that are characteristics of an open and reflexive mind in the science process or in a complex design process. This is one important component important of the design exploration process. As a matter of fact, the abductive reasoning, contrary to induction and deduction, that release universal laws from individual cases or explain individual laws from general laws gets to project desirable properties and attributes in the future by exploring new forms. It is also able to move from one concept to another at different levels of abstraction, using a deep logic similar to the one used by artists and creators to make their metaphors.

This is what we discover with Bateson (1972) when he reviews his representation models under the angle of the rhetoric of different life stories through their different variations by exploiting them or by comparing them to a similar creation pattern. None has foundations that could serve for all the other ones; it is more a sort of self-organizing inference that is accomplished in a generative and imaginative way. Bateson uses abduction and the metaphor like a practice that allows oneself to decentralize from the object and oneself, in a way to transfer or put his attributes between parentheses to emancipate oneself from his properties. This avoids the trap of existing laws and the original identity of objects.

In the traditional discourse of science and classical logic, directed by conscious intentions, we try to carry out clear and distinct Cartesian representations based on the laws of identities. We operate by induction and deduction, we try to respect the types of logic, we want to get closer to the truth of the territories we explore and map, we observe first effective causes and we expect to be effective actors who cause observable consequences. In contrast, in the metaphor discourse, we always oscillate between the temporary "as if" preoccupation of the reality we create and with which we seem to religiously play. On the other hand is the fall and reconstitution of deep logical types. This epistemological pendulum is at the heart of Warfield's FOSM (1986), who, while proposing axioms and foundation laws for the community informatics design, also questions the metaphysics of these identity laws and introduces differences that contribute to intuitive results that, even if they are still not demonstrable, they remain a tangible consequence of our interventions.

If the metaphor and abduction pave the way of the community informatics design, the individual and collective imagination become central in the forms of distributed cognition and co-production of innovation to establish the collaborative governance of complex projects and the coordination of intelligence and large-scale collective skills. Collective imagination is the playful collaborative exercise that consists of utilizing community abduction and metaphor abilities to escape and crush the past efficient causes to introduce differences in the world of knowledge that represent "a difference that makes a difference", according to the famous Bateson expression (Bateson 1972). Of course, the participative community informatics design always needs analysis and diagnostics that will allow the intervention of induction- and deduction-like research process, but it goes further than that. Indeed, in accordance with the Pierce epistemology, followed by Bateson (1972) and Warfield (1986), its practices and interventions are founded not only on the idea of logical consequences but also on the projective inferences one that, in the users'/ designers' mind and mental processes, are the equivalent of a causality generated imagination.

We could say that by injecting novelty in the world through imagination, we consciously provoke the transformation, which gives us the role of victims of the ongoing social mutations and the role of actors at the causes of these changes. The creator and the designer operate upon a research logic that seeks to consciously and collectively introduce novelty in the world, without necessarily be preoccupied by the idea of truth in the sense of classical logic, worrying instead about the ethical orientation of the future according to the desirable praxeological orientation of our future. We will retort that this represents a human potentiality that has always existed. But in the social Web era with its collaborative design platforms, the ubiquitous collective imagination, the operating capacity to collectively and massively introduce novelty in the world through telepresence mechanisms, to shatter all "ideological ready to wear", anywhere, with anyone, anytime and at a low cost, represents a unique opportunity, never seen before in history, to innovate and orientate human activities. The ubiquitous imagination represents a unique potential to imagine the virtual worlds that will accompany "idealistic" research and design for a better quality of life on Earth.

From this human capacity to imagine a new world, to play with what is real and what is not, from the representational gaps difficult to fill between the model and the represented thing, between the map and the territory, we will progressively build a new abductive science. Of these intangible simulated worlds that explode and redefine our minds, of this epistemological adventure in which things and their relations are anticipated and brought to the forefront, of this new living together transdisciplinary complexity, of the preoccupation for the deep logic, of this tyranny of inductive and deductive science, of these powerful visualization metaphors of worlds to be built "as if" like infinite innovation potential and of these open possibilities in the creative and free meanders of the social Web, we will try to build new skills, a new profession and new research trajectory based on an ubiquitous imagination that refuses domestication. Ubiquitous imagination opens unprecedented horizons and possibilities of co-creation and co-design. Like all horizons, community informatics imagination proposes points of reference and properties that are far from being opposed to reality. To the contrary, the community informatics expert practices a profession that oscillates between interaction rituals and action logic, between pure sciences and social sciences, between the traditional and the metaphorical and between the "lived" world history and its anticipation. These dialectical processes are at the heart of design situations we explore in this book.

4.1.1.6   Synthetic Thinking

The aptitude to play and articulate the ecosystem parts and the whole is an integral part of the community informatics design, just like it is necessary to be able to build exploratory tasks from the general to the particular and vice versa, going backwards a certain number of times as long as the design planning or modeling is in exploratory and intuitive mode. The research and explorations help precisely a certain number of alternative dimensions and scripts that are not rejected a priori but that are kept in reserve as potential orientations, following the collective learnings provided by the relation of dimensions and variables related to the digital social systems design. Certain facts or dimensions can seem far from the starting issue when we first "bird's eye view", analyse, but they fall into place as the practice team or community collectively identifies the variables and criteria that will serve to produce the ideal desirable concept, what we can call the "concept de design" or the to be validated prototype. This concept matured through the seven spaces of creation of the community informatics design.

The design concept possesses a very large number of properties, as we will see further along in this book. However, the reduction of these properties into fields by observation of interactions, relations and links between the concepts allow to seize them in one large expression. Furthermore, it is the role of the model and modeling of complex systems; this reduction helps the necessary decision-making along the team of users'/designers' progression in the exploratory design space, articulated in the seven spaces and various thinking modes channelled in their dialogue modes which contribute to update them.

It is strictly speaking a synthesis process that is usually realized during a visualization activity (exploratory matrix, discovery matrix, conceptual mapping and various drawings) able to capture the complexity of a design situation's aspects and to favour the mastery of a set of properties or attributes that characterizes a design situation and its particular arrangements. The divers' fields of design and their specific dimensions (needs, functionalities, tools, architectures) are no longer apprehended like accessories or indirectly related one to another, but more like a global model system of global expression as defined by Mucchielli (2005, 2006). A total ecosystem contains visible and invisible, tangible and intangible and quantitative and qualitative elements. An evolutive global system containing a series of properties and criteria integrated into a design concept overview that satisfied the starting intentions and objectives of the designers' community as well as the stakeholders.

This synthesis exercise can take place during the different phases of the life cycle or a design planning strategy, either to update relations between concepts and dimensions or simply to feed discussions to better understand the emerging alternatives or even to add educational elements to the feasible demonstration (proof of concept) or to the prototype. It allows to critically examine the links between the components of a design situation, to identify the potential vision obstacles and conflicts as well as contributing to extend the debate and democratic participation to an extended community, other teams or the entire society. Thus promoting, when the dialogue requires it, the appropriation of a participative culture capacitated by the co-design of a particular social system (education, health, cultural industries, community media, enterprise collaborative networks, etc.).

4.1.1.7   Reflexive Thinking

Reflexive thinking is in fact a "reflexive practice" as defined by Donald Schön (1983). Reflexive practice is an action mode that tries to distance itself from the design process to evaluate its development or the evolution of the entire process or even to objectify a particular practice. The evaluative processes range from the continuous evaluation of objectives to the validation effects of a given social media on co-design, including the skills evaluation. The technical and methodological tools used can be of subjective or objective nature. Several properties are rejected or accepted according to subjective appreciation or non-appreciation criteria. Other criteria contain measurable attributes, like costs to observe, the performance of the design team and the functional boundaries (functionalities to put in place or to respect). Then, we can resort to analytical tools and particular processes. In several cases of institutional development and creation of business, procedures and norm process as well as particular regulation mechanisms require a more formal evaluation in the co-design of a playful community, for example. Furthermore, when particular norms must be observed, the users'/designers' community is reminded to respect these rules or even document its actions and activities towards a future revision or a potential update made necessary by the fast evolution of the legal, cultural or socio-economical context.

However, like in any good imagination and creation process, the community informatics design of DSS does not only contain rational choices. Several choices on an ethic and aesthetic level are not guided by economics or quantitative considerations. For example, the readability of screen pages often depends on the artist/designer, his judgement, his senses and his personal preferences. The sponsors and the direction systematically trust the media designer. In Chap. 5, when we define the different aspects related to the DSS design, we will see that subjective, aesthetic and qualitative criteria of all sort can intervene in the modeling and design of various properties and attributes of a system. These "beauty" criteria and these playful or harmonious aspects are decided on the basis of an individual or group vision, and only time and use will tell us if the decision that has been made lead to the success or the failure of a project within its launch context.

Talking about context, we will admit that most of the time, the user and the designer do not have much control over it, until it is expressly to act upon the context like in the case of global democratic participation within a given society or to evaluate and modify the social roles of a university within the general state context on education. In this case, different stakeholders act upon a global expression and communication system, and their decisions could have an impact on the choices and decisions relating to a very large systemic group. However, in the case of large-scale community informatics design concerning decisions that involve large social systems (education, health, legal system) or at the cultural level of a society, the context contains its own evolutive life cycle, and the reflexive qualities of all communicational action in an exploratory and learning design space run the risk of being in conflict with other forms of thinking or vision. The stakeholders in place undertake actions susceptible to modify or orientated differently the starting intentions of each other. The thoughts, the values and the beliefs of other social actors can also inflect the basic orientations of a team of designers or a very large community of users/designers. A particular DSS design can hurt the convictions and interests of different groups, make waves and provoke changes in the context which forces other creators to answer in a reflexive, strategic or tactical way to different actions. Each one acts according to its own thinking and belief mode. A competition for the actions' legitimization is then put in place, the basic idea being that the proactive reflection is a vast learning experiential and social mechanism.

We will see these different thinking modes that helped us throughout the research process are often implicitly used in various creation processes. They can become explicit by the reflection, training and design education at various cycles of our learning systems. The set of the seven thinking modes completes the FOSM and the seven spaces methodology because their contents translate an intentional and operational reference framework that allows to directly map several of the main properties and attributes of the digital social systems (infrastructures, architectures, functionalities, socio-technologies) that can be programmed for the first time into computer systems and subsystems oriented towards the objects and aspects which will be the topic of the chapter on instantiation methodology and discovery matrices (Chap. 7). Also, properties and attributes of the group of fields involved in the modeling and visualization process will function as object/aspect agents in various reference frameworks of collaborative designs. Coupled with higher elaborated thinking modes, the fields will be developed with their respective visualization agents, and each mode will shed light on different fields that will be translated into various autonomous visualization modes in the context of intervention of a team of computer designers.

4.2   FOSM Implications and Its Various Thinking Modes for Community Informatics Design's Creation

The overview model takes its value in a series of implications. The first one is provided by a reasoning space where we can better understand the claims of a science regarding the maturity of its development, meaning we can follow the iterative and evolutive development mode through various disciplinary thinking modes. Warfield speaks of "literative" development because by combining the L of learning with "iterative", he obtains a neologism that explicitly refers to learning. We will add our own L to refer to the "languages" of the community informatics design's science and its various thinking modes that will help us elaborate terminological elements and the evolutive science vocabulary according to these various thinking modes that serve to update and evaluate it. Thus, a scientific development process can be "literative" because it integrates the social learning process of a science through natural languages, various thinking modes and specialized languages. The "literatition" represents the evolution of as well as the maturation of a science. It allows to bring conceptual and practical improvements to an aspiring science taking into consideration the contradictions or convergences discovered by applications with respect to a corpus. However, this process can only work if we examine in detail all the connections and the overview network. For that, we need all community informatics design's project stakeholder to have a sense of responsibility that transcends individual interests of practice communities associated with each block. We believe that this responsibility can be favoured by living labs and innovation put to contributions in the training about the FOSM, its seven design spaces and its seven intentional thinking modes which we will come back to. Broken connections between theory and methodology and between applications and foundations can reflect a lack of interest and even responsibility for their joint maturation in time and space of research.

The FOSM had important repercussions at the level of our own evaluation of APSI research process. Indeed, whether someone is motivated or not by the research process, as generic knowledge tied to one or the other four blocks, nor by the network between foundations, the theories, methodologies and the applications can be operationalized or improved with the help of a particular thinking mode. In the future, this model will serve as a global intervention framework, for example, in the evaluation of ICT as research support elements, at the conceptual level as well as at the level of specific methodology like modeling and society simulation. It will also help verify if certain results are disconnected from reality or if some others can be related to the corpus and to the community informatics design's data base.

In addition, the FOSM contains organizational properties that inspired our way of "disciplining" our community informatics design approach and to develop this applied science model by coupling fields that are usually disjointed, for example: the coupling between instantiation, software and architecture engineering and the idea of organizations of interactions in communication; between cooperative management and collaborative networks; between semiotics and the analysis of levels of reality involved in STS projects and the implantation of an innovation colab-type portal. We found a great utility in it for the organization of our concepts and for the presentation of our research results which helps students to develop a desire for organization in their scientific work.

The FOSM has also been useful in the presentation of various chapters of the present book and in the holistic and systemic appreciation of diverse parts of the research. It helps the researcher and the graduate studies student to present the research stages and results by taking into account the necessity of a communicational process supported within the members of a scientific practice community and various stakeholders involved in the partnership. It favours relations and important interactions for the evaluation of roles of different members involved in very different ways in a project, sometimes isolated or more at ease with separated "blocks". The model also contributes to determine the digital skills to promote in various fields and professions involved in the diverse fields of community informatics as a science, as well as the different types of sectorial leadership to develop to keep the dynamism of the iterative mechanism in its whole. It helps define and realize the task in a coordinate way, according to the plurality of thinking modes and interactive mechanisms between blocks, while continuing to integrate these processes and all people in the organizational systemic and iterative vision resulting what we have been calling communityship for several years.

With that in mind, the model contains obvious social properties for those who want to examine the distribution and coordination of activities and roles historically attributed to fundamental sciences and applied sciences. One of the great merits of the model within our team was certainly to help determine the roles of technologies and collaboration tools within the community informatics design. Our "entry" in technology through action verbs lead us to evaluate the possible alignment between modeling technologies and design instrumentalized functionalities identified by verbs in a given design situation and context: "identify", "list", "define", "classify", "rank", "link together", "interact", "model", "sketch", "draw", "simulate", "instantiate" and "facilitate". All this work of activity identification (Engenstrom 1999) and design task by verbs, under the direction of our colleague Gilles Lemire, appears in various chapters of the present book.

Finally, the model contains some important historical filiations with the pragmatic philosophy of Charles Sanders Peirce, which we will see in the next pages regarding the ontological usefulness to pave the philosophical way for community informatics design in the action (Heylighen 2007) and communicational action according to Habermas (1973, 1984). The FOSM allows to distinguish community informatics design (as well as its related sciences: social Web, computer-mediatized communication, the STS sector, collective telework, human-computer interaction, human-computer interfaces, socio-technical, interactive, participative design and, actually, the new cyber-physical systems in the Internet of Things and the Internet of Places) as a generic collaboration science as well as the technology supporting and resulting it. The idea is to keep at the same level, equal and complementary respecting humans, their resources and imagination tools, just like Kling (1973, 1996, 1999, 2000a, b, 2007; Kling et al. 2001, 2005), Moles (Moles and Rohmer 1998; Moles and Jacobus 1988; Moles 1981) and several other researchers have done before us.

4.3   Some Overall Implicit Model Restrictions

To conclude this chapter, we now consider the consequences of a limited FOSM application to community informatics design, meaning to the intervention, research or research-action models that are made of sub-models of the overall model.

At the corpus level, it could be very possible for a community to limit its interests and observations to the foundations and the theory. It is often the case for epistemologists and philosophers of sciences.

At the arena level, a practice community could very well limit its considerations to the methodology and its applications on the ground. It is often the case for the research-action specialists.

At the theory level, it is also possible to be only interested in the articulation of concepts in a given issue without worrying about the foundations. It is currently often the case in the fields of information and community informatics that very rarely questions their own foundations.

At the applications level, we realize that currently, the majority of the social Web users are only interested in the social Web tools' applications and collaborative platforms and that they do not even consider being interested in the development of the design thinking methodology.

We will evaluate this implications' assessment briefly.

The restrictions of this type have been treated widely in the scientific works dedicated to information systems and community informatics, and their implications are rather well documented. Thus, we will keep schematically reminding certain problems that happen when a team or a community limits itself to one or the other of these restrictions:

- The innovation community is quickly faced with application difficulties like the lack of supervision for the promotion of innovation, the lack of transparency between actors, the scapegoat issue, the intellectual property issue, the lack of norms and procedures and the unfounded threats and rumours.

- Students take classes and training sessions that encourage the same type of irresponsible behaviour, containing uncertain theories and unproven methodologies, without any sense of foundation because there are no foundations.
- Scientific documentation favouring articles where quantitative methods, under the multitude of curves and statistic data, hide a poor true theoretical and practical innovation. This attitude favours the interests of those who seek to obtain a promotion within their faculty, but it certainly has very little impact on the real problems of our society. In the worst case, it reaches results that contribute to increase the problems. We can ask ourselves if "our designs" really improve the life conditions for all.
- In the current explosion of the participative culture and the massive innovation, it is more and more difficult to distinguish the conclusive and structuring innovations from those who are more short-lived enterprises or researches without quality because of our incompetence to consider them in comprehensive and thorough contexts.
- It is more and more difficult to capitalize on the knowledge associated with remarkable realizations in the development of our innovative social systems and methodologies that serve to study and build them. The fact that this knowledge is not adequately reflected in the fields of applications might compromise the validation of our future social systems' performance.
- The extensive loss of knowledge due to an information overload or lack or reflection in the action might become recurrent and be more and more difficult to control.
- The teaching of appropriate thinking modes to various design situations and their contribution in the activities of the community informatics experts might be compromised. The absence of training on those various thinking modes and the forms of dialogue that support them might provoke an "improvisation without memory" that would generalize by the "digital illiteracy" of our students and the entire population.
- No matter how the innovation culture fragment itself, without real network links or without innovative structured social systems, our cultures and our society might become more and more vulnerable to other cultures that have massively decided to structure their national digital platform within vast research programs that validate massive innovation and collaborative design models. These, supported by a scientific design model which is articulated around a "reflexive process thinking mode" founded on technology.

Chapter 5
Generic Communication and Community Informatics Design: Evaluation and Validation of Socio-technical Design of a Universal Communication Platform, the Informatics Design Assistance System, Using the CAPACITÉS Evaluation Model

> *Design is primarily a thought process and communication process, transferring into action by communication. It is a natural function, expressed in the many activities we engage in. For the teleologist, design means the conscious attempt to create a better world. For the antitleologist design is the conscious part of action.*
>
> C.West Churchman

Our analysis of elements related to the development of a model of processes involved in the co-creation of socio-technical platforms seeks to result in useful norms for various types of collaborative design. The analysis is the first stags. Design rules are the synthetic result. First, the analysis allows to gather information, to measure them, to evaluate them and to incorporate them in the interactive construction, according to standardized rules, purpose of the previous operations.

This aspect allows us to justify the final "S" of CAPACITÉS and to determine the capacities of the systems thus built to generate rules, thanks to which the machine regulates its technological potential. The implementation of standardized, transcultural rules acts as a bridge between the learning process through different languages (animated images, sketches, figures or natural languages), first moments of the deployment of a learning platform by community informatics design and transcultural by these different languages, second moment of this deployment. It relies on our previous works (Harvey and Bertrand 2004; Harvey and Lemire 2001) devoted to the establishment of a communication model of the "dynamic appropriation". We take the sector of education and the learning communicational platforms as an example in order to make the abstract reality of platforms more cognitively accessible.

© Springer International Publishing AG 2017
117
P.-L. Harvey, *Community Informatics Design Applied to Digital Social Systems*,
Translational Systems Sciences 12, DOI 10.1007/978-3-319-65373-0_5

5.1   The Context

The online learning models generally contain two platforms: a technological platform and a didactic platform. The functionalities and applications of the learning
unit that allow to manage the learning uses and activities are of two orders: technological and social. The construction of a resource centre with its platforms and Web
applications around different learning communities represents a socio-technical
system (STS), meaning a social system built on a technological basis. The goal of
this chapter is to present the parameters that guide the analysis and the construction
of this socio-technical system.

A STS adds communicational and social demands from users to those of human-
computer interactions. These interactions themselves contain needs related to the
interface ergonomics and in place of the body and the body language in the didactic
space, which pose specific conditions related to the infrastructure (hardware) and
software.

A practice platform and community (experts, learners, stakeholders and partners) are dedicated to the learning of a language or another discipline, from a socio-
technical system (as defined by Whitworth and De Moor 2009a) using technology
to socially connect people through various types of communicational and didactic
tools (Harvey and Lemire 2001), for example, learning modules for vocabulary, the
animated image's grammar as well as the computer-mediated communication on
various platforms: email, social media and networks, learning exchange systems,
e-commerce, blogs, chats, etc. If technologies are often new, social interaction principles between people are not. However, lately, technological innovation values
tend to conceal sociological bases that give birth to these innovations and orientate
their development, which translates into not always happy results or even contradictory ones in regard to desired results. We can quote the negative impact of certain
video games on the concentration and conceptualization capacity of some young
people. It is a real problem with unknown consequences yet. Several questions arise
regarding the new ways of learning, reading, listening, memorizing, writing, designing, representing knowledge and interacting.[1] An important reflection is currently
taking place surrounding what we call "the computer-mediated educational
communication".

The needs and requirements of performing learning communities whether they
are mediatized by computer or by physical world data (face to face or telepresence)
contain several similarities. But we should not underestimate the impact of this bi-
modality even less the learning multi-supported by ICT. With this in mind, socio-
technical systems like distance education platforms must incorporate the
psychosocial needs and technical performance, meaning meet the needs of the community and technical functionalities. If learning communities like UQAM's My
Portal Col@b, under construction, are essentially social systems of people interact-

---

[1] See the file entitled "Pourquoi nous n'apprenons plus comme avant", dans *Philosophie magazine*,
n° 62, septembre 2012.

ing with other people in a didactic social space, then didactic communication principles must guide the implantation of the platform, instead of a design too exclusively orientated towards technology. Here, technology cannot be designed as a simple tool detached from human representation; instead, it becomes a stakeholder of the constitution of a new representation mode in various animated forms. In this case, we talk about "transformation technologies". What does this expression mean?

Transformation technologies contain a certain number or computing tools that have a major repercussion on the representation and acting mode of the human being. It transforms both the mind and the body. While technical tools have been progressively detaching themselves from the body to become technical objects, these new knowledge tools restore technology as an intermediary between the body and the mind, between the gesture and the speech. In this sense, we can consider them like mediation technologies. Technology becomes a *logos*, speech of the mind, and a *technè*, gesture of the body. Internet provokes subtle changes, even undesired ones in our brains. It also modifies our body habits by making us more sedentary. Therefore, it influences our ways of life and our daily conducts.

Community informatics design is in the line of these transformation technologies. It updates them in the preliminary learning process of the creation of transcultural or universal communication networks. It is about learning through different languages, like animation. Learning through animation is a teaching system that uses the image and animated image to try to make a bridge between languages and a new mode of transcultural communication. The animated image only makes sense according to the concept it corresponds to in the text. Learning through animation is an application of new technologies of transfers between the text and the animation related to the transformation technologies.

The evaluation tools in networking and systems theory we want to build and we want to account for in the present book constitute technological and sociological markers that allow to incorporate all the constitutive factors of this new anthropological transformation, towards which technological and current globalization processes are aiming.

UQAM's "Applied Community Informatics Lab" (ACIL) and its partners wish to contribute to the co-creation of a real learning society of online social systems' design, to the extent here the partnership will succeed in establishing a social and educational synergy that is open and ethical: people respect others' ideas without subduing their freedom nor threatening their intellectual property, their reputation or their credibility. To establish cooperation and collaboration between various agents' real or virtual (like in the Internet of Things), people must be able to communicate with each other and coordinate their activities.

The global success of learning platforms like the Colab platform in ACIL depends on the way the global design of socio-technical systems jointly optimizes technological dimensions and online interaction architecture that support social and communicational dimensions of the didactic space; this is what we call "social architecture".

5.2   Towards a Generic Communication Model

The traditional communication and didactic applied linguistics models consider their scientific analysis object as the verbal language, which is the regular language where words, phrase and texts constitute the basic entities. By keeping this objective, we avoid the fundamental contributions of the physical spaces, body language and gesture in the didactic communicational process.

We must understand where does this traditional model limitations come from in order to better comprehend the inputs of the new community informatics design's approach as design with a communicational and social nature. Here, in fact, the question is not only about linguistics. It agrees with the very own language origins and from this anthropological and cultural transformation that allowed the human thought to emancipate itself from the instinctive nature constraints and to break with the limits of the perceptive body.

The community informatics design communicational model seeks to resituate the semiotic function of the body to allow it to free itself from the salvage animality constraints that weigh heavily on the current miserable human conscience in a deep transformation. Therefore, with the different natural and visual languages of the future My Portal Col@b platform, we could be able to take into consideration the entire aspect of behaviours linked to the body language and the movement of people in the social space and time of virtual animated learning environments.

This situation is still strange because when we observe communication phenomena like where two people or members of a work group interact, it immediately appears to our senses and representations that we are facing multiple modalities of meaning creations, through actors' activities and experiences. In fact, the interactors produce holistic and generic communication acts where the linguistics part must be extracted from a larger communication act. Several studies show that the verbal language constitutes only a small part of our capacity to communicate. So why is it the dominant language? It is the fact that it belongs to the field of symbolic and abstract reason that commands the human conduct. It occupies the majority of the semantics field that makes the human being able to produce universal concepts. The word represents the concept. And until here, humanity has not been able to produce a sign system equivalent to the word system of symbolic language. This is why, by transferring the semantics function of words into images, diagrams and animated images (computer graphic objects), we will be able to create a new language that will also be invested of the semantics power of words and incorporate other dimensions of the body, especially the aesthetic dimension kept away from the semantics field of *logos* until now. Therefore, by combining the aesthetics and semantics functions of human faculties in only one representation, we could resituate this harmony of the body and the mind by reconciling the body's impulses, now focused towards a superior level of aesthetic representations (transcendental), and the capacities of the human *logos*, which would have already achieved this level of superior transcendence. This is what our social project consists of, meaning the communicational project of the socio-technical design of human activity system called the community informatics design.

The fact that we are first conceptualizing a cognition being instead of an interaction being containing multiple communicational modalities like the body, the situation and the technology is nothing new. In fact, historically, we can distinguish five sources, if we consider the mythical period when the human reason does not yet aspire to be *logos* equal to the Gods. It is the Greeks who inaugurate the reason like *logos*, measure of all things as they are and as they are not. Thus, in Western history, here is how is stretched the domination of logical reason, *logos*, on the body impulses and all that is connected to it:

1. *Ancient Greek philosophy*, which insists on the *logos* as a meaning, simultaneously rational mind and verbal language, reason discourse against rhetoric, discourse and body language art, mind cavern, prisoners of the senses.
2. *The Judeo-Christian disjunction/reduction between the body and the mind that recuperates the myth* (divine *logos*) in favour of reason (human *logos*). This is how theology is born, the science of God, as if the divine *logos* could be objects of science, submitted to the human reasoning.
3. *The Cartesian dualist rationalism*, which makes the thought the main substance, the indestructible rock of all truth. The body is the animal part, the mechanic of the human being, the temporary compartment of the spiritual mind.
4. *The formal structuralism of Saussure*, with its decentration of the individual performance, the speech and its accent on society language. Linguistics is born in this double articulation of the phenomenon language and the sense with it, the treatment of language as an autonomous structure equipped with quantitative and qualitative properties of any other phenomenon of nature or culture.
5. *Chomsky's linguistics*, with its intrinsic negligence of the body's performance and its total centration on a grammatical, ideal or mental skill. With the recent studies on the complexity and philosophy of communicational sciences orientated towards action, pragmatism or praxeology (action and activities oriented towards the emancipation of the human being) of the "incorporated mind", time has come to promote socio-technical projects where the linguistics dimension incorporates the body and gesture in total communication situations where all other parts of the communicational action are designed like dynamic communication ecosystems that incorporate cognition, biology and the body, networking technology and social and physical environment.

This means the conceptual framework and analysis practice and the construction of learning environments like My Portal Col@b, designed at UQAM like a virtual social assistance system to the construction of other online social systems, can no longer be restricted by rational aspects of the cognitive being and, instead, must be designed at various levels of society – micro, meso and macro – by integrating in its reference framework the irrational, intangible, emergent, abstract and qualitative aspects like emotions, motivations, ethics, society, group and community dimensions, etc. Another important aspect of the consequences from this orientation is that "the language faculty" of the individual (his skills and capacities) must be understood as a generic system of holistic communication containing the discourse and the behaviour, the animated language communication or the "diagrammatic" or visualization languages gathering the characteristics of verbal and non-verbal communication, the communication and learning situations and the behavioural and experiential semiotic. To synthetize our approach, we will say that My Portal Col@b is a collaborative and imaginative platform based on a communicational transdisciplinary model, a generic socio-technical communication and multimodal learning system practised by human and social organizations as an organizational and socio-communicational totality.

This generic transdisciplinary communication model (Fig. 5.1) will be succinctly and schematically presented here. It will be developed and implanted all through the experimental phase of prototyping of evolutive solutions of the "SADC platform". It will be the conceptual framework, trans-scientific, transdisciplinary and metatheoretical serving the basis of construction of the experimental framework (see the "stairs model", meaning the CAPACITÉS approach) with which we will evaluate and validate the functionalities and different applications of My Portal Col@b.

5.3   The Semio-pragmatic Communication Star

The semio-pragmatic communication approach is a generic reference framework that tries to take into account the several aspects of the human communication (bodily, verbal, non-verbal, psychological, social, technological) to incorporate them in researches and developments where several disciplines are brought in to increase the understanding of its various fields and their articulation on everyday life and the different human activities' systems. It tries to incorporate the various theories' assets like Maturana and Varela (1980, 1984) and Luhmann's (1989, 1995) autopoietic systems and Warfield's generic design foundations with its ontology and epistemology, themselves largely supported by Pierce's semiotic pragmatism, von Foerster's second-order cybernetics, Soren Brier's works on cyber-semiotic (2000, 2008, 2013) as well as Searle (1969) and Habermas's theories on collective action's intentions (1973, 1984).

Our under construction model tries to go beyond the models that have inspired design and the implantation of information systems for decades as well as the information treatment machines which are characteristic of the traditional artificial intelligence program. A pragmatic communicational model inspired by second-order cybernetics means that what is observed in the reality is not only of the same type of the observed situation, which is cognitively and communicational socio built, but that the subject observers, without being located outside like transcendental observers, are also represented like stakeholders of a collective observation and collaborative design process. The observers, users/designers, in accordance with the movement of the third phase science described in the previous chapters, are considered as living organisms involved in the observation process like bio-psycho-sociocultural human operators that partake in network social practices while researching the evolution of new modalities of science proper to the living labs and Colab movement. The appropriation of knowledge, the imagination of new human activity systems, the communicational action and the socio-technical design are devised here like collective semio-pragmatic activities. Thus this ontological position and this epistemological demand support that the observer or the researcher is not only an individual subject but an intersubjective collective of stakeholders that, more and more, incorporates university researchers, government actors and the civil society of users/designers. Also, social and economic innovation is related to this attitude since it promotes the idea of collective imagination instead of the invention of an isolated solitary genius. This is why the "I" in the discovery connects with the "we" of the collective network imagination to greatly accelerate the online social systems' design process that is a necessary condition for the massive citizen innovation by networking.

The communicational semio-pragmatic star can be represented by a seven-pointed star where languages (semiotics), design practices (pragmatic) and values (ethics and axiology) are placed at the heart of the star to feed a rising universal conscience (humans and observers' faculty to judge of their own globalized reality) (Fig. 5.1).

This way we can, from this heart, proceed with the dynamic description of the several points of the semio-pragmatic communicational star.

1. *At the heart of the star*: The boiling of dynamic quantitative relations – animated or visual language qualitative ↔ facing the universal conscience as a faculty for humans to know their own reality and to judge it. As the new languages increase like animated languages from the cultural singularities of the world, this collective consciousness develops new realities like current social transformations that need to be problematized, imagined, resolved and identified.

   "Knowing" is no longer the activity of a conscience thorn by multiple scattered objects here and there in an exterior reality and in an unfinished culture. "Knowing" becomes a semiotic, pragmatic and ethic activity at the same time.

   Around the heart: The contexts, environments, elements and properties' sphere that feed the heart of the star and project towards the exterior the transformations operated in the heart of the star:

   • *The physical infrastructures*, essential conditions indispensable for the production and the maintenance of the entire system.
   • *The worlds of social action, language and discourse* that assume the physical infrastructures and organize the communicational processes and social production, design and sociocultural development connections.
   • *The cognitive worlds*, the worlds of interfaces, architectures and superstructures, which give a sense to the basic infrastructures and orientate the existential sense of other worlds.

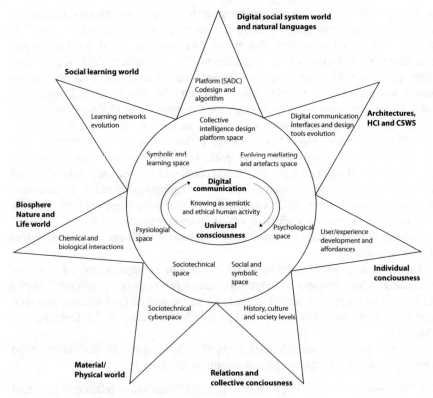

Fig. 5.1 The semio-pragmatic communicational star

- *The worlds of technological mediations* that reinforce basic infrastructures as scientific, technological, cultural and relational superstructures. These worlds provide the necessary and sufficient tools for the development of other worlds.
- *Collective and collaborative intelligence platform*, space open to the entire humanity for its transformations as a harmonized cosmic species.
- *The learning systems*, generators of new types of humans more involved in the social becoming and having more and more access to superior levels of knowledge and knowledge sharing.
- *The body's faculty development*, as an incorporated entity, at the same time individual and community subject, more and more open to the collective humanization process and the socially responsible communicational design.

2. *The seven points of the star and their external derivatives*: Of this second inter-mediary sphere are developed the seven points of the star, to give place to the constitutive external results of the semio-pragmatic star. These results mark the opening of the star to the cultural and cosmic world:

- To the physical infrastructures corresponds this emerging environment of the human world, a new place where human being activities of the life world can evolve.
  Energy, order and disorder are the outcomes of this point. They reflect the quantitative and qualitative levels of the basic infrastructures. It is the basic ecological and environmental level.
- The worlds of social action and language create universal history and culture as places for language and memorization of the entire humanity. Collective memory establishes a new dynamic of representation appropriate to the current globalization processes. The world becomes society and society is globalized through various interactions of cultural singularities.
- The cognitive worlds are the worlds of sense and experimental development as existential experience of the knowing subjects and observers.
  The conscience is an eruption of the experience of the self. It is related to the cognitive world in its quest for certainty and truth. The individual conscience is related to other consciences through languages, memory and collective imagination of more favourable words for the human being.
- The technological mediations' worlds are new development spaces for the communication interfaces.
  The technological interfaces, but also anthropological, between human and machine pave the way for this emancipation desire related to the emergence of a responsible communication, at the service of sustainable development, which is intended to set free the current humanity.
- The collective intelligence platform, which My Portal Col@b will use, with other transfer technologies: Texte $\leftrightarrow$ Visual Animation become porters as new transcultural (universal) communication tools.
  Communication networks and virtual and animated tools belong to virtual modes, always in expansion. They inaugurate these new radical transformation cycles allowing humanity to achieve, in an uncertain and undetermined future, this ubiquitous imagination concept and collective conscience looking to the future.
- Learning systems are generators of new types of cultural attitudes more and more accessible to superior levels of knowledge.
- The body's faculty development makes it an incorporated entity, at the same time individual and community subject and more and more open to collective humanization processes.

By incorporating itself in the cultural and global space-time, the boiling at the heart of the star can bring out all sorts of combinatorial variations allowing to understand the sense and trajectory of this stellar system's activities:

- Either the star is in full activity and is deployed through its intrinsic properties.
- Either it is in a degradation process, gradually losing its potentialities.

The measuring and visually evaluating mechanisms must allow at any time to diagnose the system's state of development and its components.

Furthermore, we should determine the quantitative and qualitative properties of each point of the star in order to extract the common traits and differences. Therefore, we could measure the impact values of the different constitutive components of the Un (the unit of plurality) and the way the entire stellar system moves in a given cultural and global space-time.

Our colleague Lionel Audant considers that there is an entire research to be done, from the elaboration of an algorithm point of view as well as the construction of various components in their quantitative and qualitative links, both complementary and contradictory. For now, the mathematical formulations of this algorithm are not presented here (underlying the patent on matrix function of the cosmic code), which are only providing framework elements for such research. Needless to say, it is a transdisciplinary and international research that would require the collaboration of several experts for the "algorithmic" point of view as well as the socio-technical one. The quantitative and qualitative systematization of different properties of the communication star belongs to a research that is both "quantitative" (numbers) and statistic (standard impact value).

It is a special research of magnitude that should be led, for example, by the PROMPT consortium and more specifically by UQAM's Col@b under the direction of computer and visualization experts.

5.4   The Future Colab: A Socio-technical Learning System

A socio-technical learning system is a social educational system supported by a technical base, infrastructures, middleware, software and tutorials. It is a social communication system dedicated to learning and supported by technical means. A learning community can be electronically and physically mediatized. A socio-technical learning system consists of people communicating with other through information and communication technologies. The technological, cognitive and social aspects (infrastructures and middleware) represent various autonomous systems that interact to create a global ecosystem we will model in Sect. 4.5 like conceptual stairs representing various levels of analysis at different tiers of society. Systems like UQAM's Colab are not entirely reduced to their parts or their subsystems, as long as their co-creation does not only involve these distinctive parts but also the retroactive complex interaction of the parties on the entire ecosystem and vice versa.

There is a double intentionality there that transcends and energizes the entire system. This double intentionality feeds and orientates the activities of each component of the system even if these intentionalities, in their respective deployment, can be in conflict or evolve in a contradictory manner.

Each individual represents a cognitive subsystem like each learning group or learning community is an autonomous system of people or citizens in a learning situation. A didactic socio-technical system consists of diverse subsystems that, instead of cohabiting each on their own, constitute, recreate and regenerate themselves by self-organizing and "self-maintaining" themselves. The community informatics design assistance system (SADC in French) channelled in the Colab, as a socio-technical system, is not only a system where cohabit, side by side, a social system and a technological system. It is a human activity system, a digital social system, where ethics do not come in second after software engineering activities but where creativity, educational innovation and ethics contextualize and orientate technology. Social architecture rearticulates technology and technological architecture modules and then rearticulates the cognitive and social dimensions. With this in mind, the design of an experimentation framework for the Colab is not limited to the application of sociological or didactic principles to a pre-existing technology or the application of a software infrastructure on learning various languages. It encompasses also the evaluation of the integration mode of technological and social aspects in a communicational and socio-didactic system of superior level containing emergent and evolutive properties.

5.5   Socio-semiotic, Technical and Pragmatic Levels of Didactic Experimentation

The physical systems are not alone in the learning systems' universe. The terms "information systems" and "community information systems" that represent My Portal Col@b and the SADC can be supported by several systems definitions. The philosophers suggest the idea of system in logical words and the sociologist in the social systems, the psychologists suggest the expression of cognitive systems, the community informatics expert talks shared objects and their co-construction, while economists have their economic systems, programmers their software systems, engineers their infrastructure systems and the biologists their physiological system. Which of these approaches correspond the best to the co-construction of an experimental validation framework of a universal animated language system? Paradoxically, none and all at the same time. None, because each of these approaches represents only one way of representing the systems to be built.

There is an entire methodological approach to be put into place around the double phenomenon of language and conscience boiling at the heart of the star. The explosion of sciences, each in its bubble, is also the explosion of the aesthetical conscience, the conscience in its quest for certainty, harmony and truth. The more the multiplicity is scattered, the more the conscience explodes into pieces, trying to catch up with the Un of these multiples. Human sciences, in particular, ended up emptying the human being of his singular substance singular (spiritual essence). The human being is dying. It is exploding from everywhere. And the scattered pieces of his nature, spread here and there in the particular sciences that plague him, make it more and more improbable the difficult reconversion of cultures around a central idea of the human.

The Greek antiquity had made wisdom the centre pole towards which all previous knowledge should culminate. Human wisdom was bowing in front of divine wisdom, and theology had supplanted the architectonic science of the being as a place of absolute truth governed by the Word of God.

The Renaissance inaugurates the cut between both worlds. And modernity accomplishes it by giving rise to the sciences of man next to the sciences of nature. This explosion of the concept of Man, without a special status, increases the feeling of relativity and opens the way to all sorts of deviances all more powerful than the other. Communism proclaims the supremacy of the state and relativizes the individual freedom in the name of scientific socialism. Capitalism reverses this relation and makes individual freedom the main development line in merchant relations. What man are we talking about? For what humanity social, political and technological structures governing us are put in place?

Certainly, since this original removal of the symbolic thinking of constraints of the instinct and the residual submission of the body to the savage animal appetite, it is difficult for the human to unify his conscience. But the quest is always there, more present than before in this globalization marching towards the never reached and uncertain of the planet and in these new technologies that maybe finally offer the human the possibility of reconciling his animal and his spiritual parts. For example, the work of transfer technologies between text and animation/visualization should consist of offering to singular cultures this double space of reunified knowledge and reconciliation of the body's impulses and values of the mind. As long as this original reconciliation is not accomplished, we cannot hope to achieve this unity of the conscience. The handicap is constitutive of the hybrid nature of the human being, and this nature can only be restored in the process framework proper to the liberation of the body's impulses. The "liberated" body can, at the same time, liberate the mind from residual constraints that prevent from looking further than these darken reflect of the shadows like they appear in the allegory of Plato's Cave.[2] In fact, taking into account the body's space will contribute to its own liberation as well as its mind. With the both of them, they will climb the steep hill that leads towards quality of life for all and the truth of wisdom that should guide all human intentions of development: the maturation of a universal conscience as a survival means.

Therefore we must, at all times during the deployment of the research development, be able to establish relations of correspondence and complementarity, convergent or divergent, even contradictory, that allow to find the universal knowledge Un. It is in that sense that the equations of the algorithmic and synthetic formulation must result in a Un (1), given that the quantitative and qualitative properties of various parameters have become complementary and equivalent, beyond their singular contents. This result is the necessary and essential condition to allow the conscience to finally reach this unit itself, in its endless quest for certainty and truth. Unification and correspondence and complementarity transfer's algorithms must then be designed like anthropological and cultural transformation algorithms. There too, we will need generations to achieve it, but we must start somewhere.

---

[2] Reference to Plato's *Allegory of the Cave*

The visualization of a date base or memory in a digital library only represents a facet of such information system. The semiotic and social systems vision is another one. It is important in the discovery of the meaning (semantics) according to the social vision of the system. All these disciplinary approaches are relevant if each can describe an information system in a relevant manner without contradiction with the other levels, whether it is the philosopher preoccupied by the system's ethics or aesthetics, the engineer by the performance of the infrastructures, the computer expert looking to create friendly interfaces, the biophysiologist concerned with the systems' ergonomics, the psychologist interested in the users' representation system, the sociologist interested in the psychosocial dimension of the uses and interaction patterns or the didactic expert attracted by the co-construction of learning through network socio-communication and in virtual communities (as digital social systems).

Complex systems like the Colab increase the need for a systemic and generic approach of the phenomenon we study: the creation of a SADC based on a generic model of universal communication in visualization and animation language represents a good step in that direction.

In order to explain and evaluate the communicational aspects and the use of complex solutions like the SADC incorporated in UQAM's Colab, in compliance with the analysis elements of the seven points of the communicational star, we must analyse several socio-technical uses' tiers at different levels of society.

When we do research in communication, particularly when we practise "integrative" studies that combine several disciplines like the complexity, computer and evolutive human communication sciences to build systems, we also want to be evolutive; a transdisciplinary approach is required to cover the entire elements involved in the seven points of the star. First, the semiotic approach as a logical science of sign circulation in society allows to display two analysis continuums, the human need ones and the technological solution ones likely to fulfil them. This approach, illustrated in Fig. 5.3, allows to see how physical aspects (space, time, acoustics) are related to chemical, biological and ecological aspects that start at the bottom of the stairs from an informational vision to a communicational/semiotic vision, as we rise in the hierarchy of sciences, human and social sciences and the more abstract arts, in various contexts at different levels of society with the help of different languages allowing the emergence of a collective and collaborative intelligence.

The infrastructure and the software that represent the basis of the socio-technical system are located at the first two levels. The third level, biophysical, is there to negotiate the ergonomics and ethological aspects on top of intuitive (reflexivity) and instinctual (gregarious), communicational aspects and simply to think the place of the human in nature through the mediation of these socio-technical systems. The human being records his activities in the world not only through technological innovations at the inferior level of the "stairs" but also as a human species that impacts the Earth and the world through various games of languages as defined by Wittgenstein. Languages allow exchange, content and meaning sharing in the communities. Cognitive sciences, neurology and psycho-physical sciences rely themselves on biological disciplines that allow to study the information at a micro-cellular level or between living organisms. These have to negotiate cognitive ergonomics or bodily issues, psychomotor education, related to the appropriation of messages or the sending of contents via diverse communicational signals. The human-computer interface systems rely in return on these biophysical aspects related to the brain and cognitive needs that reflect to the design of messages, the world representation and knowledge to be captured, modeled, coded and decoded.

At the fifth level, we find the sociological aspects of the socio-technical systems and the aspects of the social and public communication as well as the global conversation allowed by today's collaborative platforms and social media. These aspects cover other related aspects like ethics, aesthetics, the mind and the evolution of the conscience. The next level takes into account the connective networks that, from local to international level, cover the new needs created by the participative network culture. They account for the evolutive needs related to the community informatics design participative culture. The seventh and last level refers to the hyperconnected networks (collective and collaborative intelligence), the current and future Internet of Things where the needs for innovation and creation are channelled in an evolutive design culture we call "ubiquitous imagination", where the games of natural and expert languages are used in the configuration of tools and contents contained in the collaborative design of the community informatics type proper to the design society: they are "design games" like the ones we find in the adaptation of video games put at the service of citizen science, learning and teaching according to the gamification principle. The languages used in the identification of current global issues, in the resolution of related problems, the imagination used in innovation and the networking identity that represents a certain applied consequence (the identics), comprise the application of these languages and design games that are massively shared to human activities.

The socio-communicational autopoietic system of language games is involved in the design of virtual organizations and digital social systems we find in the CAPACITÉS model (stairs model 5.2), inspired by the seven points of the star. Between the sixth and the seventh level, we add to it, in addition to analysis levels, concrete society levels where these "language and design games" are articulated, at the micro level (individuals and groups), at the macro level (global networks) and at the meso level (virtual organizations). We will need to carry on our researches to incorporate them even more, but we believe our demonstration is developed enough at this stage to encourage more investigation in this sense. Furthermore, an upcoming book in 2018 entitled *Théories des espaces communicationnels hyperconnectés* will illustrate in part the CAPACITÉS analysis process and its potential for the design of social digital systems. A case of application of this chart to a Canadian video game enterprise will allow to start the validation.

Figure 5.2 stairs refers to a transdisciplinary analysis chart and a series of questions based on the elements of the stars, which are characterized by language and collaborative design games whose updating and implantation require more than technology or individual agents. The superior levels transcend the informational design vision to suggest a communicational, semantics, social and holistic vision of the analysis and design activities that allow a full instantiation of the current socio-technical systems.

The intersubjectivity related to cognitive worlds also requires the "ubiquitous imagination "of social and cultural worlds, themselves based on biological and technological dimensions of the continuum. It is a fractal model, telescopic even, that combines transdisciplinarity, semiotics and functional language of the collaborative design by configuration and must be understood as a sort of "universal design grammar" where combined and incorporated language and design games become a "pragmatic", even a praxeology put at the service of modeling and the implantation of emancipating socio-technical systems. Therefore, the model refers to not only the analysis chart of informational and communicational processes associated with socio-technical systems but also to the design activities collectively realized through means of various languages used in the design activities. We dedicate an entire section to this point in Chap. 5. The required communication skills for the future of the co-building of these new ecosystems that are digital social systems also cover certain computer skills that may be fulfilled through diverse stakeholders of the social system to be built (Fig. 5.2).

Indeed to do so, we must take over the communicational star analysis and build algorithmic equations according to the quantitative and qualitative criteria of the properties of each component (first level of the research). This requires a methodology preliminary to the computerization of the system's various components we call "the discovery and strategic alignment matrix"(see Chap. 9). Without going further in the programming questions we address in this book, we will now formulate a certain number of remarks to describe in more details the socio-dynamic of the stairs' levels hierarchy in connection with the seven points of the star. By doing so, we will suggest a series of questions that, in the future, will serve as an analysis chart to evaluate and design large-scale socio-technical systems.

For each systems level, we will formulate a questioning allowing to frame the algorithmic research with the quantitative and qualitative properties of the global system's components.

1. Infrastructures' systems are based on physical and material architectures and are facing energy exchanges, channel capacities, technological evolution and technological framework underlying the entire socio-technical system.

   How can we improve and consolidate these basic infrastructures? What are they made of? How many under components and elements are there in each of these components? What happened to the impact values of these main components? On which components should we act to make the system more able to support and incorporate the multiple and varied innovations of a SADC like the one in My Portal Col@b?

2. The software systems emerge from the physical infrastructure physique; they rely on various information exchange levels, data, codes and formal languages and are facing infinite loops of recursiveness and iteration of the programming and processing.

   How can we make this software accessible and easy to use? How many functionalities are there? How many are useful or necessary? How many do we need

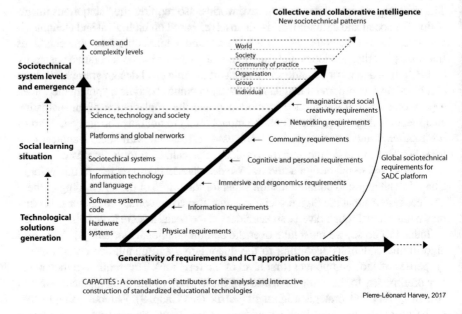

Fig. 5.2 The CAPACITÉS systems levels and society tiers

to make the navigation as efficient as possible? How many users are there? How many succeed?

3. The bio-physiological systems must face challenges at several levels such as the immersive environment, the 3D modeling, the place of the body in the educational communication, the physical and cognitive ergonomics and the user-friendliness, the bio-physiological costs like fatigue, the time devoted to learning and integration of the body into the animation, the communication by gesture and the communication sensory and perceptual organs.

    The Colab and its SADC seek to re-establish the body's cognitive function (semantics and aesthetics). How can we trace the way of this restitution? How many steps are there? How can we measure their impact in the ongoing transformation process?

4. The human-computer interface systems (human-computer interaction) emerge from the three previous systems and focus on intrapersonal communication, the representation of reality and learning worlds, on meaning exchanges between two human systems and are facing challenges like information overload, the information status at the various systems' levels and tiers of society, the understanding of visual animation language and intercultural comprehension of the users.

    How can we increase the power of apprehension and comprehension of imaginative intuition and symbolic reason? Does it require exercises and time? How much? What will be the impact of these exercises on the reason and the ubiquitous imagination? How long will it take (transformation time)?

5. The socio-technical system emerges from the human-computer interface level and is based upon the links between the community and communal level, the level of normative exchange and the division of labour, and the level of activity coordination and collaboration mechanisms between individuals, groups and learning communities. It faces problems related to trust, loyalty, faithfulness and justice.

How can we increase the communicational exchanges in a context of kindness allowing to increase the feeling of security? What are the minimum and maximum numbers of networks and users? What are the values to implement in order to favour security and exchange?

6. The level of computer-mediatized communication focuses on all the other levels, but it adds a large-scale international dimension to socio-technical systems like the SADC: a link to the entire humanity. It must face the challenge of interculturalism, the learning of the others and the world in the vast digital learning social systems and activities related to massive network innovations in the society of knowledge sharing.

How can we reach the critical mass constitutive of quantity and quality of the diverse components of the network? How can we favour the commitment, through which mechanisms or social technologies? How can we mobilize great actors' collectives? According to which values?

7. The level of collective intelligence involves levels of comprehension and intelligibility of the world that go through new paradigms, discoveries and unseen emergences.

How can we incorporate the multiples into the Un to concretely catalyse the ubiquitous imagination? How many levels of knowledge should we incorporate? How can we evaluate the quantitative and qualitative properties of these different levels of knowledge?

These are the basic questionings we need to refine and make more operational.

Therefore understood, the technology (*technè*) is made of the dynamic material and software infrastructure. The whole organization of the SADC under construction gathers a research partnership, academic and scholar organizations, computer and software applications, people, users and their relations, policies and their business models, norms and educational and didactic activities. When we say that the Colab/SADC system is a socio-technical system, this implies the seven socio-technical levels and their dynamic and evolutive interrelations. Our evaluation chart and our experimental protocol will try to ensure the harmonization of the connections between the infrastructure, the software and the middleware, between the body and the gesture, between the cognition and the human-computer interfaces and between the social and organizational systems, like the learning communities and the computer-mediatized communication level and the networks at the level of the entire humanity and the paradigms emerging from the collective intelligence and the ubiquitous imagination (the aspiring intelligence in 5.2).

Since a society embraces more its road system, its people or active organizations, the didactic Colab system will emerge as an evolutive social form that will have its longevity despite the potential changes that could happen at the individual, communicational, didactic or architectural level of its evolution.

The socio-technical system's levels also include the body, between the software informational level and the cognition level. As we have mentioned, this new dimension incorporated into our experimental plan seeks to fulfil a gap in the educational communication, knowing that in addition to the verbal language, a generic communication requires the inclusion of the physical space, the body, the non-verbal language and the gesture in the sensory creation system.

5.6   The Colab/SADC Systems Performance

The highest levels are an efficient way to describe the system but also to operationalize it. The stronger the feeling of belonging and identity to a group, the more this representation is likely to improve the group's performance, for example, the acquisition of a new language. Generally, we define the performance of a didactic system at the highest level of productivity. If a level suffers a failure, the surrounding levels also suffer from it, like a chain reaction. Likewise, when problems occur in the infrastructure, they sometimes have repercussions on the software level and so on. Therefore, the success of a system depends on all its levels, even the more abstract ones. For example, a website with a good infrastructure will not receive any visit if at the software and interface level it is full of bugs. Just like we can have technological bugs, a socio-technical system will not function if we do not take care of the cognitive, social and organizational aspects of its implantation. Even if the infrastructure, software, educational applications, social uses or the learning community cohesion failures seem different, they all have something in common: if a systems level does not work, the entire system runs the risk of failing (internal disintegration). For example, by adopting the Internet as a socialization and personalization platform supported by cloud computing, we modify the entire socio-technical system; we not only add a "human factor in the solution" like we would put a cherry on a sundae.

5.7   The Integration of Reductionism and Socio-constructivism Challenge

Our analyses reveal that the conflict of representation that seems to exist between the constructivism and the reductionism followers seems to essentially result in the fact that we consider the level of Fig. 5.3 from the either bottom-up (parts define a whole)

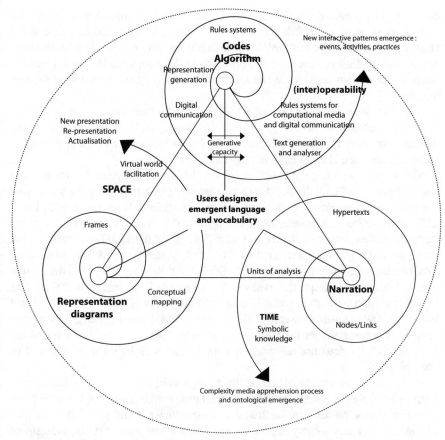

Matrix of the community informatics design in the context of the creation of a digital social didactic system.
Three major processes are at work: 1. Algorithm, the domain specific to digital communication. 2. Representation, relational
access in a semio/cognitive/social mediation process such as collaborative workspaces, simulation or visualization.
3. Narration and media apprehension process as a new science of interfaces for mastering complexity in different domains.

Pierre-Léonard Harvey, 2017

Fig. 5.3 Didactic design space: iconic symbolic process

or top-down of the system (the whole defines the parts). Constructivist psychologists like Piaget (1970), Chomsky (1986), Lemire (2008) and Maturana and Varela (1980, 1984) state that people "construct" the world and see "one" world instead of "a" world, whereas determinists like Watson, Hull (1975), Skinner and Moles (Moles and Rohmer 1998) state that the objective world creates real that define behaviour. The first ones describe behaviour from the basis, while the others adopt a top-down approach. Communication sociology usually considers individual behaviour like expression conducts and the sense resulting from external social structures, while rejecting the explanations related to the cognitive, biological and physical levels like a defective reductionism. These top-down approaches cannot exist in isolation as if, somewhere magically, all the representations of a culture and human activity were erased the same way it would be possible to eliminate them physically.

   We believe this is the heart of the problem. It is the double question of the will-fulness status: is there a transcendental willfulness (a priori) and relations between cosmic and human conscience willfulness? The first matrix function of the cosmic code poses the cosmic willfulness as a dynamic factor deciding the cohesion of the entire system. The second and third matrix functions take over this key factor quantitative and qualitative accumulation principle of the transformation to explain the status of the human conscience and its disarray regarding the meaning of its own trajectory.

It is a key issue, both as a theoretical matter and as a matter of change algorithms to be incorporated to technological tools (universal) and sociocultural networks (singular) in order to harmonize them in the Un ↔ Multiple. But we prefer not to address it here (see Harvey 2018 in reference).

Thankfully, sociology post Luhmanian technique (especially Fuchs and Hofkirchner ones, 2013, 2008, 2007) is reconnecting with psychological and cognitive roots with substantial efforts supported by the works of Habermas (1973, 1984) with social action and communicational agents; the works of Bourdieu with the "habitus" notion, based on the individual perception of the social environment; the works of Moles (Moles and Rohmer 1986, 1998; Moles 1990; Moles and Jacobus 1988) on the micro-psychology of usage (Moles and Rohmer 1976) and the human interface operator concept; the works of Giddens (1984) regarding mental models supporting the structuration social life; or even the works of Engeström (1999) and Wenger (1999) regarding the role of the subject in social learning and practice communities. Furthermore, we take into account today that the emergence of sociology from psychology does not automatically imply that sociology can be reduced to psychology.

Reciprocally, at any level, reductionist approaches tend to deny the actor's capacity of choice or decisions. For example, behaviourists define all behaviours by environmental stimulus or infrastructure contingencies while social determinists will tend to say that society articulates the cultural program, that communism or market laws (Hayek 1945) define special action from an "individual tabula rasa", or even that "only communication communicates", as declared by Luhmann (1989, 1995) when he decrees the social systems primate on cognition and agents' perception. The substitution of behaviourist engineering by social engineering can only progress with difficulty, to the extent that in those two world visions, the world is represented as a machine. Even in physics, no researcher can extract the observer outside the equation of the world, outside the cosmic matrix (Audant 2010; Hegel 2006).

The debate between constructivists and reductionists often incorporates only one disciplinary view, but the "emergence" concept allows both the derivation of idea and of "new rules", for example, the biological events derive from quantitative events but this does not transform the biology into a subdiscipline of physics. If biology coexists with physics, then sociology, communication, cognitive psychology, social cognition, computing and software engineering can also collaborate to a common creation project of a universal communication and assistance system and community informatics design. Instead of reducing all disciplines to only one reality or world, let us give the possibility to each one to overimpose, modulate itself and rearticulate itself, letting the researcher and the designer free to choose their point of view. The transdisciplinary borrowing at multiple perspectives (multi-aspectual design; Harvey 2010) can be perceived as the fact of walking around an object to observe and describe it from various angles. The creation of a universal communication and design language can greatly benefit from this programmatic culture and attitude. This experimental approach reintroduces the notion of freedom of choice while definitely abandoning the determinist isolation or reductive ↔disci-plinary. The creation of a universal communication language that is diagrammatic and dynamic involves a vision that is both individualistic and holistic of the human-machine language system. But all this shall await a later research.

Thus, the SADC/Colab design and construction spaced can be seen like a physical infrastructure's system, an information processing system, a meaning creation entity, a world representation cognitive system, a social and community structure for educational design and a universal collective and collaborative intelligence system. These perspectives do not represent different systems but the desired overlapping of various views of the same hyperspace system integrating different interconnected spaces: physical space, cognitive space, social space, cyberspace and collective intelligence space. This is why, from the beginning of this chapter, we suggest a generic applied communication model that, for now, seems capable of better taking into account the complexity of the socio-technical system we wish to build.

The SADC catalyses the interaction of all these things and probably more especially ethics and aesthetics of the collaborative and community informatics information systems. For example, it corresponds to a didactic design social space where the challenge of creating a universal diagrammatic communication language can incorporate a support technology for the creation and generation of dynamics and animated (operability and atomization algorithm), to new representation spaces by animated language (representation space) and the presentation of live stories or uses stories (narrative and story time and processes abstraction) that put in place a new type of design, a community informatics design susceptible to validate the emergence of new interactive, technological and social configurations applied to the analysis of complex issues and the design of computing and socio-technical solutions oriented towards sustainable development.

Figure 5.3 illustrates this co-creation and co-design communicational process. It is a fundamental translation process, one of the natural languages represented by information visualization languages and varied psychosocial processes we will define later. It is the fundamental constitutive structure of the main components of cyclical and iterative processes of transfer technologies Text ↔ Visualization-animation tools in the socio-technical ecosystems in transition and evolution.

What are these cycles made of? What are their quantitative and qualitative components' properties? How do they influence themselves mutually in their respective deployment? We will continue to try to answer these questions in our future researches.

5.8   Socio-technical Systems' Execution Conditions and Communication

Generally, we consider an information system does not have a high output in one or more of the following cases:

1. It does not obtain results (ineffective).
2. It is not built for usage (unusable).
3. It contains too many bugs (non-reliable);
4. It is prone to viruses (unsecured).
5. It fails when functions change (inflexible).
6. It cannot be incorporated to existing technological norms (interoperability).
7. It cannot download or import external files, documents and applications (connectivity).
8. It reveals sensitive data or personal information (privacy or indiscretion).

These eight elements will help us for the next phase of the demonstration. The attribute constellation model for the analysis and interactive construction of standardized educational technologies (CAPACITÉS) analyses five interdependent elements of a socio-technical system: the system's border, its internal structure, its effectors, the receptors and the context (the context will be addressed indirectly in the present chapter; we will come back to it in more details in this chapter and in our next book (Harvey 2018 in reference). The design of each element, according to the community informatics design approach (a collective and collaborative understanding of design), consists of reducing the risks and constraints at each level and tier. It gives rise to eight basic objectives that we complete with four "contextual" objectives because they help define the educational situation and the specific learning environment related to educational activities.

Thus the evaluation of the didactic performance of a socio-technical system like the Colab will be done from an experimental framework containing several quantitative and qualitative criteria. On one hand, these integrate risks and, on the other hand, perspectives, like in all human artefacts. Here we borrow from the works of Whitworth and De Moor (2009b).

(A) The objectives (to define for each project) are related to boundaries. This element distinguishes the platform of its environment and its context (the context is not necessarily a system).

1. *The risk:* The protection of the private life or online learning against undesired intrusions, wrong uses and personal or moral threats (security)
2. *The perspective:* The use of elements exterior from the Colab like outsourcing and cloud computing to improve a multitude of tools and learning devices

(B) Structural elements define the internal portal/SADC's operating.

3. *The risk:* The longevity of the system's operability despite the potential internal failures (reliability)

4. *The perspective:* The systems adaptation to environmental elements (flexibility) and cultural ones (cultural ergonomics) or didactics (new educational technologies)

(C) The effector elements seek to directly change the exterior world (e.g. thanks to individual or social learning).

5. *The risk:* The increase of generalized costs of educational communication
6. *The perspective:* The procurement of generalized utilities for the learning point of view, through the increase of direct action possibilities on the didactic environment, that is, a positive contribution to desirable socio-economic developments or the improvement of the animated language system (functionality)

(D) The receptor elements record the "co-creation of data visualization language world of knowledge" and receive exterior messages allowing the diagrammatic modeling of knowledge, information, culture, ethics and the cosmos (world vision and human integration through natural languages of the universe in the sensible or rational world).

7. *The risk:* Management and control of the data recording relative to an entire social system of possible and incorporated traceability of the total socio-democratic profile of people and social systems (privacy, personal information, social control)
8. *The perspective:* The creation of social and mental learning models that are more relevant by using several tools, channels, information networks and communications, data, information, cultural elements, ethical criteria and world vision sharing with other communities or other didactic systems throughout the world

These eight objectives are widely known by experts, but their combination in one protocol (experimental transdisciplinary protocol) is something new and still relatively empirically unexploited.

Analysis criteria and priorities vary according to the application context. For example, with My Portal Col@b, learning environments already validated by educational instances will reduce the importance of security criteria, whereas in new or intercultural environment, the questions of information systems ethics and the underlying axiology will give primacy to criteria that are relative to security and flexibility. The four dynamic criteria (functionality, flexibility, extensibility, connectivity) increase the opportunities, while the four passive criteria (security, reliability, privacy, conviviality) lower the risk (e.g. generalized utilities versus generalized costs related to individual and social appropriation of universal communication languages by other languages).

We can hypothesize that the tendency to communicate and act through a new didactic protocol and a new language based on information modeling and psycho-social processes will be even stronger and that the system will both jointly validate and evaluate the dynamic and active My Portal Col@b's objectives.

Even if we can think that the "functionality" elements, what the system is capable of, always have priority, the non-functional requirements of a digital social system can have a heavy responsibility in the global system's operating (all aspects related to the context). Not only code lines related to the interface can contain unexpected errors, but the entire appropriation context of the platform can depend on the actors' commitment in the use or other contingent factors that go beyond computer programming considerations. The code's strength or the technological characteristics of the tool are not the only factors for success. We too often forget that Esperanto is a powerful and universally applicable language, but its massive social appropriation is insignificant. In addition to creating the "code", we must ensure its social appropriation in several users' communities.

The SADC's conceptual foundations both suggest the appropriation of an ecosystem and of a techno-system. Current researches in neuroscience, in cognitive psychology, in communication and media and in community informatics indicate that "virtual thinking space", as supported by the community informatics design's project and My Portal Col@b, is a guarantee for human cognition validation and collective intelligence, which are currently not well understood from social sciences as well as natural and engineering sciences. However, a universal pattern communication language through dynamic visualization can be greatly updated by new types of communication and information archival. The "computing technologies", in today's broad sense (telecommunications, information systems, community information systems, social Web, social computing, 3D animation, visualization, animation and cybermetrics tools), promise to provide a wide array of tools and devices that are highly efficient for the creation of a visual, dynamic, emerging and derivative language capable of facilitating and supporting the human society. CAPACITÉS faces a crucial challenge by answering the following question: with which criteria, how and until what point can the Colab/SADC platform validate and support social and economic appropriation of new communication modes through the generalized use of a dynamic and visual information/communication and an animated diagrammatic language?

CAPACITÉS will then analyse not only the status of material and logical technology in the co-creation of the system but also the biological, cognitive and social aspects that support the creation of the visualization language. We would especially like to:

1. Analyse and validate dynamic support functions of the emerging language elements (inspired by exercises, scripts, routines, representations) at a structural level in addition to the traditional analysis of the iconic fauna, animated icons and visual sequences.
2. Incorporate elements like the perceptions, the emotions, the representations, etc. to the verbal language, and validate the gesture and non-verbal language by trying to anticipate and support the emerging and relevant communication avenues through socio-technical systems that support the creation of a universal visualization language dedicated to information.
3. Evaluate the best learning situations through animation language.

4. Support the evolutive Colab/SADC development in a dynamic process of classes
   and virtual groups in addition to virtual communities' activities of co-creation
   and interactive processes that put large groups of participants to contributions
   internationally.

5.9   The Colab/SADC Socio-technical Performance Analysis

As we just briefly saw, the complexity of a platform design dedicated to the learning
of new visualization language assisting the digital social systems' design increases
when multiple performance aspects can vary at multiple disciplinary or society levels (Fig. 5.4). For example, reliability can play at the tools' stability level but also at
the level of trust between certain software. Each level puts different problems in
interrelations. For example, the appropriation or conviviality of the platform (costs
related to use, tendency to communicate or the educational activity), as a consequence, is the reduction of learning time of certain scripts, cognitive costs related to
the appropriation of a tool or applications, the effort related to cognitive ergonomics, but also the available memory to use the software utility or the available energy
for the operating of a laptop computer. Once again, all these elements represent
different challenges for the design, especially when we think that the reliability and
conviviality dimensions can happen at more than one level.

Figures 5.5 and 5.6 show the different basic elements of CAPACITÉS (see
Fig. 5.4) as spaces for analysis, design and trial or validation per society levels and
tiers (Fig. 5.4). Theoretical and methodological details of each of these elements
will be provided in a later text after their empiric validation is performed by our
partners. Let us say for now that the compilation of attribute constellations represents the whole of the systems performance, that the shape of each constellation
represents the performance profile of a tool or an application or a service and that
the lines represent the performance tensions between the perspectives and the risks.
Knowing that the validation of a performance attribute can reduce another, for
example, and that the increase of the platform flexibility can, in return, threaten its
reliability.

Figure 6.1 allows to visualize the state of individual and cognitive performance
in the appropriation of the platform.

For the benefits of the exposé, we present a generic methodology here. However,
we will show that attribute constellations specific to the didactic experience could
be created from the following criteria: identifiability, skills, activities, frequencies
and temporality, communicability, rules and normativity, accessibility to resources
and users' profile (Fig. 6.1). Furthermore, we could create validation dimensions
and criteria to evaluate the satisfaction of users. For example, we could build analysis charts according to the following dimensions:

• *The content:* learning modules, content organization, granularity, education and
  educational scripts

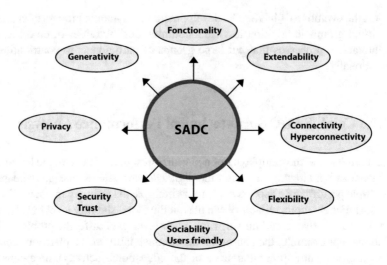

CAPACITÉS : A constellation of attribute to standardize
E-Learning technologies interacting assessment and design

Pierre-Léonard Harvey, 2017

Fig. 5.4 The basic elements of CAPACITÉS

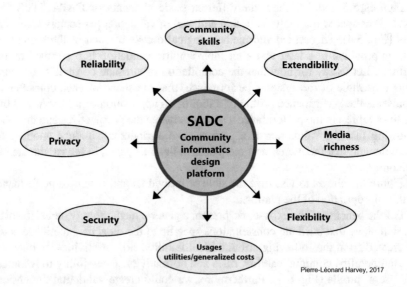

Pierre-Léonard Harvey, 2017

Fig. 5.5 Requirements and personal needs (cognition)

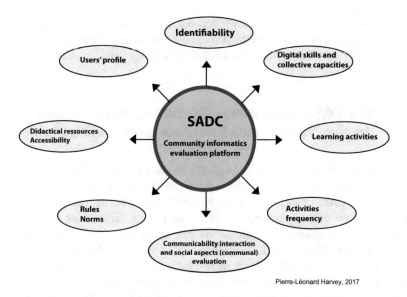

Pierre-Léonard Harvey, 2017

Fig. 5.6 The trajectories of educational uses

- *Users' commitment:* participation level, specific contributions, motivations to collaborate with the learning community, writing, reading, oral expression, pronunciation capacities and animated language mastery
- *The learners:* environment, situation, context, learning profile and cognitive models
- *Devices or software:* presentation and interface operationality, cognitive and physical ergonomics, the place of the body and gesture in immersive environments
- *Communication:* delivery and forms of content deliveries, quality of social links, sociability, tendency to communicate, appropriation of communication tools, coordination, collaboration, connectivity and interaction with the community
- *Coordination:* interactive navigation, TCAO, collaborative work, interindividual or collective interactivity, presentation of diagrams, visualization interfaces and animated tutorials
- *Collective intelligence:* constructivist and socio-constructivist activities, situated actions, distributed comprehension, shared world values and visions, collaborative work, shared skills, emergences and derivation quantities and qualities, distributed learning environment, conflicts and constraints, participative culture elements and qualities, qualitative bifurcations and complexity of the design and the appropriation of the new animated language

As the tiers change, the levels of exchange are modified: the material exchanges codes and energy, software exchanges computer code and digital information, the body exchanges signs, sounds, gestures and images, the human being exchanges perceptions and representations by the individual and distributed cognition, communities exchange meanings, knowledge and cultural elements and the networks allow the social link and the emergence of new human organization forms and collective intelligence, through diverse animation languages and visualization.

5.10 The Alignment Between Educational Solutions and the New Visualization Language Implantation Problems

The alignment between the SADC and My Portal Col@b and the learning objectives by visualization and animation require an evaluative look from the tactical point of view to the strategic one at the various levels of the analysis and society. In this section, we will expose the problems and general dimensions relative to the implantation of various cyber learning systems and techno-educational solutions in terms of design. Without exclusively focusing on the particular applications of the Colab, we will present a list of criteria serving as relevant examples for the evaluation of many platforms and the construction of indicators. Since we do not precisely know all the products and applications to come from the platform, this section is destined to give a list of fundamental elements that could help in the decision-making regarding the evaluation perspectives to take into account. We try to align the best way possible the list of dimensions and criteria on the semio-pragmatic communication model (Fig. 5.2) and the CAPACITÉS model (Fig. 5.3), even if we are conscious of the fact that we will need to improve the coherence in connection with educational objectives to be developed in our community informatics design assistance portal. These dimensions are therefore suggested as a reflexive analysis chart for the partners as well as for the APSI project: "My Portal Col@b and community informatics design". The exercise will consist of determining the indicators and criteria that can be grouped under the general particular constellation attribute dimensions, taken as an analysis chart to normalize.

1. At the infrastructure level, we will need to examine if the creation, the management and the knowledge evaluation needs are well supported by the basic structure of the Joomla platform! Here are some main evaluation categories in this chapter:

   (a) The research tools
   (b) The portal
   (c) The electronic editing tools
   (d) Learning content management systems
   (e) Classroom and learning management systems
   (f) The integration of document management systems
   (g) The integration of each partner's resource planning system
   (h) The integration of students and consumers' relations management systems
   (i) The integration of cloud computing and the updating of Internet logistics

2. At the software level, we find processes, tools and devices at three levels: training processes, training results and contents dedicated to learning.

   The Processes:

   (a) Project management
   (b) The alignment with learning objectives and the values of each community
   (c) The evaluation of needs
   (d) The continuous evaluation of the infrastructure in connection with the community's needs
   (e) The creation of contents
   (f) The prototyping pilots and results
   (g) The pilots' evaluation
   (h) The pilots' delivery and deployment
   (i) The evaluation of implantation costs

The Results:

   (a) The success rate in the completion of the exercises
   (b) The reduction of costs related to the experimentation
   (c) The number of access points to obtain information or to access to the services
   (d) The number of people who have access to the platform and learning experiences of new languages
   (e) The acquisition of new communication and innovation creation skills
   (f) The users' satisfaction
   (g) The new intuitive behaviours
   (h) The alignment of objectives and values of the various learning communities

The Contents:

   (a) The documentation quality
   (b) The references relevance
   (c) The videos and animated communication tools' quality and relevance
   (d) The support tools for the creation of contents and autonomy/user's cooperation
   (e) The quality of readings and material presented by the trainers/animators/facilitators
   (f) The accessibility to experts
   (g) The level of participative culture in the innovation and creation
   (h) Conference sessions and network learning sessions
   (i) The quality and utility of creation workshops
   (j) Personal and collective learnings (the acquisition of skills)

3. The interface level gathers the following elements:

   (a) Guidance
   (b) Incitement
   (c) The gathering and the distinction between items

    (d) Immediate feedback
    (e) Legibility
    (f) The workload;
    (g) The access and navigation brevity
    (h) The informational density
    (i) The explicit control
    (j) The explicit action
    (k) The control by users
    (l) The adaptability
    (m) The flexibility
    (n) Taking into account the user's experience
    (o) Errors' management
    (p) The protection against errors
    (q) The error messages quality;
    (r) The correction of errors
    (s) Homogeneity and coherence
    (t) The codes' meaning and denominations
    (u) The compatibility

4. At the human level, we exchange not only information but also meanings and representations so that the functionality at the software level or interfaces is replaced by the user's skills in a creation, innovation or execution task and the processing ease is replaced by the bodily, perceptive and cognitive use facility. The flexibility and the reliability of the system and its capacity to face changes that are effective of the exterior and the interior world are also featured at the human factors level. Wealth represents the degree of depth of the conveyed meanings, and confidentiality gives the individual the control of his image towards other people. Also part of this analysis level is the expansiveness of uses and security, which allows to defend against systems infiltration attempts.

5. At the community informatics level, the social Web enable connective networks of people. Groups, communities, organization or society exchanges at large are done through shared rules, norms, beliefs, memes and culture. The users of a social group system or members of a learning community develop synergies if the social unit structure obtains more results than if its members would work alone. In addition, the participative culture uses codes of ethics or social capital when conflicts, aggressiveness or language abuses occur. The capacity of a society to show tolerance requires a certain predictability or order from which we can judge the acts, while its innovation and re-creation capacity in new social space-time require autonomy and freedom. Digital social systems like virtual communities need rules to protect personal information in order to protect its members from each other. At the same time, they need transparency for people to exchange their ideas on "generativity" evolution of the system in the applications and media services. The openness means that a community lets other members of external communities act and inject new values, while identity lays the foundations of the communal "us" and the "they", which suggests a contract or

a constitutive act that prevents non-desirable or not appropriate behaviours coming from the "outside" while defining the belonging to a group and its characteristics.

In socio-technical systems like the Colab/SADC portal, it is important to address the right evaluation level and the associated factors, knowing that a socio-technical design that would not take into account the factors' diversity could have some unexpected consequences. Furthermore, in a socio-technical system devoted to the creation of a new visualization language, it becomes fundamental and necessary to take into account not only community informatics and social factors but also linguistics, pragmatic, semantics and semiotics factors:

1. Synergy
2. Ethics
3. Rules
4. Freedom
5. Privacy
6. Openness
7. Transparency
8. Identity

These important factors always incorporate this confrontation-tension dialectical between perspectives and risks. The problem the designers, researchers, managers and the political leaders are facing in the construction of a platform like a portal supporting a SADC is that the attention too specific to a particular factor can rebound somewhere else, on another problem. The right design explicitly requires innovative synthesis of conflictual goals, dialectical integration of objective often contradictory in the total design space (in the seven spaces of the evolutive and generative design spiral we have presented in the previous chapters).

5.11   The Conditions and Needs Related to Signification Exchange and the Production of Meanings

The human-computer interfaces' line between connectivity and privacy gives a social dimension to socio-technical applications based on meaning exchange. These applications emancipate at the community informatics level of the physical space, until the entire humanity, through generative and evolutive mechanisms of the collective intelligence.

Most communication exchange theories coming from the computer-mediated communication movement (Harvey 1995; Harvey and Lemire 2001; Turoff and Hiltz 1976) suppose the existence of underlying cognitive factors of the appropriation of technical solutions. The first theories were proposing a unique reference framework to analyse processes (Huber 1984; Winograd and Flores 1986) that communication between actors already seemed to overflow the simple information exchange. Furthermore, several process theories suggest interesting and relevant dichotomy: (1) the tasks versus the socio-emotional aspects, (2) the informational versus the normative, (3) the tasks versus the social and (4) the social versus the interpersonal. In 2000, Whitworth, Gallupe and McQueen combine these dichotomies by incorporating them in a unique online communication model comprising of three exchange processes:

1. *The Information Solution:* intellectual exchanges of contents originating from the literal meaning messages about the world
2. *The Relation to Others:* the emotional exchanges related to the transmitter-receiver context
3. *The Representation of the Group:* the intuitive exchange on the group position in relation to the world and the orientation and movement of the group with respect to its own meaning

Figure 5.3 summarizes the way the three meaning exchange processes try to interact through the representation of the group's identity as a first element, the relations preservation as the second one and problem solving regarding the world as a third priority. From it stem three cumulative Internet development stages likely to influence, for example, a new animation language universal system.

The First Stage: a global knowledge exchange system
This stage seems to establish itself as the Internet becomes a vast digital library containing the entire humanity knowledge in all fields with the help of tools like Google, Wikipedia and Vizster as human capacity validation and augmentation systems.

The Second Stage: a global interpersonal communication network
This stage is also in motion and in the process of being updated, as people connect with other people throughout the world, through all sorts of tools and devices, arousing the gradual proxemics law abolition.

The Third Stage: a global community and a planetary brain through the emergence of collective and collaborative intelligence supported by the ubiquitous imagination of a sustainable society guiding the Internet of Things and its cyber-physical social systems
While the development stage is still embryonic, the Internet visionaries maintain that when virtual communities come into conflict with other social structures like the leadership, democracy and justice, a battle far from being stabilized through space and time, few common structures emerge. However, throughout the world, multiple initiatives call to mind a sort of global network creativity, likely to produce generative alignments and capacities for new never seen before human and social configurations with the help of the evolutive community informatics design. It is in those human configurations that we see the digital social systems of the future. We shall come back to that point later on.

5.12   An Evaluation Framework for Communication Needs: The Observation of Socio-digital Media's Properties

One of the first attempts to classify communication media defines "media's wealth" as a "capacity of the media to facilitate common sense and shared meanings". However, according to us, the studies led in that sector are not conclusive as to whether the emergence of sense is related to the transmission capacity or as to the users' preferences when the time comes to transmit the information or knowledge. We will need to be attentive to this matter as far as the wealth is not the only factor. Other dimensions, like the shared characteristic of information, the synchronous or asynchronous characteristic of communication or the degree of communicational "continuity" allowed by a given interface, can have some influence.

Other important dimensions must be added to time and space dimensions: the communicational connection of a tool depends on the combination of transmitter-receiver patterns (one to several, several to several, several to one) and design interactivity patterns. (We will elaborate on the pattern notion in Chap. 6, when we discuss instantiation.)

The interlocutor's socio-communicational position, information and tasks to be performed can come from facial expressions, gestures, behaviours and non-verbal sounds like grunts and exclamations (2005, Mucchielli 2006).

The computer completes these individual, interpersonal and common communications by adding and subtracting attitude scales and by spreading them in lines, by presenting the statistics and by visualizing them by attribute constellations, by semantics differentials (Harvey 2018) and by factor analysis with the support of data visualization software.

5.13   A Communicational Reference Framework

In the framework of creating a visualization language communication universal system seeking to support the modeling of digital social systems, we are interested in the properties that contribute to the semantics wealth of messages; we can define as total shared meaning. However, if this perspective aims to evaluate the capacity of our SADC to support the task, actions and creation activities of the new language, we shall also focus on the system's capacity to generate innovation beyond the performances related to the task. The task is far from being the only required level of evaluation. In several respects, we expect from a SADC that it validates imagination, promotes creativity, supports the innovation capacity of individuals and groups and it opens new perspectives in fields of knowledge not yet demarcated: a collective intelligence that will guide designers with the objective of allowing creative work, nonstructured synthesis and happy and unexpected discoveries that will help achieve unprecedented results or acquire the creative skills of collaborative work in order to conquer unexplored ubiquitous imagination territories.

First, let us define the communicational framework that could contribute to define the semantics wealth, defined as the total shared meaning, in accordance to our generic communication model in Fig. 5.1.

1. *The Expressiveness:* The total meaning at a specific moment, according to the number of channels and media wealth:

    (a) *The Symbolic Position:* A simple discreet symbol, an approval or a disapproval, is not a language in itself. A public that applauds or votes is a communicational symbol.

    (b) *A Document (structured and static symbols):* The textual language is made of alphabet symbols, connected with a syntax, translated in the form of sentences that have a meaning. The diagrams have texts or graphemes, gestures and "gestèmes" that, according to the principles of the *gestalt* and the theory of action (Moles and Rohmer 1998, 1986; Moles 1990; Moles and Jacobus 1988), will form significant objects or events in the field of the individual's conscience (psychological space) or in the social fields of the identity community (social space).

    (c) *The Sound and Audio-Dynamic Objects:* The audio-dynamic communication allows the speech, the phonemes to create words and the sequence of the sentence. In music, the notes produce melodic and harmonic sequences, a polyphony that creates sequences of harmonious and emotional sounds. In the audio-dynamic timing, keys and tones translate feelings more expressively.

    (d) *Multimedia (dynamic multichannel animation):* The audio-script visual communications intervening in the creation of an animation language open multiple creation possibilities through the socio-dynamic of the multichannel. These multiple communicational modalities interact in several ways in the ecosystem to optimize the messages' wealth and the channels' combinatorics, in order to validate the socio-construction activities (Engeström 1999) of language world.

At the physical level, expressiveness can be defined as the total capacity of networks, the total number of cables connected at once.

2. *The Informational and Communicational Continuity:* The degree defining to what extent do we have continuous flows or pauses:

    (a) *Continuous communication:* The communication flow is continuous, when transmitted or received in a way that neither the transmitters nor the receivers have content editing problems, or the receiver needs to remember the message. From the transmitter's side, the flow could be unprecedented, spontaneous and authentic, while from the receiver's side, it could be short-lived. A communication flow is called "in real time" when the continuous flow exists on the transmission side as well as on the reception side of messages.

    (b) *The recording:* In recorder communication, the receiver is free to memorize the incoming communication until he decides to read it, listen to it or visualize it.

At the physical level, the continuous idea is the equivalent to the total length of time during which the entire network communicates.

3. *The Connectivity:* The number of people sending or receiving communications (Harvey 1995) in semantics link networks (Hai Zhuge 2005):

   (a) *The Broadcast Media:* the mass media, from one point to several points
   (b) *The Interpersonal Media or Self-Media:* from point to point, to point zero, the communication from self to self or from one individual to another
   (c) *The inter-Media and Community Informatics:* from several to several, multi-points, in one single transmission

   At the physical level, the connectivity can be done online, wirelessly or by radio waves.

4. *The Generalized Costs:* These costs, explicitly undefined in the present book, will be the object of a partner's decision-making process, from analysis levels as well as society levels illustrated in Fig. 5.3, for example:

   (a) At the level of creation process alignment of animation language and the platform
   (b) At the level of the shared meaning exchange
   (c) At the level of interpersonal exchange and intrapersonal communication
   (d) At the level of the community informatics exchange, its nature and the depth of the personal and community contributions

5.14   The Evolutive Generative Design, Generative Alignment and Generative Capacity: The Evaluation of Skills and Emerging Dimensions in the Future, Colab/SADC

By looking to build a communicational and socio-technical model that evaluates the Colab/SADC performance as a complex ecosystem dedicated to creation and learning a new pragmatic communication theory applied to the community informatics design, we have insisted on the fact that our reference framework, mainly communicational, could not be limited to technology or tasks. In traditional researches on information systems (IS) and on community information systems (Whitworth and De Moor 2009; De Moor 2005), our focus has been on the performances related to the alignment between the communicational star model and the tasks associated to design activities in the CAPACITÉS stairs model. The alignment concept, we have used a few times in the present text, is often used in a quantitative and qualitative evaluation to take into account the way the applications and solutions design improves the entire performance of a platform and its value in the broader sense (e.g. the one of social design). Until now, documentation on IS has focused its attention on performance evaluation criteria relying on task efficiency measures as well as precision and productivity. This is why we have suggested from the star a socio-technical framework based on a generic communicational model in order to incorporate in our future experimental plans the evaluation of abstract factors often forgotten in concrete analyses, like representations and emotions. A vision of community information systems like the one the ACIL's team will update must incorporate the human and social factors at several analysis levels. This outs us in the vision of an ecosystem where users and designers' expectations are established around the systems' capacity to favour creativity, to open new visions and to imagine new learning situations in fields of unmapped knowledge by experts' knowledge and traditional disciplines.

The connection of cyberspace ecology and the creation of a dynamic universal modeling language of psychosocial processes associated with the community informatics design will generate an invented world where ubiquitous imagination will play a big part. Since this world will be co-built with the help of all sorts of tools and devices, it was necessary to define a framework for the evaluation of physical, biological, cognitive, social and networking rules as well as for the exam of the individual and collective subjects, static and dynamic objects, design and use activities and more complex creation and innovation processes.

To take up this challenge and complete this vision without developing them in the present book, we will present here the concept of "systemic generativity", which seems particularly interesting in the development framework of a new universal communication system in community informatics design. The generativity concept will be all the more useful since it is inspired by diverse disciplines and it will allow us to explore the evaluative spaces of the attribute constellations. Like a dynamic modeling language is able to map a participatory network activity, that can be seen as an illustrated world, a representation of the world inhabited by machines along with the movement of human beings in real and virtual space and time, the concept of "generativity" will allow us to share and orientate the flow of textual, verbal, audiovisual, emotional sensing and perceptual data in collective representations channelled in the generative grammar of a new pattern language methodology.

The generativity concept, presented at the collective intelligence level, corresponds to two evolutive generative design perspectives: the generative capacity, which translates the skills of an individual or group (innovation) to produce an imaginative or ingenious object (ingenious collectivity idea), and the generative alignment concept that refers to the enabling degree allowed by an artefact or a platform to catalyse these collective imagination results (brain's alchemy), to communicate them and to further favour the generative capacity of individuals and the creation community.

In the following pages, we suggest a series of important dimensions we need to consider for the analysis of a system's performance to favour creation, for example, at the "linguistic semantic/imagination "level or "the emergence of new linguistics and dynamic visual configurations", and the demand of the alignment with the operational objectives of My Portal Col@b/SADC project (see the relations between the elements of Figs. 5.2 and 5.3), for example, to visualize the beginning of a generative design guide from the potential functionalities of the Colab/SADC platform.

From this communicational and socio-technical framework, we can now begin to define the main concepts in an operational manner, to exhaustively identify the theories, dimensions and analysis criteria by priority order and according to the most desirable action plan and to build analysis charts (questionnaires and observation tools) useful to modeling and the implantation of such systems. It is a communicational framework awareness that demonstrates the existence of very concrete transdisciplinary and communicational avenues, appropriate for digital social systems design and likely to accompany in a generative and evolutive way the design and instantiation of these ecosystems. In Table 5.1, we outline, as the conclusion of this chapter, the complementary plan of a possible alignment between the operational performance (potential performance) outlined in Table 3.1 and some relevant theories on reflection and desirable generative capacities to be put in place in different collaborative platforms (Table 5.2).

In the next chapter, we will deepen our exploration of several concepts related to the idea of evolutive and generative architecture and to its applicability to social digital and socio-technical sciences.

Table 5.1 Formative theories applied to "Generativity" concept in various disciplines' exploration

Generative design orientation	SADC potential functionalities	Generative contribution to SADC
The SACD must be representative	Visualization	The animated images and the 2D and 3D representation tools allow the cognitive and social representation of objects, situations and events of the world through multiple points of view
	Simulation	Decors, action frameworks and conversation simulation Social forms, emotivity and aggressivity situation simulation Social movements through animated language simulation
	Abstraction	Animated image "generator", translation interface "generator", speech synthesis, voice recognition
	Integration	Virtual prototyping system allowing trans-field modeling and schematization, regardless of the disciplines' boundaries, practices and professions
	Communication	Support to trans-profession exchange trans-expertise, exchange and share in the virtual communities and the CSCW (everyone has access to the works)
The SACD must be adaptative and evolutive	Personalization	Personalization of the creation interfaces for various types of users (novice, expert, seniors, families), work environments, personal preferences
	Automatization	Memorizing the texts and animated images "generators" results
The SACD must be open	Production by peers	Socio-technical extensibility of the system and capacity for the peers to use their own cloud computing applications
	Renovation	Open development norms User-friendly updating tools

Table 5.2 The exploration of formative theories that apply to the "generativity" concept in various disciplines

Discipline	Theory	Generative aspect
Psychology (Erik Erikson)	Generativity social psychology	Re-creation energy Social innovation Encouragement and guidance of the rising generation
Linguistics (Noam Chomsky)	Generative grammar	Discreet series of rules that generate infinite syntactic configurations
Organization sciences (Donald Schön)	Generative metaphor	Figurative description (or animated image production) of social events or learning situations that shape attitudes and behaviours towards them (reflexive practices)
Social psychology (Kenneth Gergen)	Generative capacity	Ability to question the status quo and transform social reality and social action
Architecture (Christopher Alexander)	Generative patterns	Simple process (algorithm) allowing the creation of a well-built artefact we can adjust to its specific context
Computing (John Fraser)	Generative design	Generation of a series of multiple and disparate design scripts susceptible to inspire users/designers (process and emerging algorithms)
Social systems design (Bela Banathy)	Generative design research	Generation of multiple aspects of the "design thinking "and appropriation of these aspects by the users
Socio-cybernetics (Kenneth Bausch)	Generative ethics	Generative and evolutive communities defining norms, values and axiological rules of social action
Social studies (Danielle Zandee)	Generative research	A recurrent hermeneutic process that generates theoretical quantic leaps

Chapter 6
Towards a Scientific Collaborative Design Approach: The Construction of a Community Informatics Design Assistance System to Support Communities and Virtual Organizations

Collaborative design has become one of the main challenges in several fields of studies, especially social and communication sciences, physics and computer sciences and even biology, architecture and ecosystems of innovation. It is part of the future research program in humanities and digital social sciences. Designers want to create systems where several entities (organizations and individuals) could collaborate to society projects in an autonomous way, on site and in their sphere of respective work. Actually this social design process occurs within the collaborative network framework. Collaborative design seeks to allow collaborators to work in a more efficient way by realizing collaborative actions beyond cultural, disciplinary, geographical and temporal barriers. However, for the system to work, we must configure it in order to meet the needs of social requests and changes. According to Lu et al. (2007), few disciplines have addressed the collaborative design study rigorously, which remains a field of the occult science or black magic. These authors grant we should transform collaborative design in a real discipline, in other words, to take it from black magic practiced by very few people to a rigorous discipline understood by all (Lu et al. 2007). Researches on collaboration found a strong resistance from the determinist philosophical tradition followers, resistance also coming from some misunderstandings created by previous works. We were wondering, for example, how to evaluate the human collaboration as an acquired social dexterity if we cannot study it scientifically. In other words, it is about presenting a community information systems design or to present the general social architecture of a collaboration platform, or in brief, the "reference architecture design and methodology for open collaboration". In this case, how to build a collaborative design that allows to generate and share the knowledge? According to Wenger and Gervais, design does not rely on a simple communication activity:

> Here, it is about unifying and coordinating the skills that exist in a practice constellation. The design challenge in organizations is not to find the form of skill that conditions all the others, but at the contrary, to coordinate multiple forms of skills in the organizational learning. (Wenger and Gervais 2005, p. 269)

© Springer International Publishing AG 2017   155
P.-L. Harvey, *Community Informatics Design Applied to Digital Social Systems*,
Translational Systems Sciences 12, DOI 10.1007/978-3-319-65373-0_6

The present chapter suggests an outline for the creation of the community informatics ecosystem's design and suggests a few leads and recommendations. It also provides a methodological framework, even a multi-methodological one, to support virtual environments. In other words, it is about experiencing a community information systems design or to present the general architecture of a collaboration software, the "reference design for open collaboration". The community informatics design assistance system (SADC) is essentially a framework presenting the adjustable design modalities according to the users' needs. It is the starting point for virtual organizations and communities that wish to implement new collaboration solutions. As an adjustable socio-collaborative platform, the SADC covers both the community informatics design's scientific bases, the design of virtual communities and the collaboration aspects. It links them in order to facilitate the information circulation and the access to knowledge and bring closer the users' communities. To a lesser degree, the SADC is also a reference model, a conceptual framework defining a middle ground and a common terminology for communication and also, a platform prototype of open service, expandable and adaptable for the structuring and integration of all sorts of online activities, socio-technical systems, personalized portals and even all sorts of collaboration platforms like virtual communities or campuses.

The SADC contains a series of models offering a complete definition of the entire essential characteristics of a collaborative work environment. It will be the first collaborative design platform in Canada and internationally that will help build the design of online socio-technical systems in order to simplify the integration of collaborative design activities as well as the evolution of the virtual systems and normalization. It will contain the following elements:

1. *A governance architecture*, containing the general architecture principles and general collaborative design strategies like the sharing of resources and the service group financing which presumes code of ethics accompanied by norms of conduct, commitment and responsibilities.
2. *A social architecture*, containing collaboration service norms as well as collaboration model that covers organizational aspects in order to support new socio-technical or community informatics designers or their virtual environment design activities.
3. *An information systems architecture* that defines a logical framework for the deployment of collaboration software that shows how the five different executing projects cover the different aspects of social systems design thinking and specifies the interfaces with components like workspaces and Web services.
4. *A technical architecture* that links the information systems components to the underlying applicative framework reflected in the standard reference models for the SADC design.
5. *A realization architecture* that defines the formal and Colab norms and their use by different application components. In other words, it questions suggesting a new methodological orientation aiming to help designers of these new virtual environments (digital social systems) to discover products, applications, functionalities and design assistance devices. We also want to indicate how it is possible to apply the multi-methodological configuration to create reference

architectures to orientate virtual communities taken in an environment that is constantly evolving when it comes to collaboration activities, online decision-making, problem-solving as well as all sorts of online human activities like virtual communities or virtual campuses.

Other works will present an open framework for the SADC updating, thus constituting an iterative process within which the users will submit reviews or suggestions for the produced architecture (online). Thus, they will contribute to the review of future publications.

6.1 The SADC's Vision

The SADC is a reference architecture for the design of collaborative software that derives from the seven reflexive and practical spaces of online socio-technical systems design. These spaces provide frameworks allowing to design the best scenarios possible in the life-cycle development of a community informatics design project. In the present book, it is a question of developing, in a diagrammatic representation, virtual environment designs as well as their exploitation for the community informatics design. The SADC will serve as practice communities' design activity planning according to an ecosystem and communication environment anchored in the socio-technical systems design associated by computers. This platform will allow the computer community informatics designers to explore the different solutions for the co-construction of knowledge and select which ones better meet their needs.

The SADC is before all a cooperation network between a plurality of platforms and social systems that seek to facilitate research, innovation and the validation of new collaboration technologies in pragmatic environments where stakeholders are the co-creators of their own collaboration environment.

The objective of the SADC is to facilitate the exploitation of a virtual platform by showing how we can use the software components, adapt them and integrate them in different contexts. The SADC intends to link organizations and virtual communities by providing them vast collaboration platforms capable of gathering thousands of users from all over the world by using the user-centred methodology promoted by European living labs and other labs focused on research and iterative design as well as the evaluation of collaborative supports.

The exploitations by users and virtual organizations are the following:

- *On a technological plan*, guides development and integration within the infrastructure of existing enterprises and virtual communities
- *On a socio-economic and socio-technical systems plan*, illustrates possible technology applications in an array of different scenarios focused on the development of project management products:

  1. The development of collaborative mechanisms of partnership validation to manage the relation with the more promising partners (coordination, concentrator, central animation for the concerted choice of collaborative tools)

2. The selection and development of generic services through the SADC (platform or virtual assistance environment for the digital social systems design generic methodology) as a socio-technical design platform of the first SADC, to manage the whole of its life cycle
3. The development of mechanisms and cybermetrics, visualization, traceability and knowledge management tools that can serve the SADC life-cycle development
4. The development of the digital library tools which can be used as memory and "patrimonial guide" for the next projects
5. The elaboration of a business model containing the methodology and support and service tools
6. The elaboration of necessary marketing tools and branding tools and the commitment of groups and My Portal Col@b communities
7. The integration and development of tools for online animation and project coordination
8. The prototyping of a database on knowledge management

After having established the ontological, epistemological, theoretical, methodological and applicative formal and semiformal framework for modeling, design and implantation of a first SADC as a digital social systems co-creation platform, we wish to favour the integration and alignment of the results of the various partners and projects in a global and evolutive architecture.

The SADC is not a rigid framework; we can use it in several ways:

• A collaboration springboard and a testing ground for users and projects that accelerates the implementation of free, punctual and easy-to-use collaboration opportunities, as well as the exploration and adoption of a virtual collaboration environment for distributed collaborative works (Budweg et al. 2006)
• A platform to lead researches and to develop and introduce new technological supports for collaboration, as a research location, together with the designers or tools and developers of commercial or non-commercial technology providers
• The pursuing of a development approach centred on the user, the maintenance of continuous communication channels and the exchanges with the user community (Appelt et al. 1999)
• An incubator for the new digital social systems models stemming from swarming, to integrate the new partners that use the collaboration and consultation les services in specific fields or to develop the functionalities of open-source code projects (Stevens et al. 2004)

We want to define a community informatics design and formal and semiformal reference models including ontology and typology associated with the development of all sorts of online human activities and generate collaborative networks and specialized digital social system divided into sectors or subfields. This operation requires a normalization of collaboration software components and interfaces. Indeed, by elaborating different models and approaches of soft systems, both to build and to accompany the imprecise or incomplete knowledge of social sciences and cyber communication (digital communication, aspect exploitation), we will reach a universal reference framework that will be a model for organizations and virtual communities.

In other words, we want to produce the design of a reference architecture that will help the enterprises and virtual organizations or users to choose an appropriate or relevant collaborative technology that corresponds to their essential preoccupations. This architecture will allow them to choose a strategic direction that meets their business needs and expectations while helping them understand the possibilities offered by collaboration software. To succeed in apprehending collaboration technology, we need a user guide or some sort of introduction that allows the users to choose the right tool and the right place to start their project or exchanges. This requirement is facilitated by the helpers who, thanks to piloting or prototyping, provide users with the necessary components for the design process associated with new collaborations by facilitating the contribution of stakeholders in the development of organizations and virtual communities by also providing training resources. First, we must build a SADC that will be used later to build other socio-economic virtual communities and other society networking business models, even other online human activity systems and other socio-technical systems that we call "digital social systems" in the service of human being.

Communication between users and technology is made easier by reference architecture. This offers a middle ground and a basic communication terminology. Indeed, it uses terms that are easily understood as well as visual models that are not too technical, not for the users nor for the virtual community, without, however, ignoring the computing aspect. This strategy should facilitate the establishment of trustful relations between the stakeholders.

This architectural platform can also support changes at the organizational and management process level by integrating the cost methods and benefits, the analysis of the gaps, the modeling of current and future elements, the collaboration parameters, mapping and risk management as well as quality control and provide the managers with high-level scenarios. Its architecture vision is translated as follows:

1. Establish principles and reference guides that can document licences, architectures, interoperability and solutions security.
2. Establish solid basis of an evolutive and collaborative architecture as well as the capacity to migrate new modules and integrate new functionalities.
3. Develop a generic open-source code socio-collaborative architecture that is user-friendly, convivial, transferable, transparent, free or very inexpensive and high-performance.
4. Develop a reference framework and user guide that is "ready to assemble" that will help all the partners to develop their own research, training and development services.
5. Define a business model containing experts, students, teachers, the public sector and the business community in order to allow the future digital social systems development with the right configuration of cognition, network coordination and collaboration tools.

6. Establish a tracking chart of tools and institutions and organize adjustment tables between tool functionalities and visualization (according to the types of tasks).
7. Define and visualize the roles of all developers.

The SADC project seeks to develop an innovative software platform in order to facilitate the creation of collaborative workspaces for users and distributed teams for the support of collaborative design and engineering tasks. This software platform provides a distributed environment, rich in knowledge, oriented towards the users as well as the adaptable and evolutive workspaces on demand, allowing a dynamic creation for the users. They will be able to establish efficient partnerships, be creative, improve productivity and adopt a more holistic approach of engineered products design. The collaborative workspaces integrated at the higher level of the software platform constitute virtual meeting locations for problem-solving, conflict resolution, knowledge sharing and on-demand access to expert advice. Software platforms are designed to facilitate software development while allowing designers and programmers to focus on the characteristics and functionalities of social systems and users' requests instead of worrying about the operating details of a system.

6.2   The Design Framework Implementation

We will start by establishing experimental communities in order to collect, link and catalogue the information, knowledge and know-how for design and necessary for their development, like we will do with a computer expert company. In the remit of this task, we will develop and execute the design, thanks to community informatics staring by defining the fundamental functional characters of support, the nature of basic users as well as the practical and theoretical knowledge captured and recorded in the SADC digital library. During the SADC design, we must optimize the conditions of this virtual environment by exploring tools, devices and ICT that support the listed design actions and activities and suggest a series of technical orientations for its design. More precisely, we will decompose the SADC in four subsystems equating to four distinctive interaction spaces: the instrumental space, the communicational space, the discursive space and the strategic space. In each space, we will try to map the respective social action and design categories in a state of progress. Accordingly, we will present a new collaborative design paradigm, the community informatics design, from which the implantation of a series of social media and Web devices that are part of the platform will be guided by social and communicational actions as well as by the human activity system the SADC seeks to support and accompany in the four interaction spaces.

We want to design a design framework in a reference architecture for collaboration software. This framework will be created from the combination of several software developed by collaborative space integrated projects (CoSpaces Integrated Project, cube ENoLL, Ning, Joomla!, Dokeos software, etc.). The SADC will use various works performed in the remit of Ecospace and Collaboration@Rural projects and other approaches, namely, the construction of worlds. In the creation of the SADC, we try to exploit existing software by illustrating diverse ways of using, adapting and integrating software components in various contexts to contribute to the construction of the knowledge world. This platform made of platforms can be exploited by user enterprises to meet the goals they had set for themselves. The SADC will contribute to achieve the following objectives:

- Guide, on the technological plan, the development and integration of information technology infrastructures within the existing enterprises.
- Illustrate the possible technology applications in an array of different scenarios for the development of project management products on the commercial plan.
- Integrate and adjust the results of different partners and projects in a global evolutive and interoperable architecture.
- Standardize the collaboration software components and the interfaces.

Currently, several researches are actively led with the goal of developing methodologies and technologies of computer-assisted collaborative systems to support designer teams that are geographically scattered, in view of the information technologies' rapid progress. However, we are mostly interested on the innovative practices and European living labs because they are centred on the human being. We are witnessing a change in paradigm where designers and engineers are not alone able to put their works in common at an international level in the context of collaborative design, because the users, which have become designers, can now closely collaborate with designers. The collaborative design system requires two types of capacities and facilities: distribution and collaboration. To support these two functions, we must develop and distribute information technologies like the Web, Java and XML languages and other technological services built as cyber-physical systems (Zhuge 2011; Ning et al. 2016). However, even with the best technologies, without a distributed architecture specifically designed to meet the requirements of performance and functionality and to establish human-human and human-computer links, there can be no effective collaboration. Therefore, by suggesting a reference architecture, we can help organizations and virtual communities to choose the technology and the type of collaboration that corresponds to essential preoccupations as well as the strategic orientation that meets their needs and business requirements and help them understand the possibilities offered by collaboration software. The success of launching a collaboration technology is made easier by helpers, who choose the right starting point, for example, with piloting and prototyping, this technology provides the necessary components for the design of new collaboration processes, it facilitates the stakeholders' mobilization in the business development and it presents itself as a resource for training.

It offers a middle ground and a basic communication terminology; in fact, it uses easily understandable terms as well as visual models that are not too technical for the user nor for the virtual communities without ignoring the computing aspect. Communication between business people, community members and technology is made easier by the reference architecture that offers a middle ground and a basic communication terminology. In fact, it uses easily understandable terms as well as visual models that are not too technical for business people without ignoring the computing aspect which should facilitate the establishment of trusting relations between stakeholders.

This architecture can also support the change management process by incorporating cost and benefit methods, gap analysis and the state of modeling and collaboration parameters, mapping and risk management as well as quality control, while providing managers with high-level scenarios.

Collaboration spaces will be developed from a distributed platform of innovative software in order to facilitate the creation of collaborative workspaces for users and distributed teams for the support of collaborative design and engineering tasks. This distributed software platform allows the users to dynamically create an on-demand collaborative workspace rich in knowledge, oriented towards the users as well as the adaptable and evolutive workspaces features that will be implemented. The users will be able to be creative and establish efficient partnerships, improve productivity and adopt a more holistic approach of engineered product design. The collaborative workspaces integrated at the higher level of the software platform constitute virtual meeting locations for problem-solving, conflict resolution, knowledge sharing and on-demand access to expert advice.

Software platforms are designed to facilitate software development while allowing designers and programmers to focus on the enterprises' direction aspects and the users' needs instead of dealing with a work device's troublesome details. Software platforms promote the reuse of all the architectures in a defined application field. They establish and optimize architecture of these applications, also in a precise field, that allows their reuse in other fields. The implantation of a good platform allows software designers to focus more on the particular current problems of a virtual community instead of the underlying infrastructure.

In the SADC, it is known that the collaboration space development within an organization or a virtual community requires an adaptation and implementation of a reference to work with the existing computing infrastructures, to manage other questions and users' needs and to support the requests for personalized workspace. It is also important that the reference implementation elaborated by the SADC evolves and expands to support additional functionalities and capacities so the organizations and virtual communities can understand the implications of new systems functionalities and make decisions regarding the adoption of new capacities.

6.3 Theoretical Vision

Our idea is to put in place a design theory that helps to better understand how, with a complex approach, a communicational complexity approach, it is possible to create a communicational design science (or community informatics) at the service of socio-technical systems developers, human activity systems supported by technology (Fig. 6.1). According to Garnham:

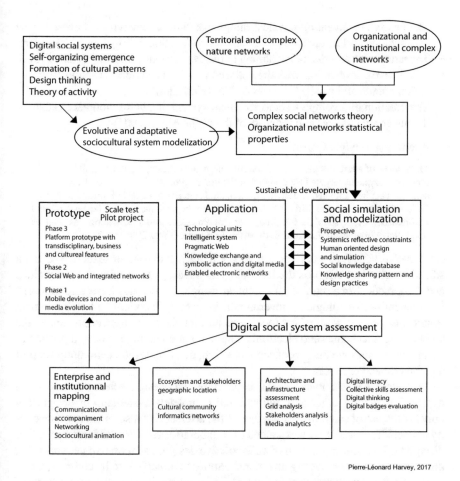

Pierre-Léonard Harvey, 2017

Fig. 6.1 Theoretical and methodological foundations for platform evaluation

Creating a public access model of the Internet requires non-commodified social spaces. Public access models are superior to market and commodity models of media, culture, and communication because it provides "all citizens, whatever their wealth of geographical location, equal access to a wide range of high-quality entertainment, information and education. (Garnham 1990, p. 120)

According to Nigel Cross (1974, 1984, 2001), the will to "scientify" design dates back to the 1920s. Buckminster Fuller was the first one to adopt the concept of design science, but it is only in 1965 that it was adopted by S. Gregory (1966) in his conference on the design method. The notion of design, until now, does not have a definition universally accepted by all; it is a polysemous term used by different researchers. Depending on the field they are in, it takes on specific properties. Nigel Cross tried to identify the frequently used definitions by researchers:

- The elaboration of action plans seeking to transform an existing situation into a preferred situation (Simon 1960)
- The beginning of changes in artificial things (J. Christopher Jones)

- The process of inventing physical things that show a new physical order, a new organization and a new form, as an answer to function (Christopher Alexander)
- The structuring argumentation aiming to resolve "serious problems" (Horst Rittel)
- A reflexive conversation with the material in a design situation (Schön 1983)
- A democratic and participative procedure (Karl Ehn)
- The creation of a complex socio-technical system that helps workers to adapt to the uncertain changes and requests of their jobs (Cross 2001)

According to Nigel Cross:

> The science of addresses the issue of determination and the categorization of all usual phenomena of systems targeted by design and the design process. The science of design also addresses applied knowledge deriving from natural sciences as suitable information for the designer's use. This definition, of course, expands beyond the "scientific design" and encompasses the systematic knowledge of des processes and methodology as well as scientific-technological functions of the artefacts design. (Cross 2001, p. 52)

As Imre Horváth supports (Horváth 2001), there is a myriad of texts that reveal a scientific reflection effort on the technological odyssey of the cultural communities and the practical exploitation of technical design. Researches have also emerged from scientific, sociological, government, industrial, historical and technological spheres. In general, researchers look more into the fields of target applications like architecture, mechanics and electronic engineering, confining the design process to problematic zones we find in conceptualization, detailed design, computing support and the realized products.

We retain Cross's idea (2001), supporting that design science refers to an approach explicitly organized, rational and completely systematic of design, not only for the use of scientific knowledge on the artefacts but also as a scientific activity in itself. This activity has expanded to collaboration networks to form a scientific discipline. It is now a question of collaborative design, collaborative networks that allow various autonomous organizational entities to be supported by computing networks. Consequently, we must find the preliminary conditions to the construction of this new discipline, to quote Luis M. Camarinha-Matos. But what is a scientific discipline? According to Camarinha-Matos, a discipline possesses six fundamental characteristics: a study centre, a paradigm, reference disciplines, principles and practices, a research program as well as a teaching program and a profession (Camarinha-Matos and Afsarmanesh 2005).

Several research projects have been performed in this field, and we identify more and more practical cases stemming from different forms of collaborative networks throughout the world. The implementation of collaborative design is a discipline. As a study centre a collaborative network scientific discipline must focus on the structure, the behaviour and the evolutive dynamic of autonomous entity networks that collaborate to better reach the common objectives. This approach must take into consideration the principles and practices for the design, the analysis, the simulation, the implementation and the operating of the digital social systems' central nervous system.

A large diversity of collaboration networks has emerged through the last years due to the difficulties experienced by the business travellers and scientists worldwide.

The advanced and highly integrated supply chains, the virtual communities and organizations, the professional virtual communities, the value constellations and the virtual collaboration labs only represent the tip of a major trend in which enterprises and professionals are seeking the complementarities and the common activities that allow them to participate in competitive business opportunities and innovative developments. Similar trends are also found in collaboration networks with lucrative purposes or oriented towards social goals (Camarinha-Matos et al. 2005a, b, c).

For Imre Horváth (2001), technical design technique is a discipline in itself since it synthesizes new information for the realization of a product. It also establishes the quality by the definition of functionality as well as the materialization and the apparition of artefacts, and it has a growing influence on the technological, economical and commercial aspects of production. Therefore, the author continues, by generating knowledge on the design and for the design, this discipline focused on scientific research which is decisive in the technical design development.

Therefore, the number of scientific publications on design's technical aspects has significantly increased since 2008 or 2009, while researches on philosophical, epistemological and teleological of design research do not seem to be developing that fast. Although some authors have conducted investigations on technical design, on several fields of interest and on university and industrial research approaches, they could not achieve a systematic analysis, confining instead to different reasoning systems. The foundation of these assessments varies from the simple chronological principle to the phenomenological classification and the contextual taxonomization.

In the case of the SADC (a sort of computer-assisted design destined for social sciences and humanities), instead of treating technical problems of the socio-technical design, our book is supported by an investigation centred on the state of the research that seeks to establish theoretical foundations, even scientific of the technical platform design and the evaluation of cultural, innovative and existing systems. Like in the living labs' methodology, we will apply an approach focused on the reconciliation with the human being and technologies. Therefore, we have explored the technical design research frontiers by trying to extract, from several studies and theories, a community informatics design theory through assembling a knowledge corpus and theories with virtual community co-construction, social systems, activity theories, cultural pattern formation and self-organizational emergence as objects. We also present the state of progress they have experienced over the past few years.

The main difference between the SADC and the other taxonomical approaches is that we introduce a model that allows the users and the virtual communities to identify the markers of their own development and to stimulate the interactivity and creativity of the users. The SADC, like the living labs' approach, incites users and virtual communities to create their own platform by seizing all sorts of experiences involving their values, success, best user practices and their own creativity in order to create a sustainable platform that will meet their needs. It allowed us not only to define a field of discourse but also to explore intrinsic relations between complex nature networks, complex institutional and organization networks and the modeling of designs oriented towards the community, communication and the dynamic of knowledge and practice activities.

So, it is virtual communities whose design corresponds to the socio-technical human activity systems we are going to build. We can already see this new design assistance systems science looming where a regional and national design is emerging as well as international social systems networks supported by new languages. These new languages will allow to apprehend not only the needs but also the direct perceptions, the shared representation, the different aspects of a communication combining the sounds and the images, the diagrammatic texts, etc. that will take us towards a social mutation more impressive than the invention of telegraphy.

The technical innovations brought by the development of communication and information technologies have been too fragmented or incomplete. For example, traditionally, the launch of technical products and services was done in a closed framework; now there is a deep division between the real market and the users that results in gaps of productivity and efficiency at the social and economic level (CoreLabs 2007). Digital social systems rise and disappear without even having enough time to occupy the social space.

In an attempt to solve this problem, virtual enterprises try to maintain an open organizational frontier because we have come to open innovation (Chesbrough 2003). In fact, we must stay away from the vertical thinking that makes an organization manage its R-D activities on itself, in order to find a horizontal way to align stakeholders and users in the co-production act (Von Hippel and Thomke 2002). Consequently, users are invited to innovate through collaboration. In this scenario, users can also be partners or stakeholders of end users. This type of collaboration can also be of interest on a more international level, having already been encouraged by European initiatives (CoreLabs 2007). These initiatives are at the heart of the European Network of Living Labs movement. Their goal is to reinforce and increase the innovative capacities within the European states by engaging the user in a co-creative manner through the entire innovation process.

Various questions arise regarding leadership, users' management, partnerships, resources, policies and strategies:

- Which norms should be implemented to ensure a good governance?
- How to provoke users and stakeholders' creation and inventiveness?
- What should I do with my ideas? Who should I address to solve my problems?
- Which system providing innovation opportunities can we create within the SADC?
- What are the available resources to help users to innovate?
- What does being creative mean?
- How to stimulate innovation?
- What are the tools, experiences and methods that better favour the exchange?

6.3.1 Collaborative Network Complexity

The collaborative networks are new complex systems. Taking diverse shapes in the different application fields, they consist of multiple facets, and their understanding requires the input of several disciplines. In fact, the diverse manifestations of collaborative networks have been studied by specialists stemming from various fields like computer sciences, computer engineering, management, economics, sociology, industrial engineering and law only, to name a few. We are now at the stage that Kuhn (1975) calls a pre-paradigmatic phase, where the phenomenon of collaborative networks is described and interpreted differently in studies according to the researcher's field of activity.

The acceptance of a new paradigm is not a pacific process (Kuhn 1975); sciences and paradigms tend to resist the introduction of a new "competitor", preferring to widen the field or the existing science rules to explain new phenomena. This tension situation is intensified by the multidisciplinary nature of phenomena, especially in the case where a plurality of traditional disciplines of organized knowledge and professional are fighting over the mastery of a new field. This is exactly what we are observing today in the case of collaborative networks. It remains to be seen if a new paradigm will emerge.

In the past, systems design research was mainly founded on the epistemology of physical sciences and humanities and on models and theories stemming from the general observation of the human behaviour and the processes and observable properties of various objects and environments. The new orientation is obvious in the growing use of designers' analysis protocols: there is a change in the construction of theories exclusively founded on external processes objectively observable that now incorporate the knowledge of internal human processes. According to Terence Love (2001), there is a substantial change in design research founded on a more detailed comprehension of the individual's functioning and his influence on the human interactions between themselves and with objects and environments. For his part Andy Dong theorizes design like a cognitive sociocultural system:

> One could express this socio-technical view on design by extending [...] a commonly accepted descriptive definition of design as: the transformation of natural processes and the "given world' through a systematic technical methodology mediated by social processes to create an artefact that achieves a set of goals established as a result of designers' shared understanding of the artefact's function, behavior and structure within a context defined by both the natural environment and human interests. (Dong 2004)

Yet, already in the mid-1990s, Love had developed a metatheoretical method to analyse the development of theories associated to research on design and more particularly on systems theories that apprehend the human being in different contexts by using various versions that were published regarding the designer, design, cognition, information systems, electronic education and the inclusion of the social qualitative. Nine layers of abstraction forming what Love calls a "theoretical chain" emerge from it (Table 6.1).

At the heart of this distinction stands the research founded on the plan that highlights the understanding of the insecurity of the real world practice, the context being an integral part of the history instead of foreign variables to be trivialized. Furthermore, the research founded on the plan implies a certain flexibility in the revision of concepts, a plurality of depending variables and the taking into account of social interactions. Participants are not considered as "subjects" affected to processes but like co-participants to the design and analysis. Finally, research highlights the characterization of situations, by opposition to control variables.

Table 6.1 The metatheoretical hierarchy of concepts and theories on human activities

Level	Classification	Description
1.	Ontological issues	The ontological basis of a design theory formulation. This level contains the human values and the researchers, designers and theory critics' fundamental hypotheses
2.	Epistemological issues	The critical study of nature, motives, limits and criteria of knowledge validity. This level contains the relations between ontology and theory
3.	General theories	These theories seek to describe the human activities and their links with the designed objects and the human environments
4.	Theories relative to the internal human processes and collaboration	Theories on motivation and cognition of the individuals participating in design and research activities, on collaboration within teams, as well as their sociocultural effects of this participation on individuals' behaviour
5.	Theories on the structure of processes	Theories on the underlying structure of design and research processes according to the culture, the type of artefacts and other attributes and similar circumstances
6.	Methods of design and research	Theories and propositions on design and research methods and techniques
7.	Theories on choice mechanism	Theories on the way designers and researchers make choices between different elements, design objects, processes, systems or other types of possibilities
8.	Theories on elements behaviour	Theories on element behaviours that can be incorporated into the design of an object, a process or a system
9.	Initial design and the labelling of reality	The level at which human descriptions of objects, processes and systems are established, for example, a vacuum cleaner, a database, the fact of sitting down at a desk, listening to a noise or observing a sunset

Terence Love Diagram (2001) adapted to community informatics design

Love's studies (2001, 2003) indicate that systems could greatly benefit from human cognition because there is a progression on the development of systems theory, where the era of the machine implies sociological epistemology that involves cognito-affective human activities. Engeström's studies on human activities could also be a good marker in the modeling and governance architecture. According to this author:

> Activity systems comprise of the subject: individual/subgroup of the community chosen as part of the analysis, tools: physical or methodological, object: problem space or product at which the activity is directed and which is transformed into outcomes, community: individuals who share the same object, division of labour: division of tasks between members of the community, rules: regulations, norms and constraints. (Engeström 1994, p. 237)

Inspired by Love's hierarchy and his metatheoretical taxonomy of design theories, we suggest to make an adaptation of it in ten levels of decreasing abstraction, in order to illustrate certain relevant theories of the community informatics design applied to digital social systems (an adaptation of Love 2001). The table below illustrates the evolution of disciplines and a way to model them in a more systematic manner to choose the most relevant ones (Table 6.2).

Table 6.2 Discipline's evolution

Foundations

The construction of the community informatics design science

Classification	Description	Reference authors
1. Ontology of cognitive and communicational design	The different ontological bases of the community informatics design field of science. Community informatics design is seen as a process of evolutive and generative co-creation, with several partners that generate a collective and collaborative intelligence. The design is multi-aspectual; it is not determinist nor linear; it cannot be reduced to the closed stages of an algorithm. It is the composition (C) of a world of knowledge	Özbekhan, Warfield, Habermas, Basden, Dooyeweerd, Banathy, Bunge, Gruber, Popper, Luhmann, Heylighen, Pierce, De Zeeuw, Von Foerster, Ackoff, Foucault, Morin, Goffman, Adorno, Manzini, Margolin, Cross, E. Laszlo, Boulding, Feng Li, Helbing, Carbone, Jantsch, Prigogine, Malone, Latour, Callon, Sloterdijk, Ashby, Maturana and Varela
2. Epistemology of communication and social and technical systems design	The representational nature of community informatics design as digital social systems design. The ways of knowing socio-technical systems and social systems design. The ways of knowing socio-technical systems and visualize them, the validity boundaries and criteria providing the basic principles for the design and co-construction of knowledge in virtual and innovation communities.	Vickers, Winograd, Fuchs, Hofkirchner, Churchman, Simon, Buckminster Fuller, De Moor, Whitworth, Checkland, Alexander, Banathy, Warfield, Heylighen, Jantsch, De Certeau, Cross, Krippendorff, Denning and Dunham, Morgan, Meadows, Broadbent
3. Social, cognitive and communicational theories applied to community informatics design	Theories of design as a creative activity and out in common representations and modeling. These theories have the objective of describing the act of social systems design and the relations they have with the design object and its environment (E). The other aspects and levels subordinate to these theories	Goldkuhl, Te'eni, Habermas, Luhmann, Giddens, Bourdieu, Marx, Brier, Banathy, Bausch, Flanagan, Nelson, Venable, Stolterman, Storkerson, Morelli, Buchanan, Dubberly, Papanek, Markus, Csiksyentmihalyi, Beer, Baudrillard, Moles, Dong, Jenkins, Ing, Toffler
4. Theories on internal collaboration, cooperation and coordination processes	Theoretical scaffolding attempting to explain the community informatics design (participative, interactive, collaborative) in terms of reflexive practices, problem-solving, construction of common representation meaning exchange between partners and partnership structures	Schön, Jonas, Carayannis, Silvermann, Jenkins, Lu, Reigeluth, Banathy, Bausch, Warfield, Senge, Weisbord, Argyris, Schein, Leydersdorff, Capra
5. Theory on the structure of the design process	Theory of social systems design analysing their life cycle and the design process updating them. Community informatics design is inspired by several models of life cycles and the sharing of theories and information systems. Furthermore, community informatics design is centred on the users' designers' commitment and the evaluation and feedback between the actors and the iterative design process. Design is often intuitive and emergent, but it can also be formal depending on the situation, the field and the culture, the type of artefact, the architecture scenario, the events and circumstances	Banathy, Sanders, Westerlund, Reymen, Dorst, De Vries, Morabito, Sack, Bhate, Flood and Romm, Flusser, Galbraith, Bausch, Midgley, Love, Stokerson, Hevner, Klein, Barab, Kling, Iaccono, Gray, Sveiby, Barton, McIntyre, Brown, Buchanan, Dunne and Martin

(continued)

Table 6.2 (continued)

Foundations

The construction of the community informatics design science

Classification	Description	Reference authors
6. Community informatics design methodologies	The systemic multi-methodologies, design techniques, ethnographic methods, human-computer interface theories, collective teleworking theories, the TCAO, theories of computer-mediatized social participation, computer-mediatized communication methodology, the guides and design kits, computer-assisted design methodologies and discovery matrices	Preece, Scacchi, Shneiderman, De Moor, Whitworth, Clegg, Jonas, A. Laszlo, Love, Dorst, Gero, Kroes, Cross, Moles, Broadbent, Glasser and Strauss, Flood and Jackson, Jones, Joseph, Eppingher, Browning
7. Theories on choice and optional field mechanisms	Theories on decision-making, optional fields, socio-technical scenarios, the type of system, the consideration of certain issues (determinism, openness), the choice between different theories, process, technologies, applications, meta-design, assistance tools for creativity and design	Banathy, Simon, Bartolomei, Afsarmanesh, Mintzberg, Hughes, Ackoff, Checkland, Christakis, Fischer et Giaccardi, Resnicks
8. Theories on the behaviour of human social elements, technological in interaction	The analysis of social networks, usage and appropriation, the interactions between the elements, the behaviour of users/designers, community ship, leadership and the interconnectivity of subsystems	Bunge, Moles, Bitterman, Cumming et Akar, Judge, Jonas, Wenger, Snyder and McDermott, Moscovici, Moreno, Harvey, Benking, Jones. Metcalf
9. The description of objects and the reality of the creation process	The mapping of processes, the rich image, the interactive scenarios, the simulation, the schematization, the diagrammatic, the mechanisms of social creativity, the study of the partners network, the establishment of control lists, the description of entities	Checkland, Chan, Berners-Lee, Cartier, Moles, Judge, Alexander, De Rosnay, Molina, Moreno, Barabasi, Johnson, Fischer and Giaccardi, Solis, Ollus
10. The initial design and the experience of new realities	The transformation of representations in real socio-technical systems, collaborative systems and innovative virtual communities, management and governance mechanisms	Wenger, Camarinha-Matos, Afsarmanesh, Morabito, Guarajedaghi, Molina, Romero, Picard, Mumford, Van Eijnatten, Trist, Whitworth, Lu

Adaptation of Love (2001)

Inspired by Love's hierarchy, we suggest a general modeling framework containing multiple criteria for the optimal design of digital social systems. This well-adapted framework favours the comprehension of disciplines and theories likely to inspire the design of ecosystems and platforms stemming from uncertain and socio-dynamic socio-technical environments. The choice of the theoretical approach to use relies on the aggregation of preference cognitive and functional functions that serve as design and base criteria for the decision-making in the mass of knowledge. These criteria help social systems' designers to optimize the use of theories and researches that are relevant to their projects. It is in that context that our lab has developed a theoretical and methodological modeling tool, inspired by Love's hierarchy and Banathy and Lemire's works (2008) in epistemology and with the basic principle of observation and evolution of disciplines according to three types of ontological elements to evaluate:

1. *The objects* and the results of the research (material aspects, tools, architectures)
2. *The actors* involved in the co-creation process and the evolutive life cycle of projects
3. *The actions* and activities, by profession and by fields, the organization of theories, communication and design process theories

Figure 6.2 illustrates this tool and processes that are associated to it. Taking into account the three fields of knowledge allows to evaluate the fields and relevant theories in various design projects.

Furthermore, the design criteria founded on reliability serve as reassurance for users and virtual communities about the structural security characteristics in view of uncertainties in modeling and seismic charges a social system can be subjected to during its life cycle. We talk about the chaos and the demands of the code, which are also easy to incorporate in this optimal process design. The methodology is illustrated by a simple example: a three-platform SADC design which overlays the open collaboration reference architecture, the integrated information reference infrastructure and the technical reference model, according to the conceptual framework architecture of The Open Group Architecture Framework (TOGAF).

A platform is presented in the form of a steel structure building for which the uncertainty of the ground movement is characterized by a probabilist answer of the spectrum that is developed from available attenuation formulas and seismic eventuality models. To paraphrase an article published in the *Health Economics* journal (Zweifel et al. 1999) fundamental design research is not a series of approaches with the intention to produce new theories, artefacts and practices that have repercussions on the learning and teaching in a natural environment. Like Cobb and his colleagues explain:

> *Prototypically, design experiments entail both "engineering" particular forms of learning and systematically studying those forms of learning within the context defined by the means of supporting them. This designed context is subject to test and revision, and the successive iterations that result play a role similar to that of systematic variation in experiments.* (Cobb et al. 2003, p. 9)

Figure 2 below, illustrate this social learning process for the digital social system design. It semi-formally habilitate the designer to study the Objects (technologies

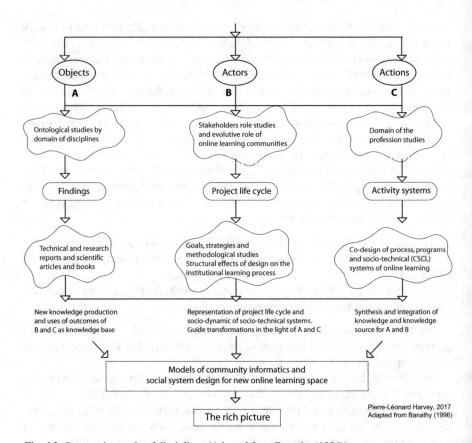

Fig. 6.2 Progressive study of disciplines (Adapted from Banathy (1996))

and artefacts), Actors (partnership helix and stakeholders) and Actions (human activity systems). It also enables us to evaluate the approaches, codes, theories to build new sociotechnical systems in an open and evolutionary way.

Collaboration is an applied field, and collaborative design researchers try to add to their program the apprehension of design technologies by trying to reproduce precise results such as the increase of user and stakeholder participation in the production of science, the creation of online communities for professional improvement, the design of organizations and virtual communities or the solving of management problems associated with preexisting users or community members' beliefs. For this reason, the SADC researchers have observed that in order to have an appropriate collaboration, we must develop technological tools, programs and mostly theories that help understand them and systematically predict the way the collaboration is executed. This research on virtual community design offers several advantages: research results that take into account the role of the social context and that have a good potential for influencing collaborative practice, tangible products, programs likely to be adopted elsewhere and a validation of results according to the use effects (Messick 1992).

6.3.2 Systems Thinking and the SADC

The phenomenon of collaborative social systems is not new. Many organizations and enterprises rise and disappear, while others greatly succeed. On our part, we will study what contributed to the success of certain organizations and the failure of some others. According to our research, several critical factors explain the success and prosperity of virtual organizations. These factors touch upon trust, the commitment of members in the innovation process, access to appropriate information and cutting-edge technology, adapted methodologies and updates as well as good governance. In this context, the SADC, in terms of various interdependent and complementary objects, feeds a collaboration mechanism in a framework of a distributed systems design architecture with the objective of satisfying the performance and functionality's requirements. Of course, there are several researches currently ongoing on collaborative design, but with the SADC, we want to develop a system and methodology prototype able to support any organization. This research will lead to a mutual comprehension of systems thinking and co-laboratory design, as well as the learning of reflection processes in place.

Systems thinking is a process that seeks the comprehension of the social systems' functioning mode. We consider design like a way to rethink virtual organization support environments and to make it a launching pad for the collectivity's prosperity in order to reinforce the entrepreneurship capacities and to promote a continuous sustainable improvement. The SADC is founded on systems thinking. It encourages the collaboration systems reflection, the innovation thinking, the strategic discovery and processes. Systems thinking, according to Checkland (1988), is a holistic analysis approach that focuses on constitutive elements of a system in correlation with the systems functioning in time and in larger systems framework. By supporting our SADC's design on a multidisciplinary and collective approach with the help of the grounded theory, the research action and the associated reflection of experimental research, we will be able to contribute to a new innovative thinking. Let us mention that an innovative thinking is linked to creative thinking and problem-solving, meaning the ability to manage a new thing or to find new ways to solve problems. We find several elements in the design thinking:

- *Collaborative thinking* includes the multidisciplinary thinking and collective intelligence.
- *Innovative thinking* that encompasses performance, communities and chains of values.
- *The discovery*, used by critical thinking, anchored theory, action research and experimental approach.
- *The treatment* that encompasses work flow, architecture, reflection in real time, risks, efficiency, maturity and information services.
- *Strategic thinking* refers to control, cause-to-effect relations and finality (Bertalanffy 1968).

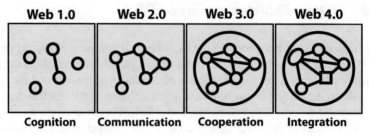

Pierre-Léonard Harvey, 2017

Fig. 6.3 Evolution of Social Software (Fuchs Adaptation)

The SADC calls on theoretical points of view and multiple research paradigms in order to build understanding of nature and learning conditions, cognition, collaboration and development. In the collaboration context, it emphasizes the way users collaborate. The design of this framework implies the development of technological tools, programs and mostly theories that will help understand and support the collaboration process. Furthermore, several researches show that collaboration, cognition, knowledge and context are irreducibly co-built, iterative and inseparable.

In his model focused on cognition, Hutchins (1995) draws a design theory like a "contextualized action model" that focuses on the emerging behaviour of human activity. Wertsch (1991), on his part, suggests an approach of distributed cognition that makes the examination of people, objects and tools they use necessary as well as the social organization factors influencing the cognition. The mediatized action theory delimits the reciprocity between agents (actions) and their tools (Fig. 6.3).

Let us remember the main objective of the SADC: Be a design platform for other platforms; serve as an assistant framework for social services design; and contribute the longevity, the quality and efficiency of virtual organizations. As a whole, we intend to:

- Create a platform for learning and exchange.
- Allow users and virtual communities to experiment.
- Support collaboration and visualization of activities.
- Use an approach founded on participative research action.

These platforms will be transformed into knowledge and exemplary practice springboard that will help to improve human cognition and extract fundamental problems and complex systems comprehension. The discovery process is supported by research process critical analyses.

6.3.2.1 Basic Concepts

Reference architecture[1] provides a proven solution model for the architecture of a particular field. It also suggests a common vocabulary to discuss the pooling, often with the objective of emphasizing standardization. A reference architecture is often

---

[1] "Reference architecture", *Wikipedia*, <http://en.wikipedia.org/wiki/Reference_architecture>.

comprised of a list of function and indications relative to their programming interfaces as well as their mutual interactions and with the external functions of the reference architecture.

Reference architectures can be defined at various levels of abstraction. At the most abstract level, a communication network links diverse pieces of equipment and each one offers different functions. At an inferior level, an architecture could, for example, illustrate interactions between procedures (or methods) of a given computer program during the execution of a very precise task.

Reference architecture provides a model that often relies on the generalization of efficient solutions. These solutions were generalized and structured for the representation of an architecture both logically and physically founded on the exploitation of models that describe observations in a certain number or successful realizations. Furthermore, it shows the way to compose these pieces to form a solution. Each reference architecture is applicable to a particular field or project.

The reference model[2] is provided with a taxonomy and a generic vocabulary and is universally applicable. A reference model is also a basic architecture. A reference architecture emphasizes more on the utility than the absolute and universal validity; it can contain concrete and specialized contents, like component samples, processes and services catalogues. The relevant reference models, like the technical reference model (Ning, Joomla!, Dokeos), the reference models for integrated information infrastructure, interconnection open systems and distributed processing open models, must, however, rely on a reference architecture.

> *The collaborative network* regroups, according to Frans M. van Eijnatten, "*self-organizing multidisciplinary cyber teams of heterogeneous human agents (individuals, groups, organizations) from different networks that intensely interact with each other – mainly through the Internet – in order to reach a common goal*". (Van Eijnatten 2005)

6.3.3   Other Common ENoLL, TOGAF and SADC Concepts and Tools

We have also identified other concepts and tools able to answer the complexity of collaborative networks like users' participation, the governance, the creation service, the infrastructure and the tools and methods.

6.3.3.1   Users' Participation

- Users' motivation
- Community management
- Type of users (users selection)
- Nature of the efforts to provide

---

[2] "Reference model", *Wikipedia*, http://en.wikipedia.org/wiki/Reference_model

- Participants' expectations and interests
- Tool performance to engage users
- Maintaining the motivation of users
- Adoption of non-obstructive methods
- Cultural empathy
- Awareness of cultural and legal differences
- Diversity of the approaches used to motivate the different types of users
- Behaviour comprehension
- Information Exchanges
- Ethical issues related to trust
- Confidentiality
- Shared mental model

6.3.3.2   The Governance

- Commitment and responsibility
- Financing, service and selection
- Social systems models
- Properties' pilots
- Management structure
- Extensions (services, partners, users)
- Management and work practices
- Sharing of resources and infrastructure
- Operational excellence
- Foundations of dynamic strategies
- Ethical issues related to trust
- Confidentiality
- Management (control) and formulation of clear objectives
- Collaboration team creation
- Creation of shared social systems models
- Creation of a common culture
- Instauration of trust and a feeling of belonging
- Resolution of political problems in the value chains
- Adoption of a holistic systems approach
- Collective learning and experimentation
- Adoption of a multidisciplinary approach
- Planning of interactive resources
- Spotting of repetitions, design of the unit and construction of a coherent whole
- Interaction, collaboration and exchange of knowledge between users and local actors
- Particular attention to initiatives and approaches coming from the basis
- Other methodologies and problem-solving tools

6.3.3.3   Creation Services

- Organization and training
- New vocabulary destined to stakeholders
- Efficient communication
- Slid partnerships between users
- Entrepreneurship
- Governance
- Management
- Management portfolio
- Ideas creation
- Support to virtual communities services
- Particular services for stakeholders, partners and users
- Market personalization
- Communication services
- Collaboration service
- Demonstration, validation and prototyping
- Contextualized activities
- Cognitive design
- Design theory
- Design stages: time period where a category of design activities happens, like conceptual design
- Technical tools and design methods: (CAO) tools and (DFX) synthesis methods
- Specific objects design at various stages
- Social process: methods and group interaction types (negotiation, cooperation, assembly)
- Cognitive process: mental process at the individual and collective level (exploration, selection, reflection, transitive memory, shared memory)

6.3.3.4   The Infrastructure

- Collaboration deployment process
- Divided infrastructure provider
- Collaborative infrastructures
- Collaborative infrastructures in the SADC
- Infrastructures adjusted to the environment
- Infrastructures adapted to other environments
- Infrastructures used in the deployment of the first phase
- Standardized and interoperable infrastructure
- Common infrastructures

6.3.3.5   Innovative Results

- Innovative expertise and skills
- Innovation preoperational phase
- Experts', stakeholders', users' and partners' commitment
- Target market (targeted social systems)
- Stakeholders value
- Optimal degree of interaction and sensitive context
- Innovative environments, supporting ideas and patents
- Optimal interaction support
- Massively distributed multi-user environments

6.3.3.6   Tools and Methods

- Methods and tool taxonomy
- Institutionalization of tools and methods
- Appropriate methods in a collaborative environment
- Exchange of methods and tools in the SADC
- Appropriate methods for the available platforms
- SADC methods
- SADC's better practice sharing projects
- Technological support to methods and tools
- Implantation of technologies
- Possibility of integrating new technologies to the SADC
- Integration system of knowledge to support the creation of data analysis, knowledge, codification and transfer
- Service systems for the creation of services required by the organizations and virtual communities
- Network system of all the actors
- Portal interface for all contributors
- Collective intelligence
- Shared vocabulary
- Ontology
- Punctual management
- Emergency management subsystem

In this chapter, we present the reference architecture for collaboration systems. This model can be used by enterprises for the construction of their own collaboration architecture, by selecting and widening the reference content. This model is based upon proven technological solutions, used at the Centre de Communication Adaptée de Montréal (CCA) and the ACIL, a band council, etc.

6.4 Methodologies

6.4.1 A Methodology to Apprehend Community Informatics Design

We did draw from several studies performed in the field of education elements that confirm the importance of community informatics design by trying to place it within the methodological paradigm to try to investigate relations between individuals, groups, learning environments and technological innovations in setting an educational designer (Barab and Squire 2004). The community informatics design field is a new discipline; therefore, it requires a method or a theory allowing users to apprehend design well. In fact, we must put in place a methodology that is favourable to collaboration, co-construction, design and innovation. By relying on adapted infrastructures and methodologies, the SADC (as a platform of design of other design platforms) enlists a great number of users from the phase of products and services design instead of only at their validation level. It benefits from talent pools, cultural creativity and diversity form different virtual organizations and groups seeking to better validate potentialities linked to users' inventiveness and imagination. By going beyond the traditional use of platform, it must allow to adapt in real time the design of new products and new services.

We have used several cases that utilize varied methodologies. In the SADC construction, it is crucial to have a global methodology that ensures its longevity. To start, we gave ourselves a reference framework in order to crystallize our reflections on the appropriation of social systems on issues related to the evolution of the SADC, its creation and its longevity. As we previously mentioned, the SADC is above all a set of complex socio-technical systems involving several objects and components in dynamic interaction that give rise to various levels of communication requiring common behaviours in the appropriation. Consequently, we are dealing with transdisciplinary concepts that, through various types of socio-technical systems, scales of observation and different disciplines, end up creating a desirable design. This design meets the requirements of Bela Banathy (2000) to rehabilitate the man at the heart of the action.

6.4.2 ENoLL's Cube Method and European Living Laboratories

This methodology allows to regroup in a coherent whole various tools and necessary methods for a maximal use of the SADC. This model (Fig. 6.4) was originally named Living Lab Harmonization Cube, but the APSI/Colab project team preferred to name it "ENoLL's cube". We will get inspired by it in part to build our SADC.

Since the living labs use a multidisciplinary and open approach and they have proven their effectiveness in several fields, with projects like *e-Inclusion*, direct democracy and the participation, we believe it plays a vital role in our design approach of services for citizens, virtual organizations and any social group that wishes to evolve, interact and represent itself within social systems.

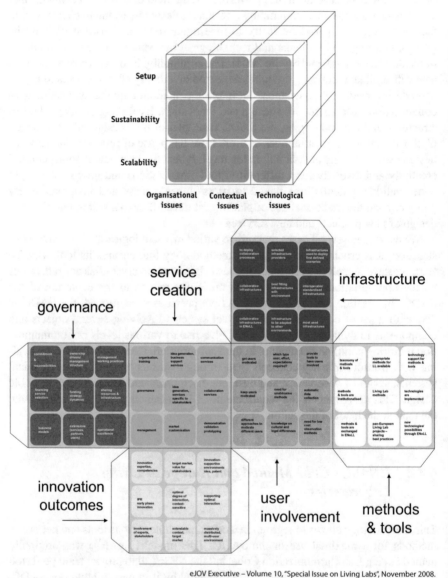

Fig. 6.4 The living lab harmonization cube's structure

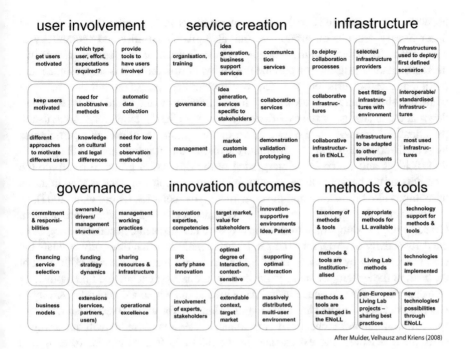

user involvement		
get users motivated	which type user, effort, expectations required?	provide tools to have users involved
keep users motivated	need for unobtrusive methods	automatic data collection
different approaches to motivate different users	knowledge on cultural and legal differences	need for low cost observation methods

service creation		
organisation, training	idea generation, business support services	communication services
governance	idea generation, services specific to stakeholders	collaboration services
management	market customisation	demonstration validation prototyping

infrastructure		
to deploy collaboration processes	selected infrastructure providers	Infrastructures used to deploy first defined scenarios
collaborative infrastructures	best fitting infrastructures with environment	interoperable/ standardised infrastructures
collaborative infrastructures in ENoLL	infrastructure to be adapted to other environments	most used infrastructures

governance		
commitment & responsibilities	ownership drivers/ management structure	management working practices
financing service selection	funding strategy dynamics	sharing resources & infrastructure
business models	extensions (services, partners, users)	operational excellence

innovation outcomes		
innovation expertise, competencies	target market, value for stakeholders	innovation-supportive environments Idea, Patent
IPR early phase innovation	optimal degree of Interaction, context-sensitive	supporting optimal interaction
involvement of experts, stakeholders	extendable context, target market	massively distributed, multi-user environment

methods & tools		
taxonomy of methods & tools	appropriate methods for LL available	technology support for methods & tools
methods & tools are institutionalised	Living Lab methods	technologies are implemented
methods & tools are exchanged in the ENoLL	pan-European Living Lab projects – sharing best practices	new technologies/ possibilities through ENoLL

After Mulder, Velhausz and Kriens (2008)

Fig. 6.4   (continued)

We find in the ENoLL cube method three primordial phases: the creation and the implementation of the living lab that allows to note the essential points before starting, the durability in order to make the approach durable and the extensibility that consists of considering from the start the future development of the lab.

The three columns of the cube correspond to the basic notions that form the whole of collaborative platform fundamental problems: the organizational, contextual and technological aspects. The co-creation and collaboration processes are covered in the organizational aspects. The co-construction of knowledge, generations of new ideas and new implementation strategies of services or products resulting from it are addressed in the contextual aspects. Finally, comes the development of technologies and design assistance systems that favour collaboration between different stakeholders (Mulder et al. 2008).

In the living lab experience, each partner or each stakeholder uses six main components in order to determine the roadmap and the needs which allow all to have a global vision of the challenges to face in order to move forwards.

However, we cannot neglect the users' participation, considered as a key element of the living lab; in fact, the users are at the heart of this concept. We must know how to both involve and motivate, gain their trust, collect and synthesize their ideas and measure their activity. According to Baecker et al. (1995), if the traditional decor favours spontaneity and realism of meetings in a specific time, the virtual decor mostly depends on groupware that also gives flexibility and spontaneity to interactions. To succeed in including users in an innovative co-creation process, we must stimulate the discussion and the creativity. Furthermore, it is important for the participants to be sufficiently varied to stimulate the discussion and the creativity while avoiding points of view that are too contradictory and could provoke a slow-down of the exchange or the experience (Bloor et al. 2001). However, a great users' participation depends on the dynamism of the group; therefore, the participants must be diversified in order to stimulate the discussion. It is not rare that the generation of ideas and concepts is intergraded in the discussion group to reinforce the creativity of the participants or to draw, by using examples of what is seen in terms of methods like brainstorm and the construction of scenarios (Bloor et al. 2001).

To ensure the SADC's durability, we must ensure the users' participation. Consequently, it is important to develop a system that takes into account the degree of the daily activity of users, for example, by using indicators that discretely evaluate the use of technology by the users. In the SADC, since we focus on the role of the user at the heart of the system, we must go beyond traditional approaches and find motivating elements that arouse an active users' participation in their social networks. A way to proceed consists of provoking a feeling of belonging for users, to establish an atmosphere that stimulates exchanges. For example, in the Colab case, we will find a way to share good practices and experiences in the field and foresee regular meeting and exchange moments according to precise modalities. This is how we manage to maintain a real circulation of ideas and give life to the community (Fig. 6.5).

At the same time, we must process the organizational aspects that might compromise the durability or longevity of the SADC. In this case, how can we motivate the users to participate in the co-creation process? We must not only find technological tools that are easy to use but also reassure the users regarding the confidentiality of their transactions and the respect of the private sphere. We must also take into account the use of social networks and the impact measuring tools have on users while taking into account the legal and cultural differences. Since the SADC is destined to serve as a framework for social systems networks beyond geographic confluences, we must take into account the cultural perspectives and relativism. These aspects will be addressed in the context of governance, which talks about management, roles and ethics. Finally, the technological tools used by users for collecting data must be the object of great attention during the construction of the SADC.

In order to create a favourable setting for exchanges and engage the users, it is primordial to define their objectives and their expectations regarding the SADC, so we must organize discussion groups and initial workshops with the potential partners to precise the expectations of each one of these partners, the efforts we demand and the form of their potential commitment. Another aspect is found in the feedback that could promote an iterative process of experienced lived within virtual communities. Besides, regarding the user's motivation, we must be on the lookout for technologies by constantly ensuring the collaborative tools are relevant and they meet the users' needs. In our initial workshops, we have asked the participants to elaborate a conceptual map of their current employment and technologies. It is important to suggest and to develop tools that will serve to vitalize the SADC's life.

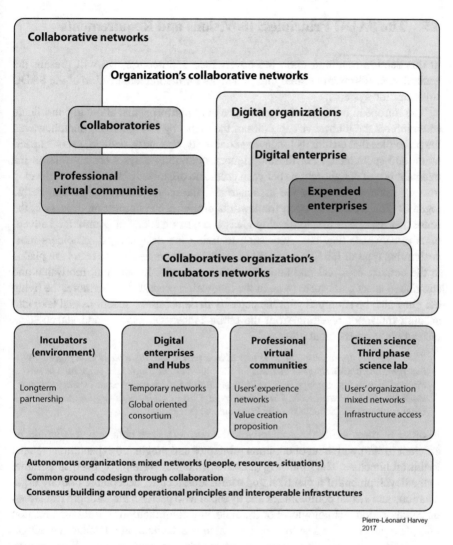

Pierre-Léonard Harvey
2017

Fig. 6.5 Collaborative networks

At the beginning, the SADC reference architecture content has been selected according to the needs of users, researchers and technology providers of the project. A pragmatic approach has been adopted. Various established or in-progress work platforms like Moodle or Sakkhai or the learning content management systems (LCMS) were discarded because of their complexity, restrictiveness and orientation on exclusive enterprise architectures instead of general reference architectures and also because they do not focus enough on collaborative technologies. Instead of that, we have followed the methodology established by Dokeos, the European living lab communities and CoSpaces, and we are determining the questions the architecture must answer and the contents to be included.

6.5   The SADC Principles: Its Visions and Requirements

In this section touching upon the governance architecture, we will present the general motivations and underlying principles for the implementation of the SADC collaboration systems.

The European living lab designers have built platforms that allow to consolidate and reinforce the innovative capacities of their labs, by taking into account, however, the principles that ensure its longevity: continuity, openness, realism, users' capacitation and spontaneity. For these designers, continuity plays a crucial role on the maintenance of collaborations between users and organizations; it allows to develop trusting relations allowing the associate and the users to accumulate knowledge together. The creation of open frameworks promotes the innovation process in the sense that users feel free to develop ideas and take on social or commercial adventures everywhere they are. According to living lab designers, stakeholders must design this type of lab like a natural or realist environment where users are placed in the context of a real and authentic life experience. In addition, motivated and stimulated users participate more in the innovation process. Furthermore, the living lab must also be equipped with the capacity to detect users' reactions and take into account the input resulting from the entire innovation process and stakeholders instead on the users input only:

> The Living Lab approach enables the user to be a part of the whole innovation process by incorporating a wide range of methods for user involvement. These take place both in traditional face-to-face settings such as focus groups and workshops and in virtual settings supported by distributed tools. The virtual settings also enable the Living Lab to reach a bigger community. (Schumacher and Feurstein 2007)

In order to meet the SADC objectives, the partners have determined it would be efficient to start with a set of common principles and pragmatic expectations related to this architecture. The following directive principles were recognized as essential to the development of a practical and useful architecture, acceptable both by organizations and virtual communities and by those who perform the in-depth researches on collaboration technologies. For example, any community or virtual organization must be equipped with a service policy which is a declaration related to the obligations, constraints and other conditions of the platform use by users. Furthermore, any architecture should have as a precise goal the increase of the efficiency of the effort and the utility of the description resulting from it. The goal determines the impact, which leads the definition of characteristics, the delays and the requirements related to the data as well as the level of detail or granularity. It must be aligned with the priorities of the community and contribute to the success of its mission's objectives.

This principle is also applied to the description of an architecture in its whole or a part of it or a view of an architecture. It also applies to architecture groups within a federation or an enterprise. For example, it will be easier to compare architectures built by different research projects in evaluation of the office work if, from start to finish, they are all built with this comparison spirit.

Any virtual architecture that is sustainable must be simple, direct and easy to understand. Without pretending exhaustiveness, we present here a few principles that contribute to ensure the longevity of an architecture.

6.5.1 A Simple and Direct Architecture

The development of an architecture that is too complex consumes a lot of time and money. It is better to pay special attention to the determination at the appropriate detail level to meet the desired objectives of the architecture design effort. We will take into consideration:

- The evaluation of the architecture impact
- The levels of the architecture decomposition
- The specificity levels in the definition of elements data architecture

In the first version of the SADC architecture, the essential architecture elements were identified; the next versions will provide additional elements given the experience acquired by working with industrial partners in the living labs and virtual community and organization setting.

6.5.2 An Architecture Well-Understood by Users

The architecture must be understandable to reinforce the applicability of information between its users. It must guide the process of human thinking in the discovery, the analysis and the problem-solving in order for designers (architects) and analysts to understand the issues quickly. The architecture must represent the information clearly by using common terms and definitions and by avoiding superfluous information.

6.5.3 Interoperability in the Entire Enterprise

The architecture must be expressive, by using a standard vocabulary with a clear semantics and a well-defined structure, to allow the comparability of data and the interoperability with other architectures of the same industrial enterprise or virtual organization. The application of this principle resorts to a set of common architectural construction elements or reference documents as a base for the architecture description. It is also essential that the architecture descriptions clearly define the external interfaces with other technologies and commercial components, in a coherent way with the method used to describe internal relations. This common basis for the development ensures the use of similar formats to display the information which allows the integration, the federation, the comparison and the reuse of disparate architectures.

6.5.4   Flexibility

The architecture must be modular, reusable and decomposable to reach a level of desirable flexibility. The architecture description is preferably composed of connected pieces that can be rearranged with a minimum of adaptation, allowing a multiple purpose use. A flexible architecture gives its users the means to function in a dynamic environment.

6.5.5   The Architecture's Vision

The architecture's vision of the SADC is taken from the CoSpaces technical objective, the creation of an innovative and distributed software framework facilitating collaborative work and the diffusion of workers and teams' knowledge in order to support collaborative design and engineering tasks. The software framework allows users to practice a dynamic creation in distributed collaborative work environments, modifiable (variable or expendable), rich in knowledge, oriented towards workers and available on demand in a way to establish efficient partnerships that can collaborate, show creativity and improve their productivity as well as adopt a holistic approach of the product phase implementation. These interactive work and collaboration environments become virtual meeting points for problem-solving, dispute resolution knowledge exchange and on-demand access to expert advice. These spaces offer a transparent and natural collaboration between workers and distributed knowledge teams. They are founded on an evolved communication, simulation services, knowledge support, innovative visualization and natural interaction; they offer a sufficient level of security, and they contribute to transform the current work practices to promote competitiveness of the entity on the global market.

The challenges to face are numerous in the sense where the architecture must allow the collaboration at multiple levels within the organization. In this case, we have to address the complexity of design by building a collaboration architecture to avoid errors and that could be costly in the design process. According to Huang et al. (2010), eight main aspects are likely to have a strong influence on a platform construction:

1. The capacity of adaptation to change or failures that occurred within the architecture network
2. The heterogeneous platforms' conviviality functioning on different exploitation systems
3. The semantics interoperability or the use of heterogeneous languages by different agents
4. The capacity to transmit the messages and modify the data (in relation with semantics interoperability)
5. A quick configuration of the implementation of the product's environment (taking into account the delays, the calendar, etc.)

6. The decrease of incidences of a service agent change
7. The preparation to a potential expansion
8. The preparation to the gaps in the information processing (Huang et al. 2010)

These elements can serve as a control list for the development of a reference architecture which is considered as a way to integrate criteria and collaboration requests to the planning process.

6.5.6   The Technological Strategy

The Office of Community and Rural Affairs (OCRA) technological strategy relies on an architecture oriented towards services (AOS). The AOS is an approach of enterprise architecture and distributed computing that allows to outsource oneself in functional applications at the local level and thanks to remote available services. More specifically, the AOS is an architectural style that guides all aspects of creation and procedure uses, presented like services all through their life cycles as well as the definition and supply of the computing infrastructure that allows the different applications to exchange data and to participate in the procedure, independently of the exploitation systems or the original programming language.

The AOS provides a general model, used by architects, whose functionality is decomposed into small distinct units (services) that can be distributed on a network or combined and reused to create commercial applications. These services communicate with each other through data from one service to another or through a coordination activity between two or several services. The SADC follows the AOS services and uses the AOS modeling to describe the different aspects or architecture views.

6.5.7   Social Systems Strategy

It is obvious that the commercial strategies are specific to each enterprise. However, we include certain general strategies to our reference architecture, like common examples of reasons to modernize the collaboration support infrastructure. The globalization of industrial activities is at the origin of the migration of design activities and production throughout the world, in order to optimize the logistics and the supply chain and to differentiate the product according to the needs and regulations of each market.

Consequently, the engineering sectors in Europe now endure strong pressures to reduce the delay of commercialization of new products and improve their quality, the clientele reaction and the market reactivity regarding the overseas enterprises with important shares in the European market, which reinforces competition. However, globalization offers European manufactures new possibilities to expand their activities in emerging countries where the current European Union penetration is limited to niche products.

The deconstruction strategies and emphasis on basic skills in place by the organizations and virtual communities promote the growth of virtual distribution enterprises. Through the last years, we have changed through an organization focused on discipline (based on the different services of a desk study) to a process (or program) more flexible based on the organization. In this context, people from several disciplines are gathered in co-located platforms (the product of integrated teams) with the representative of the production and the technical support through the product development phase. In the future, because of the great reactivity to the market demands and to get to another important step in terms of costs, cycle type and quality, it has become necessary to get orientated towards a more flexible and adaptable type of organization. In this organization, the engineering process is shared between the various teams of knowledge in a linked network. This considered organization requires punctual collaboration activities, a strong control and supervision system and appropriate and interdependent working spaces for each type of engineering or design activity.

6.5.8   Social Systems Objectives

The partners of the aeronautics and automotive industries in the design of collaborative spaces have underlined several general objectives in a collaboration architecture (Table 6.3):

6.5.9   The Stakeholders

The design of a stakeholders' card is to identify the commitment architecture's stakeholders, precise their influence in commitment and highlight questions, issues and preoccupations that need to be addressed in the architecture framework. In a reference architecture, it is favourable to stay focused on the identification of the main types of stakeholders and to let the detailed definition of their preoccupations to local enterprise architectures, because these questions are generally specific to each establishment. In particular, the most important preoccupations vary from one enterprise to another; the same happens to the most important to be grasped from the architecture point of view.

6.6   SADC Social Systems Architecture

The field of social systems architecture meets the needs of users, planners and virtual communities and organizations' managers. While the main part of the social systems architecture's content describes strategies specifically to management and

Table 6.3 The social systems objectives

Objective	Description
Personalized processing	Work methods suitable for the users' task and needs
Analysis techniques	Analysis techniques for the co-located and virtual team work
Collaborative designs	Authentic participative and collaborative and its purpose
Distributed organizations	A real distribution of the human resources organization where they are the most useful
Collaboration tools oriented towards the human	Design techniques and collaboration technologies focused on the human, with a logistics support that promotes inclusion
Participation and commitment	Support and large distribution of a strong feeling of implication and participation of the team members
Knowledge management	Deep comprehension and knowledge management and sharing promotion within the collaboration parameters
Independent collaboration site	A transparent collaboration, regardless of the collaborators' physical location
Risk management type	Efficient methods, useful to answer the needs, representations and requirements of users and contributors
Socio-technical comprehension	Models, theories and methods reflecting the complexity of socio-technical systems needs and the use of physical/cognitive objects in a social context
Flexible design factors	Requirements for the design of physical, cognitive and social support
Incorporated collaboration tools	Integrated platform software that takes over the following elements: transparent and secured access to technical simulations, data sources and on-demand computing power, the capacity to dynamically create reconfigurable workspaces, personalized with flexible entrance and exit in the collaborative workspace
Ambient interfaces	Ambient interfaces to support various engineering tasks, through transparent integration and by the improvement of technological interfaces already in place that are currently transformed in an advanced autonomous user interface (optical user monitoring, vocal commands), and the different categories of display devices (large-scale projection systems, private office systems, small mobile systems)
Change management	Change management methods for design firms (engineering) and SME, including the human factor, the processing change and the transformation of workspace infrastructure
Contextual expertise	Sensitive information related to the virtual context and experts in support to more efficient engineering and collaboration through the access to information and appropriate tools
Personalized software	Software allowing each one to create its own collaborative workspaces according to his needs
Integrated simulation	Distributed virtual environments capable to take charge of multifunctional teams and equipped with an integrated simulation
Migration	A transparent migration between different ambiance environments
Virtual community project	The creation of a common virtual space to simulate the sense of a real life for living virtual community projects, to multiply random meetings and to facilitate project management
Production workspaces	Validated collaborative workspaces capable to form the necessary collaboration within organizations of distributed production

operational aspects of the virtual community, the reference architecture can also present main preoccupations and basic concepts in order to establish a common terminology of collaboration social systems.

6.6.1   The Collaboration Model

The SADC has adopted from TOGAF and developed a varied explicative and descriptive model to reflect the various aspects of collaborative work in organizations and private and public virtual communities. It is founded on the experience of works performed with an array of industrial and social organizations, as well as the existing documentation on cooperative computer-assisted work related to distributed cognition, education and social and organizational psychology, management sciences and the collaboration within the healthcare teams (Fig. 6.6).

This model can serve as a work framework to define and structure the needs of generic users for new technologies or collaboration practice purposes. It allows the decision-makers, the designers and the developers to examine the interaction of different factors that, together, constitute a collaboration system. It also allows them to specify fields they aim in order to increase the interoperability and efficiency of the collaborative work. For example, they could develop technologies to help diminish cultural or professional differences likely to influence the group collaborative work.

The classification and the identification of design activities remain a very complicated task in the sense where they risk to bring certain structuring problems to light. The fundamental objective of design is to understand the problem structure

Fig. 6.6 Framework for collaborative practice

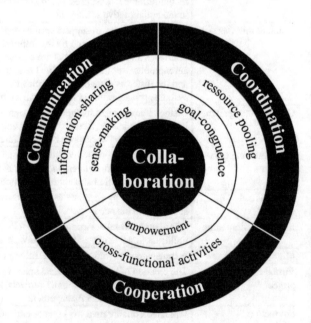

Table 6.4 The design activities

Definition activities (functions to forms/structures)	Evaluation activities (functions to forms/structures)	Management activities
Documents' analysis	Analysis	Constraint conditions
Association	Decision-making	Exploration
Composition	Evaluation	Identification
Decomposition	Modeling	Information gathering
Details	Selection, choice	Planning
Production	Simulation	Prioritization
Standardization	Trials, experimentation	Solution
Structuring/integration		Research
Synthesis		Choice
Extraction		Calendar/schedule

Adaptation of Sim and Duffy (2003)

with the solution that is in part integrated in the design effort, which is structured in a way to solve problems. The plurality of visions brings designers to spend more time trying to structure the problem instead of solving it. This is why it is important to confine the design activities before suggesting potential design solutions. Table 6.4 presents the majority of those activities.

The evaluation activities (Table 6.4 centre column) seek to find possible design solutions. These activities touch upon the analysis and the potential solutions' evaluation of the design requirements or needs. According to Sim and Duffy (2003), according to the design model, we adopt a centred approach, either on the project or on the product, inside of which planning and execution of diverse design activities are made. The approach oriented on the project is focused first on problem analysis, followed by a systematic fulfilment processing, or a series of possible solutions are generated and evaluated progressively and then decomposed to converge towards the best solution. The approach oriented on the product is more centred on the use of solution conjectures to generate a solution concept allowing to enrich knowledge and to improve the problem's definition. The great number of analyses and evaluations preformed on problem activities allows to optimize the problem's decomposition and its solution. Sim and Duffy emphasize that the solution analysis and evaluation constitute a phase of common design activities of both approaches. There is a design category that analyses and evaluates performance solutions according to certain criteria. This is what we call the evaluation of design activities or the design analysis and the activity evaluation.

The third column of Table 6.4 describes the management activities that address the relations or interdependence between the activities taking place during the design process. Designers must be able to influence the design process by performing strategic considerations. The knowledge management experts and experienced communauticians opinions are determining in the strategy selection. Several types of strategies are used at various levels of an organization, and there also are different levels of detail in the development or the process. In this case, strategic knowledge is a basis for the expertise in the fields where management or governance problems depend on the actions to undertake. This choice is problematic and requires a considerable amount of human expertise. In fact, it is knowledge that allows the strategies formation; the action plans determine the types of knowledge and tactics to use according to the problem context. That being said, there is a design activity category that encompasses the choices made by the designers to manage the design process progress. They are the management activities. Therefore, the criteria of activity category classification rely on the acquired knowledge in the design process management (Sim and Duffy 2003).

6.6.2 *Reference Enterprise Services and the Functions*

The collaboration model describes the different aspects of collaboration. In practice, these aspects are tightly linked in most collaboration environments. By drawing inspiration from the collaboration model, we have chosen to distinguish four main types of collaboration services:

- *Communication services*, they are related to the exchange of interpersonal information; they focus on the actors and group factors of collaboration.
- *Cooperation services*, collaboration relative to the use of tools to manipulate objects with the objective to produce results; they focus on the aspects that facilitate collaboration.
- *Coordination* services, they are related to the orchestration, the choreography and the emerging organization of tasks, processing and human and material resources.
- *The reference service* offers the users the production of knowledge and information that are part of the environment and are available throughout the collaboration.

These four types of services are strongly interdependent. For example, through cooperation, the coordination is often achieved thanks to communication. The inclusion of certain tools or information contents with the main basic objective of cooperation instead of in the context of collaboration, or vice versa, sometimes is a subjective judgment. We chose to apply this structure because it allows a certain organization of the great number of available services. The 3C of collaboration (communication, coordination, cooperation) are also well established in the research community in collective teleworking, while the collaboration context has been underlined as being fundamentally important by the CoSpaces users.

6.6.2.1 The Communication Services

On the collaboration model basis (TOGAF, 2009) and a survey regarding the research works, requirements and scenarios of the CoSpaces users, we have identified several generic communication services. They are related to the exchanges of

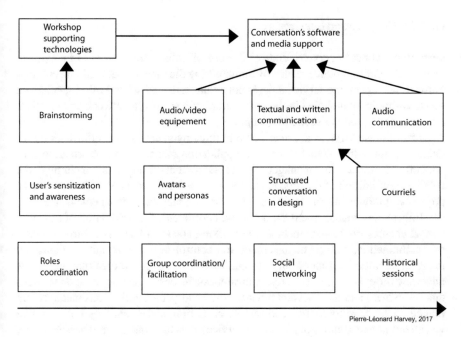

Fig. 6.7 Generic communication services

interpersonal information; they focus on the actors and group factors of collaboration. They are represented in Fig. 6.7.

The generic services presented in Fig. 6.7 and resulting from these three groups could not be considered like an exhaustive, definitive or complete list. Like the TOGAF (2009) enterprise continuum, it must be considered as a "virtual bank" of reusable architecture elements that will be elaborated, adapted and expanded by norms of the community in the context of an open living architecture.

Also, if Fig. 6.7 indicates some specialization relations between the main services, several dependency relations could have also been included. In order to preserve the generality and legibility of the models, we have, however, chosen to not present a great number of these dependencies.

Support to the conversation remains the most generic form of communication. Meetings are planned conversations likely to have a predefined program. Figure 6.7 shows more specializations of communication according to the media (text, audio and video) and the structure (brainstorm, structured conversations). The majority of other services support communication through the organization of people (role and group management) or by increasing the bandwidth or the availability of the virtual communication (avatars, population awareness, session's history). Finally, we highlight social networking like being one of the important aspects and goals of communication.

6.6.2.2   Cooperation Services

Generic cooperation services address the use of collaborative tools to manipulate objects in order to produce results by emphasizing the aspects that facilitate collaboration. Once again, the service's list is not exhaustive, and several other specialized services should be included in the architecture of a society, a network organization, a project or a particular scenario group.

Most of these services are distributed in three main categories: information production, information management and application management. Information production addresses the management of documents and data, including the collaborative edition of documents, annotations and comments and the detection of problems, product life management or PLM, product data management or PDM, etc. Information management supports and coordinates the production of information; it ensures the management of the working space and access control, specific role examination, change management, the control of versions and configuration management, the interoperability of data, reproduction and transformation. Let us underline the existence of underlying awareness, resources and notification services that serve them and meet several other needs. Finally, the applications management related to the sharing control and remote execution, screen sharing, collaborative visualization and simulation, so many services that facilitate simultaneous design, are integrated in the platform.

6.6.2.3   Generic Coordination Services

Coordination services can be supported by an explicit representation of the work to be accomplished, whether it is emerging or structured, like task management, or if they subscribe to predefined workflow like the social systems processing management. The support of information management offers a necessary overview to the exercise of a leadership supported by surveillance services and control panel. The data entry processing and the session's history can serve as foundation. The support to proactive management ensured by services allows a management by strategies and objectives, project management and planning, workforce planning, systems regulations and policies, the definition of execution constraints, etc. The horizontal coordination can very well be taken over; however, other functions like the reiteration in collaborative sessions, services and calendar planning, the entry of the best practices and their reuse (e.g. processes) are more often designed in a horizontal coordination spirit.

We can regroup the generic design activities in three main categories:

- *The definition activities:* These activities aim at the complexity management of a complex evolutive design while defining it gradually until it possesses all the details required for production.
- *The evaluation activities:* These activities consist of analysing and evaluating the feasibility of potential design solutions by rejecting unrealizable solutions; they contribute to reduce the solution space of design.

- *The management activities:* These activities manage the complexity of activity coordination associated with an evolutive design environment and its processing.
- The context of collaboration contains multiple dimensions. The organizational and personal dimensions require help to find experts, to personalize collaboration services and to use role playing for learning, exploration and skills management. The physical dimensions require an awareness to the location and distances as well as the possibility to create a virtual environment that reproduces a remote environment that generates the feeling of "being there" for the remote participants and the experts offering their services remotely during their local inspections. The dimension of information and knowledge of the context also translates through the necessity of knowledge management, training services, an understanding of the lessons learned, information exchanges and metadata management. Finally, we need a certain number of generic services to use contextual information, like navigation, filtering, visualization, multiple views as well as points of view and awareness of the supply context.

6.6.2.4   Dependencies and Orientation Analysis

In order to create a socio-technical system's architecture and a collaboration architecture at the user level, it is not enough to identify the necessary services. We must also capture the collaboration aspects and the applicable criteria to each service in order to help users solve their problems. The relations between generic aspects of the collaboration model and the services supporting them illustrate the complexity of interdependence relations between collaboration aspects and the services. Therefore, we have used this structure to guide users on technological support and analysis methods applicable to these dependency relations. The services supporting the construction team have been identified. The meetings about support and the reflection are for the construction team, while the avatars and the conversation support can improve knowledge (familiarity) and other psychological factors that will contribute to the team support and reinforcement.

In order to support a concrete collaboration scenario, constitutive elements of this generic service model must be widened, specialized and decomposed in various targeted collaboration services. The collaboration model and functional service points of view presented in this section seek to guide the solution development process by helping stakeholders to determine the levels of advanced collaboration services adapted to their situation.

6.6.2.5   Reference Needs

The user's needs, such as expressed by the CoSpaces industry partners, can serve as starting points to analyse the needs in an organization, a virtual community or an inter-organizational project. The analysis needs (requests) often face the dilemma of the chicken and the egg: users have a hard time understanding the range of needs they need to validate, while developers do not want to give them strict advice in order to limit the entry bandwidth. By providing examples of current requests, the SADC illustrates the requests' nature and form (needs) and provides a reusable request declarations catalogue (requests) a community or virtual organization can select. This strategy presents the risk of users selecting too many requests (need) less important in this preproduction data list and leaves aside the additional needs (requests) that are more important to them.

The collaboration space needs model reflects the different aspects of such methodology:

- The needs are grouped by types and by categories.
- The needs are related to the use scenarios and processing where necessary.
- The types of needs categories are related to the different aspects of the collaboration model.
- The collaboration model aspects, the types and the needs are related to collaboration services and technological elements that resolve the needs or are influenced by them (Sim and Duffy 2003).

These dependency links can be useful for the needs analysis. With more details, they complete the highest level of collaboration models and the easiest one to use. We have discovered that a great number of needs, classification relations and other dependency links make this model somewhat complex illegible. The categories and types fill a key function in the filtering of needs according to the preoccupations of the different stakeholders and the relevance of the different scenarios.

In view of a great number of specific needs, an analysis method based on the representation of direct relations between the needs and all software would be both tedious to establish and complex and difficult to use. In order to provide a simpler and easier framework to use, we have chosen to use the collaboration model as a lens to analyse the needs. By grouping the needs according to the collaboration model elements they report to, we are able to identify the relevant technologies founded on the links between architecture software and the collaboration model.

Instead of directly linking each of these numerous needs to the collaboration model, we have simplified them even more by linking them to the type of model and the need categories instead. Most of these relations reflect the specialization, which takes into account the types and the categories, by incorporating them to the elements and services of the collaboration model and vice versa. This indicates that both structures are in fact at the same level and that they play similar roles in the global architecture. Ideally, these structures should be combined, so that the types and the needs categories would be an integral part of the collaboration model. The current model reflects the historical progresses of collaborative work where the collaboration model originates from the needs. In a next revision of the architecture, all needs should be classified again according to the collaboration model instead of types and temporary categories.

6.6.2.6 Security and Communication Design

The point of view of physical technologies deals with security problems and communication. It is a challenge to support the dynamic nature of collaborative work while ensuring the appropriate processing of questions related to trust and security. A collaboration system must provide support to the information users and put at their disposal a knowledge support sub-system in addition to take into account their current activity context, like producing and sharing knowledge in a community of practice. More precisely, the security framework provides the users with a support for the selection at the participants' request, documents and necessary data for a collaboration session. This framework facilitates the integration of participants in the collaboration sessions and the access to their collaborators and applications. This requires associated devices automatically configurable for punctual collaboration purposes.

The security architecture is specifically designed for the following purposes:

- Secure communications and appropriately protect information resources used in the collaborative tools.
- Support efficient commercial transactions and secured service provisions.
- Capture the opportunities to obtain security synergies and economies of scale on the IT plan.

In a wider perspective, IT security is a continuous process where the material, software and users' knowledge are continuously the object of observations, improvements and updates. The security is analysed according to diverse points of view:

- The authentication and authorization
- The security and infrastructure process
- The network's security

A secured technical and manageable infrastructure must take into account the elements above at a precocious stage of its design regarding the new Web components. If this awareness is made possible thanks to an integration with existing applications, it will be about applying well-defined exemplary practices.

The data security includes technical procedures and measures put in place to prevent any unauthorized user to access, modify contents or use and distribute stocked or processed data by the system. Data security also includes the data integrity (the preservation of their exactness and their validity) and the system's protection against physical damages (including preventative measures and collection procedures).

The authorization control limits the access to data of each level to authorized users only. Guidelines and procedures can be established for accountability and levels as well as the control type. This obligation encompasses the possibility to specify data subgroups and to differentiate between users' groups. Furthermore, a decentralized authorization control assumes a particular importance for distributed systems.

Data protection is necessary to prevent an unauthorized user to access the data. Coding the data is one of the main methods to protect them. It is useful for stocked information on the hard drive as well as for information exchanged on the network.

Because the SADC calls for an intensive collaboration between several organizations established in various countries, the security considerations are an essential aspect. In our approach, services and application providers make authorization decisions based on the parameters affected to the user by his organization. This principle is to protect the resources without damaging the flexibility and the support of the work environment.

In the grand schemes of things, the SADC contains a set of model views that offer a complete definition of collaborative work environments. In order to simplify the integration of existing enterprise architectures as well as their evolution, potentially their normalization, its structure follows the TOGAF norm. The content includes:

- A *governance architecture,* encompassing the general principles of the architecture and the current commercial strategies focused on collaboration
- An *enterprise architecture*, with the contribution of standard services and a collaboration model on the organizational aspects of collaboration
- An *information systems architecture* that defines a logical framework for collaboration software, illustrating how to implement this framework and that specifies the component interfaces such as workspaces and Web services
- A *technical architecture* that relates the information systems components to the underlying application of the framework reflected in the standard reference models for the TOGAF technology and the integrated information infrastructure
- A *realization architecture* that identifies formal norms and collaboration industry norms as well as their use by different application components.

The SADC platform will start with the Colab that will serve as a model for virtual enterprises and organizations. The Colab will be a starting point for the enterprise wishing to implement new collaboration solutions. Like an enterprise architecture, it covers both enterprise and collaboration aspects, and it relates these two notions in order to advise enterprises in the choice of technology that better meet their commercial needs. We have explained how TOGAF's development architecture methodology (DAM) can be applied to create reference architectures in industry sectors, enterprises and collaboration projects at the architectures level, starting with the integration of the Colab.

Other works will allow to establish an open framework to update the SADC, describing the process by which other contributors could submit revisions or extensions to the published architecture and accept future revisions of a publication.

Part II
From Modeling to Implantation: the Reference Framework, Instantiation Methodology and the Discovery and Strategic Alignment Matrices

In this part, we will present a construction guide for digital social systems (virtual communities, innovation communities, collaborative platform) that contains several reference models which translate into a series of guidelines and means to support the processes and activities involved in the co-design (large-scale collaborative design, also called community informatics design) of these new virtual environments. The community informatics design guide aims to help creators of diverse types of digital social systems, the framework and the virtual environment design experts to understand well the development conditions as well as the set of mechanisms, functionalities and creativity tools to manage and operationalize their entire life cycle and the various roles of actors and partners.

Chapter 7
Reference Model, Governance Framework and Instantiation Strategy

Digital social systems can be centred on several economic activity models seeking to transform the physical creativity vision of organizations and traditional social systems (architectures and construction of buildings with well-defined borders, linear process of enterprises' value chain, university or government institutions) in a multiform and multifunctional network structure, in order to increase their chances to commit to "collaborative activities" producing value. New virtual environments co-design to assist the design of digital social systems (services portal or innovations community) that systematically uses the network and socio-digital media infrastructures. Community informatics design will take a considerable scope in the next years because the "participative social architecture" (PSA) adds a sense of location and time and an additional value to traditional notions of physical space and social time, where human activities used to take place (Harvey 2018, to be published).

Web 3.0's and Web 4.0's digital social systems (DSS) emerge thanks to the collaboration mechanisms put in place through the social Web infrastructures that must be included like social collaborative architectures. Indeed, DSS apply the common network infrastructures and the ICT in order to free themselves from the restrictive barriers of the geographical determinism, without forgetting, of course, the tangible aspect of human relations or inter-organizations. However, the infrastructure aspect does not exhaust the structuring work of the community informatics expert in the development of new collaborative spaces. Computer-mediated collaboration and communication contain several complex and abstract processes related to affiliation, trust, cohesion and resources sharing. To provide the necessary elements for social communication in the new collaborative spaces and to ensure the development of a virtual community understood as a digital social system based on inter-connectivity allowed by technology, we suggest to revisit the idea of a "socio-technical system", expression introduced by the Tavistock Institute of London that we will apply to our study object: the construction of digital social systems by the community informatics design team. This research orientation has expanded over several decades, and we shall see that in order to understand and build the future DSS, we

© Springer International Publishing AG 2017
P.-L. Harvey, *Community Informatics Design Applied to Digital Social Systems*,
Translational Systems Sciences 12, DOI 10.1007/978-3-319-65373-0_7

must drastically extend not only our theoretical foundations regarding the usual communication and social science concepts but also any praxeological foundation of a communicational action science for the construction of collaborative virtual environments. In this context, we must borrow a few concepts from management and computer sciences and community informatics design, not to formalize our approach but to give it a more systematic and operational character.

Therefore, from the design and social systems design works of Banathy (1996) and his successors, Laszlo et al. (2010), Laszlo and Laszlo (2002, 2004, 2007), Laszlo (1972), Jenlink (2004, 2009), Jenlink and Banathy (2002, 2008) and Reigeluth and Jell-Can (1998), and those of Flood and Jackson (1991) on critical social systems, Günter Ropohl's (1979, 1999) on socio-technological systems, those of Wolfgang Hofkirchner (2009) and Christian Fuchs (2004, 2008) on social sciences applied to design and knowledge management, the convergence theories of Gunilla Bradley in Sweden, the re-articulation of the collective action theory of Bruce Bimber in the United States, the works of Rob Kling (1997, 2007) and Alice Robbin (2011) on social computing and Elinor Ostrom's (Ostrom and Hess 2011) on the analysis of socio-ecological systems, we have strong theoretical foundations to analyse and build the DSS. We complete this generic approach of social systems by a socio-technical reference model included as a subsystem of human activity (Checkland and Scholes 1990; Checkland 1981), a socio-technical system. In this context, community informatics design is a design centred on the human that uses a complex system thinking, the social science one, as an explicit reference basis.

7.1 Digital Social Systems Objectives and Benefits

DSS have several objectives from an economic or organizational standpoint. Whether they are oriented towards social action, organizational design, social design, platform design, the business and innovation field, organizational change or educational activities, their main objective is to establish the trust (Luhmann 1989, 1995) between the members that wish to collaborate by decreasing the general costs of the communication action (Moles and Rohmer 1986; Moles 1981; Harvey 2008; Habermas 1973, 1984) aiming to identify partners for a particular digital social systems configuration (a virtual team, a learning community, a strategic inter-enterprise network). The DSS provides concepts, creativity tools and methods to shorten the development stage of a community or a socio-technical system through the various life-cycle phases of the community informatics design.

The DSS creation and design may contain several benefits for their members. From the network support and the infrastructures related to information technologies and communication point of view, Afsarmanesh and Camarinha-Matos (2005) and Camarinha-Matos and Afsarmanesh (2006, 2008) note ten from the most important ones that we will adapt to our context:

1. Action flexibility and promptness to help the members seize new collaboration opportunities
2. The acquisition of a widened dimension, in order compete with larger organizations
3. The influence of partners by lobbying and marketing, to expand their geographical presence in a global market's perspective
4. An increased power of negotiation in partnership purchasing situations
5. Access to a transparent collaboration infrastructure, turnkey, to facilitate collaboration and the updating of different activities between members
6. Mechanisms, processes, guidelines, design and innovation guides, assistance services, animation and support data base to facilitate creation and the deployment of a digital social system
7. Proactive profiling of members and partners and dynamic management of individual and collective skills to ensure the optimization of skills and resources likely to meet an innovation or business opportunity or to contribute to the solving of a problem or the settlement of a dispute
8. Innovation support services like questions related to copyright, learning or continuous education and tailor-made training through various types of institutional support (foundation, expertise, advice, platform design)
9. Introduction of trust consolidation mechanisms between members or between partners and the network
10. Presentation of the general principles of community informatics design and ethics guiding the development of collaborative design, like remote work, and information, knowledge and resource sharing principles

However, in order for the DSS to develop correctly and so they can generate these benefits for the community or the organization, we have prepared a series of required conditions:

1. An information technology and communication infrastructure (exclusive and open-source code) and a series of creativity tools and social media that support the management of the evolutive virtual environment prototype and the creation of the digital social system. In the "My Portal Col@b and community informatics design project", it is our portal that will fill these functions in the wider sense like a large socio-technical system (or virtual environment) assisting the community informatics design of DSS (communities and online organizations of all sorts like a corporate platform for real estate management).
2. The active involvement of members and their commitment to participate to the co-creation of the prototype, especially through the generation of updated contents and made available to the community and by the identification of their respective roles and skills.
3. The scenario of a viable community (business model, economic model, organizational design or community strategy).
4. The implementation of a global governance strategy and management strategies (people, knowledge, resources, etc.).

5. The establishment of evolutive learning strategies and digital skills management
   to improve reflexive practice, the DSS quality and life conditions of all in the
   context of a "communicational responsible act".

7.2   Community Informatics Design Social Architecture: An Evolutive Life Cycle

Several strategic approaches in organizational communication use systemic thinking and design thinking to engage the stakeholders and coordinate their activities in
diverse participative process and to consider the interconnections between the organization and its action context, for example, interactive management (Warfield
1990), the methodology of flexible systems (Checkland 1981), idealized systems
design, evolutive systems design (Laszlo 2001; Laszlo and Laszlo 2004), the intervention in total systems (Flood and Jackson 1991), management of complexity
(Gharajedaghi 1999), organizational modeling (Morabito et al. 1999), enterprise
architecture (Nadler 1981), the self-organization approach (Jantsch 1980), socio-
technologies (Bunge 1999), design thinking (Brown and Duguid 1996, 2000, 2001;
Brown and Isaacs 2005), practice communities (Wenger 1998), activity theory
(Engeström 1999) and the structured dialogic design (Christakis 1996; Christakis
and Bausch 2006), Transition Design (Terry Irwin 2015).

However, none of these changes and innovation approaches systematically takes
into consideration the role and challenges of the ICT and their impact on intentional
change and the creation of the future digital social systems, except recent initiatives
in transition design. By contrast, according to the general implicit culture of these
different approaches, social and communication sciences are not only useful to the
critic of social systems, they can also be integrated to different disciplines with
more technological perspectives, for example, information systems management,
social computing, community informatics, technology and society sciences, Internet
research, computer-assisted collaborative work, human machine interfaces that
require both a certain formalization of their approach and a short-term perspective
and problem-solving as well as researches and integrated approaches in the long
term like ethnography and participative research action (Eriksson et al. 2006; Shuler
1993) and all kinds of ecosystem innovation.

Community informatics design does not integrate social sciences before or after
the social systems design process to put the activities into context. It makes them
intervene in a critical and reflexive way throughout the co-design phases. In the next
sections, we will present a creative and reflexive framework for the DSS development while integrating an ethic and a semiformal architecture approach, which is
often lacking in social sciences, in the name of intuition, emergence and emotional-
ity. A socially responsible community informatics design cannot let fate, vagueness,
conceptual or disciplinary imprecision guide the implantation of large-scale digital
social systems.

In the society of communication, innovation, social inclusion, protection of children and elderly, dispute settlement, content organizing and knowledge sharing in communities of all sorts require digital and generic skills that must be taught at all levels of the educational system and society. It is not a phenomenon foreign to the human being or one that we can exclusively criticize from the outside or from only one discipline. In fact, several systems and social system design approaches can be put to contribution to build democratic platforms of the future. The community informatics design approach is evolutive and emerging; it operates through a semiformal social architecture, by incorporating the powerful social systems design approaches without neglecting the management sciences, cognitive sciences, business ecosystem, information systems and the complexity sciences approaches. We combine them and incorporate them in a general ethical design framework we call "community informatics axiology" (see the glossary), which are general principles and shared values in design activities.

Therefore, community informatics design can be considered as a scientific process in the classical sense of the word, containing development phases and well-identified procedures, but it is above all a culture of the reflective practice defined by Schön (1983), an open and flexible heuristic that requires creativity and imagination in the democratic vision of the socio-economic development. Heuristic and semiformalism are not opposed; they complete each other in an evolutive and generative vision of social change. However, it is not an algorithmic process where the results would be predictable and where rules and procedures would be fixed and preformatted for any type of use. Community informatics design can be motivated by problem-solving or strategic planning, but it focuses mostly on viable sociological change solutions and the suppression of social or organizational pathologies.

Community informatics design is a heuristic in the sense that it constitutes an exploratory design space where multiple creation, modeling and emergence possibilities are catalysed in a series of generative processes that involve the definition of a research frontier or the exploration of relevant processes to a specific problem. It is not about stages that are well defined and that would lead to predictable results. The heuristic aspect contains three main dimensions: (1) an ontological and epistemological component that provides the basis for the creative exploration of community information design; (2) a meta-methodology and meta-design perspective that allow the exploration of a universe of possibilities and complementary social creativity approaches (Fischer 2011, 2013a; Fischer and Konomi 2007) like in human centered design (methods and techniques collaboration and creativity tools); (3) and finally, a series of principles and consensual values that serve as quality criteria through which we can guide us to perform the design research and invent the DSS of the future. It is a responsible communication heuristic put at the service of sustainable development, an open and flexible heuristic that generates appropriate creativity processes to each situation, community and specific organization that uses it. It falls under the intuition and the generic comprehension of stages and knowledge bases (not always well defined nor fixed ahead of time) that make DSS operational. Contrary to certain approaches of traditional information systems, it does not aim data and practice codification, nor does it suggest a standardized and well-established scientific approach.

This does not translate a lack of a certain procedures' systematization nor the fact that this beginning of formalism is against the emancipation of human and social factors. It is a flexible and systematic way to begin a rigorous research process.

Understood like that, community informatics design can be defined as a heuristic approach (semiformal) seeking to support and guide researchers, practitioners and partners in the participative co-creation of sustainable, desirable and responsible DSS. Useful until a certain point for the non-initiated, it prescribes a general communicational action framework and even provides a fundamental checklist (see Chap. 10) and very detailed entities, things and structuring elements that can be incorporated and organized in DSS to make them evolve in a permanent way. Here, it is a question of team management, collaborative learning, methodology and activities. Because it is about complex activities that will have a real repercussion on individuals' activities, groups and partner organizations, we suggest a semiformal approach that lies between neopositivist formalism of information systems engineering and the more open participative research-action pragmatism of social sciences and information and communication sciences.

Social systems are varied, dynamic and unique. They represent a substantial part of the cultural heritage of our societies and economies. For this reason, we must pay a particular attention to the development of information systems (community) that, once operational, will either value or hinder social systems and existing organizations. Flexible and evolutive social architecture that supports the DSS must meet the particular members' needs. However, as architectures built for housing or the traditional construction industry, several of the entities, resources and materials that constitute it are found entirely or partially in various types of organizations and online communities. Just like we always need foundations, walls, hallways and rooms in the architecture of housing construction, for example, the DSS must be built on solid foundations, and it contains certain restrictions on access to certain services, informational spaces accessible to the public and others reserved for experts and certain partners, creativity tools and platforms that can be restrictive or convivial for the user (ref. Harvey 2018). All these elements and several others will be the object of a reflection, a collective decision-making on scenarios or alternative infrastructures on the realization phases to respect, on costs, time and the risks associated with different DSS projects. This is why the entire community informatics design process resembles an evolutive life cycle that is supported by a series of "attractors" like the value of innovation for the quality of life and the economy, responsible communication in organizations, the instrumental value of certain creativity tools and their intrinsic functional utility for the lifestyles, a value added in a new business model.

Community informatics design also suggests possible approaches (research action, ethnography of uses and practices, events or situation simulations), creativity tools and conceptual resources that can be useful for the DSS design. By no means should we let chance or improvisation dictate the development of social systems that could in certain cases contain significant strategic dimensions for the members and partners (even if creativity and spontaneity of certain initiatives sometimes require a field of larger action and imagination freedom and with fewer constraints and formalism). Participants of the DSS design process create their own community informatics design implantation approach according to the type of favoured organization or platform design. They select relevant elements, methodological approaches and collaborative tools by combining their ideas and documenting the creative solutions exploration with the appropriate resources, according to the ideal image of the digital social system they want to build for themselves. However, even if we can find as many versions of DSS as community informatics users/designers teams, they will always have a common denominator, what we call a reference model, which promotes the continuous exploration of evolutive values and principles of the community and, combined with an evolutive design ethic, will allow to continue the research in accordance with the actors mainly targeted by the new systems.

During our research process, our community informatics design approach has made explicit our commitment to improve the digital skills of users and permanent learning. Because these elements are explicit in the general research-action process in social and communication sciences, learning values the design process, and design values the learning process. Several trajectories are possible when comes the time to direct our activities towards sustainable development and socio-economic innovation, and the notion of learning and improving the skills is the driving force of this continuous process at the heart of the DSS community informatics design.

7.3   Community Informatics Design Social Architecture: A Conversation

Community informatics design is built on a basis of processes, contents and flexible technologies, but not random, that each community or organization can adapt and recreate or take the design according to its particular objectives and needs. These processes and contents are consolidated through the means of conversational design and the learning of new collaboration architectures through new platform design methodologies and tools.

We introduce here the concept of conversational design (Banathy 1996) to explain two types of dialogue that are appropriate for the non-initiated designers that need to execute community informatics design of digital social systems. From the works of Schein (1993) and Beck (2009), Banathy and Jenlink (2005) try to link the discussion on dialogue to the social systems design communication mode. Members of a practice or innovation community can now enter the universe of digital social systems design and explore the discourse method or the type of communication/animation that applies best to the DSS development. Banathy and Jenlink state that the combination of a generative dialogue and a strategic dialogue leads to a complete social communication method that is more viable to use for the members of a designer's community. They call this method "conversational design". The importance and the power of dialogue in the design of practice communities become a more and more common topic, especially when the designers' community must configure architectures or give advice on the structure of the future online community (Brown and Isaacs 2005; Bohm 1996; Wheatley 2002). Contrary to engineering practices of information systems where the conversation between designers is articulated around the formal codification language of reality and the programming of closed functionalities, conversational design uses community informatics design like a human process through which we create our institutions, our cultures and, today, our digital social systems. The great physicist David Bohm tells us that the real dialogue consists of "thinking together". Nevertheless, conversational design, as an open-decision-making process, requires certain particular skills from the participants and becomes more efficient socially when it is articulated and facilitated within certain general adaptable instructions, from both the field of information systems and the field of social sciences. Our portal will provide some precise examples.

As we illustrate it in Fig. 7.2, the semiformal community informatics design processes are the following:

1. *Generative Processes*: Processes and mechanisms by which the designing community learns to realize its aspirations and create an innovation community that becomes collaborative and responsible. Through a generative conversation, the members of the future online platform community learn to develop their individual potential and their collective and collaborative intelligence.
2. *Evolutive Learning Processes*: By progressive and evolutive learning, the members of the innovator community develop their individual, collective and digital skills that can lead them to become dynamic community informatics designers, capable to build DSS and online communities and platforms of all kinds. The evolutive learning is guided by the development life cycle that goes through the evolutive development stages, from the evolutive conscience to the evolutive praxis.
3. *Strategic Processes*: These processes catalyse the intentional, communicational and collaborative action as a creation, governance, ethics and partnership process in the community informatics design development cycle that will allow to engage the members, designers and partners in the creation of the DSS. The practice community represents innovation in itself, and at the same time, it creates a future digital social system that will help generate other social or economic innovations; in other words, it is getting ready for evolutive action.
4. *Integration Processes*: The planning and the different DSS design phases are represented in these processes that bring the innovation community to commit to a dynamic conversational design process with its environment (physical, biological, psychological, ecological, sociocultural; situations, contexts, events, partners). The conversation must be taken in the sense of actions, activities and interactions through which members commit to the conscious DSS structuring that will influence its environment and will be influenced by it in return.

The community informatics design evolutive learning program that guides the DSS construction, the learning processes in place, the collaborative design and action is built in four evolutive development stages (Laszlo et al. 2002, 2010; Laszlo and Laszlo 2004, 2007; Laszlo 1972); we can describe in the following way:

1. *The Evolutive Conscience*: This learning stage entails the passing of an individual conscience to a collective conscience, challenges to face and problems to solve that go beyond a certain "egocentric immediacy" proper to the individual apprehension of a situation, a project or a given issue. The evolutive conscience puts at risk the expansiveness and the social skills associated with the aptitude to collaborate to the co-design and to develop cognition towards a collective comprehension of problems to be solved. It is acquired in the context of interconnectivity of the worlds and the "distributed" nature of the activities to realize. It also goes through an increase of empathy for others and the knowledge of their needs in the setting of an innovation co-creation process for the participant, his community, his organization and the entire society.
2. *Digital Literacy*: This stage involves a global and systemic understanding of computer-mediatized communication and collaboration, anchored in the reality of socio-digital networks, as well as processes promoting the participation to common activities through resources sharing and the digital badges to evaluate the twenty-first century co-design skills.
3. *The Generative Skill*: This generic ability seeks to develop digital skills and abilities for a behaviour in accordance with the prescriptions of the previous two stages, the empathy and the knowledge of others. It entails a personal commitment process as a DSS community informatics designer.
4. *The Generative Praxis*: This skills stage shows an important outcome in the mutual commitment and requires a permanent effort of openness to others and real and virtual worlds as a community informatics designer participating proactively in the development of his community, organization or the entire society. Community informatics design promotes the acquisition of collaborative knowledge and skills in the virtual worlds but also in all everyday activities, whether at home, at work or in the community.

These different skills and their respective development stages establish substantial foundations, the global context, the reference model on which the interdependence of community informatics design, learning, design instantiation and action forge a systematic and intentional conversation.

7.4   The Life Cycle for the Creation of a DSS Through Community Informatics Design

In this section, we will describe the life cycle of a DSS as a methodological configuration that we started to develop in 2004. That year, following a symposium at the *Association canadienne pour l'avancement des sciences* (ACFAS), we had published an article entitled: "De l'intranet à la communautique, ou Valoriser l'entreprise interconnective pour le partage des savoirs" (Harvey 2004b). The idea was to outline the different evolution life phases or stages of a DSS and of a construction model of a knowledge management practitioner's community. Actually, a DSS emerges from its creation stage until its dissolution or, on the contrary, until the reach of a certain maturity or innovation stage. We presented in this text the communication, collaboration, leadership and technology management and innovation strategic process outlines. From the complexity and activity theories and a transdisciplinary anchoring from the technologies and information field and communication, we were suggesting then a first approach to model and implant community information systems (human-computer interfaces, collective teleworking).

Then, we broadened this perspective in successive works: in 2007 and 2008, in various conferences, we suggested, in a schematic form, the complete life cycle of community informatics design (Harvey 2008), which we had perfected over the years in our Masters and PhD classes without, however, describing the methodology in detail. It is in 2010, in an article published by Sage (Harvey 2010), that we presented a community informatics design overall approach relying on B.H. Banathy's theory (1987, 1996) of organized activity, complexity and social systems design. We were showing then that, in order to innovate in the educational social systems just like in the co-creation of learning communities, the design research could constitute a valuable alternative solution to traditional educational technologies. The co-creation of virtual communities, educational ecosystems, e-commerce communities, strategic online business alliance platforms or non-profit organization communities can benefit greatly from community informatics design as a generic construction approach for these systems.

Nevertheless, the design of digital social systems and the sustainable development strategies advocated today throughout society cannot be accomplished in the improvisation nor in a development approach that promotes old ways of doing, traditional linear management or the implantation of closed systems. The community informatics design foundations and the collaborative learning culture on which it relies on largely are basic necessary conditions for conversational design and the joint optimization of social and technological. Thus we must understand the community informatics design as a commitment approach proposition and communities' animation, in a creative process that considers not only the present or local state of a social system but also its context, as well as its interest for a specific organization or the community and its innovation potential for the economic life of future generations (e.g. by mastering new forms of organizations and digital social systems well and their possible repercussion on society).

In the following paragraphs, we will present the general description of the community informatics design architecture of the digital social systems. We will refer to you, readers or site navigators, as designers. First developed by Banathy (1996) and his successors (Laszlo and Laszlo 2004; Carr-Chellman and Savoy 2004; Laszlo et al. 2010; Jenlink and Banathy 2002, 2008; Jenlink 2001, 2004; Jenlink and Reigeluth 2000; Reigeluth 1983, 1993), social systems design can be understood as a new intellectual technology that showed relevance right away for the DSS community informatics design.

However, in addition to social systems designer's works, we add a particular three-level effort. In fact, the life cycle suggested takes into account information and communication technologies and activities (Engeström 1987, 1999) that are associated with each phase of their implantation as well as their strategic management and ethics. Thus, to the four phases stated by Banathy (1996) in his digital social systems design description (*design solution space* or DSS), we add three more that allow us to directly incorporate ICT in the system's design and instantiation spaces. Figure 7.10 illustrates the phases described by Banathy (1996). We add an exploration phase (S1) preceding the "imagine" phase related to creation and representation; a socio-technical space (S4) that allows to perform the design of creativity technologies and social media, of technological architecture and design and creation assisting tools; and finally a prototyping space (S6) and a deployment space (S7), because a DSS depends not only on the quality of the collaboration tools but also on their large-scale deployment that involves social appropriation of new technologies and a sociocultural animation strategy.

On this last note and as we have mentioned in the previous sections, this "socio-technology" is not only a creative imprecision with random results. Even if the community informatics design results are always uncertain because this form of design relies on human relations, on uncertainty associated with multiple skills and actors' roles, as well as the difficulty to establish complex partnerships, the Community Informatics Design life cycle allow an exhaustive analysis of the many dimensions in presence. It also favoured a systematic operational instantiation of the solutions adopted during any social design project. Also, as it relies on the dynamics and trust between actors, emerging interpersonal interactions as well as favoured collaboration mechanisms, we could not ignore certain design and modeling norms. This involves not neglecting certain activities, certain prerequisites, certain procedures more efficient than others according to the case and the type of system to co-build. Instantiation flexibility does not mean conceptual or operational weakness.

Our works and observations in 2012 and 2013 have led the ACIL team to think about a semiformal methodology where socio-technical creativity is instantiated in three main types of collaboration support architecture in the DSS: social, organizational and technological architecture. These three great types of architecture, the structure and the processes from Sect. 5.6 serve as the base for the community informatics design cycle updating, which is combined with the DSS life cycle, because the design process, like the life of living organisms, is never completed. In this sense, community informatics design is the way through which a DSS, as living systems, maintains its structure while evolving.

We are conscious of the fact that researchers in social sciences or practitioners in information or communication sciences consider our reference model and our methodological approach too orchestrated or its planning too formal which could damage the "sociological imagination" or stop the creativity conducive to socio-digital networks' spontaneity. Nevertheless, as mentioned earlier, the creation of a social system like an innovation platform in an enterprise cannot rely on pure improvisation nor lack a formal programming structure. Even in the case of an emerging virtual community, our experience has taught us the importance of having a project management minimum and ethical design principles to ensure the realization of a DSS project and the relevance of this new social structure. Therefore, even in the case of a temporary social structure, we will at least speak of scaffolding, and in the case of a practice community or innovation inter-enterprises that requires a more systematic overall approach, we will talk of architecture. Since this last concept is not very familiar to social or communication sciences researchers, the DSS construction project overall and collaborative networks give it a large space within the community informatics design approach.

The decision to adopt a somewhat rigorous, systematic or relatively flexible approach depends on the situation, project, the more or less authoritarian or democratic nature of the system the partners wish to establish, etc. Whether it is for a more or less temporary collaborative network scaffolding or in the context of a long-term organizational architecture construction, our reference model is one of the first to be presented in English to the co-creators of DSS and online communities of all kinds. Without being an absolute prescriptive model, it still constitutes a reference model that inspires co-creation.

7.5   The Community Informatics Design's Seven Spaces: General Principles

From design works from a first course in community informatics design we have built in 2010 for the students in the master's program in communication at the University of Bayreuth, in Germany, we present our "reference model" or the basic community informatics design architecture which is based on seven phases (or design subspaces) such as we present it in a chapter in 2014. These seven design spaces are essential to the reflection and the activities linked to the community informatics design. These reflection and action spaces seek to document the design process and its specific life cycle. This process is not dynamic or evolutive in itself, but, once fed by the members' representation, the situation analysis, problems diagnosis and the research on partner's needs and aspirations, it will provide a support and intervention tool for the members so they can commit to establish a responsible communication for sustainable development and strategic innovation management.

Other perspectives can be put to contribution thanks to more specific social innovation guides for the analysis of social appropriation of new technologies or other design elements from the enterprise architecture, organizational modeling and virtual communities design and also thanks to technology appropriation or strategic implantation of online animation technique guides and to user guides for the strategic management of innovation ecosystems implantation (that guides the most part of our research in the present book).

All this preliminary phase is destined to establish a first enriched image (Checkland) of the starting situation (intuitive problematic, non-initiated) that will be useful for the definition of each project's life cycle. Life cycles are not universal, but they can look alike from one discipline or project to another. Thus, according to the state of the situation, the needs or the budget, the life cycle could be extended by a few weeks even a few months or years and will incorporate several methods, techniques, procedures and stages. In the My Portal Col@b project setting, the life cycle was a starting point to define theories, methodologies, the community informatics and communicational reference framework and the stages to overcome, in short, the detailed architecture. The task was huge but very stimulating.

The seven exploratory design spaces were mapped in the summer of 2010 (Fig. 7.6). These design spaces schematically represented an imaginary reflection territory explored, thanks to conversation and dialogue, and creativity in the action, as a possible space for concrete activities (instantiation process) being developed through "conversational design". In Fig. 7.6 diagram, we integrate the "conversational design" theory (Jenlink 2004), Banathy's theory (1996) and the works on activity theory from Engeström (1987, 1999) and Engeström et al. (2010). This "participative research-action" territory is traversed by an evolutive, recursive and iterative spiral where the conversation and diverse thinking modes are articulated around different dialogue modes (exploratory, abductive, deliberative). Here is the representation of dialogue modes (according to Anthony Judge's works on his site *Laetus in Praesens*) incorporated to the activity theory (Fig. 7.1).

We got inspired by the entire conversational design system represented in Fig. 7.1, starting from space 1 of Fig. 7.5, "Explore", and continuing our temporal

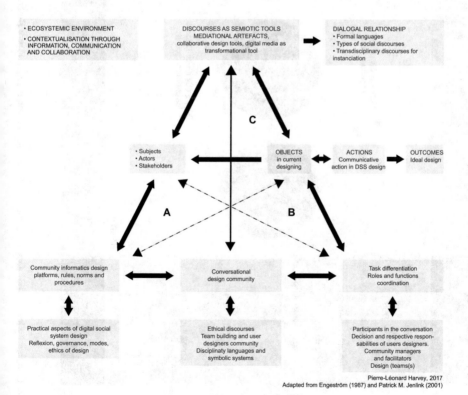

Fig. 7.1 Community informatics design, a conversational design subsystem as an ethical activities system (Adapted from Engeström (1987) and Jenlink (2001))

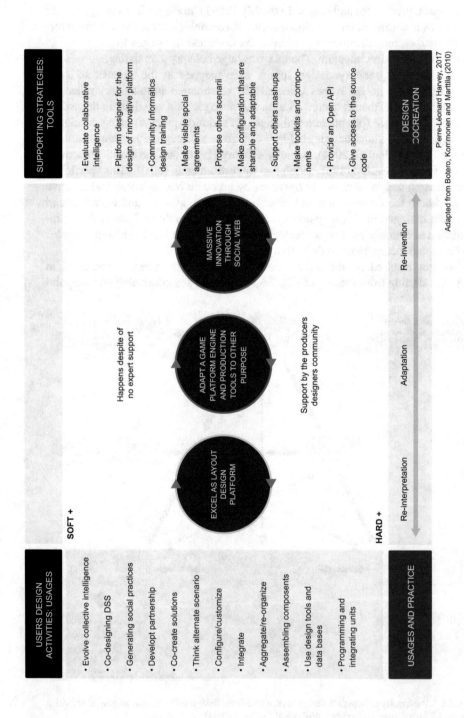

Fig. 7.2 Community informatics design's exploratory space illustration (Adapted from Botero et al. (2010))

trajectory towards the right, through space 2, "Imagine", and so on, by navigating outside and inside each space, like a film director thinks about all his project's steps, thinking about the roles, the possible scenarios, the infrastructures, architectures and processes to establish, the budgets and, most of all, the values and the ethical aspects to promote in the future design platform. Throughout this project's starting period, we have done a first reading of the situation, the possible way to improve the existing situation as well as the role of social sciences in the design and management of this type of project. We have summarily analysed existing social networks, recruited a basis team, thought of potential partners, the type of innovation (portal, SADC, business platform design) we would like to achieve and a social pathology to transcend or eradicate (job losses and need for innovation in Quebec). In short, we have started to verify the state of the situation and our own context (organization, extended family, university and colleges, local, community, global society, international network), on the members' needs, the required conditions, the preliminary activity calendar, the disciplines and fields to put to contribution, their ontology and the definition of fundamental concepts associated with the processes to implement, the roles of diverse actors, expert or citizen members and the contracts to conclude with various partners.

In this first space and with the help of the conversational design diagram, we initiated ourselves to the objects, products and services to develop, the applications to favour as well as the tools to develop, configure or establish from our first case studies. We have tried to consider the basic required digital skills to build our portal. However, we quickly realized that beyond the programming oriented towards the object by the traditional information systems approach, we should adopt a programming oriented towards the aspects (Basden 2000, 2002, 2006) or towards communication that includes various wider aspects of a community information system design problematic. For example, at the architectures' level, we had to go beyond the pure sciences technological architecture to suggest three other aspects: the seven spaces architecture, acting as a reference and reflection model, brought us to suggest technological, organizational and social architecture elements. Community informatics design, in fact, by combining social, communicational and technological aspects, must compose with the multiple aspects of a complex situation of which we will expose the main elements in the following chapters.

7.5.1   Community Informatics Design Exploratory Space

The present section is inspired by the APSI research program of the Quebec Government that works and seeks to define an analytical framework to understand the distributed and collaborative nature of what designers usually call the "design space" and that, within the APSI research of at the ACIL setting, refers to the community informatics design's exploratory space. The design space concept (Sanders and Westerlund 2011) is useful to understand the designer's act and the reflection in the action (Schön) that intervenes in design activities (Engeström 1999, 1987). With the collaborative design practice increase and the partnerships that put more and more non-initiated designers to contribution (Preece and Shneiderman 2009), our researches lead us to consider co-design space and community informatics design exploratory space concepts.

The co-design and the community informatics design space differ from the traditional "design space" concept because they can be conceptually and practically situated (Hutchins) at the very beginning of a design process (predesign), relying on the collective creativity of designers that work closely with non-expert designer communities. These designers negotiate very complex issues like social change, organizational transformations and DSS co-creation. They underline the importance of product, service and application instantiation in several fields that are more and more non-material like action and social practices. Our researches on action verbs in community informatics and in community informatics design, as noted in our different case studies and in both questionnaires, show that an analytical framework based on the notion of "community informatics design exploratory space" will substantially enrich our comprehension of community informatics design users' needs by making the experience, the exploration and the experimentation in the community informatics design seven spaces, through these spaces, from the DSS design to its instantiation in a portal.

This analytical framework is also supported by a more general one developed in the Fall of 2010, we call the attribute constellation for the analysis and interactive construction of standardized educational technologies (CAPACITÉS), and serves as a basis reference framework for the development of this more operational analytical framework. Let us remind that CAPACITÉS develops a systematic and holistic model of the appropriation phenomenon and the DSS and virtual community design. All with the help of a schematization that situates the appropriation complexity and the design generativity on two continuums: one, vertical, goes from technology (*hard*) to the social (*soft*), and the other, horizontal, situates the community's generative capacities in terms of needs and appropriation capacities of design tools. We will see later on how these modeled activities can inspire us in the creation of a concrete analytical framework, based on users' practices our theoretical and empirical studies have shown us (case studies and questionnaires).

7.5.1.1 The Design Space's Structure and Components

Therefore, from our works of the last 2 years, we suggest the community informatics design exploratory space to be conceptualized like a scenario and possibility space to realize a DSS that extends beyond the expert design concept to cover a set of design activity uses by non-expert people and communities, according to three interpretations or definitions:

1. The experiential design and navigation space in which design takes place (portal, infrastructure, social media platform).

2. The design space, in terms of activities realized by users in the work of the designer.
3. The design space of the possible futures often called "solutions space". These solutions are updated by the imagination of participants and stakeholders, with a prospective attitude that aims the participants' emancipation and the improvement of social and organizational life conditions.

The expansion of the design space (Botero et al. 2010) towards the design in use (first questionnaire) and the design in community co-creation (second questionnaire), as community informatics design suggests, goes through mapping uses and strategic practices of the community informatics design, by diagrammatically positioning the activities identified by the verbs and collaborative design possibilities offered to participants on a continuum that goes from consumption to the proactive creation. By doing so, we suggest an analytical reference framework to understand and situate the interventions for community informatics design research and a visualization tool destined to map the design activities. This represents a major result in our research because this new tool allows:

- To argue the fact that a community informatics design exploratory space is always actively co-built by a team of expert and non-expert partners and that it is explored by multiple collectives of actors through communication and social interactions and the social-mediatized participation by information technologies and communication.
- To discover the various co-design strategies through which the participants of the DSS construction conceptualize and instantiate the actors, the roles, the activities, the functionalities, the resources, the decisions, the management and governance modes as well as the strategies made explicit and available in the seven design subspaces in the community informatics design exploratory space. This design tool shows the functional and emerging relations between the seven spaces, the contemporary open innovation theories and the large perspectives offered to us to explicitly support collaboration and community informatics design activities through My Portal Col@b and its SADC. All these elements were surveyed in our questionnaires and discussion groups.

These activities are linked to the results of both our questionnaires and case studies. They are at the origin of our analytical framework and can be the object of the following questions in order to guide the action: In what type of activities are people involved in? What types of social appropriation of technologies do they favour? What are the needs to fill? What creativity, innovation and training processes could we put in place to support them? To build this framework, we had to refer to several lines of research like the collaborative ontologies, open innovation and budging theories on living labs, collaboration theories and collaborative and participative design, Gilles Lemire "verb theory", the meta-design of Fischer and Shipman (2011), Fischer (2010), Fischer and Konomi (2007), Giaccardi and Fischer (2008) and Wenger et al. (2002), on "virtual habitats", etc., which we have completed with our qualitative empirical studies and our observations on practices and digital skills in 86 practice communities in Quebec, Canada.

7.5.1.2   What People Do with the Tools

Figure 7.3 presents the basic dimensions of our analytical reference framework, the community informatics design exploratory space.

The vertical line represents the main elements of "what people do", in terms of design action verbs and expressions that translate a vision per appropriation levels similar to the different design activities illustrated by the appropriation and the CAPACITÉS community informatics design evaluation chart. Indeed, the realities of the design worlds are located on a generative continuum that go from *hard* types of appropriation (structures, infrastructures and technological architectures) to *soft* types (interactions and social practices relative to collective and collaborative intelligence), with the objective to illustrate and catalyse the different points of view to reconcile in the appropriation of the DSS tools and design because they are likely to complete each other in a co-creation and instantiation strategy. The horizontal line translates the dimensions related to the "generative capacities of tools appropriation", which seek to qualify the previous activities by letting us see they could be related differently to an evolutive continuum going from use (social media appropriation and collaborative tools) to community informatics design (co-creation, content production, tutorial guides and platform design). To elaborate more on the

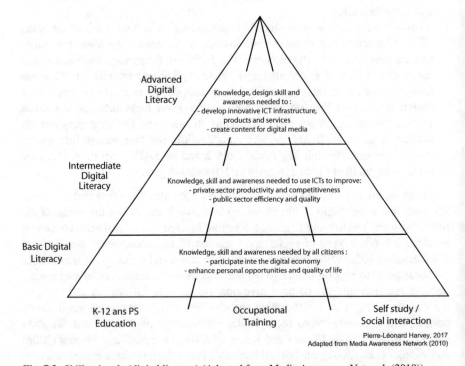

Pierre-Léonard Harvey, 2017
Adapted from Media Awareness Network (2010)

Fig. 7.3 Skills triangle (digital literacy) (Adapted from Media Awareness Network (2010))

operational vision, we illustrate the analytical framework by positioning three exemplary cases along the continuum:

1. Reconfigure Excel as a design platform device, which corresponds to the action verb "innovate in the use".
2. Adapt electronic games engines to collaborative tools creation – here we "adapt" or "divert" platform uses according to new intentions or a "wrong use" (Samuelle Ducrocq Henri).
3. Innovate in design and recreate, with the help of a collaborative platform like MediaWiki (Wikipedia), or use Joomla! as a SADC, in relation with the idea to "recreate" or "reproduce" applications by adding modules or extensions.

In this case, the particular position of a tool depends on the use conditions and the possibilities surrounding the activities to be realized, which provide users or observers with an action orientation in the exploratory design space. Let us look at it closer by defining each element expressed by a verb.

The inferior portion of these design activities refers to the composition/decomposition issues, the decision-making on material and technological resources and the infrastructure's identification/definition. It is easy to categorize alike activities usually associated with the tasks of design experts, the professional product designer or the computer expert. However, by identifying them in a socio-technical perspective, a *softer* categorization can emerge from it, if we rely on practice fields we have often relied on during our APSI researches: the science sector, technology and society (STS), human-computer interfaces, computer-assisted collaborative work, interactive American design, participative Scandinavian design, software programming, community informatics and social computing. All these disciplines address issues related to socio-digital design and collaborative technologies.

Each time an analysis level is added, the superior element aims towards the *soft* perspective that represents more organizational or social design activities. Some of the superior level activities pose a problem for certain researchers or practitioners because we consider them like real design activities if we look at them from a strict product or technological applications point of view. Yet, according to the community informatics design widened definition, which reconciles the social and the technological in the DSS construction or that considers virtual communities design as a socio-technical systems co-creation for the participative research action, these activities are considered more and more as design (Krippendorff 2007; Crilly et al. 2008), especially according to the current "design thinking" movement (Brown and Duguid 1996, 2000, 2001; Brown 1992; Dunne), which currently penetrates the field of information systems and community information systems.

To define and synthesize these *soft* design activities, we use concepts taken from previously quoted authors and the results of our research on the action verbs we have extracted from our works on case studies and two questionnaires. These two theoretical and empirical perspectives give a coherence and a concrete foundation to the suggested analytical framework, as well as the digital skills analysis framework (the skills triangle) necessary to support the passage towards the information society. Figure 7.3 illustrates these skills.

Program/Integrate/Write Modules: At the inferior level, like in the CAPACITÉS model, there is the digital and socio-technical systems design that requires a knowledge of formal programming languages and software programing algorithms (Apache, PHP, C, C++, Java, JavaScript). These activities require specialized skills in the mastery of computer languages, data processing and information management. They are performed by design decision-making, tools explorations and infrastructure integration that affect the final technological choices (platforms, software, social media). In addition, they refer to coding activities and data abstraction processes. The designs stemming from it are the product of very specialized professions and experts organizing modular reusable components for non-initiated communities. These modules provide high-level services for other design activities, especially through interface programing applications (API) users.

Using Modules and Libraries At the second software design level, software components are composed of different applications that perform relevant functions for DSS users and the community. These pro-software, tutorials and integrated community software rely on software libraries and underlying modular. These assemblies usually take place on the same computer. Their integration is performed by experts.

Assembling the Components The implementation of certain software designs does not require specialized expertise or particular skills. In the last 5 years, several user guides and tool kits have been designed, modeled and realized with the intention that the non-initiated can design their own community information systems or, at least, configure and personalize turnkey virtual environments for a given objective (e.g. the "Platform Design Toolkit 2.0", a work by Simone Cicero). However, at this stage, several applications require high-level digital skills because a programming expertise can sometimes be necessary. These various types of design activities aim to integrate new tools for personalization, the expansion of a platform by the addition of new components like plug-ins that allow the system to acquire new functional capacities.

Combine/Reorganize A complex ecosystem like the SADC evolves through communication services and design connected one another in a flexible and agile way. The addition of mashups, a recent evolution of Internet applications that represents characteristic functionalities of the Web 2.0 and 3.0, can be considered as a set of new design services created by the addition of information or applications coming from other Web services offering Web API in free source code. Today, a good part of the design activities in Quebec's virtual communities and elsewhere in the world focuses on digital skills development that combine and reorganize products and applications in a useful and innovative way. Several Web services like the ones from Google are used in the design of platforms and learning communities, according to various skills profiles we can define with the typologies and skills' verbs identified in our APSI project. Google Docs and Google Maps become prime services to manage diverse types of design applications like remote education or practice communities because they now offer standard mashups that facilitate and accompany various design types. We can also think of YouTube, Facebook and Flickr.

Integrate   Most software tools we use daily in our work devices are connected in some way to other tools, particular configurations only the user can disclose. When we think about the whole diversity of circumstances and use situations that occur in all kinds of communities from a diversity of work tools and creativity, we can only remain pensive in front of the formidable growing integration of tools we will put at the service of various designs daily and the challenges our future innovation strategies will face.

Configure/Personalize   This is an exploratory design space characteristic of the current social Web evolution where more and more non-expert users/designers engage in all sorts of design activities, products, services, applications and DSS. Sociodigital media and collaborative software usually integrate several types of configurations, virtual environments and technological assemblies that play a mediation and transformation for communications and collaboration. They also contain user guides and modes adaptable to various use contexts and personalized interaction.

Create Other Solutions   The discovery of replacement solutions designates the means users utilize to improve certain products, services or applications or perform using scenarios that transgress the collaborative platform limits. These solutions are not only creative; they are also a dynamic way to forge links together between the artefacts and the people around a common task or new ways to work as a team on a project.

Develop Partnerships and Social Agreements   A partnership is a contract between stakeholders that foresees the service provisions, the gathering of resources and the capitalization of knowledge in a collective project containing common development objectives. A social agreement represents a consensus surrounding a task or objective within a practice community or a DSS. Usually concluded at the initiative of a small leisure or work group, these agreements can evolve towards a more formal contract between two or several organizational entities (partners or stakeholders). The hashtags, the micro-blogging and the "working out loud" (Claudine Bonneau) allow to translate the collaborative work intentions or the tasks that force to "work together" and to collaborate.

Generate Social Practices   Social practices and communicational acts are human activity systems incorporated and mediatized by technological arrangement configurations of all kinds. The community informatics design seven spaces and the parameters and dimensions of the instantiation strategy represent a way to describe associations between management, design, collaboration activities and various resources, strategies or tools. Social practices and communicational acts are examined under the conversational design angle that allows to make decisions and operationalize strategies. Social practices are self-organized activities that last in various times and space horizons. Therefore, they evolve towards a set of governance and ethics, through a series of social agreements, partnership agreements, behaviour patterns and design called to evolve as the DSS communities will promote their own growth with tools, conventions, conversational design and the co-construction of new social forms and online DSS. For example, the current increase of video-sharing sites like YouTube allows to observe the phenomenal growth for the social link visualization need innovative social practices that invite members to invest and support audio-scripted visual conversations, by different types of use and visual languages, scenario annotation, visualization, etc.

The emergence of virtual design support environments and future ecosystems like the SADC creates new social situations for the design of community information systems. The analysis chart here accompanies very well the community informatics design instantiation strategy, because it refers to pragmatic activities where different actors, experts or not, are interested in concrete and relevant solutions for the future DSS construction. This means that original ideas, the imagination of new systems of human activities and the inspiration are innovation categories at the same level as technology design when we want to influence the dynamic composition and the instantiation strategy that guide the concrete articulation of the design's exploratory space made of the seven design spaces. In the same spirit, all design subsystems included in the community informatics reference model operate on an ancient tool basis as well as solutions, and new choices fall under the social and the technology. The collaboration realized with the help of this analysis chart and design guide by a good concrete instantiation strategy with tools and technology gives an enormous potential to the DSS projects in the near future.

The expansion of the traditional design space in an exploratory design space in community informatics design contains large social significations. If the "global generative capacity" of experts and non-initiated actors was increased by the open, fluid and collaborative participation of all sorts of stakeholders, in a plurality of society levels, types of use and design practices and that innovation communities would organize more DSS environments, if the traditional design space would evolve towards a continuous "design for all", the repercussions would be felt on the entire set of digital skills in Quebec's society. Thus understood, community informatics design represents, for more and more people, a powerful value added strategy of digital skills growth with the potential to positively influence the transformations that are currently happening in our society. We hope our research will contribute to this collective support of effort towards the information society.

7.6 My Col@b/UQAM Portal Project Methodology Framework and Community Informatics Design: A Reflexive, Creative and Collaborative Reference Framework

In this section, we outline several perspectives of a relevant multi-methodological configuration and a life cycle able to guide the decisions to make for the theories, the reference model, the methods and the technologies of the community informatics design (or socio-technical systems design) in My Portal Col@b project and community informatics design framework.

The management and governance system of this important research program is particularly well adapted to the co-creation of infrastructures for computational social sciences and the development of the digital communication field. It relies on the collaborative network theory of knowledge management (Camarinha-Matos and Afsarmanesh 2008), the theory of social systems design (Banathy 1996) and the Scandinavian socio-technical approach of participative design (Whitworth and de Moor 2009). It helps organize in a creative way the design activities of a practice community according to a given ecosystemic and communicational environment. We can design the future ecosystem like a DSS design space that relies conceptually on Habermas (1973, 1984), theory of social action, Engeström's activity theory (1987, 1999), on Luhmann social systems theory (1989, 1995) and Harvey's community informatics design methodology, inspired by the works of Flood and Jackson, Checkland (1976, 1981), Checkland and Scholes (1990), Ackoff (1974), Ackoff and Emery (1972), Banathy (1987, 1996, 2000), Krippendorff (2007), Moles and Jacobus (1988) and Manzini (2007, 2009).

In the present section, we will do the synthesis of a diagrammatic representation of the socio-technical systems seven spaces of design we can consider like a class of particular collaborative virtual environments seeking to support new socio-technical or community informatics designers in their design activities of virtual environments in the socio-digital media context. Community informatics design supporting virtual environments becomes collaboration platforms that are essential for a new class of contributors/designers of the free software movement and for the knowledge users/producers, in a wide array of fields like tool configuration software, online decision-making, problem-solving, social and cultural architectures and the planning of all sorts of online human activity systems like virtual communities, virtual university campus or business design platform.

We find all these activities in the heart of social sciences and the current digital communication. Mario Bunge (1999) calls them "socio-technologies" seeking social change and its planning. The implicit techniques can help to "virtualize" all kinds of projects or collaborative organizations, meaning they can support all sorts of complex projects that tend to use the media or social devices to manage, decide, perform follow-ups, realize the design, draw and work with the support of virtual environments in diverse fields and disciplines. In the case of our project, the community informatics design seven-phase spiral life cycle has served as a heuristic tool to evaluate the co-creation stages of a theoretical reference model, a governance model of the project and the semiformal instantiation framework of community informatics design, the object of the present book. Therefore, community informatics design benefits from two great development phases we expose in the following sections: a creativity phase around the seven exploratory spaces and a concrete development phase containing a specific instantiation methodology allowing to define phase by phase a series of detailed stages to follow to create and make a DSS operational during its entire life cycle.

However, like most reflections and current design, orientations are either guided by artistic approaches that contain gaps in terms of heuristic foundations, either by approaches that are too formal or too systematically oriented towards technology.

We would like to suggest an approach that takes into account design collaborative activities that occur in all sorts of socio-economic activities, like virtual communities dedicated to transformational change and in particular socio-economics (like the field of social innovation). In this context, we would like to suggest a new methodological orientation to help those new virtual environment designers (digital social systems and design platform) to discover products, applications, functionalities and assisting devices for socio-digital media design in a perspective of social innovation. Borrowing theorization elements from Checkland's (1976, 1981; Checkland and Scholes 1990) flexible systems methodology from evolutive systems design, Laszlo and Laszlo (2004, 2007) and Banathy and Jenlink's (2005) social systems design and Habermas' (1984) social action perspective, it will allow us, as a relevant programmatic questioning, to define our vision and objectives while organizing My Portal Col@b's collaborative design activities. Thus, we suggest seven iterative design spaces (Fig. 7.4) that represent the seven abstraction levels of the "design spiral", iterative, emergent and never completed, specific to community informatics design.

We have started to apply this method to My Portal Col@b co-construction that will be the first Quebec example, a first application of this original methodology that will help build the first Canadian collaborative design platform and one of the first international one that will help socio-technical systems design dedicated to innovation. The seven reflexive and practical design spaces pose a series of questions at each research phase, which will help UQAM's My Portal Col@b to incorporate their case studies, their need studies and their design patterns to design the best scenarios possible at a very early stage of the community informatics design's development life cycle. This is what we call the first creativity phase that consists of describing the seven phases in detail. The second phase, less flexible, semiformal and more logical, is called the rational phase. The exploratory phase is the first feedback loop. After successfully describing these first activities, which consists of the main flexible community informatics design's activity, the team of designers performs three other loops to get to the instantiation strategy. We will start with the first creativity loop by examining the seven design phase description.

7.7   The Community Informatics Design Spiral Process Socio-Dynamic

In Fig. 7.4 below the lines linking the spaces represent different iterative and collaborative design spirals. Each spiral is a spiral space in itself containing several entities or components that represent as many solutions or scenarios to build or to evaluate. The black arrowheads indicate the process recursive character. The white arrowheads indicate the recursive feedback process.

The first space, *Spiral 1, Explore*, is dedicated to the ontological and exploratory aspects related to theories, concepts and vocabularies that apply to our specific theme and our research object, community informatics design and knowledge

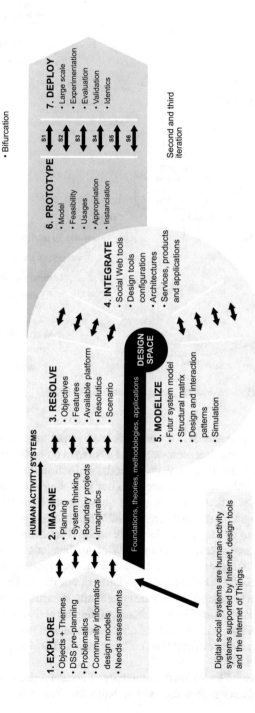

Pierre-Léonard Harvey, 2017

Digital social system codesign lifecycle : a governance system

- DSS metamorphosis
- Dissolution
- Maturity
- Bifurcation

HUMAN ACTIVITY SYSTEMS

1. EXPLORE
- Objects + Themes
- DSS pre-planning
- Problematics
- Community informatics design models
- Needs assessments

2. IMAGINE
- Planning
- System thinking
- Boundary projects
- Imaginatics

3. RESOLVE
- Objectives
- Features
- Available platform
- Resolutics
- Scenario

4. INTEGRATE
- Social Web tools
- Design tools configuration
- Architectures
- Services, products and applications

5. MODELIZE
- Futur system model
- Structural matrix
- Design and interaction patterns
- Simulation

6. PROTOTYPE
- Model
- Feasibility
- Usages
- Appropriation
- Instanciation

7. DEPLOY
- Large scale
- Experimentation
- Evaluation
- Validation
- Identics

S1 S2 S3 S4 S5 S6

Second and third iteration

DESIGN SPACE

Foundations, theories, methodologies, applications

Digital social systems are human activity systems supported by Internet, design tools and the Internet of Things.

LEGEND : RECURRENT INTERACTION
RETROACTION ⟷ READJUSTMENT

Community informatics design lifecycle: an approach aiming to enable and guide the expert and non-expert users/designers through the domain of community informatics design foundations, theories, methodologies and applications. The design space and its seven sub-spaces enable an "optional field" to guide decisions in the spirit of action-research projects.

Fig. 7.4 The seven community informatics design canvas

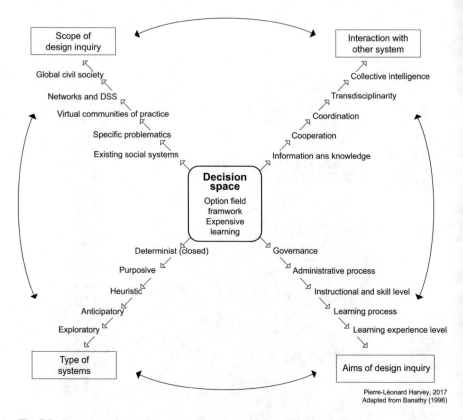

Fig. 7.5 An optional field reference creation (Adapted from Banathy (1996))

sharing in common virtual spaces. It is the analysis level where we start to examine the highest level of abstraction of a socio-technical system to co-build on a conceptual map of a type of system to build, objects to model and actions to define and the definition of the actors' role (in accordance with our modeling methodology). In this space, our research is articulated around the questions such as: Why use the "design thinking" paradigm for the design research? What theories or what methodologies would be useful to us (design platforms for social innovation, collaborative networks or knowledge management network)? What applications and what tools could be useful to us? What types of evaluation could we put to contribution (qualitative research, case studies)? What are the boundaries of our theme, our subject or object and our virtual environment? Within the community informatics design project framework and My Portal Col@b, it is about building an assisting community informatics design portal that, with the help of documentation and virtual communities case studies, aims to extract interaction, collaboration and design patterns useful for the creation of a SADC.

We will define ourselves like a virtual community of communities (a *meta mega community*) that, in a collaborative portal, will co-build one or several collaborative platforms or community informatics design assistance systems, which will later serve to build other virtual socio-economic communities and other business models of the network society, even other online and other innovation assistance socio-technical systems. Therefore, the suggested questioning reflects two parallel objects: our aspirations as a collaborative designers' community organized in partnership around a portal (My Portal Col@b) and our own intentions and needs in the construction of a community informatics design platform (the SADC). In order to make the right decisions, the team could decide to create an "optional field reference source creation" (Fig. 7.5) a sort of help tool for decision-making incorporating theoretical perspective to develop (in relation also with the hierarchy of Love's theories, in Chap. 6), as well as evaluate the society and analysis levels (with the CAPACITÉS model's help in Chap. 5), the types of interaction with the partners and other systems to consider and the system characteristics and components of the design to be realized according to the general objectives of the design process to develop.

Spiral 2, Imagine, aims to formulate the fundamental definition of a digital social system as socio-technical design ecosystem of community informatics platforms. In this spiral, research starts by asking the general questions: Why build a system dedicated itself to the construction of another community informatics design platform? More precisely, what are our intentions and our aspirations at the service of our community and the entire Quebec society? What are the aspirations of the ACIL and the colab members, their partners, the designers' communities and stakeholders, the government, citizens and enterprises? What is the common vision of all these people in the portal construction and design of an assistance community informatics design system, according to the social, economic and cultural objective our SADC will strive to fulfil? What is the objective or the common intention that will give all the members (those who serve, those we want to serve) a commitment and a clear orientation regarding our project? What is the apprehended methodological performance of community informatics design as presented in the present section? What are the other existing portals in our field? Where is the evolution of virtual environment for collaborative design assistance (or community informatics design)? From a detailed description and a synthesis of answers to these questions, we have formulated a complete definition of the future system to develop. One of the conceptual tools we have developed for this spiral is the "diagrammatic reasoning with the help of conceptual mapping" concept (Fig. 7.6).

The reflexive practice methodology illustrated by Fig. 7.6 is close to Checkland's idea of "rich image". It allows a team with a collective intention to do the design of a new digital social system and to build these "imaginatics maps" in three phases to share visions and common representations of the system to build. From these reflections made in the first space, "Explore", on the situation or the issue, the team:

1. Experiences relevant scenarios or alternatives, suitable for the design situation in order to continue the analyses
2. Observes similar systems while orientating its works on certain aspects, objects or norms to model according to the conditions, perspectives and constraints to foresee and the values of the users/designers group

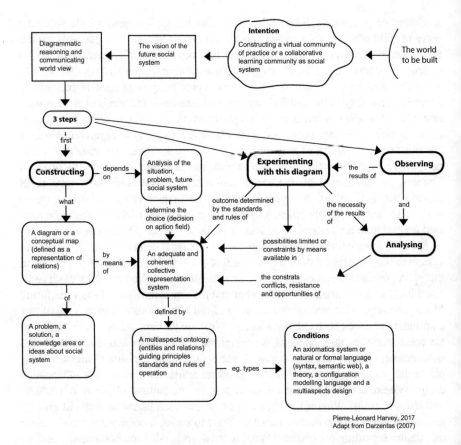

Fig. 7.6 Conceptual map representing the diagrammatic reasoning process and representations communication in a DSS project (Adapted from Darzentas (2007))

Spiral 3, Resolve, is a design space dedicated to the development of the collaborative design portal characteristics and the SADC. At the end of the project, the various basic definitions of information, technological and social architectures will merge into one single virtual design assistance environment. For now, we distinguish them, but when the designers' community will finish the platform, it will be incorporated into the UQAM My Portal Col@b. The research now gravitates around the following questions: Who will be the users of both systems? What Web and training services as well as design applications should we develop for them? What should be their characteristics and functionalities? Where, when, how, for whom, why and with what results these services should be created? To whom will the system or its different parts belong? How can we distribute the property and collaboration? What will be the rights, duties and responsibilities of each of the users and partners? How can we establish good relations with the different members, partners and the entire Quebec society?

How will the portal be managed? Who will receive the potential benefits? What economic model will satisfy everyone? The answer to these questions will allow community informatics designers to explore more in depth these scenarios and alternative techniques and methodologies and to select those answering best the definition.

In *Spiral 4, Incorporate*, the space aims to promote the coordination for the design management of the project and the general organization of the partners' communities' activities (governance), both for My Portal Col@b and the SADC, in order to obtain the best results possible for both expected realizations. The analysis of the portal's modules and the community informatics design platform functionalities will guide us in this emerging task of organizing our activities. The task now consists of executing the design of a subsystem, such as analysed and documented in the four previous spirals, and the one of another subsystem with the organizational capacity to operationalize and carry out its functions.

The management system designers seek to know what design will validate the system in the following tasks:

1. Orientate the functions
2. Energize, motivate and inspire people
3. Interact with other people, virtual designers' communities and the general socio-economic environment
4. Ensure the availability of information and resources to share in the platform
5. Engage the members of the new digital social system and the communities in a continuous organizational learning

Within the organizational design framework, we will ask ourselves the following questions: What individual, organizational and collective skills are necessary to ensure the functions identified throughout the documentation phase? What people and partners (at the technological and material resources, software, and psychological, sociological and cultural level) possess these capacities and skills? How should we organize and incorporate the material, infrastructure, technological, human and material components in a viable relational arrangement and a sustainable socio-economic model? What financial, material and human resources to allocate to which person or which groups? What communicational and organizational model promotes the construction of virtual and responsible ecosystems?

Spiral 5, Model, in the community informatics design context, is articulated on the modeling of four socio-technical subspaces, in the social action perspective of Habermas (1973, 1984), the activity theory of Engeström, the analysis framework of *Knowledge Commons* from Ostrom and Hess (2011) and communicational design (Krippendorf 2007; Harvey 2008; Crilly et al. 2008; Aakhus 2007, 2010, 2011). It suggests that the preliminary analysis of systems and subsystems of design activities has been performed in the three previous spirals. Its objective is to accompany the design and optimize the conditions of a virtual environment for collaborative design (or community informatics design platform) by exploring the tools, the devices and the ICT supporting the chosen design actions and activities and to suggest a series of technical orientations for the platform design. More precisely, we decompose the SADC in identical four subsystems with four distinct interaction spaces, each trying to map the respective categories of social action and design activities in an interaction design between designers and 3D visualization that serves to evaluate the state of progress.

Accordingly, we present a new design paradigm and digital environments co-building methodology for the new collaborative design field we call "Community Informatics Design", from which the implantation of a series of socio-digital media and Web devices will be part of the future SADC platform. It will be guided by social and communicational actions and the system of human activities for which the application's objective is to support and accompany the users/designers community in the definition of its four interaction spaces. First and at this stage of our research, we believe this approach can be used in the following activities:

• Provide several relevant elements regarding the type of actions and the different design activities that should be supported by tools with open-source code and free platforms and social media
• Guide the selection and the decision-making associated with the development and the configuration of communication collaborative tools and platform design as well as the most powerful metaphors accountable
• Align data, information, knowledge, culture and values with the tools necessary to capture them, memorize them, process them, produce them, manage them, learn them and share them while keeping in mind the ethical orientations of the project and its underlying development principles
• Report clearly the project's state of progress and inform the SADC participants and co-designers on the useful audio script visual support and on the social action and the completed design activities
• Create a matrix and a visual tool facilitating the realization of the four previous activities (Fig. 7.7)

In the SADC co-construction context, the 3D space will allow to model a complex ecosystem containing a static geometric structure, objects and dynamic entities, hypermedia conceptual maps, avatars and digital social systems simulation tools (upcoming); all these elements interact with the holistic environment of the spiral 4, which incorporates itself recursively with the six other design spirals and is, itself, as we have already announced, from four design subspaces:

• *The instrumental space*, where users/designers execute the portal and the SADC design platform
• *The communicational space*, where users/designers communicate with each other and collaborate
• *The discursive space* (or conversational), where users/designers configure their needs and requirements, modify them and make them evolve by expressing their new ideas and new concepts on the themes that interest them

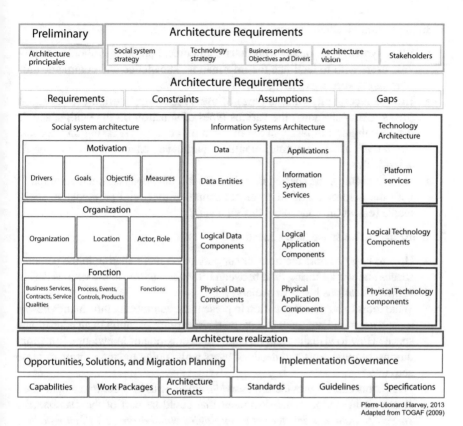

Preliminary	Architecture Requirements				
Architecture principales	Social system strategy	Technology strategy	Business principles, Objectives and Drivers	Aechitecture vision	Stakeholders

Architecture Requirements			
Requirements	Constraints	Assumptions	Gaps

Social system architecture			Information Systems Architecture		Technology Architecture
Motivation			**Data**	**Applications**	
Drivers / Goals / Objectifs / Measures			Data Entities	Information System Services	Platform services
Organization					
Organization / Location / Actor, Role			Logical Data Components	Logical Application Components	Logical Technology Components
Fonction					
Business Services, Contracts, Service Qualities / Process, Events, Controls, Products / Fonctions			Physical Data Components	Physical Application Components	Physical Technology components

Architecture realization	
Opportunities, Solutions, and Migration Planning	Implementation Governance
Capabilities / Work Packages / Architecture Contracts	Standards / Guidelines / Specifications

Pierre-Léonard Harvey, 2013
Adapted from TOGAF (2009)

Fig. 7.7 Architecture, vision and need principles (Adapted from TOGAF (2009))

- *The strategic space*, in which we define the roles of users and participants, partners and the socio-dynamic of their inter relations

In this spiral and its four activity subsystems, the questions could be the following:

1. In the instrumental space:

   - What basic elements compose My Portal Col@b and the SADC design and all their abstractions, representations and metaphors?
   - What tools (software, CAD, visualization) will best support the selection and management of the base and composition elements of the platform (My Portal Col@b and SADC)?
   - From the users'/designers' needs, case studies, documentation and the observation of competing transactional sites scenarios, how can we optimize and make more efficient the collaborative behaviour of users and their interactions with design activities and specific members' collaborative task helping tools?

2. In the communicational space:

- What synchronous or asynchronous communication devices should we provide users with to facilitate the information, knowledge and communication sharing between users/designers?
- How to incorporate various types of users'/designers' design uses to report (make them conscious) the various types of situation (in the work space, in the coordination of tasks, in the division of work, in the taking into account the situations of learning, context, particular environments of certain activities)?
- How to promote the sharing of points of view and ideas between participants with the help of a multitude of collaborative tools and participative social media (e.g. at the conceptual design level)?

3. In the discursive space (and educational):

- How to best promote the transfer support and content sharing in the personal spaces and work sharing (and between life-cycle spaces, in the various design spirals, at various levels of society)?
- What tools to put to contribution to present the community informatics design to new users and put them in a permanent learning situation in an educational space? How to visualize and manage the acquisition of knowledge from conditions, requirements and needs of users while doing the monitoring of these activities?
- What tools can we provide the users/designers with in order to annotate texts or any audio script visual document that could be part of the *Dictionnaire encyclopedique des sciences et technologies collaboratives à l'heure du Web social* (an online dictionary by Harvey will be soon available in the beginning of 2018 for the French-speaking audiences) and the construction of a collaborative ontology (especially the semantics elements associations of the instrumental space)?

4. In the strategic space:

- How to define and divide the roles and skills, duties, responsibilities and the respective rights of each group or community regarding the shared knowledge by each of the partners?
- How to follow up on the roles and tools chosen to visualize the various types of contributions according to these roles?
- How to optimize the attribution of roles and adjust them in an evolutive way (training, text and visual animation, technical follow-up, programming, integration of theoreticians, practitioners, community informatics and collaborative network experts)?

These important questions will guide the development of a generic and systematic framework in community informatics design.

Figure 7.9 illustrates the result of the answer to certain of these questions regarding the modeling space as a rich complex matrix that, by the adaptation to the life cycle of a given project containing its own architectures and basic functionalities, results in dimension monitoring matrices to take into account in digital social systems platforms. According to the team's decisions and from the options offered, certain collaborative design scenarios could be considered from these elements. Let us note that the chosen project's development cycle does not correspond exactly to the seven-phase model but that it is close since our team uses this base matrix (Harvey and Bertrand 2004) to model the evolutive architecture of the seven-phase design development cycle. It is inspired by Fig. 6.3 that describes the evolution of the disciplines intervening in the design with the help of the object/actors/actions' model (Lemire 2008) (Fig. 7.8).

Spiral 6, *Prototype*, operationalizes the models of two new systems. The portal should be prioritized in terms of systems and content architecture, whether it is the partners' ones or the ACIL ones, and the personal pages of professors and students of UQAM's communications faculty. All must start on the same line, at the same place. The examination of the existing platforms and exemplary portals in the projects similar to ours was realized in the summer of 2011, and convincing case studies were led the following fall, in particular on various European and South African living labs alongside following the SADC development.

At this stage of the project, socio-technical design is close to the final state as we complete our design description of our portal as a collaborative work space and the SADC as a design support platform for this type of online organizational structure (and also various other types of DSS). Such description can be obtained by the additional development of five models:

1. *The system/environment model*, birds' eye view of relations and interactions of our portal and its community with the environment.
2. *The structural/functional model*, the conceptual map and the objective architecture, cleared by the tools described in the second part of this present book.
3. *The activity model* (Trestini and Lemire; also incorporating Engeström 1987; Giddens 1984; Habermas 1973, 1984; Ostrom and Hess 2011; Krippendorff 2007; Aakhus 2007, 2011; Harvey 2010) and relational arrangements either the relations of communities in terms of project and governance management.
4. *The process/behaviour model* that gives the image in movement the way the inputs are transformed in outputs through community informatics design.
5. *The generic evolutive model* that simulates the transition states (Lemire 2008) and the complex transformations of the system in order to help designers understand the emerging socio-technical phenomena like the system state changes. This last model also incorporates the new tools and intelligent agents that accompany the intentional and natural SADC evolution (that we will present in the second part of this chapter).

The five first integrated models collectively represent a description both static and socio-dynamic of the ACIL's two systems (My Portal Col@b and the SADC), as well as their functional and operational integration modalities in real time and continuously: a real sociocultural representation of the new system and its environment (Fig. 7.9). They also allow to lead a series of investigations that validate

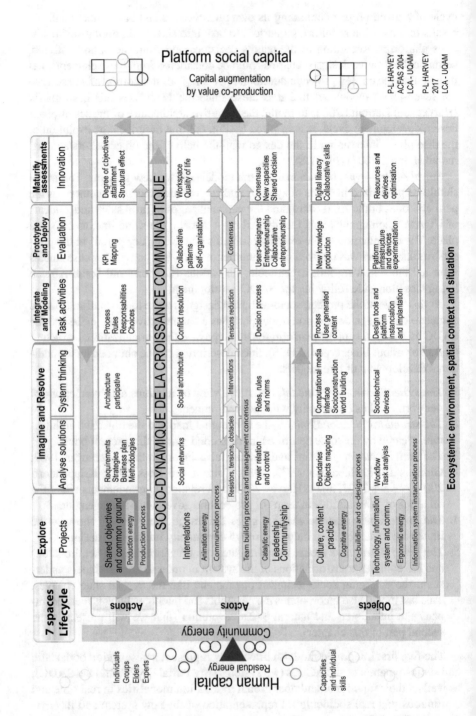

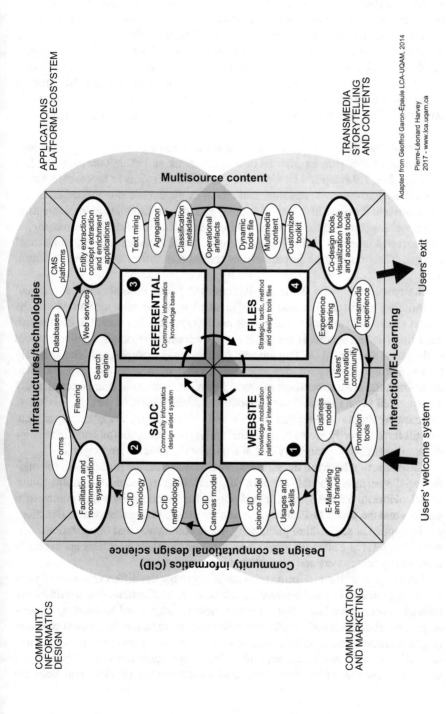

Fig. 7.9 Digital social system architecture: the SADC model (Adapted from Geoffrol Garron-Epaule LCA-UQAM (2014))

the work of designers/community informatics experts in the difficult task of evaluating and validating the equation of different subsystems of portal architectures
with the needs of users/designers and the viability of the SADC as a construction
assisting platform of such digital social systems (Hatchuel et al. (2011) call portals like the SADC "assisting platform to platform design"). The architecture
vision is another way to model the necessary functionalities for the spiral 4
model update. In accordance with our training objectives, the co-construction of
this type of architecture should be taught to our students throughout the next
years.

The last task consists of planning and formulating a prototyping and deployment plan of the various architecture subsystems and their components. The
model in Fig. 7.9 (inspired by CoSpaces and TOGAF) aims to represent a structure and a socio-dynamic development model through a socio-technical architecture similar to the one illustrated previously and to operationalize it, implementing
it in a viable prototype for all participating actors. The creation of these complex
architectures contains technological aspects but also social and organizational
aspects. Their realization is part of the community informatics expert's future
task.

The space of *spiral 6* is the penultimate task which consists of planning and
formulating a prototyping and deployment plan of the new systems from the
results obtained in spaces 4 and 5. It is not always easy nor useful to distinguish
these three design spaces. However, it is often necessary to obtain a generic model
of the portal and the SADC that are well operationally incorporated. This can only
be verified by prototyping that must be inspired by a valid experimental plan
made from different modelings of spiral 5. The various models are operationally
incorporated in one single design model, empirically valid in part. At this stage,
we know by representation that SADCs and citizen design work "on paper", but
we still have to verify their viability, their effective appropriation and their socio-
economic longevity, concretely and at a large scale, in multiple projects.

The distinction between the services, the functions and the processes of the digital social system is probably the most difficult thing to understand in this multi-
model platform. The processes that describe the functionalities like commercial
services and the user's assistance functions are anticipated and provided. Functions
can be applied at any level of granularity, while community and organizations' services are useful at a superior level where services and their interfaces are officially
managed by researchers and the partnerships organization.

The last part of the platform architecture regroups the different points of view
to be suggested to the architecture's stakeholders, as diagrams that would be too
tedious to reproduce here. The points of view are expressed to users by experts
as groups of architecture blocks schematically represented as crossed matrices
(e.g. a relations matrix and dependency links) or in a catalogue (as a checklist,
we will see an example in Chap. 10). These representation tools facilitate the
discussion on the SADC normative and ethical points of view and help the

knowledge sharing and the mutualization of meaning fields specific to the partners of the "five helices".

Spiral 7, Deploy, represents the implantation and validation space of the prototype by society tiers and the large-scale deployment one (see the society tiers and the CAPACITÉS model in Fig. 5.3). It requires additional resources to succeed in the territories or the relatively vast collaborative networks. The implantation of our solutions and applications in a large number of users/designers communities spread in virtual communities of all types or evolving in virtual environments that are the Internet's future is a task that should not leave all the space for improvisation. The current participative culture where everything is allowed must accept a design culture where the strength of network society, the information society, is channelled and catalysed in the best methodologies and in permanent learning of socio-technical design of knowledge at the service of socio-virtual systems of the future. Figure 7.10 suggests a simple model to visualize but complex and very useful for the evaluation and validation of a platform or a digital social system prototype and its design process. This diagram can help the construction of dashboards and quantitative or qualitative visualization tools.

An example of many aspects to integrate through a dashboard
enabling quantitative and qualitative data visualization

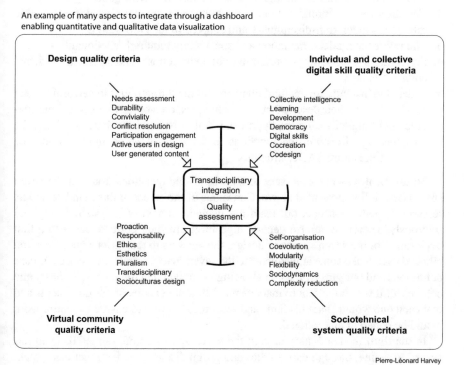

Pierre-Léonard Harvey

Fig. 7.10 Community informatics socio-technical system's evaluation criteria (Adapted from Banathy (1996))

7.7.1   The Seven Spaces Work: Towards and Instantiation Methodology

Once the first creativity phase is over and the answer to all questions serves to imagine the future system, its vision and objectives, the partners' role and their interrelations, the second creativity phase, supported by the spiral revision of the complete seven spaces cycle, has allowed us to have a preliminary idea of what portal to build and the future digital social system we would like to co-design. The first image we have obtained while doing this overview was to note the task was enormous. In fact, this first stage of planning was showing that in order to build a reference model, we had to enrich the theoretical foundations of community informatics and community informatics design. It was our first group's activity. This also allowed us to realize that we did not have norms nor an architecture to build our portal. While noting the seven space cycle spiral was a good creativity tool to start establishing solid and detailed bases of the activities to perform, we quickly realized that we imperatively needed to focus on five main tasks:

1. The situation diagnosis, through case studies and an investigation by surveys
2. The discovery of multifunctional architectures in order to develop a valuable reference model, transdisciplinary and adapted to the DSS design
3. The reference model articulation and specifically required functionalities
4. Perfecting a methodology promoting collaboration and management in virtual environments
5. A detailed instantiation methodology containing the activities to perform at each stage or phase, their description, the techniques, collaborative tools and the specific socio-digital media to support our definitions and our base ontology, the concepts' specification, the functions in the form of verbs and tools and the design of the entire SADC structure

To do so, it was not necessary to answer all the questions asked in the seven spaces description presented above. Conscious of the extent of this mandate and its research hypothesis scope, our team has decided to answer it systematically and rigorously. Therefore, after a general high-level brushing corresponding to a first exploration of the seven spaces of design, the answers to the various questions first allowed us to make some adjustments to the seven spaces spiral and precise our base definitions and our glossary, while allowing us to maintain the process's clarity and coherence. It was important to manage the different versions of our documents and that each one would share his finds and resources in order to ensure the entire work would be coherent and rational.

In the third feedback loop around the seven spaces spiral, our ACIL team has started to define, through case studies and group discussions, the functions system and functionalities that describe the precise activity articulation within a collaborative creation process aiming the creation of a DSS. The base definition of a DSS and the digital social systems typology established by our team, supported by characteristics developed in the two previous creativity loops, provided us with the necessary basis to consider the functions that our portal/SADC should incorporate and harmonize, as DSS or socio-technical entities, and to make the relevant decisions in that sense. The entire evaluation step of the existing portals, support environments for the DSS design and the "Leonardo" case studies have helped us a lot in this task.

The questions we asked ourselves, for the online case studies and the discussion groups, were similar to these: What key functions and sub-functions our DSS (portal/SADC) should have, in order to support and develop other DSS in the future? What services should we provide to the various types of users according to the types of DSS to be built? One of the keys to our reflection was, as suggested by Gilles Lemire, to think in terms of action verbs or activities to realize to provide the appropriate services and guide the activities in the two other feedback loops.

Another essential question was: To build the portal/SADC, how do these functions and their sub-functions interact and how can we organize them in a functions system? In other words, we were looking to identify the main activity categories; the main roles played by the members of our team and our partners, within each "functional universe"; and the way to link them to the various activities and class role categories to create a discrete subsystem of activities such as an organized collaborative network or a viable digital social system. A systematic and disciplinary answer made all the difference in the world, giving us the rigour of a rational method coupled with the heuristic creativity.

The fourth feedback loop around the seven design spaces consisted of giving shape to the functions defined by verbs, architectures and communicational and collaborative activity diagrams inside a schematic and generic architecture (organizational structure) favouring management, coordination and the integration of roles and activities in My Portal Col@b, as well as the community informatics design of other various types of DSS. The generic task consisted of incorporating the social and communication sciences dimensions to the management, computer sciences and public relations ones. After this final iteration in December 2011, we produced a general outline with all the components noted in our research to optimize the construction of DSS and of the portal. It is the entire DSS model, the *rich picture* (Checkland and Holwell 1998; Checkland and Scholes 1990), serving as a conceptual attractor to guide the daily, tactical and strategic DSS operations that constitutes a crucial step towards the updating of the ideal system visualized by the designers' community in space 1 and the first iterative loop.

At this stage of our presentation, it becomes more and more obvious that strategic conversational design produces language acts that generate generative detailed design processes and activity structures (analysis and research) that guide the DSS co-design. It is in that iterative modeling trajectory that the first results emerge from the first feedback loops to multiply as the conversational design gives rise to new operating concepts. This creative and iterative approach involves a trajectory that runs through the seven spaces in a transitory process, non-linear, through the overview spiral and the spirals represented by the spaces 1–7, by performing loops sometimes clockwise and sometimes counterclockwise of the conceptual map in a recursive dynamic of exploration and continuous creation.

While continuing to benefit from our readings, our document researches, our syntheses, our conceptual analyses and our results from the different spaces, we found ourselves committed in a self-generative process that is very appropriate for the reception of internal energy of the team and the lab members and to the external forces that structure the action landscape of partners and the socio-economic environment. It is the ethics conversation that makes the trust evolve between the project's partners and that contributes to the changes that promote the emancipation of each at the service of everyone's well-being. To better understand or visualize the community informatics design approach, we can compare it to rivers growing as other water courses join it, visible or invisible contributions, tangible or intangible, more or less important or relevant. The members and the partners interconnect while continuing to engage in the operational DSS aspects, progressively translating the rich starting image into programs, functionalities and activities to organize, to plan, to instantiate and to implement. This is what we will show in more detail in the following sections. We will see that between the methodological creativity phase and the rational methodological one, there is a logical link where the mind starts from the community informatics design's strange effect to enter more deeply into the more familiar methods and where the activity control processes, action verification monitoring and RD innovation capture are closer to logic than to flexibility. We will see that this only constitutes a logical passage between the implicit creativity of community informatics design, its translation into a more formal methodology and its potential passage into methodological ways or technical recipes accepted by the habit (e.g. the interview technique in social sciences or the research action). Thus, to synthetize these considerations, we will say that dynamic communities and enterprises must make a large place to creativity and innovation.

The creation of DSS is an innovation in itself, and the use of community informatics design is another one. We will take it into account in our reference model. We must, however, use these approaches to systemize more inventive methods at the beginning and that through conceptual maturation and practice become more logic and more operational in the value creation of the enterprise and designers communities. Potentially, the heuristic method evolves towards a more rational methodology (e.g. governance) to enter in the culture of a field research (social communication) and, finally, become an accepted and validated method by theoreticians and practitioners of the field make it a second nature (norms). It is in this precise sense that we can say "if you don't move forwards, you go backwards", showing that the methodological pluralism and novelty can be salutary for organizations and society. The new articulation suggested by a new philosophy of community information systems which consists of amalgamated interpretative paradigm, socio-critical approaches and neopositivism can, despite several obstacles, hold innovation and value for the entire socio-economic life.

7.8 From the Creativity Phase to the Rational Phase: A Basic Terminology

In this section, we will not come back on the theoretical and historic contributions related to the establishment of a reference model for community informatics. It is a task we will perform in other sections dedicated to the virtual organization architecture and to community informatics models. However, as we mentioned previously, a common problem in social sciences and in sciences in general is the absence of concepts and a common vocabulary as well as the introduction of new concepts coming from other disciplines to create a common conceptual base that might add even more confusion instead of clarifying things. We will therefore start with defining a basic terminology we can also find in the dictionary.

The establishment of reference models for the DSS community informatics design if often cited among the most urgent needs for the conceptual consolidation and the sustainable development of the field. Paradoxically, there does not seem to have many studies nor consensus from the community informatics fields, information systems and social computer sciences nor on what we understand as "reference model". In fact, our document study brings us to note that as for social science and communication research methods, this term represents very different notions from one researcher to the next which is translated by the varied perceptions of its utility for our researches. Therefore, it was necessary for us to reach for our dictionaries and the Internet to clarify the notion of reference models.

This task is far from being easy because confusion is king in the entire basic terminology of these fields. Knowing the creation of a field always requires basic vocabulary, we had included this important task in our research proposal of 2010 in the APSI program of MSG. For example, the terms "reference architecture", "reference structure", "system", "system architecture", "architectural structure" and several others intersperse with more or less overlaps. Without pretending to give a definitive sense to these terms, we believe it is useful to give a few definition elements and "generic orientation":

Model Environment, system or entity more or less complex from the physical, organizational, social, communicational or logical world. Traditionally, a model refers to certain particular aspects of a reality phenomenon. Two or three models of the same reality or same phenomenon can be essentially different or divergent, especially regarding the required conditions, modeling perceptions, conceptual approaches, theoretical or epistemological frameworks, ontology, aesthetic preferences, designers' experience or empirical studies. Accordingly, a model's users must understand well its underlying base intentions, its application context, its postulate and its validation criteria. There are various models at various detailed abstraction levels (it is the community informatics case), ranging from very abstract general concepts (praxeology, axiology) to representations very close to the entity to be modeled (a portal or a virtual environment) or its implantation (a collaborative design guide for the portal).

Reference Structure In the wider sense, work framework or conceptual arrangement that accompanies or frames another structure or activities subsystem. In the field of modeling (organizational or in information system), a reference structure can be considered like an "enveloping" contextual framework that may contain a certain number of subsystems, partial models, organizations or design patterns, procedures, norms, rules and tools (modeling language, DSS theory, ethics rules).

Reference Model Generic abstract representation that helps understand the entities of a system or a phenomenon (e.g. a system of human activities) and the significant interrelations of these entities (people, resources, functions) within a field and with other precise models, relevant for the particular cases of the same field. It is preferable to find reference models on a small number of unifying concepts so they can serve to other research groups to be usable online. In the case of digital environment models, as well as in education, for E-learning and for tailor-made training, to explain and analyse cases and make scenarios and most of all, to develop socio-technical human activities systems like DSS knowledge infrastructure, a well-built reference CID framework could be of great utility.

A community informatics reference model and applied science of digital social systems' construction (collaborative networks and virtual organizations) designate a generic conceptual model helping to synthesize and formalize concepts, transdisciplinary principles and better practices for the development of DSS. It is destined to have authority and provide development perspectives, design and animation guides, means to facilitate the co-creation of models centred on various aspects of the DSS as well as on the different types of architectures and implantation models useful to the development of specific DSS. A reference model is generic; its goal is not to apply itself directly to concrete cases but, instead, to serve as a base for other more concrete models, closer to the DSS construction cases, for example. It is the community informatics design instantiation methodology that gives the guidelines for the constructions of the DSS (see Sect. 7.2).

Architecture Abstract and schematic description of a system or a model; at a logical level, it tends to indicate the system's structure, functions of its components, their relations and their oppositions. Serving the development of the system, the architecture is centred on the "construction of a given system" and must be updated according to various levels of theoretical or practical levels. The word "architecture" is often used in engineering, architecture of buildings, software engineering, computer science infrastructure, in technology and management, in design of business ecosystems, in multimedia creation and in video game design. The role of architecture evolves with the professions and the fields of expertise because it depends on the various principles of development and available technologies. With community informatics design, we witness an accelerated transdisciplinary network between the Internet information technologies. Various types of expert and non-expert architectures will emerge from it in the next years as we refine our collaboration mechanisms with the creativity tools of the social Web.

An architecture can be descriptive or prescriptive. Descriptive, it helps the critic systems analysis and the evaluation of the impact of a given elements' configuration on human relations, organizational strategies and social change. Prescriptive, like in the community informatics design, the social architecture of our future virtual environments will force the possible fields with scenarios and particular forms of systemic arrangements and relational entities with emerging and original processes.

Community Informatics Design Reference Architecture   Not to be mistaken with the DSS architecture resulting from it. Channelled architecture in the seven design spaces have the objective of structuring globally and specifically the sub-architectures (participative, technological and organizational) in a particular field (here, we refer to the modelization of DSS infrastructure during co-design activity). It defines a unified particular terminology of action verbs, functionalities and roles of each system's component. By doing so, it provides elements corresponding to the different behaviour patterns or communicational activities specific to a social system, it suggests various architecture models accompanied by type scenarios or exemplary practice cases and it suggests a methodological design. The methodological configuration of community informatics design represented in the seven design spaces is the base architecture on which we can realize particular architectures' design (collaboration, decision-making, visualization, management) for a type or a category of DSS covered by community informatics and its social systems typology presented in Sect. 6.4. Thus, in the DSS field, a reference architecture for their design and management and for the virtual organizations represents the "structure", the principles and the guidelines to be followed by members to define the concrete architectures of a given DSS. The parallel creation of a data base for the reference architecture and the derived architectures (activity subsystems) also introduces the idea of exemplary practices to renew, reusable entities or reusable, "construction blocks". This helps us take our distances regarding the approaches that do not take into account the valuable theoretical ones or the ones that do not learn the lessons from experience, and this forces the designers to "reinvent the wheel" every time.

7.9   The Community Informatics Design Reference Model

The creation of a virtual community, an innovation community or any other digital social system or platform is a design and dynamic modeling process that must promote the best possible collaboration between members and partners. Community informatics design represents in itself an innovation process created by several orders' collaborative activities and at various organizations levels ranging from the largest collaboratory social system even overflowing the national borders. It must allow to create value for the stakeholders and increase their human, social, organizational, technological and financial capital. Community informatics design creates a value by offering services through a service portal, in the shape of a community informatics design assistance system. These services are provided as theories, concepts, methodologies, techniques, design reference guides or toolkit that favour the establishment of common activity grounds for the interaction, communication, cooperation, collaboration, management and the commitment of the DSS members.

After defining what a reference model in community informatics design is, we will now focus on the practical means to orientate ourselves to make it into concrete instantiation which constitutes one of our main expected realizations from the APSI program (the reference framework and the discovery of development norms that correspond to the hypothesis 2 of the research proposal). In the following sections, we will then define and present in detail the entities, elements and key components of community informatics design. These elements are the required conditions for creation, modeling, design and the management of a DSS in the entire life cycle of the community informatics design. In doing so, while presenting an approach and a complete realization architecture, we will describe the concrete architecture of My Portal Col@b and its contents that become our first guide or SADC prototype.

Let us note that we do not pretend to drain the reference model structure; we will confine ourselves to process the elements that were brought to the attention of our team to establish this first reference framework in the form of a design guide. The model could be improved and completed as part of future researches.

7.10   The Community Informatics Design Endostructure

The endogenous elements (or endostructure, the exostructure being the environment) are characteristic properties of the community informatics design that can help describe the DSS design elements and components. Initially, this modeling and DSS design vision rely on social sciences and Mario Bunge's social systems definition (1997, 2000, 2004a). Bunge situates the social system as systems that refer to the emergence concept and the emerging properties, concepts that are also related to the digital social system's concept. He states that each object of the real world is either a system, either a system's component. Accordingly, the emerging properties in the creation of social systems and digital social systems are always the properties of other systems in interaction. In accordance with this dynamic and interactionist vision of the systems he presents in the form of a symbolic equation called *CESM*, Bunge states we can model and entire complete system "s" in the following way:

$C(s)$ = Composition: the entire parts of the systems

$E(s)$ = Environment: the entire elements other than the ones contained in s and that act on some of the components s or are affected by them

$S(s)$ = Structure: the entire relations, especially the links, within the components of s or among the elements of $E(s)$

$M(s)$ = Mechanisms (or functions): the entire process that rules the behaviour of s

A mechanism is a process or a "function". Based on the precision given by Bunge (2004a), we keep the term "function" to describe the mechanisms essential to the survival of the system that constitutes the essence of its activities. For example, one of the main specific functions of a digital social system is to allow cohesion, trust and collaboration between its members which is not necessarily the function of a collaborative tool that has the purpose to build it. These functions can vary in time and in space and find themselves also in other types of systems (computer of non-human agents).

Departing from these foundations and various collaborative network modeling frameworks and DSS like the ones from ARCON and Ecolead (VBE), the works of Romero and Molina (2010, 2011) and Romero et al. (2008), TOGAF, CoSpaces, etc., the ARCON European project suggests a modeling vision that reuses elements similar to the Bunge model for the subsystem called "endostructure". Its elements are:

1. *The structure*, which includes the network structure of the DSS collaborative network and its structural topology in addition to people, their roles and their internal or external relations, structure we have named "situational topology" in another book (Harvey 2006a, b in Proulx et al. 2006) and links between the virtual spaces and the physical and human elements
2. *The composition*, which refers to all the parts of the system in terms of resources like humans and their skills, social media, creativity tools, collaboration technologies, information, knowledge basis, ontologies and specialized glossaries
3. *The function*, which, according to a DSS' characteristics, designates the procedures (code of ethics, management modes) and the methodologies (monitoring, evaluation) at the base of the functions and operations related to the seven phases of the life cycle
4. *The behaviour* (or mechanisms),which covers the entire principles, politics and management or governance rules that orientate and constrain community informatics design and the DSS, the community informatics design being the element that catalyses the DSS "socio-dynamic".

7.11   The Structural Modeling

The structural modeling helps to identify a diversity of actors, partners, social roles, relations and other structural characteristics, as well as their reciprocal links. The DSS actors are people or organizations that are members or that perform community informatics design:

1. *The business world*, which provides products, services or applications on the market and participates to the creation of organizations or virtual institutions with a lucrative objective
2. *The non-profit institutions* or NGO, which participates in the DSS construction to obtain qualitative benefits like social capital
3. *The partners' institutions* or project support, like lawyers, computing consultants or in social media information, Internet services providers, health services, insurance companies, ministries like MESRST or the *Conseil du Tresor in Quebec, Canada*, the association sector and the ecological organizations

If we go a bit further, several roles can be played by DSS actors. Here are a few of them we also find in the DSS community informatics design:

1. *The members* make up the users'/designers' core base or "design organizations" that are registered as participants in good standing with the community informatics design activities, especially the generation, sharing and the content arrangements.

2. *The administrators, executives and directors* are in charge of mobilizing and engaging the members in design activities, modeling, evolution, exploitation, animation, cooperation and promotion within the DSS. Among other functions, they determine and meet the needs in terms of skills and practical and collective abilities associated with the DSS development. They seek to recruit and invite potential partners, they ensure day-to-day management of the general DSS process, and they suggest means of settling disputes and lift the communicational obstacle in the community and the subgroups. They also detect leaders and the processes that promote communityship, they ensure the implementation of capitalization mechanisms (financial, technological, knowledge and know-how), and, finally, they define viable common policies.

3. *The director of knowledge management* is responsible for the data base or the digital library; he takes care of the production, classification, knowledge processing as well as their sharing modalities, their updating and their diffusion to various publics or target communities according to the public or private data, information and knowledge status.

4. *The collaboration broker* has the responsibilities of discovering partnership possibilities and skills to acquire through means of new collaborations, by using strategic monitoring, marketing and public relations around the community informatics design skills, and to recruit potential producers, consumers and designers.

5. *The DSS planner* is responsible for making the necessary digital skills for the DSS long-term management and expansion. Once it is built, by using strategic, commercial or technological monitoring, alliances or the useful partnerships for the evolution of the new virtual organization (identified by the broker), the planner can now think for the long-term policy options.

6. The *coordinator* is in charge of the DSS management during the co-design and throughout the construction and evolution life cycle, in order to meet the functioning and collaboration needs, to answer the emergencies with the administrators' assistance, to ensure the execution of the action plan and to organize workshops.

7. *The experts/consultants* are responsible of various specific expertise components, like the computing infrastructures, media design or the use of socio-digital media in public communication in order to assist the DSS community informatics designers and the administrators.

8. *The services providers* have the responsibility to provide an array of services like the Internet connection, collaboration support tools and development mechanisms appropriate to the various actors.

9. *The DSS ontology provider* is in charge to define, with action verbs and an appropriate terminology, tools, services and common applications to the different community or DSS members.
10. *The innovation manager* has to identify the government policies, methodologies and social innovation guides, products or processes and to ensure their appropriation in the DSS culture.
11. *The cultural animator* has the duties of planning the meetings, interventions and the cultural mediation actions and to provide the necessary tools for the members' commitment as well as establishing support and change tools promoting the emancipation of members and the quality of community life.
12. *The partner institutions* strive, as per the agreements and contracts, to maintain the DSS in place; to make it evolve by the resources service and the expertise in their field and by the upgrading of technologies, according to trends and the evolutions of the members' needs; to suggest solutions; and to provide optimal means of organizational or community development, in order to assist members and administrators in their tasks according to the specific DSS objectives.
13. *The guests* are the external organizations solicited by the DSS to play different roles in the information research and in the council related to the necessary grants for the longevity of the initiatives. They are eventually invited to be part of the DSS as full members.
14. *The accountant* is responsible for the budget, the opening of a potential common account, the respect of the costs according to a schedule and activities, the financial arrangements for grants and the respect of the norms and ethics procedures in this field.

7.12   The Community Informatics 8Cs

These different roles pose a problem in their interrelations and their complementarity in the community informatics design, in the perspective of collective intelligence and collaborative intelligence (network collaborative practices). The approach chosen by the UQAM's ACIL at first was to be inspired by the important works of Wolfgang Hofkirchner (2007, 2008, 2013) and de Christian Fuchs (2003, 2004, 2008), two theoreticians of the Ecole de Salzbourg who favour a social science approach focused on the "Internet research". These two researchers use three concept categories related to the production and management of social-mediatized information by the ICT: cognitive, communicational cooperative processes (the 3Cs). Our recent works show that these very important complex systems thinking concepts must, however, be completed with another series of integrator concepts that serve to report in a more specific way the precise "relation categories" that intervene in the DSS community informatics design. Therefore we present a brief definition of these concepts (the 8Cs) while suggesting to take it into account to describe the interdependence that takes place on the collaborative continuum occurring in the contexts of the member networking and the design partners:

1. *Connectivity*: Structure of various DSS socio-technical entities and the infra-structure process that deploys the base technological architecture for exchanges, through the ICT, allow to unify two people, a group or a community in an exchange process and creative conversation generating common benefits.

2. *Conversation*: Discursive process, widely communicational, that acts as semiotic mediation tool within the cooperative, collaborative, creative and cultural activi-ties. These activities are essential to understand and capture the interaction and interdependent design patterns in the social fabric and more particularly in the DSS construction. The use of the activity theory (Engeström 1999; Lemire 2008) as a reference framework to understand the mediation role of conversation and artefact design as a human activity system (DSS) represents one of the substan-tial inputs of our research. We will come back to it further along.

3. *Cognition (social)*: Process that, in the very wide sense, refers to the mental, especially emotions, motivations and the reflections that happen at the individual at intra-subjective level. Cognition considers the actor like an information pro-cessor. In the case of inter-individual behaviours, like in a situation of interac-tions between two partners, for example, we may talk about the beginning of a consensus building, the emergence of collective intelligence or a distributed rep-resentation. The information generation is more considered like a sense and shared meaning production. In virtual communities, if individual intelligence is the antecedent of collective intelligence, collaborative intelligence and the action intentionally oriented represent its outcome. We then talk about social cognition (Houde et al. 1998), the field of knowledge and know-how related to people that study interpersonal relations between individuals identified by personal and psy-chosocial parameters (roles and status). In the DSS case, they are in computer-mediatized interaction where the functions assumed by members within a design activity or a DSS are studied in the setting of creativity tools appropriation and computer-mediatized social collaboration that defines new social communica-tion contexts, mutual positioning, cooperation and collaboration.

4. *Communication*: Process of multiple interactions within a group of individuals or a community. These plural processes can be the object of a multi-level analy-sis of abstraction and practices at different tiers of society (see Fig. 5.3). They are information generativity and meaning evolution processes resulting from the coupling of cognitive subjects and social cognition mechanisms. For several years, they are the objects of studies, mainly in the computer-mediatized communication field (but also in the fields of Internet, social Web social, socio-digital media, the STS sector, computer-mediatized collaborative work (TCAO) and human-computer interfaces), all illuminating and stimulating fields for com-munity informatics design and the DSS.

5. *Cooperation*: Formal, evolutive and integrating process that concerns the supra-individual level and favours the information production and sharing and that emerges from synergetic effects (Fuller and Heylighen 2007) of communicating

and conversational actors. At the beginning, this research theme was the TCAO ones, computer-mediatized collaborative work and even the very important Anglo-Saxon movement of computer-supported cooperative work. In community informatics (Harvey 2008), the statement of an insufficient apprehension of technological reality incorporated to the social reality has recently led researchers to suggest the notion of user producers (*produser*) and ourselves to suggest, with other researcher groups, the term user/designer (Harvey 2010) to show the fact that humans are not only connected by computers but the real nature of this connection is human and cooperative. The consumer and designers' convergence and of the increase of the non-expert members' role in design and modeling of new virtual environments and DSS are the new Web application and social media's real underlying strength. The cooperation between actors is intense, but it only involves limited resources.

6. *Collaboration*: Process relying on mechanisms and previous processes to push cooperation further until not only the sharing of objectives and common activities but also the risks, resources, responsibilities, benefits and sanctions associated to them. Collaboration often underlies long-term activities and intangible and informal relations. It commands a common mission between partners and an exhaustive planning and commonly established. Communication channels and creativity tools are commonly identified and acquired. A collaborative structure or a particular DSS type determines the roles and the authority structure. The sharing of resources makes the leadership and power problematic an important issue. The intensity of sharing and synergies is reinforced; we are all on the same boat. Community leadership and synergy can result in communityship, a more explicit and global sharing of all constitutive elements of a virtual organization or a DSS conceptualized like a generative community. The results exceed those of individuals who act alone; in some cases, the benefits are more substantial than those of the cooperation.

7. *Culture*: In design, processes through which we favour the global creativity of a group and massive innovation in the DSS according to the values, the customs and the habitus that prevail. We can define a social creativity process like a cultural product, applications and social innovation development process. Thus, the creativity process is not the prerogative of certain genius individuals but a sociocultural generic skill to analyse, evaluate and promote at the level of an entire community or an organization. Furthermore, innovation processes must align (generative fit idea) with the strategies of other partners or stakeholders whose infrastructures, practices, habitus, technological customs, structures and creation processes harmonize in the best possible way the organizational cultures likely to converge or diverge. Then, with the help of Engeström's activity theory (1987, 1999), evaluate the sociocultural, economic, practical and distributed nature of the creation collaborative process in the context of the media and the socio-digital networks (as mediational entities). Therefore, we will monitor the exploration, commitment, clarification, semantics and representational negotiation, design conversations and the actors' argumentation, the evolutive creation mechanisms and the continuous redesign. The community informatics

designer and the community informatics expert must pay a particular attention to the individuals' commitment mode in the collaborative creativity processes according to the diversity of the partners' organizational cultures and the new ways of working in the computer-mediatized collaboration context and the computer-mediatized social participation. Ironically, social culture and creativity must also be the object of a modeling and an architecture.

8. *Contract*: A major difference between the community informatics design of DSS networking knowledge and the traditional object-oriented approach is the notion of co-responsibility of collective behaviour, common communicational acting or collective generative capacity (Van Osch and Avital 2010a, b, c). Usually, a contract exists to precise the respective obligations of a service provider and his client. In the agreement formulation, one must specify the calendar, the budget, the conditions and the methods of each of the partners. However, what is a little disturbing is that beyond the traditional characteristics, the specification notion must be processed in the most open and flexible way in the DSS environments, because community information systems that support the DSS involve fields that are a lot less formalized than the service delivery in technology or engineering in addition to put a wide diversity of roles at risk which complicates the strategic alignment of all the actors on a shared intention. Fields like social participation, culture, human relations, social creativity, innovation and the DSS structure belong more to a research and development context where everything can be put "in a contractual can" ahead of time and where the very own nature of the discovery collaborative context of activities to realize cannot be precisely defined without threatening the project's success. It is a paradox. Our APSI research seeks to increase the precision of these systems development, but at the same time, we must admit that the entire operation must play on the level of precision and abstraction of each subsystem or virtual organization or DSS' field in order to align them in a community informatics design strategy. Therefore, the collective action precision and imprecision are two benefits to reconcile in a partners' agreement.

7.13 A DSS Semiformal Typology

Finally, the community informatics design approach tries to rely on the distinction between several types of DSS which brings us to summarily propose a virtual organizations' typology (semiformal). A future research should bring us to perfect this typology from better formalized criteria of social virtual classification forms. Among the important criteria, let us mention time, space, hierarchy, heterarchy, institutionalization, generative capacity, information, entropy, the degree of freedom, the evolutive digital skills, the culture, the structuring degree, procedures and the work division/coordination, management modes, the size and the duration. Without justifying our evaluation criteria, because we will come back to it in another book, here are some DSS types that can be used as starting points for our students and the users. Our first analyses show the emergence of more stable forms in the DSS in the last few years: institutions (Wikipedia), virtual communities (Facebook), social movements (Twitter) and projects (Sun Teams). Here are a few emerging generic structures, more or less stable in time and geographic space but likely to help the structural modeling of a DSS and the decision-making:

- *The high activity team* accomplishes a certain number of intensive tasks within a certain delay.
- *The project team* accomplishes a specific cooperative project within a certain delay.
- *The collaborative work group* has formal and organizational design objectives to execute activities with an added value and to deliver products and services.
- *The informal network*'s goal is to produce and share business information, establish trust links and rekindle relations with new partners.
- *The collaborative network* is an alliance made of a wide diversity of entities (organizations, partners, people), largely autonomous, geographically distributed and heterogeneous in terms of environment, culture, social capital and goals. The cooperation is supported by the ICT.
- *The organization in collaborative networks* (online institutions) is a network of long-term partnerships collaborating to projects or common R-D. The objectives and activities are commonly defined in a "peer-to-peer network" of partners. The organization and institutionalization forms can be deep and durable. The rules and structures are well defined by a formal or relational contract, and the participants develop an identity and a strong sense of belonging on computer-assisted collaborative work platforms (e.g. Wikipedia). A strategic alliance contract between multiple actors, structured around a design platform, is a possible example. The free source code movement and the free software DSS movement are examples of global network organizations.
- *Punctual virtual community* represents a spontaneous form of unification, alliances or coalition, for a case like political activism, or as an answer to an emergency situation or a catastrophe.
- *The virtual community* is a community on the Internet or on another interactive platform of the social Web (SMS or mobile), made of a group of people interacting, sharing and using information in relation with the interests, characteristics or professional activities. A virtual community can be used for innovation products or social innovation in a community informatics design setting or in a logic of an open innovation community. This type of community does not implicitly belong to a formal enterprise network or a business.
- *The practice community* is a concept that EduTechWiki, by referring to the Wenger Gervais's book (2005), defines like a group of people working together and that is led to constantly invent local solutions to problems they go through in their professional practice. By sharing their knowledge and their expertise, these people learn together. This informal collective learning produces social practices that reflect the evolution of problem-solving and the interpersonal relations that follow. These practices also contribute to establish the necessary

vocabulary to establish tasks. Furthermore, they make a rather monotonous and repetitive work acceptable for participants by developing a pleasant atmosphere made of rituals, habits and shared stories. For Dillenbourg et al. (2003, p. 5), "a practice community regroups employees of a same organization or several organizations who collaborate outside the framework established by their organization".

- *The innovation community*: Von Hippel (2005, 2007) and his collaborator showed that very often, the technical innovation takes place in practice communities with experienced users. Even if this approach has been productive in the studies on innovation in a management perspective, it does not take into account the description of innovations implemented by the non-expert users/designers where the community development process is part of the innovation itself and where the process is a lot more spontaneous and emerging. Yet, the community informatics design project and the APSI My Portal Col@b state another alternative hypothesis. Our case studies which are about Wemotaci (the ACIL collaborative project as part of Guy Gendron doctorate studies), community informatics, CCA, Unimasoft, Cablexpert, the communication faculty and Botnia show it is not relevant to discriminate between the technical innovation and the social innovation in a practice community or the other. Our different case studies show that this development in a co-evolutive and generative "socio-technical" hardly apprehended by a causal relation and too strictly related to the formal enterprise modeling framework. We have discovered that the development of those two types of innovation can be better understood as a co-evolutive process where the technological infrastructure and the virtual practice community evolve by incorporating in their specific environment. This is why, following Van Oost et al. (2007), we suggest the innovation community concept as a way to conceptualize the type of community informatics innovation implemented from the users' experience where the community's co-design (collaborative design) becomes an integral part of the innovation.
- *The affinities community* is an important DSS archetype where the cohesion between actors and agents is motivated by a similar attitude towards certain products, services or events. The online consumer associations are typical examples of these communities that express their beliefs in social networks and act retroactively in different ways and via various media, especially by critiquing certain products in a blog, by exchanging experiences on the appropriation of certain services, by commenting the consumption's current events in the main media relayed by social media. They are the ones we call "prosumers", and these producers-consumers are sometimes very useful for an enterprise that specializes in innovation and that must launch new products and services. The experience exchange results in collective learning cycles that emerge from the collective intelligence and the digital communication.
- *The interest community* (in design) does not directly worry about problem-solving or innovation even if in practice, it sometimes does. It unites actors with a common interest like the discovery of norms for the DSS development or new innovation methods in different fields. The interested community gathers

stakeholders and partners from various horizons and practice communities. These participants meet to share information or to discuss certain common interest design problems. The interest community is a community of communities or representative of communities. Its members have a common interest in the co-construction and the global design problem-solving members that are unifying. Often temporary, the interest community is created in a specific context or environment to dissolve when the project is over. It contains a larger innovation and transformation potential than a simple practice community, professions or experts institutionally attached, under the condition to exploit the well-known "ignorance symmetry" as a social creativity source.

- *The scientists' community* represents the entire scientific core and researchers of all fields, its relations and its interactions, as an answer to the society expectations towards research centres and universities, namely, the production of reliable and viable knowledge. It is normally divided in subcategories of casts, schools and chapels more or less open, each one working in a particular field within an implacable meritocracy pyramid that reproduces itself in the light of mandarinate through symposiums, conferences and other intellectual and competitive private grounds. This functioning and the community in its whole are called into questions because of the emergence of social forces and new DSS in charge of organizing and distributing the knowledge (e.g. Wikipedia), which threatens not only the leadership of intellectuals but also the governance of the states that historically used to be in charge of producing and validating new knowledge destined to society as a whole and the training of young people. If, traditionally, scientific communities were exclusively enough related to a function an employment status or an institutional affiliation, researchers and professors of the network society must more and more associate themselves with all sorts of partner organizations and institutions organized in collaborative networks that generate new DSS like living labs, makers labs and colabs. These innovative structures invite researchers to take their expertise outside their labs to make it mature, to share it and to jointly validate it in the new fields of research of the knowledge economy at the service of sustainable development. The scientific communities go from the knowledge transfer paradigm (knowledge transmitter-receiver model) to the learning communities and community informatics design ones, responsible for a large part of the knowledge production in the network society (the dynamic knowledge appropriation and resources mutualization model). A new trust dynamic and open innovation is established and progressively replaces the authority, control and authoritarian logic of the hermetic "private clubs" of the industrial society.

- *The hypercommunity* is a hypermedia community that transcends the traditional boundaries of the enterprise, the region and the country. The current increase of global issues and borders crises favours the co-creation and management of collaborative socio-economic environments where the business world, governments, civil society and universities interact locally and globally at various society levels – micro, meso and macro – to structure common projects and establish new governance modes to lead these projects to success while allowing all actors to keep their identity, their institutional structures and their action properties according to their specific skills. However, all community partners recognize the socio-economic validation power of the "open complex networks" and the capital gains (social, financial, tangible or intangible) they are likely to cause.

By outlining this first semiformal typology of virtual organizations, we are aware of not draining the topic and to pose other important research problems, like the choice of criteria allowing to execute this typology. However, our ACIL team believes that it is the good way to show users, experts or non-experts, the necessity to better understand the online social forms in order to develop them in accordance with the social needs and, above all, to choose better structuring modeling aspects or objects to develop them.

7.14 Community Informatics Design Exostructure

The exogenous elements' modeling and their interactions with the external DSS context seek to identify the DSS interactions with its social, political and economic environment. By referring to the works done by ARCON and by relying on the works of Camarinha-Matos and Afsarmanesh (2005) and Camarinha-Matos et al. (2005a, b, c) and more specifically their book entitled *Collaborative Networks: Reference Modeling* (Camarinha-Matos and Afsarmanesh 2008), we reveal the following modeling subspaces:

1. *The market* that aims at the design with consumers'/designers' interaction and their competitors
2. *The organizational support* that refers to the various types of support services ranging from the infrastructure design to the institutions likely to support the DSS development
3. *The societal* that aims to model the interactions between the DSS and society in general and its various systems, like education, health and justice
4. *The organizational elements* that deal with potential relations with future members, the subgroups and the external group members, in innovative "morphological" arrangements or new forms of network organization

7.14.1 The Market Modeling

The vision centred on the market modeling covers an array of problems and issues related to the interactions between the communities and the consumers and those of the competitors or the potential partner institutions. The interaction of a DSS with the vast consumers market may contain elements like electronic transactions and the establishment of contracts (e.g. e-commerce), participation agreements or existing commitments and the marketing strategy, open externalization or branding.

The modeling of the competing elements may contain dimensions like the evaluation of other market strategies, equity or property policies, actors and products positioning in various markets. The account of these external elements takes us back to the intention modeling aspects, the mission and vision of the DSS and its value proposal for the socio-economic world.

7.14.2   The Institutional Support Modeling (and Potential Partners)

This modeling is related to the definition of various types of services the DSS is likely to need and that can be provided by public or private institutions or external organizations. Here, we can think about different types of entities like colabs and university research institutes, insurance companies, computing or management consultants, financial or logistics services, training institutes, certification organizations, organizational communication support enterprises and several others. We distinguish institutional support modeling that refers to the modeling of necessary services for creation and a DSS support and the partnership modeling that aims more at the economic collaboration models and strategic innovation partners in a particular field. The first one mostly aims the DSS design and the second one, the field of social or economic field in which the DSS will evolve.

7.14.3   The Societal Modeling

The societal modeling of a DSS in community informatics design refers to the strategic of the socio-technical relations structuring in the DSS (like in the virtual communities as community informatics study objects), according to an approach that is further, only in part, from the modeling management approaches to enter in a more open perspective of the innovation and participative culture. It completes the market modeling. Since the management approaches of the business process modeling (enterprise architectures) have brought a narrow vision of organizational design, community informatics design strategy, inspired by communication and social sciences, had to broaden these economy perspectives towards the non-profit organizations' – requesting a "social design" (Morelli) – to the government services, associations and community sector and the universities. We must keep in mind that the types of DSS we explained in our semiformal typology (Sect. 7.13) imply a comprehension of the field that expands to other forms of DSS, to other forms of socio-technical structuring and multiple aspects of information systems programming that are more or less tangible. This more flexible approach towards less authoritarian social forms or controls seeks to "put some network in our pyramids", without adopting an absolute approach where we would affirm it, a bit too quickly, that in cyberspace, hierarchy and control disappear. This counterproductive intellectual position is contradicted by our own experiences. The community informatics and the design only seek to enlarge the conceptual framework and the information systems discourse by adding social and communication-science concepts to it to lay the theoretical and practical foundations of information systems centred on the community and the DSS.

In fact community informatics is an emerging discipline (Stillman et al. 2009) that incorporates two orientations. From a socio-technical point of view, it borrows from the information sciences and social computing to lead researches on virtual communities design as DSS that are socio-technical systems themselves. The second orientation is communicational (with socio-political, semiotics, psychosocial and anthropological variants); it borrows largely from social sciences to understand the societal issues of the DSS implantation and formulate the sustainable development intentions that go well beyond the technological and business processes without neglecting them. For example, in addition to the technological and organizational architectures, the societal architecture modeling in community informatics design is inspired by the paradigms of a discipline we can call "community sociology" (functionalism, evolutionism, conflicts, interactionism; Harvey and Bertrand 2004), in order to evaluate their utility and their potential epistemological performance in the comprehension of technological uses and the daily relational behaviour of the members and communities. The community informatics analysis and diagnostic are enriched by the way each of the paradigms defines the community, information, communication and technology concepts.

The widened community informatics approach is distinguished from the general information systems approach because it enlightens the various ways information and social communication which are addressed in social sciences and computing while showing the similarities. Thus, for the past 10 years, information systems specialized authors such as Hevner et al. (2004), Hirschheim (1985), Hirschheim and Klein (1989), Basden (2000, 2002, 2006, 2008, 2010), Whitworth and De Moor (2009) and De Moor (2005) have shown the relevance of the Habermas communicational act theory (1984), Giddens's theory (1984) on structuring social relations, Luhmann's theory (1989, 1995) on the analysis of computing social systems and information systems and the philosophy of sciences from Dooyeweerd (1984) to establish information systems transdisciplinary bases at the frontiers of interpretative, sociocritics and positivist approaches. By widening the modeling perspectives, an entire research program opens to us in the next few years.

Even if the societal modeling aspect may contain a very wide analysis and activity that goes beyond the present connection, the basic idea is to better understand the complex interrelations between a DSS and other social systems, their repercussions, their issues and the problematic they raise for the entire society (innovation mechanisms, automation, delocalization, sustainable development, employment, regional issues, capitals attraction and investments). This perspective can help us understand the positive or negative elements of the DSS on the development of local economies, legal issues, decisional instance attitude, skills to validate, the level of education, the conflicts to resolve, the solutions to prioritize and the institutional roles to play.

7.14.4   The Institutional Modeling: Three, Four or Five Helices?

Even if community informatics design is mainly centred on the social systems, it does not forget about the entire "business strategies" that inhabits several collaborative network organizations and that is an integral part of the partnership activities. Thus, the institutional modeling includes various types of potential, individual, institutional, organizational, public or private members. In this spirit and as part of our researches on partnership models applicable in the context of the social systems construction, we were looking to identify the specific models to optimize the collaboration validation effects for the various actors aimed by My Portal Col@b services. Let us be reminded that this effort is part of our will to promote the emergence of new innovation validation mechanisms within the various actors of the Quebec society. Our research task was to explore and redefine a model we have called the "quadruple helices" that represents a flexible innovation model and multiparty strategic alliance as well as a management model aiming to explore the different roles of the stakeholders within a given ecosystem (region, local government, various organizations).

For 10 years now, several European research groups have been working on a triple helix model (Leydesdorff 2002, 2003, 2006) that incorporates the partnerships between universities, enterprises and governments. Today, we try to incorporate a fourth partnership helix to the first three by mobilizing and engaging the civil society in the start model, according to the social design philosophy centred on the user and, now, on the community. We are even discussing a fifth helix that metaphorizes and personifies a fifth innovation actor, the environment (Carayannis and Campbell 2011), or more precisely the environment ecology, in the communicational ecology sense suggested by Moles and Rohmer (1986, 1998) almost 40 years ago as founding entities of a new collaborative innovation diplomacy and a democratization of network knowledge. This stakeholders' pluralism and the diversity of the forms they can take, according to the particular intentions of the DSS builders, will be the object of our future researches.

For now, we have been looking into the quadruple helix model which focuses on the vast cooperation and collaboration projects that represent a progress even an intellectual breakthrough towards a systemic innovation policy definition, open and centred on the user and the practice community dedicated to innovation. An entire development era, linear, oriented from the top to the bottom of organizations, directed by products and services management experts rationalized in an effort and demand logic, gives way to different forms of co-production, co-creation, co-design with consumers, clients and citizens who progressively become users/designers of contents, services and applications. This transformation, highlighted in our case studies, our two questionnaires and our European living labs observation, is well illustrated in the last CEFRIO studies on social media uses (2011). It poses challenges to the university world and to public authorities in terms of new digital skills acquisition. In terms of productivity, it opens research perspectives to explore and also an important debate on the support means for a more inclusive growth centred on the ways to ensure a better connection between stakeholders and a more intelligent use of resources.

Our current works show that the concept of quadruple helices must not be used as a unique entity to be built but rather like a modeling matrix or a collaborative continuum capable of helping the decision-making in terms of DSS design and the observation of issues related to it: the communicational "holes" in actors' networks, the attractive factors for members or the informational gaps between potential collaborators, the ethics and trust issues, the construction of action plans and common meanings, membership rules, innovation marketing and sustainable DSS development, commitment and participation techniques, as well as the participation of the civil society in innovation.

Let us briefly cite four possible forms:

1. *The enterprise-university-government model*, to which we add the user/citizen designers, hence the quadruple helices
2. *The colab model* centred on the enterprise and the design of strategic alliance networks
3. *The European living lab model* centred on the public sector and the innovation research
4. *The democratic platform model* centred on the citizen

All these forms and several others are emerging in our knowledge economy. The analysis of roles, functions, design and management of these models in the socioeconomic innovated context can offer an entire array of research possibilities as winning organizational forms of the future. It could allow to shed light on the various government levels that would be very different from one social system form to another. According to the sector and production field, the structure of the value chain will also be diversified and evolutive. These models can serve as hypotheses for the DSS design in a later research.

7.15 The Community Informatics Design Reference Model

In a very simple and succinct manner, we can define the community informatics design management (CIDM) as a group of processes and functions associated with the organizational strategy and a DSS business model. The CIDM include the continuous design process and the DSS management, decision-making processes, the modeling processes and the implantation strategies that allow to validate innovation that these strategies aim the DSS creation, the innovation in terms of products, services, digital communications, social platforms and virtual environments or marketing and the brand strategy to improve the quality of the socio-economic life and to provide concrete tools favouring the success of the DSS and the organizational life (virtual and physical).

At a deeper conceptual level, the CIDM seeks to dynamically relate various dimensions attached to the life-cycle functionalities, like the DSS management processes, the partners, the design, the members, the infrastructures, the equipment and the innovation maintenance, by keeping in mind the political and sociocultural contexts and the environmental factors. The CIDM is the art and the science of using design to improve the collaboration and synergy between users, designers, experts, non-initiated, managers, administrators, researchers and citizens in order to optimize the strategy or the business process. The fundamental business processes can become central in the case of short- or long-term contracts and unavoidable for the DSS design and its competitiveness. Even in social sciences, the management dimension becomes a synonym of success and exemplary strategic practices in the conduct of projects like the current context of budget restrictions.

The design support process or the background process is strategic or business subprocesses that allow to operationalize the DSS in all its life-cycle phases and its development. The business process constitution, of a partnership contract or a business plan from a collaborative economic model, is an unavoidable activity in situations where innovation validation is performed by contracts, partnerships, collaborative networks and organization alliances. The general process underlying by the executed management is an integral part of the DSS community informatics design in order to reach a certain rationality in the definition of activities, tasks and actions associated to it. The community informatics design management process scope may vary and expand from the daily management to the tactical functionalities management of an organization's design, to the strategic activities design and collaborative ontological modeling or various processes, including operations, programming, human resources and collaboration processes modeling. The CIDM joins several types of professions, like multimedia production managers, enterprise architects and organizational designers, creation managers, design strategists, interactive and participative designers, animators, planners, administrators, marketing and branding managers, colab and living lab researchers and any manager making decisions regarding the community informatics design functioning modes at various cycles of the DSS projects.

Chapter 8
An Instantiation Methodology and Its Multiple Aspects

It is a common ground to affirm that today, all disciplines are in a crisis. Computer and social sciences are no exception. Contrary to what we diffuse in some fields, research centres and Quebec universities do not lack ideas, quite to the contrary. We experience the ideas inflation (Moles and Rohmer 1986, 1998; Moles 1990; Moles and Jacobus 1988), but it is the epistemological mechanisms and practices of ideas transition from the lab to the society that are at the heart of the storm. The crisis is also linked to the compartmentalization between disciplines, at the origin of the current view's narrowness and the difficulty to create systems that work and contribute to the quality of life of all members of society. In our field, community informatics design, an international reflection, began 6 or 7 years ago, and the *Community Informatics* journal founded by Michael Gurstein (2003) questions the theoretical foundations of information systems design and those of the related disciplines (human-computer interfaces, collective teleworking, social computing, socio-digital media, interactive design, emancipated design, human-centred design and, more recently, communicational design and community-centred design). This transdisciplinary debate is often located at a very abstract level. The present chapter aims to fulfill these gaps somehow.

In fact, for the moment, transdisciplinarity does not seem operational in the implantation of information and communication systems because we are lacking common vocabulary to exchange on our various fields. But there is more. The entire problem of field ontology or terminology refers more to a lack in the "sharing of meanings" between disciplines that do not communicate, as well as the fact that we do not have philosophical foundations to unify these disciplines, which constantly expose us to risks of useless verbosity and conflicts related to points of view. Without going too far in the epistemology and ontological questions related to our discipline, let us simply underline that we must make an effort of openness by observing the language of compartmentalized disciplines and explode the various speciality boundaries (as a reference to the Henri Laborit's new chart), to transcend boundaries and linguistics uncertain zones between psychology, with its emphasis on cognitive aspects, sociology for its social aspects, economy for its aspects related to costs

© Springer International Publishing AG 2017
P.-L. Harvey, *Community Informatics Design Applied to Digital Social Systems*,
Translational Systems Sciences 12, DOI 10.1007/978-3-319-65373-0_8

and budgets and studies in operational research on risks or aesthetics for issues related to harmony, balance, beauty and systems form. These multiple aspects, like we will see further, must be harmonized in the design and implantation of systems centred on the human. The contribution of several disciplines is a sine qua non condition of the description of fundamental dimensions of social systems and subsystems of activities evolving in interaction, through discourses, languages and artefacts. We will see a first attempt of this type of effort in the definition of transdisciplinary dimensions suggested by community informatics design and in the articulation of these dimensions in the form of a "fundamental checklist" that constitutes the heart of our instantiation strategy.

The presentation of the UQAM Colab's 8C's approach, the DSS formal typology, the metaphor of the partnership strategy quadruple helix, the activity theory and its normative transdisciplinary dimensions, the different modeling types of the endostructure and the exostructure of collaborative network systems, all that is to demonstrate the numerous aspects that concern the social or technological factors but also to push our analyses and design parameters further, approaches we need to widen while integrating them to the legal, management, biological and formative aspects of the community information systems development.

We have no idea regarding the number of aspects we had to take into account for modeling, building and commercializing a computer before a consumer could have one in front of him. So, we try to imagine the number of disciplines that must "exchange their spheres of disciplinary meanings" in order to develop a DSS. The worlds to build, the socio-construction (Lemire 2008; Harvey and Lemire (2001)) of DSS worlds to analyse, must tend to conciliate multiple meaning spheres to instantiate and develop a socio-technical system like a DSS or an innovation community. The computer expert will see a code to be used and a formal programming language to master; the psychologist will examine the interfaces appropriation's psychic aspects; the linguist will work from the information flow, the discourse analysis and conversations as well as ontologies management; the semantics Web specialist will invest himself in a vocabulary formalization; the sociologist will want to get involved in the improvement of the social link through collaboration; the manager will seek management methods of roles and resources; the ergonomist will manage backaches; and so on.

In the real world, there are no more economic or social problems than "disciplinary catastrophes". The world is not only a disciplinary procedure. Crises are lived in an "anthropocentric" and holistic way because they question the being and the communities according to several aspects especially regarding the perception, in addition to having a physical reality. Despite that, the entire world works in meaning spheres, according to various aspects, which generate numerous socio-economic repercussions and provoke interference between disciplines, practices, people and management modes and between reductionist world visions. However these world visions are intrinsically linked to real life problems, like cultural or socio-economic conflicts, they have a concrete impact on society, as they have an influence on every people's life. When we add to this the difficulty of current world crises, we can understand better why community information systems are so difficult to build and maintain, while at the same time, they represent a formidable simulation tools of social processes and an important challenge for the disciplinary evolution of social and communicational sciences in the future.

Let us look closely at these fifteen modal aspects without having to develop an entire philosophical background to explain them. From Andrew Basden's works (2008, 2010a, b, 2011), the disciple of the philosopher Dooyeweerd (1979, 1984), here is how we can divide the various aspects of a DSS, like all the meaning worlds that intervene in the design of community informatics systems. We also provide some orientations for community informatics design, accompanied by examples:

1. *The quantitative aspect:* the analysis of the number of users, attitudes, design generations, information system analysis and screen pages to create
2. *The time-related aspect:* the analysis of movement in a network, the simultaneity or the differentiation of activities, the tasks continuity and the components' parallelism of these tasks in an action plan
3. *The kinematic aspect:* the movement and transitions in the building of 3D sequences and in the construction of animated images, corporate videos and mechanisms related to acts and activities
4. *The physical aspect:* the energy, the forces, the mass; closer to us, the material resources, work environment, networking, technological infrastructure and collaborative platform
5. *The biotic aspect:* the vital functions; the human beings; the challenges related to the organism; the cognitive and physical ergonomics, illness or malaise caused by the computer; and the use of different tools, the environment ecology and any other pathology
6. *The psychic aspect:* cognition, emotion, users' psychology, interpersonal support, video or audio signals that transmit sensations, interactivity and multiple intelligences, creativity tools and reflexivity in the action and practices
7. *The analytical aspect:* the distinction in the information, the differentiation of tasks, the judgment on quality and the information relevance, the press and contents analysis tools, the discernment regarding the veracity of information sources and the knowledge classification
8. *The formative aspect:* continuous learning, schematization, processes control and monitoring, power to act, collaborative tools mastery, knowledge of remote education mechanisms or the DSS implantation/instantiation and learning organizations
9. *The linguistics, semiotic and semantics aspects:* the shared symbolic meanings; the conversational design; the mediation role and discourse transformation and of written and animated languages; the links between activities and disciplinary discourses; the integration of generative ontologies; the establishment of skills terminology; the writing of characteristics by activity field, texts and tables destined to the instantiation; the establishment of bridges between practices and disciplines; and the lifting of communication obstacles, dispute resolution, comprehension, memorizing, social and public communication and collective intelligence
10. *The social aspect:* social relations, partnerships, roles, functionalities, institutions, cooperation, collaboration, communication, connectivity, contract, the acting

together and the subsystems of activities that allow it, computer-mediatized social participation and communication and informational mechanisms of collaborative design, leadership and communityship, collaborative ontologies and social cognition and collaborative intelligence

11. *The economic aspect:* resources management, budget calculations, management sciences, sustainable development, frugality, budgets management and the respect of costs and spending, the responsible human development context, return on investment (ROI) and social capital

12. *The aesthetic aspect:* the harmonization of people, policies and values, trust, quality interfaces, educational fun social games, design and language games, attractive simulations, minimalist design approaches, colour balance, signatures and graphic chart

13. *The legal aspect:* donation, appropriation, people's rights, the Creative Commons licence, intellectual property, contracts negotiation, validation and marketing of products and services, social and strategic innovation of products, agreements in principle, partnerships conventions and fair sharing of resources

14. *The ethical aspect:* the citizen science approach, people science, third-phase science, donation culture, business deontology, culture of open-source code, gift of self, generosity, respect of people, intercultural openness, common social values, orientation towards the emancipation of men and women and recognizing minorities

15. *The vision and hope aspect:* the motivating and emancipating orientation, the actors' identity, the evolutive culture, the generative capacity of actions oriented towards the future, the members' commitment, the recognition of contributions, the lifting of uncertainties, the tolerance towards ambiguity, the capacity to settle value conflicts, the unifying optimism and the orientation towards change and innovation that requires the mobilizing of energy and resources

To conclude this presentation, we would say that DSS design and development can be done metaphorically, according to the requirements and required conditions of all their aspects like the integration and coordination of the "shared meaning spheres" (Sloterdijk 2002, 2005a, b, 2009; Basden 2000, 2002, 2008, 2010a, b) that, within collaborative networks with human and non-human components (Latour 2008), will create transformational mechanisms that, through conversational design iterative spirals (Fuller 1982; Fibonacci 2003), (Bohm 1965, 1996; Banathy 1987, 1992, 1996, 2000; Banathy and Jenks 1991; Jenlink and Banathy 2008; Luppicini 2008) will create DSS projects for the innovation under multiple aspects related to design and the community informatics instantiation methodology. We will see that these three powerful metaphors (spheres, networks, spirals) will constitute the visual metaphors of My Portal Col@b and the SADC, because they, respectively, illustrate the sense (spheres), the link (the network) and the dynamic movement (the evolutive spiral) animating them on the roads to the evolutive and generative DSS knowledge. They illustrate a sort of fundamental core, a creation matrix, a "graphic signature" and a creativity chart in community informatics design.

8.1 Instantiation Methodology Objectives

The instantiation methodology has the main objective to support the community informatics design process by the meticulous deconstruction of its multiple aspects, understood as meaning spheres or activities, whether it is management mechanisms, design processes, architectures, methodologies or resources that allow to operationalize the community informatics reference model in its various virtual and real application environments. The development of an instantiation methodology represents a great challenge for a small research team like the ACIL. This activity, which is not present or validated in social sciences, requires the combination of an array of models elaborated by a large number of authors in different fields. More specifically, projects like TOGAF, Ecolead, ARCON, CoSpaces, Botnia and Laboranova have inspired us greatly in the creation of this model and doing so under various aspects: the definition of partners' roles, the identification of information sources and knowledge, the rights and responsibilities of members, the democratic principles of development, the governance and management modes and the implantation of commitment and innovation strategies. The community informatics reference model and the community informatics design (the seven spaces) guide the creation and collaboration management process in a DSS to obtain and maintain up to date a coherent list of criteria and dimensions, as well as to define, describe, design, implant, prototype and operationalize practice communities and innovation strategies in accordance with certain communicational, organizational, social and technological requirements. We believe that these activities are greatly lacking in the social sciences and humanities and most of all in the field of virtual communities that has had several empirical studies for several years but that has not consolidated its application field theory-wise and the practice phases to reach.

The community informatics instantiation process is a semiformal approach (focused on the emergence), both heuristic and systematic, controllable in terms of time, money and validation process because it is rigorously defined and able to guide the enterprise or the community in the inference of activities' subsystems specific to the reference model or the community informatics' social architecture at three modeling levels: general, sectorial and particular levels. This process will allow to establish all the dimensions and conditions required for each modeling level: from the general required conditions (theoretical definitions) to the optimizing and specification of activities subsystems and various sectors or points of view (resources, governance, communication, collaboration, coordination, innovation) until the particular implantation in a specific field (communication software implantation or decision-making). For the purpose of the present book, the DSS instantiation process refers to the community informatics design process that characterizes the creation of the virtual environment (My Portal Col@b and the SADC's entities and components will be presented in detail in the following sections). Community informatics instantiation process describes a series of steps that supports the mechanisms, methodologies and techniques aiming at the generative specification of a DSS customizable model, by describing its components for a greater accountability towards its members and to capacitate them to realize the design of a certain type of DSS, of which the components represent the entire particular instance of the community informatics reference model.

8.2   The Community Informatics Instantiation Process

Before describing step by step the various instantiation mechanisms, methodologies and creativity tools that allow to personalize a life cycle and a particular type of DSS according to the needs of its future members, a strategy or a given business model, we will first define the generic analysis processes of activities and the basic functionalities.

8.3   The Instantiation Methodology and the Conceptual Framework Context

Community informatics design is a communicational activity by nature; it depends on the discourse as a semiotic mediation tool within cognitive, collaborative, cultural and creative activities that are essential to master the socio-economical and historical patterns that are an integral part of the society's structuring (Giddens 1984; Jenlink 2001). We will use the activity theory (Kant; Hegel 2006; Marx; Vygotsky 1978; Leont'ev; Luria; Cole; Engeström 1987, 1999; Jenlink 2009; Jenlink and Banathy 2002, 2008; Trestini and Lemire 2009) as a basic conceptual framework to understand the importance of the conversation's mediation role (and the conversational design) in the community informatics design, as a sociocultural perspective and a design perspective oriented towards research and enlightening the community informatics design relation, as a human activity system, as defined by Peter Checkland (Checkland and Holwell 1998), as well as the more general sociocultural context in which design activities take place. From Checkland and Scholes's works (1990), community informatics design can be understood as a type of human activity system, naturally intentional, which can serve to create new systems like DSS that do not exist in the real world (e.g. the SADC or any business design platform).

8.3.1   The Activity Theory

In the activity theory reference framework, the community informatics designers (the community informatics experts) and the participants of the DSS co-creation are guided by objects (what Pelle Ehn and his followers call *the Internet of Things*) or by expectations founded on their motivation to create an ideal DSS or more favourable to citizens, by addressing multiple aspects of information systems design, that go further than the traditional systems design perspectives (Basden 2010a, b). The collective creation activity is mediatized by the use of cultural artefacts that can be understood as a combination of series of rules, procedures, roles, symbols, management modes, cognitive appropriation activities, communication and language, collaboration patterns, structures and social and organizational processes, creativity tools and collaborative design platforms like a SADC. Among the important perspectives in the use of community informatics as a DSS design technology, let us mention the language systems (natural, computing, management, communication) and conversational design. We also consider like critical factors of the design orientation process, the set of sociocultural rules, to harmonize with the objects, members' motivations, their expectations, communicational requirements and the different aspects of the socio-technical design context (see the aspect theory of Andrew Basden 2010a, b). We also consider essential the entire management aspect of members in a partnership for social innovation and the entire context of stakeholders commitment that seek to realize the design of an ideal DSS, for example, in education, health or business, thus creating a designer's community. The community group composition balance between internal members and the partners is realized by a facilitator or administrator who designs the division and coordination of the work by favouring an authentic commitment of all participants in the change process. At the centre of all essential perspectives of this reference framework is the ethics perspective, the values and beliefs adopted by the participants that give a coherent social logic to the design community.

The activity theory is an essential reference framework to understand the different spheres of meanings of a human activity system like the DSS. It rests on the "relational socio-dynamic" between the subject (cognition and social appropriation of technologies), the object, the mediation artefacts (collaborative tools, social media and creativity tools), sociocultural tools, the work division and the designers' community structure as a human activity system dedicated to the DSS construction. The designers' community gathers people that share the same object, the co-creation of an ideal system. The rules refer to the explicit norms, the values, the criteria and the conventions that constrain the actions. As for the work division of action oriented towards objects and design aspects, it aims at the roles determination and the coordination of collaborative work flow.

As a sociocultural theory of human activity and learning, the activity theory focuses its attention on the interaction within the DSS and between people as the first source of communicational action, an interaction that will result in the objectification of the human subjectivity through social action. As we mentioned in the presentation of the seven design spaces (Sect. 6.5), community informatics design is based on the point of view of a "social action" concept for the identification and the intentional organization of detailed activities of collaborative design in all the phases of its instantiation and life cycle. The human activity systems are complex actions, activities and practices and interdependent design systems located in a historical, sociocultural, political and economic context (see the digital literacy triangle, Fig. 7.5).

The top triangle (C) represents an element of the activity system that helps define the relations between the subject, the object and the mediation artefacts. The subject of any activity is the people for whom the design activity is initiated. The object is the reason, the intention or the implicit or explicit result of the activity. The mediation artefacts, the tools and the media are both of cultural and technological origin and serve as "mediators" between the actions and subjects and the activities by which the object is transformed or is the object of a new design throughout the objectification process and, on the other hand, the human subjectivity (computing social or formal languages, various forms of political or socio-economic organizations, cultural or ethical norms, ideals supported by DSS projects).

The second triangle (A), at the bottom left, represents one of the interdependent elements of the activity system. This element and entities they contain describe the relations between the subjects and the sociocultural rules of the design community (related with the object, the objectives and the results) the community makes explicit, even formal.

The third triangle (B), at the bottom right, represents the relations between the objects or the intentional results, the community or the DSS in which the subject is a member of, as well as the work and tasks repartition to realize in a particular activity, in this case, the design activities for the subsystems creation. The work division should be designed in terms of description and differentiation of members or partners roles, as well as in terms of coordination and task management within the community informatics experts' community and, then, in the emerging DSS. The community informatics culture produces the DSS prototype, configures it, adapts it and transforms it as the individuals and the users/designers attend their various activities.

Connected and interdependent, the three sub-triangles (A, B and C as actions subsystems) make a reference framework for the analysis and design of a human activity system like a DSS or a community informatics designers' community. With this reference framework and the help of the seven design spaces life cycle, we will elaborate a community informatics design instantiation methodology as a complex activity subsystem and the relations that validate community informatics designers in the completion of their tasks.

In fact, the activity theory states that an activity, like community informatics design, conversational design and social change, is a social unit that involves a socially defined goal and the execution of specific social actions that have evolved in time and resulted in the achievement of this goal: a DSS co-creation. The activities contain cognition, communication, coordination, negotiation and creation patterns that interact with other patterns associated with the start of the DSS or the definition of roles, which implies the community informatics designer masters a series of creativity and collaboration tools like the symbolic ones (programming languages) to discourse tools (like communicational action, socially responsible communicational design, conversational design) and to process tools (like members management, collaborative project and community informatics design management) or a series of social media and complex collaborative platforms as illustrated in the Brian Solis (2010) conversation prism, which illustrates the use contexts of social media and its related activities. Let us note that, since the creation of its first prism in 2008, in 2013, Solis notices the extent of the conversational social media explosion that took place in 5 years (Fig. 8.1).

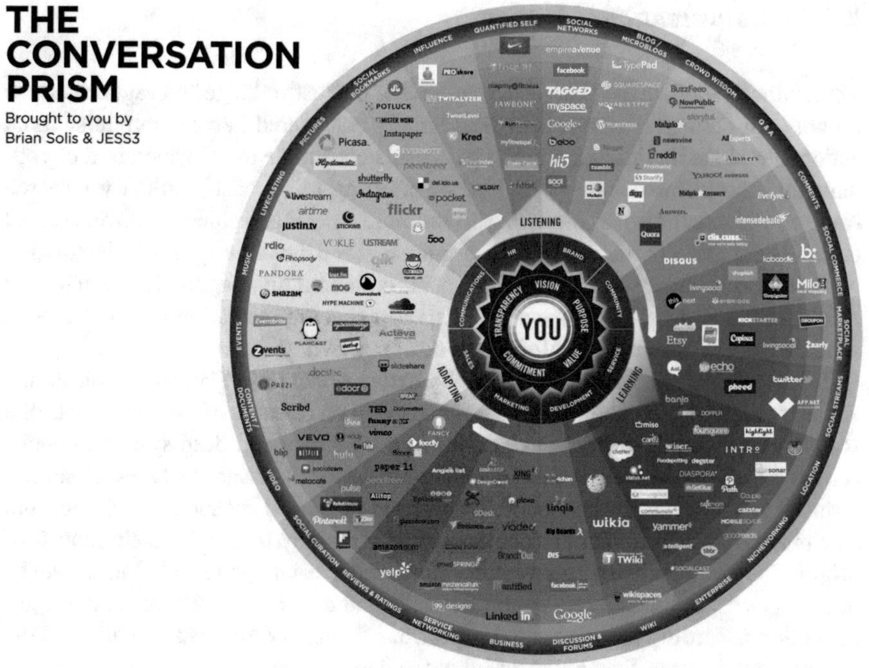

Fig. 8.1 The Solis conversation prism (Source: http://www.theconversationprism.com/ 1600x1200/)

The activity theory, applied to social media uses in the Solis prism, shows us that the social participation of people in conversational design activities is similar from one system to another. The ACIL team's point of view is that computer-mediatized social participation and collaboration contain fundamental activity patterns regardless of the tools used by the activity system to be developed. Whether it is analysing the world to inject some sense or to print new meanings with the help of various design types, we find the same fundamental simple forms. Even if each field or specific tool use contains its priorities, its components and unique mechanisms, fundamental activities come back in each field or DSS type.

Instead of different fundamental behaviours, we foresee differences in the context characteristics. Each context or field of application of a tool like Wikipedia or Facebook can produce its own research or conferences trend. Also, we could reform the Solis prism's petals with more theoretical fields, like the ones from our semi-typology (Chap. 6), and introduce activities contexts like education, health or business, collaborative network organizations, communities or synchronous or asynchronous learning networks, virtual communities, virtual organizations, social media, virtual teams, computer-mediatized communication, compute-mediatized social participation, human-computer interfaces, DSS design, etc. In all these contexts, the conversation is not just a metaphor for design: it constitutes a fundamental activity. Participation, commitment, management, negotiation and collaboration take root in the conversation.

8.3.2   Conversational Design

Thus, conversation, in the DSS design context, is not just verbiage or a vague dialogue on not well-defined issues; it is instead largely considered like a communicational action, a real media through which participants contribute to the generation of contents and the infrastructure design by committing to a transdisciplinary research leading to the creation of a new DSS in its multiple aspects and objects. Conversational design is not just a particular type of discourse, it is a dynamic system in interaction with other discourse systems (management, collaboration, negotiation), each with its objectives and its intentions and channels a specific mediation importance as a semiotic tool in community informatics design activities.

When we analyse it through the activity theory prism (Fig. 7.3), communicational action, practice discourse and orientations founded on research of various aspects of a social system, conversational design raises an important and deep system of social actions based on rules and communication mechanisms of various types, at several levels. These actions are mediated, mediatized and ruled by social languages and disciplinary discourses that are politically and culturally tainted by their context of origin. The complexity of community informatics design, as reflected in the seven design spaces, requires a wide array of fields and disciplines, reinforces our argumentation according to which we need various forms of discourse to realize all the stakeholders input as they get invested in the design process.

Community informatics design represents a series of communication and social actions that take place within a more general design activity dynamic (the exostructure). The community informatics design global activity system can be represented as a set of events, situations, project management activities, collaborative communication activities, processes, functionalities and interdependent socio-digital media. We will see in Chap. 6, a series of tables that follow the rhythm of the instantiation phases of the community informatics life cycle, that deconstruct each DSS functionality activity to transform each object or aspect into an operational and explicit intention. By doing so, we execute three tasks:

1. We transform a fundamental list of aspects, dimensions and parameters to explore into a series of intentional actions directed towards a goal.
2. We analyse languages and discourse of different fields (e.g. management, social and computing sciences) to use in order to make the design of an ideal DSS or a desired strategy.
3. We outline and create the DSS "enriched image" that would have the intention of improving social justice, equity, cultural differences, the conscience level reading various issues or even to create a socio-economic innovation strategy or a more ethical business model.

Without an in-depth exploration of the role of conversational design in community informatics design, we will say it constitutes a meta-conversation that incorporates each form of discourse, ethics or computer related, which contains each of the discourse forms associated with design activities: the natural language discourse, the strategic and generative discourse, the conversation in social media, the creativity tools that generate contents, the semiformal discourse of media design and collaborative co-design platforms and the programming languages formal discourse. The key to this conversational meta-design resides in the fact that we must train students and future professionals with the necessary skill to realize the effective transition between the discourse forms and use each discourse form in a relevant way at all stages of the design activity and life cycle. Like Gilles Lemire (2008) reminds us, as a programming tool, configuration tools, exchange and disciplinary sharing (at the same level as tools and social media), conversational design "instrumentalizes" the user, the student and the expert involved in the design activities.

8.3.2.1   Conversational Design as a Community Informatics Design Activity

In this context, members, users/designers and the stakeholders have two functions: they realize the ideal community informatics system's design and then the design and modeling of their own design process, and they redo the structure, processes and the essential social media design that are fundamental to their concrete community informatics design activities. In this sense, conversational design fulfills a mediation function that serves to mediate the activities of the community informatics system's global seven spaces of design. It constitutes in fact the meta-discourse and meta-design through which the community informatics DSS system design is created. In other words, there are two design strategies: the DSS scenario and the design strategy scenario specific to each DSS, according to the required conditions, the needs and the type of DSS to build.

Just like in the ideal concept of "social system design" put forward by Bela Banathy (1987, 1992, 1996, 2000; Banathy and Jenlink 2005), which is a central source of inspiration for the DSS community informatics design, the activity theory recognizes the importance of the mediation role of the conversation in the analysis and the multi-aspect design of these systems. Also, language is a mediation tool between the community informatics design and the activity theory. By pushing even further, several great theoreticians (Bausch and Flanagan 2013; Bausch 2000, 2001; Jones 2008, 2010; Jones et al. 2007; Christakis and Bausch 2006; Warfield 1976, 1990, 1999; Pask 1975a, b, 1976) have recognized the importance of the dialogue and the conversation in the DSS design thanks to the conversational power of the socio-digital media. We can consider that contrary to the mass communication media, social or socio-digital media, through the great interactivity and interconnectivity capacity they allow (blogs, chat rooms, online forums, videoconference, creativity, machine learning tools, cyber-physical system tools and design assistance tools), represent several modalities of the social conversation that is necessary to properly understand the mediation role in the future DSS in order to improve our skills in their design. But that is not all. The conversation instantiation incorporates socio-digital media like an operationalization chart of the exchange and collaboration between active participants in the DSS creation.

Indeed, when we observe and analyse conversational design nor only in its mediation role but also as an activity, the researcher's attention goes from the socio-digital media mediation role to the transformation role, in the reference framework of the activity theory. As an activity system (or subsystem), conversational design focuses its attention on the object and the activity aspects within the global activity system design represented by the seven spaces. More precisely, if we consider that the human activity system (e.g. a portal like the Colab, dedicated to the design of DSS) is a set of interdependent activities, the design of a community informatics system must consider the object or the particular aspects of each design activity. The discourse form, the social or technical language, formal or semiformal, the type of socio-digital media and the communicational platform collaborative design network are semiotic tools that "mediatize" or mediate the stakeholders and users/designers social actions.

These semiotic forms of technical and social discourse are largely determined by the inherent objects and aspects of each of the activity subspaces instantiated in the instantiation methodology analysis chart we will present in the next section: at each activity subspace in all the life-cycle phases, ethics rules, sociocultural norms, a social or community structure and a work distribution/coordination specific to a field which influence the design activities. The seven spaces "instantiation field" is a complex attractor of discursive activities, a conversational field that constitutes a matrix for the community informatics design conversation. In fact, each discourse form or each allowed discourse modality contains a certain number of technical and sociocultural rules, its ontology and specific terminology, its interaction and cooperation patterns and specific collaborative social actions so that each design field has its unique discourse, like the present book, for better or for worse.

Each conversation field of each sub-field of activity contributes to the evolution of the matrices that supports the conversational design and the community informatics design in all its entities, elements and world aspects to be instantiated (management, collaboration, rules). Let us note that for our students, each field of activities and each discourse field associated to it represent a series of functions and functionalities relatively well observable and classifiable. In fact, within the reference framework of the activity theory, the conversational field is generated in and through the relations between the subject, the mediational field and the language, as well as through the object and its aspects. The influence of socio-technical and sociocultural rules can allow to observe the object transformations (a DSS) and its diverse aspects on the design activity through the mediation discourse, that in return, helps to structure the social or organizational transformation processes.

One of the most important points to remember is that the type of discourse and hyper media language ("audioscriptovisual", 3D animation, schematization, process visualization) used as a modeling semiotic tool influences the object transformation in all its aspects (the DSS and its various cognitive, social, technological, functional or aesthetic aspects) into a community informatics design system dedicated to the co-creation of the ideal DSS. Once again, the double function of conversational design, as a mediation tool and an activity allowing the instantiation of concrete design activities' subsystems, refers to the double user/designer role of the stakeholders, a critical role for the understanding of conversational design as an inherent and essential activity system in community informatics design.

The attentive reader will understand that as an activity system, conversational design requires the differentiation of roles, functions and work values, and the cooperation of many proactive partners and futures DSS members' in the planning and coordination of a series of design activities mediatized by discourses and social media (see Fig. 7.1). The participation of all stakeholders (experts and non-initiated) as users/designers represents a fundamental characteristic of the conversational field construction and the instantiation methodology of the definition matrix of activities at each phase of the seven design spaces' life cycle. It is a fundamental characteristic of meta-design, which, by searching to define the forms and the different semiotic registers of the discourse in all activities subsystems sections, seeks to update and operationalize community informatics design in its various aspects.

As we will concretely see below, the conversational patterns are built by the instantiation of activities and activities subsystems specific to the design of a particular DSS type. Conversational patterns and evolutive and generative ontologies are built through the different design activities we will examine in the following section. In return, the energy and dynamic of exchanges resulting from the identification of the various forms of discourse and modeling languages make the language patterns evolve and generate a potential for creativity and transformation at a superior level. It is one of the fundamental inputs of our research, because even if the language identification is never an enclosed or premeditated exercise, it is important to define the disciplinary terms partially unified to facilitate the collaboration between people and communities of all horizons.

8.3.2.2   The Community Informatics Design Fundamental Processes: Verbs and Instantiation Activities

In this section, we will define with verbs and design activity expressions a series of operations to realize that we will find in the community informatics design instantiation methodology charts (In Chap. 6).

Manage the members and the management structure   Set of activities and support tools allowing the members integration, their accreditation, their banishment, their recruitment and the categorization of their status within a DSS. This operation is spread into mechanisms dedicated to the members' registration, the roles assignment and the work and responsibilities distribution.

Manage digital skills   Set of activities and tools helping the design and creation of digital and collective skill profiles (Le Boterf and the Canadian Alliance) of the DSS members, to identify the DSS digital skills, what we call, with Van Osch and Avital (2010b), the "collective generative capacity". It is the generic capacity of a DSS or a virtual community to collectively commit to the production of new socio-technical configurations and new creation possibilities as well as to the conceptual framework change, in order to defy the static character of certain organizations in the context of intentional communication action. This operation also contains the capacity to train members and to evaluate their collaborative skills and those of new members, as well as the discovery of new digital skills to be acquired in order to improve the DSS competitiveness structure (Harvey 2011) in a multitude of innovation fields and communication and disciplinary contexts.

Identify the collaboration possibilities Set of activities and tools helping to discover new collaboration possibilities and that could trigger the formation of a new virtual organization or DSS. The potential collaboration avenues on the dynamic between individual and collective DSS skills and the ones of potential external members in a particular field. The collaboration perspectives can come from the inside or the outside, locally or internationally. They concern a member, a community or an organization and can be discovered by a mediator or an organization dedicated to employment.

Characterize the collaboration possibilities and plan "as the crow flies" Set of support activities and tools allowing to determine and define individual and collective skills, practical abilities, capacities and aptitudes required to answer a promising collaboration opportunity as well as to schematize the approximate DSS structure from a first description of skills, at each feedback cycle of the life cycle including the desired organizational form and the partners' roles. At this stage, it is important to examine the respective DSS partners' skills according to the DSS type targeted by the co-design and the type of partnership we wish to update with contracts or cooperation agreements.

Choose partners and create partnerships Set of communicational and informational activities and series of socio-digital media promoting the scouting of partners and negotiation, their rigorous evaluation and selection by matching their skills with the required skills to meet the requirements of collaboration opportunities and face the innovation challenges associated to them. Among the relevant dimensions, let us mention the generic digital skills, the economic stability, the financial situation, the preferences, the reliability indicators, notoriety and the expertise acknowledgement.

Create partnership contracts and negotiate Set of management activities and support tools that assist people, community members and partners throughout the various iterative discussion and conversation phases with the objective of matching the needs and skills of various actors seeking to create a DSS. Community informatics design management includes agreement form design and relational and administrative contracts as well as workshops and contracts techniques. Important issues to address in this process are the following: determination of the entities and the program aspects to negotiate, the protocol or negotiation democratic mechanisms, decision process and the dimensions that correspond to it, availability of collaborative tools and socio-digital media, the sharing of resources, the use of licences, the agreement representation and their potential diffusion in the media and on the Internet. In a DSS co-design setting, the contractual process involves a great negotiation that goes beyond the parameters related to technology or objects. Other dimensions must be taken into account, especially the relational contract, the ethics contract and the social contract. All these aspects must be considered before starting the works and launch of the DSS.

Manage DSS knowledge and manage contents   Set of activities relative to the appropriation, process, production, diffusion and sharing of the information and knowledge within the DSS community and in the extended DSS and the partners. These tasks aim at the necessary elements for the DSS construction as well as the introduction of new members or partners, the update of the digital library and heritage conservation, archives and hypermedia and audioscriptovisual productions. These activities seek to support the works and development projects of the DSS at all life-cycle phases, to conserve and share the use cases, the research results, the best practices, the collaborative ontologies by fields and the lessons learned from the design of virtual organizations and previous DSS.

Establish trust   Set of design activities and tools that are useful for the evaluation of the basic trust we can give to new members (like credibility, authority, financial stability), as well as the evaluation and the subsequent monitoring, throughout the collaboration processes commanded by collaborative projects.

Evaluate collaboration (performance)   Set of evaluation activities and monitoring and analysis tools that allow to start a DSS, to follow its evolution, to qualify it and to adjust its collaborative mechanisms by using dimensions and performance indicators. A social and collaborative dashboard can be a visual support for this activity.

Making decisions   Set of management activities and software tools that contribute to support the monitoring activities of performance indicators and the visualization of DSS activities (dashboards). These tasks can be separated in various mechanisms like conflict management, levels of skills, communication obstacles, alerts, performance declines and trust issues at various levels.

8.3.2.3   Subsystems of Activities and Process

Define strategic communication and the marketing plan   Set of design and management activities and tools that support the formulation of a strategic plan and the planning of co-creation activities (including the marketing process and branding strategies), in order to promote the generative capacity of the DSS as well as the skills and abilities of its current and potential members and consumers interested by its services or applications.

Make a budget and assign resources   Set of management activities, accounting tools, responsibilities structures and accountability procedures that guarantee the DSS financial health by specifying the admissible sending or not and ensuring an efficient, effective and fair resources distribution.

Structure the governance   Set of design activities and support tools related to the global management policy of the future DSS, including internal and external operational rules, regulations, procedure and the norms supporting the daily operations of the network structure and the social processes of the DSS: members and partners, positions, roles, status, rights and responsibilities, ethic rules and their applications as well as relations between all these parameters.

Capitalize (memorize and appropriation) Set of design activities and appropriation and memorizing tools that seek to transform DSS activities into human, organizational, social and financial capital by accumulation: hypermedia documents and video to share, efficient methodologies on the epistemological and practical plans, collaborative tools and social media to share, lessons learned and exemplary practices, useful and efficient governance policies and network support contacts for the development of the DSS. These activities are divided into specific mechanisms of access rights (the public, targeted public, micro-markets, specific virtual communities, private access, limited use) for all the DSS members and partners and diffusion policies for announcements and events.

Realize the design and act in the respect of ethics Set of design activities and tools that guide change and innovation according to the future desired orientations and common values of the DSS members and partners. This set contains support functionalities of tangible and intangible, material and non-material values of the DSS community that organize the general and specific expectations and requirements of the members and partners. The general DSS co-creation activity through community informatics design relies on the self-organization and shared expectations ideas, as well as on the taking over of all activities regarding the DSS to be developed.

Ontologize Set of conversational design activities (semantic and semiotic) and software tools that support the ontological adaptation of the community informatics design and the DSS in a socio-economic field or a specific innovation sector. These activities also accompany the evolution of the DSS through the community informatics design catalysed in the seven spaces methodology of its life cycle. They contain the definition of glossary terms or a terminology specific to a field of activities or practices that constitutes the reference or instantiation architecture of the DSS. This vocabulary and these definitions also support the training, the learning and the skills acquisition process in the creation and organization of contents. They also support the global generative capacity of the DSS and members' social creativity processes. On the Internet, the words of the DSS community become the community itself.

Configure and manage information and communication technologies Set of design and management activities in community informatics that seeks to define the functions and functionalities required by a DSS that later translate into support tools. These various collaborative tools, for example digital media, design tools, open-source design platform and creativity free software, which are easily configurable, should facilitate online sociability and be inter-operational in the ICT infrastructure of each of the distributed partners. They aim to allow the different DSS users and partners to perform the design of various applications and tools obtained in the cloud in order to exchange and share the resources and the capitals of any nature (human, social, technological, financial) in a transparent and continuous way in order to collaborate to the design of innovation solutions on the Internet.

Identify supporting institutions Set of design and management activities and a series of Web design tools and methodologies allowing to identify, incorporate and facilitate supporting institutions for the DSS development. Without being socio-economic partners dedicated to the innovation, these contributors provide the necessary services for the DSS development and its activities. The information related to the supporting institutions selection and the justification of choices (tenders, Web approaches, selection criteria) are entered in the digital library through management software and recording mechanisms similar to the members registration.

Design and manage the innovation process Set of activities and tools that allows the new DSS to model and manage mechanisms and innovation forms in various activities sectors:

1. The identification of possibilities and development perspectives
2. The imagination of new worlds and ways to access them
3. The proposition of new rules and strategies that could produce new results
4. The construction of new teams and organizations of the new knowledge economy, like the innovation communities and DSS
5. The adoption of new practices and the appropriation of new tools like community informatics design
6. The development of new supporting infrastructures, collaborative platforms and the alignment of activities on new complex quality norms
7. The promotion of new values by ethics and conversational design in order to create commitment and leadership
8. The development of *communityship* through connectivity, interactivity and the presence/telepresence at the local and international level, thanks to the generalized increase of digital skills in the local communities, enterprises and in particular with young people

These processes will promote the generative capacity of communities, confrontation and the integration of points of view on innovation and the combination of co-creation efforts regarding collaborative intelligence mechanisms that will transform into products, applications, services and new digital social systems that will be manageable and favourable for Quebec's society.

Chapter 9
Toward a Discovery and Strategic Alignment Matrices for Socio-technical Systems' Design

Towards A Multi-aspect and Multi-field Modeling Architecture and Complex Social Systems and Virtual Communities' Design

In the introduction of the present book, we have underlined the fact that the socio-technical systems' complexity and extent are experiencing an exponential growth in the strong progression of global markets, technological capacities, social media platforms, consumers' and users' expectations and social needs. All these factors contribute to the complication of websites, portals, collaborative networks and virtual practice communities' co-design dedicated to human development that expands beyond the formal paradigm of traditional engineering systems. These challenges force software engineers, technology managers and the all ICT users/designers to consider technological platforms, social media and collaborative technologies like broader systems components containing not only technical aspects but also social and human aspects. The current conceptual models, coming from software engineer systems and the social science field (human-computer interaction, computer-mediatized collaborative work, Scandinavian participative design, interactive design, digital design), are limited in their perspectives, more specifically in their aptitude to represent the information and complex virtual systems' architectures. This chapter presents a conceptual structure and a modeling framework seeking to improve the existing socio-technical systems' design architectures. Returning to the notion of social architecture, we suggest an analysis and design framework that allows to jointly optimize, operationalize and instantiate architectures defined in the previous chapters (technological, organizational and informational, participative and collaborative architectures) for the DSS design as ICT-mediatized human activity systems (social media, collaborative platform creativity tools).

The value of our theoretical and practical effort will be to allow computational social science and digital communication practitioners to have, for the first time, tools and means to design and visually arrange the social informational and collaborative structure of their online activity systems while allowing engineers, managers and computer programmers to ignore the frontiers of their specialties in order to structure various types of discourses, conversations and languages to facilitate socio-technical systems design like the DSS. This chapter represents a way to increase the existing documentation by suggesting a clear generic structure for the

© Springer International Publishing AG 2017
P.-L. Harvey, *Community Informatics Design Applied to Digital Social Systems*,
Translational Systems Sciences 12, DOI 10.1007/978-3-319-65373-0_9

construction of human activity systems on the Internet, such as DSS in health, learning communities in education, virtual campuses and universities, social networks and virtual communities and cultural intervention and strategies. It does not require a special computer programming or formal language coding expertise. Based on the discovery matrix, the technique of morphology analysis, heuristic questioning matrices in the creative and imaginative thinking (Moles and Rohmer 1986, 1998; Moles 1990; Moles and Jacobus 1988) as well as on the multi-field and multi-aspect matrices (Basden 2011), our approach seeks to provide social science researchers with a qualitative and methodology that could be used by communication students and citizens/designers to identify, name and organize community information systems to better capture, memorize, treat, analyse and design complex data related to community informatics systems that will have a stronger ethical and socio-communicational character in a near future.

Community informatics design is a field of investigation that seeks practical solutions to important multi-aspect socio-technical problems. Its emergence throughout the past 20 years was answering a growing complexity of ICT uses, the insufficiencies of existing conceptual frameworks as well as gaps in the comprehension of theories and practices that guide communication and social science researchers, the policymakers, the non-expert systems design professionals, technology managers and software engineers who face important disciplinary integration challenges, like design and management of large-scale complex systems. Community informatics design can especially find an interest in the following activities:

- The co-creation of socio-technical systems like virtual communities
- The definition of government technological policies, enterprise business strategies research, platforms and grant policies
- The integration of human and social factors in the management of engineering projects, open innovation, social entrepreneurship and democratic *community-ship* in design thinking and citizen science
- Participative research action and participative in health, education and sustainable development
- The orientation of marketing and public communication strategies for community managers
- The analysis of stakeholder networks in the collective decision-making
- The development of products and services from social science theories and new communicational models to orient society's large-scale socio-technical project

9.1   The Industrial Design, the Collaborative Network Architecture and Organizational Modeling

The problems community informatics design seeks to fix are not new at all. They are not a discipline's prerogative since several fields of research are developed around tools and methods related to social appropriation of technologies, socio-technical intervention, participative design and interactive design. However, except for a few defined research fields like engineering, technology management, social computing and community informatics, few fields have adopted an extended perspective to explain and develop, in a transdisciplinary vision, systems that incorporate behaviours, organizational structures, social and human aspects, life sciences, management and socio-technical systems. Community informatics design seeks to incorporate these various disciplines in order to discover the principles, properties and fundamental processes of various technical and social systems that accomplish important functions in our societies. These social systems are human activity systems, as defined by Peter Checkland (1981), systems that are very different from purely physical systems like biologists or engineers design them. They embrace multiple aspects (particularly technologies, ethics, aesthetics, education and social interactions) of large-scale complex systems (Basden 2010a, b), for example, manufacturing systems, education practice communities, health services design, public communication policies and the development of platforms and democratic ecosystems.

In the previous chapters, we have presented several research sectors for the co-design of large-scale complex systems like socio-collaborative network and education practice communities, sustainable development studies, social change or human development. These perspectives contain the following elements:

- The optimal design of general and specific objectives for such systems
- *Hard* but mostly *soft* approaches for the social, organizational and technological architectures modeling of such systems (Chap. 6) by non-initiated managers, researchers and students in social sciences and in communications. Transdisciplinary approaches (Nicolescu 1996, 2010) allowing to represent and model the architectures and the social subsystems associated with these objectives
- Methods and tools allowing to model and understand the behaviours of use and design (conversational design, the activity theory, the DSS typology, the community informatics design exploratory space, the social media alignment matrix)
- Technical and practical means of prototyping, evaluating and testing models, development scenarios and new real digital social systems
- Approaches, methods and collaborative and social media that could help the decision-making, visualization of information and interactive social processes, an evaluation questionnaire of uses and the culture of design in virtual communities, exemplary case studies, websites analysis and a flexible and emerging life cycle that could support the DSS, instantiate them, operate them and ensure their monitoring and use them

In order to bring forward knowledge and the mastery of concepts and practices in these fundamental fields of research, university researchers in social and communication sciences must discover and suggest a philosophical examination related to these systems, like ontology (the study of the nature of these systems), epistemology (the study of ways to study these systems and to learn though them) and methodologies appropriate to their design and applications. This reminds us a few fundamental research questions:

- How can we define community informatics design and the digital social systems?
- What information or data do we need to describe and analyse digital social systems?
- Where can we find the relevant information?
- How can we observe the DSS?
- Do we have the conceptual and practical tools to develop the theories on DSS and their community informatics design?
- What are the ontological, epistemological, theoretical and practical challenges associated with the integration of social sciences, semiotic theories in communication, management, design thinking and communicational engineering?

In this chapter, we will examine these questions by going back briefly on the history of systematic thinking and design to note the current gaps of online social systems co-design like virtual community systems (human activity system including multiple socio-technical aspects) that, beyond technology and media, are presented like community or social information systems. Then, we will present an ontological community information system model likely to help the DSS construction. By using this conceptual structure, we will present a conceptual framework for the modeling and design of these systems based on the CAPACITÉS socio-technical model (Chap. 4) and called "discovery and strategic alignment matrices for the DSS community informatics design". In other aspects, we will examine the required information to describe a DSS, the location where the information is memorized, a technique that allows to find this information and instantiation methods of this information in the community informatics design.

This chapter will also provide community information systems practitioners with various means to improve the knowledge basis to facilitate community informatics design of human activity socio-technical systems like the co-design of virtual communities. In addition, for the first time, our methodology provides the social and communication sciences practitioners with an approach for the identification and organization of community information systems in order to allow the reception, memorizing, stocking, processing and analysis of these management and sharing platform and systems that we call DSS. This design methodology, by modeling design and instantiation tool configuration, represents a programming effort destined to managers that are not familiar with technology, non-expert designers in the civil society and to computational social science and communication researchers through digital social media. Far from the formal programming languages and computing codes, they allow to configure into natural language the necessary tools for the construction of community information systems specific to support DSS activities or a virtual organization.

9.2   The Foundations: The Systems Sciences as a Research Field

Regarding the applications related to human relations and the development of digital social systems and virtual organizations, the systems sciences can contribute to model and provide an online DSS construction methodology that should be a growing concern for a transformational social science and communication models oriented towards change at the service of humanity (Laszlo and Laszlo 2003). Contrary to the field of engineering systems, social sciences have not yet seriously taken into account systems sciences and social systems (Luhmann 1989, 1995; Banathy and Jenks 1991; Banathy 1987; Hofkirchner 2007, 2008; Fuchs 2003, 2008) to enrich their comprehension of the human activity systems' evolution into a large-scale network.

Community informatics design (Harvey 2008, 1996) that very early on had some interest in the systemic approaches is part of numerous fields of knowledge that have recently emerged relying on the systems' approach to organize the world and interpret it and add upon (Brill 1999). The systemic vision gives a distinct perspective on humans and nature (Laszlo 1972), without dividing them nor incorporating them without discernment. It seeks a holistic world vision; in that sense, it is a contrast with the traditional "reductionist" visions. Instead of favouring systems that are disintegrated by the obsessive analysis in more and more simple elements, reduced to their simpler expressions for the analysis commodities, the systems' approach embraces a global, holistic vision of the world (Popper 1961, 1972; M'Pherson 1974).

9.3   The Notion of a System

The notion of systems designates the manifestations of natural phenomena and processes that satisfy certain general conditions. In its wider classical design, it connotes a set of complex components in interaction, including the relations they maintain between them, which allows to identity a frontier entity and a dynamic maintenance process of this frontier. As we will see further, several definitions and different formulations have been given since the foundation of systems' sciences. For the purpose of our works, we will start by a definition based on the works of Russell Ackoff (1974) and Ackoff and Emery (1972), one of the founders of the social systems design theory (Ackoff 1974). A system represents a series of two or several linked elements that meet the following criteria:

1. Each element has an effect on the entire operating.
2. Each element is influenced by at least one other element of the system.
3. All possible element subgroups also possess both first properties.

By replacing the concept of "elements" (Laszlo 1972) by the "component" (Bunge 2003), it is possible to get to a relevant definition for the identification of any type of system, whether it is formal (mathematics, computer coding, programming language), existential (lived world of Habermas 1984), emotional (aesthetic, harmonious, emotional, imaginative, creative) or linguistics (semiotic, semantics, pragmatic). In each case, the system is a whole made of a series of elements or components in interaction. Thus, in its most fundamental definition, a system is a group of components in interaction, containing a sum of components in addition to their reciprocal relations (the system itself) by entertaining a certain form of identifiable relations with other systems.

9.4   Recent Trends in Social Sciences and Systems Sciences

The exploration of the systems sciences development by its more eminent representatives (Laszlo et al. 2002) shows us that its history can be retraced through a great diversity of intellectual activities and application efforts. For the commodity of our work, we will make here a certain number of distinctions. If we refer to the general field of theory of general systems, the first distinction to establish resides in, on the one hand, the development of ideas and the systems perspectives as such and, on the other hand, the application of the system idea in the existing disciplines (like the application of the system concept to engineering study programs, social systems design and the design of DSS and virtual organizations in communication and social sciences). This distinction allows us to distinguish two main fields of research on systems.

We can also distinguish various systemic fields in themselves: on one side, the purely theoretical development of the system's idea and their inter-relations, and on the other side, the applied perspective, with the objective to develop systemic ideas in various fields of application in the real world. The general systems theory by Von Bertalanffy (1968) represents an example of the first field while the development of engineering systems or social systems an example of the second one. There are, of course, classification examples that lead us to distinguish three kinds of systems: the *hard* systems like engineering systems, the *soft* systems that serve to characterize naturally "imprecise" problems (Moles and Rohmer 1986) and the mist systems, mainly used in operational research and socio-technical approaches.

The systems' classification between *hard* and *soft* represents an effort to attract the attention to both the degree of knowledge we have regarding a system and the systems' objectives or the underlying intentions of its development. Peter Checkland (1976, 1981), Checkland and Howell (1998) and Checkland and Scholes (1990) have developed this classification, largely taken up in the field of information systems and technology management that represents a continuum going from the formalization of a system to its semi-formalization and its openness, more or less big depending on the case.

A *hard* system like a telecommunication infrastructure or a network application is easier to define because its goals and intentions can be clearly defined. It is often the case of engineers in various fields like architecture or a software creation, to create machines, processes, smart agents, home automation systems, planes, trains or automobiles, for example. However, the intentions' simplicity and the clarity of frontiers do not guarantee the modeling, design or implantation facility. The entire current field of systems engineering is currently looking into the role of possible researches in social sciences to incorporate important factors that are a lot less quantifiable, but those are important dimensions to a system's success. A socio-technical system like the construction of a hospital contains highly complex dimensions.

At the other extreme are the *soft* systems that are characterized by human beings as main elements. These systems are difficult to define because they are blended with the existence and are often accompanied by technology. Without well-defined boundaries, they often contain vague intentions. The socio-technical systems we will mention below are part of it. At the virtual organization level and multi-person DSS and the widen elaboration in time and space, we often encounter disciplinary alignment problems, contentious visions and coordination problems that operate simultaneously. The objectives and aspects to be prioritized can then change with time. The design problems are therefore more complex.

9.4.1   Critical Systems Thinking

Recent works in the field of *soft* systems resulted in a promising thinking movement, not well known from the humanities and social science researchers that are called "emancipatory systems thinking". This field of knowledge that leads *to critical systems thinking* adopts an epistemological position that voluntarily leaves aside the ontological considerations to defend a critical and complimentary use of various systemic approaches and a disciplinary and methodological pluralism.

The critical systems thinking is a recent and solid research trend in the work studies oriented on humanist perspectives. Under the direction of pioneer researchers like Banathy (1992, 1996, 2000), Banathy and Jenks (1991), Floyd and Jackson (1991), Ulrich (1983, 1990), Ulrich and Reynolds (2010) and Romm (1996, 2002, 2006), all, to a certain point, disciples of Churchman (1968, 1971, 1974), one of the founders of emancipatory social systems thinking, this approach seeks to adapt the concept of "knowledge constitutive interests" according to Jurgen Habermas (1973, 1984), as well as Michel Foucault's interpretive analytical orientations, in a meta-methodology that incorporates a constant critical reflection. This methodology serves as a base to the generation of a new methodology that applies various critical systems thinking to problem-solving, especially critical social conscience, complementary methodology, complementary theory and the emancipation of human beings.

In social systems design, a person possessing a critical conscience is able to analyse the premises, the orientations and the underlying theoretical weaknesses to the methods and techniques used, whether in the consideration of a society tier, a systemic level or the entirety of a system. Social conscience brings into play the society environment and the organizational culture that influence the appropriation of a given system or the one of a social system through time and space. Methodological plurality and complementarity are interested in the use of various techniques and methods in order to achieve the objectives, to satisfy the intentions of a project or to realize certain activities. Finally, the notion of human emancipation seeks to create an improvement for individuals and to enhance the quality of life while being at the service of the commitment of concerned people by a cultural or organizational intervention.

9.4.2   Total Systems Intervention

One of the highly interesting subgroups of critical systems thinking is the total systems intervention. This approach starts from the principle of all problem-solving methods that are complementary. The conditions required for each problem-solving situation or design project planning gather the best applicable methods to each aspect of the problem. The selection of methods, modeling or collaboration tools and the intervention media is a particular configuration, an organization of specific elements for each project, that is accomplished by the community informatics expert, specialist of organizational collaboration supported by creativity tools, collaboration social media, project management tools and certain operational procedures. These procedures can greatly contribute to harmonize social media and the DSS strategies, according to three total systemic intervention modalities: the critical revision mode, the problem-solving mode and the critical reflection mode.

Even if critical systems thinking opens large new social sciences and communication that must contend with the development of socio-technical systems, this approach bears the imprint of a dominating rationality that serves as a conceptual structure enveloping the reality it seeks to observe and upon which it seeks to intervene. This approach seeks to emphasize the purely epistemological aspects of the system's theory. Other theories stemming from this perspective try to develop a more normative design of the system's reality. In digital social systems, we insist less on the technological information characteristics and telecommunications than on the values that guide their appropriation in change projects supported by vast technological systems (social media platforms, business ecosystem, collaboration charts).

It is especially the case of the multimodal systems thinking put forward by J.D.R. de Raadt (2000, 2001) that suggests a research perspective where human reason is part of a normative, supra-subjective and supra-arbitrary order. This normative order is supposed to precede reason and rationality and to determine the status of reason and the limits of science. In socio-technical projects, the complete control of traditional rational management and complete formalization in engineering systems collide with intuition, with the non-quantifiable, with emergence and with "enlightened improvisation".

9.4.3   The General Theory of Evolution

Since the 1990s, action systems oriented on the development of human and natural systems emerge from the study of evolutive processes in the environment and society. This approach is known as the "evolutive systems general theory". The general evolution of the universe is made of a "cosmic process" that manifests itself by event and situation sequences largely overflowing the physical or biological phenomena's framework to extend to a multitude of complex dynamic systems' evolution aspects like social systems and with Internet's advent, the DSS, through information, knowledge management and the generalized collaboration mechanisms in virtual organizations. As we have shown in our book entitled *Cyberespace et communautique* (Harvey 1995), the evolution of structures goes from atoms to stars, from great apes to the human being and from rudimentary forms of social structures to the creation of complex societies.

Today, the dominating organizational phenomenon resides in the evolution of virtual network cooperation/collaboration structures that go from the personal website to the virtual *mega-communities* of global social networks (UNESCO, OCDE, The World Bank, USAID). Human societies evolve through the convergence of organizational levels that are higher and higher to informational levels that fluctuate at various levels of society. When the flows of people, information, knowledge, energy, products and technological applications reach a certain "critical mass", they transcend the social systems' formal frontiers. In our 1993 doctoral thesis, we had shown that small tribes and neighbouring villages converge towards ethnic communities or better incorporated organizations that, in return, will become cities, regions, conurbations, countries, provinces, states, nations and, eventually, vast empires. All these evolutive states represent not only various levels of society that are in accordance with our CAPACITÉS model but also social information levels that articulate themselves at different levels of reality. These various levels of social information have been put forward by Jacques Jaffelin in *Le promeneur d'Einstein* (1991). Figure 9.1 highlights these social information levels that any social systems designer should master in order to understand better the context of uses. The different round charts illustrate an evolutive continuum of the social information complexification that has been emerging since the dawn of humanity. Each round chart contains a different level of universal impact information. Each level represents a different information status that relies on the previous round charts; it commands specific design skills like the ones that consist of aligning and organizing the information in a portal according to the various targeted publics, according to the information status and in accordance with the available media tools in various design situations. This hierarchy is not without reminding the levels of needs from the Maslow pyramid or the CAPACITÉS model's society level diagram.

Currently, we are witnessing the explosion of new forms of socialization and online social structures that go from the individual websites to the great strategic and collaborative alliances through practice communities and the innovation communities' platforms, through an organizational, cultural, economic, political and

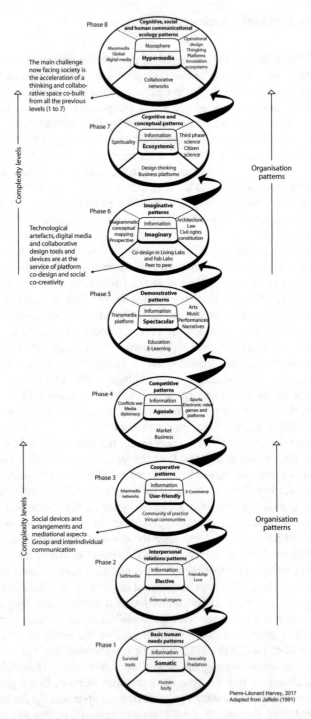

Fig. 9.1 Social information tiers

technological convergence. Together, the humanity puts in place the complex governance processes of multiple stakeholders by creating vast political and economic blocks like the European Community, NAFTA, ASEAN, UNASUR, etc.

The "bifurcation" notion (Hofkirchner), which is non-linear space and time transitions and often undetermined between the system's states (see Fig. 10.1), allows community informatics design to analyse, under the angle of the evolutive systems theory, the conditions that prevail in a social system that undergoes changes or transformations at a precise moment, in a particular space. Community informatics design reorganizes its structures to establish a new socio-dynamic regime (a new culture, policies, socio-technical design properties, the systems' state and transition) that could be founded on the previous components and past bifurcations or disintegrated in more stable individual components. The bifurcation concept refers to the revolutionary transformations our social systems, our systems and social virtual organizations and the entire society endure. The reins of power change hands, the work division design and its coordination are redone; virtual communities are born, thanks to networking; new ideas emerge, like the open massive transborder innovation; new social movements rely on technology; and new behaviours and lifestyles appear and take the initiative. When the order is re-established, transformational chaos disappears leaving room for a new, more stable system state.

Immanuel Wallerstein (quoted in Harvey 2004a) teaches us that bifurcations can be calm and continuous but also explosive, catastrophic, abrupt and absolutely unpredictable. This is why we must try to anticipate the future of our societies in a sense that is favourable and that ensures the future of the specie. Thus, facing uncertainties and global disruptions in our current world, the community informatics expert and the systems designer must be attentive to the bifurcation our social systems are experiencing, by exploring and selecting scenarios and alternative solutions likely to give a satisfying answer to periods of indetermination and large-scale disruptions.

The general theory of evolutive systems is founded on the fundamental transdisciplinary orientations, on the integration of principles of the general systems theory, cybernetics and systemics, information and communication theories, the complexity and chaos theory, the theory of dynamic systems, the thermodynamics and all relevant science for the analysis, modeling and design of a DSS. Community informatics design, by using these sciences as a foundation, gives itself tools and means to understand underlying laws, rules and the socio-dynamic that govern the evolution of complex social systems in various fields of investigation. The basic concepts of these new disciplines can be developed in a way to show the dynamic and rapid evolution of digital social system and socio-technical systems.

9.4.4 Social Systems Design

Open social systems design represents a field of research that is relatively new and unknown among the communication and social science researchers. Yet, its integrator framework based on the systemic approach makes it an interesting transdisciplinary approach, able to bridge the gap between disciplines like computing, information systems and community information systems, management and technology. Among the pioneers of the first wave are Simon (1969), Jones (1970), Churchman (1971), Jantsch (1976, 1980) and Warfield (1976). The memorable year for this approach was 1981, marked by contributions from Ackoff (1974), Ackoff and Emery (1972), Checkland (1981), Nadler (1981), followed by Argyris (1982, 1993a, b), Ulrich (1983), Cross (1974, 1984, 2001) and Banathy (1984, 1996, 1999, 2004). More recently, researchers like Laszlo and Laszlo (2004), Reigeluth and Jenlink (2008), Fuchs (2008) and Hofkirchner (2008, 2013) have continued Banathy's work in similar directions, with the creation of "evolutionary systems design" we will see in the next section.

Social systems design has emerged recently as a manifestation of open systems thinking corresponding to the soft systems approaches. As a research discipline oriented towards the anticipation and the creation of the future, it incorporates both a component focused of the results and a component focused on the decision-making. We will see that these two components are important for the DSS community informatics design. The first is related to research in the classical sense of the word with a strong component in social and communication sciences. It uses various disciplinary, interdisciplinary and transdisciplinary approaches. The second perspective is less interested in research results than in the knowledge application results; in this sense, it tends more concrete problems' investigation, a way to create pragmatic knowledge and applications favouring intentional social change.

This last idea is important for the communication research or the social science practitioner dealing with new digital fields. While the "information systems" and the "organization theory" traditional methods, including the "organizational communication" one, have failed or, at least, were tardy to offer a clear vision of virtuality, virtual communities, collaborative network organizations containing horizontal organizational architectures and new forms of governance put in place by stakeholders and partners groups, the information community and socio-technical systems methods (Whitworth and De Moor 2009), pragmatic Web and the languages/action theories (Goldkuhl and Lind 2010; Te'eni, 2006; Winograd, 2006) and symbolic action perspective in information systems (Aakhus 2014) have wanted to fill this gap since the beginning of the century. All the works, more and more known on "organizational semiotics" and "cybersemiotics" (Brier 2000, 2008, 2013), can also help us in the design of digital social systems and community information systems by incorporating the social, pragmatic and semantics levels (Krippendorff 2007).

In fact, the social systems design approach seeks to understand a creation and collaboration situation (e.g. the creation of a scientific collaborative portal on social Web's platforms or a business design platform) as a set of interconnected, interdependent and interactive processes. Therefore, solutions they seek to suggest (alternatives, design resumption, reuse, planning emerging from a vision that incorporates multiple aspects; Basden 2000) go well beyond the traditional information systems approach that went from an information technology application paradigm to an opportunity to build a new social field: the social Web, media and socio-technical networks that support the co-creation and design of new social systems and collaborative virtual organizations; in short, community informatics design is the social systems design to which human factor perspectives, socio-technical systems (Clegg 2000) and social computing are added (Kling 1973, 1999, 2007; Kling et al. 2005). These research orientations favour the design of future virtual social ecosystems thanks to a holistic comprehension better documented of the dynamic governing online social systems as living and organic systems. This means that all citizens can and must take the responsibility of socio-technical systems design for the co-creation of our future, in interdependence with all the involved stakeholders in the co-development of a system. These are the computing enterprise participating citizens as users/designers (Harvey 2010), the universities' colabs, the democratic living labs and the responsible policies of various government levels.

By its nature, DSS design is a participative activity: it is not the business of experts, and the significant changes currently required in our societies are led to terms only by communities that are affected at the first degree by these new systems that solicit them and choose their orientations and the way to implant them. If we consider that the information systems in the enterprises and in the current electronic commerce industry and the services can be considered like digital social systems, we will admit that people and communities represent the critical factor and the main beneficiaries of their potential socio-economic validation effects. Furthermore, we will concede that it is essential that it be them to undertake the changes and transformations and that we should incorporate them in our efforts. This process is everyone's business; it gives a fundamental role to social science researchers in modeling, design, virtual communities and Internet socio-critical systems implantation.

In accordance with the basic social systems design philosophy (Banathy 1987), DSS community informatics design, realized with the help of social Web collaborative creativity tools and the open-source code, support the "participative democracy" through which people directly engage in the issues and activities that mainly concern them. It is a fundamental orientation that will guide the implantation of a citizen portal in the setting of the research focus works 3, entitled "Online Democracy", from the *Commission citoyenne sur les droits et l'harmonisation des relations interculturelles*'s project funded by the *Conseil de recherche en sciences humaines du Canada* (under our colleague's direction: Mireille Tremblay). To understand this research orientation well from a scientific point of view, we take our inspiration from the systems' theoretician Bela Banathy (2000, 2001) and Banathy and Jenks (1991) that characterizes the systems as follows: "Science focuses on the natural world's study. It seeks to describe what exists. Centred on the research of problems, it studies and describes problems in various fields. Humanities focus on comprehension and the discussion of the human experience". In design, we focus on the research of solutions and the creation of objects and value systems that do not yet exist.

The scientific methods include controlled experiments, classifications, acknowledgement models, analyses and deductions. In humanities, we apply the analogy, the metaphor, the critic and the evaluation. In design, we divide alternative situations, we create models, we make synthesis and we use situations and solution models.

Science promotes objectivity, rationality and neutrality. It cares about the truth. Social sciences validate subjectivity, imagination and commitment. It cares about justice. Design validates pragmatism, ingenuity, creativity and empathy. (And we add abduction.) It cares about the alignment equity and the impact of design on future generations.

9.4.5   *Evolutive Socio-technical Systems Design: Community Informatics Design as a New Digital Skill*

Recent efforts to apply the general evolution theory to the design of social systems mediatized by and through social media and collaborative platforms as socio-technical systems (Trist and Bamforth 1951; Trist 1953; Emery 1993; Weisbord 1992; Badham et al. 2000; Fischer and Konomi 2007; Whitworth and de Moor 2009; De Moor 2005) mark the rise of community informatics design as one of the social intelligence technologies allowing the computer-mediatized social participation (Fischer 2010, 2013a, b; Giaccardi and Fischer 2008) with the help of "innovation colabs". Evolutive socio-technical systems design is a praxeological field (Moles and Rohmer 1986, 1998; Moles 1990; Moles and Jacobus 1988; Le Moigne 1979a, b, 1983) oriented on the creation of evolutive crossroads for the sustainable development of life on Earth. As a research discipline, it tries to validate the work of social science and information and communication science practitioners to define what could be "socially responsible communicational design". The evolutive community information systems designer is called a community informatics expert (or a "communitician"). He has the responsibility to strategically align systems, like social, organizational and technological architectures he creates through socio-dynamic means (Moles and Rohmer 1998; Moles 1967), cultural change and patterns and behavioural interaction models and collaboration that intervene in the development of virtual environments put at the service of our societies' sustainable development.

Relying on the general evolution theory (Laszlo 2004; Heylighen 2007) as well as on their methodological concepts of social systems' design approaches (organizational semiotics, semio-pragmatism, cybersemiotics, the activity theory, conversational and multi-aspect design), as well as on the new field of computer-mediatized social participation, the evolutive community informatics design faces challenges arisen until now by an intentional strategic monitoring of decision assistance systems dedicated to the environment and the sustainability of our planet ecosystems. This implies that we would engage in the co-creation of our future in an evolutive interdependence (Harvey 1995) with our social and natural environments.

This approach is based on the belief that we are able, on one hand, to configure our future in a way that it would be favourable, thanks to our self-organizing capacity to understand multiple aspects, characteristics and required conditions by our environment and, on the other hand, to realize it according to an ethical design approach that respects our values, our aspirations and our expectations. The orientations of this praxeology and this pragmatic philosophy have been elaborated for 40 years already from the pioneer researchers program from The Club of Rome (Ozbekhan 1969; Christakis 1987, 2010) and is currently ongoing within the objectives of the European projects called FuturICT Flagship, which seeks to understand and manage socially interactive, complex and global systems by highlighting durability and resilience (Bishop et al. 2011; Lukowicz and Conte 2011). According to researchers that promote this pilot project, to reveal the hidden laws and processes that underlie the "evolution" of our societies represents the biggest and more urgent scientific challenge of our century (Helbing 2010, 2011, 2012a, b).

According to the promoters of this approach that unites researchers from all horizons and various countries, the integration of three fundamental fields, information and communication technologies, complexity sciences and social sciences, will lead to a change in paradigm that will facilitate the symbiotic co-evolution (De Rosnay 1975) of ICT and society. Large-scale monitoring systems will provide massive data and information coming from our global complex information systems. This data is collectively generated from the global data base in order to develop durable models of socio-technical and economic systems. The results will allow to better understand the global functioning of our social systems and to document the design and development of a new generation of ICT systems that are socially adaptive, self-organized and co-built in, by, for and through energy and intelligent collaboration of vast collectives of actors. "Having become conscious about the evolution, we must make the evolution conscious now. If this is what we want, the next step in the development of human societies can be intentionally guided" (Laszlo and Laszlo 2003).

To do so, we will have to multiply, for Quebec, Canada and the rest of the world, disciplinary crossroads and trans-profession practice fields, where individuals and communities will collaborate, according to their own desire to get involved in new socio-political contracts, in the reflexive co-design of knowledge representation systems put at the service of the creation of flexible social, resilient, open and favourable systems to the human being.

Community informatics design of evolutive social systems supports an "anticipatory democratic philosophy" where people and civil society apply their digital socially and ecologically responsible multi-skills by becoming active participants in the conscious definition of our future. Innovative ICT practice communities engaged in community informatics and evolutive socio-technical design make an evolutive learning user/designer community (Harvey 2010; Laszlo et al. 2010), and this type of local or extended community by telepresence (Moles 1973) and remote collaborative networks favour the emergence of an "evolutive design culture". This process is destined to the improvement of "evolutive socio-technical skills" of all citizens: a universal and generic appropriation mechanism leading to an improvement of digital literacy. Digital literacy refers to a desirable state of individuals update, human communities and vast collectives of actors involved in large-scale socio-technical projects, a state that is marked by the cognitive and social ICT mastery, through the knowledge capacities, practical abilities of media and social platform appropriation, by a critical attitude towards emancipation tools and methodologies and by the required values for collaboration and ICT-mediatized design activities. Digital literacy validated by digital badges represent a whole program of research based on our UQAM's Applied Community Informatics Laboratory (ACIL), in Montreal.

Along with literacy, digital literacy should be promoted and taught at all levels of the education system and society as a whole. It is an essential condition for massive innovation and the pursuit of more sustainable modes of existence. It is the duty of social science oriented towards the improvement of life quality and a socially responsible communicational design to favour the emergence of such an emancipation culture for all, where large-scale technological projects intervene (see the next section). These modes of life and survival for our societies join the co-creation of products, services, applications and change processes in terms of numerous social systems aspects that can be socially desirable, culturally emancipatory, psychologically validating, economically sustainable, technologically feasible, operationally viable, environmentally friendly and generationally sensible.

The analysis, monitoring and evaluation of all these aspects simultaneously exceed the skills of a single individual and require the implementation of robust virtual environments (Darzentas and Spyrou 1995) where creativity and collaboration tools can help develop adaptative and evolutive alignment strategies that will ensure the longevity and maintenance of new ecosystems at various levels of society (individuals, groups, organizations, practice communities, collaborative networks, social systems, global network systems).

In accordance with our CAPACITÉS modeling approach, based on De Moor theories (2005) and Whitworth and De Moor (2009), community informatics design of evolutive systems seeks to identify opportunities to increase the dynamic stability and the self-creation of social systems through various levels of society, in interaction with an array of components that are larger than in traditional engineering systems, according to different temporalities and spaces (e.g. the efforts of Léo Semashko in tetrasociology).

In the image of expressed aspirations by the vast FuturICT Flagship European project, we would like to suggest a project where vast fields of knowledge could illustrate the evolutive and emancipatory potential associated with various fields and where society in its whole could benefit from the different investing efforts in the complex dynamic systems that globally limit the scientific field of community informatics design of the future social systems (we will present this project at the end of the present chapter). The strategic monitoring and the technological intelligence of literacy and digital skills of all citizens become, in accordance with the results of our APSI research realized with the financial help of *the Secrétariat du Conseil du Trésor du Québec*, one of the main objectives of evolutive community informatics design.

Thanks to the implementation and the experimentation of democratic socio-technical platforms that promote the involvement of individuals and communities in the co-creation of "crossroads" specific to the sustainable evolutive development and the harmonization of international efforts for the balance between the human being and nature, we seek in the present book to define the foundations and practices of evolutive learning communities in community informatics design in the field of general science and in the field of social and communication sciences in particular. In the next section, we will examine large-scale technological projects from the tetrasociology, socionics and sociocybernetics angle.

In the context of a citizen commitment process in the sociological imagination (C. Wright Mills) and the creation of transdisciplinary bridges (or "crossroads"), the current research on evolutive community informatics design seeks to promote and adapt synthetic models of evolutive learning communities in community informatics design in the real world, for example, "the intelligent worlds" (Abdoullaev 2011), collaborative virtual environments, innovation co-design in virtual communities (Brandtzaeg et al. 2010) and the intelligent cities (Komninos and Tsarchopoulos 2013; Komninos 2003). Alexander and Katia Laszlo (Laszlo et al. 2010) define an evolutive learning community like a group of two or several individuals possessing a common intention, a common identity as well as a commitment in the co-creation of spheres of meaning seeking to develop evolutive skills through the co-design "learn-to-learn" (Nicolescu 1996, 2010), in harmony with the dynamics of their own physical and sociocultural environment. Evolutive learning communities in community informatics design do not want to adapt the environment to the members' needs nor to unilaterally adapt the members' needs to the environment. Instead, they jointly mature the major issues of our time by the harmonization of co-creation and co-design processes, a socio-dynamic of sharing resources that aim the sustainable co-development. Problems are transformed into issues, uncertainty situations are considered like perspectives and individual dreams become collective projects. From these dynamics and activities, digital and social skills are increased, which allows to validate the comprehension of organizations and change models and patterns associated with any complex dynamic system through energetics and informational transformation.

In connection with social and communication sciences, complexity sciences and the ICT transdisciplinary field, community informatics design of evolutive social systems provides theoretical foundations and evolutive governance principles of coordination/collaboration/evolutive communication and ethics. It makes us think that the harmonization of human activities and the balance of human future can be entrusted to the citizen and the civil society as long as it is possible to create today the necessary skills for the use of creativity and design tools at the service of strategies, alignments and harmonization platform through which we could, together, guide the sustainable and desirable development of our societies and organizations.

The fact that community informatics design of evolutive social systems can currently rise is related to substantial advances in several fields, especially social and collaborative Internet platforms, social systems design and conversational design, modeling and human activity visualization tools and the research of a form of critical systems thinking that gives it an emancipatory and harmonizing interest that relies on soft systems approach, critical systems approach, emancipatory systems approach, massive educational orientations of remote and permanent education and the learning communities in community informatics design supporting these orientations. The result is a DSS approach supported by the ICT, oriented in a humanist way, understood as a meta-methodology, a meta-design (Fischer 2013a), that accompanies and facilitates the critical application of various aspects of socio-technical systems to the numerous situations of the real world.

9.4.6   The Socio-technical Design Culture

The 2009 publication of the book by Brian Whitworth and Aldo de Moor entitled *Handbook of Research on Socio-Technical Design* is an important turning point in the research issues and approaches on evolutive socio-technical systems. The social interaction and action are at the heart of this approach. Socio-technical systems are described as computing technologies that validate social interactions of all types, whether for email or blog conversations, chat groups, collective writing (wikis), e-commerce (eBay), online learning (Web City, Moodle, Dokeos), social networking (LinkedIn, Facebook), co-design or modeling (mind maps, Cmap). Whitworth and De Moor note that the Internet has evolved from the content generation and static data base applications hosting towards global communication platforms. According to them, like ICT that become an integral part of social life, the social world should also be part of technical design. Without it, a "socio-technical gap" emerges, which translates to a deficit between what society considers desirable and what makes technology.

Socio-technical systems rise when social systems emerge from technical systems that can expand from small collaborative groups to great technological systems (GST) documented by Hughes (1983, 1987, 1990), with components that can be physical, legal, organizational, institutional, community or societal (Ostrom and Hess 2011). They contain complex interaction patterns encompassing invention, discovery, economic development and social innovation systems. Whitworth and De Moor (2009) consider the socio-technical field as transdisciplinary; they believe no university discipline can avoid this field nowadays. From the communication and social sciences stand point, the socio-technical systems approach transcends the human-computer interaction, the community information systems, the computer-assisted collaborative work and the computer-mediatized communication (Harvey 2010). Depending on the situation or the project, we will resort to communication theories or the perspectives of the language-action movement, the pragmatic Web or the cognitive sciences, the engineering systems, computing, health and education sciences, sociology, business management and more recently the symbolic action perspective.

Krippendorff (2007), great communication and human-centred design specialist, assures the movement we tend to call human-centred design unites all these approaches.[1] The assumption is that technology or the infrastructures are not "defi-

---

[1] Voir le site Web d'IDEO Design <www.ideo.com>

nite static data" but entities co-created by humans for their own use instead of from technology for its own purposes. In this sense, two authors join the promoters of evolutive design:

> In the end, the global humanity must control guide and define computing, la technology that is transforming humanity and maybe we need to change what is changing us in order to survive. If society is the context of technology and not the other way around, we have to define the conditions, designs and measures technology will have to follow. (Whitworth and De Moor 2009)

This is why in our conceptualization of community informatics design, as socio-technical problems are put in context and resolved, it becomes important for the citizens and the society in general to consider the critical systems thinking to envision socio-technical questions. A highly "technologized" society like ours is affected by the growing innervation of the social fabric by technologies, but it can also "socialize" the technology it contributes to create. Conversely, technological designs exist within a social context; they must integrate this context in their modeling to grow in harmony with social requirements.

Thus, socio-technical systems are essentially hybrids: they contain a mix of socio-cognitive structures, complex social structures, hard infrastructures and soft architectures that are difficult to model. The development of technical systems and DSS by community informatics design is a complex socio-technical approach and is difficult to realize since it tries to balance and harmonize human and social aspirations (Harvey 1995) with the constraints and challenges brought by technologies. We do not think this is an easy task to realize at first, but we hope that the matrix and combination model we present in this chapter will answer most of the requirements expressed by different users/designers having different worldviews and many types of digital skills.

9.4.7   The Socio-technical Interaction Network Methodology

In this spirit and according to this approach, one of the most eminent of social computing, referred to by Whitworth and De Moor (2009), is Rob Kling (1973, 1996, 1999, 2000a, b, 2007; Kling et al. 2005), and Kling et al. (2001), according to whom information and communication do not exist separately on the social or technological plan (Lamb; Sawyer; Kling 1973, 1996, 2000a, b, 2007; Kling et al. 2001, 2005). According to Kling, several assumptions underlie a new social computing and community informatics research strategy called the socio-technical interaction network or STIN. Kling's approach (2003) is an emerging conceptual structure aiming to identify, organize and analyse social interaction models, to develop systems and configure the components of an information system. Therefore, it is not a mature theory by an approach that seems promising. This is why we allow ourselves to add some theoretical elements, especially, as we will see further, Hughes's elements on great technological systems (Scacchi 2006). Since 1991, Kling has considered the information systems foundations as network models designed like a set of equipment, applications and techniques, containing identifiable capacities of information processing as replacement solutions to "engineering systems" that are centred on the infrastructure and equipment components, on their information processing components and the formal organizational arrangements as "social action" base.

The socio-technical interaction network approach relies on the social construction of technology and on socio-technical approaches associated with researchers like Bijker and Pinch (1987), and we add Hughes and his large technological systems (1987, 1990, 1998). This last approach retains technical artefacts, legislative constraints, organizational structures and natural resources. Hughes defines large technological systems like open intentional systems that exist to solve problems and that interact in an environment containing two types of factors: the independent ones and those that depend on the systems. A large technological system distinguishes itself from its environment by control limits applied by other components of the system. These limits define the system's frontiers.

Hughes talks about components by mentioning the concept of "system's structures" that are both technical and socio-technical components in dynamic interaction. He designs these systems like a hierarchical structure that seems to be the inventors, innovators, organizers and information systems' managers' preference. In the image of the complexity hierarchy evolving at various levels of the system and levels of society that compose our CAPACITÉS model presented in Chap. 4, Hughes defines and understands the structure of great technological systems like socio-technical systems in dynamic interaction. He informs researchers to be attentive to the level of analysis often forgotten by the followers of traditional engineering hard approaches. Hughes introduces several tiers of analysis that translate various behaviours of systems, understood as evolutive models of large technological systems. In this sense, his approach is compatible with Kling's (1973, 1996, 1999, 2000a, b, 2007; Kling et al. 2001, 2005) and the great evolutive systems one presented in the previous sections. It helps to better understand the dimensions involved in the design of great DSS that is currently exploding on the Web. It is also based on the actor-network theory associated with Latour (2008), Law and Callon's works, from l'École des Mines in Paris.

All these approaches can differ from one another but all equally help to understand the role of the social behaviour in the creation and use of technological artefacts. From the actor-network theory, the socio-technical interaction network maintains the concept of actors that can be a human or a non-human participant. In addition to assure that technology and the social are inseparable, Kling (1999, 2007) states that social behavioural theories should influence the choices related to technical design that the participants are incorporated in multiple interrelations intertwined and non-mediatized by technology and that they consequently possess multiple contradictory commitments where sustainable development, routine and operating procedure questions are critical. In this context, the socio-technical interaction network and the great technological systems make two relevant approaches for the analysis, the development and design of multiple "inter-actor" network systems such as DSS that we define as large-scale socio-technical human activity systems that require important decision-making to ensure their development according to flexible, open, operational and evolutive options or scenarios.

9.4.8   Systems Oriented by the Context

All these approaches validate the postulate according to which the attention given to people, their uses and their socio-technical design skills is a rare resource and a lot more important than the information system in itself, even a community one. The American researcher Gerhard Fischer, one of this movement's leaders, calls these "human-centred computing systems". In a recent article, he develops a multidimensional conceptual framework, the "context-oriented systems", one that relies on a particular attention to the many dimensions of the context and that seeks to face this challenge by transcending the current socio-technical systems, which neglect certain aspects of the context without paying attention to the problems this negligence could create. This structural and process framework is based on an array of different systems, developed and evaluated by for 20 years to explore different dimensions of the context we will examine closely in Sect. 9.6.2, by presenting 15 socio-technical systems aspects of Andrew Basden (2000).

Fischer (2010, 2013a) tries to define the context elements more precisely, its aspects that would allow to provide the right information, at the right moment, at the right place, in the right way, to the right person. We add to it the requirement to provide the right knowledge to the members of a given virtual practice community. Thus, Fischer poses the challenges, the orientations and the "design negotiations" (potential dangers, gaps and promises). He gets an innovative conceptual framework out of it for the design of the future generation of systems oriented by context. These systems will support the advanced interactions (collaboration processes), to assist people and practice communities in the appropriation of network knowledge, to make them more productive, more creative and more innovative, by insisting on several aspects that had been neglected until then by computer experts and engineering systems experts.

Therefore, according to Fischer (2012), a first important aspect of the context definition depends on the way to obtain information elements that concern them, among the following:

1. In this new approach and in accordance with our DSS approach, open-source code software, ubiquitous computing and computing clouds allow people to commit to virtual environments that accompany them in the design, the implantation, the surveillance and the monitoring that provide them with a myriad of information on these activities.
2. In design activities, the context is not a static entity with fixed properties but an entity with multiple aspects that are emerging and without definite boundaries. Some context aspects can be inferred with partial designs (interfaces, plans, drawings, project planning), but the designer might have to explicitly articulate his intention by precising more systematically the nature of certain components.
3. Certain context parameters are determined by information and knowledge coming from outside the virtual environments, for example, the members of a learning community that discuss around an interactive white board. Such environment

sometimes requires appropriation mechanisms to map external events and translate them into computing objects; people can also provide this information explicitly, alone or in a group.

The second important context element is the way to design it, model it and represent it. One important challenge at this level is to infer high-level objectives from the observation of lower-level operations. For example, if the users must collectively generate information on the context, the question of the objective consists of knowing who among the partners or the stakeholders is volunteering to realize these activities.

The third important question is to know to which project objectives or specific intentions the context aspects and information are destined. Instead of generating useless or too many contents, it is better to proceed by strategic alignment between the context, tools, methods and techniques and to ask questions like: Who says what? To whom? By which means? What for? With what intention? The creation of different discovery and strategic alignment matrices between a project's objectives and socio-digital media may constitute an important design and creativity tool. While being careful of not creating an addition problem of "informational overload", taking into account the context should contribute to optimize the planning of contents and knowledge for different groups and users' communities.

Taking into account the context of design leads us to suggest a multidimensional research framework (Chap. 6), where the active users' support becomes our priority intention for many tasks, for example: the design is centred on the users' needs and aspirations; the contexts are differentiated and customized with their help; same with the articulation of the design intentions that are built with the 8C's approach; the access to information and knowledge is realize through the sharing of several analysis tools and collaboration open-source code software. In all these activities, conversational design and co-design are seen as social learning activities coming from the cooperation between experts and non-experts, in different aspects of the programming and tools' configuration context. And, finally, all the actors work on the alignment of all the elements around the DSS project. The underlying idea is to analyse community information systems with the angle of "participative culture" contexts.

In front of global and pressing systemic problems our world is facing, we must try to transcend the cognitive level of individual spirit to better apprehend the challenges of collective intelligence and mobilize the collaborative comprehension in the discovery of solutions that are favourable to man. We have seen that the solving of this problem requires network virtual social structures (like the DSS) that favour the human knowledge, organizations, capacities and their application to various fields of human activities, at work or elsewhere. The creation of collaborative virtual environments aiming at the planning of large-scale projects and the solving of problems to promote the work of virtual communities to analyse, synthesize and share knowledge in order to support the collective generation of contents, community informatics design, networking, citizen democracy as well as various activities of common knowledge around sustainable development. These knowledge-updating activities seek to put the new co-design social structures at the service of the human being and require to promote a participative "design culture" like our two APSI questionnaires and our case studies have revealed the growing importance in Quebec and globally.

From this brief reminder and various elements mentioned above, we will now suggest a conceptual framework based on the ACIL works within the APSI program, where we have led our research projects for 2 years. This semiformal conceptual framework will allow us to analyse and operationalize the instantiation strategy we have suggested in Sect. 7.2.

9.5   A Digital Social Systems Conceptualization: The Foundations

Let us remind that a conceptualization is a simplified world vision, represented towards a certain intention. It provides a base for a field of knowledge formally represented (or semiformally in social sciences), to represent the objects, concepts, aspects and other entities and elements we presume that exist in a given field of knowledge. Explicitly or implicitly, each socio-technical system relies on a certain conceptualization that describes its concepts, its class of components, its typology of values, its interactions and its relations.

In Sect. 7.2, we described and defined several elements of a conceptual framework under construction for the analysis and design of socio-technical systems applicable to the structuring and development of digital social systems. This framework aims to meet the challenge of better understanding the collaborative design assistance virtual environments and to suggest a practical design framework that expands well beyond the existing according to a conversational ontological co-design model. From Bunge's works (1983, 2000, 2003, 2004a, b), our framework systematizes and semi-formalizes the identification and the definition of common fields to all DSS considered like socio-technical systems of a particular type. Our approach also incorporates philosophical foundations of complex evolutive systems that underlie the transdisciplinary works of the UQAM's ACIL team.

These fields contain the following elements:

1. The foundations of community informatics "design thinking" (ontology, metaphysics, futurology, axiology, praxeology, epistemology) we have seen in Sects. 2.9 and 2.10.
2. The context (the multiple aspects) and the multiple design situations, at various levels of society and at various complexity degrees
3. The environment and the exogenous (exostructure) and endogenous (endostructure) components
4. The social and communication field (social network, social media-mediatized social network that consists of describing human and social dimensions, the DSS type of social structure and the interrelations between these two elements)

5. The functionalities (including objectives and the intentions of the socio-technical system or the DSS and its organizational, social and collaborative architectures
6. The ICT that incorporates the physical and material architecture and the other DSS non-human components, especially the material, software, the infrastructure and the community information system
7. Processes (methodologies, techniques, design and modeling sub-process, the activities realized by the socio-technical system, people, communities and machines).

9.6   DSS for Users: Design Oriented Towards Everyday Life (A Praxeological Ontology)

The practical objective is to remind the foundations of a general theory of communicational design processes destined to build collaborative DSS that, as we have seen, we wish to contribute to the design of a conscious evolutive design (Banathy 1996; Laszlo and Laszlo 2003; Fuchs and Obrist 2010; Harvey 2010) that incorporates the technological and human aspects in a semiformal operational process resulting in the emergence of new social structures more favourable to man.

The design of a participative culture and a collaborative society requires not only a basic conceptual framework but also the construction of a transdisciplinary methodology that incorporates nature, society, conscience and technology according to a cooperative mode. To do so, we must incorporate various levels of reality (Harvey 1996) into an ecosystemic theory understood like a field of interactions that contains significant human relations and collaborative management modes focused on the quality of life of many as well as on social computing and natural sciences.

Our comprehension of systems reality, our society model, is not naturalist nor culturalist, reductionist or dualistic but praxeological (Brier et al. 2004). Our vision of reality is based on a non-reductionist, multidimensional and complex approach as suggested by Edgar Morin (1982, 1984, 1985, 1990) in his various books dedicated to system's complexity. We represent the various aspects of reality from the angle of social and semiotics practices (Brier 2000, 2008, 2013; Gazendam 2001; Stamper et al. 2000). These semiotics design practices are represented in the problem-solving process of the 8C, which is focused on three aspects: survival and evolution, social roles and power issues and balanced and a fulfilling life. In Chap. 4, we suggested a visual model of these various levels of reality the "semio-pragmatic communication star". We have coupled this model with a hierarchical vision of complex systems, the CAPACITÉS model. The semio-pragmatic ontological vision of the 8C, the CAPACITÉS model and the communication star form a series of seven great dimensions taken into account for a communicational design approach.

9.6.1 The Multiple Aspects Contextualizing Community Information Systems

Based on a 2500-year-old critic of philosophical thinking, the Dutch philosopher Herman Dooyeweerd (1984) suggests an atypical approach of reality that allows us to address and build information systems and their connection to everyday life, in the image of de Habermas' life world (1984), but in a more extensive way. Dooyeweerd (1984) suggests a deep critic of the theoretical, analytical, scientific and philosophical thinking. However, he shows that we must not abandon these formal forms of thinking like the anti-rationalist do because we can find promising links with their daily activities. We lack space to present in detail such an important approach. Our effort will consist of showing that an aspect-oriented approach could complete the object-oriented approaches in the design of community information systems seeking a sustainable information society. We will see that by linking them to relevant articulated questions in a discovery matrix, we can transform these elements into prodigious a creativity and reflection tool.

Mario Bunge, from McGill University, like several other contemporary thinkers, pre-suggests the possibility to adopt a theoretical attitude to understand the world. We fully adopt this attitude, even if other postures may differ from it. Thus, Dooyeweerd (1979) considers that this philosophical attitude constitutes a problem in itself, by adopting an attitude based on the flow of everyday life in order to reflect the various aspects the experience acquired day to day, within which he sees a curious coherence. Let us examine this closer. It is a contrast regarding the world to build, but not a contradiction. Basden (2000, 2002, 2006, 2008, 2010a, b) quotes, as an example, the elements (things) like a manufacture, a book and a trip to Mars, where we find aspects (multiple modalities), particularly physical, logical and legal, which cannot be processed each against the others. The physical causality strongly reverberates in the logical relation antecedent consequence and in the legal relation between intellectual property and afferent sanctions. We will examine these 15 aspects in detail in Sect. 9.6.2.

On the basis of this experience modality, Basden argues that the logical aspect (or analytical) does not have a privilege position "above" other aspects, but it is not only one aspect among many, without any significance. If we recognize the historical importance of the analytical aspect in sciences and in philosophy, it is not to elevate it as a modality superior to the others but instead to differentiate the roles it can play in our behaviour as human beings. This is why it offers an important model that promotes the input of social sciences in the representation and modeling of basic concepts associated with information systems destined to online communities and DSS, as knowledge sharing systems for the innovation and the sustainable development.

The most popular knowledge representation approaches in the object-oriented models are the objects, the attributes, the qualitative and quantitative values that feed these attributes, methods and procedures, messages and languages and a limited number of relations between these various entities. For each of these elements, we must ask ourselves questions like: Why such component was chosen to represent knowledge related to a specific field? To what extent is this choice appropriate in practice? Wand and Weber (1990a) have tried to root their information systems approach in the philosophical ontology of Bunge (2003, 2004b), as seen in Chap. 6, because they thought his works could directly apply to information systems. Wand and Weber retain the following grammatical concepts to map Bunge' philosophical concepts:

- Things, properties, states (stable or unstable), events (internal or external, precisely defined or not), transformations, stories, couplings, class systems and types
- The relative laws: the state of the laws, the appropriate legal state spaces, the legal event spaces and the legal transformations (e.g. the sociocultural law evolution cycles according to Abraham Moles 1967)
- The concepts associated with the evolutive systems theory: the composition, the environments, the structure, the subsystems, the deconstruction and the structure level, to which we add the mechanisms or processes

The Wand and Weber (1990a) data model contains a vaster extent than the previous object-oriented computing models and an extended capacity to include appropriate elements to the knowledge representation in complex systems like DSS. But it does not go far enough to analyse the current context of "free source code" the innovation users/designers one that requires the use of natural language instead of strictly formal programming languages to represent the knowledge of the world we lived daily. The multimodalities of the Dooyeweerd model (1979, 1984) incorporate not only the formal science languages but also those of social sciences, letters and arts. Multiple languages can take into account and validate the programming skills of non-initiated and users in their role as developers of digital social systems in the spirit of "citizen science" and "social design". By neglecting certain important aspects and plurality of the "lived world" of the user mass, we might end up with big mistakes and important socio-technical problems, like digital skills deficiency for the appropriation of information systems destined to the development of virtual communities and DSS. The world, the worlds, is not strictly representable like things around the Internet of Things and cyber-physical systems or independent like fields of meaning; we must analyse these things in relation with the world and its multiple dimensions.

In every day's attitude (by opposition with the abstract world of experts' data) and the lived world, multiple aspects can be taken into account. We can use an information systems to compile socio-demographic data (logical aspect), as well as to share and comment them in a group setting (social aspect), or to keep confidential data (ethical aspects). In the types of activities relative to the procedures, the analytical-logical aspect specific to computing experts could be dominating, while in the DSS, where knowledge sharing is generalized within a widen community, we could incorporate more diversified aspects like ethical principles. We could evaluate the social and cultural aspects of a given design situation, reflect on its legal and physical aspects and observe the linguistics and communication behaviours. In the transdisciplinary approach of community informatics design, it is important to understand that the aspects cannot be modeled and understood as autonomous, abstract and independent modalities. It is important to consider that formal languages and science's analytical perspectives are only an aspect, a modality of the world to socio-build and make evolve into complex interrelation complexes, within systems containing several transitional, emerging and dynamic systems.

9.6.2   A Proposal to Represent DSS Activities and Knowledge

We could use the study of aspects in relation with the requirements of community information systems from the linguistics modality that scans all aspects of social systems to model. For each aspect, conversational design and linguistics can provide a series of complementary dialogue modes encompassing their symbols that can any express potentially significant activity or knowledge within each aspect of a social system. In accordance with the approach we have adopted for a decade, we will discuss the aspects in terms of "worlds to build" or "meaning spheres" as Basden calls them (2000, 2002, 2006, 2008, 2010a, b) inspired by Dooyeweerd (1979, 1984) and Habermas.

For Dooyeweerd (1979, 1984), the aspects are meaning spheres and rules that allow any reality to be and to occur. The type of content we can extract from each aspect includes all what aspects validate in terms of reality production (or conscience). The set of aspects validates or creates the following properties:

- The spheres are distinct modes of being (things, entities, elements, components, events, processes).
- The spheres are distinct types of property basis.
- The spheres are distinct types of rationality or inference.
- The spheres define distinct ways to link things and people's communities.
- The spheres are distinct types of rules, laws, procedures or significant constraints.
- The spheres define distinct ways to function and act.

The worlds to build, the DSS and the socio-technical systems like the virtual communities command appropriate representations and modeling to the users'/designers' needs. The concrete proposition we formulate in the present section goes towards the sense of a multi-aspect representation that could be suitable for the modeling and design of DSS. It is not exhaustive nor definite, but it is an illustration of the community informatics approach that favours the "primitive aspectual multi-modality" useful to the representation of knowledge in evolutive systems (adaptation of Dooyeweerd 1979, 1984; de Basden 2002, 2006, 2008, 2010a, b).

The following list's goal is to present examples of aspects to take into account in the design of community information systems, instead of imposing a systematic model to follow. It suggests a series of primitive elements to validate for the potential integration of different meaning spheres in the users/designers' everyday experience.

1. **The Quantitative Aspect (Discreet Number)**

   The Being: The number of instructors, the ratios, the fractions, the proportions, the statistics and the types that anticipate the other aspects like the real numbers for the space aspect and utilities and generalized costs for the economic aspect.

   The Properties: The precision, measure, approximation, dimensions and duration.

   The Inferences: Mathematics, statistics and factorial analysis.

   The Relations: Larger than…, smaller than…, according to…, the series and the tool assortments.

   The Constraints: The statistics laws where, for example, a given quantity remains constant as long as a change does not occur.

   The Activities: Increase, scaling and the statistics functions.

2. **The Spatial Aspect (Progressive Extension)**

   The Being: The space in itself, shapes, spaces and virtual environments, cyberspace "furniture", the network space, straight or curvy lines, areas, regions, society levels and dimensional lines.

   The Properties: The size, orientations, trajectories, the action landscape, the distance, the type of indirect experience, the side (interior/exterior, left/right), the psychosociological aspects of space, the interaction and communication context, the types of social matrices and forms of life, the navigation process and the movement in the virtual space, the imaginary space of virtual territory, the distribution of individuals, virtual urbanization, the types of connection to the environment, the topology of clickable spaces, the arrangement of work and leisure spaces, the creation and explanation of socio-technical spaces and the structuring of forms of conduct.

   The Inferences: The geometry, topology, situational topology, psycho-sociology of space and psychological ecology.

   The Relations: Spatial alignments and arrangements, pages-screen suites, the mock-up, the schematization, touching, crossing, overlapping, parallelizing, surrounding, the topology of actions and the activities to realize.

   The Constraints: The boundaries must possess certain markers, must not overload a pages-screen, a graphic chart and colours and must read from left to right.

   The Activities: Join, link, transgress, click, roll-down, deform, jump, develop, make a rotation, energize, activate, program and perform the design.

3. **The Kinematic Aspect (Soft or Radical Movements)**

   The Being: The typology of acts, movements, flow, trajectories, mandatory passages, labyrinths, the rotation centre, the evolution of images and animations.

   The Properties: The velocity, speed, direction, divergence or convergence, curvature, the duration of movement and the activity time.

The Inferences: The theory of acts, psychology of space and quantum mechanics.

The Relations: Rapid, slow, front/back, individual or collective navigation, travel or make music together and work alone or in a team, in practice communities or large scale.

The Constraints: The rules of a happily constraining labyrinth.

The Activities: Start, follow, activate, energize, stop, move, roll, draw and follow a trajectory or a creation procedure.

4. **The Physical Aspect (Energy, Mass, Matter, etc.)**

The Being: Waves, particles, forces, fields, causality, impacts, the material, components, mechanisms, chemical particles, alloys, solutions, liquids, fluids, gas and crystals.

The Properties: The mass, the energy, the density, the charge, the frequency, the spectre, the force, the solidity, the weight, the height and the power.

The Inferences: The various energy functions and the materials' chemistry.

The Relations: From cause to effect, attraction or repulsion.

Constraints: The balance, mass conservation, energy, initiative and thermodynamic laws.

The Activities: The physical interaction, the expansion of a field by an inverse square law, dissolvement, catalysis and the chemical reaction.

5. **The Organic Aspect (Biotics and Integrity of the Organism)**

The Being: The organisms, organs, the system's boundaries, the biological mechanisms, the dissipative structures, the organizational fence, the tissues, food, life, population, the environment, the ecosystem, the dysfunctions, the genome and biotechnologies.

The Properties: Health, illnesses, pathologies, age, endurance and the statistics in video role games.

The Inferences: A bad exploitation of nature entails an overdevelopment and a neglected hygiene entails pathologies.

The Relations: Between parents and children, the family, the tribe, networks, the food chain, symbiosis, osmosis, the structure or the ecosystem.

The Constraints: The necessity for a sustainable development and a safe environment.

The Activities: Regulate, save, grow, incorporate, manage, reject, reproduce, recreate, emerge and disappear.

6. **The Psychic Aspect (Feel and Be Touched)**

The Being: The sensations, perceptions, feelings, signals (colours, sounds, touch), cerebral functions, mental states, cognition, emotions, memories, reflection, attention, imagination and creation.

The Properties: Colours, sounds, message intelligibility, readability, cognitive ergonomics, volumes, satisfaction or dissatisfaction and happiness or sorrow.

The Inferences: The psychological theories, the non-stimulation of the psychological field entail boredom, stress or anxiety, the information overload entails the saturation of the mind, an insufficient level of skill entails an under-use of the innovative mind, etc.

The Relations: Between stimulus and response, collective intelligence, collaborative intelligence, the tendency to communicate, the indirect experience, telepresence and constructivism.

The Constraints: The level of perception organ sensitivity, the Weber-Fechner law, the Zipf law of least effort, attention, retention and selective perception.

The Activities: Imagine, solve, build, develop, create, memorize, forget, learn and plan.

7. **The Analytical Aspect (Differentiate, Distinguish Types and Formalize)**

The Being: Distinct and defined concepts, objects, elements, entities, structures, situations, design processes, name and identify things and design activities.

The Properties: Current, desirable, cybernetic, structural characteristics, values, principles, differences and similarities, typology, classes, combinatorics, the representation of an entity, the current state and the desirable state.

The Inferences: A sequence of the design process, life-cycle phases, a design situation, the design activities and sub-activities.

The Relations: The partner and stakeholder roles, complementarities and divergences, technological convergence and governance modes.

The Constraints: The non-contradiction principle, entity integrity, the respect of procedures and rules, collaborative governance rules, contracts and coordination mechanisms.

The Activities: induce, deduce, distinguish, perform classes and typologies and evaluate pages-screen or the efficiency of educational communication.

8. **The Formative Aspect (Learning Power and Skills Acquisition)**

The Being: The structure, infrastructure, relations, communication, design process, modifications, transformations, innovations, plans, drawings, system in transition, means and purposes, tools, the instrumentalization, objectives, intentions, the power and hierarchy/heterarchy.

The Properties: Formalism, semiformalism, openness or closure of the system, the emphasis, feasibility, efficiency, desirability, versions control, relations and social media strength and network analysis.

The Inferences: The process analysis, data or social media visualization, objectification of the design approach and skills acquisition.

The Relations: Means and purposes, shared intention of a change project, the maturation of a consensus, sociometry and the graph research, phases and operations sequences, the deconstruction of activities, tasks and subtasks, the state of the systems and the subsystem transition and the articulation between the whole and the parties.

The Constraints: The referential integrity, transdisciplinary integration, convergence and divergence of fields, the synthesis of activities, the planning process, the constraints and the institutional procedures.

The Activities: Construct/deconstruct, form, solve problems, plan projects, link, redo the design, research, change, create an evolution though significant changes, change a state, monitor, manage and evaluate.

9. **The Linguistics Aspects (Symbolic Meaning)**

The Being: Information and communicative aspects, the parts of the discourse (names, verbs, etc.), words, expressions, sentences, lists, tagging, titles, crossed references, quotes, roots, words etymology, formal and natural languages and language codes.

The Properties: Time, space, the world, fields, emphasis, denotation and connotation, organizational culture, sense, meaning, symbolic, iconic, sound objects, image grammar, schematic, diagrammatic and translation and discovery matrices.

The Inferences: Semantics, semiotics, syntax, pragmatic, the language/action perspective, the communication and information theory, media writings, electronic editing, interactive screenwriting, symbolic action perspective and transmedia storytelling.

The Relations: Combine ideas, connect complementary modes of dialogues and conversation, compare world visions and solve collective problems for sustainable development.

The Constraints: The law of least effort, conceptual mapping rules, the image grammar, discourse processes, the typology of dialogue modes and their possibilities and constraints in design.

The Activities: Speak, write, understand, draw, animate, receive and send messages, socio-build worlds, search texts, define concepts, find consensus, translate, construct/deconstruct, instantiate, and converse.

10. **The Social Aspect (Interaction, Social Systems and Social Networks)**

The Being: The person, the small group, the practice community, the virtual community, the human activity system, the socio-technical system, the strategic alliance of partners, the collaborative network and the institutions.

The Properties: Roles and status, social position, leadership and community-ship, formal or informal structure, openness or closure of the digital social system, the types of frontiers, socio-demographic data, behavioural characteristics, the activity types and the field of cultural intervention.

The Inferences: Social systems theory and methodology, socio-cybernetics theory, evolutive systems theory, social network types and communicational consequences, the types of virtual institutions and challenges for work.

The Relations: Friendship, complicity, communication, collaboration, cooperation, coordination, contracts, consensus, convergence and divergence, subscription, identity, belonging, collaborative networks, alliances and partnerships, organizational culture, conflicts and animation.

The Constraints: The administrative contract, the moral contract, management modes, ethics rules, rules of conduct, intellectual property, norms and procedures, work distribution, typology of dialogue modes and communication ecology.

The Activities: Build collaborative networks, develop DSS, communicate with different public through mass communication or socio-digital media, identify, name, associate, recognize, answer, formulate an intention, initiate a change, implant, instantiate, ensure, support, maintain, monitor, evaluate, react, recreate, self-organize and take charge.

11. **The Economic Aspect (Consumption, Sustainable Resource Development and Management)**

The Being: Human resources, material and natural, consumption, conservation, exchange, markets, telecommunications infrastructures, platforms, collaboration charts, applications and services.

The Properties: Limits, types of goods, products, virtual services and applications, sectors, fields, prices, revenues, economic models, governance models, collaboration models and partnership types.

The Inferences: The social systems models dedicated to sustainable economy, strategic perspective, evolutive design strategies development, offer and demand management, social responsibility of organizations and public communication.

The Relations: The new economic models, users/designers/experts, the development of cyber services in partnership, composed with limited resources, business ethics in virtual worlds and validation of innovation with multiple stakeholders.

The Constraints: The distribution of wealth rules in a sustainable human development perspective, business ethics, types of contracts and collaborative governance modes.

The Activities: Create new economic models, develop DSS in the knowledge economy, distribute though networks, electronically commercialize and develop collaborative networks and fractal partnerships (quadruple or quintuple helix).

12. **The Aesthetic Aspect (Harmony, Happiness and Quality of Life)**

The Being: Beauty, nuances, design, feelings, emotions, humours, pleasure, harmony, leisure, sports, games, arts, attitudes and aesthetics.

The Properties: Harmony, well-being, quality of life, imbalance, image's grammar, types of space, the paradox, special effects, colour chart, attributes and perception dialectics dipole (interesting/uninteresting, familiar/strange, erotic/austere, close/distant) and the types of menus.

The Inferences: The roles of visual contents and animations on the creation perceptions and the appropriation of interfaces-screens and websites, the importance of aesthetics for cyber learning, readability criteria and information and aesthetic perception theories.

The Relations: Space and cyberspace relations, institutional graphic chart, colours and organizational culture, users and interfaces-screens, navigation modes, hyperlinks, visual fatigue, cognitive ergonomics and users' retention, the theory of relations, etc.

The Constraints: The *gestalt* laws, sensation and perception processes, cognitive sciences laws, social systems design laws, the needs for the harmonization of action and human activities, human-computer interfaces rules and educational communication.

The Activities: Harmonize, incorporate, regulate, play, perform, co-design, co-create, promote the being together and learn to plan the information and the communication.

13. **The Legal Aspects (Optimization and Wealth Distribution)**

The Being: The cyberspace reality legal setting, responsibilities and roles, sociocultural evolution of the law in cyberspace, the Internet law, intellectual property, regulation, patents, inventions, innovations, policies, rules, procedures, contract, systems security measures, hacking, spying, trade secrets, social justice and legal and sociocultural values.

The Properties: The type and nature of the law violation, the level of security, the elements to secure, protection of personal information, the appropriation rate, market laws, organizational or institutional rules, equity and company's laws.

Inferences: Transformations of the Internet laws and the ICT effects, applications and new norms on production, cultural diffusion and intervention and emergence and application modalities of normativity and labour law.

The Relations: The impacts on the artistic and cultural production, media regulation mechanisms, regulatory phenomena and new knowledge economy, new professions and new organizational relations, strategic alliance legal aspects, collaborative networks and DSS, rules and human relations and national legislation and media laws.

The Constraints: Intellectual property rules; cyberspace law; telecommunication law; regulation organizations like the Charter of Human Rights and dissidence; convergence processes; information circulation; the sharing and diffusion of sensitive knowledge; the analysis of existing legal paradigms in other countries; the protection of personal data, children and senior citizens; and participative democracy.

The Activities: Realize agreements and contracts, reflect upon network governance mechanisms, study cases, judge, remunerate, reward, share risks, fight injustice and elaborate a regulation.

14. **The Ethic Aspect (Norms and Design's General Direction)**

The Being: Attitudes, codes, values, beliefs, axiology, inclusion and social justice.

The Properties: The degree of self-realization, the social responsibility level, elements of ecological responsibility, evolutive responsibility, multilevel values at various levels of society, (generosity), the commitment level, concern for the entire social system, the quality of feedback mechanisms and monitoring in order to satisfy the starting intention, balance between individual and collective needs, between community action the technology used and the justification of the approach, fair socio-organizational behaviours, the stakeholders respect and civility, etc.

The Inferences: The code of ethics, the equity theory in social psychology, the cultural evolution cycle, sociocultural intervention rules and the studies of the impact technology has on customs and the global culture.

Les Relations: The culture of giving, knowledge sharing and active participation in networks, fair exchanges, the respect of others, the distribution of collective wealth, collaborative networks ethics and beneficial alliances for all.

The Constraints: The respect of rules and fair and responsible ways to do a DSS design and to conduct human business.

The Activities: Give, share, include the less fortunate, perform design for all in the lived world, commit, and forgive.

15. **The Trust Aspect (Participation, Trust and Commitment)**

The Being: Commitments, beliefs, values, principles, rituals and trust.

The Properties: The degree of certainty or uncertainty, ambiguity, legitimacy, credibility, authority, representations, shared values and beliefs.

The Inferences: The qualities of participative design and partners and partner's commitment, the level of trust and the project's objectives, the *PAT-Miroir* method, the nature and the concrete elements of commitment and mobilization, the value orientations and the theories of computer-mediatized social participation.

The Relations: The respect of commitments and contracts, partners' respect, un-hacked identity and community belonging and supported mobilization.

The Constraints: Not respecting contracts, partnership procedures, supported commitment, business rules and respect of laws and codes of ethics.

The Activities: Give his word, commit, adopt an ethical behaviour, trust and be trustworthy and prove his skills with experience.

Chapter 10
The Fields and the Definition Taken into Account for the Construction of the Multimodal and Multi-aspect Discovery and Strategic Alignment Matrices (2MDSAM) for the DSS Design

From the reference framework described in the previous chapter and the whole entities defined as modalities or aspects to be taken into account in the DSS instantiation and implantation, in this chapter, we present the definition of the multimodal and multi-aspect discovery and strategic alignment matrices (2MDSAM) for the DSS design. The 2MDSAM provides an operational reference framework to organize and model the elements in interaction and the dynamic DSS components as well as a way to describe the design process and activities. It seeks to fulfil the gaps of current modeling systems in information systems through the input of multiple disciplines and fields to the DSS modeling. The evolution of the Web in the past 10 years took us from the design of information and communication systems dedicated to content production and planning to digital social systems supporting community, family, organizational and social life at a large scale. Social sciences have remained quiet until now in front of this major phenomenon of the third millennium. In this chapter, we wish to fulfil this gap by suggesting a concrete representation and modeling tool while showing the potential for universal design (generic) centred on the human. The 2MDSAM operationalize the DSS conceptualization (its instantiation) while facing the challenge of pushing back the framework limits existing in the design of organizations and DSS. It provides a way to organize the information on various modalities and several DSS aspects in order to facilitate the co-creation and cognition distributed for the development of better DSS.

10.1 Community Informatics Design Systems' Conceptualization

We can visualize the 2MDSAM like a cross containing row entries and identical columns (Fig. 10.2). The diagonal represents the system's components, and the cells other than the ones from that diagonal (off-diagonal cells) represent the relations

© Springer International Publishing AG 2017   313
P.-L. Harvey, *Community Informatics Design Applied to Digital Social Systems*,
Translational Systems Sciences 12, DOI 10.1007/978-3-319-65373-0_10

between components. The cells on that diagonal represent a graph of a particular class of knots. Each knots class "is aligned with" one of the DSS fields. The block of cells from the diagonal represents the multimodal and multi-aspect relations that connect a diversity of knots classes.

The readers familiar with the IEEE standards could interpret the 2MDSAM as a collection of models referring to the totality of the digital social system. Each row or column in the 2MDSAM represents a "vision", a point of view, a particular aspect and a series of concerns or questions related to the system being studied or under construction. In addition, the 2MDSAM lays the foundations for the "face-to-face" interactions between elements, which give the entire DSS a more systematic perspective founded on the theory.

The 2MDSAM is modeled according to an enriched data structure able to represent the social information and contents for community informatics design and the management of the digital social systems project. The 2MDSAM is both a hypergraph and a multigraph. A hypergraph contains various graphs that contain different classes of knots. There are interactions between the different types of knots (e.g. between the stakeholders and the infrastructures, between certain social aspects and socio-technologies). A multigraph may contain several types of cross checking or boundaries between knots. For example, two practice communities could possess reciprocal relations, like communications through socio-digital media and economic links.

Each knot and each social system and sub-social system under development relation can be described as properties and attributes of these properties. For example, a property related to quantitative aspects can be described by an attribute (binary, abstract, scaling up, digital) or by a statistic function. Furthermore, the 2MDSAM allows to represent the temporal evolution of the social system (knots, relations, properties), in accordance to our adaptation of the "systems in transition state" theory.

The 2MDSAM data structure is made of seven classes of knots that correspond to seven fields connected to the DSS development: the exostructure, the endostructure, the design activity processes, the socio-communicational processes, the functionalities, the socio-technologies and ethics. It is the modeling of a type of complexity architecture, according to Simon's expression (1960, 1962), that represents an effort of entities definition to appreciate the wealth of its interrelations, in order to analyse the community information systems and the realization of creative DSS scenarios. Before presenting the discovery matrix, here is an attempt to synthesize and semi-formalize the present components. An entire work of fundamental and applied research must be performed to validate these operational definitions and to instantiate them in systems that would be more favourable for us. Let us examine the fields identified by our team within the APSI research.

10.1.1   The Exostructure (Exogenous Elements or Environment)

The exostructure encompasses the modeling of exogenous elements and their inter-actions with the external context of DSS design; the identification of the DSS inter-actions with its social, political, economic and cultural environment; the market modeling; the support and organizational and institutional support modeling; the societal; the partnership helix modeling; the evolutive criteria and sustainable devel-opment modeling; as well as ethics principles.

10.1.2   The Endostructure (Endogenous Elements)

The endostructure brings together the elements that describe a series of properties specific to community informatics design while taking into account the relations between components in interaction in a DSS: the network structure, its infrastruc-ture topology, the stakeholders, the identification and the negotiation of their roles, the procedures and constraints, the management and governance rules and the socio-communicational aspects (the 8C approach, the aspects philosophy, the quin-tuple helix theory, the activity theory, the conversational design theory of various dialogue modes, the processes diagrammatic, etc.).

10.1.3   The Community Informatics Design Activities: Process, Collective Creation Mechanism and Sociocultural Design

The main global aspects of the community informatics design activities are: the type of social system to co-build; the philosophical modeling position according to themes and situations; the design process (design activity sequences, the life cycle, the phases, the tasks, the subtasks realized by the DSS or within it, the basic termi-nology); the design context; the relations between aspects, properties and attributes; the relations between aspects and objects (especially between the resources level and the project's objectives' ambition level); time and the calendar; transitory states; the system's boundaries to model or develop; design ethics; entities' representation modes; an entity state; the description of the entity state; past and current DSS properties; desirable properties; the design situation (a DSS state combination, the process state and the context state at a precise moment); the description of the design situation (the values of all properties); the scenarios; the alternatives; the determination of activities; tasks and subtasks to realize; transformations; muta-tions; the design process objectives and the choice of elements to represent; model-ing methodologies; and the design space and reality modes of representation (at a certain moment in time).

10.1.4   Socio-communicational Structure and Processes

The main socio-communicational aspects are: the social and organizational architecture; the analysis of the network sociometrics structures (made of people, peers networks, partner communities, stakeholders and organizations); people's interests and needs in the DSS co-construction, workshops and dialogue; resources to investigate community informatics design activities, understand them and engage multiple actors in network collaborative practices; the analysis of social networks; the participative architecture for user's content generation and contributions management; the participants' identity and the participation mechanisms in various interaction patterns; dialogue modes and their interaction (collateral commitment and resources sharing); pragmatic and cybersemiotics; communication dedicated to action and activity coordination and conflict management; the language action perspectives; "organizing" and "sense making"; the community informatics design consequences on the relations between people and partner users/designers and the evaluation of these consequences, communication values and principles; the procedures; the research-action methodology, cultural intervention phases and reflexive practice; as well as the epistemology of design thinking and community informatics design thinking modes, virtual communities types and online collaborative networks platforms.

10.1.5   Functionalities

Functionalities encompass what the system does in relation to goals, objectives, reasons and the social DSS justification, motives of various actors, stakeholders and the DSS intentions. It is the functional incorporated architecture of the set of three architectures, especially through the identification of action verbs and DSS planned activities in order to combine tools, applications and services to validate and accompany what the DSS wants to do (its intentions and objectives). For example, functionalities at the content production and communication level consist of sharing, standardizing, diffusing and virtualizing processes, to unite resources and intranets with the help of Web research tools, RSS feeds, Atomz and folksonomy. At the collaboration level, it is about sharing; coordinating; managing; making collective decisions through blogs, wikis, social networks, platforms and instant communication systems like Skype; as well as developing its collective identity and collective efficiency, to stand out, to produce, to innovate and to co-create. At the applications accompanying workspaces level, functionalities seek to personalize, facilitate, visualize, adapt work spaces according to professions, simplify life, draw, model, schematize by composite apps and open and free suites. At the collaborative processes and the free services level, functionalities must make fluid, accompany, optimize, motivate to promote collaboration between actors (people, communities, organizations, partners, stakeholders), optimize the capture and collective information visualization, train participants to the modeling and familiarize them with the instantiation and implantation processes of favourable solutions for the community or the organization, such as modeling applications like SMART or matrix navigators, or even decrease the administrative delays through the use of online simplified forms, contract types, self-service applications and creativity tools that are lower cost and user-friendly.

10.1.6 Socio-technologies

The main socio-technologies are the technological architecture and its norms, the physical aspects of the DSS infrastructure and components and non-human DSS elements, including the infrastructure, the interfaces design, the smart agents, the socio-digital functionalities and the commitment strategies of the participants oriented towards social communication and collaboration. Socio-technologies contain a large part of the social and socio-communicational architecture, and they are incorporated into marketing, governance, optimization of numerous communication processes, public communication and public relations, design support through collaborative tools, artificial intelligence and smart agents, modeling, simulation, decision-making, investigations and participative research action.

In social sciences and in community informatics, the social architecture and socio-technologies refer more and more to the community informatics experts work that applies the analysis principles and social media design and information architecture (content generation, contact strategies, viral marketing, open externalization, ubiquitous computing, social applications, business models and processes, knowledge economy, community development, communication for development, the user's experience and the users/designers commitment). They now encompass the construction of platforms and digital environments, modeling and simulation of complex social processes, transmedia platforms and, in the present book, the DSS design assistance platform. The technologies, methodologies and various approaches of all nature are the ones seeking to introduce new aspects in the world, to change it or to improve it. Socio-technologies are the art and the science of making things happen in order to improve everyone's quality of life.

10.1.7 Ethics

Community informatics design, in the way we address it in this book, refers to the fundamental orientations a collective of users/designers wants to offer to the evolution of its future social systems. Community informatics design ethics refer to the norms designers and multiple stakeholders decide to adopt to learn to live together and to make consequent collective decisions for the future rising generations. Ethics in the deep and more generic sense we can give consists of determining the sought-after qualities of the final result according to the actors' objectives and intentions. For example, to understand the functionalities in relation to sustainable development ethics criteria (self-realization, the respect of culture and identity, the learning of others, economic durability, economic feasibility, operational viability, institutional and social validation, the respect of the environment, the motivation of all generations or the inclusion of various social classes).

10.1.8   Community Informatics Design's Activity System Time and Transition States

The seven DSS community informatics design components and their environment change through time and their development. The components (elements, entities, people, intentions and norms), their properties and their attributes can be modified: we add some, we remove some, and we modify their characteristics. A DSS contains emerging properties that result in interactions between the social and socio-technological components. In Chap. 4, we have presented the CAPACITÉS model's "flexibility" property; we implicitly tried to introduce this concept like an evolution degree measurement of a social system through time, as an emerging property of a socio-technical system that can be understood by examining social and technological fields that jointly interact in a DSS to evaluate and measure a DSS's flexibility; a community informatics expert must understand its changing sources, grasp the influence of new components on different parts and the whole and determine who is responsible of the implementation and management of these changes.

By getting inspired by the works of Isabelle Reymen et al. (2001, 2003, 2006), we have chosen to represent a community informatics design system by using the transition state systems. This complex system modeling theory inspires us because it has a general impact to take into account the similar design processes in the various disciplines we have examined through our case studies and the document research realized within the APSI research (project life cycles, software engineering architectures, in building architecture, in technologies management and in participative research action in social sciences). We see here an interesting heuristic approach because it can help the realization of the seven modeling fields of the DSS community informatics design's evolution and to socio-dynamically model an array of "design situations" (Reymen et al. 2001, 2003, 2006) and "design activities". It helps define the imprecise but fundamental concept of "situational topology" by describing the interactions between spaces and time, infrastructures, behaviours and resources that intervene at various moments and various levels of analysis in systems modeling. It finally helps the operationalization of various transdisciplinary combinations to model DSS involving several specialities and professions.

In the state of transition systems theory, a state is defined as the situation at a given moment in time, a state modified by transitions. A community informatics design situation corresponds to a state; a community informatics design activity corresponds to a transition. Descriptive and normative modeling of large-scale complex systems, we suggest in our book, uses the transitions state concept to describe the various design processes in a DSS discovery and strategic alignment matrices. Only observable users/designers behaviours are taken into account. Furthermore, only basic transition state systems concepts help us describe the users/designers behaviour. The mathematics aspect and the formal notation of these systems have not been retained for obvious reasons, linked to the impossibility of measuring the phenomena in the strict applied sciences sense and also facilitating the process comprehension by a more general audience of university professors and practitioners that are less keen about mathematics (which is our case and most of our students' case as well). Let us finally note that the basic terminology of transition state systems modeling is extended to the terminology and the common use concepts in technical sciences and that we have used to describe the community informatics design seven fields of modeling as notions of representation, property, attributes of these properties, activities, structures, relations and processes (with several conceptual extensions and by analytical prolongation towards social sciences, even sciences of the imprecise (Moles 1967, 1992).

10.1.9   System's Boundaries

DSS have difficult boundaries to determine since they are built in networks that can expand to several levels of complexity in an "evolutive social geography" with sometimes imprecise origins. For our purposes, DSS design and for modeling needs, let us say that the boundaries are temporarily defined by components control that constitute the systems (in various fields) and by their strategic alignment with the system's intentions (its current or anticipated functionalities). The DSS components make a unified whole that interacts with the environment (exostructure) as an open and evolutive systems oriented towards the improvement of various ecosystems.

Often, a socio-technical system like a DSS incorporates components that do not contribute to the system's objective anymore and remain passive. Certain components can even provoke the system's inertia and weight constraints or require exaggerated procedures and rules. Others make it divert from its objectives. Because social systems are systems in permanent evolution, the system must adjust, adapt to face social pathologies (Yolle), dysfunctions and conflicts threatening it. Even if certain members of a DSS or a collaborative network are disagreeing on a procedure or certain elements of a project plan, the system will self-regulate or the facilitator/designer will find a way to adjust the components by realigning them on the objective and the system's intentions. We can think of the components replacement, their modification, the modification of policies or other modes of change adaptation. In certain cases, the omission to make these adjustments might lead to the system's death. Mutations and transformations are the nature of living systems; like the DSS, we can consider like self-adaptive complex systems capable of recreating their own existence conditions.

10.1.10   Other Properties: Complexity Levels, Society Tiers and Their Relationships

The interdependence between parties and the components constitutes another property of the socio-technical systems, therefore the DSS. The current state of a design, a system and a community informatics design system depends on the previous states. We may think the social construction of a DSS is the result of hundreds of decisions made throughout its development. The DSS depends on the choice of several types of knowledge and theoretical contributions, which changes our way of observing, analysing and evaluating these systems through time. Therefore, the comprehension efforts of human decisions, impromptu events and other types of information on behaviours require a deep knowledge of each of the seven fields.

As we have demonstrated in Chap. 8, socio-technical systems like DSS exist through various levels of complexity (see the CAPACITÉS model) and at various society tiers while containing multiple entities and components in dynamic interaction. Figure 10.1 represents the characteristics of complex socio-technical systems according to a space-time plan containing various technologies mediatized dynamic interactions which favours evolution and social systems generativity, for better or for worse.

Even if our conceptualization of the DSS fields centralizes its attention on large-scale complex socio-technical systems, our basic socio-technical systems analysis and design model design DSS from different degrees of complexity, from the more technical to the softer one, from the infrastructure to the global social networks and from a simple individual interacting with an artefact for an intention or a need to the global collective networks capable of interacting with millions of people (LinkedIn, Facebook, Twitter). The infrastructure, architectures and structure of the socio-technical system set of components should reflect those of its social organization. This is why the CAPACITÉS schematic representation reflects various levels of social complexity, supported or accompanied by a physical and software infrastructure and by the appropriate analysis levels. The social field and the relations between partners or stakeholders have the priority on socio-technologies and help define the inferior complexity levels. It is difficult and even less desirable to trace well-defined limits between levels; it is not necessary to also have opaque boundaries between each of the seven modeling fields.

10.2   Multimodal and Multi-aspect Discovery and Strategic Alignment Matrices Co-construction for the DSS Design (2MDSAM)

10.2.1   Exogenous Components Matrix

By starting with the top left corner of Fig. 10.2, the exogenous components matrix (exostructure) represents the environmental field of the DSS. It contains dimensions and factors that interact on the system or that are influenced by its development.

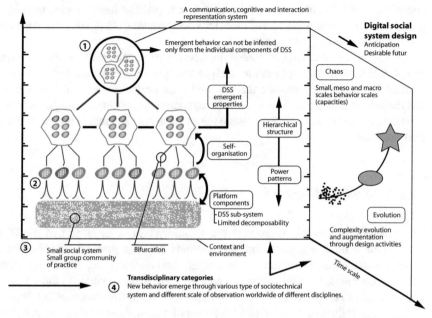

① Digital social system are complex sociotechnical systems involving ② many objects and components dynamically interaction give birth to various ③ communication levels which are asking for ④ new participative behaviors.

Fig. 10.1 Complex socio-technical system characteristics

ASPECTS ➡	ECOSYSTEM ENVIRONMENT	SOCIAL SYSTEM	DIGITAL SOCIAL SYSTEM, DESIGN PROCESS AND FEATURES	SOCIAL AND COMMUNICATIONAL RELATIONS	DSS AND PLATFORM FONCTIONS	MEDIASPHERE DESIGN TOOLS	AXIOLOGY AND SHARED VALUE
DOMAINS ➡	EXOSTRUCTURE	ENDOSTRUCTURE	OBJECTIVES AND DESIGN PROCESS	SOCIO-COMMUNICATIONAL PROCESS	FEATURES	SOCIAL TECHNOLOGIES	ETHICS
EXOSTRUCTURE		ENDO X EXO	OPD X EXO	SCP X EXO	FEA X EXO	SoT X EXO	ETH X EXO
ENDOSTRUCTURE	EXO X ENDO	**ENDO X ENDO**	OPD X ENDO	SCP X ENDO	FEA X ENDO	SoT X ENDO	ETH X ENDO
OBJECTIVES AND DESIGN PROCESS	EXO X ODP	ENDO X ODP	**ODP X ODP**	SCP X ODP	FEA X ODP	SoT X ODP	ETH X ODP
SOCIO-COMMUNICATIONAL PROCESS	EXO X FEA	ENDO X FEA	ODP X SCP	**SCP X SCP**	FEA X PSC	SoT X SCP	ETH X SCP
FEATURES	EXO X FEA	ENDO X FEA	ODP X FEA	SCP X FEA	**FEA X FEA**	SoT X FONC	ETH X FONC
SOCIAL TECHNOLOGIES	EXO X SoT	ENDO X SoT	ODP X SoT	SCP X SoT	FEA X SoT	**SoT X SoT**	ETH X SoT
ETHICS	EXO X ETH	ENDO X ETH	ODP X ETH	SCP X ETH	FEA X ETH	SoT X ETH	**ETH X ETH**

LEGEND
EXO : EXOSTRUCTURE (environment)
ENDO : ENDOSTRUCTURE (stakeholders)
ODP : OBJECTIVES AND DESIGN PROCESS
SCP : SOCIO-COMMUNICATIONAL PROCESS

FEA : FEATURES (of the platforms as DSS)
SoT : Social technologies
ETH : ETHICS (shared value)

Pierre-Léonard Harvey, 2017
Adapted from Bartolomei (2007) and Moles (1990)

Fig. 10.2 Exogenous components' matrix (as part of 2MDSAM) (Adapted from Bartolomei (2007) and Moles (1990))

The main environmental components are the political, social, cultural, economic and technological factors that promote, force or modify the DSS characteristics. Each of these exogenous elements and contain properties and attributes that describe the characteristics of each of the components. For example, for the practitioner's community of a hospital, the governance and regulation mechanisms, the city's goods and services and the cost of electricity and science state of advancement constitute environmental components.

Let us start by observing the interactions between exogenous elements and exogenous. It is sometimes important to analyse this type of interaction. For a hospital, it could be interaction between the fair medication price (exogenous component) and the help and the government grants (exogenous component), or the gap between government norms and policies guiding the medical acts and real practices of clinician communities.

10.2.2   Stakeholders

The stakeholder's matrix represents the social system, a large part of the DSS endostructure field, encompassing the relations between partners and the social appropriation of collaboration technologies. Stakeholders are the components (entities, elements, for a modeling abstract purpose) that contribute to the system's objective and that control the various systems' resources (the community) dispose of them. The influence of the network's power of action, spatial extension or cyberspace and the mastery of action landscape and various elements of the endostructure (organization, DSS, partnership contracts, collaborative network) represent the system's boundaries. To identify the stakeholders of a DSS project, it is useful to ask the following questions: Who benefits from it? What are the concrete benefits? Who finances the project? Who provides the 2.0, 3.0 or 4.0 media or collaborative platforms? Who loses? What are the constraints and norms in effect with each partner?

Interactions between stakeholders make the collaborative social network mediatized by technology. These multiple interrelations can be analysed and synthesized in different ways. In the setting of a health agency and its regional partners, for example, the analysis of social networks can facilitate the comprehension of interactions between a hospital and the various healthcare partners, for example, or between the departments and the associative communities of a region in order to organizational design of the care continuum, to verify the information relating to the best collaborative practices or to optimize the care efficiency for certain types of illness through the exchange of inter-professional expertise.

10.2.3   DSS Objectives

The objectives matrix represents a part of the functionalities field that defines the often complex combinatory between the various actors' intentions and the general and specific objectives of the project. The objectives contain the explicit and implicit DSS needs and the communication requirements and conditions specific to each participating member (within or outside the institution or responsible organization). A hospital objective can be to create practice communities in metal health in order to improve daily patients monitoring. Properties and attributes can include quantifiable needs, performance indicators and analysis tools for social media's performance in the patient's evaluation and monitoring, concerning the increase of family doctors according to the communities to serve, the number of emergency admissions, the structuring degree of an ambulatory shift or the relief of an emergency regarding the level of collaboration of various partner communities.

The objectives × objectives interaction matrix allows the modeler or the community informatics expert to represent the interactions between various objectives. For example, if a hospital seeks to reduce its operating costs and optimize the quality of life of its personnel, there might be some enormous contradictions in the system. Likewise, if we wish to maximize contacts between patients while putting all the clinical actors in distant geographical networks, certain contradictions might occur. Or if we try to make certain practices transparent that could potentially harm the expertise exclusivity of certain doctors. Finally, the simultaneous desire to cut in all the healthcare services and increase the number of doctors in remote regions will create problems at the healthcare administration level.

The objectives × objectives interactions are essential to all complex projects because they reveal obvious important contradictions or paradoxes at the beginning and throughout DSS projects.

10.2.4   Functionalities

Functions (or functionalities) describe the actions the DSS performs to meet the objectives. Described by verbs in the community informatics design model, they are accomplished in priority by humans but also by smart machines (robots), collaborative platforms and creativity tools. Each function must have a link or a relation with an objective or another function. Like in the APSI project, it was about creating instantiation norms to build a SADC; several functions of our DSS nominally seek to coordinate and create governance modes and respect ethics modes to maintain the trust and reputation. They may contain properties and attributes easily identifiable, measurable like socio-demographic or socio-professional information of the members of a community (or even the list of components to instantiate by fields). They can also be connected to certain forms of DSS or favour certain particular aspects and attributes of a field. Each community informatics design socio-technology or activity is connected to a particular form of DSS to co-build, hence the importance to link the functionalities to the fields of activity (see our DSS typology essay in Chap. 6).

The ethical or cultural aspects are sometimes more difficult to seize, but these heuristic methods very well serve to apprehend them qualitatively, even if we need to equip them with a more systematic evaluation measure later on. For example, how can we guarantee the security of all patients' electronic files in a hospital? What tools or platforms can meet the users of a hospital website trust needs and security? What types of mobile applications can satisfy the physiotherapists acting in emergencies at the level of any administrative region while accessing the information contained in the patients' files? What information, communication and collaboration tools can accompany knowledge sharing (functionalities) in a virtual community tribe of diabetics with international ramifications? In a hospital, functionalities related to the personnel and patients training or to the collaboration between community organizations and the hospital professional services could be retained for more general functionality purposes of the healthcare services' coordination.

As for the functionalities × functionalities interactions, our group has identified various types of functionalities between different functions associated with the creation of a DSS, for example, the respective knowledge of the members of a healthcare community and the necessity to share certain knowledge, discuss and talk about the healthcare service planning, simulate costs and its specific governance modes and debate the ethics factors to consider and the service modeling procedures and needs. There can be various types of more abstract social relations to consider (socio-communicational aspects). For example, the type of network according to existing hierarchies, relations between services (between human resources and the members training formation). In fact, we can deconstruct social relations into sub-functions like extra training units, actors collaboration in diverse sub-tasks, emergency services to improve users' well-being, information services to create and social networks to promote.

10.2.5   Socio-technologies (Technological Architectures and Collaborative Tools)

Socio-technologies' matrix brings into play the platforms' physical infrastructure components, software tools and collaborative technologies for design support. It is also the field of study that observes social media associated with the analysis, research, research action and R-D relative to the improvement of computer-mediatized social participation technologies, in all sorts of fields and for all sorts of activities, in practice or innovation communities. These components are destined to create technological infrastructures and non-human physical entities that support design and research for the benefit of stakeholders, users/designers of civil society, universities, enterprises and organizations, the government and its agencies.

Socio-technologies' matrix supports the efforts of one or several practices, virtual or not, communities in the realization of their objectives according to the functionalities identified by the team in charge and the stakeholders. For the APSI project, the Colab infrastructure has been hosted at the UQAM's Sciences Pavillon by our colleagues Guy Gendron and Abderraman Ourahou. The platform choice (infrastructure) was the latest version of the Joomla! platform, from a series of criteria elaborated in a previous project funded by our partner Clarica/Sun Life through the researches we were conducting at Hexagram/UQAM (a research and art creation and media technologies centre based in Montreal), we have been members for 12 years and where we have developed the virtual communities design and socio-technical systems foundations. The ACIL houses educational software and tools for cyber learning in the spirit of digital literacy. The multi-criteria analysis chart guiding the choice of a platform will be presented later.

Socio-technologies × socio-technologies interactions, interactions between various types of technological objects, like infrastructures, the material and software, social media and creativity tools (modeling, simulation, visualization), have been the object of an important reflection the present book wants to acknowledge. Instead of adopting a classical techno-centred approach or reject it completely, the entire reflection about technological structures was made around socio-technical systems in order to find an instantiation method focused on the human that could take into account the various types of architectures, like the technological systems and the organizational architectures (technologies management approaches and institutional governance, enterprise architectures and organizational design) to which we have added an important analysis and design perspective we call "social and participative architectures" (closer to the social science theories and methodologies and participative research action our researchers were more familiar with).

Therefore, the interaction between diverse technological components cannot ignore the human-machine interfaces that are at the heart of the mediation and media coverage of collaborative social links. The socio-technologies × socio-technologies interaction is distancing itself from the pure machine × machine or infrastructure × infrastructure interaction, even if it necessarily keeps several aspects form it since infrastructures modeling accompanies the more abstract interactions promoted by platforms and social media. We focused our attention on problems like applications compatibility, systems interoperability between stakeholders, social appropriation of applications destined to the evolution of the community depending on the professions, the mastery of tools by professionals and clinicians, training needs and the cost of licences acquisition regarding open-source code software. In healthcare, for example, the evaluation of existing platforms of each of the partners according to professional activities and skills of various departments is an unavoidable socio-technical issue. We will give an example of the alignment matrix between objectives, functionalities and the social Web 2.0 tools.

10.2.6   Community Informatics Design Activities (As an Evolutive Process)

10.2.6.1   What Is a Design Situation?

The activities, as defined by Engeström's activity theory (1987, 1999), associated with community informatics design represent the dynamic field of analysis and the implementation of socio-communicational processes according to two models:

1. A *descriptive model* of the generic activity, based on the activity theory, serving to identify the best design activity model for a specific field ecosystem or a specific form of DSS (e.g. a business platform or an enterprise collaborative network). This model also helps describe the DSS in terms of media and collaborative tools, individual and community intention, the distribution and coordination of work, tasks and sub-tasks to perform, norms, procedures to respect and expected results as well as contradictions between socio-communicational processes and within each of them.

2. A *normative model* (Reymen 2001) seeking to accompany users/designers and community informatics experts thanks to a reflexive structure on the design process that contains seven phases of an iterative and open life cycle made of the following generic elements:

   - A *design situation* that contains the DSS to be co-created, because they do not yet exist, the properties and attributes of the DSS influencing the design process, for example, the seven phases of community informatics design that could be increased, decreased or modified depending on the case (the number of phases of the life cycle potentially creating different tasks and sub-tasks), depending on a more or less finished suite of steps or sequences of activities to be realized, as well as factors describing the exostructure and the endostructure influences (or socio-communicational processes) on design activities (properties and attributes of various aspects of objects, products, applications and services of the DSS that can evolve during its construction and the dependent factors of the people or community determining them).
   - The *relations in community informatics design* that unite properties and factors (limiting or rewarding) and express the influence of a property, an attribute or a factor on another property in a given design situation. For example, the relations in a practice community in hospitals could be of hierarchical, heterarchical or lateral; causal relations could be the object of hypothesis; we could also discover dependence or interdependence relations by analysing certain types of behaviours or conducts, appropriate or not, ethical or not. Relations could also be noted between the tools, the requirements and the needs of people, for example, telepresence workshops regarding social media and video-conferencing tools available in various patient communities, tools limiting or enhancing the workshops.

- *The representation of an entity* (components and elements), that is, the DSS undergoing modeling and design, a design process like the community informatics design seven phases spiral is the reproduction of a series of properties, attributes and factors of this entity in a mental image, an enriched image, a drawing, a collective representation model, a theoretical model, a graph, a diagram, a visualization or a 2D or 3D model, a prototype or a discovery or alignment matrix. For example, we could visualize the co-design activity process of doctors and nurses in a department, represent the members of a network with drawings and diagrams, describe the dialogue modes or conversational design according to certain functionalities to be created and make the enriched image of a DSS practice community project with all its components. The representation of a software can be its open-source code or an information flow diagram. Different representations of a same entity or technological object can be suggested and found in various sections of a digital library or a design assistance website. The cognitive or mental representations of various actors can be different on several aspects. The design intentions can be represented according to a variety of thinking modes, language types (formal or informal) and dialogue or animation modes. Representation modes can be aligned, contradict, oppose and complete themselves.
- *The state of an entity*, or the series of values, identified for all properties and factors that influence this entity (related to the DSS or the community informatics design process) at a certain given moment in time. The state of an entity can also be considered, in Dooyeweerd's aspects definition (1984), like a specific property of this entity. It also describes a particular portrait of this identity according to the project's state of advancement or DSS maturation. Its value is represented by a series of values.
- *The description of the state of an entity*, or a specific representation of a subseries of values (monetary, ethics, cultural) of the state of the entity, based on the general terminology of state transition systems. A state description by the concepts text must be put to contributions. Therefore, to represent dynamic phenomena, concepts can be represented by images, videos, animations and various types of diagrams.
- *Current properties* of a social system of a design process at a certain moment in time.
- *Desirable properties* related to intentions and objectives of the community or the community informatics expert. Current properties are determined or influenced by the users/designers community (eventually based on expert designers experts' opinions) and by the design context. Users/designers can identify the desirable properties but factors related to the exostructure or emerging factor scan also be determining for the design elements articulation. The desirable properties rely on questions and concepts generally used in various design professions, such as needs, constraints, procedures, conditions, specification, modeling and instantiation.

- *The current state* of the DSS under design or under a community informatics design process is a series of values for all current properties.
- *The desirable state* of a DSS under construction or under a community informatics design process, represented by different series of values for all desirable properties.

From these definitions, we will admit that a design situation, at a precise moment, can be defined as a combination of the state of advancement of the DSS being designed, the community informatics design process state and the state of the design context at this moment. According to Reymen et al., this means the design situation includes:

1. The series of values of all properties of the different aspects describing the DSS under construction
2. The series of values of all properties serving to describe the design process
3. The series of values of all factors influencing the DSS being designed and its community informatics design process

This means that during the design process, community informatics experts build the representations of the DSS to co-build, the design process (inspired by the life cycle and classical design phases or by developing their own imaginative model) and the design context. The representation fabrication entails the modeling of reality from a particular point of view, by neglecting certain non-relevant aspects while validating others. Therefore, we will define the description of a community informatics design situation like the specific representation of relevant aspects' subcategories, the series of values and the series of all properties serving to describe the DSS being co-designed as well as the design process and the series of values influencing the DSS under co-construction and its community informatics design process. The description of a design situation is greatly improved by using entities' discovery and strategic alignment matrices (components, elements, communication phenomena) that allow to identify and describe the relations between the aspects properties and the DSS characteristics and the factors involved in the design situation.

Reymen's team and co-researchers suggest a way to make a difference between an entity, its representation, the state of an entity and the state of the description of this entity. Therefore, an entity exists in the realty (its aspects and its aspects' properties). Just like Reymen, we have chosen to model our entities (component s and reality elements) through the state concept (more relevant than the static entity concept) by including the values concept (and attributes) for properties and factors; a state is an "objective" because it is defined by the users/designers (e.g. a subjectivity shared in a distributed cognition). An entity can be represented in various ways (texts, diagrams, information flows, photos, video, animations). The representation of an entity is realized by a person, a community or an intelligent agent, according to a limited list of properties and factors. We do not insist on the values and properties in mathematical terms because they pose problems to large segments of the population. Large-scale design for all can today take advantage of several modeling tools combining texts and graphic elements, but where the entire computational aspect has been "algorithmed" in user-friendly software for a wide community of users.

In the community informatics design process supported by discovery and strategic alignment matrices and containing several types of aspects, properties and states, the concept of "interactive scenario" becomes important. The values of a certain property contain "relations" (e.g. costs regarding the resources to mobilize for a project) that can lead to a scenario or several possible scenarios when we analyse various types of aspects, properties and values combinations linked to each of the scenarios. For each possible scenario, the various properties of an entity can be more or less important. These scenarios can emerge in current design properties or in desirable properties.

10.2.6.2 What Is a Design Activity?

A community informatics design situation can be transformed into another design situation by one or several actions. Users/designers can change the current state of a DSS under development as well as the design process and its activities. Stakeholders can also change the design context. Let us remind that stakeholders are actors or partners that have an interest in a DSS products, applications or services. Users/consumers, users/designers in civil society, elected in charge of governance, administrators planning innovation policies and production or logistics managers can make the decisions at various stages of the development time continuum. The design context can also be modified by certain interactions between community informatics experts and stakeholders.

We call "transformation" an action oriented towards a goal. An action put in place without an explicit goal is a "mutation"; this happens spontaneously, without any intervention of the human conscience. This distinction is important in order to avoid language abuse and fakes. Therefore, a design activity is a transformation according to a design objective at a given moment and space, initiated by a user/designer or a community informatics expert that provokes a state transition of the DSS under construction or under the design process. For example, for the construction, in a hospital, of a virtual campus that adds to the traditional training given by the human resources direction (the type of university offering computer training), the implementation of a new training course like the one of Moira Allen' socio-constructivist healthcare approach and the implantation of a collaborative learning community will constitute a design activity. The change is triple since three new properties are added to the system in place. In fact, we go from:

1. A linear knowledge diffusion system (computer training) to a learning system by project
2. A bank of courses to teach to collaborative design activities by social learning

3. A group of users in individual training to a learning community by collaborative project (a new knowledge sharing mode, by socio-constructivist exercises in a learner community)

Transitions in the design context are described by transformations. Unplanned and emerging changes that occur during the deployment of the new solution are described as mutations. Community informatics experts and users designer of a virtual community of a DSS can modify the properties of the DSS under design and the community informatics design process (life cycle, phases, improvisation of actions to implement, occasional adaptations). The current properties and the desired properties can be modified, and other scenarios can be suggested. These could be articulated as prototypes to be experimented, social media to be configured on the hospital virtual campus platform, or simply a new concept to try according to a design objective and the functionalities related to it.

These new experimentations are helping to take calculated risks. Unheard properties emerge from new inputs or new knowledge brought in the DSS or the design process. Existing properties can be deconstructed into several sub-properties. The acts and actions seeking to modify the DSS state or the ongoing design process are translated by a new under design DSS representation or by design process modifications containing properties changes or new factors influencing the DSS structure or the design process. We can also modify the design process, its life cycle, its stages and tasks and sub-task sequences by carrying out changes on the entire process or at the level of certain specific sub-processes.

The production of a representation means either the creation or the co-creation of a new representation or the modification of an existing representation. For example, going from a conceptual mapping and the semantics network relying on the theory to a representation of living knowledge of the nursing personnel by the representation of objects, actions and people that Moira Allen's approach entails, it represents a transition between two types of representation. The transition of experts' theoretical concepts to the co-creation in conceptual maps teams, taking into account the real nursing personnel's practices, shows another transition, a radical one, in the way of seizing and sharing knowledge in order to produce more interactive online training scenarios and more iterative mock-ups.

The objective of a design activity is to create, with the help of Engeström's activity theory (1999) and his triangle "representing" an activity system at a moment in time, a modeling of the current social system (or the ecosystem), in other words, to create a representation of the desirable DSS state according to the desirable objectives we had set. The DSS under design must respect the desired DSS properties conditions, and the DSS representations must respect the desired properties for a given representation. In this spirit, the representation must respect the requirements of a representation media (a written description, the transcription of a dialogue, a photo, a 3D modeling, a video presentation, a schematization, an animation with or without a text) as well as the stakeholders' needs, depending on the utilities or the general costs related to a solution or a given scenario.

Often, the final goal of a design activity is not explicit. For example, it could mean to make the desired use of a website research tools more convivial. For the DSS desired state, functionalities × collaborative research tools mock-ups could be produced as double-entry discovery matrices where information research systems' convivial properties, like learning time, cognitive costs and tool appropriation efforts, would be defined by values or arbitrary or symbolic measures, thus translating more or less accurately their conviviality degree. The representation could contain text, symbolic equations and transactional video scenarios on the Internet allowing to determine the level of tools' ease of use and to help the design of potential replacement scenarios.

10.2.6.3   A Descriptive Design Process

In accordance with the semiformal approach we have adopted throughout the present book, we do not define the design process like a formal programming and planning algorithm, what would be contrary to community informatics creativity and imagination. Nor do we define it as a completely informal system where we would have a total creativity freedom. In the first case, it is a more closed-up process, containing well-defined stages. In the second one, it is about the emergence, even improvisation, without the capacity to seize all the interaction and design patterns, an operation made impossible by the lack of traces. Furthermore, this second approach is not really interesting for us, because the lack of stages or of a scaffolding of semi-open or semiformal sequences would prevent us from carrying out approaches that are specific to the grounded theory, for example, by learning from the ground experience or by feedback and a process evaluation (lack of process). The heuristic does not mean an unbridled creativity but a discovery and imagination process characterized by a semiformal approach and catalysed by animation and well-identified governance mechanisms.

Without coming back to the definition and design theories addressed in the first part of the book, with modeling in mind, let us remind that we can consider the design process like a more or less finished sequence (because sometimes it ends in the project's computing section) of design activities necessary to meet a need, a result fulfil an intention or meet an objective. Theories, research process, quantitative or qualitative methods, collaborative tools and platforms, DSS time spaces and their various arrangements, the three levels of skills and digital literacy are all examples of design situations.

A designer, a community informatics expert or an important collective of users/ designers can perform design activities according to more or less linear sequences, iterative circular processes or more or less parallel applications incorporated during a phase of designs consolidation. In fact, the community informatics design process, as collaborative and participative design, can be realized by various teams and in different time spaces. The change objects, aspects and subjects sometimes command a different co-design life cycle from one community to another. The design process properties can also be different from one team to another and act on the

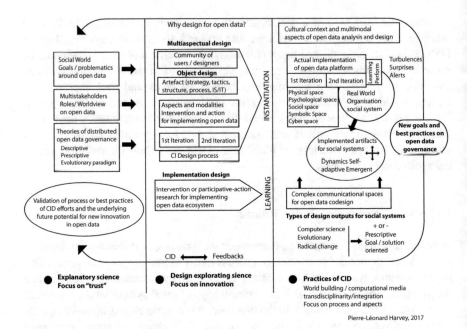

Pierre-Léonard Harvey, 2017

Fig. 10.3 A community informatics design (CID) process and activities: a project architecture for the governance of open data

causes of these changes, which could modify the activity sequence and the tasks to realize.

During the entire community informatics design process, community informatics experts can focus in turn on the under design DSS, on the design process (in seven, eight or nine phases or depending on the various aspects to model), on the design context or on the current and desired design properties. Series of properties and values (e.g. various modes of co-creation) can be added, deleted or modified according to new experiences, the context evolution or the collective maturation of an issue. The development and evaluation of design propositions or alternative scenarios constitute ways to realize social learning or experiences during a design process. In fact, it is a highly creative process that entails a "sociological imagination", the exploration of new knowledge worlds with open data and prospective efforts in the research of future development solutions based on new goals and best practices outcomes (Fig. 10.3).

The goal of a design process is to create one or several under design DSS representations, giving an ideal image of its properties, and its future desirable state, like discovery and exploration matrices, can allow us to do so. The DSS must also meet the members and the stakeholders' needs in terms of desirable design process properties. Often, the goal of a design process entails its desired properties (e.g. the alignment of goals with certain functionalities). These desired properties can be formulated at the level of the final design process state (like the budget and the project completion) or focus on the process state during the design (like the schematization of certain design process states, the adoption of a certain type of modeling matrix, the appropriation of a software tool to manage the projects or visualization, the planning of various types of presentation or workshops seeking to present stages reports and intermediate results, instructions for the documentation or bibliography or the creation of a glossary). The design goal can then be formulated and articulated as a product co-creation, a task or a specific application during a particular process (choosing a decision-making for remote teams' works). The design goals are then jointly defined by stakeholders and users/designers, usually with the help of a community informatics expert or a computing designer whose skills allow configuration and the integration of any software applications at all level. Users/designers and computing experts collaborate to define the properties of the DSS to build; they have the power to determine the desired representations with the technical advice of computing experts.

Let us remind that the current and desired properties, as they are modeled with discovery and exploration matrices, can be added, modified and deleted during the entire DSS co-creation process. It is both a natural evolutive change process and an intentional cultural process. In the evolutive systems theory like in the social systems one, the simultaneous evolution of current properties and desired properties are called "co-evolution". We can then create in a community of practice one or several representations of a system (e.g. for the UQAM's Colab, we started from a schematic representation of the system's global architecture by text zones and arrows to get to present the various versions of the portal's architecture as a table of contents that describes the portal structure in a linear way, Chap. 6). We could rescue these modules in the modules in a table of contents' tree view ("home page", various sections like "projects", "members", "tutorials", "collaborative tools") and present them as text to later transform them into more educational synthetic texts succinctly describing modules that can be incorporated into an action plan to represent the design steps and facilitate programming and Web planning.

A design task at a certain moment is a task that aims at the design goals at this moment of the development, starting with the current design situation. One or several users/designers, sometimes scattered in various stakeholders, perform a task by carrying out design activities. Another way to express this design task concept is to say that it is made of a series of actions seeking to transform the current state of the DSS being co-designed or the characteristics and properties of the community informatics design process by taking into account the context elements at the micro-, meso- and macrosocial level. This evolution at the tasks level is often related to the design process goals, which, at the beginning of the project, are often vague and intangible. Certain constraints or procedures associated with design activities force the users/designers and the community informatics experts to modify their strategy, to plan differently their creation processes and refine their goals and objectives. The end of the co-design process (according to the design maturity criteria determined by a team) occurs when the state of the under design DSS and its multiple representations (properties, attributes, instantiation modes) aligns with the design project goals. In the daily practice, let us remind that tasks are not always well explained.

A community informatics design task can be made of several sub-tasks when the discovery and strategic alignment matrices reveal its properties in a more precise way or an appropriate questioning on the ways to proceed, in relation to the DSS objectives, show the usefulness. A sub-task at a certain moment is a task that simply seeks to reach the design objectives at a precise moment in the DSS development. For example, it could be about creating a collective under-construction DSS representation at a certain level of detail or analysis or at a certain society tier, by focusing on certain DSS co-design aspects at a precise moment of the community informatics design life-cycle process. For example, during phase 1 of the design's seven-phase life cycle, a community could decide to create a list of useful concepts for the design of a certain form of DSS under design and agree to divide this operation into sub-tasks mediatized by a wiki, by distributing it to the team in charge and the network partners in order to reduce the burden of defining the terms related to the entire task and, therefore, improve the concepts comprehension connected to the study of the design situation and the co-design process. Also, we could decide to adopt a specific dialogue mode, to use this communication mode for the implementation of design workshops and organizational coordination sub-tasks for various members or teams.

The evolution of properties, representations and positive or negative feedback on design activities can influence the design objectives. At the end of a DSS process, new sub-tasks (e.g. theoretical concepts to define by the grounded theory technique) require other new modeling and modification sub-tasks leading to a renewed design process. This is what happened to our team, during the APSI project, when the examination of our reference architectures properties like TOGAF, ARCON, Zachman framework and CoSpaces empirically convinced us of the necessity to add two additional phases to the life cycle seven original ones, and furthermore, these phases could be replaced by "metamorphosis", a phase when an important transition forces the team to adopt a wide array of the DSS properties or representations, or, also, by a *dissolution* phase when, on an ad hoc basis, a virtual practice community must stop its works or dissolve the team or simply because we have reached the end of a funded research project.

The execution of a sub-task creation can be the work of a manager in charge of collaboration, the facilitator of a practice community or the director in chief of knowledge management. Carrying out sub-tasks is articulated around several factors, a certain duration in time, the team composition and its various professions and transdisciplinary expertise, the DSS and form DSS favoured by the team and the operational objectives, social media and collaborative tools available or really mastered by the team's members and the stakeholders' respective responsibilities. Work distribution and general sub-task coordination related to the community informatics design seven spaces and their scheduling in precise sub-tasks can be considered as a strategic design activity, with a verification list of entities (elements and component) established from Engeström's activity theory triangle (1999) modeled through the stakeholders discovery and strategic alignment matrices and social networks, objectives and properties matrices and social media matrices and functionalities).

Each design task at each life-cycle stage, for each type of architecture (technological, organizational, social) identified in our DSS model, has a specific design context; each design context is in turn defined in connection with a specific design context. Users/designers and community informatics experts performing a design task and afferent sub-tasks can interact with other stakeholders, other professions and specialists of various disciplines involved in the projects. According to a specific design context, they can exchange different types of social information (Jaffelin 1991, 1995; Harvey 2005, 2006a, b, 2008), from various modes of computer-mediatized communication and social participation devices. Namely, they can share knowledge regarding the under-construction DSS desired properties, refine the design process properties with the help of concepts expressed in this chapter, precise and validate the desire properties, evaluate the values of different factors like in the social appropriation of various collaborative modeling tools. They can also influence and modulate these factors by various dialogue modes (Banathy and Jenlink 2005; Christakis and Bausch 2006; Judge 2008a, b) and coordinate their negotiation/deliberation on global and local solutions to add to the various types of issues and challenges related to DSS design/implantation.

A "design space" or a "co-design exploratory space", at a precise moment, is a design activity space that contains the current state of the social system to transform as well as a series of all possible states directed towards a goal and motivated by the under-construction DSS design intentions and its articulation, its feedback and its potential effect on the ongoing design process. The design space in the various community informatics is modeled like the global architecture of a design system represented by the community informatics design's seven spaces with entities that are evaluated by the community informatics design analysis matrix and by the "design space concept", matrix which contains the modeled design process entities in the present section and the questions and programs in the following sections. The first one indicates the types of design that occur in an experts' practice community or non-initiated and their state at a given moment of the DSS development. The second one helps us identify all the future desired states by people in charge and stakeholders with the help of a design process.

We will see that the global architecture schematized by the seven spaces allows to collectively generate analysis of use and the types of design to adopt to accompany and model the future desirable or desired states according to the three main types of community informatics architecture: technological, organizational and social. These future states of architectures as well as the identification of their properties and their values are channelled in the current design state, for input activities, removal or modifications of properties and values related to them. The states of the environment and the design context belong only partially or indirectly to the design space, because designers of any level and expertise have no real influence on them, unless the DSS has the explicit goal of influencing the environment (the exostructure) and the design context with a particular attention to social architectures (e.g. by the animation and the large-scale cultural or socio-political intervention strategies).

The design space concept as defined by Elizabeth B.-N. Sanders and Bo Westerlund (2011) is useful for the comprehension of the design act and tasks related to it and for the reflection in the action (Schön 1983), intervening in design activities (Engeström 1999). With the multiplication of collaborative design practices and partnerships involving more and more the non-specialist designers' contribution (Preece and Shneiderman 2008, 2009), our researches lead us to consider the co-design space concept and the community informatics design exploratory space as more precise than the traditional design space done on the drawing table or on a microcomputer of a single designer. Taking into account the social media growth, the citizen science rapid evolution, like in the fab labs and the living labs concepts, society becomes a sort of innovation co-laboratory where players are not defined ahead of time nor once and for all. To the contrary, community informatics imagination plays a great role because our models have a hard time adapting to all these changes.

In this spirit, the co-design or community informatics design space differs from the traditional "design space", because it can be conceptually and practically located (Hutchins 2000, 2010) at the very beginning of the design process (pre-design or pre-planning of sub-space 1, "Explore") which relies on the collective creativity of designers working together with non-specialist designers communities. They negotiate and deal very complex issues like social change, organizational transformations and the DSS co-creation through various dialogue modes. They empathize the importance of products, services and applications instantiation, in fields more and more immaterial like social action and practices and social systems design. From there, emerges the need to evaluate a "design space" in terms of change or transition, not only at the level of its properties but also at the best practices level of the design process of future desirable states.

Our researches on action verbs in community informatics and in community informatics design, as revealed in our various case studies and two questionnaires, show that an analytical framework based on the notion of an evolutive community informatics design exploratory space in transition state can substantially improve our comprehension of users' needs by experiencing, exploring and experimenting in, by and through the moments illustrated by community informatics design seven spaces, the DSS design to its instantiation in a portal open to change.

Community informatics design is a transformation activity of the existing social system or DSS's current state serving to validate an existing community or to create new institutions and to "digitalize" them as communities or virtual organizations through a communication reframing of the design process oriented by the DSS objectives. To practise their profession and their skills, community informatics designer, new essential figures in the computational social sciences, root their practices in the design situation at a precise moment and perform their various tasks and sub-tasks to achieve the design objectives. The interaction modeling task between expert designers, users/designers, stakeholders and peer networks in the design context is a complex task made necessary so that all DSS co-creation participants are informed of the representations by all members and ontologies of other partners, in order to debate important factors of the design context and to deliberate on the influences of important DSS characteristics and properties as well as on the adoption and negotiation of design processes and activities to favour. Sometimes, these discussions bring practice communities to modify the design goals, just like a context change can occur because of unexpected exogenous factors influencing the design objectives in a completely different way than the objectives formulated by the partners.

By developing a community informatics design model process, our team has defined concepts and terms as parts of reality (entities, components, elements, properties of these elements, values of these elements studied by the philosophy of sciences) and others as representations of reality (signs, discourse symbols, meaning studied by semantics and semiotics). In the table of the following page, our concepts are presented in the left column and channelled in a matrix that, row by row, presents the general questions we can formulate in a communication research context.

10.3 A Normative Design Process Guiding the Critical Thinking

We can define the reflection upon the community informatics design process like a critical thinking process structured around the community informatics design seven spaces, according to a descriptive model developed in Sect. 5.6. The normative community informatics design model is only summarily elaborated here for exploratory matrix modeling process purposes. The detailed seven spaces instantiation process has been presented in the previous section. In Chap. 7, we presented a list of concepts based on this operational strategy that could be supported by discovery and strategic alignment matrices. In Chap. 8, we presented a list of terms aligned on the example of the adaptation of a life cycle supported by the seven spaces generic methodology. Supported in this task by our colleagues Marie Kettlie André and Hassane Beidou, we will present a fictitious instantiation and modeling strategy that relies on the theoretical definitions of the community informatics instantiation and modeling and on the list of terms defined and presented in the last two chapters, especially within the aspects theory framework and the transition state's systems theory. The concepts focused on critical thinking rely more specifically on the descriptive model terminology.

Let us note that we try to identify and define all the concepts of the study well. If this model can eventually throw off certain researchers who are not familiar with several of our concepts, they at least are accompanied by references and the research teams' mention that created them, often by relying on numerous transdisciplinary researches. We simply wish to put a little rationality where certain researchers only see improvisation, emergence, unbridled creativity and artistic freedom. Science rises more from rigor than from debonair behaviours. In addition, an online glossary will eventually accompany our definitions (Harvey's online site 2018), which represents another effort towards the inter-comprehension between disciplines and professions.

10.3.1 Community Informatics Design Reflection Process

The main descriptive model concepts presented in Sect. 5.6 are the design situation and the design activities. Community informatics experts start from a design situation in space 1 of the design spiral at certain moment. We define the "design process reflection" like an activity seeking the critical examination of designers' perceptions on the collaborative design situation and on what they cognitively master from the design activities. This process is done through various philosophical design thinking modes (as seen in Chap. 3) that offer a reflection basis to systematically consider the ways a community informatics expert guide himself on certain principles, of which he analyses, interprets and develops a thinking oriented by a goal and intentions, and all these acts (once again channelled in the verbs) are articulated together. We will come back to it further along in this chapter. The design process reflection will be defined than as a combination of "reflexive thinking mode on the design situation" and the reflection about design activities retained or memorized in a data base.

The design situation gives a static base to the design process, while the design activities give a dynamic perspective of the process. The analysis of discourses and representation modes on the design situation brings to light the following elements:

1. The difference perceived between the current situation and the desired properties of the future DSS to develop must be known in order to verify if all the important aspects to model and instantiate are taken into account, individually and collectively.
2. The real difference between the current system state and its desired state through the design process, which is useful to judge and evaluate the project's progression or maturation.
3. The discovery of important factors in the exostructure or the design context that is useful to determine the future interactions with the design context entities and elements.

Different discovery and strategic exploration matrices can be built by teams that will later analyse the interaction patterns to extract from the social practices related to design. According to our vision, the seven spaces reflection (at least) should answer several essential questions: Are we trying to resolve essential problems or are we entangled in the sub-optimization of processes that have no incidence on the change or innovating objectives? Are the partial results satisfying or should we do more iterations or other feedback loops? Is our way of performing the design satisfying or efficient for all members? Is the seven spaces process a satisfying one? In other words, do the matrices allow to discover interactions between components and properties that are really relevant for our issues?

10.3.2   Community Informatics and Participative Reflection Process

The thinking process contains three main activities: the analysis, the synthesis and the reflection in action. These three activities have direct links with the basic seven spaces of the community informatics design life cycle (Harvey et al. 2013), with the basic mechanisms of the reflexive practice as suggested by the important works of

Donald Schön (1983) and Schön and Bennett (1996) for the main phases of problem-solving creative processes described in the works of Daudelin (1996), as well as with the generic interactions specific to various design processes as revealed by the discovery and strategic alignment matrix.

The analysis stage which corresponds to Space 1 called, "Explore", consists of documenting the subject, collecting the facts, preparing the start questions of the entire project and doing the critical analysis of the facts as revealed by a variety of tools, use case studies, questionnaires, group discussions and discovery matrices. In the preliminary analysis context, the facts are those we bring to light by returning to the properties; the factors connected with the various aspects of the issues identified by the discovery matrix; the relations between the design situation properties and factors, in the sense we described in this chapter; and the design activities performed throughout the design process itself. Evaluation criteria like coherence; project boundaries' identification; the approach and stage complementarity; the work consistency; the feasibility, the fidelity and the validity of the analysed facts; etc. could be of great utility.

The synthesis stage is a representation, vision and image formation stage that suggests a synthesis of analysis facts, either by mapping or by schematization of an image enriched as defined by Checkland or by other visualization, modeling or simulation software tools. To be equipped with an enriched image of facts and processes under study seeks to select elements (entities, components, properties) and to give ourselves an image of the DSS to build as globality, as a total ecosystem containing our instantiation concepts supported by discovery matrices analysis elements as well as concrete facts from the self-reflection done at the analysis stage.

During the stage of reflection in the action, the community informatics expert analyses the image obtained at the synthesis stage. He asks the following questions: Why is the situation represented this way? What can I learn? What should we change? What should be the next steps? Should we keep the same objectives?

10.3.3   Structured Reflection

The structured reflection is a community informatics design process; in the sense we understand it in this chapter, it is a combination of a reflection that is rigorous and systematic (we call it semiformal) and a reflection that leads on an ad hoc basis, as the collaborators team evolves in its reflections and practices in the action. The systematic approach (not scientific nor completely formal like in pure sciences) contributes to reduce the risks of avoiding certain important elements of the design process. The regular team reflection allows to bring potential changes and to suggest modifications to adjust the objectives. The structured reflection on the seven stages indicates what changes could be made and when and how they could be implemented. In the following pages, we will briefly focus on the "how", knowing it would be possible to answer the other questions in the next research or another book.

10.3.4   Reflection Regarding the Design Situation and the Activities

Towards the end of the APSI project, we had the idea to obtain an overall view of important facts regarding several facts from our theoretical models and of a beginning of acquired experience. This exercise ended up in three interrelated lists. The first list is an exhaustive description of the community informatics design situation, based on the questions relative to the DSS properties and the community informatics design process. The second list suggests a theoretical point of view; it is the intention of this chapter to give instantiation elements to carry out as well as the design process, exploration, alignment properties to do the first stage and the analysis one. The third list is meant to present the basic concepts and to define the fundamental terms associated with DSS properties, in order to extract the forms, boundaries, characteristics and attributes; the relations between properties and factors, in a design situation; the activities really performed; and the planned activities according to goals by including a strong communication perspective, in other words, the relations and interactions cartography between all these entities, must they be tangible and intangible (Verna Allee 1998, 2002), formal and semi-formal, artistic and emotional, quantifiable and qualifiable.

During the APSI mandate and through all the co-design processes, whether they are workshops, group discussions, modeling or decision-making regarding collaborative tools or the choice of social media that are useful for the community informatics design process, our forms took the configuration of tables, sheets of paper and task list to fulfil in the management software Communa4 suggested by the researcher Abderraman Ourahou, members and partners directory, basic and common ontologies vocabulary in the philosophical sense of the word. The conservation of all these elements is to allow us to come back on certain computer-memorized elements or to keep on file the fundamental texts destined to the post-project reflection (which is the goal of the present book) and to the identification of important contents for subsequent publications. The entire chapter seeks to connect the practice and the theoretical models.

The second list was channelled in the metaphorical expression of "Hassane's boxes", taken from the list of elements to instantiate by the researcher Hassane Beidou, and we had to systematically analyse the conceptual and practical interactions. To make that list, largely inspired by the important work of Luis M. Camarinha-Matos and Hamideh Afsarmanesh et al. (2008), we have put together a new smaller team of three people and defined, from the first iteration of our own works, our reference models and our research results, a list of elements, entities to take into account, by keeping in mind the elements surveyed in our questionnaire (the socio-demographic characteristics, the types of virtual and innovation communities, design, governance, ethics, the project's closure or expansion activities, etc.), the case studies results and the enormous documentation on living labs. This list, and its results exposed in the following chapter, helps to take into account a good number of elements to maintain in various design situations and in the design activities associated them. It also helps define an instantiation or research framework, in other words, design boundaries, by making an inventory of the aspects to be retained by the community informatics experts. It finally must be made up to date with current sociological, managerial and technological evolution.

For community informatics design as envisioned by the present design proposition, this list is an example to take into account in the community informatics instantiation process presented in the first part of this chapter. It helps to establish norms, sections, functionalities and the entities' properties to instantiate from the description and the synthesis of the seven fields to model: the exostructure, the endostructure, the community informatics design activities, communication structures and processes, functionalities, socio-technologies, ethics and values.

The third list, presented as questions, was created by our colleague Marie-Kettlie André. This detailed list is presented in a text, first inspired by community informatics design "seven spaces", that suggests a "verification list" for the scaffolding of the technological, organizational and social architectures and overall entities in the design process. In doing this task, with the help of the Camarinha-Matos and Afsarmanesh framework (2008), and by analysing the precise community informatics design situation we have followed, it rather suggests a "nine spaces" nomenclature, and that, after a reflexive process of return on our situation (and our activities) during several months, in early 2012. This list incorporated to a strategic exploration text is presented in Chap. 5. (We can also find long excerpts in the Colab website.) It is a fictitious modeling example (instantiation) after the completion of the research and development My Portal Col@b mandate realized within the APSI project. These nine steps are aligned with the seven initial steps of the community informatics design exploratory space, and they complete it by adding two more.

Therefore, from a checklist organized as terms and questions and coming from a methodological questioning related to the creation of the seven spaces, several questions related to the three main architecture types (TOGAF, Ecolead, Zachman) suggested in the present book and a list of questions related to the creation of questions contained in "Hassane's boxes" from the ARCON project, we end up with a scenario example containing the entire elements and research or design activity questions, as well as two additional stages. Hassane Beidou and Marie Kettlie André wanted to answer the generic following questions: What are the Colab or a DSS desired properties? What part of the effort and the budget should be dedicated to this stage? (Let us remind that the costs and the budget and action plan realization evaluation go through an appropriate terminology definition and by the identification of concrete realization steps appropriate to each design situation.) What are the project's stakeholders and what are their needs? What are the generic entities to take into account? What are the important steps of the life cycle to determine, to keep, to modify and to add? These questions seek to show that users/designers can answer to these questions in team while performing an important and interesting approach of the life cycle in the light of budget time as presented in Chap. 6 dedicated to the presentation of transition state systems theory.

These lists seek to show the feasibility of an instantiation inspired by a reference framework norms aiming to explore more concrete possibilities of a project. These work propositions for the definition and classification of systems should be evaluated in the next few years in workshops, classes and concrete realizations (longer ones). They could, and it is our dearest wish, inspire our future students dealing with DSS development during their undergraduate or graduate studies.

10.3.5   Reflection Regarding the Design Situation

The description of a design situation entails that we model reality as we have done here, from a certain point of view, of a certain world vision of this reality by neglecting certain characteristics. To do so, we asked ourselves the following questions, based on our foundations, our ontological definitions, our definitions of aspects, properties, etc. One of the good methods consists of making checklists and forms specific to help designers in making decisions on the important elements of a given design situation.

To describe a design situation is like explaining the state of a design task to a person involved or removed from the project. The problem is formulated in terms of reference frameworks and instantiation strategy; the needs to meet are described just like the desired solutions, the design process state (in part) and the activities associated to it. The means, tools, methodologies and techniques to achieve it are also drawn. Social media are described by functionalities, from the life cycle and the co-creation process related to it. The desired results are also stated; the fields of representation are brought out in order to show the coherence between the life cycle, the aspects and the fields to be modeled.

How to describe a design situation? We suggest to do a textual description of a set of relevant elements, by giving references of other types of representations: matrix, process diagrams, modeling software, specific governance techniques or information research and prototypes. The description is a complex combination, created in an exhaustive way for a given situation while knowing that at each phase of the project, the personalized list of elements to model and instantiate can change. The description may contain elements from various disciplines, with skills from different fields of expertise or university departments, tangible or intangible elements, quantitative or qualitative information and more or less specialized knowledge. Let us remind that the exercise does not aim at exhaustiveness at all cost; it is instead about making a design proposition that maintains the aspects, their most important properties and factors. It is important to realize that the main goal of the element list described in this chapter is the reflection and the non-formalization of a completely document process of the issue relative to a solution. We cannot say which aspect is the most important, because it depends of each discipline, each task to execute and skills more or less specialized of each designer.

10.4   A Fictitious Case Study: Informatics Design Project Planning and Its Monitoring by Creating Entities Lists Through a Transdisciplinary Interaction Matrix

In the present section, which serves as an introduction for the next chapter, we rely on the works performed by researchers David Romero and Arturo Molina (2010) described in their article "Virtual organization breeding environment toolkit: Reference model, management framework and instantiation methodology". Our goal is not to systematically use their work but get inspired by it and adapt it. In this spirit, we will show how to use it in the context of community informatics strategies in terms of project structuring, diffusion, innovation, management and planning community informatics design that can create a DSS within an organization or a territory community or cross-borders.

Therefore, the community informatics design process that we will try to demonstrate contains a vision oriented towards several conceptual categories described in our reference model, with the support of our methodological and systematic iteration process, that refer to the seven fields to model (endostructure, exostructure, etc.) within the seven spaces design life cycle presented in the previous chapters. One of the first elements of this strategy is to proceed to a first complete iteration of the seven phases and by keeping in mind the seven fields to model, but without systematically taking them in a fixed way, in other words, by referring to it in terms of checklist elements to take into account during the design realization. This list will vary according to each specific project. Therefore, at each of the seven design spaces ("explore" "imagine", "resolve", "incorporate", "model", "prototype", "deploy"), we will examine the design tasks to accomplish as well as the terms and concepts referring to them, in terms of reference framework and action to undertake. We start the process by keeping in mind our seven spaces and our seven fields, and we reorganize them according to large modeling lines that correspond to the open and flexible nature of the community informatics design process. These guidelines, widely inspired by our reference framework, endure adjustments from our own experience during the reflection on our APSI research design process. These modeling lines for a DSS instantiation are:

- *The composition* that refers to the available resources for the community informatics design development as a technological innovation platform.
- *The functionalities* that are made of verbs surrounding the design or that take part of its definition (communicate, collaborate, cooperate, innovate, etc.).
- *The behaviours*, to see the approaches and roles attributed to designers by various stakeholders.
- *The ontology*, the implementation of governance, ethics and innovation notions.
- *The DSS dissolution or evolution*, the metamorphosis or state transition in terms of a virtual community life cycle deploying or dissolving.
- *The business strategy*, also called "organizational strategy (business models and platforms)".
- *Ethics*, a few aspects will also be on the agenda.

To reach the short-term objectives of a DSS oriented towards the finalities and perspectives at the basis of the collaboration in network systems, community informatics design commands previous co-creation of a good development environment. In other words, skills and the capacity to provide the essential conditions and mechanisms for a quick and flexible community informatics design configuration. In fact, this research presents a community informatics design reference model as a reference guide for design initiators, designers managers, experts in practice communities and users/designers in charge of the creation and the functioning of virtual and applicative environments.

Therefore, within the community informatics design reference model, the management aspect is also presented as a set of management activities and support tools to ensure a community informatics design will fulfil all the necessary tasks and functionalities to reach its objectives. The seven spaces can be considered as a governance system, and the community informatics design instantiation method is presented like a controlled process and monitoring until a certain point, addressing the systematic entities, with a series of evaluation measures and then with qualitative and semiformal measures, supported by various means (e.g. creativity and modeling tools and methods) to help establish management functionalities and operating of a design during its complete life cycle, on the community informatics design reference model basis.

In fact, once again, we remind that this section dedicated to the operationalization of a DSS by community informatics design is inspired by Romero and Molina (2010, 2011) and is an adaptation and a reappropriation of several concepts discovered during the APSI research and at the heart of our community informatics design researches, which gives its highly illustrative value since it combines both approaches. In this spirit, this chapter is widely dedicated to create an illustration of the way to use the seven iterative spaces of community informatics design while adapting them to several elements of our seven fields of modeling (exostructure, endostructure, functionalities, resources, etc.) and by the description of entities to model contained in a checklist. We will focus on this type of modeling through the creation of these lists in the next chapter.

Chapter 11
The Organization and Governance of an Incubation and Learning Environment with the Help of Tool Boxes: Reference Model, Community Informatics Design Framework and Instantiation Methodology

For 30 years, a wide variety of long-term strategic alliances have generated organizations such as the industrial clusters (Norman and Porter 2007; Porter and Karmer 2006), the industrial districts (Becattini et al. 1990) and network organization ecosystems such as collaborative enterprise networks and interconnective universities. These alliances have emerged in common regions (technology hub) gathering organization groups ready to cooperate with the objective of creating group opportunities within organizations that taken individually would not have benefited from the same development capacities, especially regarding the level of cost.

These alliance strategies have been limited on the long term, either because of the geographical proximity of the members making up this group, either because of the lack of adequate telepresence or convivial tools. Retroactively, this limitation presents a certain advantage, to energize the local cultures common to a group of given partners, which facilitates the establishment of a trusting environment and a sense of community. Let us think here about the case of the *Cité du multimédia* and the *Cité du commerce électronique* in Montreal. However, with the ICT, globalization, the market in constant movement and new virtual forms' progress over the past few years, these strategic alliances are more and more focused on the virtual industries (Molina et al. 1998) and on the organization of a virtual gathering of community informatics design environments.

These technological trends arouse the interest of organizations, especially the small and medium enterprises (SME), in order to overcome their geographical situation and to join in collaboration with one or several of these organizations in the global landscape. Community informatics design and its SADC, which we can define as an open-source code innovation ecosystem, to support users or managers of online communities and design assistance for interaction websites, are in the long-term an interactive design platform that will promote strategic alliances between the organizations seeking to offer multimodal conditions (human, financial, social, infrastructural and organizational) necessary to support the quick and fluid configuration of collaborative platforms useful to organizations and society. Therefore, community informatics design, defined by the UQAM's ACIL as

© Springer International Publishing AG 2017
P.-L. Harvey, *Community Informatics Design Applied to Digital Social Systems*,
Translational Systems Sciences 12, DOI 10.1007/978-3-319-65373-0_11

"socially responsible communicational design", mainly focuses on the creation of a suitable environment for the establishment of an adaptation, an appropriation, a cooperation and a collaboration, with the help of different technological supports, facilitating the implementation of an efficient environment for user/designer practices.

However, the DSS are coalitions and organization dynamics created in the short term and more or less well adapted to a maturation and collective commitment environment (gathering, incubation or learning environment that often commands long-term activities) to take advantage of a collaboration opportunity between designers and virtual environment users. This long-term intersectorial integration for collective action should done while incorporating the basic skills and necessary resources to reach, alongside with the quality frameworks and the evaluation of the delays and the costs expected by the recipient users whose cooperation is supported by computer networks (Camarinha-Matos and Afsarmanesh 2007) and digital media.

We have seen in the previous chapters that the present research offers an array of tools made of socially responsible design, oriented by seven design phases, a reference model, a management framework and an instantiation methodology, constituting a set of guidelines to support the processes and activities involved in the creation and functioning of new virtual environments. The community informatics design toolkit (the SADC) seeks to help design initiators and managers to understand the requirements and the planning mechanisms of the ICT tools and functionality management.

11.1   Community Informatics Design Characterization

The traditional organizations' design is generally focused on the linear and iterative transformation of the point-by-point value chain, towards the organization of a network structure known under the name of value network, aiming to increase the chances to take advantage of the collaboration opportunities. Community informatics design completes this perspective without rejecting it, based on the efficient ICT infrastructures to overcome the geographical constraints, in order to provide the common basis to instantiate the interaction between its members and with the finality of facilitating the configuration and the implementation of DSS.

The design then focuses on the introduction of new approaches and reinforcement mechanisms of trust as prerequisites for any collaboration. Therefore, community informatics design seeks to improve the members' preparation to join the community, the potential of future DSS defining a common ICT infrastructure stand and commercial rules of cooperation between autonomy and heterogeneity of communities of practice through electronic means (e.g. the information on systems and data bases; Afsarmanesh and Camarinha-Matos 2005).

11.2 Community Informatics Design's Aim and Benefits

As we have mentioned above, community informatics design seeks to establish a trusting basis between users and designers collaborating in a DSS, by reducing the costs and unnecessary delays to find suitable partners and to perform well-integrated architectural configurations, while providing the appropriate assistance (e.g. for methods, resources and tools) in order to reduce the complexity of the implementation and management throughout the digital social system creation process (Camarinha-Matos et al. 2005a, b, c). However, a community informatics design process development can provide various benefits to its users (e.g. in a creative way and to join a group environment that meet their requirements).

The most relevant benefits, according to researchers like Camarinha-Matos and Abreu (2005), Afsarmanesh and Camarinha-Matos (2005) and Camarinha-Matos and Afsarmanesh (2006), are:

1. *The flexibility in the leveraging of fundamental perspectives*, to create a virtual system to facilitate the emergence of a possible collaboration in terms of organization
2. *The increase of the apparent size*, to compete with big enterprises
3. *Influential lobbying and marketing*, to widen the geographic presence coverage and the access to occasional global markets
4. *An increased negotiation power*, for joint purchases
5. *ICT infrastructure system access*, transparent, easy to use and affordable, serving as a catalyser of interoperability between designers
6. *The performance of mechanisms, directives and services* destined to facilitate the creation of the virtual system process
7. *Proactivity*, community informatics design facilitating the member profiling and skills management in order to ensure the availability of skills and resources to take advantage of the collaboration possibilities
8. *Support to the provision of services*, such as insurance, guidance and training, through support institutions
9. *The introduction of mechanism-establishing trust* between community informatics design users
10. *General guidelines for the collaboration*, especially regarding work and sharing between DSS users

Nevertheless, Afsarmanesh and Camarinha-Matos (2005) list a set of requirements with respect to community informatics design to function properly and generate all these benefits:

1. A strong ICT infrastructure, providing a set of tools to support community informatics design in the management and the digital social systems creation process
2. An active participation of community informatics design users including updating the information on basic skills

3. The establishment of a viable modeling system of community informatics design organization
4. The establishment of community informatics design management strategies and governance rules

11.3 Community Informatics Design Value Creation Perspectives

Generally, community informatics design represents real organization ecosystems where trust is progressively built and where virtual environment dynamics are created each time collaboration opportunities are present or identified. In fact, community informatics design creates value for its users by offering a set of services, including various tools and methodologies, for the creation of a field of interaction and common cooperation between users and designers, aiming towards their involvement in a real virtual system dynamic. Also, community informatics design creates value for the market, mainly, thanks to the dynamic resulting from the creation processing seeking to select the most suitable virtual system in the eyes of the partners and according to their basic skills. The main goal here is to exploit the unique capacities and the strategic assets to deliver a product, a service or an application respecting time, cost and expected quality constraints.

In sum, in terms of value creation, the community informatics design strategies aim to help their users discover and develop new ways to promote technological innovation and economic growth through collaboration means (Romero et al. 2006).

11.4 The Community Informatics Design Life Cycle

A community informatics design life cycle constitutes all the phases of an incubation environment of collective network activities, where we can cross all stages from the creation phase (space 1, "Explore") until the representation of a possible dissolution, going through the organization processes performed by community informatics design managers during all these stages. We explore, we analyse, we document and we diagnose communicational needs and requirements. The creation stage, "Explore", can be divided in two substages: the initiation and recruitment:

1. *The initiation phase* is interested in various themes like strategic pre-planning, issues and initial incubations of the maturation environment (gathering, incubation or learning environment).
2. *The project launch phase* (not the DSS launch as planned in stage 7, "Deploy") is the constitution and the launch of the community informatics design process.

The first substage could be about the generic exploitation of the community informatics design reference framework and its object and themes to develop; whereas at this evolution stage, we process small daily changes in community informatics design, as functioning principles, in order to start the design process.

The second substage is the metamorphosis, big changes made to the community informatics design functioning principles that result in a new operating form. Partnerships are examined and the recruitment and partner commitment process is initiated. We explore possible avenues and solutions.

11.5   The Community Informatics Design Reference Model

We have seen in Chap. 6 that a reference model is a generally well-known conceptual framework. The comprehension all designers have of certain design concepts, entities and relations must be significant, in order to facilitate the implementation of guidelines and the creation of specific models in the field of virtual communities. The "holistic" reference model described in the present book is not really well known, but it relies on several common terms, documented from an abundant review of the literature, whether in systems theory, in design, in management and technology or in social and communicational sciences.

The community informatics design reference model seeks to synthesize and formalize basic concepts, principles and long-term practices of collaboration networks. Therefore, the community informatics design reference model framework suggested in this study sought to provide a common framework for traditional reproduction environments (oriented towards production and services), like living labs and fab labs, industrial clusters, organization ecosystems like technopoles as well as new aspects like emergency networks in case of disasters and colab virtual networks (Camarinha-Matos and Afsarmanesh 2006).

The community informatics design reference model mainly consists of presenting a complete overview of the key elements and components of an incubation and learning environment and formulating the main requirements allowing to create and manage the course of its entire life cycle in seven phases.

Tables 11.1, 11.2, 11.3, 11.4, 11.5, 11.6, 11.7, 11.8, 11.9, 11.10, 11.11, 11.12, 11.13, 11.14, and 11.15 constitute a checklist of entities to take into account in a normalized design approach. They present a community informatics design based on a reference model from the ARCON modeling, defining two subspaces each equipped with four types of modeling representing the point of view on DSS to build, inspired by our seven fields to model. These modelings give an abstract representation of a community informatics incubation and learning environment from its interior environment (endogenous elements or endostructure) and exterior ones (the exogenous or exostructure interactions).

At this stage, it is important to mention that the community informatics design reference model containing seven fields to model only aims to give a first synthetic overview of the environment's key elements as described in various chapters of the

Table 11.1 Description of a design situation: the innovation and appropriation of community informatics design and the DSS

Structural design (DC3.1.1)	Compositional design (DC31.2)	Functional design (DC3.1.3)	Behavioural design (DC3.1.4)
Actors	*Physical resources*	*Fundamental processes*	*Prescriptive behaviour*
Private organizations	Machines	Management composition and structure	Cultural principles
Government institutions	ICT resources	Registration of new CID users	Regional traditions
NGO	Material	CID users' roles, rights and management of responsibilities	Company culture
Roles	ICT infrastructure	CID rewarding user management	NGO culture
Design users	Software	Profile and skills management	CID culture
DSS support provider	CID management system	Profile management	"Commitment"
Opportunity broker	*Human resources*	Skills management	"Leadership"
DSS planner	Personalized CID	Trust management	"Trust"
DSS coordinator	*Information/resource knowledge*	Among CID members	"Self-learning"
Community informatics design (CID) manager	The CID, the DSS, CID users' profile and information skills	Among CID managers and users	"Long-term global vision"
CID support provider	CID information governance	Between CID/DSS and the clientele	"Efficient communication"
Ontology provider	CID value information system	Productivity management	"Innovation"
Services provider	CID support institutions' information	CID performance	Governance principles
Support institution	DSS information	DSS performance	Honesty, trust and integrity
Public (guests)	Containing CID actives	User performance	Openness
CID advisor	Documents, books, directives pamphlets	Decision-making management	Orientation towards performance
Relations	Contracts processing accelerated model	CID skills analysis	Responsibility and empowerment
Networking	Information of interest	Performance ignorance	Mutual respect
Coordination	Links towards other sources of information	Trust ignorance	CID commitment
Cooperation	Learnt lessons	Creation and identification of collaboration opportunities management	Members acceptability principles (users)
Collaboration	Documentation inherited from the CID	Collaboration opportunities	Leadership role principles
Typology network	Documentation inherited from the DSS	DSS rigorous planning	Contract execution policy
		Research, selection and suggestion of partners	
Long-term network strategy: virtual	FAQ	Negotiation of agreements and contracts	Brokerage principles

	Resource ontology		
Size	CID ontology (the top, the basis and the levels of field)	DSS information management	Decision criteria
Location		DSS registrations management	Sanction and reward principles
Field		Management of the DSS inherited information	Interoperability principles
Collaboration pilots		*Background process*	*Mandatory behaviours*
Orientation (values systems)		Strategic management	Rules
Dynamism		Marketing and brand management	Rights and duties policy
Outputs		Financial management	Accession policy
		Resource management	Security issues
		Governance management	Conflict resolution policy
		Active management	Financial policy
		Value information system management	Rule modifications
		Ontology management	Intellectual property right policy
		ICT management	Internal rules
		Management institution support	ICT use instructions
		Innovation management	Sanction principles
		Procedures	*Constraints and conditions*
		CID creation procedures	Accession agreement
		CID initiation and recruitment	Agreement modification
		CID foundation	*Contracts and agreements*
		CID functioning procedures	Confidentiality constraints
		CID evolution procedures	Imposed legal constraints
		CID dissolution procedures	Legal contracts, "CID consortium contract", "DSS contract"
		Methodologies	Normative internal constraints
		CID management methodologies	Physical constraints
		DSS creation methodologies	*Incitements and sanctions*
			Incitement and reward policy
			Sanction policy

Table 11.2 Innovation and appropriation: the reference model adaptation

Market	Input	Society	Constituency
Design identity declaration	*Social network nature*	*Legal identity network*	*Attraction factors*
CID mission statement	Benefit	Legal status	CID reason of existence
Cid vision statement	Non-profit	Legal entity	Attraction and recruitment strategy
CID general strategy	Government	Informal entity	Advertisement
Objectives (in the long term)	NGO	Principles and values	Industry shows
			Community participation motivation
References and testimony design profile	*Support entities*	*Impacts*	Incitements
Who are we?	Certification entities	Field of advertisement and design skills	
	National institutions	DSS creation	*Accession rules*
How to contact us?	International institutions	*Legal questions*	The foundation charter
Marketing and advertisement strategy	Insurance entities	Dispute resolutions	Reward mechanisms for registration
Diffusion	Private institutions	Intellectual property rights	Notice of activity termination
Direct marketing	Public institutions	*Public interactions*	*Potential members (users)*
Brand strategy	Logistics entities	Government organizations:	Company associations
Market interactions	Norm register	Social security	Private institutions
Clients (CID and DSS)	Compensation centres	City hall	Public individual experts
Strategic clients	Data provider issues	Civil defence	Institutions
Potential clients	Financial entities	Associations	*Durability factors*
Competitors	Banks	Interest groups	Research members (teams)
Direct competitors	Investors	Supporters	Invitation
Indirect competitors	Sponsors	Opponents	Solicitation
Provider (potential)			

	Support entities	Regulation limits	Reward
Other partners	Advisors	Other entities	
Sponsors	Individual experts	*Public relations*	
Interactions and transactions	Training organizations	Political relations	
Auctions	Advisors	Support research	
Request processing	Professional associations	Information transfer	
Contract (with clients)	Individual experts	Diffusion	
	Research organizations	Direct	
	Universities	Social relations	
	Research institutes	Cultural	
	Acquisition services	Patronage	
	Financial relations	Build a reputation	
	Technological services	Build successful cases	
	Training action		
	Support action		
	Guarantee action		
	Knowledge transfers		
	Advisory service		
	Creation agreement		
	Agreement		
	Contracts		
	Pacts		

Community informatics design (CID) reference model adaptation with Romero et al.'s (2008) exogenous subspace

Table 11.3 The community informatics design or DSS innovation and appropriation: the environmental analysis

CID1.	Space 1: Explore
Community informatics design seven spaces	Stage A: creation, innovation and appropriation
	Pre-planning
	Constitution of a first reference framework guiding the action
Process	1. **Issue**: environmental analysis use of the FOSM

Objective	
Identification of the pilots to create DSS through the CID	**Skill**
	The activity applies when an entity (organization) wants to create a CID or a DSS
Identification and classification of business attractors (the reasons) for the organizations joining the CID.	The activity presents the economic and technological market analysis

No.	Activities	Description	Responsibilities	Directives	Tools
CID.1.1	Economic and technological market analysis	Identify the main objectives and benefits: what is the main reason of a CID or a DSS?	CID initiator	Perform a market analysis	**Procedures and methodologies**
		Identify, classify and analyse the needs to be met by a CID	CID manager or supervisor	Identification of the market trends	Market study
		Economic needs	CID advisor	Identification of the CID strengths, weaknesses, perspectives and threats	Five strength model
		Social needs	Support institutions	Evaluation of the competing scenario for a CID business model	Success key factors
		Technological needs		Classify the CID potentials, the DSS products and the services according to the complexity and the uncertainty (e.g. products, perishable goods or equipment)	Competitive sustainable benefits of information systems

	Identification of the sustainable competitive benefits for a CID value proposition (products/services): offer a distinctive value	Basic knowledge in organizational and systems intelligence
	Identification of critical factors in market success for the CID value proposition (products/services): market share	
	Perform an economic analysis	**Procedures and methodologies**
	Identification of economic trends	Research in market economy
	Identification of the CID's success critical economic factors	Key success factors
	The industry's key sectors	Sustainable competitor benefits
	The industry's participation in the gross domestic product (GDP)	
	Imports and exports	**Information systems and directory**
Identify the potential sectors of the industry and organizations (not limited to geographical proximity) that could be involved in the CID	Tax rate	Basic knowledge in organizational and systems intelligence
Identify the ICT interoperability needs and service support providing or allowing efficiency in terms of business and collaboration	**Perform a technological analysis**	**Procedures and methodologies**
Identify the fundamental skills and resources of the organization that will contribute to the creation of a CID or a DSS in an initial phase		

(continued)

Table 11.3 (continued)

	Identification of technological trends	Research in techno-market
	Identification of success technological factors for the organization model in CID	Key success factors
	ICT interoperability	Competitive sustainable benefits of information systems
		Basic knowledge in organizational and systems intelligence
Resources		
	Human resources: individuals or teams with knowledge and skills in market studies, strategic planning and the ICT development infrastructure	
	Financial resources: usable funding mechanisms	
	Physical resources and ICT resources: basic knowledge in organizational and systems intelligence	

The results of this phase

Potential client list of the market to serve

Industrial sectors to cover

List of potential organizations (members, users) that could belong to the DSS or contribute to the CID

Transparency of the needs and requirements, ICT infrastructure and easy-to-use software, affordable and open-source code, free software

Comments

The community informatics design designers or the DSS initiators must refer to organizations involved in a DSS creation process to be inspired, consult experts or university researchers for the CID process initiation

Table 11.4 Community informatics design or DSS innovation and appropriation: the strategic planning

CID2. CID or DSS seven spaces	Space 2: : **Imagine**
	Creation, innovation and appropriation by the design thinking modes
	Define the conceptual and practical project boundaries. Think of various applicable scenarios for our situation

Process	2. **Imaginatics:** strategic planning – scenario options and decision-making

Objectives	**Skill**
According to various thinking modes, establish the CID objectives, analyse the strategy and formulate strategies as possible scenarios	The activity introduces the first stages of the CID organizational model definition

No.	Activities	Description	Responsibilities	Directives	Tools
CID 2.1	Establishment of objectives Analysis strategy	*Objective definition* Mission Vision Objectives	DSS initiator CID supervisor CID advisor CID support institutions	*Answer the following questions* Why are we creating a CID (mission)? What does the CID seeks to achieve (vision)? What are the specific CID objectives? What would be the strategy for the CID creation and operating?	**Procedures and methodologies** Strategic design tools Organizational model tools Organizational formulation plan tools **Information systems and directory** Basic knowledge in organizational and systems intelligence
CID 2.2	Strategy formulation	**Business plan formulation** Marketing and branding strategy Financial and operational strategies DSS creation and operating plan	CID initiator CID supervisor CID advisor Support institutions	Creation of a strategic and action plan, marketing and branding, for users or target groups – market and demand demographics Range of products and services Advertisement and promotion Price scale and budget Brand strategy Public relations Differentiation value Other markets and brand questions	**Procedures and methodologies** Commercial logistics strategy: the 4Ps (product, price, place, promotion) Relational market Brand alliance strategies Price strategy **Information systems and directory** Basic knowledge in organizational and systems intelligence
				Creation of a strategic financial action plan Budget proceedings General responsibility Accession (in terms of costs) Other financial questions	**Procedures and methodologies** Decision-making financial tools (return on investment, added value, net present value, internal rate of return, etc.), ICT validation effects on processes and return on collaboration

(continued)

Table 11.4 (continued)

			Creation of a strategic operational action plan	**Procedures and methodologies**
			Governance	Project management tools (Gantt diagram)
			Definition	Contract models
			Contracts and agreements	Provision catalogue
			Organizational structure	Laws of the commerce information system
			Principles, status (policies) and rules	Assistance system on agreements, contracts and negotiation
			Roles, rights and responsibilities	
			Compliance with the profile definition	
			Definition of work procedures	
			Support service offer for the CID users	
			Support service offer to for the DSS creation and registration	
			Resources	
			Human resources: individual or team, with market strategy, branding operational and planning knowledge and skills	
			Financial resources: mechanism used for financing	
			Physical and ICT resources	
			ICT resources: strategic CID, project CID, agreement, contract, tools, negotiation and systems (e.g. software)	

The results of this phase

Launch and diffusion strategy suitable to our needs. Resources for the DSS maintenance and longevity.

Animation and social action facilitation mechanisms

Comments

CID strategy guiding and monitoring the implementation of the market, coordination and collaboration, brand creation, financial strategy, operational strategy and strategic maintenance plans during the CID creation and functioning

Table 11.5 Community informatics design or DSS innovation and appropriation: the strategic application

CID 3. Seven design spaces' stage	Space 3: **Resolve**: creation, innovation and appropriation of innovative solutions				
Process	Implementation of strategy and problem-solving at various society levels of tiers				
Objective	Adaptation of the CID implementation strategy in terms of the enterprise or the organization's problem-solving, ICT infrastructure and governance levels. Identification of basic DSS functionalities			The activity presents the finale stages towards the CID definition as an organizational model	
No.	**Activity**	**Description**	**Responsibilities**	**Directives**	**Tools**
CID.3.1	A DSS definition, process, functionalities	Characterization of organizational processes for the CID management	CID initiator (researcher)	**Definition of CID process functionalities through successful management**	**Procedures and methodologies**
		Scenario establishment	CID supervisor (designer)	Organization processes classification in order to perform specific actions on the CID actors (users, designers)	Frameworks, architectures, platforms and reference models
			CID advisor (webmaster or manager)	CID taxonomy	Enterprise Architectures
			Support institutions	CID actor management	PERA (enterprise reference architecture)
				CID structure accession	TOGAF's open architecture system
				Skills profiling and management	Zachman (IBM architecture)
				DSS creation and user registration	
				Identification of collaboration opportunities	GERAM (reference architecture and generalized methodology for enterprises)
				Strong characterization and planning	FEAF (federal enterprise architecture framework)

(continued)

Table 11.5 (continued)

				Partners search and suggestions	Organization architecture
				Contract negotiation assistance	Information systems architecture
				Information management in a DSS	Information and applications architecture
				General DSS direction	Technical architecture
				Strategic market management	Design architecture
				CID governance	CID organization process
				CID creation	Social architecture
				Performance management	**Organization taxonomy process**
				Information management and institution support	ENAPS (European network on productivity advanced studies)
				ICT management	ISO (International Standardization Organization)
				Value system management	**Diagrammatic**
				Ontology management	Graphic effects
				Decision management assistance	Functional diagram
					CBE diagram
					Work flow diagram
CID4. Seven design spaces' stage	**Space 4: Integrate ICT** infrastructure's definition, social Web tools and technological architectures	Characterization of the ICT infrastructure used as intermediate interface between the CID users, information systems and support of a provider services	CID initiator (researcher)	Definition of information systems support and referential for the CID process	**Information and directory systems**

CID supervisor (designer)	Management system for CID use
CID advisor (webmaster or manager)	User registration
Support institutions	Enriching functionalities for users
Support service	Roles, rights and responsibilities in terms of user's management
	Characteristics
	Profiling and systems and skills management
Access providers	**Discovery and research of new functionalities and skills in terms of collaboration perspectives' determination**
	Characterization of collaboration opportunities
	Planning systems
	Search for partners and collaborators
	Suggestion systems
	Contract negotiation
	Assistance system
	DSS information management system
	DSS registration functionalities
	DSS information characteristics

(continued)

Table 11.5 (continued)

CID5. Seven community informatics design spaces' stage	Space 5: Model				
	Create discovery matrices to help define the governance structure of the CID or DSS process	Characterization and simulation of the governance structure	CID initiator (researcher)	**CID governance structure definition**	Trust towards design systems Performance management systems Support institutions for data management systems Institution characteristic registration support Value systems **DSS management** Ontology management systems **Design decision assistance system** Analysis characteristics of gaps and skills Lack of performance alert Low level of trust characteristic
		Future social system model	CID supervisor (designer)	Piloting committee definition	

Use creativity, modeling or visualization tools to represent various processes involved in the CID	CID advisor (webmaster or manager)	CID authorities (board of directors)
	Support institutions	**CID user role definition**
	Support service	CID users
	Access providers	CID management (responsible for the website)
		Trajectory planner and integrator or DSS organization
		DSS coordinator
		CID advisor
		Support services
		Ontology provider
		Support institutions
		Definition principles
		User eligibility principles
		Leadership role principles (authorities)
		Contract execution policy
		Definition rules: behaviour
		Code of ethics and culture
		Functional and operational design rules according to the community's values
		Definition regulations
		Accession policy
		Incitement policy
		Safety policy
		ICT use policy

(continued)

Table 11.5 (continued)

		Intellectual property rights policy
		Rights and duties policy
		Dispute resolution policy
		Rule modifications
		Contracts and agreements definition
		CID consortium contract
		Projects with user contract
		Contracts with subcontractors
	Definition of functions, roles and rights and CID or DSS user responsibilities	

Resources
Human resources: individuals or teams with knowledge and skills in design process management, ICT evolution, governance and legal issues
Financial resources: financing mechanisms to use
Physical and ICT resources: ICT infrastructure – material and software

The results of this phase

CID process definition

Implementation and execution of ICT infrastructures

Definition of the governance structure for data, information and knowledge

Use of simulators, social process dashboards and visualization tools useful to the representation of various processes

Comments

Definition of the structure, positions, roles, principles, rules, regulations, contracts, agreements, rights and responsibilities in terms of CID or DSS management

Table 11.6 Community informatics design foundations: implementation and execution of the governance structure, infrastructure and configuration of ICT

CID6	
Seven spaces' stage	Space 6: **Prototype.** Mock-up production stage where we proceed to a feasibility demonstration. We evaluate uses and the tools, methods, solutions and application appropriation. We make sure to have a good governance structure and project management and a good business platform
Process	1. Governance configuration in terms of ICT innovation serving the DSS
Objective	

Focus on the implementation and prove the CID's or DSS's proper functioning | The activity focuses on the implementation of the ICT infrastructure (platform) and the DSS governance structure

No.	Activities	Description	Responsibilities	Directives	Tools / Procedures and methodologies
CID 6.1	Configuration and execution of the ICT infrastructure	DSS configuration and execution in terms of ICT infrastructure	CID initiator (researcher)	Required software for interoperability between the CID users	**Procedures and methodologies**
	Prototype and feasibility demonstration	Ontology downloading	CID supervisor (designer)	All necessary support services for the organization and collaboration efficiency	Mechanisms of implementation and functioning of CID subsystems and ICT infrastructure
		Creation of information referential	CID advisor (webmaster or manager)	Security	Mechanisms and parameters in place for links between the CID various parts
		Implementation of administrative data	Support institutions	Web services	Mechanisms of ontology collecting and downloading
			Support service	Blogs	Mechanisms of transfer form a CID to a new one
		Founding members registry (researchers and designers)	Access providers	Forum	
			Community managers	Videoconference	
				Messaging	
				Creation of personalized pages	
				Billing	
				Information exchange	
				Other support services	

(continued)

Table 11.6 (continued)

DC6.2	Configuration of a governance structure and prototyping pursuit	Creation of a piloting committee (authority structure)	CID initiator (researcher)	All questions related to the governance structure must be documented for the CID use and distributed to all DSS users	Procedures and methodologies
		Publication of principles, rules and regulations that will rule the CID or the DSS	CID supervisor (designer)		Governance principles, rules, regulations, roles, rights and responsibilities measured in terms of CID
			CID advisor (webmaster or manager)		**Information systems**
			Support institutions		Company portals (e.g. bulletin boards)

The results of this phase

ICT infrastructures and current information systems

Resources

Human resources: individuals or teams with knowledge and skills in design process management, ICT evolution, governance and legal issues

Financial resources: financing mechanisms to use

Establish a governance structure

Physical and ICT resources

Creation of a prototype and uses identification

ICT infrastructure (material and software)

Comments

The future members must read and accept the principles, rules and regulations governing the CID or the DSS before the accession process request

The definition of design in terms of management, position, roles, principles, rules, regulations, contracts, agreements, rights and responsibilities must be documented and published. We review the entire structures, architectures, models and DSS process to make a strong demonstration of feasibility

Table 11.7 Community informatics design foundations: the group of users as a constituent DSS

CID7					
The seven spaces' stage	Space 7: **Deploy** 1 – innovation – deployment foundations in the community or large-scale deployment from lessons learnt and evidence-based practices during the prototyping phase				
Process	**Identics:** progressive institutionalization of the DSS constituent. Evaluation of user group. Development of the organizational and commercial identity and institutionalization. Evaluation of training, incubation and learning mechanisms in the DSS and the development of identities at various levels of society through the CAPACITÉS model				
Objectives					
The designers DSS must now give way to the commitment and registration users' process			The activity focuses on recruitment, accreditation and user registration		
No.	**Activities**	**Description**	**Responsibilities**	**Directives**	**Tools**
CID7.1	Accession requests reception invitation to potential CID users	**Registration of new users**	CID initiator (researcher)	Receive or ask for the relevant data for the user accreditation process	**Procedures and methodologies**
		Organization of DSS accession requests	CID supervisor (designer)		CID user registration stages: collecting the provided information on functionality management systems and CID users
		Invitation sending (requests) to CID preselected users	CID advisor (webmaster or manager)		User registration
		Organization according to requirements and skills	CID candidates (users)		

(continued)

Table 11.7 (continued)

DC7.2	Evaluation and accreditation of candidate user accession	Accession candidate evaluation accession application	CID initiator (researcher)	**Evaluation of a collaboration preparation**	**Procedures and methodologies**
		Accreditation of the provided information	CID supervisor (designer)	Skills, trusts and performance criteria profile	Potential CID user registration stages
			CID advisor (webmaster or manager)	**Accreditation documents to examine**	Validation of the provided information
			CID candidates (users)	Accreditations and certificates	Information systems trust evaluation basis
				Financial notation	User management systems
				Recommendation and reward letters	User registration characteristics
				Licences and patents	
				Articles (journals and magazines)	

CID.3	Acceptance and rejection of candidate user accession	Acceptance and rejection of accession requests		Basic criteria for applications acceptance or rejection	Basic criteria for candidates' acceptance or refusal
			CID initiator (researcher)		**Procedures and methodologies**
			CID supervisor (designer)	Basic information and validation profile of factual information	Main steps of the CID users' roles, rights and responsibility assignment
			CID advisor (webmaster or manager)	Trust-level base	Information and directory systems
			CID candidates (users)	Conformity with the CID field of skills	CID user functionalities and systems management
				If a candidate is accepted, he becomes a CID member (user) that will have responsibilities and initial rights according to his role	
				If a candidate is rejected, he will receive comments for self-improvement and will have the possibility to make another accession request	User registration
				An organization of CID users or a community of practice can play various roles	Roles, rights and responsibility management of CID users

(continued)

Table 11.7 (continued)

				Group CID user profile and skills data	Procedures and methodologies
CID7.4	Roles, profiling and skills for CID user accession	Assignment of roles, rights and responsibilities to CID users	CID initiator (researcher)	General information	Information validation and verification mechanisms provided by users during the registration and their profile update
		Definition of users' profiles and skills	CID supervisor (designer)		New applicant management mechanisms
			CID advisor (webmaster or manager)	Organization name	
		General skills and information		General description	Information systems
			CID users	Information	Functionalities and user management systems
		Information related to skills		Activity sector	User registration
		Financial information		Legal status	CID and DSS management process profiling and skills
				Strategy	
		Information validity proof (visibility)		Organization number	
				Skills-related information	
				Process	
				Products and services	
				Resources	
				Human resources	
				ICT resources	
				Material resources	
				Practical	
				Associated	

The results of this phase	Resources
List of real CID users including their roles, rights and responsibilities	Individual human resources or in teams with knowledge and skills in terms of profiling and skills identification
List of real CID users, including their profile and a complete description of their skills	Financial resources: financing mechanism to use
	Physical resources and ICT resources
	System management and user profiling
	System management of CID user skills

Comments

Registration requests and CID user's accreditation process

CID accession request from other design organizations or other collaborative platforms

The future DSS users must read and accept the principles, rules and regulations governing the CID before their accession to the institution (DSS) under development

Table 11.8 Community informatics design foundations: support to the selection of establishments

CID 7.2	**Deploy 2 – suite:** pursuit of large-scale deployment and concern for the longevity of the initiative				
Seven spaces' stage					
Process	3. Support to selection institutions helping the platform deployment				
Objectives					
Selection of support institutions in order to help users in their CID activities				Activity focusing on the support for recruitment, accreditation and user registration institutions	
No.	**Activities**	**Description**	**Responsibilities**	**Directives**	**Tools**
CID7.2.	Support institutions	Simplified institution support in charge of new user registration	CID initiator (researcher)	Selection and support of institutions that could provide CID with ICT services	**Procedures and methodologies**
	Registration	Support institutions can also become CID actors and members	CID supervisor (designer)	Change of role, duties and rights when a user becomes a DSS or CID member	Validation and validity mechanisms of the information provided by new members during their registration and profile update
			CID advisor (webmaster or manager)		Management mechanisms of new user accession levels
			Institutional support		**Information systems**
					Management system and user functionalities
					Member registration
					Profiling system and skills management
					Support institutions to CID user information systems management
					Registration of CID portal characteristic support

The results of this phase

	Resources
Real list of support institutions with profiles, the complete description and the CID user skills	Individual human resources or in teams with knowledge and skills in terms of profiling and skills identification
The identics is the socio-technical institutionalization process of models and scenarios suggested by reference user's communities in the previous phases and spaces	Financial resources: financing mechanism to use
	Physical resources and ICT resources
	System management and user profiling
	Skills system management

Comments

The institution support must be conditioned by the acceptance of principles, rules and regulations governing the field of CID before the beginning of any design activities and relations with the communities of users

Table 11.9 Community informatics design foundations: the launch

CID 7.3	Deploy 3: the DSS launch					
The seven spaces' stage						
Process	4. PR process: DSS launch					
Objectives	DSS launch and innovation and researcher invitation and all community informatics stakeholders (e.g. a quintuple-helix partnership) during the CID launching meeting			DSS activities must focus on the functioning of the CID organizations		
No.	**Activities**	**Description**	**Responsibilities**	**Directives**	**Tools**	
CID7.3.1	CID launch	CID form and launch	CID initiator (researcher)	Founding members' invitation (researchers) in CID during a DSS launch	**Procedures and methodologies**	4Ps market strategy (product, price, place, promotion)
			CID supervisor (designer)	Announcement of the CID operations starts in various media (internet, TV, newspapers, radio, LinkedIn, twitter, etc.)		
			CID advisor (webmaster or manager)	Execution of a strategic plan in terms of market and brand	**Tools**	
			Institutional support			Relational design
			Service provider support			Co-design strategy
						Design strategy
						Interaction design
						Transition design
						Ideal design
Output				**Resources**		
CID operational stage				Human resources: all CID users		
				Financial resources: the use of financing mechanisms		
				Physical resources and ICT resources (material and software)		
Comments						
The CID supervisor (webmaster) must announce the beginning of the CID operations						
The focus must be on the partners' commitment and mobilization						

Table 11.10 Community informatics design's functioning and evolution: management actors

CID 7.4

The seven spaces' stage: deploy 4

Process: marketing, brand strategy

Objectives: recruitment pursuit

Creation of complete CID users' profiles for skills management and DSS creation support			Concentration of the activities on user management and CID designers			
No.	**Activities**	**Description**		**Responsibilities**	**Directives**	**Tools**
CID7.4.1	Accession	**CID user management**		CID initiator (researcher)	**User registration**	**Procedures and methodologies**
	Design structure	Integration		CID supervisor (designer)	Reception or sending of accession requests	Validation and validity mechanisms of the information provided users in their profiles during their registration as new user designers
			Accreditation			Management mechanisms of new user accession
		Disintegration		CID advisor (webmaster or manager)	Evaluation of a potential collaboration	
		Enrichment		Institutional support	Production of accreditation documents of requesting users	**Information systems and directory**
		Categorization		Service provider support	Acceptance and refusal of accession	Management system and user functionalities
		Activity divided in three mechanisms			Giving out rights, roles and responsibilities to CID users	User registration
		Member registration			**Enriched registrations of users**	Enriching functionalities for designers
		Member acknowledgement			CID user performance acknowledgement for their good participation in the CID process and the DSS creation	Design function in terms of responsibilities, roles and user's rights
		User responsibilities in terms of rights and roles			CID user reward for their initiative in the multiple roles played within the DSS	
					Acknowledgement of active CID user input	

(continued)

Table 11.10 (continued)

CID7.4.2	Skills profiling and management	Creation and maintenance of a CID user self-profile system	CID initiator (researcher)	Profile management: create, update and delete CID and DSS users' self-profiles	**Procedures and methodologies**
		Activity divided in three stages	CID supervisor (designer)	Skills evaluation: validate CID users' skills according to "perceptibility" processes, capacities and resources' skills	Validation and validity mechanisms of the information provided by new members during their registration and profile update
		Profile management	CID advisor (webmaster or manager)	New skills discovery: collective CID users' skills	Management mechanisms of new user accession levels
					Information systems and directory
		Skills evaluation	Institutional support		Profiling and skills management system
		New skills discovery	Service provider support		Discovery and functionality research of new skills
					Creation of a digital badge system (or ecosystem platform)

Resources

Human resources: all CID users

Financial resources: the use of financing mechanisms

Physical resources and ICT resources

Profiling and CID users' skills management system

The results of this phase

Real list of CID user designers with their socio-professional profile and the complete description of their skills profile through a digital badge system List of the DSS members and skills cartography

Comments

Skills management and digital badge system are accompanied by the collaboration pattern identification, incubation and learning mechanisms, the creation of tutorials and community informatics design guides such as CID training tutorials and a SADC guide

Table 11.11 Community informatics design's functioning and evolution: the creation of a DSS and registration management

CID7.5	Deployment 5. Manage the members and the participants			
Seven spaces' stage				
Process	2. Creation of a DSS and registrations management			
Objectives				
Support the DSS and the creation of registration activities towards a quick configuration of the CID dynamic in response to identified collaboration possibilities			The concentration activity of the DSS activities on the registration creation	
No.	**Activities**	**Description**	**Responsibilities**	**Directives**	**Tools**
CID7.5.1.1	**Revise the CID's 8Cs framework:**	Detection and collaboration opportunities research	Broker	**Identification and categorization of collaboration opportunities in CID**	**Procedures and methodologies**
	1. Connectivity		DSS users	Detect and research collaboration opportunities (tenders in newspapers, electronic boards, Web pages, Internet, forums, chats, messaging, social media and social networks)	Governance measures and principles, rules, regulations, roles, rights and responsibilities of a DSS
	2. Conversation		Support service	Find the required skills to meet user's needs	**Information systems and directory**
	3. Cognition		Providers	Research skills in the field of CID	Collaboration, opportunity and identification system
	4. Communication			**Output: general CID information**	
	5. Cooperation			Contact	
	6. Collaboration			Title	
	7. Culture			Description	
	8. Contract			Deadline	
	Opportunities			URL or website address	
	Identification			Other relevant data	

(continued)

Table 11.11 (continued)

CID7.5.2	Always from the 8Cs	Characterization of collaboration opportunities and definition of DSS strategic plans d	Designer	Selection of collaboration possibilities	Procedures and methodologies
	Collaboration		DSS planner	Selection of collaboration modalities:	Governance measures and principles, rules, regulations, roles, rights and responsibilities of a DSS
					Interoperability principles
	Cooperation		Support service	Organization or DSS processing a collaborative model	
	Contracts		Provider	Distributed cognition in an organizational process	**Information systems and directory**
	Communication			Collaboration project:	Characterization of CID collaboration possibilities
	Coordination			(Occurs at the project level when activities are performed by humans only)	Planning system
				Collaborative problem-solving	
	Creation			Ad hoc collaboration in fast response for emerging countries in a crisis situation	
				Characterization in terms of skills:	
				Identification of necessary skills and capacities	
	Opportunities			Product characterization	
				Service characterization	
	DSS characterization and detailed planning			Planning strategies	
				Definition of a detailed DSS structure	
				Topology of the organization in terms of form, level, associated roles and governance rules	
				Definition of the partnership form:	
				Cooperation contracts and agreements	
				Representation of the descending CID model (planning) and ascending (emerging countries)	
				Evaluation of various configuration simulations	
				Ideal DSS ending or metamorphosis configuration	

CID7.5.3	Partner research and selection	Identification, evaluation and selection of potential CID partners		Selection of the majority of loyal CID users	Procedures and methodologies
			Designer		Principal stage of the attribution of roles, rights and responsibilities to CID partners
		Partner research	DSS planner	Requirements of a possibility of a given collaboration	
		Potential partners' evaluation (preference specification)	Support service	Partner evaluation and selection according to defined criteria	
		Partner selection	Provider	Accessibility	Rights and duties of the partner policy
		Peers network		Use time	
		Stakeholder network (helix)		Participation level	
				Assessment and performance indicators	Measures, rules, regulations and principles of the CID governance
				Other criteria	Accession policy
				Output: list of potential DSS partners based on the skills required to perform a task corresponding to a CID	Users' acceptability principles
					Leadership role principles
					Information systems and directory
					Partner research and suggestion system

(continued)

Table 11.11 (continued)

CID7.5.4	Agreement and contract	Computer-assisted communication	Designer	Negotiation	Procedures and methodologies
	Negotiation assistant (WizAN)	Support to negotiations and agreements during the creation of a DSS: co-foundation	Planner	Negotiation protocol definition	Measures, rules, regulations, and principles of the CID governance, decision-making principles
		Type of contract: specifications and general definitions according to a CID requirements	CID coordinator	Decision and corresponding parameter process	
		Structure and topology	CID users	**Contracting representation of agreements**	Reward and sanction principle
		Contract under negotiation and negotiation process	Support service	Formulation and modeling of contracts and agreements	DSS governance principles
		DSS registration: agreement and contract signature	Providers	Contract type identification	Functional and operational DSS rules
				Definition of mechanisms and contract execution institutions	Internal rules used for benefit distribution within a DSS
				Definition of legal issues	Intellectual property policy
				Types of contracts	Problem-solving policy
				CID contracts (with actors and CID users)	Regulation modifications
				DSS contracts (with DSS partners and users)	**Information systems and directory**
				Output: agreements concluded and signed DSS contract	Agreement and contract negotiation
					Assistance system

CID7.5.5	DSS information management	Designer	DSS registration	Procedures and methodologies
	DSS registration: profile creation	Planner	Once a DSS is configured and ready to work, the user must manifest his interest in CID creation by creating his own profile	Principal DSS registration steps
		CID coordinator	The DSS creation notice must be communicated to all users involved	Provided information collection
	Information on previous DSS researches: active immaterial recovery facilitating the DSS creation and exploitation while foreseeing the potential CID dissolution	CID users	**Previous DSS research management**	Validation of the provided information
				Information systems and directory
		Support service	Once a DSS is dissolved, precious knowledge (lessons learnt) could ensure the DSS durability; outside the CID, it must be transferred again within a knowledge management task	Profiling and skills management system
			DSS management challenges	DSS information management system
		Providers	Select relevant information lessons learnt and successes	DSS registration functionalities
				Procedures and methodologies
			Interpret, analyse, filter, store and organize the DSS model for the implementation of the CID context in order to systemize and display decision-making information	DSS and CID previous research transfer mechanisms
				Measures, rules, regulations, and principles of the CID governance
				Intellectual property policy
				DSS information management system
				DSS previous research information characteristics
				Heritage management system

(continued)

Table 11.11 (continued)

	Knowledge management system
	Intelligence in the organizational system
	Technological data warehouse, data base

Resources

| Human resources: broker, DSS planner, DSS coordinator and CID manager, partners and providers of DSS support services |
| Financial resources: financing to be used |
| Physical and ICT resources: |
| Creation of DSS registration system (tools) |
| Co-foundation of tools |

The results of this phase

- Negotiations command (brokerage) identification
- Characterization and rigorous planning of negotiations between DSS partners
- Partnership and suggestion research for accession requests (access towards DSS creation)
- Contract models (flexibility in terms of contract negotiation in order to come to an agreement)
- Registration of DSS created within CID platforms
- User designer accession
- Mechanism and institutionalization patterns (Hess and Oström 2011)

Comments

The multiple DSS partners can also be asked to become DSS long-term members or register as CID user expert or not; eventually, organizations or diversified practice communities, outside the CID, could be widened to other territories

Table 11.12 Community informatics design's functioning and evolution: the general direction

CID 7.6	Support CID operations and the DSS evolution				
The seven spaces' stage					
Process	3. General CID governance				
Objectives					
Support, maintain and accompany the CID self-management during its functioning and evolution				The activity focuses on the CID self-management	
stage					
No.	**Activities**	**Description**	**Responsibilities**	**Directives**	**Tools**
CID7.6.1	Strategic management and promotion	Execution of strategic management processes of a virtual community informatics environment (or strategic network management), in a collaborative spirit	Designer	**Design strategic management process**	**Procedures and methodologies (strategy)**
		Execution of the promotion, co-creation strategy and CID identity development	Planner	Objective establishment	Design (formulation of the strategy as a design process)
			CID coordinator	Strategy formulation	Analysis and monitoring through the CAPACITÉS model (usability, openness, security, sociability, etc.; strength, weakness, perspectives, threats)
			CID users	Strategy implementation	Planning (formulation of the strategy as a formal process)
			Support service	Control strategy	Theory of organizational system
			Providers	**Problems in the CID collaboration strategy formulation**	Scenario planning
				Frictions	Theoretical positioning (formulation of the strategy as an analysis process)

(continued)

Table 11.12 (continued)

Dilemmas	Entrepreneurship (formulation of the strategy as a visionary process)
Tensions	Enterprise government
	New leadership style
Challenges in the CID collaboration strategy formulation	
Negotiation process	Distributed cognitive (formulation of the strategy as a mental process)
Reach of a consensus	Organizational learning, social power and hierarchical distance basis
Common objectives (win-win relations)	Partnership value perspective
Combination of brands, prestige and the organization reputation in the unique CID and DSS setting for strong users' visual practices	Culture (formulation of the strategy as a collective process)
	Appreciative research, cultural dimensions, collaborative intelligence culture
	Environment (formulation of the strategy as a reactive process)
	Contingency theory
	Situational leadership
	Configuration (formulation of the strategy as a transformation process)
	Configuration of chaos organization
	Catastrophe theory

Innovation system		
Information systems and directory (for the strategy)		
Knowledge basis		
Intelligence system for organizational matter		
Procedures and methodologies (design marketing)		
Mix marketing for the design		
Advertisement		
Marketing chain		
Inter-enterprise commercialization		
Inter-consumer commercialization		
Co-design corporation		
Events and promotions		
Public relations		
Segmentation and targets		
Product development		
Information systems and directory (for the marketing)		
User/designer relations management system		

(continued)

Table 11.12 (continued)

			Designer	Financial affairs	Procedures and methodologies
CID7.6.2	Financial activities, accounting and resource management in all the design spaces	Financial affairs management			
		Accounting maintenance	Planner	CID cost	Accounting conventions and procedures
		Deployment of the CID resources through the support process of resources management	CID coordinator	Taxes	Active costs to pay for the CID use
			CID users	Investments	Capitalization and amortization of a DSS goods and equipment
					Contingency
			Support service	**Accounting affairs**	CID revenue
			Providers	Price to pay for a CID use	CID endowment
				Rewards of a CID use	CID use cost
				Resources related affairs	Revenues generated from the CID use
				Design management directory	Taxation policy
				ICT management	**Information systems and directory**
				CID value management system	Enterprise and resources planning system
					Accounting system
					Inventory system
CID7.6.3	Governance management	Surveillance of CID user behaviour (rights, roles and responsibilities) and the DSS performance through use and exploitation policy of this platform	Designer	**CID principles**	**Procedures and methodologies**

Four perspectives of responsibility	Planner	Honesty, trust and integrity in the use	Measures, rules, regulations, and principles of the CID governance
Strategic perspective	CID coordinator	Transparency in activities	**Information systems and directory**
Strategic vision	CID users	Orientation towards performance	Design portals (e.g. bulletin boards)
Strategic alignment	Support service	Responsibility and imputability	
Strategic insurance	Providers	Mutual respect and CID commitment	
Resource perspective (good use)		Acceptability and belonging principles	
Human resources		Leadership roles principles	
Technological resources		Contracts execution policies	
Physical resources		Brokerage principles	
Financial resources		Decision-making principles	
DSS or **organizational perspective**		Reward and sanction principles	
Structure		Interoperability principles	
Policies		Network and governance principles	
Decision-making		**CID regulations**	
Service perspective		Accession policy	
Systems		Security issues	
Procedures		Sanctions and inventive principles	
Methodologies		Financial policies	
Responsibilities services		Use the ICT directives	
		Policy on intellectual property rights	
		Policy on rights and duties	
		Conflict resolution policy	
		Administrative regulations modification	

(continued)

Table 11.12 (continued)

CID7.6.4	Trust management		Designer	Basic trust perspectives and criteria	Procedures and methodologies
		Define user trust (equity between CID users)			
		Define trust criteria	Planner	Chart	Methodology for basic trust management
					Information systems and directory
		Define and manage trust relations	CID coordinator	Skills	Trust management systems
		Trust between users and designers	CID users	Expertise and experience	
		Trust of a user towards the CID administrative management	Support service	Social aspects	
		Trust of a CID or a DSS user	Providers	Sense of community	
		Perform a quantitative evaluation of a CID management process reliability		Financial and economic aspects	
				Financial ratios	
				Technology	
				Broadband	
				Interoperability	
				Availability	
				Norms	
				Security protocols and norms	
				Software and material norms	
				Management and behavioural norms	
				Behavioural management structure (collaborative alliance)	

CID7.6.5	Performance management	Execution of performance management cycle	Designer	Follow the life and management cycle of CID performance	Procedures and methodologies
		Execution of performance management cycle			**Procedures and methodologies**
		Planning	Planner	Planning	Score sheet model
		Setting objectives	CID coordinator	Surveillance productivity measure	Engineering organization process
		Establishment of elements and norms communication	CID users	Evolution	Excellence model
		Surveillance productivity measure	Support service	Note	Quality system
		Performance measure	Providers	Define a select key indicators ad performance norms	Public service excellence model
		Feedback		Measurable	Mastery of statistic processes
		Progression		Understandable	Value management
		Evolution		Verifiable	**Information systems and directory**
		Reaction to suboptimal performances		Fair	Performance management systems
		Maintenance of a good performance		Realizable	Indicator system
		Note		Manage key performance indicators through an indicator system and present them in dashboards to facilitate control and interpretation	Dashboard system
		Summary of the performance			
		File quotation			
		Reward			
		Good performance acknowledgement and reward			

(continued)

Table 11.12 (continued)

			CID asset directory common goods	Procedures and methodologies
CID7.6.6	Asset directory management	Designer	**CID asset directory common goods**	**Procedures and methodologies**
	Sharing of CID valuable assets that could be interesting and useful to share with other CID users	Planner	Documents, books, CID practice assistance pamphlets	Organizational memory taxonomy
			Contract models	Principles and motivational measures
		CID coordinator		**Information systems and directory**
		CID users	Acceleration of the procurement phase	Asset management directory system
		Support service	General legal questions related to this sector	Content management system
		Providers	Specific CID sector interest information	
			Links towards other sources of information	
			Lessons learnt, best practices	
			FAQ	
CID7.6.7	Support institution information management	Designer	Select and support institutions able to provide technological services to the CID	**Procedures and methodologies**
	The institution support will take the shape of a simplified user registration process	Planner	If a support institution becomes a CID member, it must then modify its role and have new rights and duties	Verification mechanisms of the information validity provided by users during the registration and profile update
	Support institutions can become full CID members			Management mechanisms in terms of accessions
		CID coordinator		**Information systems and directory**
		CID users		User functionality management system
		Support service		CID user registration
		Providers		Profiling and skills
				DSS management
				DSS support institutions and management
				Registration support of institutions characteristics

					Procedures and methodologies
CID7.6.8	ICT management	ICT infrastructure management based on DSS	Designer	Define the guidelines for planning, delivery and management of the IT services, especially for the information technology infrastructure library (ITIL)	
		Good practice guide:	Planner	**ICT management services**	Information systems architecture
		Identification of the enterprise needs	CID coordinator	Network management services	Information architectures
		Planning deployment, design, trials and exploitation	CID users	Operation management	Application architectures
		Technical support and ICT services management and technological components	Support service	Local processors management	**Information systems and directory**
			Providers	Computer installation	Security
				System acceptance and management	Networks and data base applications
CID7.6.9	Value systems and information management	Active management of material elements and CID immaterial values in order to model and evaluate their use for the co-creation and co-production of value for the CID and DSS users	Designer	**Taxonomy's use for the processing and classification of CID verbs and concepts**	**Procedures and methodologies**
			Planner	Financial capital (corporate assets in terms of design use)	CID tangible and intangible evaluation methods and models
			CID coordinator	Intellectual capital (intangible assets in terms of design use)	**Methods**
			CID users		Intangible value calculation
			Support service	Social capital (intangible assets in terms of design use)	Added value of the intellectual coefficient for users and designers
			Providers		Intellectual capital
					Measure
					Models
					Organization navigator
					Intellectual assets and monitor of the intellectual capital index
					Technological model
					DSS excellence model
					Information systems and directory
					Knowledge management system

(continued)

Table 11.12 (continued)

CID7.6.10	Levels of ontology management	Designer	Ontology construction stages	Procedures and methodologies
Ontology's management				
	Superior level	Planner	Learning	Ontology pattern design
	Inferior level	CID coordinator	Design	**Information systems and directory**
	Field level and application level	CID users	Engineering	Ontology discovery management system
	Ontology relations management	Support service	Fusion (collaborative construction)	Dictionary, glossary, lexicon, etc.
	Superclass	Providers	Evolution	
	Subclass		Evaluation	
	Partial		Recommended by the W3C for ontology norms	
	Equivalent			

CID7.6.11	Decision-making and management assistance	Decision-making as a process leading to the selection of the action plan among alternatives	Designer	Some guidelines for the decision-making	Procedures and methodologies
			Planner	Decision-making must be done in full awareness	Scenario analysis
			CID coordinator	Decision-making must take users' needs into account	Analysis and objective research
			CID users	Identify the options available for the decision-maker	Design analysis
			Support service	Identify the factors influencing the decision	Comparison analysis in pairs (between the various CID users)
			Providers	Collect information on factors influencing the participants	Analysis chart
					Strength analysis
					Analysis of costs and benefits related to the design use
					Monte Carlo simulation
					Information systems and directory
					Decision management assistance system
					Characteristics of skills and gap analysis
					Alert functionalities in case of suboptimal performance
					Low characteristics trust levels

The results of this phase

Notification issuing. Modifications and realignment of practices during the deployment, recruitment, evaluation, validation and institutionalization (identics)

Warnings and reports on CID performance management

Contribution to the structuring of a common vocabulary and a glossary

Resources

Human resources: all CID users

Financial resources: financing mechanisms to use

Physical resources and ICT resources: CID management systems

Comments

Discovery of the most suitable mechanisms for the CID management process and corresponding procedures

Improvement of DSS design methods and community information systems

Specialized or general directories must be adapted to each management structure and CID policies

Table 11.13 The community informatics design dissolution: the sharing of the assets

CID7.7	Deploy 5. Potential dissolution stage			
The seven spaces' stage				
Process	1. Sharing of the assets resulting from the dissolution			
Objectives			The activity focuses on the dissolution of assets from the CID directory	

Return and sharing of the goods in the CID directory and the assets owners

No.	Activities	Description	Responsibilities	Directives	Tools
CID7.7.1	Dissolution of the shared assets	Executive CID directory and dissolution of CID users' assets and goods	CID manager CID coordinator CID users	Identification of the CID users' good property that have been shared to create the CID assets directory	**Procedures and methodologies** Methodology for the nomination or the selection of users taking care of the previously existing CID researches Methodology to define new rights and roles beyond the CID existence **Information systems and directory** Asset management system directory Content management system

Results		**Resources**	
None, only the experience acquired by partners at the level of the organizational or societal level. Certain less tangible capitals		Human resources: CID manager, CID webmaster, CID users Financial resources: financing mechanism to use Physical resources and ICT resources: user/designer asset management system	

Comments

The dissolution entails all the assets shared by the CID users/designers; the main person in charge of this process is the CID manager. In the university context, it is all about the research result sharing, their diffusion and the sharing of products and potential applications. In the context of an enterprise, various types of intellectual, human, social, financial, material or organizational capitals can be shared within a platform (a business platform or a design platform as DSS). See
CID 7.7.2 below

Table 11.14 The community informatics design dissolution: the legacy

CID 7.7.2	Stage D: dissolution			
The seven spaces' stage				
Process	2. CID legacy (knowledge transfer)			
Objectives				
Capture, transfer and appropriation of the knowledge collected throughout the CID seven phases' life cycle		The activity focuses on the basic knowledge and creation of the CID legacy		
Transfer of brands and other branding assets generated during the CID life cycle		The activity focuses on the brand's transfer and other user/designer assets		
No.	**Activities**	**Description**	**Responsibilities**	**Directives**	**Tools**
CID7.7.2.1	CID legacy (knowledge transfer and sharing)	Knowledge available for all actors (users, designers and learners) of the CID construction	CID manager	Identification of suitable knowledge elicitation and transfer techniques to be used by each CID user identification of a suitable mechanism for the transfer of intellectual property rights on brands and other user brand assets	**Procedures and methodologies**
		Basic knowledge of the experiences collected throughout the CID life cycle (best practices)	CID coordinator		
		Legacy of brands and other branding assets from users and designers	CID users		User nomination or selection methodology to be in charge of the post-CID legacy
					Methodology to define new rights and roles in the post-CID
					Knowledge elicitation techniques
					Interviews, protocols
					Analysis triage concept
					Decomposition techniques
					Goals
					Information task limits
					DSS learning
					Application techniques
					Knowledge transfer techniques
					Information systems and directory
					Knowledge management system

(continued)

Table 11.14 (continued)

The results of this phase	Resources
Legacy: CID knowledge basis	Human resources: CID manager, CID portal webmaster, CID users
Brands and other immobilizations and brands legacy in terms of CID	Financial resources: financing mechanisms to be used
	Physical resources and ICT resources: legacy management system and knowledge management system

Comments

Knowledge sharing and transfer process to all actors (users, designers, learners and design researchers, community managers, webmasters) involved in the CID activities; the main person in charge of this process is the CID manager

Knowledge of the future CID documentation transfer process

Table 11.15 The community informatics design dissolution: the closing

CID7.8	Deploy 8. Dissolution			
The seven spaces' stage				
Process	3. CID closing			
Objectives				
End of business and research contracts with all the CID actors (including users)	The activity focuses on finalizing contracts with all CID actors (including users and learners)			
Stop of information systems and CID referential	The activity focuses on the closing of information systems and CID referential			
CID closing announcement	The activity focuses on the closing communication with all CID actors			
	The activity focuses on the CID closing			
No.	**Activities**	**Description**	**Responsibilities**	**Directives**	**Tools**

CID7.8.1	Planning the CID closing and the relevant documentation	Contract termination plan with all the CID actors, users and learners
		Information systems and CID referential stopping plan
		Documentation of useful information for a CID legacy
			CID manager
			CID coordinator
			CID users
				Contract termination plan with all the users, support institutions, support services, providers, the CID webmaster, brokers and the CID members
				Back-up data in the information systems and CID referential
				Information on the CID legacy
				CD or DVD back-up units, for removable hard drive CID legacy takeover by documenting the CID closing process or any other precious information
					Procedures and methodologies
					Nomination or selection methodology of the members in charge of the post-CID legacy
					Methodology to define new roles and rights in the post-CID
					Back-up strategy
					  Complete system back-up
					  Incremental back-up
					Information systems and directory
					Data back-up system

CID7.8.2	Communications related to the CID closing	Public announcement of the CID closing to all actors involved in the design	CID manager CID coordinator CID users	Announce and manage a CID closing by leaving good future perspectives	**Procedures and methodologies** Contract termination CID closing announcement **Information systems and directory** Role of the media: Internet, Web, social media, social networks, messaging, blogs, forums, television, newspapers, radio, written press, etc.

(continued)

Table 11.15 (continued)

CID7.8.3	CID stop	ICT infrastructures stop	CID manager Support service provider	Final control of information systems and CID referential back-up Information systems and CID referential stop	**Procedures and methodologies** Nomination or selection methodology of the members in charge of the existing post-CID legacy

Resources

Human resources: CID manager DC, CID portal webmaster, CID users	
Financial resources: financing mechanisms to be used	
Physical resources and ICT resources: legacy, knowledge and content management system	

The results of this phase

The DSS will cease to exist and the online site will be shut down

Comments

All actors/designers are involved in the CID management process present book. Nevertheless, it cannot be considered as finished or exhaustive since new elements can be added to it or removed from it depending on the needs and requirements specific to each project while respecting the concerns raised by designers, design managers, virtual communities and communities of practice (COP) experts as well as the characteristics of the design situation according to its application field, its environment and the intervention contents. Therefore, the seven fields are not static but heuristic and dynamic.

11.5.1   Community Informatics Design Endostructure

In this spirit, the endogenous elements making up community informatics design endostructure aim to identify a set of specific properties and characteristics to capture a design practice and to constitute the elements and suggest different modeling framework like ARCON that promotes modeling of this subfield. Therefore, from our reference framework comprised of seven fields, we can realize the design of a set of elements and entities and describe them from various modeling angles. Each developers' team can choose the fields and elements to model, the types of representation and modeling as well as the analysis level of depth or detail. These elements and their modeling angle are divided into four subfields:

1. *The structural elements*, referring to the community informatics design's structure from the network and constituent elements such as actors, roles, relations as well as the network topology of a community of practice
2. *The compositional elements*, referring to the community informatics design's composition of human and material resources, users, socio-technologies, infrastructures, information, knowledge and ontologies
3. *The functional elements*, to assist the community informatics design process implementation, as well as procedures, methodologies and basic functions and operations associated to the various stages of the community informatics design life cycle
4. *The behavioural elements*, encompassing principles, policies, community informatics design governance and ethics rules for designers making them adapt their behaviour to the pre-established norms regarding the use of community informatics design

11.5.2   Community Informatics Design Structural View

Structural modeling allows to identify a plurality of actors, roles, relations and other community informatics design structural characteristics. In fact, community informatics design actors and users are the organizations registered in the DSS environment. First of all, we observe the commercial entities, private organizations and government institutions that offer products and services on the market instead of getting involved in the organization of digital and online communities to enjoy quantitative benefits, such as durability and economic aspects. The second aspect to remember refers to the non-profit institutions like NGOs and support institutions involved in the organization of the virtual environment to make enormous qualitative benefits. Here we can talk about social prestige or social capital. Finally, the last community informatics design structural element refers to legal services, contractual service providers and enterprises ensuring the maintenance of individuals' lives. It is important to mention at this level the entire aspect of access to new clients, for example, insurance and training companies, ministries, associations in the ICT and design sector, chambers of commerce as well as environmental organizations campaigning for a healthy sociobiological ecosystem.

Furthermore, different roles can be played by community informatics design actors, designers and users. These roles are taken into account in the incubation and learning environment specific to each DSS. Stakeholders negotiate their participation rules from their respective meaning fields they later put in common for future action and activities. Together, they determine the envisioned challenges. Thus, we find:

- *The members* (users) of community informatics design, forming the basis of the role played by design organizations or online practices that are ready to participate in design activities.
- *The administrator or director* (manager) of community informatics design, playing a role of the person in charge of the platform's functioning and evolution as well as the role of promoter of the cooperation between the members possessing design skills. He also has the mandate of recruiting new organizations or inviting them to participate in the daily management of general community informatics design processes. Alongside these functions, the manager ensures and facilitates dispute resolutions as well as the preparation of active tools to make the community informatics design policies common to all design users.
- *The broker*, in charge of identifying and acquiring new collaboration opportunities through marketing and promotion strategies, also possesses negotiation skills with community informatics design potential clients.
- *The digital social system planner* (organization or community), assuming the responsibility of identifying the necessary skills and the virtual systems partners' potential in terms of new virtual organizations structuring.
- *The virtual system's coordinator* (organization or community), in charge of the virtual community management throughout its life cycle, in order to fulfil the objectives set within a collaboration opportunity.
- *The community informatics design advisor* also playing the role of advisor in charge in the specific expertise fields of collaborative design assists community informatics design users, members and managers in their daily tasks.
- *The services related to community informatics design*, focused on contributors responsible to provide or transmit a wide variety of services, support tools and mechanisms to various community informatics design actors.

- *Community informatics design ontology provider*, responsible for providing common services to various design actors and support institutions.
- *Institutional support supervisor*, keeping community informatics design up to date by incorporating the trends and the new technologies of his field of expertise, in order to suggest optimized solutions to help users or design managers accomplish their mission.
- *Community informatics design's guests*, organizations located outside the community informatics design process and interested to find general information on the learning environment to potentially become members of a community informatics design team.

In other words, different relations can be established between community informatics design actors (members, users, designers, peers, stakeholders), each entailing different degrees of interdependence that go from collaboration networks to coordination and cooperation networks in order to trace a collaboration continuum towards the multiplication of inter-organizational relations. These relations and interactions are described in the discovery and strategic alignment matrices that, by reusing the elements of an instantiated concepts list, examine several important interactions between the fields to model: the exostructure, the endostructure, the community informatics design activities, the communicational structures and processes, the functionalities, the socio-technologies and the ethics.

As clearly described by Camarinha-Matos and Afsarmanesh (2006), it is a networking involving a communication and an information on the benefits of mutual exchanges by comparing generalized utilities and collaborative actions (Moles and Rohmer 1986; Harvey 1996). As for coordination, which constitutes the second element of reflection of these researchers, in addition to activities they consist of aligning or modifying, the goal is to wait for more efficient results. Finally, the notion of cooperation extends and explains the interdependencies associated with resource sharing between design actors to reach compatible objectives.

In sum, these important concepts represent constituent elements of a generic social architecture seeking a good collaboration between design users. This collaboration is considered, as previously mentioned, like a process where risks, resources, responsibilities and rewards are shared by these actors in the achievement of a common objective.

Finally, in order to distinguish a new community informatics design features, researchers Camarinha-Matos and Afsarmanesh (2007) suggest a semi-typology, in order to identify and postulate the specific attributes of the existing and emerging properties of a design oriented towards the determination of skills profiles and relevant characteristics (the design situation). This semi-typology can be summarized in four community informatics design types or fields. They are the stable field of products and services (available in open-source code on the market or online), the one-of-a-kind stable domain like electricity or citizen services, the emerging field (the type of DSS to build) and a field led by innovation (new process, new work methods, new forms of production or applications, etc.).

From these first checklists of entities to model, we can make sub-lists by examining the entities to model according to the seven spaces of design. Therefore, in the following tables, we make a list of entities by using the action verbs corresponding to the activities contained in these seven design spaces (Camarinha-Matos and Afsarmanesh 2007, 2008) (Tables 11.3, 11.4, 11.5, 11.6, 11.7, 11.8, 11.9, 11.10, 11.11, 11.12, 11.13, 11.14 and 11.15).

The examination of this checklist for a DSS community informatics instantiation allows to discover the complexity of the structures and the decision-making that intervene in the development of numerous types of digital institutions and environments. We believe it resolves a certain number of issues but it also creates new ones. Let us simply think about ethics and aesthetics concepts and questions we have not addressed until now. It is only the beginning of a complex process that will need the support of creativity, simulation and visualization tools. In the next section, on the first checklist basis, we will show the utility of crossing all these fields in a first trans-field discovery matrix (non-exhaustive) related to the healthcare field.

11.6   Trans-field Interactions

In this section, we present an illustration of the relations' evaluation between entities from the need and utility to constitute checklists in the healthcare field.

We will use here some of the several elements of the checklist presented in the previous section in order to examine and illustrate with examples the interactions between several fields with entities, properties and components that could be essential to the start of a new community informatics design project. In compliance to our first chapters where we insisted on the relevancy and importance to identify relations (between fields, between entities, between domains) in order to help the reflection and decision-making about design, we are connecting here the creation of the list and the relations between the fields in the healthcare sector.

In the present section, we will use certain elements of our checklist while comparing their contents, which helps the decision-making. The majority of these examples are the results of our own modeling experience and virtual community implantation at the Centre Hospitalier Pierre-Le-Gardeur, within a project we carried out with our colleagues Albert Lejeune and Gilles Lemire as well as several UQAM students. The project that took place between 2003 and 2006 was entitled "community informatics and distributed learning". Here are interaction examples corresponding to several relations between fields already identified in the present chapter. Let us be reminded that the objective of the exercise is not to drain the subject of be exhaustive but to show the utility of making element checklists (entities, components) and to evaluate the performance of the 2MDSAM matrix for a team of users/designers and community informatics experts containing degrees of skills and various expertise:

- *The Exogenous Element Interactions* × *Stakeholders*: The exostructure elements can affect entities (properties, components, elements) of certain endostructure parts like the stakeholders. It is the case of the computerization of electronic patient files in a hospital where socio-demographic characteristics command the reorganization of trainings, because of dissimilar skills levels of actors and specialities to implement in this upgrade.
- *The Exostructure* × *Objective Interactions*: The exogenous elements often influence the setting of objectives. The increase of a beneficiary population affects the profitability of hospital services.
- *The Exostructure* × *Functionality Interactions*: The exostructure (the market) can influence the development of information services and the knowledge level with respect to the planning of contents. A hospital could be tempted to add new functionalities like management services and knowledge sharing in response to certain cultural or socio-demographic characteristics or from a market (exogenous factors).
- *The Exostructure* × *Socio-technology Interactions*: An exogenous element can affect technological objects or their acquisition, if it concerns policy and government infrastructure acquisition and appropriation procedures. This case requires consultation by the hospital informational resource department, websites and government documentation regulation policies on infrastructures used by the hospital and its regional partners.
- *The Exostructure* × *Design Activity Interactions*: The exogenous elements can influence the situation and the design activities as well as the necessary changes for the hospital system, because some information can be publicly revealed while others must be kept strictly confidential and can only be shared by the professional body. The state of science and best medical practices can also play an important role.
- *The Stakeholder* × *Exostructure Interactions*: Even if we noticed earlier that in most cases, individuals and stakeholders do not have any influence on political or cultural environment factors, they can have some influence at certain moments through democratic means like voting, protesting or committing to large-scale projects. The medication cost takeover by the state or certain organizations; the increase of virtual healthcare communities in a region, the number of family doctors in a province; the training of clinical communities of practice in a particular sector like mental health, blood banks and artificial insemination; and ethics in biotechnologies are all examples where a plurality of stakeholders or participants must obtain consensus for the design decision-making or have constructive citizen dialogues.
- *Stakeholder* × *Objective Interactions*: The structures, properties and components of stakeholders (endostructure) influence the DSS design objective definition. For example, if the hospital management suggests a service reorganization or a new strategic plan, it can face opposition or inertia, or on the contrary, obtain the support of social or organizational groups depending on the process and structure characteristics that could feel threatened by the new structure or strategy. A DSS multi-field matrix could cross the entities of the new strategic policy with the

policy positions of different actors in a data base in order to document a serious theoretical multi-gamer model to analyse opinion divergence, to analyse the flow of positive or negative actions for the project and try to align the interests.

- *Stakeholder × Functionality Interactions*: This matrix allows to map the sociometric influences the stakeholders have over the corresponding functionalities. For example, a hospital functionality in the issue of knowledge network diffusion in practice communities that will be related to stakeholders interested by this functionality.

- *Stakeholder × Socio-technology Interactions*: DSS stakeholders generally wish to make the decisions regarding social media platforms and collaborative and creative tools that concern the DSS to co-build or destined to accompany the design process. There are "socio-constructivist" interactions between stakeholders and the choices of infrastructures, software and tools. During the implantation of home care services, a community of "nomadic therapists" might want to choose the best mobile tools for diagnosis and the sharing of knowledge by network between the members on the ground and professional services at a hospital.

- *Stakeholder × Activity (Design) Interactions*: The human elements contribute to an array of tasks and sub-tasks within a DSS project. In a practice and learning community social media functionalities in the hospital environment, they can model the tasks by conceptual mapping (e.g. a rich picture), describe the medical acts, carry performance studies, contribute to the redaction of charts and forms, mediatize all sorts of files related to the execution of their tasks, make mock-ups of learning scenarios and imagine new ways of doing.

- *Objective × Exostructure Interactions*: The populational objectives of a DSS can influence the dimensions, properties and endogenous values associated to it. In a hospital system, the creation of virtual communities can question the traditional role of the doctor and his expertise, confronted to the new reality of tribes and communities of practice progression or healthcare learning. The healthcare DSS objectives can affect the public perception regarding the real doctor's skills or his real and exclusive expertise to provide cares.

- *Objective × Stakeholder Interactions*: DSS objectives can affect the stakeholders. The creation of virtual professional communities can affect the professional relations or the departments and their relations with their patients. These new relations can also affect the questioning about doctors' and nurses' remuneration since they see their tasks diminish with the progression of preventative cares provided by the community.

- *Objective × Functionality Interactions*: The functional composition and decomposition of a DSS start with the objectives pursued by the community in charge of the DSS co-creation. For example, if a community of practice objective is to support the clinical service efforts of a hospital, the relations hypotheses, the ones diagnosing an illness, which ensures the best response for specific or urgent cares in a given field that received a complaint and processes it, refer to functionalities such as the reception of hospital admission messages, the responsibility in answering such messages and ensuring the patient transport and the priority treatment of the patient and so on and so forth.

- *Function × Objective Interactions*: From the moment where designers' work tries to align or directly direct the entire or a part of the functions to the DSS objectives, several interactions are occurring between functionalities and the DSS objectives. An example consists of aligning the structure of communities of practice with the hospital management process: an analyst could measure the cost of resources and workforce allocated for each DSS objective to meet (patient support, clinical service support, document writing for prevention).
- *Functionality × Socio-technology Interactions*: The attribution of functionality maps each functionality specific to an element or certain DSS properties. Each functionality is corresponded with a physical component, an infrastructure element or a particular social media. For example, the functionalities to "memorize information corresponding to patients' files" and "model relations between various services" will be associated with modeling capacities from Cmap or mind map.
- *Functionality × Activity Interactions*: There are several interactions between the design activity system and the functionalities the DSS has to assume. The "distribution of an appropriate medication to various groups of patients" function corresponds to activities, norms and procedures occurring in the task chain associated with the delivery of the right medication to each patient.
- *The Socio-technology × Exostructure Interactions*: There are numerous interactions within socio-technologies and between them and the environment of socio-technical projects like DSS for the innovation. The existing hospital infrastructures can constitute new material, just like the lack of skills can slow down the appropriation of new telecommunication infrastructures. Some needs like large diagnosis devices (scanners) cannot be met because of a lack of resources from the government to the hospitals.
- *The Socio-technology × Functionality Interactions*: All ICT and all infrastructures can be described by a functionality. However, in the case of a hospital or another public establishment like a university, the acquisition cost represents a property containing attributes (different prices can change quarterly) likely to prevent the purchase of necessary material and the obtainment of a functionality. Open-source code software configurable by available local teams can represent an alternative solution. For example, the acquisition cost of an exclusive community information system (e.g. a business platform or a social design platform) has a direct link with the sub-functionalities of knowledge management.
- *The Socio-technology × Activity (Design Process) Interactions*: Most activities related to a DSS and socio-technical systems generally require suitable technologies. Several DSS designs contain processes, tasks and sub-tasks that require technologies: the modeling process, highly complex and specialized, that requires computing modeling tools, crossed matrices between functionalities to create with the technologies accompanying them which has an important incidence on the activities related to the design process. In certain cases, these constraints have a decisive impact on modeling and the feasibility of complex digital social systems.

406 11 The Organization and Governance of an Incubation and Learning Environment...

- *The Activity (Design)* × *Exostructure (Environment) Interactions*: The activities related to a particular design situation interact with exogenous elements. For example, an analysis of the procedures on the cycle of adopting the best sterilization practices in a hospital can reveal that excellent practices occurring every day might not appear in the government portal and are never used as exemplary practices in the entire hospital system even if empirical scientific data validate this data. The problem of updating all members' knowledge occurs regarding the great trends or best practices (exostructure) undergoing in a hospital or a given community.

- *The Activity (Design Process)* × *Stakeholder Interactions*: A feedback targeting certain stakeholders can be useful, for example, to notify the interested parties the slowness or the stop of a computing system and the success rate of the new tool appropriation of the satisfaction level of patients regarding the implantation of a service prototype or even to remind an administrator the non-respect of a commitment or a contract.

- *The Activity (Design Process)* × *Socio-technology Interactions*: A socio-technical system the scope of a DSS dedicated to knowledge management in a hospital can cost hundreds of thousands of dollars, even 10 or 20 million of dollars. Therefore, it is important to identify socio-technologies related to design processes and activities that will support hospital DSS activities because the automation of certain functions at great costs may harm the hospital or partner institutions instead of helping them if a strategic alignment analysis matrix of micro-, meso- and macro-care acts performed by the hospital is not correctly carried out (it is the fine analysis of what people do in their everyday task).

11.7 Construction Guide of a Discovery and Strategic Alignment Matrix (2MDSAM)

The 2MDSAM is a useful collaborative tool to develop different modes of thinking and relations in a wide diversity of analysis fields, namely, service design, great socio-technical systems, business platforms and innovation communities, collaborative project management and the analysis of many types of digital social systems design. A 2MDSAM co-construction, like a community informatics design lifecycle process, is a circular, iterative and non-linear process, because it does not take place according to a sequence of predefined stages. The community informatics expert has the latitude to add, subtract or modify the information on DSS fields and properties throughout the seven design spaces' process. Before building a 2MDSAM, the analyst/designer and his team have to determine the project's goals, define the type of DSS to model and determine the information sources and data useful to the first decision-making. Table 11.16 reproduces a first exploratory matrix we have created for a team we are part of at UQAM (the Citizen Commission group, under the direction of Mireille Tremblay). This matrix serves to identify the priority

Table 11.16 Cyberdemocracy and alignment matrix

Formulate strategic motives of the group's portal	Give our priority goal	What are the main aspirations of our team? What values do we share?
Create our mission statement	Develop a few clear and short sentences summarizing the issue and the means to articulate it	What type of support or mission? Why use this or that media? For what solution or what change?
Give clear objectives	Say how we will meet them with social media or design tools	What services would we like to offer through certain communication tools? (see CIEL in Canada, Tassi in Italy, FING in France)
Perform researches	Document review, bibliography, site visit, exemplary sites, studies, reports, case study, animation types	What types of methodological processes, techniques and tools that could be useful? What types of messages or networks will have an impact? What type of social participative architecture?
Identify our users, partners and participating communities of practice	Who are the leaders interested in our issue? What roles could they play? What type of collaboration?	What interest communities would we like to see to take part in various stages of our project? Commitment, marketing, culture, basic training, coordination, management, attitudes, media trajectories, geo-/demography, etc.
Create dynamic and mobilizing messages	What communicational guideline to favour? What creative, simple, relevant, engaging messages?	What information for which channel? What message and media diffusion and appropriation modalities? How to define social multimodal communication? With what goals?
Strategically align media and tools with the objectives	What are the convivial useful media that will accompany our objectives and our issue? Create an alignment diagram from activity verbs: communicate, coordinate, animate, vote, survey, dialogue, debate, deliberate	What good media format to adopt for our audience? To manage and mobilize the members? To coordinate the research and convince stakeholders to take action? To think, understand, give ideas, train? Through what tactics can tools be acquired and promoted? How to facilitate workshop?
Create the alignment diagram	Start with priority objectives, for example, animate the site, the partners, the communities, the public, the international publics	How to define our type of interaction and contact points with our users or our various types or animation modalities? Make decisions on tools. Create various types of double-entry tables according to objectives and activities to realize, for example, verbs, functionality, tools, benefits, constraints, measures and evaluations (ref.: Stephen Thorpe animation support tools)
Ensuring security and privacy	Take care to preserve the safety and life of people in case of a delicate situation, warning, risk and catastrophe	How to secure the information of our partners and our own team? What criteria to define as an information must be kept secret, confidential, shared with a small group or a wider audience or at large? How to fight against the informational or delinquency overload?

Source l Pierre Léonard Harvey June 14, 2012 Version 1

information before making deeper decisions about the DSS to build, thanks to detailed discovery matrices. It corresponds to space 1, "Explore", and also allows to review the elements related to the six other design spaces by favouring a first iteration of the complete cycle, in the first analysis. We believe it is a simple and efficient starting tool.

After answering these types of question in a particular workshop or at the beginning of any DSS projects (for example in using these questions in Space 1 "Explore"), and according to the nature and complexity of each project, a group of users/designers or a group of diverse stakeholders could take the decision of not modeling certain fields and abandon certain others in a clear manner. They could also decide to proceed differently if time, cost or skills constraints could hinder the process. In other cases, it will be necessary to model all domains for different reasons like security, the exhaustiveness needs, the aesthetics or artistic aspects or the particular requirements of a sponsor.

In the case of a DSS community informatics design, a project manager using a 2MDSAM could start by suggesting to use the simplified matrices presented above to a list of stakeholders involved in the project in order to explore the orientations and to proceed to a bird's-eye view analysis. Certain participants involved in the design and potential users of the service, the application or the DSS could also be part of it. Then, this social matrix made of stakeholders, partners, communities and potential users could be organized in a more detailed way by gathering the needs, roles and possible relations' information between various parties, what we call the "stakeholder matrix". It is the first matrix to build.

The second matrix to build is the objective matrix. Generally, the objectives are formulated by action verbs. The different information sources that constitute it could include the first matrix participants' conditions and requirements; the marketing data obtained from interviews, discussion groups or questionnaires; data obtained on the Web; as well as other sources. While building the objective matrix, the community informatics experts and the user/designer community of practice could put in relation each objective with each stakeholder identified in the Stakeholder × Objective matrix. All users/designers or participants of a project can infer a good amount of important knowledge of these three matrices, schematically the main stakeholders and their objectives. This information is vital to each seven design spaces' life cycle because it helps designers to understand the roles of partners, in order to know which one is influencing what aspect of the life cycle and which ones are affected at what moment and for what reason.

Then, the members could build the DSS functionality matrix by decomposing the DSS under construction and its constituent functions. The objective action verbs can be reused or diversified in order to attribute the functions. The attribution of functions relates the functionality matrix to the socio-technology matrix (Functionalities × Socio-technologies) as well as the activity matrix (Functionalities × Activities) as the digital social systems designers (communitician) ensure the suggested designs support the entire DSS functionalities.

The socio-technology matrix, more specifically, represents the portion channelled in socio-technical design. It examines relations between technical subsystems (social media, collaborative and design tools, platforms) and other fields and their components (objectives, functionalities, activities). The activity matrix observes the relations between the DSS processes (activities) and the tasks and sub-tasks to realize while aligning them. The 2MDSAM also allows users/designers and community informatics experts to link each relevant part to the design activities (Stakeholders × Activities) and the socio-technology components to the activities (Socio-technologies × Activities), in order to capture information and important knowledge on the interaction and the interconnectivity between fields.

The designers/analysts can identify and memorize the factors related to the endo-structure and the exostructure, thanks to the construction of the environment matrix that considers the exogenous and the endogenous elements. This aspect we have greatly developed in the present chapter through an important checklist presentation helps them capture important information on the social and human aspects that are too often forgotten by computing specialists and traditional information sciences. As the DSS community informatics design matures through the stakeholder communication throughout its life cycle, the 2MDSAM records the transitions of state and the evolution of components between the fields.

For the collaborative management of DSS design projects, community informatics experts as well as non-experts people can easily follow a procedure similar to the one we are proposing in the 2MDSAM framework. Our component listing from the previous section is an example. It all depends on the developing DSS maturity; the elements and sources and the quality of the information necessary for the construction of a DSS will vary within each project.

For example, a simple spreadsheet software like Microsoft Excel can generally be used to build a simple 2MDSAM and offer a variety of statistics and very valuable mathematical tools. Simple double-entry similarity matrices can be used to master the complexity of fields to take into account in order to improve the DSS design. However, in the future, analysis and visual modeling tools will have to be used or created in order to realize the full 2MDSAM potential.

Chapter 12
The Conclusion: Towards a Computerized Modeling Tool for a 2MDSAM with Fully Qualified and Assigned Functionalities

The future tasks we need to accomplish to create a 2MDSAM with fully qualified information represent a highly complex socio-technical modeling. However, to simplify this task, our team will use software like the systems modeling and the representation tool created at MIT by Jason Bartolomei's team. Among the new tools, the systems modeling and representation tool (SMART) is one of the best for the construction of systems models, like the 2MDSAM, from the documentation system and text systems (Bartolomei et al. 2012). He performs this task by using a new process, the qualitative knowledge construction (or QKC). SMART records the information for different classes of the matrix's knots, relations and properties (attributes) over time and facilitates the extraction of information and knowledge by allowing to export them and translate them into mathematical formulas (Bartolomei 2007).

The QKC process is a technique of qualitative information incorporation in systems models. We would like to use such tools to instantiate the qualitative information in systems models, in our case, DSS models and their various fields. The information could be gathered by interview, questionnaire or discussion groups and by different types of observation. It is converted into text that is subsequently coded or tagged by content analysis categories (knots, relations, reports, properties and attributes). Once coded or inserted in an image grammar, the data is automatically incorporated to an enriched data structure (organized to increase the intelligibility) that uses colour, geometric shapes and movement languages to catalyse the information and represent it. The system or the social system targeted by the analysis is then visually represented by distribution of values in a cell; the data rendering that supports the representation is contained in the cells. By developing a program aiming to translate textual observations reports and coded data interviews likely to be systematically and quantitatively analysed, the communication or social science researcher can translate the qualitative information into quantitative information.

By establishing a transparency and an obvious traceability in the qualitative and quantitative translation process, this type of tool fulfills Warfield's promise stated in the first chapter when we wanted to bring precision without necessarily be confronted

© Springer International Publishing AG 2017
P.-L. Harvey, *Community Informatics Design Applied to Digital Social Systems*,
Translational Systems Sciences 12, DOI 10.1007/978-3-319-65373-0_12

by the mathematics barrier. While doing their data processing work, human and social researchers do not need to be mathematics and statistics experts to identify, observe and model DSS. Software like QKC lifts these epistemological barriers, paving the way to the construction of better social systems models, better application designs and a collaborative complexity management.

The demonstration of a 2MDSAM construction can be performed here without a longer development. Let us simply remind that such models offer enormous benefits for the analysis, monitoring, simulation and imagination of new DSS. The 2MDSAM we present here represents a substantial effort from our team to offer a framework containing a deep logic allowing to organize and represent knowledge related to large-scale socio-technical systems as presented in the first chapter, according to the meaning and definition Warfield gives.

12.1   Towards a Universal Generic Visual Language Model

Modeling and visualization tools like Stella and the *Métaphore universelle inc.* (visualization and representation software of complex data with the help of metaphors like spheres, colour, shapes and movement) could help establish a visualization prototype of the transition state structure of activities during a DSS, thus providing a feasibility demonstration for design activity analysis and psychosocial processes involved in the construction of DSS. Let us briefly examine a possible research scenario where the challenge is to examine the interesting generic functionalities to represent the co-construction of online organizations and DSS. The argument here is to use 3D modeling software for the complex political planning and implementation of new governance mechanisms of large-scale socio-technical projects. First, we have insisted on the fact that any type of large-scale project required design ads implementation of suitable governance processes. Any governance type represents a challenge for cognitive mastery and comprehension of organizations complexity and DSS. The use of traditional project charts, electronic acetates and simple cognitive maps are not suitable for the capture of DSS complexity and evolution. We will need extra coherence in the analysis. Here, we will use as an example the precursory works of Anthony Judge (2008a). This researcher, in his website and through various works and conferences, has explored at length the use of polyhedrons to represent the complexity and the way to computerize this process to facilitate the emergence, representation and transformation of "psychosocial organizations", his own expression, which correspond to our DSS. Inspired by very important authors, like Atkin, Fuller and D. Alexander, the Australian researcher Anthony Judge considers that polyhedrons, especially those that refer to a high complexity, offer representation devices on which system's complexity can be represented in a way to improve mnemonic possibilities and to validate a sense of transformational potential, especially when these validation factors are reinforced by regularity, symmetry, movement and transition properties and by a palette of suitable colours.

Our statement will be to consider the possibilities and functionalities offered by the use of visualization metaphors like the polyhedrons as conceptual support, cognitive help or support to collaborative works of practice communities.

Here, we pick up some elements suggested by Judge who utilizes the Stella software functionalities (Robert Webb 2000) that can represent today and in the future complex 3D and 4D phenomena in various governance contexts of vast collaborative design projects. We focus here on certain applications that can be commonly used in this optic and on the way we could extend them as support to certain fields and identified functionalities in our instantiation strategy and discovery matrix process in particular. Our use of the Stella software is justified by the fact that it is very well-known of our French-speaking colleagues and that this imaginative attitude could be applied to other similar visualization software for modeling assistance. Our succinct development simply seeks to show the feasibility of transfer of such toll configuration process towards other visualization tools at the service of designers. Implicitly, we wish to explore if such application can suggest unexpected approaches likely to facilitate the emergence, representation and transformation of virtual organizations and DSS, whether for remote work groups, virtual teams, network organizations, collaborative inter-enterprise alliances, large-scale issues, cultural intervention strategies or concepts and values related to the planning of great socio-technical systems.

Our outlook on DSS facilitation, their emergence and their representation depends on the confluence and transdisciplinary convergence of independent research fields that unfortunately have remained unexplored during several years, especially because of intellectual property issues or a lack of managers training, for example:

- The purely geometric representation of the polyhedron upon which rely the symmetric tensegrities: in a virtual network organization or a DSS, tensegrity (attributed to Buckminster Fuller) is a metaphor made of the words "tension" and "integrity"; we define it temporarily as the study of tensions, harmony, balance or unbalance between the various structures of a social network taken as a group of unities (technologies, humans, agents) in dynamic interaction (the characteristics of an ecosystem).
- The analysis of the non-linear dynamic that characterizes the tensegrities.
- The challenge of tensegrity for the architects in the industry of construction.
- The implications of the training concept associated with the works of the conversation and interaction of actors theory based on the tensegrity theory.
- The implications of spatial metaphors in the physical space on the design of cognitive spaces and social systems.
- Private visualization software (our input)
- The relevancy of these fields, examined by Judge:

  – For the new governance forms (2008a) that it would allow to analyse and model
  – For the observation of new forms of organization in which cybernetics of third order is considered as significant (2007)

– For the emergence and support of new forms of virtual organization within
  social networks and video game environment, regarding their potential for the
  rapid cognitive mastery of a phenomenon and their dynamic development
– To encourage their use where the issue of intelligence and collective and
  collaborative imagination is important (2005)
– For the cognitive relevancy of the spherical metaphor applied to various
  modes of dialogue (2011, 1998), in the organization of knowledge (1994), in
  learning spaces and problem-solving (1996)

What are the relevant functionalities of the Stella visualization software
(Webb 2000) in various fields of interest for the DSS design and implantation?
In the following lines, we will briefly examine these functions while underlining
that other types of modules and visualization devices could be evaluated in the same
spirit. Here are a few schematic comments on the Stella functionalities likely to
improve the mnemonic function which could be very relevant in institutional design
and varied strategic situations for the following purposes:

• *Select/deselect:* The polyhedrons' faces and edges could be selected independently for subsequent operations.
• *Mapping 2D/3D networks:* The polyhedrons and visual languages can be represented as solid 3D forms; we can pivot and move from left to right and top
  to bottom. The 2D networks can represent all sorts of network structures and
  relations. These two representation modes can be combined by modifying the
  window or the interface.
• *Use colour:* A complete colour spectrum like the universal spectrum of traffic
  lights can serve to distinguish values, interests, opinions or attitudes, in accordance with different schemes of information qualification.
• *Choose images:* The application of images at various faces of the polyhedron is
  excellent in various applications like Stella. We can represent:

  – The logos of the organizations collaborating in a coalition of design partners
  – The portrait of the representatives, stakeholders, sponsors and collaborators
    involved in the planning of a collective project
  – The portrait of the organization members, contacts and friends in a collabora-
    tive network like it is the case in several current social networks
  – The portrait of the participants and the facilitator of a workshop

• These functionalities are only a small example of the basic possibilities offered
  for any Web page relevant for a project and that allows to represent different organizations or different DSS and explore them with a virtual reality navigator.
• *Qualify/label:* We can convert a text into images or present it under various formats
  and use the rotation function to identify them. Traditional labelling can contain:

  – People (contacts, collaborators, friends, partners)
  – Organizational units, virtual communities, networks and collaborative organi-
    zations and various types of DSS
  – Problems and elements of a problem
  – Various planning and community informatics design strategies and the
    properties and components related to them

- The fundamental values of a design project from an ethic chart
- Multi-aspect and multifunctional dashboards to follow a project
- Qualitative and quantitative information syntheses

- *Transform:*
  - Structures between them; go from one structure to the other in different ways that are useful for a project. To be explored since Stella does not have this function.
  - A 2D representation into a 3D representation in order to improve the images or diagrams strength to map the strategic challenges of the Quebec digital platform. In the context of sustainable development projects, we can also capture variables such as P for "population and security", H for "health and well-being", L for "learning and education", C for "commerce and production", E for "environment and impacts" and R for "regulation and norms of equity".

- *Capture the various fields of an instantiation strategy* and the challenges related to the identification of properties and their reciprocal connections in order to make decisions that are better founded in a field option or better articulated scenarios.
- *Use colours, shapes and movement* to distinguish the complex arenas and the heterogeneous fields in order to discover the models of conduct or behaviour considered like "virtual dialogue environments", where some text or image analyses can favour the synthesis, the conciliation of points of view or the mastery of a situation's complexity.

- We could continue at length in this direction, and this exercise will be done in our future research projects. We simply want to signal here the great possibilities of the current visualization tools to better master the collaborative management of complex projects. These visualization activities go beyond the information visualization; they expand to all sorts of psychosocial processes while showcasing the great importance of this process of information related to community informatics design qualification in connection with the computing possibilities of several tools available on the market. For now, we will not go any further in the practical aspect of the computerization of this process, because our statement could become too technical for the non-expert readers. We will simply identify the various possible applications of visual modeling software applied to the DSS.

12.2 The Potential Applications of Visual Modeling Languages to the DSS

Let us take, for example, various elements taken from the virtual practice communities associated with various DSS development strategies.

- *The integration of virtual teams:* One of the possible application fields of languages and model visualization is the construction of online teams. One of the important theoretical inputs we can refer to is the Stafford Beer one and the "viable systems".

The central statement in this application is constituted by the creation of social structures based on 3D tools to validate the socio-organizational characters or roles, compatible or not (Beer 1985; Espejo and Harnden 1989).

- *The social networking:* An important variant of the previous application is an extension of the fields of the media and social networks, considering the current interest for the validation of visualization and conceptual mapping of the social networks that currently have the shape of friend networks and personal contacts or family networks. The question is if more coherent commitment and participation structures, based on a suitable suite of 2D and 3D visual interfaces, can serve as catalysers or DSS organization models. This could be the proof that this type of tool represents an additional option to master the complexity of great projects as a complement to lists of partners belonging to different networks we can classify by name, activity type, in any relevant order or from criteria serving to build an analysis chart or a discovery matrix. Furthermore, one of the main reasons to favour such computing development is beyond the simple list of names or roles, and from the works related to the construction of discovery matrices, we can discover new qualities and important characteristics on the relations between stakeholders, so many elements are taken into account in the construction of practice communities associated with the development of a DSS dedicated to innovation. This exercise could be a big step towards taking into account the various qualities and values more or less visible or tangible associated with the development of more coherent or performing communities.

- *The online games guilds:* Another favoured application of the visualization use and various modes of activity representation and design process is the guilds (practice communities, associations, circles, tribes) that are devoted to collaborative design and online interactive games management. We especially think about the design situations that have hidden aspects, secrets, badly mastered because they contain intangible coherence and cohesion factors that would be relevant to discover in order to guide certain activities. Analysis observation and evaluation charts which allow to better understand the structuring and operating of the online gaming communities could constitute a fundamental input to evaluate the strategies and offer competitive benefits. In this esprit, the growing overlap between strategic simulations and electronic scenarios of a game could offer in a few years a mastery of a more suitable complexity by revealing the "secrets" of all sorts of training strategies in various fields like health, education and the environment, which could lead to the success of reality in these activities fields.

- *The research colabs, the living labs, the excellency centres and collaborative research networks:* Because of the transdisciplinary challenges such DSS design environment pose, sociometric mapping and the schematization of various design processes or playful activities through 2D and 3D visualization tools, under various forms of "organized complexity" apprehension, could be fruitful in the identification of qualities and factors intervening in the integrative nature of such DSS, at their rising stage, their growth or their metamorphosis, dissolution or access to maturity. We can easily imagine all the utilities of such modeling tools can bring to the structuring of excellency centres of the federal government or to the Quebec government innovation validation activities.

- *Digital social systems:* In a more generic way, we consider the mapping of stakeholders and the necessary functionalities to meet their expectations (e.g. the translation of the discovery matrices results in an evolutive 3D model) through various representations and modeling interfaces that can improve in a relevant manner the "visualization sense of a group's integrity", which could bring a concrete and operating complement to the comprehension of the structuring and the functioning of these groups. Analysis charts built in groups and mediatized in 3D modeling suitable tools would contrast with simplistic diagrams usually used in this type of activity, in particular in the communication through social media. In particular, we would need suitable analysis and media validation tools to identify and characterize the levels of additional complexity to take into account to improve the efficiency of the virtual work teams and online training. Beyond the psychosocial analysis, the real interest of using modeling tools resides in the possibilities offered by a series of "visual and design interaction models" that could constitute a sort of "visual mirror" of the directory of strategies useful for design, the implantation and the deployment of DSS, especially in the competitive ubiquitous contexts. Another advanced possibility would be two innovation communities wanting to create a collaborative network that could visualize their interrelations around the same models.

- *The relations complementarity and unbalance:* Another functionality of the DSS co-construction and innovation communities is the development of stakeholder communities in terms of coalition and strategic alliance between multiple partners where we must ensure the required variety of elements and complementary components (people, organizations, technological resources, design strategies, shared values concepts or functionalities). The possibility to identify symmetries and differences offered by different types of interfaces like Stella could help distinguish even more the elements of a field (cognitive, social, legal aspects), its multiple aspects, its properties and their relations and connections, through colours, shapes or movement. The use of this grammar of the 3D image applied to the mediatization of the strategic alignment and discovery matrices results could also greatly help showcase the potential unbalance between stakeholders.

- *Mapping and coding of socio-communicational functionalities:* Beyond the quantification of more measurable objects (like socio-demographic aspects, degrees of ICT appropriation or the attitudes ladder), the value of 3D modeling software's language models could be clearly associated with their "cognitive qualitative meaning", which could be usefully mapped in different aspects of a design strategy (exostructure, endostructure, community informatics design activities, communicational structures and processes, functionalities, socio-technologies, ethics and values) in a way to showcase the convergences and divergences, contrasts and complementarities in the various relations and connections between stakeholders. This could be useful in the exploratory activities related to spaces 1 and 2 of the seven spiral design spaces, in the exploration of a common vision, or even in the simulation of context more favourable to action, for a small interest group or a large innovation community. It could also be the development of a communicational or educational device, the symbolic comprehension of a project and the monitoring of the members' perceptions dealing with a complex activity.

The projections and the imagination of a new virtual territory scope are directed towards the desired and desirable values. In its more obvious shape, the visualization of complex systems issues resides in the identification and informational typologies and the distinction of psychosocial functionalities specific to a design project, whether it is values or principles that guide activities, action and intervention programs, quantities, qualities or properties associated with various fields to be modeled or developed. If the presentation of a series of element list by fields, accompanied by their discovery matrix process, represents an important step in the more systematic DSS design, we should consider the connections between these series of elements more. The visualization of these connections and their operating arrangements for the planning can be of a considerable importance for the rigor, the integrity and the viability when we try to apply them to design situations. The example of vast social systems like the healthcare system in Quebec illustrates the arrangement of elements often disparate and badly processed, like documents, reports, articles and policies not considered in a holistic manner. The dynamic conceptual mapping of systems and subsystems of activities could contribute to ask better research and development questions when the observation of complex reports between elements is done in a more systematic way, through the discovery and representation of interaction models and graphic design. In our case, the community informatics field, the particular interest resides in the series of aspects and modeled fields we have identified and defined in an entire instantiation strategy by trying to reduce the numerous fields to seven great types (exostructure, endostructure, etc.) to make the typology of their elements as a checklist in order to appreciate the connections and arrangements through discovery matrices with the objective of computationally translating them in visual languages with two, three, four or even more dimensions.

12.3   Future Researches

The use of the entire community informatics design methodology supported by new modes of visual representations will be the topic of our next works on complex social systems governance, in particular we are thinking of: the empowerment of the civil society in design problematics, the organizational transformation through the co-creation of many kinds of digital design platforms, the perspectives opened by the proliferation of all kinds of computerized artwork and visualization tools and their related cognitive issues, the overcoming of obstacles and the resolutions of conflicting worldview, the results of consensus building in conversational workshops, the assessment of psychosocial impacts of various modes of dialogue and the responsible communication at the service of innovation ecosystems and sustainable digital social systems.

The ubiquitous imagination in a complex design world is only the beginning. The concrete FOSM contribution to community informatics design and the 2MDSAM in the apprehension and implantation of DSS systems has yet to be proven. We would need several important socio-technical projects to validate their foundations, their theories, their methodologies and their applications. Even if we believe that the conceptual scaffolding, reference framework and instantiation strategies presented in this book are sufficient to describe several complex social systems of interest for our society, we do not know yet if the seven design spaces and the seven fields of modeling presented represent a design methodology suitable for the DSS development and, if so, to what extent. In particular, we need to better define the fields of exostructure, design processes and applied ethics.

Important researches have started and are realized everyday in the world in order to explore the interactions between several socio-technical systems of human activities. To move towards more rigorous approaches in the comprehension and implantation of these systems, we shall create "design and knowledge catalysers" like the SADC and 2MDSAM, to be able to represent complex ecosystems where each of the systems or subsystems interacts with the exostructure or the endostructure of the other. The first apprehended results of these researches, combining complexity sciences, computing and social and communicational sciences, already promise the discovery of unexpected facts with an organizational behaviour we badly master and with governance modes and integration mechanisms we do not explore enough in the context of disparate and diversified social systems.

We believe the conceptual model presented in this book, with its methodology, as well as our first APSI research results on the social appropriation of methodologies and design collaborative tools will contribute to improve the existing systems but also to provoke the appearance of a strong social interest for modeling and the implantation of social systems that will be more favourable in the future. They provide a wider model to scientifically and methodologically represent socio-technical systems we call digital social systems. The invaluable free open-source code software input frees the imagination for a new movement of "design thinking" free of the limits provided by the use of private software. This movement makes possible a larger amount of programming and modeling systems that, once integrated in an analytical framework and a semiformal instantiation methodology, promise us social systems that will accompany human activities in all sorts of socio-economic activities spheres.

Finally, the heaviest task consists of developing partners' commitment and implantation strategies especially at the level of future research policies. The data visualization strategies and the development of exhaustive criteria in order to determine when and how the modeling of complex social systems should be applied here are research subjects really worth exploring.

The FOSM, community informatics design and its seven exploratory spaces as well as the 2MDSAM now allow users/designers, expert or not, to reflect and represent each scientific block of socio-technical systems design and the fields associated to them. Users can contribute to map the interactions within and between these fields as well as to "configure" their relations and connections through discovery matrix and modeling tools. They can also represent the DSS evolution through time and their various states of transition, in terms of structure – evolution of the knots and relations between fields – and the properties of elements and components of various aspects of the systems to build. The approach is systematic enough to be programmable and translated into visualization tools with n dimensions to assist various users/designers audiences. From qualification of information and knowledge, we come back to a quantification that will also command and new qualification, according to fields and never-ending knots of the global scientific conversation.

Finally, the FOSM of community informatics design, its seven design spaces and the 2MDSAM allow us to process for the first time, in a unified manner, social interactions and techniques in the context of the social Web under construction. This will allow us to direct the ubiquitous imagination and the participative culture of users towards the construction of DSS, innovation communities and social networks at the service of our society's development and to study them with the bets theoretical, methodological and technological tools.

References

Aakhus, M. (2007). Communication as design. *Communication Monographs, 74*(1), 112–117.

Aakhus, M. (2011). Crafting interactivity for stakeholder engagement: Transforming assumptions about communication in science and policy. *Health Physics, 101*(5), 531–535.

Aakhus, M. (2013). Deliberation digitized: Designing disagreement space through communication. Special issue of argument in context on political deliberation. *Journal of Argumentation in Context, 2*(1), 101–126. 26p.

Aakhus, M., & De Moor, A. (2013). It's the conversation, stupid! Social Media Systems Design for Open Innovation Communities. http://www.communitysense.nl/papers/2012_De_Moor_Aakhus_It's_the%20Conversation_Stupid.pdf. Consulté le 6 décembre 2013.

Aakhus, M., & Jackson, S. (2005). Technology, interaction, and design. dans K. Fitch & R. Sanders (dir.), *Handbook of language and social interaction* (pp. 411–435). Mahwah: Erlbaum.

Aakhus, M., & Jackson, S. (2014). Becoming more reflective about the role of design in communication. *Journal of Applied Communication Research*, (2, 2), 125–134.

Aakhus, M., & Rumsey, E. (2010). Crafting supportive communication online: A communication design analysis of conflict in an online support group. *Journal of Applied Communication Research, 38*(1), 65–84.

Aakhus, M., et al. (2014). Symbolic action research in information systems: The introduction to the special issue. *MIS Quarterly, 38*(4).

Abdoullaev, A. (1999). *Artificial intelligence.* Moscou: Encyclopedic Intelligence Systems.

Abdoullaev, A. (2008). *Reality, universal ontology, and knowledge systems: toward the intelligent world.* Hershey: IGI Global.

Abdoullaev, A. (2011). Creating the future: Building tomorrow's urban World: Intelligent Nations and Smart Cities of the future. http://eu-smartcities.eu/sites/all/files/blog/files/WHAT_ARE_SMART_CITIES%20%26%20COMMUNITIES.pdf. Consulté le 23 novembre 2013.

Abowd, D., Atkeson, G., Bobick, F., Essa, A., Macintyre, B., Mynatt, D., & Starner, E. (2000). Living laboratories: the future computing environments group at the Georgia Institute of Technology. http://www.cc.gatech.edu/fce/pubs/fce-org.pdf. Consulté le 11 novembre 2013.

Ackoff, R. L. (1974). *Redesigning the future: A system approach to societal problems.* New York: Wiley.

Ackoff, R. L., & Emery, F. E. (1972). *On purposeful systems.* Londres: Tavistock.

Afsarmanesh, H. & Camarinha-Matos L. M. (2005). A framework for management of virtual organizations breeding environments. In dans L. M. Camarinha-Matos & H. Afsarmanesh (Eds.) *Proceedings of 6th PRO-VE'05 - collaborative networks and their breeding environments*(pp. 35-48) New York: Springer. 26-28 Sept 2005.

Afsarmanesh, H., & Camarinha-Matos, L. M. (2008). The ARCON modeling framework. In *Collaborative networks reference modeling*. ISBN: 978-0-387-79425-9 (pp. 67–82). New York: Springer.

Afsarmanesh, H., Camarinha-Matos, L. M., & Ollus, M. (2008). *Methods and tools for collaborative networked organizations*. New York: Springer.

Agbobli, C., & Hsab, G. (2011). *Communication internationale et communication interculturelle*. Québec: Presses de l'Université du Québec.

Alexander, G. C. (2003). Interactive management: An emancipatory methodology. *Systemic Practice and Action Research, 15*(2), 111–122.

Allee, V. (1998). *The knowledge evolution: Expanding organizational intelligence*. Oxford: Butterworth-Heinemann.

Allee, V. (2002). *The future of knowledge: Increasing prosperity through value networks*. Oxford: Butterworth-Heinemann.

Ama, S. (2006). Using moodle to build social capital. http://www.cvc.edu/2006/05/using-moodle-to-build-social-capital/. Consulté le 11 novembre 2013.

Anderson, T. (2004). Toward a theory of online learning. dans T. Anderson & F. Elloumi (dir.), *Theory and practice of online learning*. Athabasca: Athabasca University. http://cde.athabascau.ca/online_book/ch2.html. Consulté le 11 novembre 2013.

Annerstedt, A. (2007). Living labs: or, user-driven innovation environments in the information society. http://www.oii.ox.ac.uk. Consulté le 5 mai 2007.

Appelt, W., & Manbrey, P. (1999). Experiences with the BSCW shared workspace system as the backbone of a virtual learning environment for students. In *Proceedings of ED Media'99* (pp. 1710–1715), Charlottesville.

Argyris, C. (1982). *Reasoning, learning, and action: Individual and organisational*. San Francisco: Jossey Bass.

Argyris, C. (1993a). *Knowledge for action: A guide to overcoming barriers to organizational change*. San Francisco: Jossey-Bass.

Argyris, C. (1993b). *On organizational learning*. Cambridge, MA: Wiley.

Argyris, C., & Schon, D. (1978). *Organisational learning: A theory of action perspective*. Reading, Mass: Addison Wesley.

Argyris, C., & Schun, D. (1982). *Reasoning, learning and action*. San Francisco: Jossey-Bass.

Ashby, W. R. (1952). *Design for a brain*. New York: Wiley.

Ashby, W. R. (1956). *An introduction to cybernetics*. Londres: Chapman and Hall.

Atkin, R. H. (1974). *Mathematical structure in human affairs*. New York: Crane Rusak.

Atlas, C., & Le Moigne, J. -L. (1984). *Edgar Morin: science et conscience de la complexité*. Aix-en-Provence: Librairie de l'Université.

Audant, L. & Audant, P. L. (2010). APPRENTISSAGE PAR ANIMATION ET super langage interactif de communication universelle. Cahier du Colab,Automne 2010, numéro 1. Travaux du Laboratoire de communautique appliquée (LCA), Faculté de Communication, UQAM.

Badham, R. (2000). Sociotechnical design. dans W. Karwowski et al. (dir.), *Handbook of human factors and ergonomics* (pp. 1031–1040). New York: Wiley.

Baecker, R. M., Grudin, J., Buxton, W. A. S., & Greenberg, S. (1995). *Readings in human-computer interaction: Toward the year 2000*. San Francisco: Morgan Kaufmann.

Banathy, B. H. (1971). *Instructional systems*. Belmont: Fearon.

Banathy, B. H. (1984). *Systems design in the context of human activity systems: An introductory text: Try-out version*. San Francisco: International Systems Institute.

Banathy, B. H. (1986). A systems view of institutionalizing change in education. dans S. Majumdar (dir.), *1985–86 Yearbook of the National Association of Academies of Science*. Columbus: Ohio Academy of Science.

Banathy, B. H. (1987). Instructional systems design. dans R.M. Gagné (dir.), *Instructional technology: Foundations* (pp. 85–112). Hillsdale: Erlbaum.

Banathy, B. H. (1988). Systems inquiry in education. http://link.springer.com/article/10.1007/BF01059858#page-1. Consulté le 11 novembre 2013.

Banathy, B. H. (1992). *A systems view of education*. Englewood Cliffs: Educational Technology.

Banathy, B. H. (1996). *Designing social systems in a changing world*. New York: Plenum.

Banathy, B. H. (1999). Systems thinking in higher education: Learning comes to focus. *Systems Research and Behavioral Science, 16*(2), 133–145.

Banathy, B. H. (2000). *Guided evolution of society: A systems view*. New York: Kluwer Academic/ Plenum.

Banathy, B. H. (2001). The evolution of systems inquiry, part 1 & part 2, a Special Integration Group (SIG) of the International Society for the Systems Sciences (ISSS) originally SGSR, Society for General Systems Research. http://www.isss.org/primer/evolvel.htm et http://www. isss.org/primer/004evsys.htm. Consulté le 30 novembre 2013.

Banathy, B. H. (2008). A taste of systemics: Why a systems view? A Special Integration Group (SIG) of the International Society for the Systems Sciences (ISSS), originally SGSR, Society for General Systems Research. http://www.isss.org/taste.html. Consulté le 11 novembre 2013.

Banathy, B. H., & Checkland, P. (1996). *Designing social systems in a changing world, Contemporary systems thinking; language of science*. New York: Springer.

Banathy, B. H., & Jenks, C. L. (1991). *The transformation of education by design*. San Francisco: Far West Laboratory.

Banathy, B. H., & Jenlink, P. M. (2003). Systems inquiry and its application in education. http:// learngen.org/~aust/EdTecheBooks/AECT%20HANDBOOK%202ND/02.pdf. Consulté le 11 novembre 2013.

Banathy, B. H., & Jenlink, P. M. (2004). Systems inquiry and its application in education. dans D. H. Jonassen (dir.), *Handbook of research for educational communications and technology* (2nd éd., pp. 37–57). New York: Macmillan Library.

Banathy, B. H., & Jenlink, P. M. (2005). *Dialogue as a means of collective communication*. New York: Plenum.

Barab, S. A., & Squire, K. (2004). Design-based research: Putting a stake in the ground, *The Journal of the Learning Sciences, 13*(1), 1–14.

Barab, S. A., Kling, R., & Gray, J. H. (2004). *Designing for virtual communities in the service of learning*. Cambridge (R.-U.): Cambridge University Press.

Barker, R. G. (1968). *Ecological psychology*. Redwood City: Stanford University Press.

Barnes, M. (2004). *Value chain guidebook: A process for value chain development*. Nisku: Agriculture and Food Council of Alberta—Value Chain Initiative.

Bartolomei, J. E. (2007). *Qualitative knowledge construction for engineering systems: Extending the design structure matrix methodology in scope and procedure*. Boston: Massachusetts Institute of Technology, Engineering Systems Division.

Bartolomei, J. E., Hastings, D. E., De Neufville, R., & Rhodes, D. H. (2012). Engineering systems multiple-domain matrix: An organizing framework for modeling large-scale complex systems. *Systems Engineering, 15*(1), 41–61.

Basden, A. (2000). On the multi-aspectual nature of information systems. dans J. M. Heimonen & M. Ruohonen (dir.), *Pertti Jarvinen—60 years work for science* (pp. 49–60). Tampere: University of Tampere, Department of Computer and Information Sciences.

Basden, A. (2002). The critical theory of Herman Dooyeweerd? *Journal of Information Technology, 17*(4), 257–269.

Basden, A. (2006). Aspects of knowledge representation. dans S. Strijbos & A. Basden (dir.), *Search of an integrative vision of technology: Interdisciplinary studies in information systems* (pp. 19–38). New York: Springer.

Basden, A. (2008). *Philosophical frameworks for understanding information systems*. Hershey: IGI Global.

Basden, A. (2010a). Towards lifeworld-oriented information systems development. dans H. Isomaki & S. Pekkola (dir.), *Reframing humans in information systems development*. New York: Springer.

Basden, A. (2010b). On using spheres of meaning to define and dignify the IS discipline. *International Journal of Information Management, 30*(1), 13–20.

Basden, A. (2011). A presentation of Herman Dooyeweerd's aspects of temporal reality. *International Journal of Multi-aspectual Practice, 1*(1), 1–28. Available at IJMAP.

Bateson, G. (1972). *Steps to an ecology of mind.* New York: Random House.

Bausch, K. C. (2000). The practice and ethics of design. *Systems Research and Behavioral Science, 17*(1), 23–51.

Bausch, K. C. (2001). *The emerging consensus in social system theory.* New York: Kluwer Academic/Plenum.

Bausch, K. C., & Flanagan, T. R. (2012). *Body wisdom in dialogue: Rediscovering the voice of the goddess.* Riverdale: Ongoing Emergence Press.

Bausch, K. C., & Flanagan, T. R. (2013). A confluence of third-phase science and dialogic design science. *Systems Research and Behavioral Science.* Wiley Online Library. doi:https://doi.org/10.1002/sres.2166.

Becattini, G. (1992). Le district industriel: milieu créatif. Restructurations économiques et territoires. *espaces et sociétés,* 1992/*1*(66), 147–164. doi: 10.3917/esp.1992.66.0147. https://www.cairn.info/revue-espaces-et-societes-1992-1-page-147.htm

Becattini, N., Cascini, G., & Rotini, R. (2011). Correlations between the evolution of contradictions and the law of identity increase, *Procedia Engineering, 9,* 236-250.

Beck, U. (2009). World risk society. dans J. K. Berg Olsen, S. A. Pedersen & V. R. Hendricks (dir.), *A companion to the philosophy of technology* (pp. 495–499). Hoboken: Wiley.

Beer, S. (1985). *Diagnosing the system for organizations.* Chichester: Wiley.

Benking, H. (1993). *Visual access strategies for multi-dimensional objects and issues: A new world view, based on the hyperlink ECO-CUBE for better understanding and communication about multi-disciplines like ecology.* FAW Technical Report - 93019, WFSF - World Futures Studies Federation, Turku.

Benkler, Y. (2006). *The wealth of networks: How social production transforms markets and freedom.* New Haven: Yale University Press.

Benneth, W., & Segerberg, A. (2013). *The cogic of connective action: Digital media and the personnalization of contentious politics.* Cambridge (R.-U.): Cambridge University Press.

Bennett, W., & Segerberg, A. (2013). *The logic of connective action: Digital media and the personalization of contentious politics.* Cambridge (R.-U.): Cambridge University Press.

Bieber, M., Mcfall, B., Rice, R. E., & Gurstein, M. (2007). Towards systems design for supporting enabling communities. *The Journal of Community Informatics, 3*(1). http://ci-journal.net/index.php/ciej/article/view/281/313. Consulté le 11 Novembre 2013.

Bijker, W. E., & Pinch, T. (1987). *The social constructions of technology systems: New directions in the sociology and history of technology.* Boston: Massachusetts's Institute of Technology.

Bishop, S., Helbing, D., Lukowicz, P., & Conte, R. (2011). The European future technologies conference and exhibition 2011 FuturICT: FET flagship pilot projectFuturICT: FET flagship pilot project. *Procedia Computer Science, 7,* 34–38. Elsevier. doi:10.1016/j.pocs.2011.12.014. Available online at www.sciencedirect.com.

Bloor, M., Frankland, J., Thomas, M., & Stewart, S. (2001). *Focus groups in social research.* Londres: Sage.

Bohm, D. (1965). *A special theory of relativity.* New York: W.A. Benjamin.

Bohm, D. (1996). *On dialogue.* Londres: Routledge.

Bohm, D. (1998). *On creativity.* Londres: Routledge.

Bonk, C. J., & Cunningham, D. J. (1998). Searching for learner-centered, constructivist, and sociocultural components of collaborative educational learning tools. dans C. J. Bonk & K. S. King (dir.), *Electronic collaborators: Learner-centered technologies for literacy, apprenticeship, and discourse* (pp. 25–50). New York: Erlbaum.

Bonneau, C. (2012). *La co-configuration intra-organisationnelle d'une technologie à code source ouvert en tant que lien entre son développement et ses usages [ressource électronique]: le cas de Moodle dans une université québécoise, thèse de doctorat en communication.* Montréal: Université du Québec à Montréal.

Boronowsky, M., Herzog, O., Knackfub, B., & Lawo, M. (2006). Wearable computing: an approach for living labs. http://www.wearitat work.com. Consulté le 10 septembre 2008.

Botero, A., & Saad-Sulonen, J. (2008). Co-designing for new city-citizen interaction possibilities: Weaving prototypes and interventions in the design and development of urban mediator. In *Proceedings of the tenth anniversary conference on participatory design* (pp. 266–269). Indianapolis: Indiana University.

Botero, A., Kommonen, K. -H., & Marttila, S. (2010). *Expanding design space: Design-in-use activities and strategies*. Proceedings of the DRS conference on design and complexity, Montréal, Design Research Society. http://www.designresearchsociety.org/docs-procs/DRS2010/PDF/018.pdf. Consulté le 12 décembre 2013.

Boulding, K. E. (1956). General systems theory: The skeleton of science. *Management Science, 2*(3). http://emergentpublications.com/eco/ECO_other/Issue_6_1-2_18_CP.pdf?AspxAutoDetectCookieSupport=1. Consulté le 11 novembre 2013.

Bourgeois, D. T., & Horam, T. A. (2007). A design theory approach to community informatics: community-centered development and action research testing of online social networking prototype. *Journal of Community Informatics, 3*(1). http://ci-journal.net/index.php/ciej/article/view/308/333. Consulté le 11 novembre 2013.

Brandtzaeg, P. B. (2010). Towards a unified media-user typology (MUT): A meta-analysis and review of the research literature on media-user typologies. *Computers in Human Behavior, 26*(5), 940–956.

Brier, S. (2000). Trans-scientific frameworks of knowing: complementarity views of the different types of human knowledge. *Systems Research and Behavioral Science, 17*(5), 433–458.

Brier, S. (2008). *Cybersemiotics: Why information is not enough!* Toronto: University of Toronto Press.

Brier, S. (2013). Cybersemiotics: A new foundation for a trans-disciplinary theory of consciousness, cognition, meaning and communication. In *Origins of mind* (pp. 97–126). Berlin: Springer.

Brier, S., Donacheva, A., Fuchs, C., Hofkirchner, W., & Stockinger, G. (2004). Fuschl conversations: foundations of information science towards a new foundation of information-, cognitive- and communication-science. http://fuchs.uti.at/wp-content/uploads/infoso/Fuschl_FIS.pdf. Consulté le 11 novembre 2013.

Brill, H. J. (1999). Systems engineering—a retrospective view. *Systems Engineering, 1*(4), 258–266.

Brown, J. S. (1992). The role of habitat selection in landscape ecology. *Evolutionary Ecology, 6*, 357–359. http://download.springer.com/static/pdf/355/art%253A10.1007%252FBF02270697.pdf?auth66=1387048563_6ccd303bd15a6fedbfc663575b71543b&ext=.pdf. Consulté le 12 décembre 2013.

Brown, J. S., & Duguid, P. (1996). Organizational learning and communities of practice: Toward a unified view of working, learning, and innovation. dans M. D. Collen & L. S. Sproull (dir.), *Organizational learning* (pp. 58–82). Thousand Oaks: Sage.

Brown, J. S., & Duguid, P. (2000). *The social life of information*. Boston: Harvard Business School Press.

Brown, J. S., & Duguid, P. (2001). Knowledge and organization: A social-practice perspective. *Organization Science, 12*(2), 198–213.

Brown, J., & Isaacs, D. (2005). *The world café: Shaping our futures through conversations that matter*. San Francisco: Berrett-Koehler.

Bruner, J. (1996). *The culture of education*. Cambridge, MA: Harvard University Press.

Budweg, M., Bock, G., & Weber, M. (2006). The Eifel plume-imaged with converted seismic waves. *Geophysical Journal International, 166*(2), 579–589. doi:https://doi.org/10.1111/j.1365-246X2005.02778

Bunge, M. (1983). *Treatise on basic philosophy: Epistemology and methodology I*. Dordrecht: D. Reidel.

Bunge, M. (1997). Mechanism and explanation. *Philosophy of the Social Sciences, 27*, 410–465. https://doi.org/10.1177/00483931 9702700402.

Bunge, M. (1998). *Philosophy of science: From problem to theory*. New Brunswick: Transaction Publishers.

Bunge, M. (1999). *The sociology-philosophy connection.* New Brunswick: Transaction Publishers.

Bunge, M. (2000). *Social science under debate: A philosophical perspective.* Toronto: University of Toronto Press.

Bunge, M. (2003). Philosophy of science and technology: A personal report. dans G. Floistad (dir.), *Philosophy of Latin America* (pp. 245–272). Dordrecht: Kluwer Academic.

Bunge, M. (2004a). How does it work? The search for explanatory mechanisms. *Philosophy of the Social Sciences, 34*(2), 182–210.

Bunge, M. (2004b). Clarifying some misunderstandings about social systems and their mechanisms. *Philosophy of the Social Sciences, 34*(3), 371–381.

Burnette, C. (2009). A theory of design thinking. http://www.independent.academia.edu/charles-burnette. Consulté le 11 novembre 2013.

Camarinha-Matos, L. M., & Abreu, A. (2005). Performance indicators based-on collaboration benefits. In *Collaborative networks and their breeding environments, IFIP* (pp. 273–282). New York: Springer.

Camarinha-Matos, L. M, & Afsarmanesh, H. (2004). In: L.M. Camarinha-Matos, H. Afsarmanesh (Eds.) *Collaborative networked organizations -A research agenda for emerging business models.* 1st time published by Kluwer Academic Publishers in March 2004, and 2nd time published by the Springer in December 2004. ISBN 1-4020-7823-4.

Camarinha-Matos, L. M., & Afsarmanesh, H. (2005). Collaborative networks: A new scientific discipline. *Journal of Intelligent Manufacturing. 16*(4–5), 439–452.

Camarinha-Matos, L. M., & Afsarmanesh, H. (2006a). Collaborative networks: Value creation in a knowledge society. dans *Knowledge enterprise* (Vol. 207, pp. 26–40).

Camarinha-Matos, L. M., & Afsarmanesh, H. (2006b). Results assessment and impact creation in collaborative research - An example from the ECOLEAD project. *International Journal of Technology Innovation.* Entrepreneurship and Technology Management - TECHNOVATION, Elsevier, Electronic version of the Journal.

Camarinha-Matos, L. M., & Afsarmanesh, H. (2007a). *Virtual organizations breeding environment: Key results from ECOLEAD, IFAC-CEA, 07.* Monterrey: Mexique.

Camarinha-Matos, L. M., & Afsarmanesh, H. (2007b). A framework for virtual organization creation in a breeding environment. *International Journal Annual Reviews in Control, Elsevier publisher, 31*(1), 119–135.

Camarinha-Matos, L. M., & Afsarmanesh, H. (2008). *Collaborative networks: Reference modelling.* New York: Springer.

Camarinha-Matos, L. M., Silveri, I., Afsarmanesh, H., & Oliveira, A. I. (2005a). Towards a framework for creation of dynamic virtual organizations. dans L. M. Camarinha-Matos, H. Afsarmanesh & A. Ortiz (dir.), *Collaborative networks and their breeding environments* (pp. 69–80). Boston: Springer.

Camarinha-Matos, L. M., Afsarmanesh, H., & Ollus, M. (2005b). *Virtual organizations: Systems and practices.* Boston: Springer.

Camarinha-Matos, L. M., Afsarmanesh, H., & Ollus, M. (2005c). Ecolead: A holistic approach to creation and management of dynamic virtual organizations. dans L. M. Camarinha-Matos, H. Afsarmanesh & A. Ortiz (dir.), *Collaborative networks and their breeding environments* (pp. 3–16). Boston: Springer.

Campbell, D. T. (1952). The Bogardus social distance scale. *Sociology and Social Research, 36*(5), 322–326.

Capra, F. (1997). *The web of life: A new scientific understanding of living systems.* New York: Random House.

Capra, F. (2004). *The hidden connections: A science for sustainable living.* New York: Random House.

Capra, F. (2008). *The science of Leonardo: Inside the mind of the great genius of the renaissance.* New York: Random House.

Carayannis, E. G. (2013). Campbell DFJ: Mode 3 knowledge production in quadruple helix innovation systems: Quintuple Helix and social ecology. In E. G. Carayannis, I. N. Dubina, N. Seel, C. DFJ, & D. Uzunidis (Eds.), *Encyclopedia of creativity, invention, innovation and entre-*

preneurship (pp. 1293–1300). New York, NY: Springer. [http://link.springer.com/reference-workentry/10.1007/978-1-4614-3858-8_310] [http://www.springerreference.com/docs/html/chapterdbid/378732.html].

Carayannis, E. G., & Campbell, D. F. (2009). "Mode 3" and "quadruple helix": Toward a 21st century fractal innovation ecosystem. *International Journal of Technology Management, 46*(3), 201–234.

Carayannis, E. G., & Campbell, D. F. (2011). Open innovation diplomacy and a 21st century fractal research, education and innovation (FREIE) ecosystem: Building on the quadruple and quintuple helix innovation concepts and the "Mode 3" knowledge production system. *Journal of the Knowledge Economy, 2*(3), 327–372.

Carayannis, E. G., & Campbell, D. F. J. (2012). *Mode 3 knowledge production in Quadruple Helix innovation systems: Twenty-first democracy, innovation, and entrepreneurship for development, Springerbriefs in business*. New York: Springer.

Carr-Chellman, A., & Savoy, M. (2004). Follow the yellow brick path: Finding our way home via Banathy's user-design. *Systemic Practice and Action Research, 17*(4), 373–382.

Cartier, M. (2002). *Les groupes d'intérêts et les collectivités locales: une interface entre le citoyen et l'État*. Québec/Paris: Presses de l'Université Laval/L'Harmattan.

Cartier, M. (2011). Éducation, quand tu nous tiens. dans *Éducation comparée verticale: images d'enseignement* (pp. 51–64). Paris: U Harmattan.

Castells, M. (2011). *The rise of the network society: The information age—economy, society and culture* (Vol. 1). Oxford: Blackwell.

CEFRIO. (2011). L'engouement pour les médias sociaux au Québec. *L'Enquête NETendances 2011*. http://www.cefrio.qc.ca/media/uploader/2_medias_sociaux.pdf. Consulté le 7 septembre 2012.

Chalmers, A. F. (1999). *What is this thing called science?* Brisbane: University of Queensland Press.

Checkland, P. (1976). Science and the systems paradigm. *International Journal of General Systems, 3*(2), 127–134.

Checkland, P. (1981). *Systems thinking; systems practice*. New York: Wiley.

Checkland, P. (1988). Information systems and systems thinking: time to unite? *International Journal of Information Management, 8*, 239–248.

Checkland, P. (2000). Soft systems methodology: A thirty year retrospective. *Systems Research and Behavioral Science Syst. Res, 17*, S11–S58.

Checkland, P., & Banathy, B. H. (2000). *Guided evolution of society: A systems view*. New York: Springer.

Checkland, P., & Banathy, B. H. (2005). *Dialog as a collective means of design conversation* (pp. 187–203). New York: Springer.

Checkland, P., & Holwell, S. (1998). *Information, systems and information systems*. Chichester: Wiley.

Checkland, P., & Scholes, J. (1990). *Soft systems methodology in action*. New York: Wiley.

Chesbrough, H. W. (2003). *Open innovation: The new imperative for creating and profiting from technology*. Boston: Harvard Business Press.

Chesbrough, H., Vanhaverbeke, W., & West, J. (dir.) (2008). *Open innovation: Researching a new paradigm*. Oxford: Oxford University Press.

Chomsky, N. (1986). *Knowledge of language: Its nature, origin, and use*. New York: Praeger.

Christakis, A. N. (1973). A new policy science paradigm. *Futures, 5*(6), 543–558.

Christakis, A. N. (1987). High technology participative design: The space-based laser. dans J. A. Dillon Jr. (dir.), *General systems* (Vol. 30, pp. 69–75). New York: International Society for the Systems Sciences.

Christakis, A. N. (1988). The Club of Rome revisited. dans W. J. Reckmeyer (dir.), *General systems* (Vol. 31, pp. 35–38). New York: International Society for the Systems Sciences.

Christakis, A. N. (1993). The inevitability of demosophia. dans I. Tsivacou (dir.), *A challenge for systems thinking: The Aegean seminar* (pp. 187–197). Athènes: University of the Aegean Press.

Christakis, A. N. (1996). A people science: The CogniScope system approach. *Systems: Journal of Transdisciplinary Systems Sciences, 1*(1), 16–19.

Christakis, A. N. (2004). Wisdom of the people. *Systems Research and Behavioral Science, 21*, 317–330.

Christakis, A. N. (2005). *Dialogue for the information age.* Greenwich: Information Age.

Christakis, A. N. (2007). The spread of obesity in a large social network over 30 year. *New England Journal of Medicine, 357*, 370–379.

Christakis, A. N. (2010). The anthroposphere. dans J. Brockman (dir.), *This will change everything* (pp. 225–228). New York: Harper.

Christakis, A. N., & Bausch, K. C. (2006). *How people harness their collective wisdom and power to construct the future in co-laboratories of democracy.* New York: Information Age.

Christakis, A. N., & Brahms, S. (2003). Boundary-spanning dialogue for 21st-century agoras, *Systems Research and Behavioral Science, 20,* 371–382

Christakis, A. N., & Dye, K. M. (1999). Collaboration through communicative action: Resolving the systems dilemma through the CogniScope. *Systems: Journal of Transdisciplinary Systems Sciences, 4*(1-2), 9–32.

Christakis, A. N., & Flanagan, T. R. (2010). *The talking point: Creating an environment for exploring complex meaning.* Charlotte: Information Age Publishing, Inc.

Christakis, A. N., & Harris, L. (2004). Designing a transnational indigenous leaders interaction in the context of globalization: A wisdom of the people forum. *Systems Research and Behavioral Sciences, 21,* 251–261.

Christakis, A. N., Warfield, J. N., & Keever, D. (1988). Systems design: Generic design theory and methodology. dans M. Decleris (dir.), *Systems governance* (pp. 143–210). Athènes-Komotini: Publisher Ant. N. Sakkoylas.

Churchman, C. W. (1968). *The system approach.* New York: Dell.

Churchman, C. W. (1971). *The design of inquiring systems: Basic concepts of systems and organizations.* New York: Basic Books.

Churchman, C. W. (1974). *Qu'est-ce que l'analyse par les systèmes?* Paris: Dunod.

Churchman, C. W. (1979). *The systems approach and its enemies.* New York: Basic Books.

Clegg, C. W. (2000). Sociotechnical principles for system design. *Applied Ergonomics, 31*(5), 463–477, https://doi.org/10.1016/S0003-6870(00)00009-0, consulté le 12 novembre 2013.

Clement, A., Gurstein, M., Longford, G., Moll, M., & Shade, L. R. (2012). *Connecting Canadians: Investigations in community informatics.* Edmonton: Athabasca University Press.

Cloutier, J. (2001). *Petit traité de communication: EMEREC à l'heure des technologies numériques.* Gap: Atelier Perrousseaux.

Cobb, R., Stephan, M., Mcclain, K., & Gravemeijer, K. (2001). Participating in classroom mathematical practices. *The Journal of the Learning Sciences, 10*(1-2), 113–163.

Cobb, P., Disessa, A., Lehrer, R., & Schauble, L. (2003). Design experiments in educational research. *Educational Researcher, 32*(1), 9–13.

Collins, A. (1992). Toward a design science of éducation. dans E. Scanlon & T. O'Shea (dir.), *New directions in educational technology* (pp. 15–22). New York: Springer.

Collins, A. (1999). The changing infrastructure of education research. dans E. C. Lagemann & L. S. Shulman (dir.), *Issues in education research: Problems and possibilities* (pp. 289–298). San Francisco: Jossey-Bass.

CONSEIL DES SCIENCES, DE LA TECHNOLOGIE et DE L'INNOVATION. (2011). De l'imagination à l'innovation: le parcours du Canada vers la prospérité. L'état des lieux en 2010: le système des sciences, de la technologie et de l'innovation au Canada, http://publications. gc.ca/pub?id=450668&sl=0/, consulté le 9 février 2014.

Coppola, C., & Neelley, E. (2004). Open source - opens learning: Why open source makes sense for education, http://www.fkm.utm.my/~kasim/cad/OpenSourceOpensLearningJuly2004.pdf, consulté le 12 novembre 2013.

CORELABS. (2007). Building sustainable competitiveness: Living labs roadmap 2007-2010. Recommendations on networked systems for open user-driven research, development and innovation, http://www.ami-communities.eu/pub/bscw.cgi/d421846/CoreLabs_D2.3_RoadMap. pdf, consulté le 12 novembre 2013.

COSPACES. (2007), http://www.cospaces.org/downloads/cospaces_brochure.pdf, consulté le 12 novembre 2013.

Courbon, J. C., & Tajan, S. (1997). *Groupware et Intranet: application avec Notes et Domino*, Paris: Masson.

Craig, R. T. (1999). Communication theory as a field. *Communication Theory, 9*(2), 119–161.

Craig, R. T. (2006). A practice. dans G. J. Shepherd, J. St. John & T. Striphas (dir.), *Communication as... perspectives on theory* (pp. 38–47), Thousand Oaks: Sage.

Creswell, J. W. (2008). *Research design: Qualitative, quantitative, and mixed methods approaches*. Thousand Oaks: Sage.

Crilly, N., Good, D., Matravers, D., & Clarkson, P. J. (2008). Design as communication: Exploring the validity and utility of relating intention to interpretation. Design Studies. *29*(5), 425–457.

Cross, N. (1974). *Redesiginng the future*. New York: Wiley.

Cross, N. (1984). *Developments in design methodology*. New York: Wiley.

Cross, N. (1994). *Engineering design methods: Strategies for product design* (2e éd.). Chichester: Wiley.

Cross, N. (2001). Designerly ways of knowing: Design discipline versus design science. *Design Issues, 17*(3), 49–55.

Cross, N., Christiaans H., & Dorst, C. (1996). *Analysing desigti activity*. Chichester: Wiley.

Danilda I., Lindberg M., & Torstensson B-M. (2009). Women resource centres. A Quattro Helix innovation system on the European Agenda. Accessed 31 March 2012 http://www.hss09.se/own_documents/Papers/3-11%20-%20Danilda%20Lindberg%20&%20Torstensson%20-%20paper.pdf Paper.

Darzentas, J. (2007). Exploring creativity in the design process: A systems-semiotic perspective. *Cybernetics and Human Knowing, 14*(1), 37–64.

Darzentas, J., & Miesenberger, K. (2005). Design for all in information technology: A universal concern. In *Database and expert systems applications* (pp. 406–420). Berlin: Springer.

Darzentas, J., & Spyrou, T. (1995). Designing a designers' decision aiding system (DDAS). *Journal of Decision Systems, 4*(1), 9–22.

Daudelin, M. W. (1996). Learning from experience through reflection. *Organizational Dynamics, 24*(3), 36–48.

De Moor, A. (2005). *Towards a design theory for community information system*. présenté à la 11th International Conference on Human Computer Interaction, Las Vegas.

De Moor, A., & De Cindio, F. (2007)* Beyond users to communities: Designing systems as though communities matter. *The Journal of Community Informatics, 3*(1), http://ci-joumal.net/index.php/ciej/article/view/434/312, consulté le 12 novembre 2013.

De Raadt, J. D. R. (2000). *Redesign and management of communities in crisis*. s.L: Universal Publishers.

De Raadt, J. D. R. (2001). *A method and software for designing viable social systems*. s.L: Universal Publishers.

De Rosnay, J. (1975). *Le macroscope: vers une vision globale*. Paris: Seuil.

De Zeeuw, G. (1996). *Second order organizational research*. Working Papers in Systems and Information Sciences. Hull (R.-U.): University of Humberside.

De Zeeuw, G. (1997). Three phases of science: A methodological exploration, http://www.academia.edu/618520/THREE_PHASES_OF_SCIENCE_A_METHODOLOGICAL_EXPLORATIONl, consulté le 12 novembre 2013.

Demailly, A. (2004). *Herbert Simon et les sciences de conception*. Paris: L'Harmattan.

Dewey, J. (1938). *Logic, the theory of inquiry*. New York: Holt.

Dillenbourg, P., Poirier, C., & Carles, L. (2003). Communautés virtuelles d'apprentissage: e-jargon ou nouveau paradigme?. dans A. Taurisson & A. Sentini (dir.), *Pédagogies.Net* (pp. 11–48). Québec: Presses de l'Université du Québec.

Dong, A. (2004). *Design as a socio-cultural cognitive system*, présenté à la 8th International Design Conference, Dubrovnik, 18-21 mai.

Dooyeweerd, H. (1979[1963]). *Roots of western culture: Pagan secular, and christian options [trad. J. Krayy]*. Toronto: Wedge.

Dooyeweerd, H. (1984[1953-1958]). *A new critique of theoretical thought* (vol. 1–4). Jordan Station: Paideia.

Dougiamas, M. (1998). A journey into Constructivism, http://go.web assistant.com/wa/upload/users/ul000057/webpage_20553.html, consulté le 12 novembre 2013.

Dougiamas, M. (1999). Moodle-A web application for building quality online courses, http://scholar. google.com/citations7view_op=view_citation&hl=fr&user=AIS_XfgAAAAJ&citation_for_view =AIS_XfgAAAAJ:Y0pCki6q_DkC, consulté le 12 décembre 2013.

Dougiamas, M. (2006). Moodle: A case study in sustainability. Retrieved from the Open Source Software, dans Advisory Service (JSC OSS WATCH), http://oss-watch.ac.uk/resources/cs-moodle, consulté le 12 décembre 2013.

Doxiadis, C. A. (1968). *Ekistics: An introduction to the science of human settlements*. Londres: Oxford University Press.

Dron, J. (2007). Designing the undesignable: Social software and control. *Educational Technology & Society, 10*(3), 60–71.

Ducrocq, S. (2011). Les Tribus ludiques du "Lan Party": Perspectives d'apprentissage et de socialisation en contexte de compétition de jeux vidéo en réseau local, thèse de doctorat publiée en ligne, Montréal, Université du Québec à Montréal, http://www.archipel.uqam.ca/3826/, consulté le 17 novembre 2012.

Dye, K. M. (1997). Collaborative design process science, Boston, Working Papers at MIT.

Einstein, A. (1989). Comment je vois le monde. Flammarion

Emery, F. E., & Trist, E. L. (1975). *Towards a social ecology: Contextual appreciations*. Londres: Plenum.

Engestrom, Y. (1987). *Learning by expanding: An activity-theoretical approach to developmental research*. Helsinki: Orienta-Konsultit.

Engestrom, Y. (1994). Learning by expanding: The years after, http://lchc.ucsd.edu/mca/Paper/Engestrom/expanding/intro.htm, consulté le 12 novembre 2013.

Engestrom, Y. (1999). Activity theory and individual and social transformation. dans Y. Engestrôm, R. Miettinen & R. L. Punamaki (dir.), *Perspectives on activity theory* (pp. 19–38). Cambridge (R.-U.): Cambridge University Press.

Engestrom, Y., Sannino, A., Fischer, G., Morch, A., & Bertelsen, O. (2010). Grand challenges for future HCI research: Cultures of participation, interfaces supporting learning, and expansive learning, Proceedings of NordiCHI'2010, Reykjavik, octobre, pp. 863–866, http://l3d. cs.colorado.edu/~gerhard/papers/2010/nordichi-panel.pdf, consulté le 12 novembre 2013.

Enh, P. (2008). *Participation in design things*. Malmô: School of Arts and Communication, Malmô University.

Espejo, R., & Harnden, R. (1989). *The viable systems model-interpretationsand applications of Stafford Beer's VSM*. Chichester: Wiley.

Etzioni, A. (1998). *The essential communitarian reader*. Washington, DC: Rowman and Littlefield.

Etzioni, A. (2009). *New common ground: A new America, a new world*. Washington, DC: Potomac Books.

Etzkowitz, H., & Leydesdorff, L. (2000). The dynamics of innovation: From National Systems and "Mode 2"to a Triple Helix of university-industry-government relations. *Research Policy, 29*(2), 109–123.

Fallman, D. (2003). *Design-oriented human-computer interaction*, Proceedings of conference on human factors in computing systems, CHI Letters, (Vol. 5(1)), Fort Lauderdale, avril, http://cowbell-4.cc.gatech.edu/hci-seminar/uploads/1/Design-Oriented%20Human-Computer%20Interaction.pdf, consulté le 12 novembre 2013.

Feenberg, A. (1999). *Questioning technology*. Londres: Routledge.

Fibonacci, L. (2002 [1202]). Fibonacci's Liber Abaci: A translation into modem english of Leonardo Pisano's Book of Calculation [trad. L.E. Sigler], New York, Springer.

Fischer, G. (2006). Learning in communities: A distributed intelligence perspective. *The Journal of Community Informatics, 2*(2).

431

Fischer, G. (2007). *Designing socio-technical environments in support of meta-design and social creativity*, Proceedings of the conference on computer supported collaborative learning (CSCL 2007) (pp. 1–10), New Brunswick (N.J.), Rutgers University, juillet.

Fischer, G. (2009a). *Cultures of participation and social computing: Rethinking and reinventing learning and education*, Proceedings of the International conference on advanced learningtechnologies (ICALT) (pp. 1–5), IEEE Press, Riga. http://l3d.cs.colorado.edu/~gerhard/papers/2009-ICALT-paper.pdf, consulté le 30 mars 2011.

Fischer, G. (2009b). *Democratizing design: New challenges and opportunities for computer-supported collaborative learning*, Proceedings of CSCL 2009: 8th international conference on computer supported collaborative learning (pp. 282–286), Rhodes, University of the Aegean. http://l3d.cs.colorado.edu/~gerhard/papers/2009-CSCL-paper.pdf, consulté le 12 novembre 2013.

Fischer, G. (2010). End-user development and meta-design: Foundations for cultures of participation. *Journal of Organizational and End User Computing, 22*(1), 52–82. http://l3d.cs.colorado.edu/~gerhard/papers/2010-JOEUC.pdf, consulté le 12 novembre 2013.

Fischer, G. (2011). *Social creativity: Exploiting the power of cultures of participation*, Proceedings of SKG 2011: 7th International conference on semantics, knowledge and grids (pp. 1–8), Beijing, octobre. http://l3d.cs.colorado.edu/~gerhard/papers/2011/SKG-China.pdf, consulté le 12 novembre 2013.

Fischer, G. (2012). Context-aware systems: The "right" information, at the "right" time, in the "right" place, in the "right" way, to the "right" person". dans G. Tortora, S. Levialdi & M. Tucci (dir.), *Proceedings of the conference on advanced visual interfaces (AVI 2012), ACM* (pp. 287–294). Capri: mai. http://l3d.cs.colorado.edu/~gerhard/papers/2012/paper-AVI-context-aware.pdf, consulté le 12 novembre 2013.

Fischer, G. (2013a). A conceptual framework for computer-supported collaborative learning at work. dans S. Goggins, I. Jahnke & V. Wulf (dir.), *Computer-supported collaborative learning at the workplace* (pp. 23–42). Heidelberg: Springer. http://l3d.cs.colorado.edu/~gerhard/papers/2011/book-cscl-work.pdf, consulté le 12 novembre 2013.

Fischer, G. (2013b). *From Renaissance scholars to Renaissance communities: Learning and education in the 21st century*, International conference on collaboration technologies and systems (pp. 13–21), San Diego, IEEE, mai, http://l3d.cs.colorado.edu/~gerhard/papers/2013/CTS.pdf, consulté le 12 novembre 2013.

Fischer, G., & Giaccardi, E. (2006). Meta-design: A framework for the future of end user development. dans H. Lieberman, F. Paternô & V. Wulf (dir.), *End-user development* (pp. 427–457). Dordrecht: Springer

Fischer, G., & Herrmann, T. (2010). Socio-technical systems: A meta-design perspective. *International Journal of Sociotechnology and Knowledge Development, 3*(1), 1–33, http://l3d.cs.colorado.edu/~gerhard/papers/2010/journal-socio-ts.pdf, consulté le 12 novembre 2013.

Fischer, G., & Konomi, S. (2007). Innovative media in support of distributed intelligence and lifelong learning. *Journal of Computer Assisted Learning, 23*(4), 338–350.

Fischer, G., & Shipman, F. (2011). Collaborative design rationale and social creativity in cultures of participation. *Human Technology: An Interdisciplinary Journal on Humans in ICT Environments (Special Issue on Creativity and Rationale in Software Design), 7*(2), 164–187. http://l3d.cs.colorado.edu/~gerhard/papers/2011/journal-dr-cop.pdf, consulté le 12 novembre 2013.

Fischer, G., Rohde, M., & Wulf, V. (2006). Spiders in the net: Universities as facilitators of community-based learning. *The Journal of Community Informatics, 2*(2). http://ci-journal.net/index.php/ciej/article/view/337, consulté le 13 mars 2014.

Fischer, G., Jennings, P., Maher, M. L., Resnick, M., & Shneiderman, B. (2009). Creativity challenges and opportunities in social computing, Proceedings of CHI 2009 (Boston) (pp. 3283–3286). ACM, New York. http://l3d.cs.colorado.edu/~gerhard/papers/2009-CHI-panel.pdf, consulté le 12 novembre 2013.

Flanagan, T. R., & Bausch, K. C. (2011). *A democratic approach to sustainable futures: A workbook for addressing the global Problématique*. Riverdale: Ongoing Emergence.

Flanagan, T. R., & Christakis, A. N. (2010). *The talking point: Creating an environment for exploring complex meaning*. Charlotte: Information Age.

Flanagan, T. R., & Christakis, A. N. (2011). Referential transparency for dialogic design science. *International Journal of Applied Systems Science*.

Flanagan, T. R., Mcintyre-Mills, J., Made, T., Mackenzie, K., Morse, C., Underwood, G., & Bausch, K. C. (2012). A systems approach for engaging groups in global complexity: Capacity building through an online course. *Systemic Practice and Action Research, 25*(2), 171–193.

Flood, R. L., & Jackson, M. C. (1991). *Creative problem solving: Total systems intervention*. Chichester: Wiley.

Flores, M., & Molina, A. (2000). Virtual industry clusters: Foundation to create virtual enterprises, in advanced in networked enterprises - Virtual organizations. dans L. Carmarinha-Matos, H. Afsarmanesh & Heinz-H. Erbe (dir.), *Balanced automation and systems integration* (pp. 11–120). Boston: Kluwer Academic Publishers.

Forrester, J. W. (1961). *Industrial dynamics*. Cambridge, MA: MIT Press.

Forrester, J. W. (1968). *Principles of systems*. New York: Wright-Allan.

Fourez, G. (1974). *La science partisane, Essai sur les siginfications des démarches scientifiques*. Paris: Duculot.

Fox, S. (2002). Studying networked learning: Some implications from socially situated learning theory and actor network theory. dans C. Steeples & C. Jones (dir.), *Networked learning: Perspectives and issues* (pp. 1–14). London: Springer.

Frielick, S. (2004). Beyond constructivism: An ecological approach to e-learning. dans R. Atkinson, C. McBeath, D. Jonas-Dwyer & R. Phillips (dir.), *Beyond the comfort zone: proceedings of the 21st ASCILITE conference* (pp. 328–332), Perth, 5-8 décembre, http://www.ascilite.org.au/conferences/perth04/procs/frielick.html, consulté le 12 novembre 2013.

Fuchs, C. (2003). Globalization and self-organization in the knowledge-based society. *Journal for a Global Sustainable Information Society, 1*(2), 105–169.

Fuchs, C. (2004). Knowledge management in self-organizing social systems. *Journal of Knowledge Management Practice, 5*, 351–356.

Fuchs, C. (2008). *Internet and society: Social theory in the information age*. New York: Routledge.

Fuchs, C. (2010). Social software and Web 2.0: Their sociological foundations and implications. dans S. Murugesan (dir.), *Hand- book of research on Web 2.0, 3.0; and X.0: Technologies, business, and social applications* (Vol. 2, pp. 764–789). Hershey: IGI Global. http://fuchs.uti.at/wp-content/uploads/2009/12/Web2.pdf, consulté le 12 novembre 2013.

Fuchs, C., & al. (2010). Theoretical foundations of the web: Cognition, communication, and co-operation. Towards an understanding of Web 1.0, 2.0, 3.0. *Future Internet, 2010*(2), 41–59. https://doi.org/10.3390/fi2010041.

Fuchs, C., & Hofkirchner, W. (2005). Self-organization, knowledge and responsibility. *Kybernetes: The International Journal of Systems & Cybernetics, 34*(1-2), 241–260(20). Publisher: Emerald Group Publishing Limited DOI: https://doi.org/10.1108/03684920510575825.

Fuchs, C., & Obrist, M. (2010). HCI and society: Towards a typology of universal design principles. *International Journal of Human Computer Interaction, 26*(6), 638–656. doi:https://doi.org/10.1080/10 447311003781334.

Fuchs, C., Hofkirchner, W., & Klauninger, B. (2002) The Dialectic of Bottom-up and Top-down Emergence in Social Systems (September 30, 2002). INTAS Project "Human Strategies in Complexity" Research Paper No. 8. Available at SSRN: https://ssrn.com/abstract=385300 or https://doi.org/10.2139/ssrn.385300.

Fuller, R. B. (1975). *Synergetics*. New York: Macmillan.

Fuller, R. B. (1982). *Critical path*. New York: St. Martin's Press.

Fusaro, M., et al. (2005). Rapport du Comité institutiomtel sur les plateformes d'apprentissage en ligne, travaux du Vice-rectorat aux services académiques et au développement technologique, Université du Québec à Montréal, 14 décembre.

Gallupe, B. (2001). Knowledge management systems: Surveying the landscape. *International Journal of Management Reviews, 3*(1), 61–77.

Garnham, N. (1990). *Capitalism and communication: Global culture and the economics of information.* Londres: Sage.

Garon, G. (2006). L'appropriation d'un système d'information communautique par les membres d'une communauté de pratique en santé mentale: le cas du Centre hospitalier Pierre-Le Gardeur, travaux du Laboratoire de communautique appliquée, Département de communication sociale et publique, Université du Québec à Montréal.

Garrety, K., Robertson, P. L., & Badham, R. (2004). Integrating communities of practice in technology development projects. *International Journal of Project Management, 22*(5), 351–358.

Gazendam, H. W. (2001). Semiotics, virtual organisations, and information systems. dans K. Liu, R. J. Clarke, P. Bogh Andersen & R. K. Stamper (dir.), *Information, organisation and technology* (pp. 1–48). New York: Springer.

Genoud, P., & Schweizer, A. (2009). Living Lab e-Inclusion: rapport de pré-étude, version 30.09.09, http://www.ict-21.ch/com-ict/spip.php?article87, consulté le 12 novembre 2013.

Germain, M., & Malaison, C. (2004). *L'intranet dans tous ses états: une approche interculturelle de ses multiples dimensions.* Québec: Isabelle Quentin.

Gharajedaghi, J. (1999). *Systems thinking: Managing chaos and complexity.* Boston: Butterworth-Heinemann.

Giaccardi, E. (2005). Metadesign as an emergent design culture. *Leonardo, 8*(4), 342–349.

Giaccardi, E., & Fischer, G. (2008). Creativity and evolution: A metadesign perspective. *Digital Creativity, 19*(1), 19–32, http://13d.cs.colorado.edu/~gerhard/papers/digital-creativity-2008. pdf, consulté le 12 novembre 2012.

Gibbons, M., et al. (1994). *The new production of knowledge: The dynamics of science and research in contemporary societies.* Stockholm: Sage Publications.

Giddens, A. (1984). *The constitution of society: Outline of the theory of structuration.* Berkeley: University of California Press.

Goldkuhl, G. (2004). Design theories in information systems: A need for multi-grounding. *Journal of Information Technology, Theory and Applications, 6*(2), 7.

Goldkuhl, G., & Lind, M. (2010). A multi-grounded design research process. In *Global perspectives on design science research* (pp. 45–60). Heidelberg: Springer.

Greenfield, A. (2007). *Everyjware: la révolution de l'ubimédia [trad. Cyril Fiévet de Everyware: The Dawning Age of Ubiquitous Computing].* Limoges: FYP.

Gregory, S. A. (1966). A design science. dans S. A. Gregory (dir.), *The design method* (pp. 323–330). Londres: Butter worth.

Gurstein, M. (2000). *Community informatics: Enabling communities with information and communications technologies.* Hershey: IGI Global.

Gurstein, M. (2003). Effective use: A community informatics strategy beyond the digital divide. *First Monday,* 8(12), http://firstmonday.org/ojs/index.php/fm/article/view/1107/1027, consulté le 12 novembre 2013.

Gurstein, M. (2006). Editorial: Sustainability of community ICTs and its future. *The Journal of Community Informatics. 1*(2), http://ci-journal.net/index.php/ciej/article/viewArticle/230/185, consulté le 10 décembre 2013.

Gurstein, M. (2007). *What is community informatics (And why does it matter)?* Milan: Polimetrica.

Gurstein, M. (2008). Community informatics: What's in a name. *The Journal of Community Informatics, 4*(3), http://www.ci-journal.net/index.php/ciej/article/viewArticle/521/433, consulté le 12 décembre 2013.

Habermas, J. (1973 [1971]). *Theory and Practice [trad. J. Viertel].* Boston: Beacon.

Habermas, J. (1984). *The theory of communicative Action [trad. T. McCarthy].* Boston: Beacon.

Hall, A. (1962). *A methodology of systems engineering.* Princeton: Van Nostrand.

Hall, E. T. (1969). *The hidden dimension.* New York: Anchor Books.

Hall, E. T., Mesrie, J., & Niceall, B. (1984). *Le langage silencieux.* Paris: Seuil.

Harris, L., & Wasilewski, J. (2004). Indigenous wisdom of the people forum: Strategies for expanding a Web of transnational indigenous interactions. *Systems Research and Behavioral Science, 21*(5), 505–514.

Harvey, P. -L. (1993). La parole communautique: interactionnisme méthodologique et écologie des besoins psychosociaux des usagers de médias interactifs, thèse de doctorat, Montréal, Département de sociologie, Université de Montréal.

Harvey, P. -L. (1995). *Cyberespace et communautique : appropriation, réseaux, groupes virtuels.* Québec: Presses de l'Université Laval/L'Harmattan.

Harvey, P. -L. (2003). Rapport Col-et-Gram. La communauté de pratique des chercheurs d'Hexagram (Institut de recherche et création en arts et technologies médiatiques), travaux du Laboratoire de communautique appliquée (LCA), Hexagram axe de recherche "Télévision interactive et communautés virtuelles", Montréal.

Harvey, P. -L. (2004a). *La démocratie occulte: rapport de force, gouvernance et commmunautique dans la société de l'information.* Québec: Presses de l'Université Laval, coll. "Laboratoire de communautique appliquée".

Harvey, P. -L. (2004b). De l'intranet à la communautique, ou valoriser l'entreprise interconnective pour le partage des savoirs. dans M. Germain & C. Malaison (dir.), *L'intranet dans tous ses états* (pp. 89–110), Montréal: Isabelle Quentin.

Harvey, P. L., & Bertrand, N. (2004a). Virtual Communities. In A. Distefano, K. L. Rudestam, & R. J. Silverman (Eds.), *The encyclopedia of distributed learning.* Santa Barbara: Fielding Graduate Institute. Sage Publications, Inc.

Harvey, P. -L. (2005). La communautique: un paradigme transdisciplinaire pour l'étude des arts, des sciences et des métiers de la communication médiatisée par ordinateur. dans J. Saint-Charles & P. Mongeau (dir.), *Communication: horizons de pratique et de recherche.* Québec: Presses de l'Université du Québec.

Harvey, P. -L. (2006a). Les îlots de vie communauticiels: topologie situationnelle des commu- nautés de pratique. dans S. Proulx, L. Poissant & M. Sénécal (dir.), *Communautés virtuelles: penser et agir en réseau.* Québec: Presses de l'Université Laval.

Harvey P. -L. (2006b). Design communautique et coopération organisationnelle : une théorie du design communautique pour les systèmes d'information collaboratifs qui supportent les pro- cessus émergents de la connaissance. dans J. -M. Penalva (dir.), *Intelligence collective: rencon- tres 2006* (pp. 81–108). Paris: Presses de l'École des mines.

Harvey, P.-L. (2008a). Community Informatics and Social System Design for Raising Collective Intelligence in Society: Toward a framework for a Generic Design Science. Summer School, Minds and Society, Cognitive Sciences Institute, Montreal, Quebec, Canada, 4 juillet 2008.

Harvey, P. L. (2008b). Applying social systems thinking and community informatics thinking in education: Building efficient online learning design culture in universities. In K. E. Rudestam & J. Schoenholtz-Read (Eds.), *The hanbook of online learning: Innovations in higher educa- tion and corporate training.* California: Sage Publications.

Harvey, P. -L. (2010). Applying social systems thinking and community informatics thinking in education: Building efficient online learning design culture in universities. dans K. E. Rudestam & J. Schoenholtz-Read (dir.), *The handbook of online learning.* Thousand Oaks: Sage.

Harvey, P.-L. (2011). Design communautique, réseaux sociotechniques et e-learning. Conférence internationale prononcée dans le cadre du Colloque 626 du 79ième Congrès de l'ACFAS, Curiosité, Diversité, Responsabilité. Tenu du 9 au 13 mai 2011 à l'Université de Sherbrooke et à l'Université Bishop's, Sherbrooke. Conférence prononcée le 13 mai 2011. Partenaires: LCA, Services Gouvernementaux du Québec, Secrétariat du Conseil du Trésor, Université de Bayreuth Allemagne, Université de Lille, Unima Logiciel, Hexagram et UQAM.

Harvey, P.-L. (2014) *Design Communautique appliqué aux systèmes sociaux numériques. Fondements communicationnels, théories et méthodologies* (pp. 648). Presses de l'université du Québec: Quebec.

Harvey, P.-L. (2016). Community informatics design for digital social systems: The ultimate tool for a human democratic open data age. In *Open data, Le Réseau international des Chaires Unesco en communication, communication and information sector.* ORBICOM, UQAM: Université ibéro-américaine de Mexico.

Harvey, P. -L., & Andre, M. K. (2003). Ubiquitous computing and gaming: Building platforms like mobile communityware for gaming to support millions of gamers. dans H. Twaites (dir.),

Proceedings of the ninth international conference on virtual systems and multimedia. Montréal: VSMM/3Dmt Center/Hexagram Institute.

Harvey, P. -L., & Bertrand, N. (2004b). Virtual communities. dans A. DiStefano, K. E. Rudestam & R. J. Silverman (dir.), *The encyclopedia of distributed learning, fielding graduate institute.* Santa Barbara: Sage.

Harvey, P. -L., & Ho, T. P. (2014). La recherche intervention à l'âge des médias sociaux:design communautique, transmédia storytelling et compétences numériques. Conférence et PPT prononcée dans le cadre du Colloque annuel du Réseau International des Chaires UNESCO en Communication, ORBICOM, Université Bordeaux-Montaigne, les 6 et 7 novembre 2014.

Harvey, P. -L., & Lemire, G. (2001). *La nouvelle éducation: NTIC, transdisciplinarité et communautique.* Québec: Presses de l'Université Laval/L'Harmattan.

Hatchuel, A., Le Masson, P., Reich, Y., & Weil, B. (2011). *A systematic approach of design theories using generativeness and robustness*, International conference on engineering design, Copenhague, août, 2011.

Hayek, R. A. (1945). The use of knowledge in society. *The American Economie Review, 35*(4), 519–530.

Haythornthwaite, C., Andrews, R., Kazmer, M. M., Bruce, B. C., Montague, R., Preston, C. (2007). Theories and models of and for online learning. *First Monday, 12*(8), http://journals.uic.edu/ojs/index.php/fm/article/view/1976/1851, consulté le 13 novembre 2013.

Hegel, G. W. F. (2006). *Phénoménologie de l'esprit.* Paris: Vrin.

Helbing, D. (2010). The future ICT knowledge accelerator: Unleashing the power of information for a sustainable future, Ithaca, Cornell University Library, http://arxiv.org/ftp/arxiv/papers/1004/1004.4969.pdf, consulté le 21 novembre 2013.

Helbing, D. (2011). FuturICT - new science and technology to manage our complex, strongly connected world, Cornell University Library, http://arxiv.org/pdf/1108.6131.pdf, consulté le 13 novembre 2013.

Helbing, D. (2012a). Modeling of socio-economic systems. dans D. Helbing (dir.), *Social self-organization* (pp. 1–24). Heidelberg: Springer.

Helbing, D. (2012b). Accelerating scientific discovery by formulating grand scientific challenges. *The European Physical Journal Special Topics, 214*(1), 41–48.

Helbing, D. (2013). Globally networked risks and how to respond. *Nature, 497*(7447), 51–59.

Hess, C., & Ostrom, E. (Eds.). (2007). *Understanding knowledge as a commons.* Cambridge, MA: MIT Press. Portions of the book are available OA at http://mitpress.mit.edu/catalog/item/default.asp?ttype=2&tid=11012.

Hevner, A. R., March, S. T., Park, J., & Ram, S. (2004). Design science in information systems research. *MIS Quarterly, 28*(1), 75–105.

Heylighen, F. (2001). The science of self-organization and adaptivity. *The Encyclopedia of Life Support Systems, 5*(3), 253–280.

Heylighen, F. (2007). Accelerating socio-technological evolution: From ephemeralization and stigmergy to the global brain. dans G. Modelski, T. Devezas & W. Thompson (dir.), *Globalization as an evolutionary process: Modeling global change* (pp. 286–335). Londres, Routledge.

Heylighen, F. (2011). Self-organization of complex, intelligent systems: An action ontology for transdisciplinary integration, http://pespmc1.vub.ac.be/papers/ECCO-paradigm.pdf, consulté le 13 novembre 2013.

Heylighen, R (2013). Self-organization in communicating groups: The emergence of coordination, shared references and collective intelligence. dans A. Massip-Bonet & A. Bastardas-Boada (dir.), *Complexity perspectives on language, communication and society* (pp. 117–149). Heidelberg: Springer.

Hirschheim, R. A. (1985). Information systems epistemology: An historical perspective. dans G. Fitzgerald, R. A. Hirschheim, E. Mumford & A. T. Wood-Harper (dir.), *Research methods in information systems* (pp. 9–33). Amsterdam: Elsevier Science.

Hirschheim, R., & Klein, H. K. (1989). Four paradigms of information systems development. *Communications of the ACM, 32*(10), 1199–1216.

Hoadley, C. (2002). Creating context: Desigti-based research in creating and understanding CSCL, http://tophe.net/papers/cscl02hoadley.pdf, consulté le 13 novembre 2013.

Hochheiser, H., & Lazar, J. (2007). HCI and societal issues: A framework for engagement. *International Journal of Human Computer Interaction, 23*(3), 339–374.

Hofkirchner, W. (2007a). A critical social system view of the Internet. *Philosophy of the Social Sciences, 37*(4), 471–500. http://pos.sagepub.eom/cgi/reprint/37/4/471, consulté le 13 novembre 2013.

Hofkirchner, W. A. (2007b). Critical social systems view of the internet. *Philosophy of the Social Sciences, 37*(4), 471–500.

Hofkirchner, W. (2008a). How to achieve a unified theory of information. dans J. M. Nafria & F. Salto Alemany (dir.), *¡Qué es información?, Actas al Primer Encuentro Internacional de Expertos en TeorJas de la Información, un enfoque interdisciplinary.* 6-7 novembre, Leon: Universidad de Leôn.

Hofkirchner, W. (2008b). How to achieve a unified theory of information. In J. M. Díaz Nafría & F. Salto Alemany (Eds.), *¿Qué es información?* León: Universidad de León.

Hofkirchner, W. (2009). Community-Where to from here? From 'networked individualism' towards 'community networks'. *Journal of Sociocybernetics, 7*, 62–72.

Hofkirchner, W. (2010). How to design the infosphere: The fourth revolution, the management of the life cycle of information, and information ethics as a macroethics. *Knowledge, Technology, and Policy, 23*(1-2), 177–192.

Hofkirchner, W. (2013). *Emergent information: A unified theory of information framework.* Londres: World Scientific.

Hofkirchner, W., & Fuchs, C. (2003a). *The dialectic of bottom-up and top-down emergence in social systems. tripleC, 3*(2), 28–50, http://triplec.at, consulté le 18 novembre 2013.

Hofkirchner, W., & Fuchs, C. (2003b). The architecture of the information society. Gray litterature from the Institute of Design and Technology Assessment, Vienna University of Technology, Favoritenstr. 9, A-1040 Wien, Austria.

Hofkirchner, W., & Fuchs, C. (2008). Autopoesis and critical social systems theory. dans R. Magalhaes & R. Sanchez (dir.), *Autopoesis in organization theory and practice* (pp. 111–129), http://fuchs.uti.at/wp-content/uploads/2009/12/autopoesis.pdf, consulté le 20 novembre 2013.

Hofkirchner, W., Fuchs, C., Raffl, C., Schafranek, M., Sandoval, M., & Bichler, R. (2007). *ICTs and society: The Salzburg approach: Towards a theory for, about, and by means of the Information Society.* Salzburg: ICT&S Center Research Paper Series.

Horvâth, I. (2001). A contemporary survey of scientific research into engineering design. dans S. Culley, A. C. McMahon & K. Wallace (dir.), *Proceedings of ICED 01, 21-23 août* (pp. 13–20), Bury St. Edmonds/Londres: Professional Engineering.

Houde, O., et al. (1998). *Vocabulaire de sciences cognitives : neuroscience, psychologie, intelligence artificielle, linguistique et philosophie.* Paris: Presses universitaires de France.

Huang, C. Y., Yang, T. T., Chen, W. L., & Nof, S. Y. (2010). Reference architecture for collaborative design. *International Journal of Computers, Communications and Control, 5*(1), 71–90.

Huber, G. P. (1984). *Issues in the design of group decision support systems.* Austin: University of Texas.

Hughes, T. P. (1983). *Networks of power: Electrification in Western Society.* Baltimore: Johns Hopkins University Press.

Hughes, T. P. (1987). The evolution of large technological systems. dans W. E. Bijker, T. P. Hughes & T. J. Pinch (dir.), *The social construction of technological systems.* Cambridge, MA: MIT Press.

Hughes, T. P. (1990). *American genesis.* Baltimore: Johns Hopkins University Press.

Hughes, T. P. (1998). *Rescuing Prometheus.* New York: Pantheon Books.

Huhns, M., & Ghenniwa, H. (2006). eMarketplace model: An architecture for collaborative supply chain management and intégration. dans B. Chaib-draa & J. P. Muller (dir.), *Multiagent based supply chain management* (pp. 29–62). Heidelberg: Springer.

Hull, R. E., & Mohan, M. (1975). *Teaching effectiveness: Its meaning, assessment, and improvement.* Englewood Cliffs: Educational Technology Publications.

Hutchins, E. (1995). *Cognition in the wild-issue.* Cambridge, MA: MIT Press.

Hutchins E. (2001). Distributed cognition. In: *The International Encyclopedia of the Social and Behavioral Sciences*, pp. 2068–2072.

Hutchins, E. (2010). Cognitive ecology. *Topics in Cognitive Science, 2*(4), 705–715.

Illich, I. (1973). *Tools for conviviality.* New York: Harper and Row.

Irwin, T. (2015). Transition design: A proposal for a new area of design practice, study, and research. *The Journal of the Design Studies Forum, 7*(2), 229–246.

Isaac, L. W. (1997). Transforming localities: Reflections on time, causality, and narrative in contemporary historical sociology. *Historical Methods, 30*(1), 4–12.

Jackson, M. C. (1985). Social systems theory and practice: The need for a critical approach. *International Journal of General Systems, 10*(2), 135–151.

Jackson, M. C. (1995). Beyond the fads: Systems thinking for managers. *Systems Research and Behavioral Science, 12*(1), 25–42.

Jaffelin, J. (1991). *Le promeneur d'Einstein: vers une théorie de l'information générale.* Le Cerf/Méridien: Paris/Montréal.

Jaffelin, J. (1995). *Critique de la raison scientifique, ou Une nouvelle manière de penser.* Paris: L'Harmattan.

Jakobson, R. (1963 [1960]). *Essais de linguistique générale [trad. N. Ruwet].* Paris: Minuit.

James, W. (1907). *Pragmatism: A new name for some old ways of thinking.* New York: Longman.

Jantsch, E. (1969). *Perspectives of planning.* Paris: OECD.

Jantsch, E. (1976). *Design for evolution.* New York: Braziller.

Jantsch, E. (1980). *The self-organizing universe.* Oxford: Pergamon.

Jenkins, H. (2006a). Confronting the challenges of participatory culture: Media education for the 21st century (part two). *Nordic Journal of Digital Literacy, 2,* 97–112. http://www.idunn.no/ts/dk/2007/02/confronting_the_challenges_ofparticipatoryculture_-_media_education_for_the, consulté le 13 novembre 2013.

Jenkins, H. (2006b). *Convergence culture: Where old and new media collide.* New York: New York University Press.

Jenkins, H. (2009). *Confronting the challenges of participatory culture: Media education for the 21st Century.* Cambridge, MA: MIT Press.

Jenlink, P. M. (2001). Activity theory and the design of educational systems: Examining the mediational importance of conversation. *Systems Research and Behavioral Science, 18*(4), 345–359.

Jenlink, P. M. (2004). Discourse ethics in the design of educational systems: Considerations for design praxis. *Systems Research and Behavioral Science, 21*(3), 237–249.

Jenlink, P. M. (2006). Activity theory as a framework for designing educational systems. dans J. L. Kincheloe & R. A. Horn Jr. (dir.), *The praeger handbook of education and psychology* (Vol. 2). Westport: Greenwood Publishing Group.

Jenlink, P. M. (2009). Preparing democratic educational leaders: An equity-based approach. dans P. M. Jenlink (dir.), *Equity issues for today's educational leaders: Meeting the challenge of creating equitable schools for all* (pp. 33–51). Lanhan: Rowan & Littlefield.

Jenlink, P. M., & Banathy, B. H. (2002). The Agora project: The new agoras of the twenty-first century. *Systems Research and Behavioral Science, 19*(5), 469–483.

Jenlink, P. M., & Banathy, B. H. (2008). *Dialogue as a collective means of design conversation.* New York: Springer.

Jenlink, P. M., & Reigeluth, C. M. (2000). A guidance system for designing new K-12 educational systems. dans J. K. Allen & J. Wilby (dir.), *The proceedings of the 44th annual conference of the international society for the systems sciences,* Toronto, 16-22 juillet.

Jenlink, P. M., Reigeluth, C. M., Carr, A. A., & Nelson, L. M. (1998). Guidelines for facilitating systemic change in school districts. *Systems Research and Behavioral Science, 15*(3), 217–233.

Johannessen, J. A., & Olsen, B. (2011a). Projects as communicating systems: Creating a culture of innovation and performance. *International Journal of Information Management, 31*(1), février, 30–37, http://www.sciencedirect.com/science/article/pii/S0268401210000617, consulté le 11 décembre 2013.

Johannessen, J. A., & Olsen, B. (2011b). What creates innovation in a globalized knowledge economy? a cybernetic point of view. *Kybernetes: The International Journal of Systems & Cybernetics, 40*(9-10), 1395–1421(27). https://doi.org/10.1108/03684921111169459.

Jones, C. (1970). *Design methods*. New York: Wiley.

Jones, P. H., (2008). Socializing a knowledge strategy. dans E. Abou-Zeid (dir.), *Knowledge management and business strategies: Theoretical frameworks and empirical research*. Hershey: IGI Global.

Jones, P. H. (2010). The language/action model of conversation: Can conversation perform acts of design? *Interactions, 17*(1), 70–75.

Jones, P. H., Christakis, A. N., & Flanagan, T. R. (2007). Dialogic design for the intelligent enterprise: Collaborative strategy, process, and action, Proceedings of INCOSE 2007, San Diego, 25-29 juin.

Judge, A. (1995). Envisaging the art of navigating conceptual complexity: In search of software combining artistic and conceptual insights. *Knowledge Organization, 22*(1), 2–9.

Judge, A. (1998). Typology of Twelve Complementary Dialogue Modes Essential to Sustainable Development. Internet Paper. Retrieved from the Anthony Judge website, «Laetus in Praesens», 20 November 2017 (Creative Commons License).

Judge, A. (2007). Imagining the real challenge and realizing the imaginai pathway of sustainable transformation, http://www.laetusinpraesens.org/docsOOs/real.php, consulté le 13 novembre 2013.

Judge, A. (2008a). Configuring global governance groups: Experimental visualization of possible integrative relationships, http://www.laetusinpraesens.org/docsOOs/globgov.php, consulté le 13 novembre 2013.

Judge, A. (2008b). Polyhedral pattern language: Software facilitation of emergence, representation and transformation of psycho-social organization, http://www.laetusinpraesens.org/docs00s/stella.php, consulté le 13 novembre 2013.

Judge, A. (2017). Enabling a 12-fold Pattern of Systemic Dialogue for governance. Internet paper. Retrieved from the Anthony Judge website, «Laetus in Praesens», 20 November 2017 (Creative Commons License).

Katz, E., & Lazarsfeld, P. F. (2006). *Personal influence: The part played by people in the flow of mass communications*. Piscatawa: Transaction.

Kerlinger, F. N. (1973). *Foundations of behavioral research* (2nd ed.). New-York: Holt, Rinehart and Winston\American Problem Series.

Klein, H. K. (2009). Critical social IS research today: A reflection of past accomplishments and current challenges. dans C. Brooke (dir.), *Critical management perspectives on information systems* (pp. 249–272). Oxford: Butterworth Heinemann.

Kling, R. (1973). *Toward a person-centered computing technology*, Proceedings of the 1973 Fall Joint Computer Conference, Atlanta, août.

Kling, R. (1996). Synergies and competition between life in cyberspace and face-to-face communities. *Social Science Computer Review, 14*(1), 50–54.

Kling, R. (1999). Can the "next generation Internet" effectively support "ordinary citizens"? *The Information Society, 15*(1), 57–64.

Kling, R. (2000a). Social informatics: A new perspective on social research about information and communication technologies. *Prometheus, 18*(3), 245–264.

Kling, R. (2000b). Learning about information technologies and social change: The contribution of social informatics. *The Information Society, 16*(3), 217–232.

Kling, R. (2003). Critical professional education and information and communications technologies and social life. *Information Technology & People, 16*(3), 394–418.

Kling, R. (2007). What is social informatics and why does it matter? *The Information Society, 23*(4), 205–220.

Kling, R., Crawford, H., Rosenbaum, H., Sawyer, S., & Weisband, S. (2000). Learning from organizational and social informatics: Information and communication technologies in human contexts, NSF Workshop Report, http://www.social-informatics.org/uploadi/editor/SIjreport.pdf, consulté le 13 décembre 2013.

Kling, R., Kraemer, K. L., Allen, J. P., Bakos, Y., Gurbaxani, V., & Elliott, M. (2001). Transforming coordination: The promise and problems of information technology in coordination. dans

T. Malone, G. Olson & J. Smith (dir.), *Coordination theory and collaboration technology* (pp. 507–534). Mahwah: Erlbaum.

Kling, R., Mckim, G., & King, A. (2002). A bit more to it: Scientifc multiple media communication forums as socio-technical interaction networks. *Journal of the American Society for Information Science, 54*(1), décembre, 47–67.

Kling, R., Rosenbaum, H., & Sawyer, S. (2005). *Understanding and communicating social informatics: A framework for studying and teaching the human contexts of information and communication technologies.* Medford: Information Today.

Kommonen, K. H., & Botero, A. (2013). Are the users driving, and how open is open? Experiences from Living Lab and user driven innovation projects. *The Journal of Community Informatics, 9*(3), http://ci-journal.net/index.php/ciej/article/view/746/1026, consulté le 13 mars 2014.

Komninos, N. (2003). *Intelligent cities.* Londres: Spon.

Komninos, N., & Tsarchopoulos, R. (2013). Toward intelligent Thessaloniki: From an agglomeration of apps to smart districts. *Journal of the Knowledge Economy, 4*(2), 149–168.

Koohang, A., & Harman, K. (2005). Open source: A metaphor for e-learning. *Informing Science Journal, 8,* http://inform.nu/Articles/Vol8/v8p075-086Kooh.pdf, consulté le 13 novembre 2013.

Krippendorff, K. (2007). The semantic turn: A new foundation for design. *Artifact, 1*(1), 56–59.

Krohs, U. (2008). Co-designing social systems by designing technical artifacts: A conceptual approach. dans P. E. Vermaas, P. Kroes, A. Light & S. A. Moore (dir.), *Philosophy and design* (pp. 233–245), Delft: Springer.

Kuhn, T. S. (1970). *The structure of scientific revolutions* (2e éd.). Chicago: University of Chicago Press.

Lacasa, P., Martinez, R., Mendez, L., & Cortes, S. (2007). Classrooms as "Living Labs": The role of commercial games, http://web.mit.edu/comm-forum/mit5/papers/Lacasa%20%20 Games%20and%20Folk%20culture%2026%2004%2007%20MIT.pdf, consulté le 13 novembre 2013.

Landry, M. (1988). Les problèmes organisationnels complexes et le défi de leur formulation. *Canadian Journal of Administrative Sciences, 5,* 34–48.

Laouris, Y., & Christakis, A. (2007). Harnessing collective wisdom at a fraction of the time using structured design process embedded within a virtual communication context. *International Journal of Applied Systemic Studies, X*(X), 000–000.

Laszlo, E. (1972). *The systems view of the world: The natural philosophy of the new developments in the sciences.* New York: Braziller.

Laszlo, A. (2001). The epistemological foundations of evolutionary system design. *Systems Research and Behavioral Science, 18*(4), 307–321.

Laszlo, E. (2006). *Science and the reechantment of the Cosmos: The rise of the integral vision of reality.* Inner Traditions: Rochester.

Laszlo, A., & Laszlo, E. (2003). *The connectivity hypothesis: Foundations of an integral science of quantum, cosmos, life, and consciousness.* Albany: State University of New York (SUNY) Press.

Laszlo, K. C., & Laszlo, A. (2004). The role of evolutionary learning community in evolutionary development: The unfolding of a line of inquiry. *Systems Research and Behavioral Science, 21*(3), 269–280.

Laszlo, K. C., & Laszlo, A. (2007). Fostering a sustainable learning society through knowledge-based development. *Systems Research and Behavioral Science, 24*(5), 493–503.

Laszlo, K. C., Laszlo, A., Romero, C., & Campos, M. (2002). Evolving development: An evolutionary perspective on development for an interconnected world. *World Futures: The Journal of General Evolution, 59*(2), 105–119.

Laszlo, A., Laszlo, K. C., & Dunsky, H. (2010). Redefining success: Designing systemic sustainable strategies. *Systems Research and Behavioral Science, 27*(1), 3–21.

Latour, B. (2008). A cautious Prometheus? A few steps toward a philosophy of design (with special attention to Peter Sloterdijk), Proceedings of the 2008 annual international conference of the design history society (pp. 2–10). Keynote lecture for the Networks of Design*meeting of the Design History Society. Falmouth, Cornwall, 3rd September 2008.

Lazarsfeld, P. F., & Merton, R. K. (1971). Mass communication, popular taste and organized social action. dans P. Marris & S. Thornham (dir.), *Media studies: A reader* (2e éd., pp. 18–30). New York: New York University Press.

Le Moigne, J. -L. (1977). *La théorie du système général: théorie de la modélisation*. Paris: Presses universitaires de France, coll. "Systèmes-Décisions".

Le Moigne, J. -L. (1979a). "Systémique et épistémologie: Aix-en- Provence", rapport de recherche, GRASCE, Université de droit, d'économie et des sciences d'Aix-Marseille, Faculté d'économie.

Le Moigne, J. -L. (1979b). "La systémographie: pour mieux maîtriser les modèles", texte présenté au colloque sur la problématique. Québec: Faculté des sciences de l'administration, Université Laval.

Le Moigne, J. -L. (1983). *La théorie du système général: Théorie de la modélisation* (2e éd.). Paris: Presses universitaires de France, coll. "Systèmes-Décisions".

Lejeune, A., & Harvey, P. -L. (2007). L'analyse des systèmes d'activités, l'apprentissage extensif et le co-design en communauté: une approche alternative à la réingénierie du système de santé au Québec. *Revue Gestion 2000, 24*(5), 143–159.

Lemire, G. (2008). *Modélisation et construction des mondes de connaissances*. Québec: Presses de l'Université Laval.

Leydesdorff, L. (2002). The communication turn in the theory of social systems. *Systems Research and Behavioral Science, 19*(2), 129–136.

Leydesdorff, L. (2003). *A sociological theory of communication: The self-organization of the knowledge-based society*. s.l.: Universal Publishers.

Leydesdorff, L. (2006). The triple helix and knowledge-based innovation systems. dans M. Rebernik, M. Mulej, M. Rus & T. Kroslin (dir.), *Cooperation between the Economie, Academie and Governmental Spheres: Mechanisms and Levers. Proceedings of the 26th Conference on Entrepreneurship and Innovation Maribor, 30-31 mars 2006* (pp. 143–152).

Lhotellier, A., & St-Arnaud, Y. (1994). Pour une démarche praxéolo- gique. *Nouvelles pratiques sociales, 7*(2), 93–109, http://id.erudit.org/iderudit/301279ar, consulté le 13 novembre 2013.

Lï, W. D., Lu, W. F., Fuh, J. Y. H., & Wong, Y. S. (2005). Collaborative computer-aided design-research and development status. *Computer-Aided Design, 37*(9), 931–940. doi:https://doi.org/10.1016/j. cad.2004.09.020.

Living Labs Europe. (2007). http://www.livinglabs-europe.com, consulté le 20 septembre 2007.

Long, P. D., & Erhmann, S. C. (2005). Future of the learning space: Breaking out of the box. *Educause Review, 40*(4), 42–58.

Love, T. (2001). *Changes to theory making about systems involving people: Meta-theoretical analysis and brain research*, Systems in Management 7th annual ANZSYS Conference 2001, Perth, Edith Cowan University, http://www.love.com.au/PublicationsTLminisite/2001/2001%20 ANZSYS01%20People%20Sys%20NTA%20and%20Brain.htm, consulté le 13 novembre 2013.

Love, T. (2003). Beyond emotions in designing and designs: Epistemological and practical issues. dans D. McDonagh, D. Gyi, P. Hekkert & J. van Erp (dir.), *Design and emotion* (pp. 387–391). Londres: Taylor and Francis.

Lovink, G. (2007). Blogging, The Nihilist Impulse. In *Zero comments: Blogging and critical internet culture* (pp. 1–38). Londres: Routledge.

Lovink, G., & Rossiter, N. (2010). Urgent aphorisms: Notes on organized networks for the connected multitudes. dans M. Deuze (dir.), *Managing media work*. Londres: Sage.

Lovink, G., & Schneider, F. (2002). A virtual world is possible: From tactical media to digital multitudes, http://makeworlds.net/node/22, consulté le 13 novembre 2013.

Lu, S. C-Y., Elmaraghy, W., Schuh, G., & Wilhelm, R. (2007). A scientific foundation of collaborative engineering. *CIRP Annals - Manufacturing Technology, 56*(2), 605–634.

Luhmann, N. (1989). *Ecological communication*. Oxford: Polity Press.

Luhmann, N. (1995 [1984]). *Social systems [trad. J. Bednarz Jr. & D. Baecker].* Redwood City: Stanford University Press.

Luppicini, R. (2008). *Handbook of conversation design for instructional applications.* Hershey: Information Science Reference.

M'Pherson, P. K. (1974). A perspective on systems science and systems philosophy. *Futures, 6*(3), 219–239.

Macpherson, I. (2004). Remembering the big picture: The co-operative movement and contemporary communities. dans C. Borzaga & R. Spear (dir.), *Trends and challenges for co-operatives and social enterprises in developed and transition countries* (pp. 39–48). Trente (Italie): Edizioni31.

Majumdar, S. (1986). *1985-86 yearbook of the National Association of Academies of Science.* Ohio Academy of Science: Columbus.

Manzini, E. (2007). Design research for sustainable social innovation. In *Design research now* (pp. 233–245). Bâle: Birkhauser.

Manzini, E. (2009). New design knowledge. *Design Studies, 30*(1), 4–12.

Martin, J. L. (2008). Imagining new futures: The simple power of story. *Journal of Futures Studies, 13*(1), 113–124.

Maturana, H., & Varela, R. (1980). Autopoiesis and cognition: The realization of the living. Dordrecht: D. Reidel.

Maturana, H., & Varela, R. (1987). *The tree of knowledge: The biological roots of human understanding.* Boston: Shambhala.

Mckey, P., & Ellis, A. (2007). Three design principles for predicting the future of the web, http://ausweb.scu.edu.au/aw07/papers/refereed/mckey/paper.html, consulté le 13 novembre 2013.

Media Awareness Network (MNet). (2010). Digital Literacy in Canada: From Inclusion to Transformation. A Submission to the Digital Economy Strategy Consultation July7, Digital Economy Consultation, Minister of Industry Canada, May 10, 2010.

Mehlenbacher, B. (2007). Triangulating communication design: Emerging models for theory and practice, Proceedings of the 25th Annual ACM international conference on design of communication, ACM (pp. 87–94). SIGDOC'07, October 22–24, 2007, El Paso, TX, USA.

Mehlenbacher, B. (2008). Communication design and theories of learning. SIGDOC'08: The 26th ACM International Conference on Design of Communication Proceedings, Lisbon, Portugal, 139–146. doi:https://doi.org/10.1145/1456536.1456564.

Mehlenbacher, B. (2009). Multidisciplinarity and 21st century communication design, Proceedings of the 27th ACM international conference on design of communication, ACM (pp. 59–66). SIGDOC'09, October 5-7, 2009, Bloomington, Indiana, USA.

Mélèze, J. (1972). *L'analyse modulaire des systèmes de gestion A.M.S.* Puteaux: Hommes et Techniques.

Messick, S. (1992). The interplay of evidence and consequences in the validation of performance assessments. *Educational Researcher, 23*(2), 13–23.

Metcalf, G. S. (Ed.). (2014). *Social systems and design translational systems sciences.* Tokyo: Springer. 2014th Edition.

Miller, J. G. (1978). *The living systems.* New York: McGraw-Hill.

Ming Fen, L. (2000). Fostering design culture through cultivating the user/designers design thinking and system thinking, Annual Proceedings of selected papers presented at the national convention of the association for educational communications and technology, Denver, Margareth Crawford et Michael Simonson, pp. 25–28.

Mingers, J., & Brocklesby, J. (1997). Multimethodology: Towards a framework for mixing methodologies. *Omega, 25*(5), 489–509, https://doi.org/10.1016/S0305-0483(97)00018-2, consulté le 11 décembre 2013.

Mink, L. O., Fay, B., Golob, E. O., & Vann, R. T. (1987). *Historical understanding.* Ithaca: Cornell University Press.

Mitroff, I. I., & Blankenship, L. V. (1973). On the methodology of the holistic experiment: An approach to the conceptualization of large-scale social experiments. *Technological Forecasting and Social Change, 4*(4), 339–353.

Moles, A. A. (1957). *La création scientifique*. Genève: Kister.

Moles, A. A. (1967). *Sociodynamique de la culture*. Paris: Mouton.

Moles, A. A. (1973). *La communication*. Paris: Les dictionnaires Marabout.

Moles, A. A. (1981). Pensée rigoureuse et sciences du vague: du bon usage des mathématiques dans les sciences sociales, Cahiers internationaux de sociologie, vol. 71, juillet-décembre, pp. 269-287.

Moles, A. A. (1988). Design and immateriality: What of it in a postindustrial society? [trad. D.W. Jacobus]. *Design Issues, 4*(1-2), 25–32.

Moles, A. A. (1990). *Les sciences de l'imprécis*. Paris: Seuil.

Moles, A. A. (1992). *Théorie de l'information et perception esthétique*. Paris: Flammarion.

Moles, A. A., & Rohmer, E. (1973). *Micropsychologie et vie quotidienne*. Paris: Denoël.

Moles, A.A. & Rohmer, E. (1976). Micropsychologie. Denoël, Coll. Médiations, Paris.1976.

Moles, A.A. & Rohmer, E. (1978) Psychologie de l'espace. Casterman

Moles, A. A., & Rohmer, E. (1986). *Théorie structurale de la communication et société*. Paris: Masson.

Moles, A. A., & Rohmer, E. (1998). *Psychosociologie de l'espace*. Paris: L'Harmattan.

Molina, A., Panetto, H., Chen, D., Whitman, L., Chapurlat, V., & Vernadat, F. (2007). Enterprise integration and networking: Challenges and trends. *Studies in Informatics and Control, 16*(4), 353–368.

de Moor, A. (2017). CommunitySensor: towards a participatory community network mapping methodology. *The Journal of Community Informatics, 13*(2), 35–58.

Moor, Y., Tholander, J., Holmberg, J. (2005). *Designing for Cross cultural Web-based knowledge building*, présenté à la 10th Computer Supported Collaborative Learning (CSCL) Conference, Taipei, juin.

Morabito, J., Sack, I., & Bhate, A. (1999). *Organization modeling: Innovative architectures for the 21st century*. Upper Saddle River: Prentice Hall.

Morgan, G. (1986). *Images of organization*. Beverly Hills: Sage.

Morin, E. (1973). *Le paradigme perdu: la nature humaine*. Paris: Seuil.

Morin, E. (1977). *La méthode 1. La nature de la nature*. Paris: Seuil.

Morin, E. (1980). *La méthode 2. La vie de la vie*. Paris: Seuil.

Morin, E. (1982). *Science avec conscience*. Paris: Fayard.

Morin, E. (1984). *Sociologie*. Paris: Fayard.

Morin, E. (1985). On the definition of complexity, The science and praxis of complexity: Contributions to the symposium held at Montpellier, France, 9-11 May, 1984, The United Nations University, p. 62.

Morin, E. (1990). *Introduction à la pensée complexe*. Paris: ESF.

Mucchielli, A. (2005). *Étude des communications: approche par la contextualisation*. Paris: A. Colin.

Mucchielli, A. (2006). *Étude des communications: nouvelles approches*. Paris: A. Colin.

Mulder, I., Velthausz, D., & Kriens, M. (2008). The Living Labs harmonization cube: Communicating Living Labs' essentials", eJOV Executive, vol. 10, numéro spécial, novembre.

Nadler, G. (1981). *The planning and design approach*. New York: Wiley.

Nadler, G. (1985). Systems methodology and design. *IEEE Transactions on Systems, Man, and Cybernetics, 15*(6), 685–697.

Nelson, H. G. (1993). Design inquiry as an intellectual technology for the design of educational systems. dans C. M. Reigeluth, B. H. Banathy & J. R. Olson (dir.), *Comprehensive system design: A new education technology* (pp. 145–153). Stuttgart: Springer-Verlag.

Nelson, H. G., & Stolterman, E. (2003). *The design way: Foundations and fundamentals of design competence*. Englewood Cliffs: Educational Technology Publications.

Nicolescu, B. (1996). *La transdisciplinarité: manifeste*. Monaco: Éditions du Rocher.

Nicolescu, B. (2010). Methodology of transdisciplinarity: Levels of reality, logic of the included middle and complexity. *Transdis- ciplinary Journal of Engineering and Science, 1*(1), 17–32.

Nicolescu, B. (2011). The need for transdisciplinarity in higher education in a globalized world. In A. Ertas (Ed.), *Transdisciplinarity: Bridging natural science, social science, humanities*

& *engineering*. Texas: The Academy of Transdisciplinary Learning & Advanced Studies (ATLAS) Publishing.

Ning and al. (2016). Cybermatics: Cyber–physical–social–thinking hyperspace based science and technology. *Future Generation Computer Systems, 56*, 504–522.

Norman, S., & Porter, D. (2007). Designing learning objects for online learning, Knowledge Series, http://dspace.col.org/bitstream/123456789/155/l/KS2007_Designing-Learning-Objects.pdf, consulté le 14 novembre 2013.

O'Neill, M., Giddens, S., Breatnach, P., Bagley, C., Bourne, D., & Judge, T. (2002). Renewed methodologies for social research: Ethno-mimesis as performative praxis. *The Sociological Review, 50*(1), 69–88.

Oliveira, A., Fradinho, E., & Caires, R. (2006). From a successful regional information society strategy to an advanced living lab in mobile technologies and services, http://ieeexplore.ieee.org/xpl/login.jsp?tp=&arnumber=1579456&url=http%3A%2F%2Fieeexplore.ieee.org%2Fstamp%2Fstamp.jsp%3Ftp%3D%26arnumber%3D1579456, consulté le 14 novembre 2013.

Ostrom, E. (1990). *Governing the commons: The evolution of institutions for collective action*. New York: Cambridge University Press.

Ostrom, E., & Hess, C. (2011). *Understanding knowledge as a commons: From theory to practice* (2e éd.). Cambridge, MA: MIT Press.

Owen, C. (2008). *Design thinking: On its nature and use* (pp. 26–31). Rotman: hiver.

Ôzbekhan, H. (1969). Toward a general theory of planning. dans E. Jantsch (dir.), *Perspectives of planning* (pp. 47–155), Paris: OCDE.

Ôzbekhan, H. (1970). The predicament of mankind: Quest for structured responses to growing world-wide complexities and uncertainties, http://sunsite.utk.edu/FINS/loversofdemocracy/Predicament.PTI.pdf, consulté le 14 novembre 2013.

Pallot, M. (2006). Living Labs, http://www.ami-communities.eu, consulté le 20 septembre 2007.

Papanek, V., & Fuller, R. B. (1972). *Design for the real world*. Londres: Thames and Hudson.

Pask, G. (1975a). *Conversation, Cognition and learning: Cybernetic theory and methodology*. New York: Elsevier.

Pask, G. (1975b). *The cybernetics of human learning and performance*. Londres: Hutchinson.

Pask, G. (1976). *Conversation theory: Applications in education and epistemology*. New York: Elsevier.

Peeters, M. A. G., et al. (2006). The big five personality traits and individual satisfaction with the team. *Small Group Research, 37*(2), 187–211. https://doi.org/10.1177/1046496405285458.

Peirce, C. S. (1935). *The collected papers, vol. I-VI, par C. Hawthorne et P. Weiss; vol. VII et VIII, 1958, par W. Burks*. Cambridge, MA: Havard University Press.

Pettenatti, M. C., & Cigognini, M. E. (2007). Social networking theories and tools to support connectivist learning activities. *Inter- national Journal of Web-Based Learning and Teaching Technologies, 2*(3), 39–57. http://elilearning.files.wordpress.com/2007/09/ijwltt2007_pettenati_cigognini.pdf, Retrieved, November 20 2017.

Piaget, J. (1970). *Genetic epistemology*. New York: W.W. Norton.

Pinch, T. J., & Bijker, W. E. (1987). The social construction of facts and artifacts: Or How the sociology of science and the sociology of technology might benefit each other. dans W. E. Bijker, T. P. Hughes & T. J. Pinch (dir.), *The social construction of technological systems: New directions in the sociology and history of technology* (pp. 17–50). Cambridge, MA: MIT Press.

Ponce De Leon, M., Eriksson, M., Balasubramaniam, S., & Donnelly, W. (2006). Creating a distributed mobile networking testbed environment through the living labs approach, http://repository.wit.ie/645/l/TridentCom2006_miguelpdl_sasib_LivingLabApproach_final.pdf, consulté le 12 novembre 2013.

Popper, K. R. (1961). *The poverty of historicism*. Londres: Routledge and Kegan Paul.

Popper, K. R. (1965). *Conjectures and refutations: The growth of scientific knowledge* (2e éd.). New York: Basic Books.

Popper, K. R. (1972). *Objective knowledge*. Oxford: Clarendon Press.

Popper, K. R. (2002[1959]). *The logic of scientific discovery,* New York: Psychology Press.

Porter, M. E., & Kramer, M. R. (2006). Strategy and society. *Harvard Business Review*, *84*(12), 78–92.

Preece, J., & Maloney-Krichmar, D. (2005). Online communities: Design, theory, and practice. *Journal of Computer-Mediated Communication*, *10*(4).

Preece, J., & Shneiderman, B. (2008). Copernican challenges face those who suggest that collaboration, not computations are the driving energy for socio-technical systems that characterize Web 2.0. *Science*, *319*, 1349–1350.

Preece, J., & Shneiderman, B. (2009). The reader-to-leader framework: Motivating technology-mediated social participation. *AIS Transactions on Human-Computer Interaction*, *1*(1), 13–32. Available at: http://aisel.aisnet.org/thci/vol1/iss1/5.

Preece, J., Abras, C., & Maloney-Krichmar, D. (2004). Designing and evaluating online communities: Research speaks to emerging practice. *International Journal of Web Based Communities*, *1*(1), 2–18.

Prigogine, I., & Stengers, P. (1984). *Order out of Chaos*. New York: Bantam.

Proulx, S. (2006). Communautés virtuelles. Penser et agir en réseau (codirection avec Louise Poissant et Michel Sénécal), Presses de l'Université Laval

Ranjan, M. P. (2005a). *Creating the unknowable: Designing the future in education*, EAD06 Conference, Brême, février.

Ranjan, M. P. (2005b). Lessons from Bauhaus, ULM AND NID: Role of basic design in PG education. Paper submitted for the DETM Conference at the National Institute of Design, Ahmedabad in March 2005.

Ranjan, M. P. (2007). Lessons from Bauhaus, Ulm and NID: Role of basic design in PG education, Design education: Tradition and modernity, scholastic papers from the international conference, DETM 2005, p. 8, Ahmedabad, India, National Institute of Design.

Ranjan, A., & Ranjan, M. P. (Eds.). (2007). Handmade in India: A Geographic Encyclopedia of Indian Handicrafts (New York: Abbeville Press, 2009). A. Ranjan and M.P. Ranjan (Eds.) Handmade in India: Crafts of India (New Delhi: Council of Handicraft Development Corporations (COHANDS).

Rasmussen, T. (2003). On distributed society: The history of the Internet as a guide to a sociological understanding of communication and society. dans G. Liestol, A. Morrison & T. Rasmussen (dir.), *Digital media revisited* (pp. 443–467). Cambridge, MA: MIT Press.

Reigeluth, C. M. (1983). *Instructional-Design theories and models: A new paradigm of instructional theory* (Vol. 2). Mahwah: Erlbaum.

Reigeluth, C. M. (1995). *A conversation on guidelines for the process of facilitating systemic change in education*. Englewood Cliffs: Educational Technology Publications.

Reigeluth, C. M. (2008). Chaos theory and the sciences of complexity: Foundations for transforming education. In B. Despres (Ed.), *Systems thinkers in action: A field guide for effective change leadership in education*. New York: Rowman & Littlefield.

Reigeluth, C. M. (2009). Instructional theory for education in the information age. dans C. M. Reigeluth & A. A. Carr-Chellman (dir.), *Instructional-Design theories and models: Building a common knowledge base* (Vol. 3, pp. 387–400). New York: Routledge.

Reigeluth, C. M., & Carr-Chellman, A. (2008). *Instructional Design theories and models, vol. Ill, Building a common knowledge base*. Mahwah: Lawrence ERlbaum Associates.

Reigeluth, C. M., Banathy, B. H., & Olson, J. R. (1993). *Comprehensive systems Design: A new educational technology*. Stuttgart: Springer Verlag.

RESEAU EDUCATION-MEDIAS (dir.). (2010). La littératie numérique au Canada: de l'inclusion à la transformation, mémoire présenté dans le cadre de la Consultation-stratégie sur l'économie numérique du Canada, Ottawa.

Reymen, I. (2001). Improving design processes through structured reflection: Case studies, SAI Report 2001/3, octobre, Eindhoven, Pays-Bas, http://www.researchgate.net/publication/.../9fcf d5112bda954aa9.pdf/, consulté le 9 février 2014.

Reymen, I., Andries, P., Mauer, R., Stephan, U., & Van Burg, E. (2012). Dynamics of effectuation and causation in technology-based new ventures (interactive paper). *Frontiers of*

Entrepreneurship Research, *32*(6), article 25, http://digitalknowledge.babson.edu/fer/vol32/iss6/25/, consulté le 9 février 2014.

Rheingold, H. (1993). *The virtual community: Homesteading on electronic frontier reading.* Boston: Addison-Wesley.

Rico de Sotelo, C. (n.d.). Communication Internationale et Développement. Itinéraires et problématisations, Cahiers COLAB, Observatoire de la Communication Internationale et Interculturelle, Travaux du Département de Communication sociale et publique, UQAM 2011®.

Rico de Sotelo, C. (2008). Regards croisés sur la diversité culturelle: entre la production matérielle et l'intégration citoyenne. Une perspective du Sud. In David contre Goliath. La Convention sur la protection et la promotion de la diversité des expressions culturelles de l'UNESCO, sous la dir. de Yves Théorêt. Montréal: Hurtubise HMB.

Rittel, H., & Webber, M. (1984). Planning problems are wicked problems. dans N. Cross (dir.), *Developments on design methodology.* New York: Wiley.

Robbin, A. (2011). Embracing technology and the challenges of complexity, http://www.triple-c.at/index.php/tripleC/article/view/245, consulté le 14 novembre 2013.

Roberts, D. (1973). *The existential graphs of Charles S. Peirce.* La Haye: Mouton & Co. N.V.

Romero, D., & Molina, A. (2010). Virtual organisation breeding environments toolkit: Reference model, management framework and instantiation methodology. *Production Planning and Control, 21*(2), 181–217. doi:https://doi.org/10.1080/09537280903441963.

Romero, D., & Molina, A. (2011). Collaborative networked organisations and customer communities: Value co-creation and co-innovation in the networking era. *Production Planning and Control, 22*(5-6), 447–472. doi:https://doi.org/10.1080/09537287. 2010.536619.

Romero, D., Galeano, N., Giraldo, J., & Molina, A. (2006). *Towards the definition of business models and governance rules for virtual breeding environments* (Vol. 224, pp. 103–110). Network-Centric Collaboration and Supporting Frameworks, IFIP, New York: Springer Publisher.

Romero, D., Galeano, N., & Molina, A. (2008). A virtual breeding environment reference model and its instantiation methodology. dans L. M. Camarinha-Matos & W. Picard (dir.), *Pervasive collaborative networks* (pp. 15–24). Boston: Springer.

Romm, N. R. A. (1996). Systems methodologies and intervention: The issue of researcher responsibility. dans R. L. Flood & N. R. A. Romm (dir.), *Critical systems thinkmg* (pp. 179–194). New York: Plenum.

Romm, N. R. A. (2002). A trusting constructivist approach to systemic inquiry: Exploring accountability. *Systems Research and Behavioral Science, 19*(5), 455–467.

Romm, N. R. A. (2006). The social significance of Churchman's epistemological position: Implications for responsible conduct. dans J. Mclntyre-Mills (dir.), *Rescuing the enlightenment from itself: Critical and systemic implications for democracy* (Vol. 1, pp. 68–92). New York: Springer.

Ropohl. (1999). Philosophy of socio-technical systems. *Techné: Research in Philosophy and Technology, 4*(3), printemps, 186–194, doi:https://doi.org/10.5840/technel9994311.

Ropohl, G., & Lenk, H. (1979). Toward an interdisciplinary and pragmatic philosophy of technology. dans C. Mitcham & R. Mackey (dir.), *Research in philosophy and technology.* New York: The Free Press.

Rosenbloom, D. H. (2013). Reflections on "Public Administrative Theory and the Separation of Powers" David H. Rosenbloom. *The American Review of Public Administration, 43*(4), 381–396.

Sack, W., Detienne, F., Ducheneaut, N., Burkhardt, J. -M., Mahendran, D., & Barcellini, F. (2006). A methodological framework for socio- cognitive analyses of collaborative design of open source software, http://arxiv.org/ftp/cs/papers/0703/0703009.pdf, consulté le 14 novembre 2013.

Sage, A. (1977). *Methodology for large-scale systems.* New York: McGraw-Hill.

Saint-Arnaud, Y. (1989). *Les petits groupes: Participation et communication.* Montréal: Presses de l'Université de Montréal.

Sanders, E. B. N., & Westerlund, B. (2011). Experiencing, exploring and experimenting in and with co-design spaces. dans I. Koskinen, T. Hàrkâsalmi, R. Mazé, B. Matthews & J. J. Lee (dir.), *Proceedings of the Nordic design research conference 2011: Making design matter.* (pp. 298–302). Helsinki, Finland.

Scacchi, W. (2006). Socio-technical design. dans C. Ghaoui (dir.), *The encyclopedia of human-computer interaction* (pp. 656–659). Hershey: Idea Group Reference.

Scardamalia, M., & Bereiter, C. (1994). Computer support for knowledge-building communities. *The Journal of the Learning Sciences, 3*(3), 265–283.

Schein, E. H. (1993). *On dialogue, culture, and organizational learning* (pp. 40–51). Winter: Organizational Dynamics.

Schein, E. (2012). Corporate culture. dans J. Vogelsang, M. Townsend, M. Minahan, D. Jamieson, J. Vogel, A. Viets, C. Royal & L. Valek (dir.), *Handbook for strategic HR: Best practices in organization development from the OD network* (pp. 9–16). New York: The Organizational Development Network.

Schoenfeld, A. H. (1992). On paradigms and methods: What do you do when the ones you know don't do what you want them to? *The Journal of the Learning Sciences, 2*(2), 179–214.

Schôn, D. A. (1983). *The reflective practitioner: How professionals think in action.* New York: Basic Books.

Schôn, D. A. (1992). Designing as reflective conversation with the materials of a design situation, http://www.cs.uml.edu/ecg/pub/uploads/DesignThinking/schon-reflective-conversation-article-1992.pdf, consulté le 14 novembre.

Schon, D. A., & Bennett, J. (1996). Reflective conversation with materials. dans T. Winograd (dir.), *Bringing design to software.* New York: ACM.

Schuler, D., & Namioka, A. (1993). *Participatory design: Principles and practice.* Londres: Taylor & Francis.

Schumacher, J., & Feurstein, K. (2007). *Living Labs - A new multistakeholder approach to user integration,* présenté à la 3rd International Conference on Interoperability of Enterprise Systems and Applications (I-ESA'07), Funchal, Madère.

Searle, J. R. (1969). *Speech acts: An essay in the philosophy of language.* Cambridge (R.-U.): Cambridge University Press.

Senge, P. M. (1990). *The fifth discipline.* New York: Doubleday.

Senge, P. M. (2006). *The fifth discipline: The art and practice of the learning organization.* New York: Random House.

Senge, P. (2013). Learning organizations. dans E. Sallis & G. Jones (dir.), *Knowledge management in education: Enhancing learning and education* (pp. 77–98). New York: Routledge.

Senge, P., Scharmer, C. O., Jaworski, J., & Flowers, B. S. (2005). *Presence: An exploration of profound change in people, organizations, and society.* New York: Crown Business.

Shannon, C. E., & Weaver, W. (1949). *A mathematical theory of communication* (2e éd.). Urbana: University of Illinois Press.

Shneiderman, B. (2007). Creativity support tools: Accelerating discovery and innovation. *Communications of the ACM, 50*(12), 20–32.

Shneiderman, B. (2010). *Designing the user interface: Strategies for effective human–computer interaction* (1st ed). Addison-Wesley, 1986; 2nd ed. 1992; 3rd ed. 1998; 4th ed. 2005; 5th ed. 2010; 6th ed., 2016.

Shneiderman, B. (2011). Technology-mediated social participation: The next 25 years of HCI challenges. dans J. À. Jacko (dir.), *Human-computed interaction: Design and development approaches, Part I* (pp. 3–14). Berlin: Springer Verlag.

Shneiderman, B., & Pleasant, C. (2010). *Designing the user interface: Strategies for effective human-computer interaction* (5e éd.). Boston: Addison-Wesley.

Shneiderman, B., & Preece, J. (2009). The reader-to-leader framework: Motivating technology-mediated social participation, University of Maryland, http://www.cs.umd.edu/~ben/papers/Jennifer2009Reader.pdf, consulté le 12 décembre 2013.

Shneiderman, B., & Preece, J. (2011). Realizing the value of social media requires innovative computing research. *Communications of the ACM, 54*(9), septembre, doi:https://doi.org/10.1145/1995376.1995389.

Siemens, G. (2005a). Learning development cycle: Bridging learning design and modem knowledge needs, http://www.elearnspace.org/Articles/ldc.htm, consulté le 14 novembre 2013.

Siemens, G. (2005b). Connectivism: Learning as network creation. e-Learning Space.org website. http://www.elearnspace.org/Articles/networks.htm.

Sim, S. K., & Duffy, A. H. B. (2003). Towards an ontology of generic engineering design activies. *Research in Engineering Design, 14*(4), 200–223.

Simon, H. A. (1960). *The new science of management decisions*. New York: Harper and Row.

Simon, H. A. (1962). The architecture of complexity. *Proceedings of the American Philosophical Society, 106*(6), décembre, 467–482, http://www.stor.org/sici?sici=0003-049X%2819621212 %29106%3A6%3C467%3ATAOC%3E2.0.CO%3B2-1&., consulté le 13 décembre 2013.

Simon, H. A. (1969). *The science of the artificial*. Cambridge, MA: MIT Press.

Simon, H. A. (1974). *La science des systèmes, science de l'artificiel*. Paris: EPI.

Simon, H. A. (1996). *The sciences of the artificial* (3rd ed.). Cambridge, MA: MIT Press. Orig.

Simon, H. A. (2005). Darwinism, altruism and economics. In G. Dopfer (Ed.), *The evolutionary foundations of economics* (pp. 89–104). Cambridge: Cambridge University Press.

Sloterdijk, R. (2002). *Sphères I. Bulles: microsphérologie [trad. O. Mannoni]*. Paris: Pauvert.

Sloterdijk, P. (2005a). Foreword to the theory of spheres. dans M. Ohanian & J. C. Royoux (dir.), *Cosmograms* (pp. 223–240), New York: Lukas and Sternberg.

Sloterdijk, P. (2005b). *Sphères III. Écumes: sphérologieplurielle [trad. O. Mannoni]*. Paris: M. Sell.

Sloterdijk, P. (2009). Geometry in the colossal: The project of metaphysical globalization. *Environment and Planning D: Society and Space, 27*(1), 29–57.

Smith, A. (2006). An inquiry into the nature and causes of the wealth of nations, http://www2. hn.psu.edu/faculty/jmanis/adam-sniith/wealth-nations.pdf, consulté le 14 novembre 2013.

Smith, J., & Brown, A. (2005). Building a culture of learning design: Reconsidering the place of online learning in the tertiary curriculum, http:www.ascilite.org.au/conferences/brisbane05/ blogs/proceedings/71_Smith.pdf, consulté le 14 novembre 2013.

Solis, B. (2010). *Engage: The complete guide for brands and businesses to build, cultivate, and measure success in the new web*. Hoboken: Wiley.

Spyrou, S. S., Berler, A. A., & Bamidis, P. D. (2003). Information system interoperability in a regional health care system infrastructure: A pilot study using health care information standards. *Studies in Health Technology and Informatics, 95*, 364–369.

Stamper, R., Liu, K., Hafkamp, M., & Ades, Y. (2000). Understanding the roles of signs and norms in organizations: A semiotic approach to information systems design. *Behaviour & Information Technology, 19*(1), 15–27.

Stephan, P. F. (2006). Le design cognitif: une perspective pour la recherche en design, http:// archive.peterstephan.org/fileadmin/website/05_publikationen/PFS_Le_Design_cognitif.pdf, consulté le 14 novembre 2013.

Stewart, J., & Williams, R. (2005). The wrong trousers? Beyond the design fallacy: Social learning and the user. dans H. Rohracher (dir.), *User involvement in innovation processes: Strategies and limitations from a socio-technical perspective*. Munich: Profil Verlag.

Stillman, L. (2005). Participatory action research for electronic community networking projects. *Community Development, 36*(1), 77–92.

Stillman, L., & Linger, H. (2009). Community informatics and information systems: How can they be better connected?. *The Information Society, 25*(4), 1–10.

Stillman, L., Kethers, S., French, R., & Lombard, D. (2009). Adapting corporate modelling for community informatics. *Vine, 39*(3), 259–274.

Storkerson, P. (1997). Defining design: A new perspective to help specify the field, http://www. communicationcognition.com/Publications/ConstructivistDesign.pdf, consulté le 14 novembre 2013.

Storkerson, P. (2006). Communication research: Theory, empirical studies and results. dans A. Bennett (dir.), *Design studies: Theory and research in graphic design* (pp. 158–178). New York: Princeton Architectural Press.

Storkerson, P. (2008). Is disciplinary research possible in communication design? *Design Research Quarterly, 3*(2), 1–8.

Sunstein, C. R. (2006). *Infotopia: How many minds produce knowledge*. New York: Oxford University Press.

Sunstein, C. R. (2009). *Republic.com 2.0*. Princeton: Princeton University Press.

Susi, T., & Ziemke, T. (2001). Social cognition, artefacts, and stigmergy: A comparative analysis of theoretical frameworks for the understanding of artefact-mediated collaborative activity. *Cogtntive Systems Research, 2*(4), 273–290.

Sveiby, K. E. (1997). *The new organizational wealth: Managing and measuring knowledge-based assets*. San Francisco: Berrett-Koehler.

Sveiby, K. E., & Skuthorpe, T. (2006). *Treading lightly*. Adelaide: Griffin.

Tapscott, D., & Williams, A. D. (2008). *Wikinomics: How mass collaboration changes everything*. New York: Penguin.

Tapscott, D., & Williams, A. D. (2010). Innovating the 21st century university: It's time. *Educause Review, 45*(1), 17–29.

Taylor, J., Rodden, T., Anderson, A., Sharples, M., Luckin, R., Conole, G., & Siraj-Blatchford, J. (2004). An e-Leaming Research Agenda, http://www.epsrc.ac.uk/ResearchFunding/Programmes/e-Science/eLeamingRAgenda.htm.Workshop, consulté le 11 novembre 2007.

Te'eni, D., Carey, J. M., & Zhang, P. (2006). *Human-computer interaction: Developing effective organizational information system*. Hoboken: Wiley

TOGAF. (2009). TOGAF certification for people, exam eligibility guidelines for ATTC providers, The Open Group, http://www.opengroup.org/togaf9/cert/docs/TOGAF_Exam_Eligibility-guidelines.pdf, consulté le 11 décembre 2013.

Trestini, M., & Lemire, G. (2009). Environnements Constructivistes d'Apprentissage: quand les activités collectives et individuelles permettent aux apprenants de construire leurs connaissances. *Education Canada*, 1–56.

Trist, E. L. (1953). Temporary withdrawal from work under full employment: The formation of an absence culture, http://www.moderntimesworkplace.com/archives/ericsess/sessvoll/Hillp494.opd.pdf, consulté le 13 décembre 2013.

Trist, E. L., & Bamforth, K. W. (1951). Some social and psychological consequences of the long-wall method. *Human Relations, 4*(1), 3–38.

Turoff, M., & Hiltz, S. R. (1976). Meeting through your computer: Information exchange and engineering decision-making are made easy through computer-assisted conferencing, http://web.njit.edu/-turoff/papers/mtyc.pdf, consulté le 11 novembre 2013.

Ulrich, W. (1983). *Critical Heuristics of social planning: A new approach to practical philosophy*. Berne: Haupt.

Ulrich, W. (1987). Critical heuristics of social systems design. *European Journal of Operational Research, 31*(3), 276–283.

Ulrich, W., & Reynolds, M. (2010). Critical systems heuristics. dans M. Reynolds & S. Holwell (dir.), *Systems approaches to managing change: A practical guide* (pp. 243–292). Londres: Springer.

Underhill, A. R. (2006). Theories of learning and their implications for on-line assessment. *Turkish Online Journal of Distance Education, 7*(1), http://tojde.anadolu.edu.tr/tojde21/articles/anthony.htm, consulté le 15 novembre 2013.

University of Southern California, USC. (2013). USC Stevens Center for Innovation, http://stevens.usc.edu/index.php.

Valaskakis, K. (1988). At the crossroads of "futurism" and "prospective": Towards a Canadian synthesis ? *Technological Forecasting and Social Change, 33*(4), 339–353.

Valaskakis, K. (2010). Notes on relativity in future studies. *Technological Forecasting and Social Change, 77*(9), 1464–1468.

Van Eijnatten, F. M. (2005). A chaordic view of collaborative networked organisations, http://www.chaosforum.com/docs/nieuws/CSTCN01.pdf, consulté le 15 novembre 2013.

Van Oost, E., Verhaegh, S., & Oudshoorn, N. (2009). From innovation community to community innovation: User-initiated innovation in Wireless Leiden. *Science, Technology & Human Values, 34*(2), 182–205.

Van Osch, W., & Avital, M. (2010a). The road to sustainable value: The path-dependent construction of sustainable innovation as sociomaterial practices in the car industry. dans T. Thatchenkery, D. L. Cooperrider & M. Avital (dir.) *Positive design and appreciative construction: From sustainable development to sustainable value* (pp. 99–116). Bingley (R.-U.): Emerald Group.

Van Osch, W., & Avital, M. (2010b). From Green IT to sustainable innovation, AMCIS 2010 Proceedings, note 490.

Van Osch, W., & Avital, M. (2010c). Generative collectives, ICIS 2010 Proceedings, note 175.

Von Bertalanffy, L. (1968). *General systems theory, foundation, development, applications.* New York: G. Braziller.

Von Foerster, H. (1984). *Observing systems.* Salinas: Intersystems.

Von Hippel, E. (2005). Democratizing innovation: The evolving phenomenon of user innovation. *Journal fur Betriebswirtschaft, 55*(1), 63–78.

Von Hippel, E. (2007). *The sources of innovation.* Oxford: Oxford University Press.

Von Hippel, E., & Thomke, S. (2002). Customers as innovators: A new way to create value, HarvardBussiness Review, http://web.mit.edu/evhippel/www/papers/HBRtoolkitsaspub.pdf, consulté le 28 novembre 2013.

Vygotsky, L. S. (1978). *Mind and society: The development of higher psychological process.* Cambridge: Harvard University Press.

Wand, Y., & Weber, R. (1990a). Toward a theory of the deep structure of information systems, International Conference on Information Systems (pp. 61–71). Wand, Y. and Weber, R. "TOWARD A THEORY OF THE DEEP STRUCTURE OF INFORMATION SYSTEMS" (1990).ICIS1990 Proceedings. 3. http://aisel.aisnet.org/icis1990/3

Wand, Y., & Weber, R. (1990b). An ontological model of an information system. *IEEE Transactions on Software Engineering, 16*(11), 1282–1292.

Warfield, J. N. (1976). *Societal systems.* New York: Wiley.

Warfield, J. N. (1986). The domain of science model: Evolution and design, Proc. 30th Ann. Mtg., Society for General Systems Research, Salinas, Intersystems, H46-H59.

Warfield, J. N. (1990). *A science of general design: Managing complexity through systems design.* Salinas: Intersystems.

Warfield, J. N. (1999). The problématique: Evolution of an idea. *Systems Research, 16*, 221–226.

Warfield, J. N. (2006). *An introduction to systems science.* Washington, DC: National Academies Press, World Scientific.

Warfield, J. N., & Cardenas, A. R. (1994). *A handbook of interactive management.* Ames: Iowa State University Press.

Warfield, J. N., & Christakis, A. N. (1987). Dimensionality. *Systems Research, 4*(2), 127–137.

Watzlawick, P. J., Helmick Beavin, J., & Jackson, D. D. (1972). *Une logique de la communication.* Paris: Seuil.

Weaver, W. (1948). Science and complexity. *American Scientist, 36*, 536–544.

Webb, B. R. (1995). Opinion: Educational research and computer supported co-operative learning. *Programmed Learning, 32*(2), 139–146.

Weick, K. E. (1995). *Sensemaking in organizations.* Thousand Oaks: Sage.

Weick, K. E., Sutcliffe, K. M., & Obstfeld, D. (2005). Organizing and the process of sensemaking. *Organization Science, 16*(4), 409–421.

Weinberg, G. M. (1975). *An introduction to general systems thinking.* New York: John Wiley.

Weinberger, D. (2011). The machine that would predict the future. *Scientific American, 305*(5), 52–57.

Weisbord, M. R. (1992). *Discovering common ground: How future search conferences bring people together to achieve breakthrough innovation, empowerment, shared vision, and collaborative action.* San Francisco: Berrett-Koehler.

Weisbord, M. R., Weisbord, M., & Janoff, S. (2000). *Future search: An action guide to finding common ground in organizations and communities.* San Francisco: Berrett-Koehler.

Wellman, B. (2002a). The networked nature of community: Online and offline, It & Society, *1*(1), juin, 151–165, http://homes.chass.utoronto.ca/~wellman/publications/Networked_Nature_of_Community/Vol01-1-A10-Wellman-Boase-Chen.pdf, consulté le 9 décembre 2013.

Wellman, B. (2002b). Little boxes, glocalization, and networked individualism. In M. Tanabe, P. van den Besselaar, & T. Ishida (Eds.), *Digital cities II: Computational and sociological approaches* (pp. 10–25). Berlin: Springer.

Wenger, E. (1998). *Communities of practice: Learning; meaning and identity*. Cambridge (R.-U.): Cambridge University Press.

Wenger, E., & Gervais, F. (2005). *La théorie des communautés de pratique*. Québec: Presses de Université Laval.

Wenger, E., Mcdermott, R. A., & Snyder, W. M. (2002). *Cultivating communities of practice: A guide to managing knowledge*. Boston: Harvard Business Press.

Wertsch, J. V. (1991). *Voices of the mind: Sociocultural approach to mediated action*. Cambridge: Harvard University Press.

Wheatley, M. J. (2002). *Turning to one another: Simple conversations to restore hope to the future*. San Francisco: Berrett-Koshler Publishers. http://www.ode.state.or.us/opportunities/grants/saelp/willing-to-be-disturbed.pdf, consulté le 10 décembre 2013.

Whitworth. (2009). The social requirements of technical systems. In B. Whitworth & A. De Moor (Eds.), *Handbook of research on socio-technical design and social networking systems*. IGI Global: Hershey. at http://brianwhitworth.com/STS/STS-chapter1.pdf.

Whitworth, B., & Aldo de Moor (Eds.). (2009). *Handbook of research on socio-technical design and social networking systems, vol. II*. Information Science Reference: Hershey.

Whitworth, B., & de Moor, A. (2009). In B. Whitworth & A. De Moor (Eds.), *Handbook of research on socio-technical design and social networking systems*. Hershey: IGI Global. at http://brianwhitworth.com/STS/STS-chapter1.pdf.

Whitworth, B., Gallupe, B., & Mcqueen, R. J. (2000). A cognitive three-process model of computer-mediated groups: Theoretical foundations for groupware design. *Group Decision and Négociation, 9*(5), 431–456. doi:https://doi.org/10.1023/A:1008780324737.

Wiener, N. (1961). *Cybernetics: Or control and communication in the animal and the machine*. Cambridge, MA: MIT Press.

Wikipedia. (2008). Performance management, Wikipedia Foundation, http://en.wikipedia.org/wiki/Performance_management, consulté le 14 novembre 2013.

Wilson, B. (1984). *Systems: Concepts methodologies and applications*. Londres: John Wiley.

Wilson, A. (2006). *Marketing research: An integrated approach*. Gosport (R.-U.): Financial Times Prentice Hall.

Winograd, T. (2006). Shifting viewpoints: Artificial intelligence and human-computer interaction. *Artificial Intelligence, 170*, 1256–1258. http://hci.stanford.edu/winograd/papers/ai-hci.pdf, consulté le 10 décembre 2013.

Winograd, T., & Flores, F. (1986). *Understanding computers and cognition: A new foundation for design*. Norwood: Ablex Publishing Corporation.

Ye, Y., & Fischer, G. (2007). Designing for participation in socio-technical software systems. dans C. Stephanidis (dir.), *Proceedings of the 4th international conference on universal access in human- computer interaction, partie* 1 (pp. 312–321). Heidelberg: Springer.

Zhuge, H. (2009). Communities and emerging semantics in semantic link network: Discovery and learning. *IEEE Transactions on Knowledge and Data Engineering, 21*(6), 785–799.

Zhuge, H. (2010). Interactive semantics. *Artificial Intelligence, 174*, 190–204.

Zhuge, H. (2011). Semantic linking through spaces for cyber-physical-socio intelligence: Amethodology. *Artificial Intelligence, 175*, 988–1019.

Zweifel, P., Felder, S., & Meier, M. (1999). Ageing of population and health care expenditure: A red herring?. *Health Economics, 8*(6), 485–496.

Index

A

Aakhus, M., 24, 79, 229, 233, 290

Abductive thinking, 24, 103

Activity theory, 46, 204, 213, 223, 229, 248, 249, 262, 266–272, 281, 292, 315, 326, 330, 334

Afsarmanesh, H., 21, 23, 32, 164, 171, 202, 223, 254, 340, 341, 346, 347, 349, 401, 402

Algorithm, 7, 40, 44, 48, 73, 100, 126, 128, 131, 136, 137, 154, 170, 205, 220, 329, 331

Applications, 5, 7, 8, 10, 12, 15, 16, 19, 24–26, 28, 30, 32, 35, 36, 51, 52, 54, 55, 58, 61–67, 70, 73, 80, 87, 89, 91, 93–95, 97, 99, 100, 103, 104, 113, 115, 116, 118, 122, 133, 134, 138, 141, 144, 146, 147, 151, 153, 156, 157, 161, 162, 164, 171, 187, 194, 197, 198, 215, 216, 219–221, 224, 226, 228, 237, 245, 247, 249, 257, 275–277, 282–284, 287, 290, 294, 296, 297, 310, 311, 316, 317, 324–326, 329, 331, 333, 336, 365, 391, 394, 401, 413–415, 419

Applied Community Informatics Lab (ACIL), 1–3, 30, 32, 51, 58, 67, 78, 79, 82–85, 87, 90, 93, 101, 119, 152, 178, 211, 215, 227, 233, 238, 247, 252, 254, 265, 269, 294, 301, 325, 345

Appropriation, 1, 3, 5, 8, 12, 14, 27, 32, 40, 50, 51, 55–57, 64, 65, 68, 74, 75, 82, 85, 92, 93, 96, 97, 101, 103, 105, 111, 117, 123, 130, 139–141, 143, 147, 154, 171, 179, 211, 212, 216–218, 236, 247, 248, 252, 253, 262, 264, 267, 275–277, 280, 286, 293, 299, 300, 304, 310, 311, 322, 325, 331, 333, 335, 344, 346, 354, 357, 359, 365, 395, 403, 405–407, 417, 419

APSI, 1, 2, 4, 12, 16, 27, 53, 71, 74, 86, 87, 93, 113, 144, 179, 215, 219, 220, 241, 244, 250, 252, 294, 301, 314, 318, 323, 325, 334, 340, 341, 343, 344, 419

Architecture, 10, 16, 20, 27, 28, 41, 46, 91, 92, 94, 98, 100, 114, 119, 127, 153, 155–162, 164, 168, 169, 171, 173–175, 178, 183–188, 193–198, 204, 206, 210–213, 215, 233, 236, 238, 239, 241–244, 248, 250, 256, 276, 279, 285, 302, 314, 316–318, 333–335, 341, 359, 360, 391, 407

Aspects, 4, 6, 8, 15, 20, 24, 26–31, 40, 41, 43, 44, 47, 48, 51, 54, 61, 62, 68, 69, 75, 77, 85, 104, 105, 107, 111, 112, 121, 122, 126, 127, 129, 130, 134, 140, 141, 148, 154, 156, 159, 162, 165, 166, 169, 170, 181, 182, 186, 187, 190, 192–196, 198, 215, 224, 227, 236, 240–242, 254, 255, 261–267, 270, 272–274, 279, 281, 282, 285–287, 290, 292, 294, 296, 299–306, 309, 311, 313–317, 323–329, 331, 332, 334, 337–339, 341–343, 349, 388, 400, 408, 409, 416, 417, 420

Australia, 72

Axiology, 64, 67, 68, 123, 139, 154, 205, 241, 301, 311

Axioms, 26, 62, 70–74, 77, 109

© Springer International Publishing AG 2017
P.-L. Harvey, *Community Informatics Design Applied to Digital Social Systems*,
Translational Systems Sciences 12, DOI 10.1007/978-3-319-65373-0